Marketing Management: Text and Cases

Robert J. Dolan
Harvard Business School

McGraw-Hill
Irwin

Boston   Burr Ridge, IL   Dubuque, IA   Madison, WI   New York   San Francisco   St. Louis
Bangkok   Bogotá   Caracas   Kuala Lumpur   Lisbon   London   Madrid   Mexico City
Milan   Montreal   New Delhi   Santiago   Seoul   Singapore   Sydney   Taipei   Toronto

McGraw-Hill Higher Education

A Division of The **McGraw-Hill** *Companies*

MARKETING MANAGEMENT: TEXT AND CASES
Published by McGraw-Hill, an imprint of The McGraw-Hill Companies, Inc. 1221 Avenue of the Americas, New York, NY, 10020.

Case material of the Harvard Graduate School of Business Administration is made possible by the cooperation of business firms and other organizations which may wish to remain anonymous by having their names, quantities, and other identifying details disguised while maintaining basic relationships. Cases are prepared as the basis for class discussion rather than to illustrate either effective handling of an administrative situation.

domestic   1 2 3 4 5 6 7 8 9 0 CCW CCW 0 9 8 7 6 5 4 3 2 1
international 1 2 3 4 5 6 7 8 9 0 CCW CCW 0 9 8 7 6 5 4 3 2 1

ISBN   0-07-249980-X

Publisher: *John E. Biernat*
Executive editor: *Linda Schreiber*
Developmental editor: *Nina McGuffin*
Editorial Assistant: *Sarah L. Crago*
Marketing manager: *Kim Kanakes Szum*
Project manager: *Natalie J. Ruffatto*
Production associate: *Gina Hangos*
Producer, media technology: *Todd Labak*
Designer: *Matthew Baldwin*
Supplement producer: *Erin Sauder*
Photo research coordinator: *David A. Tietz*
Cover design: *Proof Positive/Farrowlyne Associates, Inc.*
Interior design: *Proof Positive/Farrowlyne Associates, Inc.*
Typeface: *10/12 Minion*
Compositor: *Proof Positive/Farrowlyne Associates, Inc.*
Printer: *Courier Westford*

Library of Congress Cataloging-in-Publication Data

Dolan, Robert J.
    Marketing management : text and cases / Robert J. Dolan.
      p. cm. — (McGraw-Hill/Irwin series in marketing)
    Previously published: Homewood, IL : Irwin, c1993.
    Includes bibliographical references and index.
    ISBN 0-07-249980-X (alk. paper)
    1. Marketing—Management. 2. Marketing—Management—Case studies. I. Title. II. Series.

HF5415.13 .Q45 2001

2001045238

www.mhhe.com

MCGRAW-HILL/IRWIN SERIES IN MARKETING

Alreck & Settle
The Survey Research Handbook
Second Edition

Anderson, Hair & Bush
Professional Sales Management
Second Edition

Arens
Contemporary Advertising
Eighth Edition

Arnould, Price & Zinkhan
Consumers
First Edition

Bearden, Ingram & Laforge
Marketing: Principles & Perspectives
Third Edition

Belch & Belch
Introduction to Advertising & Promotion: An Integrated Marketing Communications Approach
Fifth Edition

Bernhardt & Kinnear
Cases in Marketing Management
Seventh Edition

Berkowitz, Kerin, Hartley and Rudelius
Marketing
Sixth Edition

Bowersox and Closs
Logistical Management
First Edition

Bowersox and Cooper
Strategic Marketing Channel Management
First Edition

Boyd, Walker & Larreche
Marketing Management: A Strategic Approach with a Global Orientation
Fourth Edition

Cateora & Graham
International Marketing
Eleventh Edition

Churchill, Ford, Walker, Johnston, & Tanner
Sales Force Management
Sixth Edition

Churchill & Peter
Marketing
Second Edition

Cole & Mishler
Consumer and Business Credit Management
Eleventh Edition

Cravens
Strategic Marketing
Seventh Edition

Cravens, Lamb & Crittenden
Strategic Marketing Management Cases
Sixth Edition

Crawford & Di Benedetto
New Products Management
Sixth Edition

Duncan
IMC: Building Relationships that Build Brands
First Edition

Dwyer & Tanner
Business Marketing
Second Edition

Dolan
Marketing Management: Text and Cases
First Edition

Eisenmann
Internet Business Models: Text and Cases
First Edition

Etzel, Walker & Stanton
Marketing
Twelfth Edition

Futrell
ABC's of Relationship Selling
Sixth Edition

Futrell
Fundamentals of Selling
Seventh Edition

Hair, Bush & Ortinau
Marketing Research
First Edition

Hasty and Rearden
Retail Management
First Edition

Hawkins, Best & Coney
Consumer Behavior
Eighth Edition

Hayes, Jenster & Aaby
Business To Business Marketing
First Edition

Johansson
Global Marketing
Second Edition

Lambert & Stock
Strategic Logistics Management
Fourth Edition

Lambert, Stock & Ellram
Fundamentals of Logistic Management
First Edition

Lehmann & Winer
Analysis for Marketing Planning
Fourth Edition

Lehmann & Winer
Product Management
Second Edition

Levy & Weitz
Retailing Management
Fourth Edition

Mason & Perreault
The Marketing Game
Second Edition

McDonald
Direct Marketing: An Integrated Approach
First Edition

Moloan & Graham
International and Global Marketing Concepts and Cases
Second Edition

Mohammed, Fisher, Jaworski, & Cahill
Internet Marketing
First Edition

Monroe
Pricing
Second Edition

Patton
Sales Force: A Sales Management Simulation Game
First Edition

Pelton, Strutton, Lumpkin
Marketing Channels: A Relationship Management Build Brands Approach
Second Edition

Perreault & McCarthy
Basic Marketing: A Global Managerial Approach
Thirteenth Edition

Perreault & McCarthy
Essentials of Marketing: A Global Managerial
Eighth Edition

Peter & Donnelly
A Preface to Marketing Management
Eighth Edition

Peter & Donnelly
Marketing Management: Knowledge and Skills
Sixth Edition

Peter & Olson
Consumer Behavior and Marketing Strategy
Sixth Edition

Rangan
Business Marketing Strategy: Cases, Concepts & Applications
First Edition

Rangan, Shapiro & Moriaty
Business Marketing Strategy: Concepts and Applications
First Edition

Rayport, Jaworski & Breakaway Solutions
Introduction to e-Commerce
First Edition

Rayport & Jaworski
e-Commerce
First Edition

Rayport & Jaworski
Cases in e-Commerce
First Edition

Stanton & Spiro
Management of a Sales Force
Tenth Edition

Sudman & Blair
Marketing Research: A Problem Solving Approach
First Edition

Ulrich & Eppinger
Product Design and Development
Second Edition

Walker, Boyd and Larreche
Marketing Strategy: Planning and Implementation
Third Edition

Weitz, Castleberry and Tanner
Selling: Building Partnerships
Fourth Edition

Zeithaml & Bitner
Services Marketing
Second Edition

PREFACE

For four years, through the spring of 2000, I had the good fortune to be the course head for the first-year marketing course at Harvard Business School (HBS). When I joined Harvard in 1980, then-course head Professor Ben Shapiro told me that he had the best job at the school. Since he was saddled with the responsibility of transforming neophytes like myself into first-rate case developers and teachers, I did not understand his statement. Sixteen years later, when I became course head, I began to understand a glimmer of what he meant.

A typical teaching group at HBS involves about seven professors—a mix of senior and junior levels—all dedicated to delivering the best marketing course we can in about 35 sessions. Our students make meeting this goal a challenge—and, they also make it fun. All of them are smart and hard-working, but none of them could be described as a typical student. They are mathematicians, artists, and historians; come from many different countries and work experiences; and have a variety of aspirations. All have cleared a very high hurdle in terms of individual accomplishment and leadership potential in order to be admitted to the MBA program at HBS.

Heading the teaching group charged with the task of teaching thousands of these people over a four-year period turned out to give me what all of us seek in our work—a great deal of personal satisfaction and challenge. I learned a lot. Over four years, I and the professors in my teaching groups developed much new material, developing cases and accompanying notes that worked together to communicate key concepts. We tried them all out. Some of them worked very well and have already migrated from HBS, becoming integrated into courses at other leading business schools. Others did not work quite as planned and will probably have a hard time getting out of the file cabinet and into the classroom again. Through the process of development, experimentation, and critical review, I think we have identified the best material and the best way to organize it. This book reflects that thinking. It mixes some "classic" cases, which present seemingly enduring marketing challenges, with recently developed material. Included in each of the five parts of the book is at least one case relating to electronic commerce issues.

Compared to previous versions of this book, the notes that head each part are no longer simply "notes." Now they are designed to be fairly comprehensive as they set out many of the fundamentals that will be encountered in the cases in that part.

While developed specifically for a required course in the first year course in Harvard's MBA Program, the materials in this text are appropriate for both upper-level undergraduate and successful executive courses as well. The text requires no previous formal training in marketing, but the materials have proven to have a high level of value-added, even to individuals with extensive educational exposure and work experience in the field.

Marketing Management: Text and Cases is the product of many whose efforts take place in the environment of Harvard Business School. HBS provides us the stimulus of high expectations but also provides the resources required to meet such expectations. In particular, I wish to thank Dean Kim Clark and the members of the division of research for their support of my own efforts. Second, I want to thank the members of my teaching groups over the four years: Ruth Bolton, Sam Chun, John Deighton, Susan Fournier, David Godes, John Gourville, Kip King, Ajay Kohli, Rajiv Lal, Youngne Moon, Walter Salmon, and Luc Wathieu.

I am also indebted to the many professors who have allowed me to include their materials in the book. In addition to my teaching group colleagues, these include Mark S. Albion, Frank V. Cespedes, Patrick J. Kaufmann, Rowland T. Moriarty, Das Narayandas, John A. Quelch, V. Kasturi Rangan, Benson P. Shapiro, Hirotaka Takeuchi, and George Wu. Thanks also to my assistant of the past year, John Higgins, for all the help in the production of the book. Finally, thanks to Shiela Linehan for going through First Year Marketing with me four times and keeping all the pieces of that experience together. Her organization skills made bringing the four-year experience together in a book fun, rather than a chore.

Marketing is a great subject—a simple and elegant combination of science and art. The materials in this text are designed to present the important marketing problems of today in such a way as to foster development of the knowledge and skills required to discover implementable solutions for such problems.

CONTENTS

Introduction to the Marketing Process

Part I consists of two notes and five cases that introduce key concepts of marketing management. The first note, "Note on Marketing Strategy," describes the process by which we conceptualize and analyze marketing problems. Figure A of that note is a key process diagram, around which the book is organized. The second note, "Note on Low-Tech Marketing Math," presents useful quantitative analysis methods that are "low-tech" in the sense that at most a calculator is required to execute them. The simple, "back of the envelope" calculations presented in this note will regularly help provide insight in case analyses.

The five cases in the module span a wide variety of contexts and types of marketing problems. "Sealed Air Corporation" opens the module with a business-to-business situation in which a strong incumbent is being attacked by a low-cost rival. Written in 1982, this case is one of the best-sellers in the history of Harvard Business School because the classic issue it discusses—a profitable pioneer finding its business jeopardized by a new entrant—is as prevalent in today's high-technology era as it was when the case was written.

"Tweeter etc." then takes us to the world of retailing, where a small consumer electronics company seeks to prosper through an innovative pricing plan.

The next case, "Warner-Lambert Ireland: Niconil," moves us to an international setting, as the company seeks to introduce a new product in Ireland. The product's success will depend on its acceptance by a number of different players: end users, doctors, and pharmacists. What marketing plan will win the necessary support?

We then consider a services marketing issue, as the "The Aravind Eye Hospital, Madurai, India: In Service for Sight" raises the question of the significance of marketing in eradicating blindness in India.

Finally, "The Black & Decker Corporation (A): Power Tools Division" closes the module as Black & Decker, the leader in power tools for consumers, considers its plight in the tradesman segment. Here a Japanese competitor has gained a commanding lead over Black & Decker. Some market research information helps diagnose the cause of the problem as we consider some potentially bold actions that may help the company gain share leadership in the tradesman segment.

Part I reveals the scope and nature of marketing problems and begins building an analytical approach to diagnosing and defining problems, developing and evaluating alternative plans of action, and constructing implementation plans.

NOTE ON MARKETING STRATEGY

Long ago, Peter Drucker wrote that any business enterprise has only two basic functions: marketing and innovation.[1] All else, he implied, was detail. The central role of marketing in the enterprise stems from the fact that marketing is the process via which a firm creates value for its chosen customers. Value is created by meeting customer needs. Thus, a firm needs to define itself not by the product it sells, but by the customer benefit provided.

Having created the value for its customers, the firm is then entitled to capture a portion of it through pricing. To remain a viable concern, the firm must sustain this process of creating and capturing value over time. Within this framework, the plan by which value is created on a sustained basis is the firm's Marketing Strategy. Marketing Strategy involves two major activities: (i) selecting a target market and determining the desired positioning of product in target customers' minds and (ii) specifying the plan for the marketing activities to achieve the desired positioning. Figure A presents a schematic describing a general process of marketing strategy development. As shown, five major areas of analysis underlie marketing decision making. We begin with analysis of the 5 C's—customers, company, competitors, collaborators, and context. We ask:

Customer Needs	What needs do we seek to satisfy?
Company Skills	What special competence do we possess to meet those needs?
Competition	Who competes with us in meeting those needs?
Collaborators	Who should we enlist to help us and how do we motivate them?
Context	What cultural, technological and legal factors limit what is possible?

This leads first to specification of a target market and desired positioning and then to the marketing mix. This results in customer acquisition and retention strategies driving the firm's profitability.

This note develops this framework. We organize the presentation by first setting out the major decisions to be made; then we elaborate on the 5 C's analysis required to support effective decision making. As an overview note, we do not provide depth in presenting the actual analytical techniques. However, throughout the note we provide references to textbooks which contain in-depth coverage of the issues.[2]

Target Market Selection and Product[3] Positioning

Marketing strategy development begins with the customer. A prerequisite to the development of the rest of the marketing strategy is specification of the target markets the company will attempt to serve. Marketers have generally been moving from serving large mass markets to specification of smaller segments with customized marketing programs. Indeed, a popular phrase today is "markets of one" suggesting that marketing campaigns can and should be customized to individuals. In the days of "you can have any color you want as long as it's black," production capabilities and limited information on consumers' varying wants acted as constraints on the development of programs customized to individual consumers. Now, new technologies enable firms to practice customized marketing on an economical basis in many situations.[4]

Professor Robert J. Dolan prepared this note as the basis for class discussion.

[1]Peter F. Drucker, *The Practice of Management* (New York: Harper, 1954)

[2]The idea for a note of this type as a useful adjunct to studying marketing originated with Professor Raymond E. Corey in his "Marketing Strategy: An Overview," written in 1978, HBS No. 579-054.

[3]Throughout this note, we will use the term "product" although the logic conveyed applies equally to situations in which customer value is delivered by a product/service bundle or a service alone.

[4]The development of customization strategies is covered in B.J. Pine II, *Mass Customization* (Boston, Mass.: Harvard Business School Press, 1993), and D. Peppers and M. Rogers, *The One to One Future* (New York: Currency/Doubleday, 1993).

Figure A Schematic of Marketing Process[5]

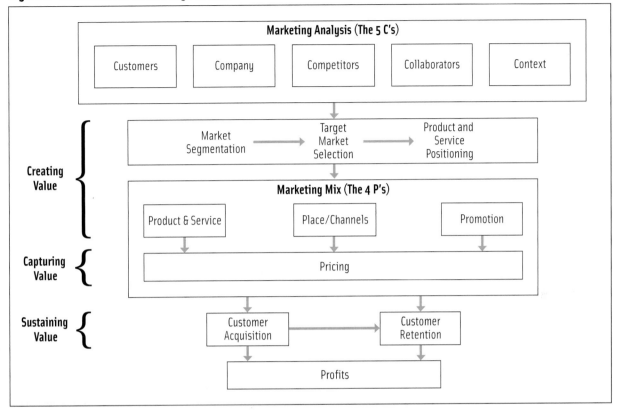

The two key questions are:

1. Which potential buyers should the firm attempt to serve? To answer this, the firm must first determine the most appropriate way to describe and differentiate customers. This is the process of segmentation.

2. How much customization should the firm offer in its programs, i.e., at which point on the continuum from

Mass Market - Market Segments - Market Niches - Individuals

will the firm construct plans?

Markets can be segmented in a variety of ways.[6] Among the most widely used bases are:

- demographic (e.g., age, income, gender, occupation)
- geographic (e.g., nation, region of country, urban vs. rural)
- lifestyle (e.g., hedonistic vs. value oriented).

These three types of bases—demographic, geographic, and lifestyle—are general descriptors of consumers. Often, a useful segmentation of the market is derived by using segmentation bases which describe a customer's behavior or relationship to a product, e.g.,

User Status	Non-User vs. User
Usage Rate	Light, Medium, Heavy User
Benefits Sought	Performance-Oriented vs. Price-Oriented
Loyalty Status	None, Moderate, Strong, Totally Loyal
Attitude Toward Product	Unsatisfied, Satisfied, Delighted

For example, a personal computer manufacturer segmenting the market on the basis of user status might

---

[5]This figure derives from similar representations developed over the years by HBS marketing faculty and other academics.

[6]A good reference on the process of segmentation is in V.R. Rao and J.H. Steckel, "Segmenting Markets: Who Are the Potential Buyers," *Analysis for Strategic Marketing* (Reading, Mass.: Addison-Wesley, 1998), Chapter 2.

choose to target first-time home-use computer buyers; another may target mainly those who already owned but wish to "trade-up." The firms' explicit choice of target markets has obvious, important implications for both the features to include in their computers and their communications efforts. Segmentation schemes yielding these clear implications for marketing are most useful. There is little point in using a segmentation basis to define groups to be marketed to in the same way.

The process of selecting the segments to serve is critical because ultimately the customer has the right to dictate the rules via which the marketing game will be played, i.e., a customer uses the purchase criteria he or she decides to use and these in effect are the "rules of the game." Thus, the firm's selecting a target market is tantamount to choosing the rules of the game, and consequently target market selection should consider:

- The firm's comparative strengths and weaknesses vis-a-vis competition given the target market's purchase criteria.
- The firm's corporate goals and the fit of the segment with these goals.
- The resources necessary to market successfully to the target segment.
- The need for/availability of appropriate collaborators to market successfully.
- The likely financial returns from the segment.

As part of the segmentation and target market selection process, the firm has to play out scenarios, i.e., consider the question: if we pursue this segment, how would we approach it and how would we want potential buyers to see us? The answer should be formalized in a "positioning statement" specifying the position the firm wishes to occupy in the target customers' minds.[7] The precise form of a positioning statement can vary but a form typically quite useful is to fill in:

_____	is	_____
Our Product/Brand		(single most important claim)

_____	_____
among all	(competitive frame)

_____	_____
because	(single most important support)

In some cases, the positioning cannot be sufficiently well captured via a focus on "single most important" claim, e.g., a computer manufacturer may want to be seen as both "easy-to-use" and "fast," so the positioning statement form can be adjusted. But, an explicit statement of the positioning idea is critical.

The absolute importance of target market selection and positioning is well conveyed in a best-selling marketing textbook:

> "The advantage of solving the *positioning problem* is that it enables the company to solve the *marketing mix problem*. The marketing mix—product, price, place, and promotion—is essentially the working out of the tactical details of the positioning strategy."[8]

The Marketing Mix

Neil Borden[9] of Harvard Business School used the term "marketing mix" to describe the set of activities comprising a firm's marketing program. He noted how firms blend mix elements into a program and how even firms competing in a given product category can have dramatically different mixes at work. He specified 12 mix elements, viz.

1. Merchandising–Product Planning
2. Pricing
3. Branding
4. Channels of Distribution
5. Personal Selling
6. Advertising
7. Promotions
8. Packaging
9. Display
10. Servicing
11. Physical Handling
12. Fact-Finding and Analysis–Market Research

Over time, an aggregation and regrouping of these elements has become popular. As shown in Figure A, the "4 P's" of Product, Price, Promotion and Place are often

---

[7]This conception of "positioning" has been popularized by Ries and Trout in *Positioning: The Battle for Your Mind*, 1st ed. (Revised, McGraw-Hill, 1986).

[8]P. Kotler, *Marketing Management: Analysis, Planning, Implementation and Control*, 8th ed. (Englewood Cliffs, N.J.: Prentice-Hall, 1997), p. 310.
[9]N.H. Borden, "The Concept of the Marketing Mix." Reprinted in R.J. Dolan, *Strategic Marketing Management* (Boston, Mass.: Harvard Business School Press, 1991).

used to set out the "marketing mix" in an easy to recall way. We now discuss the major issues in setting the "4 P's" in the following sequence:

1. Product
2. Place (Channels of Distribution)
3. Promotion (Communications Strategy)
4. Pricing

Product

(a) Product Definition

Product decisions start with an understanding of what a product is, viz. the product offering is not the thing itself, but rather the total package of benefits obtained by the customer. This idea has had a number of names, e.g., the "total product concept," "the augmented product," or "the integrated product." For marketing strategy development purposes, the product has to be considered from the point-of-view of value delivered to the customer. Value can be delivered simultaneously by a number of vehicles, e.g.,

- the physical product itself
- the brand name
- the company reputation
- pre-sale education provided by salespeople
- post-sale technical support
- repair service
- financing plans
- convenient availability
- word-of-mouth references provided by earlier adopters of the product
- reputation of outlet where purchased

For example, a shirt from the Lands' End Catalog is not just a shirt but one shipped within 24 hours of order and unconditionally guaranteed.[10] This broad conception of a "product" is key to seeing possible points of differentiation from competitors.

---

[10]This example is offered by Regis McKenna as an illustration of an "integral product" in his "Marketing in an Age of Diversity," *Harvard Business Review*, September-October 1988.

(b) Product Line Planning Decisions

A taxonomy of product line planning decisions is best developed by considering examples of some product planning decisions firms face.

- *Product Line Breadth:* A desktop computer manufacturer considers also selling laptops; a maker of men's golf attire considers adding a women's line; an automobile manufacturer considers a mini-van or sport utility vehicle. Product line *breadth* decisions are how many different lines will the company offer. A guiding principle in answering breadth questions is the company's position on desired consistency or similarity between the lines it offers. Some firms focus, e.g., "we market only products which draw on our skills in small motor technology" while others are more broad: "we sell products which draw on our superior consumer products marketing skills."

- *Product Line Length:* A beer producer in the mass part of the market is considering if it should develop an entry in the premium segment; the high-end computer manufacturer considering the product line breadth issue above also has to decide if it wants to compete in the emerging "under $999" market sector. These are product line *length* decisions, i.e., how many items will there be in a line providing coverage of different price points.

- *Product Line Depth:* The men's golf attire manufacturer considers whether to offer its $110 crew neck sweater in five colors or just three. Thus, a product line *depth* decision, i.e., how many types of a given product.

These are the three major types of product line planning decisions. Important considerations in making these decisions are:

- Does the product satisfy target customer wants in a way that is profitable for the firm?

- Does it offer opportunity for differentiation from competitors when the "product" is appropriately viewed as the total set of benefits delivered to consumers?

- What is the impact of this product on the rest of the line? Will it be a *complement* to other products, enhancing their value to the customer (e.g., a color-coordinated sweater enhancing the value of the matching golf shirt) or will it be a *substitute* possibly cannibalizing sales (e.g., an entry in the low-end of the personal computer machine taking sales from the same manufacturer's high-end, higher-margin items)?

- What is the impact of the items on the brand and company's reputation? The brand's equity is often a key asset and the product may enhance it or it may detract from it. A key issue is whether there would be damage to the brand, e.g., did Lipton Soup detract from the equity as a tea supplier, did Sears Financial Network hurt Sears' retail operations?[11]

(c) Individual Item Decisions

As reflected in the discussion above, decisions on individual items need to be considered within the context of the firm's full product line due to item interrelationships. At the individual item level, decisions to be made are whether to undertake efforts to:

- delete an item from the line
- reposition an existing product within the line
- improve the performance of an existing product to strengthen its positioning
- introduce a new product within an existing line
- introduce a product to establish a new line

(d) The New Product Development Process

Generally, a proactive approach to new product development follows some form of a sequential process, e.g., a five-step process of:

1. Opportunity Identification
2. Design
3. Testing
4. Product Introduction
5. Life Cycle Management[12]

In the Opportunity Identification stage, the firm identifies a customer problem which it can solve. In addition, it identifies the concept for a product to ensure both a product/market fit (the product fits the needs of the customer) and a product/company fit (it fits with the manufacturing and operational skills of the firm).

The next two stages of Design and Testing are linked in an iterative process. For example, the firm might first embody the product idea in a concept statement which is tested via presentation to potential customers. Given a favorable reaction, the concept could then be developed into a mock-up to permit more effective communication of what the product would look like when actually marketed. An unfavorable reaction from consumers in any testing results in an iteration back to the design stage.

Testing with consumers can be done via a number of procedures,[13] e.g., surveys, taste tests, simulated test markets (in which mock stores are set up and consumers recruited to shop in the mock store environment), and actual test markets for consumer goods and beta tests for industrial goods. Testing is appropriate not only for the product itself but also for the supporting elements of the marketing mix, such as the communication strategy and price.

After the firm has settled on the product and a supporting plan, it reaches Product Introduction. Decisions at this stage involve the geographic markets to which the product will be introduced and whether markets will be approached at the same time or sequentially over time (e.g., a regional rollout).

After introduction, a process of Product Life Cycle Management begins. First, the firm should continually be learning more about consumers from their reactions to the introduced product. This added learning may suggest product repositioning or marketing mix changes. Second, the marketing environment is always changing. For example, customer wants are not static; market segment sizes change; competitive offerings change; technology impacts the firm's capabilities and costs. Thus, managing the product line is a dynamic process over time.

Place: Marketing Channels

The marketing channel is the set of mechanisms or network via which a firm "goes to market," i.e., is "in touch"

---

[11]These examples are offered and this topic is considered in detail in D.A. Aaker, *Managing Brand Equity* (New York: Free Press, 1991), particularly Chapter 9.

[12]This particular model is presented by G.C. Urban and J.R. Hauser in *Design and Marketing of New Products,* 2nd ed. (Englewood Cliffs, N.J.: Prentice Hall, 1993).

[13]These methods are described in C.M. Crawford, *New Product Management,* 5th ed. (Homewood, Ill.: Irwin 1997) and R.J. Dolan, *Managing the New Product Development Process* (Reading, Mass.: Addison-Wesley, 1993).

with its customer for a variety of tasks ranging from demand generation to physical delivery of the goods. The customer's requirements for effective support determine the functions which the members of the channel must collectively provide. Kash Rangan[14] of Harvard Business School has identified eight "generic" channel functions which serve as a starting place for assessing needs in a particular context:

1. Product Information
2. Product Customization
3. Product Quality Assurance
4. Lot Size (e.g., the ability to buy in small quantities)
5. Product Assortment (refers to breadth, length, and width of product lines)
6. Availability
7. After-Sale Service
8. Logistics

An important point with respect to channel design is that while there are options about whether a particular institution (e.g., a distributor) is included in the channel or not, the setting implicates specific tasks which need to be accomplished by someone in the channel. One can eliminate a layer in the chain but not the tasks that layer performed. The popular phrase "we've cut out the middleman and passed the savings on to you" seems to indicate that the middleman represent all costs but no value-added. The functions done by the middleman now have to be done by someone else. Thus, the recommended approach is to develop "customer-driven" systems assessing the channel structure and management mechanisms that will best perform the needed functions.[15]

The two major decisions in channels are:

(i.) channel design
—which involves both a length and breadth issue

(ii.) channel management
—i.e., what policies and procedures will be used to have the necessary functions performed by the various parties.

[14]V.K. Rangan, "Designing Channels of Distribution," HBS No. 594-116, also reprinted in V.K Rangan, B.P. Shapiro, and R.T. Moriarty, *Business Marketing Strategy: Concepts and Applications* (Homewood, Ill.: Irwin, 1995).

[15]This approach is advocated and described in detail in L.W. Stern, A.I. El-Answry and A.T. Coughlan, *Marketing Channels*, 5th ed[.].
(Englewood Cliffs, N.J.: Prentice-Hall, 1996); particularly Chapter 5.

(a) Channel Design

With an understanding of customer requirements in place, a primary question in channel design is whether distribution will be "direct," "indirect" or both, i.e., some customers served one way and others another. In direct distribution, there is no independent party between the firm and its customers, e.g., the "blue suits" of the firm's salesforce visit the customer premises and sell computer mainframes. Through 1980, this was the only way IBM sold its products. In indirect distribution, there is a third party. This party may operate under contract to the firm (e.g., as in a franchise system) or it may act independently (e.g., as in a situation where a retailer pays for and takes title to the firm's goods and then is free to sell them at whatever price and in whatever fashion it desires).

Through the 1960s, the conventional wisdom was that a firm should either go to market direct or indirect, but not both because of the channel conflict which would result. The bias was toward going direct as soon as sales volume justified it, because it provided more control and direct contact with customers.

By the early 1980s, more firms began simultaneously serving different target markets, each requiring different channel functions (e.g., one segment needed intense pre-sale education; another did not). Thus there came a need to manage "dual distribution" wherein different systems are used to reach each market segment efficiently and effectively. A firm salesforce served some segments; a distributor served others. This move away from only one method of "going to market" has accelerated. Now a firm may sell through retail outlets and via direct mail; use its own salesforce to call on some accounts; rely on distributors to call smaller ones; and rely on other customers to find the company's 800 number, Web site, or submit an order directly to the firm through some Electronic Data Interchange System. In many firms, the economics of reaching the full set of its chosen target segments are such that a single approach for all customers simply won't work. Thus, rather than making one decision, the firm needs to make a coordinated set of decisions by market segment recognizing and preparing to manage the conflicts that may arise across the different channel types.

In addition to customer requirements, the major considerations in channel length issues are:

—*account concentration:* If a few customers represent the bulk of sales opportunities (e.g., jet engines), a direct selling approach can be cost effective. If the target group is larger in number and more diffuse (e.g., toothpaste), then the services of someone like a retailer who can spread the costs of an account relationship over many products is warranted.

—*degree of control and importance of direct customer contact:* One reason to go direct may be the lack of intermediaries from whom the firm could secure adequate attention, i.e., the firm lacks the power to gain some control over the intermediaries to ensure the necessary tasks are performed. Also, direct customer contact may be seen as a critical way to gain market understanding as an input to future product development efforts.

The second part of the channel design issue is channel breadth, i.e., how intense should the firm's presence be in a market area? Does the firm wish to intensively distribute its product, making for maximal customer convenience (e.g., placing the product "within arm's reach of desire," as Coca-Cola terms it,) or does it wish to be more selective? More selectivity may be warranted if there is a market education or development task to be done. Thus, some automobile manufacturers, typically high-end (e.g., Infiniti), limit the number of dealers in an area to reduce the dealer's concern that the benefits of developing potential customers in a given area would accrue to another dealer "free-riding" on these efforts.

In general, the strength of the argument for limiting distribution to selective or exclusive levels increases with

- the customer's willingness to travel and search for the good,
- the unit cost of stocking the good,
- the amount of true "selling" or market development which needs to be done.

As a product becomes more well known, there is a tendency to become less selective in distribution. For example, personal computers moved from computer specialty stores to mass merchants and warehouse clubs over time as customer education requirements decreased. Thus, the right channel structure changes over time. This presents a significant challenge as the firm seeks to maintain flexibility in channels while complex legal and other relationship elements tend to cement distribution arrangements.

(b) Channel Management

Conflict between "partners" in a distribution system is not uncommon—more than a few litigations have been filed over issues like:

- "we provided a great product, but they never sold it the way they agreed to"
- "we developed the market, but they were never able to supply the product on a reliable basis"
- "they began distributing through a discounter right in the middle of the territory we spent years developing"

Many conflicts do not result in litigation but color the relationship, e.g., a beer distributor lamenting "somehow their [the manufacturer's] view is that every time sales go up, it's their great advertising; when sales go down, it's our lousy sales promotion." In a general sense, all parties in the marketing system want the product to "do well." But conflicts can arise from:

1. lack of congruence in goals, e.g., the manufacturer's #1 priority may be to "build the consumer franchise," while the distributor's is to make money this quarter.
2. lack of consensus on who is doing what, e.g., who is to perform certain functions such as after-the-sale service; who handles small accounts; who handles global or national accounts when assignments were originally made along a smaller geographic basis.

Channel management is a day-to-day "work-on-it" task rather than a solve-it-once situation. Attention to proper design of contracts and other explicit understandings can help to reduce the potential for conflict. Good communications, e.g., through dealer panels, can help facilitate development of understanding and trust which will almost always be necessary to resolve issues since contracts cannot typically anticipate all the situations which may arise.

Promotion: Marketing Communications

The next element of the marketing mix is deciding the appropriate set of ways in which to communicate with customers to foster their awareness of the product, knowledge about its features, interest in purchasing, likelihood of trying the product and/or repeat purchasing it. Effective marketing requires an integrated communications plan combining both personal selling efforts and non-personal ones such as advertising, sales promotion, and public relations.

(a) Tasks and Tools

A useful mnemonic for the tasks in planning communications strategy is the 6 M's model:

1.	Market	To whom is the communication to be addressed?
2.	Mission	What is the objective of the communication?
3.	Message	What are the specific points to be communicated?
4.	Media	Which vehicles will be used to convey the message?
5.	Money	How much will be spent in the effort?
6.	Measurement	How will impact be assessed after the campaign?

The marketing communications mix is potentially extensive, e.g., including "nonpersonal" elements such as: advertising, sales promotion events, direct marketing, public relations, packaging, trade shows, as well as personal selling.[16]

A key to developing an effective communications strategy is understanding of the people involved in the purchase decision making, the roles they play, and their current perceptions of the situation. Those involved, the so-called Decision-Making Unit (DMU) for a product, can vary from very few (even just the user himself or herself) to many. Hundreds may be involved in major industrial purchases.

Members of the DMU differ in the role played, their desires, and perhaps their perceptions; consequently, the need is for an integrated communications plan which uses different elements of the communication mix to address different issues pertinent to DMU members. Each element has particular strengths and weaknesses.

(b) Nonpersonal Vehicles

Advertising in media is particularly effective in:

- creating awareness of a new product
- describing features of the product
- suggesting usage situations

- distinguishing the product from competitors
- directing buyers to the point-of-purchase
- creating or enhancing a brand image.

Advertising is limited in its ability to actually close the sale and make a transaction happen; sales promotions may be an effective device to complement the favorable attitude development for which advertising is appropriate.[17]

One trend in advertising is the movement to more precisely targeted media vehicles. For example, whereas the three major TV networks were once the only choices for television advertising, highly specialized channels like The Nashville Network (featuring country music) and the Golf Channel are now available. Direct marketing to households is another option. A direct mail piece can be customized to the household receiving it based on some demographic data available on mailing lists or even purchase histories. A catalog can both describe the firm's products and provide ordering information. Like a direct mail piece, the catalog can be customized to the household receiving it.

Sales promotions include things such as samples, coupons, and contests. These are usually most effective when used as a short-term inducement to generate action.

The three major types of sales promotions are:[18]

- *consumer promotions:* used by a manufacturer and addressed to the end consumer, e.g., a cents-off coupon sent in the mail or contained in print media or a continuity program such as collecting proofs-of-purchase to redeem for a gift.

- *trade promotions:* used by the manufacturer and addressed to the trade, e.g., temporary off-invoice price discounts or cooperative advertising allowances.

- *retail promotions:* used by the trade and addressed to the end consumer; often this is stimulated by a trade promotion. Examples include offering a discount and displaying or advertising the brand.

---

[16]This categorization is given by P.W. Farris and J.A. Quelch in *Advertising and Promotion Management: A Manager's Guide to Theory and Practice* (Chilton, 1983).

[17]A good reference on advertising is D.A. Aaker, R. Batra, and J.G. Myers, *Advertising Management*, 4th ed. (Englewood Cliffs, N.J.: Prentice-Hall, 1992), wherein the need to consider advertising in the overall context of the communications mix is stressed.

[18]R.C. Blattberg and S.A. Neslin, *Sales Promotion: Concepts, Methods, and Strategies* (Englewood Cliffs, N.J.: Prentice-Hall, 1990), uses this categorization. This book includes important information on the types and design of sales promotion events and empirical evidence on their impact.

Public relations refers to non-paid communication efforts, such as press releases, speeches at industry seminars, appearances by firm executives on radio or TV programs. These efforts do entail a cost to the firm, but generally are distinguished from advertising by virtue of the fact that the firm does not pay for space in the media vehicle itself. For example, in some industries, new product reviews in the trade press are very influential with consumers. However, the output of public relations activities is somewhat less controllable than is the case with either advertising or sales promotion. Purchasing a TV spot pretty much guarantees that the firm's desires with respect to message and timing of delivery will be met. That level of control is not generally attainable with public relations since other parties decide whether or not to pick up a press release, write favorable or unfavorable things about the product in a review, and so forth.

(c) Personal Selling

A salesperson as the communication vehicle presents the advantage of permitting an interaction to take place between the firm and a potential customer rather than just the broadcast of information. The salesperson can develop an understanding of the particular customer's perceptions and preferences and then tailor the communications message to the particulars of the situation. The importance of personal selling in the communications mix typically increases with the complexity of the product and the need for education of potential customers. For example, pharmaceutical companies maintain large field sales forces because nonpersonal media would not do an adequate job of educating doctors about new drugs.

It is critical to identify precisely the tasks of a salesperson. In some cases, the primary role is to take an order generated primarily by other elements of the marketing mix. In other cases, demand generation is a key task as the salesperson prospects for new accounts and/or performs consultative selling solving customers' problems. A salesperson can also have a role after-the-sale, providing technical support or transmitting customer data to the firm as a form of market research. Understanding the tasks to be done is a prerequisite to specifying skills and desired behaviors of salespeople. Recruiting, selecting, and training programs can be designed to provide the needed talents; and evaluation, compensation, and motivation plans constructed to induce the necessary effort.

(d) Constructing the Communications Mix

The proper allocation of dollars across the various media vehicles varies greatly depending upon the market situation. A fundamental decision is whether to focus on a "push" or "pull" strategy. In a push strategy, focus is on inducing intermediaries, such as a retailer, to sell the product at retail. Advertising's job may be to make the consumer aware of the product, but the closing of the deal is left to the intermediary. Alternatively, a "pull" strategy means the end consumer develops such an insistence on the product that he or she "pulls" it through the channel of distribution, and the retailer's role is merely to make the product conveniently available.

As the number of feasible communication vehicles has increased (e.g., to event sponsorship, telemarketing, one's own Web site, a posting on someone else's Web site, and infomercials), the job of specifying the right communications mix has grown more complex simply due to the number of options and permutations and combinations to be considered. However, the growth in options also creates the possibility of gaining competitive advantage via superior performance in this task.

Pricing

To a large extent, the combination of the 3 P's—product, place (channel), and promotion (communication mix)—determine the target customer's perception of the value of the firm's product in a given competitive context. Conceptually, this perceived value represents the maximum price which the customer is willing to pay. This should be the primary guide to pricing the product. Once the firm has created value for customers, it is entitled to capture some of that value for itself to fund future value-creation efforts. This is the role of effective pricing.[19]

(a) Pricing Basis and Objective

In most situations, cost should act as a floor on pricing. In some circumstances, a firm intentionally sells at a loss for a time to establish a position in the market, but it is often difficult to increase prices later due to the customer's use of the introductory price as a reference point.

---

[19]This view is developed in R.J. Dolan and H. Simon, *Power Pricing* (New York: Free Press, 1996).

With perceived value in mind, the first question is what is the marketing objective and how does the pricing objective derive from that? For example, the perceived value of the product typically varies by customer. Thus, the higher the price, the lower the sales rate, and vice-versa. The price that would maximize short-term profit is thus typically higher than the one which would maximize market penetration subject even to making some profit on each item.

Some have described this as a choice between a "skim" and "penetration" pricing strategy. In a skim strategy, the focus is on those customers with high value—skimming-the-cream off the top of the market. The classic example of this is hardcover books at $30 initially for the impatient and dropping to $7 for the identical book in softcover about a year later. In penetration pricing, the firm sets a lower price to generate lots of sales quickly. This "leaves money on the table" with the high-value customers, but is designed to preempt competition and gain a significant number of customers early on. The appeal of a penetration strategy increases to the extent that (1) customers are sensitive to price, (2) economies of scale are important, (3) adequate production capacity is available, and (4) there is a threat of competition.

(b) Price Customization

Since customers typically place different values on the product, the firm should consider whether it is worth trying to capitalize on these value variations by charging different customers different prices. In some cases, legal constraints and logistical practicalities can make this infeasible. However, many firms owe their economic well-being to their ability to customize prices. For example, the yield management systems used by airlines and car rental companies have been a major source of profit, as prices are varied depending on when the buyer is booking, for how long, for what days of week, and so forth. These characteristics are used as indicators of the value the customer places on the product. Price customization can be achieved by

- developing a product line—such as the hardcover/softcover book situation described above.

- controlling the availability of lower prices, e.g., by making them available only in certain locations.

- varying prices based on observable buyer characteristics, e.g., software suppliers charge lower prices to "upgraders" than to new customers; the logic in

new customers paying a higher price is they value the product more highly since they do not have the option of sticking with the current version. "Upgraders" identify themselves by turning in some proof of ownership, such as support manuals.

- varying prices based on observable characteristics of the transaction, e.g., quantity discounts could be offered if the situation were that big-volume buyers valued the product less than small-volume buyers.

(c) Price Leadership

Some industries feature a large degree of pricing interdependence in an industry, i.e., competitors react to pricing moves. Thus, any pricing decision has to reflect anticipated competitive reaction.

In some industries, legal and effective price leadership has been displayed as firms avoided price cutting in pursuit of share gains. In other industries, price wars have destroyed the profitability of nearly all the players. The tendency toward excessive price competition is particularly acute when

- firms have high fixed, but low variable costs,

- there is little differentiation among competitors' products, and thus consumers largely buy on price,

- industry growth rate is low,

- there are barriers to capacity adjustment, and economies of scale are important.

Thus, a key decision is how to ensure that the firm's actions do not have a negative impact on industry profitability by setting off a round of price cuts.

Analysis Underlying Marketing Strategy Formulation

As reflected at the top of Figure A, the major areas of analysis to be conducted in developing marketing strategy are the "5 C's":

- Customers
- Company
- Competitors
- Collaborators, e.g., channel partners and suppliers
- Context

Customer Analysis

Effective marketing requires in-depth understanding of customers' purchase and usage patterns. As noted above, areas to be considered are

- The Decision Making Unit (DMU)
  - who is involved in the process?
  - what role does each play?

Researchers have identified five major roles in buying situations and it should be understood who assumes each role (more than one individual can play each role and one individual can play more than one role). These roles are

- Initiator(s) – recognize value in solving a particular issue and stimulate search for product.
- Decider(s) – make the choice.
- Influencer(s) – while not making the final decision, have input to it.
- Purchaser(s) – consummate the transaction.
- User(s) – consume the product.

For example, in a decision to purchase a computer for the home, the initiator role may be held by the oldest child who saw value in it for her school assignments; the decider on brand was a relative with computer knowledge; parents and all children influenced the product features and price point; the purchaser was the same as the decider; and the user was all family members.

The second major area is

- Decision-Making Process (DMP)
  - is there search for information?
  - how?
  - what criteria are used to evaluate alternatives?
  - how important are the various attributes, such as price and performance?
  - how did DMU member interact?

Other considerations include:

- where do customers wish to buy?
- how is the product to be used?
- how frequently/intently will it be used?
- how important is the problem which it solves?

These questions need to be addressed at a disaggregate level so market segments can be identified.

Company Analysis

Corporate strengths and weakness need to be understood since the fit of the product to the company is important as well as the fit to the market. Assessing product/company fit requires an understanding of the finances, R&D capability, manufacturing capability, and other assets of the firm.

Competitive Analysis

Marketers need to identify both current and potential competitors. Competitors' strengths and weaknesses must be understood as the firm seeks differentiation possibilities. Similarly, in order to be able to predict and shape competitive reactions, the firm must assess competitors' objectives and strategies.

Collaborator Analysis

To the extent that there are important partners in the marketing system, their positions and goals need to be assessed. Frequently, two key collaborators are the downstream trade (e.g., retailers) and upstream suppliers. With respect to the trade, the firm must understand their cost structure; expectations about margins and allocation of tasks; support and training requirements; and the nature of their relationship with the firm's competitors.

Increasingly, suppliers are being seen as critical collaborators in making marketing strategy work. What is their ability to supply quality product on a reliable basis? How much lead time is required, especially relative to the delivery time commitment to downstream customers?

Context Analysis

Marketing strategy can take very little for granted. The context shapes what is possible and it is always changing. Indeed, spotting important changes in context before a competitor is a reliable path to competitive success. This point is vividly illustrated by the disruption that the Web is producing on 'facts' about distribution and communication that generations of businesspeople took for granted. Clearly, then, marketing strategy analysis must be alert to technological context. What threats, vulnerabilities, opportunities and resources does the technological frontier pose for the firm?

Culture, like technology, can shift and bring surprise unless carefully monitored. As many fortunes are made by anticipating cultural trends as technological trends, as Coca-Cola, McDonalds and Nike attest. Products and services acquire meaning from their place in a culture, and they acquire economic value from that meaning. Value, then, is vulnerable to shifts in the culture (what we call trends and fashions.) The systematic analysis of cultural trends (popularized recently as 'coolhunting' and 'consumer ethnography') is increasingly an integral part of strategy formulation.

Similarly, politics, regulation, law, and social norms are not fixed features of the marketing landscape, but factors to consider and monitor for signs of disruption. Markets such as banking, television and pharmaceuticals operate in particularly unstable settings. It is dangerous to design marketing strategy for such environments without a carefully developed point of view on the regulatory context.

The 5 C's analysis is input to the construction of the marketing strategy. In the end, an economic analysis needs to be done to ensure that everything adds up to a viable business proposition. What are the fixed dollar commitments? What level of unit contribution can be attained, and what is the anticipated associated sales level?

Summary

Devising an effective marketing program requires in-depth analysis to support decision making on a host of interrelated issues. Textbooks have been written to address this general topic[20] and to provide in-depth information on specific topics given in this note. This note's objective was to contribute by bringing together the issues and analyses underlying marketing strategy development to provide a general overview and provide guidance to resources which could be usefully consulted if needed.

---

[20]For general marketing management issues, good texts are T.K. Kinnear, K.L. Bernhardt, and K.A. Krentler, *Principles of Marketing*, 4th ed. (New York: Harper Collins, 1995) and P. Kotler, *Marketing Management: Analysis, Planning, Implementation and Control*, 9th ed. (Englewood Cliffs, N.J.: Prentice-Hall, 1997).

NOTE ON LOW-TECH MARKETING MATH

The Note on Marketing Strategy (9-598-061) describes the scope of marketing analysis needed to provide the basis for the development of a marketing strategy and the supporting implementation plan. The type of in-depth understanding of factors described there is often usefully supplemented by numerical analysis; at times, we need relatively complex, computer-supported analysis. At others, a low-tech approach utilizing the proverbial "back of the envelope" and maybe a calculator does the job.

This note defines key terms and basic calculations useful in both case analysis and real-life marketing decision-making. To accompany this knowledge, one needs to develop some intuition about which type of numbers to look at when. A program of case studies offering repeated exposure to and practice in these issues is a good mechanism for developing skill in using quantitative analysis to develop and support your argument.

Basic Terminology

(a) Types of Cost

Most of the time, a seller hopes to get a price which more than covers his or her cost. In everyday conversation, we might simply say they are trying to make a profit. We would measure that profit as the difference between the revenues taken in and the costs incurred.

It is often useful to make a distinction between two kinds of costs, fixed and variable. We define *fixed costs* as those that remain at a given level regardless of the

Professor Robert J. Dolan prepared this note as the basis for class discussion rather than to illustrate either effective or ineffective handling of an administrative situation. Professor Luc Wathieu provided helpful comments and input.

amount of product produced and sold. An example of a fixed cost would be the firm's expenditure on an advertisement. Regardless of how much Budweiser beer or Nike athletic shoes are sold, the media outlet gets the same fee from the takers of its advertising time or space.

In contrast, *variable costs* are those that change depending upon the amount of product produced and sold. For example, the more beer Budweiser sells the greater are its packaging costs, shipping costs, raw material cost and so forth.

Often in marketing case studies the *variable cost per unit* will be given. For example, the Sealed Air Corporation case (9-582-104) tells us Sealed Air's variable cost for a unit of its SD-120 product (where a "unit" is defined as 1,000 square feet) is $36.31—comprised of two components: manufacturing ($28.38) and transportation ($7.93). In the Warner-Lambert Ireland Case (9-593-008), the company's variable cost for producing a 14-day supply of its Niconil product is 12 Irish pounds.

In reality, the variable cost per unit may depend on the total output produced. Figures 1a and 1b present two different situations which arise.

In both panel (a) and panel (b), we show the fixed cost which is incurred regardless of volume produced. In panel (a), the total cost line, which is the sum of the fixed cost and total variable cost, is a straight line meaning that it increases at a *constant* rate with increases in volume. This means the variable cost per unit is constant. Panel (b) shows the same fixed cost, but the shape of the total cost curve is different. It increases at a *decreasing* rate with volume. This means the variable cost per unit decreases the more the firm produces. This could happen for a number of reasons, e.g. the firm gets more efficient in its manufacturing process or gets a better deal from raw material suppliers as it buys larger amounts from them. In most marketing case studies, we assume that panel (a) represents a reasonable approximation to the reality and take variable cost per unit to be a constant.

(b) Margin Calculations

The Sealed Air case also tells us that the company sells its SD-120 product for $65.35 per unit. We call the difference between the per unit revenue received by firm and the variable cost per unit the *unit margin*. If it's clear from the context, we sometimes drop the "unit" part and simply call this the margin. Another term sometimes used to represent the same quantity is *unit contribution*. We can calculate Sealed Air's margin as $65.35−$36.31=$29.04.

Sometimes, it is useful to state the margin in percentage terms. To get this, divide the unit margin in dollars by the revenue per unit. For example for Sealed Air, this is:

$$\frac{\$29.04}{\$65.35} = .444$$

To put this in percentage terms, multiple by 100, in other words swing the decimal point two places to the right, i.e. Sealed Air's *percent margin* is 44.4%.

Note that in calculating the percent margin we do not divide by the firm's cost, but rather by the revenue it receives. This is something one has to be careful about. For example, consider a retailer and let's say that this retailer gets a 50% margin on jewelry. For an item that costs the retailer $100, this means the selling price is $200. This situation is as shown in Figure 2.

The margin % is defined by (A) ÷ (C), not (A) ÷ (B).

Given this, you figure a selling price given a cost and a % margin like this. (Appendix 1 provides the derivation of this for those interested.)

$$Selling\ Price = \frac{Cost}{1 - [Percent\ Margin/100]}$$

We sometimes look at the margin structure for a channel of distribution. For example, consider Figure 3 which shows the channel for a producer/manufacturer of a "Beginning to Golf" instruction tape.

The manufacturer sells through a wholesaler, who in turns sells to retailers, who then sell to the public. Each of the three members of the channel of distribution (manufacturer, wholesaler, retailer) performs a function and is compensated for it by the margin it receives:

Manufacturer's margin ($3.50)	=	Manufacturer's selling price to distributors ($7.50)	−	Manufacturing cost ($4.00)
Wholesaler's margin ($1.20)	=	Wholesaler's selling price to retailers ($8.70)	−	Price paid to manufacturer ($7.50)
Retailer's margin ($1.30)	=	Retailer's selling price to consumer ($10.00)	−	Price paid to wholesaler ($8.70)

Figure 1a Constant Variable Cost Per Unit

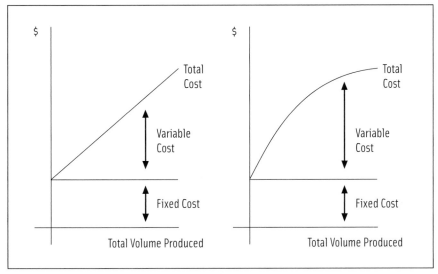

Figure 1b Cost, Margin, Selling per Relationship

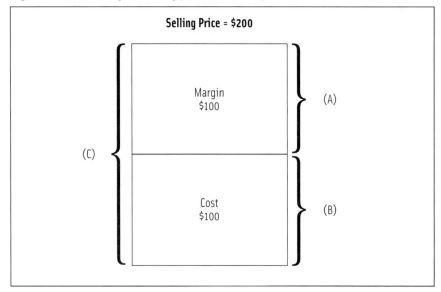

So the dollar margin is a measure of how much each organization makes per unit sold.

In this example, the retailer's percentage margin is 13% margin ($1.30 on his $10 selling price to consumers). The manufacturer's and wholesaler's percentage margins are 46.67% and 13.79% respectively.

Break-Evens

(a) Recovering Fixed Costs

What the organization makes in margins helps it to cover its fixed costs and hopefully produce a profit. We

Figure 2 Price and Cost at Levels in the Channel of Distribution

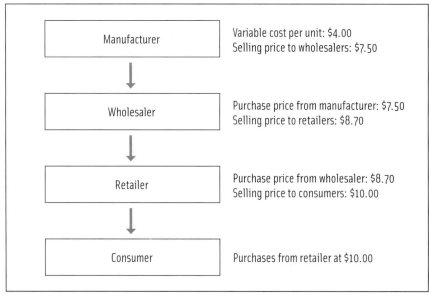

term the number of units sold which just enables the company to cover its fixed costs, its *break-even volume* (BEV). Mathematically, this BEV is given by:

$$BEV = \frac{\text{Fixed Costs in Dollars}}{\text{Dollar Margin per Unit}}$$

For example, say the "Beginning to Golf" tape manufacturer had $700,000 in costs to produce the tape. These costs are fixed because they would not change with the number of tapes he sells. Given the $3.50 margin per tape, to recover his $700,000 investment, he would have to sell the break-even volume of:

$$BEV = \frac{\$700,000}{\$3.50/unit} = 200,000 \ units$$

(b) Changes in Fixed Cost

We can also use this type of calculation to see what other potential investments would have to yield to be worthwhile. For example, suppose a noted golf pro will endorse the tapes for a one-time payment of $175,000. This would be worthwhile if the manufacturer believed that the endorsement would result in added sales of:

$$\frac{\text{Added Costs}}{\text{Dollar Margin per unit}} = \frac{\$175,000}{\$3.50/unit} = 50,000 \ units$$

(c) Changes in Margin Per Unit

Similarly, we can examine the impact of changes in the unit margin. Suppose our noted golf professional did not require a $175,000 fixed payment for his endorsement, but instead wanted a $1 royalty per tape sold. This would cut the manufacturer's margin from $3.50 to $2.50 per tape and we can assess the change in the break-even volume:

$$BEV = \frac{\$700,000}{\$2.50/unit} = 280,000 \ units$$

This represents a 40% increase in the break-even volume from 200,000 units with no endorsement.

Market Size and Share

We would have to know a lot more about the market and the quality of the products before we could make any decisions using these numbers. That is, we don't really know if the 200,000 units required to break-even (assuming we did not go for the endorsement) is a "big number" or one that should be easily attainable for the firm. We really have to assess all the factors set out in the Note on Marketing Strategy to assess that.

In conjunction with that, it is sometimes useful to convert the break-even units number into a share of market number. For example, suppose that some research showed that a total of 5,000,000 golf instruction videos were likely to be sold annually. Then, we could calculate our break-even market share:

$$\begin{array}{l}\text{Break-Even Share of} \\ \text{Golf Video Market}\end{array} = \frac{200,000 \ units}{5,000,000 \ units} = 4\%$$

This might yield added insight. Note however that how we want to define "the market" is a question to consider.

Suppose our research further showed that of the 5,000,000 tapes sold, only 1,000,000 were of the "beginner" variety. It might be more appropriate to look at the share we would need of this market, i.e.

$$\begin{array}{l}\text{Break-Even Share of} \\ \text{Beginner Golf Video} \\ \text{Market}\end{array} = \frac{200,000 \ units}{1,000,000 \ units} = 20\%$$

We also need to select the time horizon which is most appropriate for us. This will vary with the specific situation. The two share figures we calculated here implicitly assumed that we were looking to recover our fixed costs in one year.

Impact of Price Decisions

Figure 3 shows the drivers of profit. To this point, we have largely focused on the right-hand branch of this profit tree. Simple calculations also can help in assessing price decisions shown on this left-hand branch.

Consider a manufacturer selling at $100 per unit and achieving sales of 1 million units per year. Assume variable cost per unit is $60 and, thus, his unit margin is $40. Panel (a) of Figure 4 shows this situation. The shaded rectangle represents the total margin of $40 million (1 million total units times $40 unit margin). The total contribution or margin can always be represented as a rectangle on a price and unit volume graph since it is the product of the unit margin (rectangle width) and sales volume in units (rectangle height).

Suppose management questioned whether the current $100 price yielded the highest possible total margin and was considering alternative prices in the range of plus or minus 20% from the current price. As a first step,

Figure 3 The Drivers of Profit

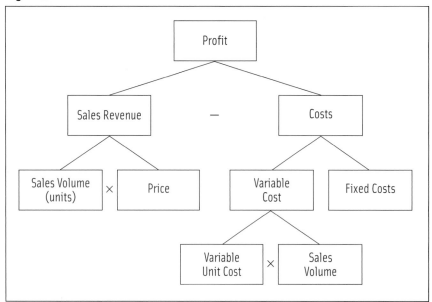

one might want to know the unit sales volume required to maintain the $40 million total margin with alternative prices.

Consider the 20% price cut alternative. This is shown in panel (B). An $80 price with unchanged variable unit cost of $60 reduces the unit margin from $40 to $20. Thus, the company now has to sell twice as many units as it did at a price of $100 to achieve the same total margin and profit. With 2 million units sold at $80, sales revenue would increase to $160 million, but total margin remains at $40 million. Since the total margin is unchanged, the area of the shaded rectangle is the same as in panel (a). While the price reduction is only 20%, the reduction in unit margin is 50%. The sales increase required to compensate for this smaller margin accordingly is 100%. We can always think of the volume adjustment needed to keep contribution the same as a problem of keeping the area of the shaded rectangle the same. As we decrease price, the rectangle gets thinner and so must get taller. As we think about price increases, the rectangle gets fatter and hence can get shorter and still have the same area.

The 20% price-increase scenario is summarized in panel (C) of the figure. With a $120 price, unit margin increases to $60, thereby requiring only 666,666 units to be sold to generate $40 million total margin. Thus, a 33.3% decrease in volume will have total margin unchanged. If unit sales decline by less than 33.3%, the price increase would drive total margin and profit up.

As we see, price decreases and increases have highly leveraged effects. A seemingly small reduction in price can have a large negative impact on unit contribution, requiring a tremendous increase in sales volume to generate the same profit. A small percentage price increase can have a strong positive effect on unit margin, creating a large acceptable decrease in sales volume while still retaining the margin level. These effects are most pronounced when variable costs are high and unit margins small.

Using the Numbers

In this note we have shown how one can calculate a quantity given other quantities. Essentially, we showed how to translate some facts or estimates into other facts/estimates. This translation process is useful if the end result is an accurately derived fact/estimate which is suggestive of what one should do as a manager.

The key point is this: numbers often become significant in an argument when there is some benchmark to compare them to. In marketing, such benchmarks are developed from understanding the market size, growth rate, and competitive activity. Calculations in and of themselves are useless unless combined with other information to provide a meaningful context.

As noted at the outset, useful numbers work requires intuition about what quantities to calculate. That

Figure 4 The Effect of Price on Total Margin

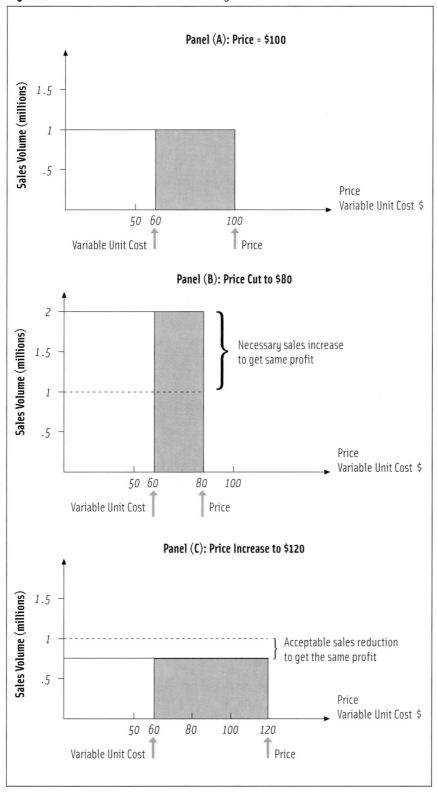

intuition will develop through practice on bringing numbers to bear on arguments in a well-connected way. This short note does little to develop that intuition. Our goals were more modest, i.e., to specify terminology, mechanics, and suggest potential applications. The goal of the quantitative analysis must always be kept clear: to help in making marketing policy decisions.

APPENDIX 1

Suppose we know a firm's unit cost C and its percentage margin M. Let P = price it receives. By definition of the percentage margin we know:

$$[M / 100] = \frac{P - C}{P} \qquad (1)$$

We want to take equation (1) and solve it for P. As a first step, multiply both sides of (1) by P to get:

$$P[M / 100] = P - C \qquad (2)$$

Subtract P from both sides:

$$P[M / 100] - P = -C \qquad (3)$$

Factor out the P on the left-hand side:

$$P[M / 100 - 1] = -C$$

Multiply both sides by: $\frac{-1}{[M / 100 - 1]}$

$$P = \frac{C}{[1 - M / 100]}$$

Example: A firm's cost is $25 and it wants to make a margin percentage of 40% (M=40). Therefore, its price has to be:

$$\frac{\$25}{1 - 40/100}$$

$$= \frac{25}{.6} = \$41.66$$

To check: at $41.66, the margin is $41.66 − $25 = $16.66. Thus, the percentage margin is $\frac{\$16.66}{\$41.66} \times 100 = 40\%$ as required.

SEALED AIR CORPORATION

The president and chief executive officer of Sealed Air Corporation, T. J. Dermot Dunphy, explained the firm's 25% average annual growth in net sales and net earnings from 1971 to 1980:

> The company's history has been characterized by technical accomplishment and market leadership. During the last 10 years we built on our development of the *first* closed-cell, lightweight cushioning material, introduced the *first* foam-in-place packaging system, and engineered the *first* complete solar heating system for swimming pools. We intend to follow the same management guidelines in the 1980s. We intend to seek market leadership because market leadership optimizes profit, and foster technological leadership because it is the only long-term guarantee of market leadership.

In July 1981 Barrett Hauser, product manager of Sealed Air's Air Cellular Products, was reflecting on Dunphy's management philosophy as he considered how Sealed Air should respond to some unanticipated competition in the protective packaging market. As product manager, Hauser was responsible for the closed-cell, light-weight cushioning material that Dunphy had mentioned. Sealed Air's registered trademark name for this product was AirCap.[1] AirCap cushioning materials had always faced a variety of competitors in the protective packaging market. More recently, however, several small regional producers had invented around Sealed Air's manufacturing process patents and begun to market cheap imitations of AirCap in the United States.

Robert J. Dolan, associate professor, prepared this case as the basis for class discussion rather than to illustrate either effective or ineffective handling of an administrative situation. Certain nonpublic data have been disguised.

AirCap Cushioning and Its Competitors

AirCap cushioning was a clear, laminated plastic sheet containing air bubbles of uniform size (see Exhibit 1). The feature that differentiated AirCap cushioning from all other bubble products was its "barrier-coating": each AirCap bubble was coated on the inside with saran. This greatly increased air retention, meaning less compression of the material during shipment and, consequently, better protection. Barrier-coating and its customer benefits had been the central theme of Sealed Air's AirCap cushioning selling effort for 10 years.

Between 1971 and 1980 Sealed Air and Astro Packaging of Hawthorne, New Jersey, were the only air bubble packaging material producers in the United States. Sealed Air licensed Astro to use Sealed Air's patented technology. Astro produced two types of bubbles: a barrier bubble similar to AirCap,[2] and an uncoated bubble. Its sales were split about evenly between the two. In 1980 Astro's total U.S. sales were approximately $10.5 million, compared with $25.35 million in U.S. sales for AirCap cushioning. Sealed Air's market education had made customers aware of the advantages of coated bubbles; consequently, uncoated bubbles had never achieved greater than a 15% dollar share of the U.S. market before 1980.

In July 1981 uncoated bubble operations were being set up in Ohio, California, and New York. GAFCEL, which served the metropolitan New York market, was the only competitor yet to achieve significant sales volume. Two GAFCEL salespeople—one full time, the other about half time—had reached a $1 million annual sales rate. Several of AirCap's distributors had taken on the GAFCEL line.

Hauser was preparing to recommend Sealed Air's reaction to these somewhat unanticipated competitors. The firm could produce an uncoated bubble as cheaply as GAFCEL within a month with no major capital investment; it could run on machines used for another

---

[1] Sealed Air, AirCap, and Instapak are registered ® trademarks of Sealed Air Corporation. Solar Pool Blanket is a TM trademark of the same corporation.

[2] Astro's barrier bubble and the AirCap bubble differed in both manufacturing process and coating material. Astro used nylon rather than saran. The basic idea of reinforcing the polyethylene bubbles to improve air retention was, however, the same.

Sealed Air product. If Hauser were to recommend that the historic champion of barrier-coating offer an uncoated bubble, he would have to specify timing, the marketing program for the new product, and any adjustments in policies for AirCap cushioning and Sealed Air's other products. As Hauser thought about his options, he again flipped through the training manual recently distributed to Sealed Air's sales force: "How to Sell against Uncoated Bubbles."

The Protective Packaging Market

The three major use segments of the protective packaging market were:

1. Positioning, blocking, and bracing: These protective materials had to secure large, heavy, usually semi rugged items in a container. Typical applications included shipment of motors and computer peripherals.

2. Flexible wraps: These materials came under less pressure per square foot. Applications included glassware, small spare parts, and light medical instruments.

3. Void fill: These materials were added to prevent movement during shipping when an item and its protective wrap (if any) did not fill its carton.

The positioning, blocking, and bracing market was unique because of the heavier weights of items shipped. Flexible wrap and void fill were sometimes hard to separate because it was convenient to use the same product for both functions. The key distinction was that loose fills (for instance, polystyrene beads) dominated the void fill market but provided no cushioning protection and, hence, did not qualify as flexible wrap.

Until 1970 most materials used for protective packaging were produced primarily for other purposes. Heavy, paper-based products had dominated the market. Sealed Air was one of the first companies to approach the market with a customer orientation, i.e., it began product development with an assessment of packagers' needs. Since then a variety of products specifically designed for protective packaging had appeared.

Sealed Air served these markets with two products:

1. Instapak® foam-in-place systems (1980 worldwide sales of $38.8 million) could accommodate any application, though their most advantageous use was for heavy items. In this process two liquid chemicals were pumped into a shipping container. The chemicals rapidly expanded to form a foam cushion around the product. Instapak's comparative advantage resulted in a majority of applications in positioning, blocking, and bracing.

2. AirCap bubbles (1980 worldwide sales of $34.3 million) primarily served the flexible wrap and void fill markets.

In addition to coated and uncoated polyethylene air bubbles, there were two major competitors in these markets: paper-based products (cellulose wadding, single-face corrugated, and indented kraft), and foams (polyurethane, polypropylene, and polyethylene).

An excerpt from an AirCap promotional brochure in Exhibit 2 shows how Sealed Air positioned AirCap as a cost-effective substitute for these competitive products and loose fills. The brochure first pointed out the cost savings from AirCap cushioning, then presented results of "fatigue" and "original thickness retention" tests to demonstrate AirCap's protective superiority. Exhibit 3 compares products competitive with AirCap cushioning and Exhibit 4 gives their U.S. list prices, which represent relative costs for any order size from an end user. Quantity discounts were offered on all materials.

Buying Influences

The proliferation of packaging products and the lack of easily demonstrable universal superiority caused confusion among end users. For example, products such as pewter mugs were shipped around the United States in AirCap cushioning, Astro coated bubbles, or even old newspapers.

Users were a varied lot. Some bought on a scientific price/performance basis. They understood "cushioning curves" such as those in Exhibit 5. Sealed Air could provide independently measured cushioning curves for competitive products as well as its own. Regardless, many firms did their own testing.

At the other end of the spectrum were firms with "a purchasing-department mentality," as some packaging materials suppliers put it. Price per square foot was their first consideration, delivery their second. As one Sealed Air executive commented, "To these people, cushioning curves are like accounting numbers. They think you can make them say anything you want."

There were no systematically collected data on the buying process or the extent to which price dominated performance in the purchase decision. Based on his experience as a district sales manager and now product manager, Hauser guessed that a packaging engineer influenced about 40% of the material purchase decisions.

The U.S. Market

In 1980, dollar sales by segment in the U.S. protective packaging market were:

- *Positioning, blocking, and bracing:* $585 million
- *Flexible wrap:* $126 million
- *Void fill:* $15.6 million

Exhibit 6 breaks down total sales for the flexible wrap market by product type for 1975, 1978, and 1980.

AirCap cushioning annual sales in the United States since 1972 were:

Year	Gross Sales (in millions)	Year	Gross Sales (in millions)
1972	$7.7	1977	$16.4
1973	10.0	1978	18.4
1974	13.0	1979	21.2
1975	12.8	1980	25.3
1976	14.6		

Despite the high cost of coated bubbles relative to the uncoated product, Sealed Air had kept most of the U.S. air bubble market. Key factors were Sealed Air's patent protection and licensing of only one competitor, extensive market education, and the packaging mentality in the United States. Packaging engineers enjoyed a status in U.S. organizations not accorded them elsewhere. Packaging supplies were viewed as a productive, cost-saving resource. In contrast, recent research by Sealed Air indicated that many European firms viewed packaging supplies as "expendable commodities."

The European Market

Sealed Air had manufacturing operations in England and France and a sales organization in Germany.[3] It was the only company selling a coated product in these countries. Sales figures for 1980 were:

Country	Total Bubble Sales	AirCap Sales
England	$3,649,000	$2,488,500
France	4,480,000	592,200
Germany	7,688,000	404,600

England. Sealed Air had developed the protective packaging market here and had good distribution. Later on, Sansetsu, a Japanese firm, began marketing a high-quality uncoated product made in Germany. Prices for the uncoated bubble were 50% less than the cost of comparably sized AirCap cushioning. Sansetsu and other uncoated bubble manufacturers had chipped away at Sealed Air's one-time 90% market share. The most pessimistic Sealed Air distributors estimated that the firm would lose 50% of its current market share to uncoated bubbles within three years.

France. Here, Sealed Air owned an uncoated bubble manufacturer SIBCO, with sales of $750,000 in 1980. In 1972 SIBCO was the only marketer of uncoated bubbles in France. Two major competitors, one with superior production facilities, had entered the market. Uncoated bubbles were priced about 40% lower than AirCap, and price was the key buying determinant. The major French distributor of AirCap cushioning had a 50-50 mix of coated and uncoated sales in 1978. In 1980 the mix had changed to 70-30 (uncoated over coated), with 90% of new bubble applications being uncoated.

Germany. AirCap cushioning was a late entrant (1973) to the German market and never held commanding share. Moreover, from 1978 to 1980, it had lost share at a rate of 20% to 30% per year. Sansetsu had an efficient manufacturing facility in Germany and sold approximately $6 million of uncoated product in 1980. (The price for uncoated was about 35% less than for coated.)

AirCap Cushioning

Grades and Sales

AirCap cushioning grades differed in bubble height and thickness of the plastic films. Bubble heights were designated by a letter code, and the plastic films came in four thicknesses (see Table A). Sealed Air produced eight differ-

Table A Differing Grades of AirCap Cushioning

Bubble Heights	
SB:	$\frac{1}{8}$ in. high, used for surface protection when cushioning requirements were minimal.
SC:	$\frac{3}{16}$ in. high, used primarily for wrapping small, intricate items, possibly for larger items if not very fragile.
ST:	$\frac{5}{16}$ in. high, used in same kinds of applications as SC grade, except with slightly greater cushioning requirements. Also used as a void fill.
SD:	$\frac{1}{2}$ in. high, used for large, heavy, or fragile items or as a void fill.
Plastic Film Thicknesses	
Light duty (110):	each layer of film was 1 mil (^{1}/1,000 of an inch) thick; used for light loads.
Regular duty (120):	one layer of 1 mil and one layer of 2 mils; for loads up to 50 lbs. per sq. ft.
Heavy duty (240):	one layer of 2 mils and one of 4 mils; for loads up to 100 lbs. per sq. ft.
Super duty (480):	one layer of 4 mils and one of 8; for loads over 100 lbs. per sq. ft.

[3]The firm also had a manufacturing facility in Canada and a sales organization in Japan. Sealed Air licensees operated manufacturing facilities in Australia, Mexico, South Africa, and Spain.

ent height/thickness combinations (see Table B). Some of the known end uses for each grade are shown in Exhibit 7.

Sales by grade for the last six months of 1979 and the first six months of 1980 are shown in Table C.

Pricing

All AirCap cushioning was sold through distributors. Prices reflected Sealed Air's costs and the prices of competitive products. Variable costs and prices to the distributor are shown in Table D.

Sealed Air's suggested resale price list is shown in Exhibit 8. Largely because of its selective distribution policy, distributors generally followed this list. The price schedule entailed quantity discounts for end users. Thus, distributor margins varied with the size of the customer's individual order. (Quantity price was determined by the total square footage of a single order, combining all grades,

ordered for shipment at one time to a single destination.) In some major metropolitan areas, up to 50% of AirCap business was truckload/railcar orders by end users. In this event Sealed Air shipped the material from its plant directly to the end user; the distributor received a 10% margin and handled user credit and technical service. In some markets the percentage of direct shipments was as low as 10%.

Selling Effort

Sealed Air's U.S. operation consisted of 7 regional manufacturing operations, 62 salespeople (each selling AirCap cushioning, Instapak, and other Sealed Air products), and 370 distributors. To control the shipping cost of its bulky product, Sealed Air had regional manufacturing operations in three eastern states, Ohio, Illinois, Texas, and California. The regional presence, however, had proven to be an effective sales promotion device as well.

Table B Eight Different Height/Thicknesses by Sealed Air

Height (inches)	Thickness			
	110	120	240	480
SB-$\frac{1}{8}$	X			
SC-$\frac{3}{16}$		X	X	
ST-$\frac{5}{16}$		X	X	
SD-$\frac{1}{2}$		X	X	X

Table C AirCap Sales by Grade

Grade	Sales in 1,000 Square Feet	
	July–December 1979	January–June 1980
1/8 in.		
SB-110	59,128	48,513
3/16 in.		
SC-120	76,349	81,014
SC-240	5,036	4,426
5/16 in.		
ST-120	31,912	42,234
ST-240	4,369	3,914
1/2 in.		
SD-120	44,252	43,624
SD-240	25,202	21,799
SD-480	3,138	1,358
Total sales	249,386	246,882

Note: In addition, because SB-110 could not compete in price against foams for many surface protection applications, Sealed Air introduced an A-100 grade in January 1980. The A-100 bubble was 3/32 in. high—the shortest coated bubble Sealed Air could make with available technology. January to June 1980 sales of A-100 were 17,802,000 sq. ft.

Table D AirCap Variable Costs and Distributor Prices (in dollars per 1,000 sq. ft.)

Grade	Manufacturing	Freight	(1) Total Variable Cost	(2) Price to Distributor for Truckload Delivery[a]	(2) - (1) Sealed Air Dollar Margin
A-100 ($\frac{3}{32}$ in.)	$12.46	$1.32	$13.78	$20.60	$6.82
SB-110 ($\frac{1}{8}$ in.)	14.02	1.99	16.01	30.25	14.24
SC-120 ($\frac{3}{16}$ in.)	17.92	2.64	20.56	43.50	22.94
SC-240 ($\frac{3}{16}$ in.)	29.83	2.64	32.47	56.30	23.83
ST-120 ($\frac{5}{16}$ in.)	25.36	5.29	30.65	51.40	20.75
ST-240 ($\frac{5}{16}$ in.)	32.83	5.29	38.12	65.35	27.23
SD-120 ($\frac{1}{2}$ in.)	28.38	7.93	36.31	65.35	29.04
SD-240 ($\frac{1}{2}$ in.)	36.52	7.93	44.45	78.60	34.15
SD-480 ($\frac{1}{2}$ in.)	62.88	7.93	70.81	140.90	70.09

[a]Less than truckload shipments were priced 15% to 20% higher. Consequently, distributors almost always ordered in truckload quantities. They were allowed to mix grades within an order. Depending on the grade ordered, a truckload could contain 70,000 sq. ft. (all SD-480) to 420,000 sq. ft. (all A-100).

Before Instapak was acquired in 1976, 28 salespeople devoted 90% of their time to AirCap cushioning products. In 1981 the 62-person force was expected to allocate time as follows: 60% to Instapak systems, 35% to AirCap cushioning, and 5% to other Sealed Air products. (Exhibit 9 shows Sealed Air sales by product line and other financial data.)

Part of Sealed Air's market share leadership philosophy was a consultative selling approach. Salespeople spent about half their time making cost studies at end-user locations. With the help of Sealed Air's packaging labs, salespeople attempted to show how their products could save on material and labor cost and reduce damage in the end user's particular situation. Distributors' salespeople took orders on AirCap cushioning but did little to demonstrate AirCap use and application to customers. If a distributor's salesperson identified a potential AirCap account, he or she would inform the Sealed Air salesperson and a joint call would be arranged. In this way the potential account learned about the product and ordering procedures simultaneously.

Distributors sometimes complained to Sealed Air about the level of AirCap selling effort. Since distributor's margins on AirCap cushioning were generally higher than the 10% to 12% for Instapak sales, distributors were not happy with Sealed Air's greater allocation of salesperson time to Instapak. Some distributors said they would be content if the salesperson in their area really allocated 35% to AirCap; some claimed the actual AirCap selling effort amounted to only 20%. Instapak's sales growth had been impressive, but some Sealed Air executives felt this had cost them some distributor satisfaction.

Both distributors and end users regarded Sealed Air's salespeople as among the best trained and most knowledgeable in the packaging industry. Sales force salaries were above average. They were composed of a base salary plus commissions of 2% on net AirCap sales and 1% on net sales of all other products, including Instapak. (As an added incentive Sealed Air gave salespeople $75 for each Instapak dispenser placed. It took back $75 for each one removed.) In a typical week a salesperson called on 20 end users and checked in with two or three distributors.

U.S. Distributors

During the 1970s Sealed Air invested heavily in developing a selected distributor network. The firm had 370 distributors by 1980. Sealed Air considered 135 of these their "first-line distributors" because they collectively handled over 80% of its business. The 20 largest AirCap distributors handled about 35% of the business. Larger distributors typically carried both Instapak foam-in-place and AirCap cushioning. The largest distributor of Sealed Air products had 1980 Sealed Air sales of approximately $2 million, just about half of which were AirCap.

Distributors traditionally tried to be full-line houses—capable of meeting each customer's complete packaging needs—so they carried a broad range of products. A survey of Sealed Air's first-line distributors showed that 83% carried loose fills, 65% carried polyethylene foam, and 29% carried Du Pont's polypropylene foam. Although most carried competitive products, distributors had displayed loyalty to Sealed Air and AirCap

Table E GAFCEL's Distributor Prices per 1,000 Sq. Ft.

	SO-22 ($\frac{3}{16}$ in.)	LO-22 ($\frac{1}{2}$ in.)
Distributor truckload	$31.63	$36.03
Suggested resale by order size:		
1,000 sq. ft	$56.54	$75.24
20,000 sq. ft	47.12	62.70
40,000 sq. ft	42.84	57.07
100,000 sq. ft	39.40	44.68
Truckload	34.79	39.63

cushioning. Sealed Air, in turn, had kept to its selective distribution policy.

Competing Uncoated Bubble Cushioning

Sealed Air considered both types of bubbles made by Astro as inferior products. GAFCEL, the new regional producer, made a "decent product" in Hauser's estimation; he felt that its success to date came largely at Astro's expense.

The New York metropolitan market was ideal for the new producer. It was not customer- or distributor-loyal, and price was a key variable. Sealed Air's estimate of GAFCEL sales rates was $750,000 per year for the $\frac{1}{2}$-in.-high uncoated bubble and $250,000 per year for the $\frac{3}{16}$-in. bubble. Both had two layers of film 2 mils each.

GAFCEL's distributor prices for truckload shipments and suggested resale prices to end users for the metropolitan New York market are shown in Table E. (Astro's uncoated bubble prices are in Exhibit 4.)

Sealed Air had not yet extensively tested the GAFCEL uncoated bubble. Although it was better than Astro's uncoated, its performance would not be dramatically different from that found in previous uncoated testing (see Exhibit 2). In terms of cushioning curves, the $\frac{1}{2}$ in. GAFCEL bubble was comparable to Sealed Air's ST-120 or SD-120 for very light loads, not greater than 0.15 lbs./sq. in. pressure. At greater loads, however, the accelera-tion curve would increase rapidly, moving above even the SB-110 by pressures of 0.25 lbs./sq. in. (see Exhibit 5).

Sealed Air Decisions

Sealed Air had conducted a good deal of research on manufacturing uncoated bubble products. It knew the best production process would be similar to that currently used for its Solar Pool Blankets™. Thus, the firm could begin manufacture of an uncoated product quickly in its New Jersey plant. Likely distributor response to a Sealed Air uncoated product was difficult to predict. Some distributors had requested it, but others regularly complained that there were already too many coated grades.

Preliminary estimates of the variable costs for producing Sealed Air uncoated bubbles were $19 per 1,000 sq. ft. for $\frac{3}{16}$ in. height, $20 per 1,000 sq. ft. for $\frac{5}{16}$ in., and $21 per 1,000 sq. ft. for $\frac{1}{2}$ in. Freight cost depended on bubble height and distance shipped. Although GAFCEL's production process was completely different, its production costs were believed to be comparable.

Hauser now had to decide whether to recommend that Sealed Air enter the uncoated bubble market (with an about-face on its previous exclusive emphasis on coated bubbles), or whether to suggest some other reaction to its new competitors.

Exhibit 1 AirCap® Products and Uses

Cushioning

AirCap® air bubble cushioning protects products against shock and vibration during handling and shipping by literally floating them on a cushion of air. This material offers consistent performance because our unique *barrier-coating* guarantees air retention. AirCap withstands repeated impact since it will not fatigue or take a compression set. Cushioning applications include a range of products from lightweight retail items to delicate power supplies weighing several hundred pounds. Choose the grade that best fits *your* cushioning application!

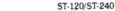

SC-120	ST-120/ST-240	SD-120/SD-240/SD-480
Regular Duty	Regular, Heavy Duty	Regular, Heavy, Super Duty

Protective Wrap/Interleaving

AirCap is an excellent "protective wrap" material and ideal for "interleaving" between similarly shaped items. It is clean, non-abrasive, easy to use and provides superior surface protection. Lay your product on AirCap sheeting, fold it over and your product is fully protected! Typical protective wrap/interleaving applications include china, glassware, printed circuit boards, and spare parts.

SB-110	SC-120/SC-240	ST-120
Light Duty	Regular, Heavy Duty	Regular Duty

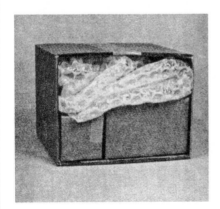

Void Fill

When a void in a package is not completely filled, the cushioned product may migrate within the shipping container. This movement is a major cause of damage in transit. Since large *regular-duty* AirCap bubbles do not compress, they fill voids effectively and eliminate product movement. Simply stuff AirCap sheeting into the carton, (left) or use an economical rolled "log". It's easy, clean, lightweight and cost efficient!

ST-120	SD-120
Regular Duty	Regular Duty

Exhibit 2 Sealed Air Presents AirCap as Cost-Effective Substitute

Typical Cost-Savings Comparisons

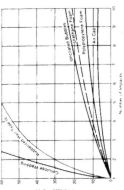

AirCap Vs. Corrugated Inserts

A manufacturer using corrugated inserts, cellulose wadding and polyethylene bags eliminated the need to inventory many packaging components (right), and reduced labor 84% by switching to AirCap (left).

Item	Corrugated Package	AirCap Package
Carton	$ .55	$ .55
Inner packaging	.80	1.05
Labor	.83	.13
Freight	2.60	2.40
Total cost	$4.78	$4.13
Savings using AirCap		$ .65

AirCap Vs. Loose Fills

A distributing firm found that it needed an excessive amount of flowable to prevent product migration. A new AirCap package (left) using a simple criss-cross technique resulted in reduced material, shipping, labor and carton costs.

Item	Loose Fill Package	AirCap Package
Carton	$ .73	$ .47
Inner packaging	.75	.54
Labor	.42	.25
Freight	3.02	2.72
Total cost	$4.92	$3.98
Savings using AirCap		$ .94

AirCap Vs. Thin-Grade Foams

An electronic service center employing the use of a thin-grade foam (right) required many layers of wrapping to protect against shock and vibration. Large AirCap bubbles (left) provided superior performance and lower packaging costs.

Item	Foam Package	AirCap Package
Carton	$ .46	$ .38
Inner packaging	1.33	.87
Labor	.66	.33
Freight	4.09	3.94
Total cost	$6.54	$5.52
Savings using AirCap		$1.02

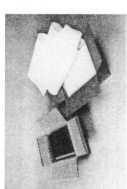

AirCap Vs. Cellulose Wadding

A metering firm discovered it needed only half as much AirCap to achieve the same performance that cellulose wadding provided (right). In addition to lowering material costs, AirCap (left) is clean, lint free, non-abrasive and lightweight.

Item	Cellulose Wadding Package	AirCap Package
Carton	$ .30	$ .22
Inner packaging	.22	.12
Labor	.25	.08
Freight	1.35	1.20
Total cost	$2.12	$1.62
Savings using AirCap		$ .50

Resists Fatigue

In the transportation environment, packages are subjected to many jolts, bumps and shocks that can potentially cause damage. To function effectively, a cushioning material must retain its ability to protect over a series of repeated impacts. The loss of protective ability during repeated impact is termed "material fatigue".

This graph (left) indicates the increased shock an average product (0.25 psi) will receive during a ten-drop sequence from 24 inches. Test results show barrier-coated AirCap outperforms all materials tested.

BARRIER-COATING
Each individual AirCap bubble is barrier-coated to retain the air

Retains Original Thickness

When a load is placed on a cushioning material two things occur that may contribute to a deterioration in its performance. First, is the immediate compression of the material. Second, is the additional, more gradual loss of thickness, termed "creep". Generally, excessive thickness loss of a material results in increased material usage in cushioning and dunnage applications. Creep may contribute to product damage as the loss of thickness creates a void in a package, allowing the product to move, shift or migrate.

This chart (left) demonstrates how barrier-coated AirCap retains its original thickness better than all materials tested and provides product protection throughout the entire packaging, shipping, handling and storage cycle.

Material Tested	Initial Thickness Loss Upon 0.4 psi Load	Gradual Thickness Loss After 30 Days	Total Thickness Loss
AirCap SD 240	7%	7%	14%
Polypropylene Foam	19%	11%	30%
Polyethylene Foam	16%	24%	40%
Cellulose Wadding	26%	12%	38%
Rubberized Hair IV	24%	27%	51%
Uncoated Bubbles (Large)	14%	50%	64%
Urethane Foam (1.25 pcf)	53%	—	—
Embossed Polyethylene (Max)	54%	—	—

*30 day evaluation not conducted due to excessive initial thickness loss

IMMEDIATE THICKNESS LOSS (CREEP)
AirCap retains its original thickness upon the immediate application of a load. (See Below).

UNLOADED   LOADED
BARRIER-COATED AirCap (0.4 psi)

UNLOADED   LOADED
CONVENTIONAL CELLULOSE MATERIAL (0.4 psi)

GRADUAL THICKNESS LOSS (CREEP)
AirCap's unique barrier-coating retains the air more effectively than uncoated bubbles, eliminating creep.

DAY 1   DAY 30
BARRIER-COATED AirCap (0.4 psi)

DAY 1   DAY 30
UNCOATED BUBBLES (0.4 psi)

Exhibit 3 Competitive Product Information

1. *Cellulose wadding (a paper-based product which tries to trap air between piles of sheeting)*
   - Major suppliers:
        Jiffy Packaging, Hillside, N.J.
        CelluProducts Co., Patterson, N.C.
   - Sizes available:
        Thickness of 0.17 in., 0.25 in., 0.37 in., 0.50 in.
   - Advantages/disadvantages:
        Much cheaper than AirCap in thin grades; will not mark item wrapped; heavier than AirCap (3–4 lbs. per cu. ft. vs. less than 1 lb. for AirCap) meaning higher shipping cost; excessive compression under heavy loads (see test results, **Exhibit 2**).
2. *Corrugated products (sheets of ribbed cardboard, often cut and perforated to specific sizes)*
   - Major suppliers:
        About 800 firms manufacturing in 47 states, including larger paper companies.
   - Advantages/disadvantages:
        Single face (cardboard with ribs on one side) appreciably cheaper than AirCap on square-foot basis; labor cost of using corrugated usually very high; poor cushioning.
3. *Polyethylene foam (thin, smooth, rigid sheets of low-density foam)*
   - Major suppliers:
        Sentinel Foam Products, Hyannis, Mass.
        CelluProducts Co., Patterson, N.C.
        Jiffy Packaging, Hillside, N.J.
   - Sizes available:
        48 or 68 in. wide rolls of thickness $\frac{1}{16}, \frac{3}{32}, \frac{3}{16}, \frac{1}{4}$ in.
   - Advantages/disadvantages:
        Appreciably cheaper than AirCap in thin grades on square-foot basis; does not mark item wrapped; rigid product means hard to work with; tendency to tear; cushioning inferior to AirCap; more expensive than AirCap in thicker grades.
4. *Polypropylene foam (thin, coarse, rigid sheets of low-density foam)*
   - Major supplier:
        Du Pont Microfoam
   - Sizes available:
        Standard 72 in. wide rolls of thickness $\frac{1}{6}, \frac{3}{32}, \frac{3}{16}, \frac{1}{4}$ in.
   - Advantages/disadvantages:
        Basically the same as for polyethylene foam.
5. *Loose fills (expanded polystyrene beads, peanuts, etc.)*
   - Major suppliers:
        Many small firms
   - Advantages/disadvantages:
        50% cheaper than AirCap on cubic foot basis; messy; poor cushioning.
6. *Uncoated bubbles (sheets of small air bubbles made of polyethylene film)*
   - Major producer:
        Astro, Hawthorne, N.J. (Sealed Air licensee)
   - Sizes available:
        48 in. wide roll standard, bubble heights $\frac{3}{16}, \frac{1}{4}, \frac{1}{2}$ in. Bubbles also varied in the thickness of the films used. Generally, thicknesses were 1, 2, 3, or 4 mils with increasing film thickness giving greater strength.
   - Advantages/disadvantages:
        Cheaper than comparable height coated bubble; excessive air loss over time (about 65% height loss under 50 lbs. per sq. ft. pressure over 30 days vs. 15% for AirCap).
7. *Competitive coated bubble (essentially the same as uncoated bubble except nylon film coating added)*
   - Major supplier:
        Astro, Hawthorne, N.J. (Sealed Air licensee)
   - Sizes available:
        48 in. wide roll standard, bubble heights $\frac{1}{8}, \frac{3}{16}, \frac{1}{4}, \frac{1}{2}$, 1 in.
   - Advantages/disadvantages:
        Under heavy loading, nylon barrier holds up better than Sealed Air's saran barrier; poor quality control (bubble heights generally 13% less than specified).

Exhibit 4 Suggested End User Prices (in dollars) for Major Competitive Products

1. Paper-Based

Cellulose Wadding (Jiffy Packaging)		Single-Face Corrugated
Thickness (in.)	Price	
0.17	$27.70	$22.75
0.25	37.40	
0.37	50.60	
0.50	65.00	

2. Foams

Thickness (in.)	Jiffy Packaging (polyethylene)	Sentinel Products (polyethylene)	Du Pont Microfoam (polypropylene)
$\frac{1}{16}$	$20.30	$18.20	$17.20
$\frac{3}{32}$	25.90	24.00	25.17
$\frac{1}{8}$	34.15	32.70	34.90
$\frac{3}{16}$	53.35	49.40	53.86
$\frac{3}{8}$	na	na	109.72

3. Competitive Bubbles (Astro)

Coated Nylon			Uncoated—Polyethylene		
Bubble Height (in.)	Film Thickness[a] (mils)	Price	Bubble Height (in.)	Film Thickness[a] (mils)	Price
$\frac{1}{8}$	1 and 1	$35.25			
$\frac{3}{16}$	1 and 2	49.50	$\frac{3}{16}$	2 and 3	$47.00
$\frac{1}{4}$	1 and 2	57.00	$\frac{1}{4}$	2 and 3	54.50
$\frac{1}{2}$	1 and 2	71.75	$\frac{1}{2}$	2 and 4	65.75
$\frac{1}{2}$	2 and 4	87.75			
1	1 and 2	90.00			
1	2 and 4	110.00			

Note: Prices are per 1,000 sq. ft. based on a 50,000 sq. ft. order.

a. Each bubble is made of two layers of film. Thicknesses shown are for individual layers in mils. Thicker film produces a stronger product.

Exhibit 5 Comparative Cushioning Performance by Grade

Engineered To Provide Superior Cushioning

The test data on the graph below was developed by the Lansmont Corporation, an independent testing laboratory. The test method used closely simulates actual shipping conditions, and employs the use of an enclosed test block and shock machine. Five bottom drops were executed from 24 inches at each static stress. The last four drops were averaged to arrive at data points used to develop each cushioning effectiveness curve. This data illustrates AirCap's superior performance over a wide range of loadings, and may be used for comparison and to specify the best Air-Cap grade and thickness for your cushioning requirements. (SD-240 curves taken from data provided in Military Handbook 304-A).

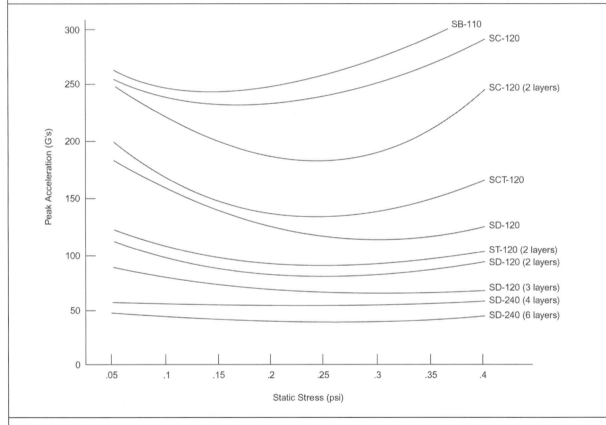

Source: AirCap brochure

Note: To be read: For a product exerting 0.25 lbs. per sq. in. of pressure on the packaging material while at rest, the peak acceleration (a measure of shock to the product) when dropped from 2 ft. is 118 g. if SD-120 is used, 260 g. if SB-110 is used.

Exhibit 6 U.S. Market—Flexible Wraps by Product Type (in millions of manufacturers' dollars)

	1975	1978	1980
Paper-based			
Cellulose wadding	20	23	23
Single-face corrugated	20	25	27
Indented kraft	1	1	1
	41	49	51
Foams[a]			
Polyurethane	10	11	12
Polypropylene	4	5	7
Polyethylene	1	6	25
	15	22	44
Polyethylene air bubbles[b]			
Coated and uncoated (combined)	15	22	31
Total	71	93	126

Source: Company records
a. Sales figures exclude nonpackaging uses, such as construction and furniture industries.
b. Figures are for flexible wrap market only and are therefore less than AirCap's and Astro's total U.S. sales.

Exhibit 7 AirCap Applications by Grade

Grade	Package Contents	Packaging Material Displaced (if known)
SB-110	Furnace thermostats Shorthand machines Taco shells Tempered glass sheets	 Corrugated $\frac{1}{16}$-in. polypropylene foam
SC-120	Clocks	Shredded paper
SC-240	Wooden picture frames	Corrugated
ST-120	Light fixtures Overhead projector lenses Computer components Telephone bell ringers Amplifiers Saucepans Two-way radios	Corrugated Corrugated $\frac{3}{32}$-in. polyethylene foam Corrugated Urethane foam pads
ST-240	Exit alarms Mixers Fryers Carbonless paper rolls	
SD-120	Oven burners Pharmaceutical bottles Candleholders Recorders Carburetors	Shredded paper Polypropylene foam
SD-240	Lamps Gallon jugs Computer terminals Printed circuit boards Foil wallpaper Blood coagulation timers	 Corrugated Foam pads and corrugated Corrugated
SD-480	Leaded glass windows Custom motorcycle seats Motor controls	 Astro uncoated bubble LP-24

Exhibit 8 Suggested U.S. Resale Price List, Effective March 1980

Item (thickness in inches)	Sq. Ft. per Order per Single Destination	Price per 1,000 Sq. Ft.
A-100 ($\frac{3}{32}$)	1,000 or more 5,000 " " 10,000 " " 30,000 " " 50,000 " " Truckload/railcar	$34.30 30.85 27.45 25.70 24.75 22.80
SB-110 ($\frac{1}{8}$)	1,000 or more 5,000 " " 10,000 " " 30,000 " " 50,000 " " Truckload/railcar	50.00 45.40 40.90 38.10 37.05 33.50
SC-120 ($\frac{3}{16}$)	1,000 or more 5,000 " " 10,000 " " 30,000 " " 50,000 " " Truckload/railcar	71.70 64.55 57.40 53.75 52.60 47.65
SC-240 ($\frac{3}{16}$)	1,000 or more 5,000 " " 10,000 " " 30,000 " " 50,000 " " Truckload/railcar	93.40 84.40 74.95 70.20 68.60 62.25
ST-120 ($\frac{5}{16}$)	1,000 or more 5,000 " " 10,000 " " 30,000 " " 50,000 " " Truckload/railcar	85.30 77.10 68.50 64.25 62.75 $57.25
ST-240 ($\frac{5}{16}$)	Same price per 1,000 sq. ft. as SD-120	
SD-120 ($\frac{1}{2}$)	1,000 or more 5,000 " " 10,000 " " 30,000 " " 50,000 " " Truckload/railcar	$107.85 97.70 87.55 81.40 79.35 72.40
SD-240 ($\frac{1}{2}$)	1,000 or more 5,000 " " 10,000 " " 30,000 " " 50,000 " " Truckload/railcar	130.75 118.30 105.95 98.55 95.70 87.25
SD-480 ($\frac{1}{2}$)	1,000 or more 5,000 " " 10,000 " " 30,000 " " 50,000 " " Truckload/railcar	232.75 210.55 188.35 175.55 171.25 $155.60

Exhibit 9 Selected Financial Data ($ thousands)

	1976	1977	1978	1979	1980
Net sales by class of product					
Air cellular packaging	$18,872	$21,422	$25,028	$29,996	$34,330
Foam-in-place packaging	3,049	15,489	21,133	29,056	38,802
Other packaging	4,553	3,595	3,453	3,432	3,688
Recreational and energy prod.		2,682	4,644	7,951	11,777
Total worldwide	$26,474	$43,188	$54,258	$70,435	$88,597
United States	–	35,765	43,410	54,325	67,344
Costs and expenses					
Cost of sales	$16,451	$24,270	$31,111	$43,199	$54,125
Marketing, administration, development	6,696	12,093	14,527	16,855	21,485
Other income (expense)	32	(816)	(738)	(278)	(119)
Earnings before income tax	3,359	6,009	7,882	10,103	12,868

Source: Sealed Air Annual Reports 1979, 1980

TWEETER ETC.

On August 16, 1996, Sandy Bloomberg, founder and CEO of Tweeter etc., reflected on the recent history of his small, upscale New England retailer of consumer electronics. Tweeter had grown from a 13-store chain with $35 million in annual sales in 1991 to a 21-store chain with $82 million in annual sales in 1996. Bloomberg had always attributed part of this growth to Tweeter's "Automatic Price Protection" policy, which had been implemented in 1993. Under Automatic Price Protection (APP), Tweeter monitored local newspaper ads and automatically mailed a refund check to a consumer if an item purchased at Tweeter during the past 30 days was advertised for a lower price by a competitor.

Two recent developments in the marketplace gave Bloomberg reason to reflect on APP, however. First, on May 16, 1996, Tweeter ventured outside its traditional New England base and purchased a controlling interest in Bryn Mawr Stereo, another small, high-end consumer electronics chain based in suburban Philadelphia. One year earlier, Bryn Mawr had adopted Tweeter's "Automatic Price Protection" policy, but up to the time of Tweeter's purchase, had failed to see any significant impact on sales. Second, on June 16, 1996, Nobody Beats the Wiz ("The Wiz") opened a 50,000 square foot electronics retail outlet in suburban Boston, the second of ten outlets planned for the New England market and the first in Greater Boston. The Wiz, a nationally recognized New Jersey-based discount retailer, threatened to change the playing field in the already highly competitive New England audio and video consumer electronics market.

Three years earlier, Tweeter's introduction of APP had received national press coverage in *The Wall Street Journal* (see Exhibit 1). Now, Bryn Mawr's seeming lack of

success with the policy gave Bloomberg cause to question the impact of APP. Moreover, whatever its past impact, Bloomberg wondered how effective the policy would be in a market increasingly dominated by large discount retailers such as The Wiz.

The Consumer Electronics Industry

The United States Market

In 1995, consumer electronics was a $30 billion industry in the United States, as measured by manufacturer sales (see Exhibit 2). The previous ten years had seen the market grow at a 5.6% compound annual rate, with future growth projected to be strong through 1998. While industry data on retail sales was unavailable, it was widely believed that retail margins averaged about 30% across product categories.

At the retail level, consumer electronics were distributed through a variety of channels, including specialty electronics stores (e.g., Tweeter), electronics/appliance superstores (e.g., Circuit City), mass merchants (e.g., Wal-Mart), warehouse clubs (e.g., Sam's Club), department stores (e.g., Macy's) and mail order houses (e.g., Sound City). Exhibit 3 provides an overview of these channels. Exhibit 4 shows the distribution of sales across channels for select categories of consumer electronics.

The New England Market

With a population of 13.2 million, New England represented 5% of the U.S. consumer electronics market. In 1996, there were 8 retailers in this region with market shares in excess of 2% (see Exhibit 5). By far the two largest were Lechmere (35% share) and Circuit City (19%).

For decades, Lechmere had been the region's most popular retailer of consumer electronics and home appliances, growing to 28 stores (averaging 50,000 square feet) throughout New England and northern New York by 1995. Selling televisions and stereos since the 1960s, Lechmere had become, for many New Englanders, the only place to consider when buying video

Professors John Gourville and George Wu prepared this case with research assistance from James Evans as the basis for class discussion rather than to illustrate either effective or ineffective handling of an administrative situation. Some nonpublic data have been disguised.

and audio equipment. Historically, such attitudes had been reinforced with well-informed salespeople, good customer service and fair pricing on a wide variety of entry and middle-level products. In 1994, Lechmere was purchased for $200 million by Montgomery Ward, a privately-owned, national mass merchant with approximately $6 billion in annual sales. While Lechmere stores continued to operate under the Lechmere name, many consumers believed that the level of customer service and salesperson knowledge had decreased appreciably under Montgomery Ward's control.

In contrast to the regional legacy of Lechmere, Circuit City, the nation's largest consumer electronics retailer, only arrived to the New England market in early 1993. However, their New England presence quickly grew to 15 full-sized stores (approximately 30,000 square feet) and 6 smaller "Circuit City Express" stores (approximately 3,000 square feet). With a reputation for knowledgeable salespeople and good service, Circuit City topped $5.5 billion in sales across more than 350 stores nationwide in 1995. Although Circuit City's offerings included personal computers, medium to large home appliances, audio tapes and compact discs, approximately 60% of their total sales were derived from the sale of video and audio equipment.

At the other end of the spectrum was Cambridge Soundworks, with less than a 1% share of the New England market. Founded in 1988, Cambridge Soundworks specialized in the design, manufacture and sale of their exclusive line of medium to high-end stereo and home theater speakers. Accounting for 69% of their total revenues in 1995, these speakers regularly received positive reviews in the audio and consumer electronic magazines and were often rated as a good value for their $200 to $600 per set price tags. The bulk of Cambridge Soundworks' remaining sales consisted of popular brand-name audio electronics, such as receivers by Harman Kardon and CD players by Sony, which complemented the sale of their private label speakers. While still only a niche player in the region, Cambridge Soundworks had grown appreciably in recent years, with revenues increasing from $14.3 million in 1993 to $26.9 million in 1995. Having traditionally relied on catalog sales (67% of total sales in 1993), much of this growth was due to the opening of a series of small retail outlets in 1994 and 1995. By the end of 1995, Cambridge Soundworks had 23 retail locations throughout New England (15 stores) and Northern California (8 stores), and revenues were divided between catalog (32%), wholesale (13%) and retail sales (55%).

Tweeter etc. Company History

The Formative Years: 1972 to the Mid-1980s

The competitive environment was quite different when Tweeter first arrived upon the consumer electronics scene in 1972. In the early-1970s, 21-year-old Sandy Bloomberg had been working at Audio Lab, a hi-fi repair shop and components dealer located in Harvard Square in Cambridge, Massachusetts. While at Audio Lab, Bloomberg became entranced by high quality audio components.[1] At that time, the high-end stereo market was only just developing in the United States, with few consumers beyond the hobbyists and avid audiophiles even aware of the increasingly high quality of stereo components available to the general public. In 1972, Bloomberg traveled to Europe where he witnessed and was encouraged by a more mainstream acceptance of high-end stereo components. Shortly afterward, Bloomberg opened his first Tweeter etc. in the storefront of his cousin's industrial music business located near Boston University.

Within a few years of Tweeter's founding, the U.S. stereo components market tripled and the Boston market became littered with a number of small independent retailers, of which Tweeter was only one. At the time, there were two major stereo retailers in the Boston area—Tech Hi-fi, started in 1963 by two MIT dropouts, and Lechmere. Tweeter avoided direct confrontation with either retailer by initially focusing on the student market, serving their more sophisticated tastes for higher quality stereo components. Bloomberg's business philosophy was built on a commitment to value, quality, and service.

By 1979, Tweeter had expanded to six stores in the Boston area and one in Rhode Island (see Exhibit 6 for a chronology of Tweeter's expansion). These stores averaged 6,000 square feet in space, although some, such as the Harvard Square store at 2,000 square feet, were significantly smaller. At about this time, Tweeter expanded its product line to take on high-end video equipment, principally in the form of color televisions.

---

[1]Stereo components are separate audio devices that can be combined to form a single stereo system. For example, a component system might consist of a receiver, a CD player, a cassette deck, and one or two pairs of speakers, all separately purchased to obtain the best of what each manufacturer has to offer. Typically, component systems are more flexible (components can be added or upgraded with ease) and capable of higher quality sound than "rack systems" or "compact systems," which offer prepackaged componentry.

Much as Bloomberg had anticipated, the general population's knowledge of and demand for high-end stereo and video equipment continued to grow through the mid-1980s. This growth was aided by strong regional and national economies and by the introduction of new technologies (e.g., Video Cassette Recorders [VCRs], Compact Disc [CD] Players). These conditions helped to solidify Tweeter's positioning at the high-end of the audio and video market.

By the end of 1986, Tweeter had grown to 13 stores throughout eastern Massachusetts and Rhode Island and by the late-1980s, Tweeter's share of the New England consumer electronics market had grown to almost 2% overall, and close to 5% in the Boston area.

During this period, Tweeter continued to be recognized as a retailer of high quality, high-end audio components and video equipment, with knowledgeable salespeople who offered high levels of customer service. Two of their advertising slogans during this period were, "We don't carry all the brands, only the ones that count" and "Some hi-fi salesman can sell you anything, and often do." Tweeter customers generally perceived that they were paying a premium price for the products they purchased, but were receiving the best customer service in the region for that premium.

The Shake-Out Years: Mid-1980s to 1993

The euphoria of the mid-1980s was short lived, however, as three factors contributed to an overall decline in the New England electronics market in the late-1980s and early-1990s.

First, the market growth of the mid-1980s led to new competitive entrants, especially at the lower end of the retail market. In 1985, for instance, two Michigan-based chains, Fretter Superstores and Highland Superstores, both warehouse-like electronics chains, opened four stores each in the Boston area. Second, by the late-1980s, household penetration for color televisions, VCRs and many other home electronics had grown appreciably, thereby limiting future growth in those product categories. Third, the once growing U.S. economy came to a screeching halt in 1987 and 1988, with New England among those geographic regions hardest hit.

These factors combined to have two major consequences. First, not all retailers survived. The first to falter was Tech Hi-fi, which found itself financially overextended just as competition was heating up. In 1985, it declared bankruptcy and closed its 11 Massachusetts

stores. The demise of Tech Hi-fi was followed six years later by Highland Superstores (10 New England stores) and in 1995 by Fretter (15 stores), both of whom also suffered from being financially overextended.

The second major result of the increasingly competitive environment of the late-1980s was increased price promotion. Traditionally, the New England electronics market had been characterized by four major "Sale" periods during which retailers discounted certain products to draw consumers into their stores—a Presidents' Day Sale in mid-February, a Father's Day Sale in June, a "Back to School" Sale in early-September, and a "Wrap it up Early" or "Pre-Holiday" Sale in mid-November. For the remainder of the year, product prices remained relatively steady, with only limited advertised price discounting.

Beginning in 1988, however, as the Boston economy bottomed out and consumer electronics sales growth flattened, Lechmere initiated an ongoing series of weekend "Sale" campaigns in which they would cut prices on select items on Friday, Saturday and Sunday. In order to retain their market shares, Tweeter and most other major retailers followed suit. As a result, the weekend "Sale" became a commonplace event, and consumers began to expect price discounts when purchasing audio and video equipment. In some cases, sales people would even tell customers not to buy on Wednesday, but rather to wait until Saturday when the desired item would be 20% off. During this period, it was not uncommon for 60% to 80% of a retailer's sales to occur on Saturday and Sunday.

As consumers increasingly focused on price in their purchasing process, Tweeter's profitability suffered. Noah Herschman, Tweeter's vice president of Marketing, described the problem in the following fashion:

> The consumers just wanted price, price, price. But, we didn't carry entry-level products, like a $139 VCR or a $399 camcorder. We carried the middle and high-end stuff. So people would look at our ads and they would look at Lechmere's ads. Lechmere would advertise a $139 VCR, and we would advertise a $199 VCR. They'd have a $399 camcorder, and we'd have a $599 camcorder. Even though their middle and high-end equipment sold for the same price as ours, we seemed to be more expensive to the inexperienced consumer. Our print advertising was actually driving people away—doing more damage to our business than if we never ran it.

In response to the profitability downturn, Tweeter attempted to compete on price as well as product quality and customer service. For instance, Tweeter began to carry Sherwood audio components, an entry-level brand comparable in price to the low-end offerings of Lechmere, Fretter and others. In addition, Tweeter began to stock the lower-end models of brands it had been carrying only at the middle and high-end, such as Sony. Nevertheless, the majority of Tweeter's product line was still in the middle to high-end and included brands such as Denon, Alpine, Kenwood, Klipsch and Boston Acoustics.

To further aid in this price-based competition, Tweeter joined the Progressive Retailers Organization in 1988, a buying consortium founded in 1986 that consisted of small high-end consumer electronics retailers throughout the United States which combined for over $1 billion in annual sales. As a result, Tweeter was able to obtain prices from manufacturers that were comparable with those obtained by its larger competitors.

Despite these efforts, the public perception of Tweeter remained unchanged. Customers continued to view Tweeter as more specialized and more expensive than Lechmere and the other New England retailers. While most consumers still recognized the high level of service Tweeter provided, many believed that such service came at the expense of higher prices, something they were increasingly less willing to accept. As a result, Tweeter's sales and profitability began to deteriorate starting in the early-1990s (see Exhibit 7). Tweeter's plight was exacerbated by Circuit City's entrance into the New England market in the spring of 1993. Circuit City's media-blitz advertising and fierce price competition further focused consumers' attention on price as the primary determinant of product choice.

A Change in Strategy: August 16, 1993

Frustrated by Tweeter's financial performance, Sandy Bloomberg, Jeff Stone (Tweeter's recently hired president and COO), Noah Herschman and the rest of the Tweeter management hashed out possible competitive responses at a management retreat in the spring of 1993.

In preparation for this retreat, Tweeter had conducted a number of focus groups in the months leading up to the retreat. Herschman boiled down the results of these focus groups into the two sets of insights.

First, individuals shopping for consumer electronics in the New England area displayed the following general characteristics and behavior:

- On average, consumers actively thought about purchasing a new product one to two months before actually making the purchase.

- On average, consumers visited two to three retailers prior to purchasing a desired product. The factors most cited by consumers in their selection of stores to visit include newspaper advertisements (cited by 70% of consumers), past experience with the store (50%) and recommendations of friends and family (40%).

- Eight out of ten consumers checked newspaper advertisements for product availability and price information when in the market for consumer electronic equipment. Virtually all of these consumers delayed purchase until they saw the desired product or class of product advertised in a newspaper circular.

Second, individuals who were familiar with or considered purchasing at Tweeter displayed the following specific characteristics and behavior:

- Four out of five consumers viewed Tweeter as being more expensive than the major competitors in the market (i.e., Lechmere, Fretter). However, most of these consumers reported that if price were not an issue, they would prefer to purchase their desired product from Tweeter.

- Of all consumers who visited Tweeter in search of a product, 60% also visited Lechmere, 45% also visited Fretter and 20% also visited Sears in the course of their product search.

- One in three consumers specifically came to Tweeter to figure out what to buy and then went to Lechmere or Fretter, believing they could get a better price there.

These focus groups also allowed Tweeter to characterize four types of electronics consumers in the New England market: the "entry-level customer", the "price biter", the "convenience customer", and the "quality/service customer":

Entry-Level Customers The *entry-level customer* was interested in buying the cheapest item in a given category and was relatively indifferent to product quality and customer service.

The Price Biter The *price biter* was very cognizant of price, but was also concerned with product quality and customer service. Price biters were more focused on getting the "absolute best deal" than on getting the "absolute lowest price" in a particular category.

The Convenience Customer For the *convenience customer,* price, service and product quality were of secondary importance to shopping convenience. A convenience customer tended to shop in a store such as Lechmere or Sears because it was familiar and/or because they could purchase products in many different categories (e.g., luggage, jewelry, camera equipment, housewares, etc.) on the same shopping trip.

The Quality/Service Customer For the *quality/service customer,* high levels of product quality and customer service were of primary concern and price, while still important, was of secondary concern. Some retailers referred to these consumers as "BBCOs"—"Buy the Best and Cry Once".

Herschman estimated that while this final group represented only 10% of the total New England customer base, it accounted for 70% of Tweeter's clientele. Exhibit 8 provides Herschman's estimates for the distribution of customers for Tweeter as well as for the other major competitors in the New England market.

Armed with these insights, Bloomberg and his team used the spring management retreat to completely revamp the marketing strategy for Tweeter etc. This new strategy was announced to the public on August 16, 1993 and was referred to by Herschman as a "three-pronged attack" to restore price credibility at Tweeter.

Abandonment of the "Sale"

First, in a radical departure from the practices of its competitors and from their own historic behavior, Tweeter eliminated the use of the "Sale" to build store traffic and promote consumer spending. Herschman explained:

> We were getting killed by the big players—Lechmere, Circuit City and Fretter. Every weekend, everyone was having a sale, but on different makes and models of product. This made it almost impossible to compare prices across retailers. This worked in favor of the big stores, who were already perceived as low priced, but it was killing us. Even though we were competitively priced, because of our high-price image, no one was listening. And even more frustrating was the fact that our increasing reliance on the weekend "Sale" drew attention away from our unique selling proposition—high quality products and great customer service.

Thus, as part of Tweeter's new strategy, Sandy Bloomberg and Jeff Stone decided to do away with the weekend "Sale" and move to an "Every Day Fair Pricing"

strategy. They vowed to set Tweeter's prices competitively and to look to policies other than the "Sale" to communicate its price competitiveness to potential customers.

Automatic Price Protection

As the primary means to communicate their price competitiveness, Tweeter instituted "Automatic Price Protection" as the second prong of their "three-pronged" strategy. "Price Protection" or "Price Guarantees" were an oft-used retailing tactic intended to assure customers that they were receiving the best price available on any given product. In its typical form, if a consumer purchased a product at one store and later found it for a lower price at another store, the consumer could return to the first store with proof of that lower price and get reimbursed for the difference. Typically, these price protection policies were in effect for 30 days from the time of purchase and promised to refund 100% of the price difference, although some retailers promise refunds of 110%, 150% or even 200% of the price difference.

Over the years, this form of price protection had led to some interesting battles amongst retailers. In New York City, for instance, the consumer electronics retailer Crazy Eddie advertised "We will not be undersold. Our prices are the lowest—guaranteed. Our prices are insane." At the same time, its primary competitor, Newmark and Lewis, advertised a "Lifetime low-price guarantee" which promised to rebate 200% of the price difference if a consumer found a lower price at any time during the life of the product. Both stores declared bankruptcy in the 1980s.

As of 1993, most of the major consumer electronics retailers in New England practiced some form of price protection. For instance, Lechmere, Circuit City and Fretter all offered a 110% refund for a period of 30 days. In contrast, Tweeter offered a 100% refund for 30 days. Jeff Stone, president of Tweeter, estimated that Tweeter refunded $3,000 to $4,000 per month to its customers under this price protection strategy. One industry expert estimated that across all price protection programs, only about 5% of consumers entitled to a rebate actually followed through and redeemed that rebate.[2] Often cited reasons for this low rebate redemption included the effort needed to physically track newspaper ads and to travel back to the retailer to obtain the refund.

---

[2]*The Wall Street Journal,* August 17, 1993, p. B6.

On August 16, 1993, Tweeter took price protection one step further. Under Automatic Price Protection, Tweeter took it upon itself to track the local newspapers and send out rebates. If a consumer purchased an item at Tweeter and it was advertised for less in a major local newspaper within 30 days, Tweeter automatically mailed that consumer a check for the difference. Tweeter's APP covered individual items priced at $50 or more and applied to price differences of $2 and greater (see Exhibit 9 for Tweeter's advertised explanation of their policy). In addition to APP, Tweeter retained and extended their former price protection policy to 60 days and renamed it "Regular Price Protection."

Operationally, APP was administered by a specialized department at Tweeter's corporate headquarters in Canton, Massachusetts. A staff member would physically check every issue of eight major newspapers in the New England area for price advertisements from Tweeter's competitors. These papers included *The Boston Globe, The Boston Herald, The Cape Cod Times, The Danbury News Times, The Hartford Courant, The New Haven Register, The New London Day* and *The Providence Journal.* If any product carried by Tweeter was advertised by a competitor, the price and model number of that product and the date of the advertisement were entered into the Tweeter database. This information was then cross matched against Tweeter sales data to check for purchases of that product at a higher price within the past thirty days. If any such purchase was found, the computer generated a check for the difference and automatically mailed it to the purchaser within five days.

A Change in the Marketing Mix

The third prong of Tweeter's "three-pronged" strategy to restore price credibility was a shift in their marketing mix away from print advertising and toward television and radio advertising as well as direct mail and product catalogs.

Over the years, Tweeter's marketing budget had typically run at about 8% of gross sales. Under their old "Sale" based promotional strategy, the vast majority of this marketing budget was dedicated to newspaper advertising in the form of weekly "Sale" announcements. In FY 1993, for example, 80% of their $3.1 million marketing budget was spent on newspaper advertising, with the remaining 20% split between radio advertising, direct mail, market research and in-store promotions. With the elimination of their Sale-based strategy, the Tweeter marketing mix changed significantly (see

Exhibit 10). Most noticeably, the choice of media and message shifted from newspaper advertising which focused on "Sale" prices to radio and television advertising which focused on Tweeter's price competitiveness and Automatic Price Protection policy.

In conjunction, Tweeter instituted a direct marketing campaign which revolved around a 50- to 100-page seasonal "Buyer's Guide", which provided product descriptions and prices for all of Tweeter's major products. Produced four times per year, by 1996 this guide was mailed to approximately 325,000 individuals. Herschman estimated that of these 325,000 recipients, 270,000 had made a purchase at Tweeter within the past 18 months. It was believed that 90% of those who purchased some item at Tweeter ended up on this catalog mailing list for at least a period of two years. Buyer's Guides were also made available to consumers at each of Tweeter's retail locations as well as at various musical events sponsored by Tweeter, such as the summer outdoor concert series at Great Woods in Mansfield, Massachusetts.

August 1996

By most accounts, Tweeter's shift in strategy had a positive effect on financial performance. Sales almost doubled in the three years since the institution of the new strategy, from $43.7 million in FY 1993 to a projected $82.3 million in FY 1996. A breakdown of 1996 sales across major product categories, by percentage, is shown in Exhibit 11. Part of this recent growth could be attributed to an increase in sales per store, with same-store sales increasing by 50% between 1993 and 1996, and part could be attributed to an increase in the number of stores from 14 to 21 over the same period.

The Impact of Automatic Price Protection

Immediately after the announcement of Tweeter's new strategy, the media response to APP was extremely positive, with articles in *The Wall Street Journal, The Boston Globe* and *The Boston Herald* all extolling the virtues of the Tweeter's unique price guarantee. There were a few skeptics, however:

> . . . most suppliers sell retailers products that are not available elsewhere in the market. Thus, there is little chance that many items will qualify for the refunds.[3]

---

[3]*The Boston Globe,* August 17, 1993, p. 35

... the impact will be more one of perception than of massive price refunds, in part because Tweeter's moderate to high-end products don't overlap with many other retailers.[4]

Other observers disagreed. Edgar Dworsky, the Massachusetts assistant attorney general for consumer protection commented:

> It's a brilliant idea. The problem with price protection guarantees has been that it's the consumer's burden to find a lower price somewhere else. Tweeter's going to do the watching for you. I just hope they don't lose their shirts.[5]

By the end of 1995, Tweeter had mailed a total of 29,526 APP checks totaling over $780,000 (see Exhibit 12). It was not clear to Sandy Bloomberg what to make of this number, however. For instance, if Tweeter's prices were competitive, why were they sending out any checks?

An added concern for Bloomberg and his management team was whether Tweeter's message of price competitiveness was reaching potential customers. While routine price comparisons suggested that Tweeter was competitive on price relative to its major competitors (Exhibit 13), some recent surveys indicated that many customers still perceived Tweeter as being more expensive (see Exhibit 14). In addition, few consumers seemed to understand the essence of APP and most were unaware of that it was Tweeter who offered it (see Exhibit 14). In looking at this data, Herschman noted the difference in customer attitudes between those who were aware of Tweeter's APP policy and those who were not.

The Purchase of Bryn Mawr Stereo and Video

APP was only one of the things on the mind of Tweeter management in spring and summer of 1996. On May 16, after several years of friendly discussions, Tweeter finalized the purchase of Bryn Mawr Stereo and Video, a privately-owned consumer electronics chain headquartered outside of Philadelphia, in King of Prussia, Pennsylvania. Using a similar high-end, high-service strategy as Tweeter, Bryn Mawr had grown to approximately $35 million in annual sales over 13 stores located in eastern Pennsylvania, New Jersey, Delaware and Maryland.

Tweeter planned to retain the Bryn Mawr name to capitalize on its brand recognition, while merging management across the two chains.

Not surprisingly, Bryn Mawr faced many of the same competitive challenges as Tweeter. Long known for its high-end merchandise and superior service quality, many consumers held the perception that Bryn Mawr was not price competitive with the large electronic superstores operating in the Mid-Atlantic region, such as Circuit City, Best Buy and Nobody Beats the Wiz. To fight this perception, at Bloomberg's urging, Bryn Mawr adopted Tweeter's Automatic Price Protection in September of 1995. Unlike Tweeter, however, Bryn Mawr failed to see any appreciable increase in sales through the time of their purchase by Tweeter. While some at Tweeter attributed this shortcoming to Bryn Mawr's less aggressive campaign to advertise APP and its features, it gave others cause to question the role of APP in building sales.

Nobody Beats the Wiz

Another issue that concerned Tweeter management in the summer of 1996 was the recent entry of Nobody Beats the Wiz into the local market. On June 16th, The Wiz opened a sleek new 50,000 square foot retail outlet in Saugus, Massachusetts, their first store in the Greater Boston area and their second in Massachusetts. In total, The Wiz had plans to open ten stores in the New England market over the next several years. Lon Rebackin, vice president of real estate for The Wiz, noted:

> This is a priority market for us. In the short term and the long term, we will be a player in New England.[6]

A privately held company with over $900 million in sales in 1994, the Wiz was the third largest consumer electronics retailer chain in the United States, offering a wide selection of audio and video electronics, as well as personal computer hardware and software. The Wiz operated a total of over 50 stores in New York, New Jersey, Connecticut, Pennsylvania and most recently, Massachusetts.

The Wiz was known for its monstrous marketing campaigns touting rock bottom prices, a strategy they had used with great effectiveness in the New York metropolitan market. These campaigns often included noted sports stars as football's Joe Namath and basketball's Julius Irving. In addition, The Wiz was generally recognized as offering intensive customer service. They also

---

[4]*The Boston Herald*, August 17, 1993, p. 1
[5]*The Wall Street Journal*, August 17, 1993, p. B6

[6]*The Boston Globe*, June 7, 1996, p. 38

offered 110% price protection for 30 days on all items except camcorders and cellular telephones.

Publicly, the competitive reaction to the entry of The Wiz was understated. Harlan Platt, a professor of finance at Northeastern University commented:

> They're marvelous at creating the perception that they're giving customers the best deal of all. But the New England consumer is more worldly and wise. I wouldn't be surprised to see The Wiz withdraw and seek greener pastures.[7]

In commenting for Tweeter, Noah Herschman claimed:

> It's a great time to be in Boston when The Wiz comes in. They only generate interest in the product category. But the people we sell to are enthusiastic about what we have. Our niche is more the personal touch.[8]

Privately, however, Tweeter's management was concerned that the entry of The Wiz could lead to a new round of price wars, much like those of the late 1980s and early 1990s. Bloomberg could not help but wonder whether APP would continue to be an effective policy under those circumstances.

The Future

Having reviewed the events of the recent past, Sandy Bloomberg found himself back where he had started. He had always believed that Automatic Price Protection had played a major role in Tweeter's growth, but now Bryn Mawr gave him reason to question that belief. Even if he could attribute Tweeter's recent success to APP, however, the entry of The Wiz had the potential to reshape the competitive playing field in the increasingly crowded New England market. Sandy wondered what role Automatic Price Protection would play in Tweeter's future competitive positioning.

---

[7] *The Boston Globe,* March 1, 1996, p. 65
[8] Ibid.

Exhibit 1 *The Wall Street Journal* Article, August 17, 1993

Tweeter's Customers Told: 'Your Check Is in the Mail'

* * *

New England Retailer Says Its Computers Shop the Ads Of Rivals to Ensure Refunds

By WILLIAM M. BULKELEY

Staff Reporter of THE WALL STREET JOURNAL

Tweeter etc., a New England stereo and television retailer, is going a step beyond its rivals by promising to automatically mail customers a refund check anytime a competitor advertises a lower price.

Most companies in the competitive electronics field will give refunds to customers who buy a product, then see it advertised for less and bring in the ad within 30 days. Tweeter says it will save customers the trouble of monitoring ads and returning to the store.

"In electronics, everyone has a low-price guarantee. But then, it's try and catch them," said Jeffrey Stone, president of Tweeter. "This time, the check really is in the mail."

Nothing Under $50

Based in Canton, Mass., Tweeter, a unit of closely held New England Audio Co., sets some limits. It said it will monitor one or two daily newspapers in each of its markets. Any time a competitor within 25 miles of one of its stores advertises a lower price, the "automatic price protection" program goes into effect. Radio, television and direct mail ads don't count. And the guarantee applies only to items over $50.

When Tweeter's competitive marketing staffers see a rival's ad quoting a price, they enter it in Tweeter's computer. A program then checks to see if anybody has bought that item from Tweeter for a higher price in the past 30 days. If so, the computer spits out a check for the difference.

Edgar Dworsky, Massachusetts assistant attorney general for consumer protection, said: "It's a brilliant idea. The problem with price protection guarantees has been that it's the consumer's burden to find a lower price somewhere else. Tweeter's going to do the watching for you. I just hope they don't lose their shirts."

Volume Discounts Available

Tweeter, with $40 million a year in sales at 14 stores, is a medium-sized player in the increasingly competitive New England market. It sells name-brand stereos, televisions, car radios and car phones. It doesn't compete at the very low end of the market. However, Tweeter says that because it is part of the Progressive Retailers Organization Inc., a Palm Springs, Calif., buying group, it can get the same volume discounts available to national chains.

Mr. Stone of Tweeter estimates that the company mails $3,000 to $4,000 a month in refund checks to sharp-eyed customers. He says the amount could double under the new program.

Retail consultants say the total may be far higher. "I'd guess 5%" of customers actually check competitors' ads, says Robert Kahn, a retail consultant in Lafayette, Calif. But he says, "This will build customers because somebody who gets a check will say something exceptional about Tweeter to his friends."

Banking on 'Incremental Sales'

That's what Tweeter is counting on. "A few incremental sales will more than pay for the program," said Sandy Bloomberg, chief executive and founder of Tweeter.

Tweeter officials said the company worked to build a high-price, high-quality image during the 1980s. But focus group research showed it needed to reverse that image for the '90s. "People used to boast about how much they paid for something. Now they boast about how much they saved on it," said Mr. Stone.

Source: Company records

Exhibit 2 Annual Domestic and Import Manufacturer Sales of Consumer Electronics in the United States by Category[a] (in millions of dollars)

	1990	1991	1992	1993	1994	1995	1996 (est.)
Video							
Direct view color TV	$ 6,247	$ 6,035	$ 6,651	$ 7,376	$ 7,285	$ 6,969	$ 7,100
Projection TV	626	683	714	841	1,117	1,398	1,720
Monochrome TV	132	92	79	73	70	65	62
TV/VCR combo	178	265	375	599	710	729	816
VCRs	2,504	2,525	2,996	2,912	2,933	2,859	2,716
Camcorders	2,269	2,013	1,841	1,958	1,985	2,160	2,183
Laserdisc players	72	81	93	123	123	105	92
Home satellite	421	370	379	408	900	1,265	1,479
Sub-Total	$12,449	$12,064	$13,128	$14,290	$15,123	$15,550	$16,168
Audio							
Rack systems	$ 804	$ 667	$ 614	$ 545	$ 595	$ 537	$ 507
Compact systems	466	597	756	919	1,108	1,242	1,335
Separate components	1,935	1,805	1,586	1,635	1,686	1,940	2,100
Portable equipment	1,645	1,780	2,096	2,187	2,495	2,749	2,724
Home radios	360	310	324	307	306	298	298
Sub-Total	$ 5,210	$ 5,159	$ 5,376	$ 5,593	$ 6,190	$ 6,766	$ 6,964
Mobile Electronics							
Car stereo equipment[b]	1,192	1,232	1,467	1,604	1,898	1,935	1,975
Cellular telephones	1,133	962	1,146	1,257	1,275	1,431	1,620
Sub-Total	$ 2,325	$ 2,194	$ 2,613	$ 2,861	$ 3,173	$ 3,366	$ 3,595
Blank Media	$ 1,638	$ 1,661	$ 1,568	$ 1,486	$ 1,436	$ 1,413	$ 1,442
Accessories & Batteries	$ 2,167	$ 2,145	$ 2,253	$ 2,974	$ 3,286	$ 3,475	$ 3,745
Total	$23,789	$23,223	$24,938	$27,204	$29,208	$30,570	$31,914

Sources: U.S. Consumer Electronics Sales & Forecasts 1991–1996; Consumer Electronics Manufacturers Associations, January 1996

[a]Excludes home office equipment (e.g., telephones, fax machines, personal computers), and electronic gaming equipment.
[b]Excludes factory installed car stereo equipment.

Exhibit 3 Channels of Distribution for Consumer Electronics

Specialty Stores and Boutiques
Characterized by good to excellent customer service, high salesperson knowledge and moderate selling pressure. Medium- to high-end product lines, especially in terms of audio components (e.g., Sony, . . .). Limited use of promotional sales. Typically smaller in size with good facilities (e.g., sound-proof listening rooms). Examples include Tweeter, Cambridge Sound Works, and Bryn Mawr Stereo.
Electronic/Appliance Superstores
Hectic, high-volume selling machines. Moderate to good customer service, varied salesperson knowledge, and strong selling pressure. Carry a wide selection of all the major product lines (e.g., Sony, Pioneer, JVC, . . .). Heavy use of promotional sales. Large, open facilities with listening rooms common, but not a certainty. Examples include Circuit City, Best Buy, Nobody Beats the Wiz and Lechmere.
Department Stores
Poor to moderate customer service, limited salesperson knowledge and low to moderate selling pressure. Carry a more limited product line, mainly entry and middle level products. Prone to promotional sales. Examples include Sears and Macy's.
Mass Merchants
Little to no customer service, little salesperson knowledge and little selling pressure. Limited product line, geared toward "value" brands, such as Sound Design and Yorx. Unlikely to find audio components at these stores. Examples include Wal-mart and K-Mart.
Warehouse Clubs
No customer service and no selling pressure. Price, not service or ambiance, is the reason people shop at warehouse clubs. Product selection is varied and limited and selection changes all the time. On occasion, good values on good quality equipment can be found. Examples include Costco and Sam's Club.
Mail Order Houses
Advertise in stereo and video magazines as well as via their own catalogs. No service and no selling pressure. No ability to sample equipment. Prices are sometimes attractive, but shipping can be expensive. Returns are difficult. Examples include Crutchfield and Sound City.

Source: Consumer Reports, February, 1996, pp. 18–27

Exhibit 4 1995 Market Share by Channel for Select Consumer Electronics Categories

	Direct View Color TV's	Video Camcorders	Portable Audio[a]	Audio Components	Blank Media[b]
Specialty Stores/Electronic Superstores	49.0%	46.0%	37.0%	64.0%	17.0%
Mass Merchants/Warehouse Clubs	25.0%	25.0%	32.0%	14.0%	45.0%
Department Stores	6.5%	7.5%	17.0%	6.5%	16.0%
Mail Order Houses	3.0%	6.5%	5.0%	3.5%	2.0%
Other	15.0%	15.0%	9.0%	12.0%	20.0%
Total	100.0%	100.0%	100.0%	100.0%	100.0%

Source: Dealerscope Merchandising, July 1996, pp. 46–50
[a]Portable Audio includes Walkman and Discman-type portable systems
[b]Blank Media includes blank audio cassettes, VCR cassettes and Camcorder cassettes

Exhibit 5 New England Market Share—1992 to 1996[a]

	1992	1994	1996
Lechmere	33.0%	36.0%	35.6%
Circuit City	0.0%	7.4%	18.6%
Sears	7.8%	7.4%	8.7%
Radio Shack	4.9%	5.8%	3.9%
Wal-Mart	n/a[b]	n/a[b]	3.9%
Tweeter	2.8%	2.7%	3.6%
Bradlee's	2.2%	2.5%	2.4%
Service Merchandise	4.1%	3.0%	2.1%
Fretter	5.0%	4.9%	1.7%
BJ's Wholesale Club	2.5%	2.3%	1.2%
K-Mart	0.6%	0.4%	1.2%
Costco	n/a[b]	0.7%	0.6%
Jordan Marsh	1.3%	0.4%	0.6%
Cambridge Sound Works	n/a[b]	n/a[b]	0.6%
Other	35.8%	26.5%	15.3%

Source: Company records; Based on research conducted by WCVB-TV, Boston, MA.
[a]Based on an annual telephone survey of approximately 1,000 adults in the New England market in response to the question, "In the past 2 years, at which store did you make your LAST purchase of home electronics equipment?".
[b]Market share not reported separately, but included in "Other".

Exhibit 6 Tweeter Store Openings

1972	Commonwealth Avenue, Boston, MA
1973	Harvard Square, MA
1974	Newton, MA
1976	Burlington, MA
1977	Framingham, MA
1979	Dedham, MA; Warwick, RI
1982	Peabody, MA
1984	Hyannis, MA
1985	Waterford, CT; Hanover, MA
1986	Danbury, CT; Seekonk, MA
1990	Newington, CT
1993	Avon, CT
1994	Manchester, CT; Salem, NH
1995	Boylston Street, Boston, MA; Milford, CT
1996	Holyoke, MA; Nashua, NH

Source: Company records

Exhibit 7 Tweeter etc. Income Statement: FY 1990 to FY 1996[a]

	FY 1990	FY 1991	FY 1992	FY 1993	FY 1994	FY 1995	FY 1996 (est.)[b]
Gross Revenues	$39,500	$35,660	$41,140	$43,714	$55,164	$70,305	$82,400
Cost of Goods Sold	26,228	23,586	27,209	28,485	35,739	45,299	52,300
Total Gross Margin	$13,272	$12,074	$13,931	$15,229	$19,425	$25,006	$30,100
Total Expenses	15,146	14,085	13,894	15,890	18,038	22,304	26,500
Net Income	($1,874)	($2,011)	$37	($661)	$1,387	$2,702	$3,600

Source: Company Records
[a]Fiscal Years are from October 1 of the previous year through September 30 of the year indicated.
[b]Figures for FY 1996 are based on midyear projections and do not include the purchase of Bryn Mawr Stereo and Video.

Exhibit 8 Makeup of Customer Bases Across New England Retailers

Customer Segment	Total Market	Tweeter	Lechmere	Circuit City
Entry Level	50%[a]	5%[b]	40%	35%
Price-Biter	15%	20%	10%	35%
Convenience	25%	5%	40%	15%
Quality/Service	10%	70%	10%	15%
	100%	100%	100%	100%

Source: Tweeter Company Estimates
[a]To be read, 50% of all New England consumer electronics customers are Entry-level customers.
[b]To be read, 5% of all Tweeter customers are Entry-level customers.

Exhibit 9 Tweeter Automatic Price Protection

Only Tweeter <u>Automatically</u> Mails You A Check For The Difference!

If you buy something at Tweeter and it's advertised for less in a major local newspaper within 30 days, we'll <u>automatically</u> mail you a check for the difference!

It's been more than two full years since we introduced Automatic Price Protection.^{SM} And to date, Tweeter remains the only retailer in the country (world?) to provide such a service.

Needless to say, customers who have received APP^{SM} checks in the mail have been delighted by the fact that they didn't have to shop around for a better price. INSTEAD, TWEETER DID THE PRICE SHOPPING FOR THEM <u>AFTER</u> THE SALE!

Here's How APP™

Step 1

Staff memebers in the Automatic Price protection Department go through each consumer electronics ad in every edition of the major local newspaper.
When we find an item advertised that Tweeter sells, we record the model#, price, and date of the ad in our computer.

Step 2

Our Management Incormation Department then finds every customer who purchased that item from Tweeter within the 30-day period preceding the ad.

Step 3

The names and addresses of customers who paid more than the advertised prices are separated and spooled.

Step 4

Checks are cut for the difference between what the custormer paid and the price advertised. They are mailed within five days.

Common Myths about Automatic Price Protection^{sm}

Myth: That APP doesn't work because most retailers havemodel numbers that are unique to them, so we can't compare prices.

Reality: The truth is, that Tweeter has no unique model numbers. In fact, we share all of out TV, VCR, Camcorder, and Portable Audio models with the other big retailers like Lechmere, Circuit City, and the Wiz. And we share most of our Car Stereo models, and many of our Home Stereo models with them as well.

Myth: That Tweeter only mails out checks for large amounts and that small price protection amounts are omitted.

Reality: Tweeter mails out APP checks for amounts of $2 and over.

Myth: That Tweeter only Price Protects items that are high-priced.

Reality: Tweeter Price Protects items priced $50 and over.

Myth: That the APP checks Tweeter mails out are only redeemable for merchandise at Tweeter.

Reality: The APP refunds that Tweeter mails out are bonafide checks. You can cash them anywhere.

Exhibit 10 Tweeter Marketing Mix

	FY 1993		FY 1996	
	$ (000s)	**As % of Sales**	**$ (000s)**	**As % of Sales**
Print	$2,500	7.1%	$ 300	0.3%
Television	0	0.0	1,150	1.4
Radio	375	1.1	2,750	3.3
Direct Mail[a]	125	0.3	1,000	1.2
Music Series[b]	0	0.0	225	0.3
Pre-Openings[c]	0	0.0	275	0.3
Other[d]	125	0.3	1000	1.2
Total	$3,125	8.9%	$6,700	8.0%

Source: Company Records
[a]Includes quarterly Buyers Guides and other one-time only direct mail campaigns   [c]Includes promotional efforts related to new store openings
[b]Includes sponsorship of Great Woods Concert Series   [d]Includes Marketing Research, Public Relations and Cellular Telephone Promotions

Exhibit 11 Tweeter Product Mix: 1996

Product Category	% of Dollar Sales
Video	
TV's 40″ and Under	14%
TV's Over 40″	10%
Video Cassette Recorders (VCRs)	6%
Camcorders	4%
Direct Satellite Systems (DSS)	1%
Sub-Total	35%
Audio	
Speakers	14%
Receivers	9%
CD Players	7%
Personal Portable	4%
Tape Decks	2%
Other Audio Electronics[a]	5%
Sub-Total	41%
Car Stereo	14%
Other[b]	10%
Total	100%

Source: Company Records
[a]Includes Amplifiers, Preamplifiers, Boom Boxes and Compact Systems
[b]Includes Cellular Phones, Cables, Blank Tapes, Warranties and Labor

Exhibit 12 Automatic Price Protection Rebates by Month (in dollars)

		Number of Checks		$ Value of Checks	
		Month	Cumulative	Month	Cumulative
1993	August	89	89	$ 1,816	$ 1,816
	September	268	356	5,105	6,921
	October	549	905	15,718	22,639
	November	843	1,748	25,595	48,234
	December	1,571	3,319	31,229	79,463
1994	January	433	3,751	10,295	89,758
	February	341	4,093	9,188	98,945
	March	403	4,495	12,410	111,355
	April	475	4,970	10,600	121,955
	May	591	5,561	13,714	135,669
	June	690	6,251	14,331	150,000
	July	483	6,734	11,350	161,350
	August	529	7,263	12,014	173,364
	September	581	7,844	9,354	182,718
	October	681	8,525	14,949	197,666
	November	1,594	10,119	39,003	236,669
	December	4,249	14,368	104,260	340,929
1995	January	1,528	15,895	36,389	377,318
	February	849	16,744	17,751	395,069
	March	850	17,594	20,154	415,223
	April	561	18,155	12,656	427,879
	May	610	18,765	12,636	440,515
	June	1,108	19,873	25,583	466,098
	July	160	20,033	3,236	469,334
	August	675	20,708	16,614	485,948
	September	628	21,335	16,498	502,445
	October	1,078	22,413	27,881	530,326
	November	2,403	24,815	72,038	602,364
	December	4,711	29,526	181,499	783,863

Source: Company records

Exhibit 13 Product Line and Price Comparisons Across Major New England Retailers—27" Color Televisions

Model	Lechmere	Circuit City	Wiz	Tweeter
GE-27GT600	320 (Sale)			
GE-27GT616	280 (Ad)			
Hitachi-27CX1B		450		
Hitachi-27CX5B	480 (Sale)	500 (Ad)		
Hitachi-27CXSB		440		
JBC-AV27720	450	430		
Magnavox-TP2770	500			
Magnavox-TP2782C	500	450		
Magnavox-TS2743			400	
Magnavox-TS2752C	350 (Sale)			
Magnavox-TS2753C	370	350 (Ad)		
Magnavox-TS2775C		380 (Sale)		
Magnavox-TS2779			400 (Ad)	
Mitsubishi-CS27205	500 (Ad)		479	500
Mitsubishi-CS27305	670		598	600
Mitsubishi-CS27407	920		850	850
Panasonic-CT27G11	400 (Sale)	430	430	
Panasonic-CT27G21	430 (Sale)	480	497	480
Panasonic-CT27SF12	650 (Sale)	630		
Panasonic-CT27SF21	700 (Sale)			650
Panasonic-CT27SF22	700 (Sale)			
Panasonic-CT27SF23	750		750	750
Panasonic-CT27SF33	900			
ProScan-PS27108		600 (Ad)	548	600
ProScan-PS27113		630 (Sale)	578	
ProScan-PS27123				750
ProScan-PS27160		870		
RCA-F27204BC	530 (Ad)			
RCA-F2240WT	350 (Sale)		380	
RCA-F27638BC				400
RCA-F2767SBC		450	395 (Ad)	
RCA-F2767BC	430 (Sale)			
Sharp-27GS60	330 (Ad)			
Sharp-27HS120			330 (Ad)	
Sony-KV27S20	500 (Ad)	500		550
Sony-KV27S25	550 (Sale)	550	550	
Sony-KV27V20	590	550 (Sale)	550	550
Sony-KV27V25				650
Sony-KV27V35	840		750	750
Sony-KV27V55	800		750	
Sony-KV27XBR45	900 (Sale)		970	1000
Toshiba-CF27E30	400 (Ad)			
Toshiba-CF27F50	470 (Sale)		497	
Toshiba-CF27F55	500 (Ad)	500		
Zenith-SM2789BT	650	500		
Zenith-SR2787DT	650 (Sale)			
Zenith-SR2787DT	550 (Sale)			
Zenith-SY2772DT	480			
Zenith-SY2773DT		450 (Ad)		

Source: Comparison of products and prices in the week of September 16, 1996
Notes: (Ad) indicates a price advertised in the local paper; (Sale) indicates an unadvertised, in-store markdown.

Exhibit 13 Product Line and Price Comparisons Across Major New England Retailers—Mulitple CD Players (continued)

Model	Lechmere	Circuit City	Wiz	Tweeter
Adcom-GCD700				700
Admiral-MWDK1	90 (Sale)			
Denon-DCM360				330
Denon-DCM460				400
Fisher-DAC503			158	
Fisher-DAC6005			219 (Ad)	
Harmon-Kar.-FL8300		300 (Sale)	299 (Ad)	
JVC-XLF108BK	120 (Ad)	120		
JVC-XLF152BK		180 (Sale)	180	
JVC-XLF252BK		200 (Ad)	180 (Sale)	
JVC-XLM418BK			220 (Sale)	
Kenwood-DPJ1070		300 (Ad)		300
Kenwood-DPJ2071		500		
Kenwood-DPR3080	200	170	199	180
Kenwood-DPR4070		180 (Ad)	188	
Kenwood-DPR4080	220		230	200
Kenwood-DPR5080		220		
Kenwood-DPR6080				300
Onkyo-DXC320	350			
Onkyo-DXC330	270	300	280	
Onkyo-DXC530	330			
Onkyo-DXC606	400 (Sale)			
Pioneer-PD65				800
Pioneer-PDF59				300
Pioneer-PDF79				400

Model	Lechmere	Circuit City	Wiz	Tweeter
Pioneer-PDF109				800
Pioneer-PDF505	220	200 (Ad)	200	
Pioneer-PDF605	200 (Sale)	240	220	
Pioneer-PDF705		300 (Ad)		
Pioneer-PDF901		180		
Sony-CDPC425				
Sony-CDPC445	200 (Ad)			
Sony-CDPC545			279	
Sony-CDPCA7ES				350
Sony-CDPCA8ES				550
Sony-CDPCE405		200 (Sale)	200	200
Sony-CDPCE505		250	270	
Sony-CDPCX153	350 (Ad)	300	377	
Sony-CDPCX200		350 (Sale)		350
Sony-CDPCX270				450
Sony-CDPXE500	160			160
Technics-SLMC400			299 (Ad)	
Technics-SLMC50	230 (Ad)		248 (Ad)	
Technics-SLPD687	150 (Sale)	170 (Sale)		
Technics-SLPD787			168	
Technics-SLPD887	170 (Ad)	140	168 (Sale)	
Yamaha-CDC555			230 (Ad)	220
Yamaha-CDC755				350
Yamaha-CDC845				450

Source: Comparison of products and prices in the week of September 16, 1996
Notes: (Ad) indicates a price advertised in the local paper; (Sale) indicates an unadvertised, in-store markdown.

Introduction to the Marketing Process ▼ 53

Exhibit 13 Product Line and Price Comparisons Across Major New England Retailers—Camcorders (continued)

Model	Lechmere	Circuit City	Wiz	Tweeter
Canon-ES80		470		
Canon-ES90		560		
Canon-ES100		500		
Canon-ES200		600	598	
Canon-ES900		800	898	
Hitachi-VM1900A		500		
Hitachi-VM2900A		600		
Hitachi-VMH710A		800		
Hitachi-VMH720A		800 (Ad)		
Hitachi-VMH825LA		1200		
JVC-GRAX310			498 (Ad)	
JVC-GRAX350		550 (Ad)	648	
JVC-GRAX410U	500	550 (Sale)	498 (Ad)	
JVC-GRAX510U	500			
JVC-GRAX710U	600 (Ad)	630 (Sale)	648	
JVC-GRAX810U		700 (Sale)		
JVC-GRAX910U	730 (Ad)	800	798	
JVC-GRAX1010U		900		
Panasonic-PVA206	550 (Ad)	570	528 (Ad)	
Panasonic-PVA306	600 (Sale)	680		700
Panasonic-PVD406	800	800	800	800
Panasonic-PVD506	900	900 (Ad)	900	900
Panasonic-PVL606	1000 (Ad)	1000 (Sale)	998 (Ad)	1000
Panasonic-PVIQ295			600	
Panasonic-PVIQ305		600		
Panasonic-PVIQ475		630 (Sale)		
Panasonic-PVIQ505			798	
RCA-CC431	500 (Ad)			
RCA-CC436	600			
RCA-CC616	700 (Sale)			

Model	Lechmere	Circuit City	Wiz	Tweeter
RCA-PRO800	300 (Ad)	300 (Ad)	370	
RCA-PRO844		500	500	
RCA-PRO847		600	600	
RCA-PROV712		600 (Ad)	648 (Ad)	
RCA-PROV714		850 (Ad)	798 (Sale)	
RCA-PROV949HB		800 (Ad)		
Sharp-VLE37U	600 (Ad)	580		
Sharp-VLE39U	600 (Sale)		700	
Sharp-VLE47U	800 (Ad)	850	998	
Sharp-VLL65U	450 (Ad)			
Sony-CCDFX730		900 (Sale)		
Sony-CCDTR44	500 (Ad)	500 (Ad)		
Sony-CCDTR54		500 (Ad)		500
Sony-CCDTR64	600 (Ad)	600 (Ad)	598	
Sony-CCDTR74	650	650 (Sale)	648	650
Sony-CCDTR78			650	
Sony-CCDTR82	650 (Ad)			
Sony-CCDTR83	850 (Ad)	750 (Sale)		
Sony-CCDTR84	770		700	700
Sony-CCDTR88			748	
Sony-CCDTR94	800	800 (Ad)	800 (Sale)	800
Sony-CCDTR600	1150 (Sale)	1100 (Ad)		
Sony-CCDTR910				1300
Sony-CCDTRV11	700 (Ad)	700 (Ad)	698 (Sale)	700
Sony-CCDTRV21	900 (Ad)	900 (Ad)	898	900
Sony-CCDTRV29		1000 (Ad)		
Sony-CCDTRV30		800	998	
Sony-CCDTRV40	1190 (Sale)	1100	1198	
Sony-CCDTRV41	1200	1200 (Ad)		1200
Sony-CCDTRV81	1500 (Ad)	1500 (Ad)		1500

Source: Comparison of products and prices in the week of September 16, 1996
Notes: (Ad) indicates a price advertised in the local paper; (Sale) indicates an unadvertised, in-store markdown.

Exhibit 13 Product Line and Price Comparisons Across Major New England Retailers–Full-Sized Speakers (continued)

Model	Lechmere	Circuit City	Wiz	Tweeter	Model	Lechmere	Circuit City	Wiz	Tweeter
Advent-ADVAmber			299		KEF-Q50				600
Advent-ADVHeritage			350		KEF-Q70				900
Advent-ADVLaureate			250		Klipsch-Heritage				1000
BOSE-100		75			Klipsch-KG.5			198 (Ad)	200
BOSE-151		120			Klipsch-KG1.5				300
BOSE-201 Series 1VB	100 (Ad)	100 (Ad)			Klipsch-KG2.5				400
BOSE-301 Series 1VB	160 (Ad)	159 (Ad)			Klipsch-KG3.5V				500
Compact Reference-CR6				200	Klipsch-KG4.5V				600
Compact Reference-CR7				260	Klipsch-KG5.5V				800
Compact Reference-CR8				340	Klipsch-KLPKS3			800	
Compact Reference-CR9				420	Klipsch-Series				1300
Infinity-REF20001		100			Lerwin-VS80	130			
Infinity-REF20003		160			Lerwin-VS100	180			
Infinity-REF20004		200			Lerwin-VS120	200			
Infinity-REF20005		280 (Ad)			Lerwin-VS150	370			
Infinity-REF20006		350			Lerwin-CVEAT10BK			230	
Infinity-RS20002C	280				Lerwin-CVEAT12BK			250	
Infinity-RS20003C	330				Lerwin-CVEAT15BK			400	
Infinity-RS200SL	300				Lynnfield-VR20				550
Infinity-RS225BL	220				Lynnfield-VR30				500
Infinity-RS325	200 (Sale)				Lynnfield-VR40				1400
Infinity-RS625	250				Mirage-M90IS				200
JBL-ARC30		130			Mirage-M290IS				450
JBL-ARC50		170 (Sale)			Mirage-M5901				600
JBL-CM42		130			Mirage-M8901				700
JBL-L1		260 (Ad)			Mirage-M10901				1200
JBL-L3		400			Mission-731	180			
JBL-L5		500			Mission-732	300			
KEF-Q10				250	Mission-735	450			
KEF-Q30				400	Polk-M3lIB			250	
					Polk-S8B			200	

Source: Comparison of products and prices in the week of September 16, 1996
Notes: (Ad) indicates a price advertised in the local paper; (Sale) indicates an unadvertised, in-store markdown.

Exhibit 14 1995 Customer Survey Data[a]

Q1: Home electronic stores are offering price protection plans.
What is AUTOMATIC PRICE PROTECTION?

Response	% of Responders (n=1286)
Buy item/Receive a Refund by Mail *	17.8%
Guaranteed Lowest Price *	14.2%
Buy item/Pickup Refund Check	9.7%
Item Covered under Warranty	8.9%
Buy Item/Pickup Refund Check + 10%	4.4%
Other	4.4%
Don't Know	40.6%

*Considered a correct response to the question.

Q2: Automatic Price Protection is after you buy an item, if the store sees the item advertised
for less, the store mails you a refund check. Which one store sells home electronics and
offers the Automatic Price Protection plan?

Response	% of Responders (n=1286)
Tweeter etc.	22.1%
Circuit City	13.4%
Lechmere	10.3%
Fretter	5.8%
Radio Shack	1.2%
Sears	1.0%
Other	4.6%
Don't Know	37.9%
None	3.9%

Q3: Compared to the big chains, like Lechmere and Circuit City, do you think that Tweeter's prices are . . .

Tweeter Prices are . . .	% of Responders (n=1286)	Aware of Tweeter's APP Policy (n=284)	Unaware of Tweeter's APP Policy (n=1002)
Lower	4.7%	5.1%	4.6%
About the Same	25.3%	36.1%	22.2%
Higher	16.0%	14.5%	16.4%
Don't Know	54.0%	44.3%	56.8%

Source: Company records; Based on research conducted by WCVB-TV, Boston, MA
[a]Data are based on a random telephone survey conducted in the Greater Boston area.

WARNER-LAMBERT IRELAND: NICONIL

Declan Dixon, director of marketing for Warner-Lambert Ireland (WLI), examined two very different sales forecasts as he considered the upcoming launch of Niconil®, scheduled for January 1990. Niconil was an innovative new product that promised to help the thousands of smokers who attempted to quit smoking each year. More commonly known simply as "the patch," Niconil was a transdermal skin patch that gradually released nicotine into the bloodstream to alleviate the physical symptoms of nicotine withdrawal.

Now in October of 1989, Dixon and his staff had to decide several key aspects of the product launch. There were different opinions about how Niconil should be priced and in what quantities it would sell. Pricing decisions would directly impact product profitability as well as sales volume, and accurate sales forecasts were vital to planning adequate production capacity. Finally, the product team needed to reach consensus on the Niconil communications campaign to meet advertising deadlines and to ensure an integrated product launch.

Company Background

Warner-Lambert was an international pharmaceutical and consumer products company with over $4 billion in worldwide revenues expected in 1989. Warner-Lambert consumer products (50% of worldwide sales) included such brands as Dentyne chewing gum, Listerine mouth wash, and Hall's cough drops. Its pharmaceutical products, marketed through the Parke Davis Division, included drugs for treating a wide variety of ailments, including heart disease and bronchial disorders.

Research Associate Susan P. Smith prepared this case under the supervision of Professor John A. Quelch as the basis for class discussion rather than to illustrate either effective or ineffective handling of an administrative situation.

Warner-Lambert's Irish subsidiary was expected to generate £30 million in sales revenues in 1989:[1] £22 million from exports of manufactured products to other Warner-Lambert subsidiaries in Europe and £4 million each from pharmaceutical and consumer products sales within Ireland. The Irish drug market was estimated at £155 million (in manufacturer sales) in 1989. Warner-Lambert was the sixteenth-largest pharmaceutical company in worldwide revenues; in Ireland, it ranked sixth.

Dixon was confident that WLI's position in the Irish market would ensure market acceptance of Niconil. The Parke Davis Division had launched two new drugs successfully within the past nine months: Dilzem, a treatment for heart disease, and Accupro, a blood pressure medication. The momentum was expected to continue. The Irish market would be the first country launch for Niconil and thus serve as a test market for all of Warner-Lambert. The companywide significance of the Niconil launch was not lost on Dixon as he pondered the marketing decisions before him.

Smoking in the Republic of Ireland

Almost £600 million would be spent by Irish smokers on 300 million packs of cigarettes in 1989; this included government revenues from the tobacco sales tax of £441 million. Of 3.5 million Irish citizens, 30% of the 2.5 million adults smoked cigarettes (compared with 40% of adults in continental Europe and 20% in the United States).[2] The number of smokers in Ireland had peaked in the late 1970s and had been declining steadily since. Table A presents data from a 1989 survey that WLI had commissioned of a demographically balanced sample of 1,400 randomly chosen Irish adults. Table B shows the numbers of cigarettes smoked by Irish smokers; the average was 16.5 cigarettes.

Media coverage on the dangers of smoking, anti-smoking campaigns from public health organizations such as the Irish Cancer Society, and a mounting array of legislation restricting tobacco advertising put pressure

---

[1]In 1989, one Irish pound was equivalent to US$1.58.
[2]*Adults* were defined as those over the age of 15, and *smokers* as those who smoked at least one cigarette per day.

Table A Incidence of Cigarette Smoking in Ireland (1988–1989)

Of adult population(16 and over)	30%	(100%)
By Gender		
Men	32	(50)
Women	27	(50)
By Age		
16–24	27	(17)
25–34	38	(14)
35–44	29	(12)
45–54	29	(9)
55+	27	(19)
By Occupation		
White collar	24	(25)
Skilled working class	33	(30)
Semi- and unskilled	38	(29)
Farming	23	(17)

Note: To be read (for example): 27% of Irish citizens aged 16–24 smoked, and this age group represented 17% of the population.

Table B Number of Cigarettes Smoked Daily in Ireland (based on 400 smokers in a 1989 survey of 1,400 citizens)

More than 20	16%
15–20	42
10–14	23
5–9	12
Less than 5	4
Unsure	3

on Irish smokers to quit. Promotional discounts and coupons for tobacco products were prohibited, and tobacco advertising was banned not only on television and radio but also on billboards. Print advertising was allowed only if 10% of the ad space was devoted to warnings on the health risks of smoking. Exhibit 1 shows a sample cigarette advertisement from an Irish magazine.

Smoking as an Addiction

Cigarettes and other forms of tobacco contained nicotine, a substance that induced addictive behavior. Smokers first developed a tolerance for nicotine and then, over time, needed to increase cigarette consumption to maintain a steady, elevated blood level of nicotine. Smokers became progressively dependent on nicotine and suffered withdrawal symptoms if they stopped smoking. A craving for tobacco was characterized by physical symptoms such as decreased heart rate and a drop in blood pressure, and later could include symptoms like faintness, headaches, cold sweats, intestinal cramps, nausea, and vomiting. The smoking habit also had a psychological component stemming from the ritualistic aspects of smoking behavior, such as smoking after meals or in times of stress.

Since the 1950s, the ill effects of smoking had been researched and identified. Smoking was widely recognized as posing a serious health threat. While nicotine was the substance within the cigarette that caused addiction, it was the tar accompanying the nicotine that made smoking so dangerous. Specifically, smoking was a primary risk factor for ischaemic heart disease, lung cancer, and chronic pulmonary diseases. Other potential dangers resulting from prolonged smoking included bronchitis, emphysema, chronic sinusitis, peptic ulcer disease, and for pregnant women, damage to the fetus.

Once smoking was recognized as a health risk, the development and use of a variety of smoking cessation techniques began. In *aversion therapy,* the smoker was discouraged from smoking by pairing an aversive event such as electric shock or a nausea-inducing agent with the smoking behavior, in an attempt to break the cycle of gratification. While aversion therapy was successful in the short-term, it did not prove a lasting solution, as the old smoking behavior would often be resumed. Aversion therapy was now used infrequently. *Behavioral self-monitoring* required the smoker to develop an awareness of the stimuli that triggered the desire to smoke and then to systematically eliminate the smoking behavior in specific situations by neutralizing those stimuli. For example, the smoker could learn to avoid particular situations or to adopt a replacement activity such as chewing gum. This method was successful in some cases but demanded a high degree of self-control. While behavioral methods were useful in addressing the psychological component of smoking addiction, they did not address the physical aspect of nicotine addiction that proved an insurmountable obstacle to many who attempted to quit.

Niconil

Warner-Lambert's Niconil would be the first product to offer a complete solution for smoking cessation, addressing both the physical and psychological aspects of nicotine addiction. The physical product was a circular adhesive patch, 2.5 inches in diameter and containing 30mg of nicotine gel. Each patch was individually wrapped in a sealed, tear-resistant packet. The patch was applied to the skin, usually on the upper arm, and the nicotine was absorbed into the bloodstream to produce a steady level of nicotine that blunted the smoker's physical craving. Thirty milligrams of nicotine provided the equivalent of 20 cigarettes, without the cigarettes' damaging tar. A single patch was applied once a day every morning for two to six weeks, depending on the smoker. The average smoker was able to quit successfully (abstaining from cigarettes for a period of six months or longer) after three to four weeks.

In clinical trials, the Niconil patch alone had proven effective in helping smokers to quit. A WLI study showed that 47.5% of subjects using the nicotine patch abstained from smoking for a period of three months or longer versus 15% for subjects using a placebo patch. Among the remaining 52.5% who did not stop completely, there was a marked reduction in the number of cigarettes smoked. A similar study in the United States demonstrated an abstinence rate of 31.5% with the Niconil patch versus 14% for those with a placebo patch. The single most important success factor in Niconil effectiveness, however, was the smoker's motivation to quit. "Committed quitters" were the most likely to quit smoking successfully, using Niconil or any other smoking cessation method.

There were some side effects associated with use of the Niconil patch, including skin irritation, sleep disturbances, and nausea. Skin irritation was by far the most prevalent side effect, affecting 30% of patch users in one study. This skin irritation was not seen as a major obstacle to sales, as many study participants viewed their irritated skin areas as "badges of merit" that indicated their commitment to quitting smoking. WLI recommended placement of the patch on alternating skin areas to mitigate the problem. Future reformulations of the nicotine gel in the patch were expected to eliminate the problem entirely.

Niconil had been developed in 1985 by two scientists at Trinity College in Dublin working with Elan Corporation, an Irish pharmaceutical company specializing in transdermal drug delivery systems. Elan had entered into a joint venture with WLI to market other Elan transdermal products: Dilzem and Theolan, a respiratory medication. In 1987 Elan agreed to add Niconil to the joint venture. Warner-Lambert planned to market the product worldwide through its subsidiaries, with Elan earning a royalty on cost of goods sold.[3]

Ireland was the first country to approve the Niconil patch. In late 1989 the Irish National Drugs Advisory Board authorized national distribution of Niconil, but stipulated that it could be sold by prescription only. This meant that Niconil, as a prescription product, could not be advertised directly to the Irish consumer.

Health Care in Ireland

Ireland's General Medical Service (GMS) provided health care to all Irish citizens. Sixty-four percent of the population received free hospital care through the GMS, but were required to pay for doctor's visits (which averaged £15 each), and for drugs (which were priced lower in Ireland than the average in the European Economic Community). The remaining 36% of the population qualified as either low-income or chronic-condition patients and received free health care through the GMS. For these patients, hospital care, doctor's visits, and many drugs were obtained without fee or co-payment. Drugs paid for by the GMS were classified as "reimbursable"; approximately 70% of all drugs were reimbursable in 1989. Niconil had not qualified as a reimbursable drug; although WLI was lobbying to change its status, the immediate outlook was not hopeful.[4]

Support Program

While the patch addressed the physical craving for nicotine, Dixon and his team had decided to develop a supplementary support program to address the smoker's psychological addiction. The support program included several components in a neatly packaged box which aimed to ease the smoker's personal and social dependence on cigarettes. A booklet explained how to change behavior and contained tips on quitting. Bound into the booklet was a personal "contract" on which the smoker

---

[3]A royalty of 3% on cost of goods sold was typical for such joint ventures.
[4]None of the products in the smoking-cessation-aid market was reimbursable through the GMS. Reimbursable items excluded prescriptions for simple drugs such as mild painkillers and cough and cold remedies.

could list his or her reasons for quitting and plans for celebrating successful abstinence. There was a diary that enabled the smoker to record patterns of smoking behavior prior to quitting and that offered inspirational suggestions for each day of the program. Finally, an audio-tape included instruction in four relaxation methods which the smoker could practice in place of cigarette smoking. The relaxation exercises were narrated by Professor Anthony Clare, a well-known Irish psychiatrist who hosted a regular television program. The tape also contained an emergency-help section to assist the individual in overcoming sudden episodes of craving. A special toll-free telephone number to WLI served as a hot line to address customer questions and problems. Sample pages from the Niconil support program are presented as Exhibit 2.

While studies had not yet measured the impact of the support program on abstinence rates, it was believed that combined use of the support program and the patch could only increase Niconil's success. It had proven necessary to package the Niconil support program separately from the patch to speed approval of the patch by the Irish National Drug Board. A combined package would have required approval of the complete program, including the audio-tape, which would have prolonged the process significantly. If separate, the support program could be sold without a prescription and advertised directly to the consumer. Development of the support program had cost £3,000. WLI planned an initial production run of 10,000 units at a variable cost of £3.50 per unit.

The support program could serve a variety of purposes. Several WLI executives felt that the support program should be sold separately from the nicotine patches. They considered the support program a stand-alone product that could realize substantial revenues on its own, as well as generating sales of the Niconil patches. Supporting this position, a pricing study completed in 1989 found that the mean price volunteered for a 14-day supply of the patches and the support program combined was £27.50, and for the patches alone, £22.00. The mean price for the support program alone was £8.50, suggesting a relatively high perceived utility of this component among potential consumers. There was a risk, however, that consumers might purchase the Niconil support program *instead* of the patches, or as an accompaniment to other smoking cessation products—thus limiting sales of the Niconil patches.

Another group of executives saw the support program as a value-added point of difference that could stimulate Niconil patch sales. This group favored wide distribution of the support programs, free of charge, to potential Niconil customers. A third group of WLI executives argued that the support program was an integral component of the Niconil product which would enhance the total package by addressing the psychological aspects of nicotine addiction and improve the product's success rate, thereby increasing its sales potential. As such, these executives believed that the support program should be passed on only to those purchasing Niconil patches, at no additional cost.

Two options, not necessarily mutually exclusive, were under consideration for the distribution of the support programs. One option was to distribute them through doctors prescribing Niconil. A doctor could present the program to the patient during the office visit as he or she issued the Niconil prescription, reinforcing the counseling role of the doctor in the Niconil treatment. Supplying the GPs with support programs could also serve to promote Niconil in the medical community. A second option was to distribute the support programs through the pharmacies, where customers could receive the support programs when they purchased the Niconil patches. A disadvantage of this option was that a customer might receive additional support programs each time he or she purchased another package of Niconil. However, these duplicates might be passed on to other potential consumers and thus become an informal advertising vehicle for Niconil.

Pricing

Because all potential Niconil customers would pay for the product personally, pricing was a critical component of the Niconil marketing strategy. Management debated how many patches to include in a single package and at what price to sell each package. In test trials, the average smoker succeeded in quitting with Niconil in three to four weeks (i.e., 21 to 28 patches); others needed as long as six weeks.[5]

As Niconil was essentially a tobacco substitute, cigarettes provided a logical model for considering various packaging and pricing options. The average Irish smoker purchased a pack of cigarettes daily, often when buying the morning newspaper. Fewer than 5% of all cigarettes were sold in cartons.[6] Because the Irish smoker rarely

---

[5]Smokers were advised not to use the patch on a regular basis beyond three months. If still unsuccessful in quitting, they could resume use of the patch after stopping for at least a month.
[6]A carton of cigarettes contained 20 individual packs of cigarettes; each pack contained 20 cigarettes.

purchased a multi-week cigarette supply at once, he or she was thought likely to compare the cost of cigarette purchases with the cost of a multi-week supply of Niconil. WLI thus favored packaging just a 7-day supply of patches in each unit. However, Warner-Lambert subsidiaries in continental Europe, where carton purchases were more popular, wanted to include a six-week supply of patches in each package if and when they launched Niconil. Managers at Warner-Lambert's international division wanted to standardize packaging as much as possible across its subsidiaries and suggested as a compromise a 14-day supply per package.

Following the cigarette model, two pricing schemes had been proposed. The first proposal was to price Niconil on a par with cigarettes. The average Irish smoker smoked 16.5 cigarettes per day and the expected retail price in 1990 for a pack of cigarettes was £2.25. WLI's variable cost of goods for a 14-day supply of Niconil was £12.00.[7] Pharmacies generally added a 50% retail mark-up to the price at which they purchased the product from WLI. A value-added tax of 25% of the retail price was included in the proposed price to the consumer of £32.00 for a 14-day supply. In addition, the consumer paid a £1.00 dispensing fee per prescription.

Under the second pricing proposal, Niconil would be priced at a premium to cigarettes. Proponents argued that if the Niconil program were successful, it would be a permanent replacement for cigarettes and its cost would be far outweighed by the money saved on cigarettes. The proposed price to the consumer under this option was £60.00 for a 14-day supply.

Competition

Few products would compete directly with Niconil in the smoking cessation market in Ireland. Two small niche products were Accudrop and Nicobrevin, both available without a prescription. Accudrop was a nasal spray that smokers applied to the cigarette filter to trap tar and nicotine, resulting in cleaner smoke. Anticipated 1990 manufacturer sales for Accudrop were £5,000. Nicobrevin, a product from the U.K., was a time-release capsule that eased smoking withdrawal symptoms. Anticipated 1990 manufacturer's sales for Nicobrevin were £75,000.

The most significant competitive product was Nicorette, the only nicotine-replacement product currently available. Marketed in Ireland by Lundbeck, Nicorette was a chewing gum that released nicotine into the body as the smoker chewed the gum. Because chewing gum in public was not socially acceptable among Irish adults, the product had never achieved strong sales, especially given that its efficacy relied on steady, intensive chewing. A second sales deterrent had been the association of Nicorette with side effects, such as mouth cancer and irritation of the linings of the mouth and stomach.

Nicorette was sold in 10-day supplies, available in two dosages: 2mg and 4mg. Smokers would chew the 2mg Nicorette initially, and switch to the 4mg gum after two weeks if needed. In a 1982 study, 47% of Nicorette users quit smoking, versus 21% for placebo users. A long-term follow-up study in 1989, however, indicated that only 10% more Nicorette patients had ceased smoking, compared with placebo users. The average daily treatment cost to Nicorette customers was £0.65 per day for the 2mg gum and £1.00 per day for the 4mg gum. Nicorette, like Niconil, was available at pharmacies by prescription only, so advertising had been limited to medical journals. Anticipated 1990 manufacturer sales of Nicorette were £170,000; however, the brand had not been advertised in three years.

Forecasting

Although Nicorette was not considered a successful product, WLI was confident that Niconil, with its less-intrusive nicotine delivery system and fewer side effects, would capture a dominant position in the smoking cessation market and ultimately increase the demand for smoking cessation products. Precise sales expectations for Niconil were difficult to formulate, however, and two different methods had been suggested.

The first method assumed that the percentage of smokers in the adult population (30% in 1990) would drop by one percentage point per year through 1994. An estimated 10% of smokers attempted to quit smoking each year, and 10% of that number purchased some type of smoking cessation product. WLI believed that Niconil could capture half of these "committed quitters" in the first year, selling therefore to 5% of those who tried to give up smoking in 1990. Further, they hoped to increase this share by 1% per year, up to 9% in 1994. Having estimated the number of customers who would purchase an initial two-week supply of Niconil, WLI managers then had to calculate the total number of units purchased.

---

[7]This cost of goods included Elan's royalty.

Based on experience in test trials, WLI anticipated that 60% of first-time Niconil customers would purchase a second two-week supply. Of that number, 20% would purchase a third two-week supply. About 75% of smokers completed the program within six weeks.

A more aggressive forecast could be based on WLI's 1989 survey, which showed that of the 30% of [the 1,400] respondents who were smokers, 54% indicated that they would like to give up smoking, and 30% expressed interest in the nicotine patch. More relevant, 17% of smokers indicated that they were likely to go to the doctor and pay for such a patch, though a specific purchase price was not included in the question. A rule of thumb in interpreting likelihood-of-purchase data was to divide this percentage by three to achieve a more likely estimate of actual purchasers. Once the number of Niconil customers was calculated, the 100%/60%/20% model used above could then be applied to compute the total expected unit sales.

Production

Under the terms of the joint venture with Elan and using current manufacturing technology, production capacity would be 1,000 units (of 14-day supply packages) per month in the first quarter of 1990, ramping up to 2,000 units per month by year-end. WLI had the option to purchase a new, more efficient machine that could produce 14,000 units per month and reduce WLI's variable cost on each unit by 10%. In addition, if WLI purchased the new machine and Niconil was launched in continental Europe, WLI could export some of its production to the European subsidiaries, further expanding its role as a supplier to Warner-Lambert Europe. WLI would earn a margin of £2.00 per unit on Niconil that it sold through this channel.[8] Estimated annual unit sales, assuming a launch of Niconil throughout Western Europe, are listed in Table C. Warner-Lambert management aimed to recoup any capital investments within five years; the Niconil machine would cost £1.2 million and could be on-line within nine months.

Marketing Prescription Products

Prescription products included all pharmaceutical items deemed by the Irish government to require the professional expertise of the medical community to guide consumer

Table C Estimated Unit Sales of Niconil in Western Europe

Year 1	100,000 units
Year 2	125,000 units
Year 3	150,000 units
Year 4	175,000 units
Year 5	200,000 units

usage.[9] Before a customer could purchase a prescription product, he or she first had to visit a doctor and obtain a written prescription which specified that product. The customer could then take the written prescription to one of Ireland's 1,132 pharmacies and purchase the product.

The prescription nature of Niconil thus created marketing challenges. A potential Niconil customer first had to make an appointment with a doctor for an office visit to obtain the necessary prescription. Next, the doctor had to agree to prescribe Niconil to the patient to help him or her to quit smoking. Only then could the customer go to the pharmacy and purchase Niconil. This two-step purchase process required WLI to address two separate audiences in marketing Niconil: the Irish smokers who would eventually use Niconil and the Irish doctors who first had to prescribe it to patients.

Niconil's potential customers were the 10% of Irish smokers who attempted to give up smoking each year (2% of the total Irish population). Market research had shown that those most likely to purchase Niconil were aged 35-44 and in either white-collar or skilled occupations (18% of Irish smokers). Smokers under the age of 35 tended to see themselves as "bullet proof": because most were not yet experiencing the negative health effects of smoking, it was difficult to persuade them to quit. Upper-income, better-educated smokers found less tolerance for smoking among their peers and thus felt greater pressure to quit. Research had also indicated that women were 25% more likely to try Niconil as they tended to be more concerned with their health and thus more often visited the doctors from whom they could learn about Niconil and obtain the necessary prescription.

The most likely prescribers of Niconil would be the 2,000 General Practitioners (GPs) in Ireland. The average

---

[8]Warner-Lambert's European subsidiaries were likely to consider purchasing this new machine themselves as well.

[9]Drugs and other pharmaceutical products that did not require a written prescription from a doctor were called "over-the-counter" or "OTC" drugs.

GP saw 15 patients per day and eight out of ten general office visits resulted in the GPs writing prescriptions for patients. Although 10% of Irish doctors smoked, virtually all recognized the dangers of smoking and rarely smoked in front of patients. A *Modern Medicine* survey of 780 Irish GPs indicated that 63% formally gathered smoking data from their patients. GPs acknowledged the health risk that smoking posed to patient health, but they were usually reluctant to pressure a patient to quit unless the smoker was highly motivated. Unsolicited pressure to quit could meet with patient resistance and result, in some cases, in a doctor losing a patient and the associated revenues from patient visits. Smoking cessation was not currently a lucrative treatment area for GPs. Most would spend no longer than 15 minutes discussing smoking with their patients. To the few patients who asked for advice on how to quit smoking, 92% of GPs would offer "firm, clear-cut advice." Fewer than 15% would recommend formal counseling, drug therapy, or other assistance. GPs were not enthusiastic about Nicorette due to poor results and the incidence of side effects.

WLI was confident that Niconil would find an enthusiastic audience among Irish GPs. As a complete program with both physical and psychological components, Niconil offered a unique solution. In addition, the doctor would assume a significant counseling role in the Niconil treatment. It was anticipated that the GP would initially prescribe a 14-day supply of Niconil to the patient. At the end of the two-week period, the patient would hopefully return to the doctor for counseling and an additional prescription, if needed.

Marketing Communications

WLI intended to position Niconil as a complete system that was a more acceptable alternative to existing nicotine replacement therapy for the purpose of smoking cessation. Niconil would be the only smoking cessation product to address both the physical dimension of nicotine addiction through the patch and the psychological dimension through the support program. Compared with Nicorette gum, Niconil offered a more acceptable delivery system (Niconil's transdermal system vs. Nicorette's oral system) and fewer, less severe side effects. WLI planned to promote these aspects of the product through a comprehensive marketing program. The Niconil launch marketing budget, detailed in Exhibit 3, followed the Warner-Lambert standard for new drug launches. Several WLI executives felt that this standard

was inadequate for the more consumer-oriented Niconil and pressed for increased communications spending.

Advertising

Because Irish regulations prohibited the advertising of prescription products directly to the consumer, Niconil advertising was limited to media targeting the professional medical community. Three major publications targeted this audience: *Irish Medical Times, Irish Medical News,* and *Modern Medicine.* WLI planned to advertise moderately in the first year to raise awareness of Niconil in the medical community. After that it was hoped that the initial momentum could be maintained through strong public relations efforts and personal testimony to the product's efficacy. Exhibit 4 summarizes the proposed 1990 media advertising schedule for Niconil.

WLI's advertising agency had designed a distinctive logo for Niconil that would be used on all packaging and collateral materials such as "No Smoking" placards. These would feature the Niconil logo and be distributed to doctors' offices, hospitals, and pharmacies to promote the product. Ideally, the logo would become sufficiently well recognized that it could be used eventually on a stand-alone basis to represent Niconil to the end consumer without the brand name. This would allow some flexibility in circumventing Irish advertising restrictions to reach the end consumer. Sample logos and packaging are illustrated in Exhibit 5. The agency had also developed the following four concepts for a Niconil medical journal advertisement:

- "Day and night I crave cigarettes. I can't stop. I'm hooked." When they ask for help, give them the help they need—new Niconil nicotine transdermal patches.

- Where there's smoke, there's emphysema, throat cancer, angina, lung cancer, sinusitis. Now a way to break this deadly addiction. Introducing Niconil nicotine transdermal patches—all they need to succeed.

- Emphysema, lung cancer, peptic ulcer, angina, sinusitis, throat cancer. Help end their deadly addiction. One-a-day instead of a pack-a-day. Introducing Niconil nicotine transdermal patches.

- "How many of your patients are dying for a smoke?" Help them break the cycle of addiction. Introducing Niconil nicotine transdermal patches. A better way to stop.

Direct Mail

A direct mail campaign to Ireland's 2,000 GPs was planned in conjunction with the Niconil product announcement. Two weeks prior to launch, an introductory letter would be mailed with a color photo of the product, a reply card offering a support program, and additional product information. The support programs would be mailed in response to the reply cards, arriving just prior to the launch. A response rate of at least 50% was anticipated based on past direct mail campaigns.

Public Relations

The formal Niconil product announcement was scheduled to occur in Dublin at a professional event that WLI had dubbed the "Smoking Cessation Institute Symposium." The symposium would be chaired by Professor Anthony Clare (the narrator of the Niconil audio-tape), Professor Hickey (an expert in preventive cardiology), and Professors Masterson and J. Kelly from Elan Corporation. Open to members of the medical profession and media, the event was intended to focus attention on the dangers of smoking and to highlight Niconil as a groundbreaking product designed to address this health hazard.

WLI had sought endorsements from both the Irish Cancer Society and the Irish Heart Foundation, two national health organizations that actively advocated smoking cessation. Because both nonprofit institutions relied on donations for financing and were concerned that a specific product endorsement would jeopardize their tax-exempt status, they refused to endorse Niconil directly. Representatives from each institution had, however, stated their intention to attend the launch symposium.

In advance of the symposium, a press release and supporting materials would be distributed to the media. Emphasis would be placed on the role that Niconil would play in disease prevention. It would also be noted that Niconil had been developed and manufactured locally and had the potential for worldwide sales. Other planned public relations activities included a roundtable dinner for prominent opinion leaders in the medical community. Publicity in the media was planned to coincide with key "commitment to change" times such as New Year's and Lent.[10]

---

[10]Lent was an annual penitential period during spring of the Roman Catholic religious calendar that was still observed by many of the 95% of the Irish who were Roman Catholic.

Sales Strategy

WLI Ireland had a sales force of 16 representatives whose average annual salary, bonus, and benefits amounted to £25,000 in 1988. They focused their selling efforts on 1,600 Irish GPs who were most accessible geographically and most amenable to pharmaceutical sales visits. The sales staff was divided into three selling teams of four to six representatives. Each team sold separate product lines to the same 1,600 GPs. The team that would represent Niconil was already selling three other drugs from Elan Corporation that were marketed by WLI as part of their joint venture. These four salespeople would add Niconil to their existing product lines. Sales training on Niconil would take place one month prior to the product launch.

The pharmaceutical salesperson's challenge was to maintain the attention of each GP long enough to discuss each item in his or her product line. Because Niconil was expected to be of great interest to GPs, the salespeople were keen to present Niconil first during the sales visit, followed by the less exciting products. Normally, a new product would receive this up-front positioning. However, Dixon argued that Niconil should be presented last during the sales call to maximize the time that a salesperson spent with each GP and to prevent the sales time devoted to the other three Elan products from being cannibalized by Niconil. Based on revenue projections for all four products, salespeople would be instructed to spend no more than 15% of their sales call time on Niconil. On average, each WLI salesperson called on six to seven doctors per day. The goal was for each sales team to call on the 1,600 targeted GPs once every three months. In the case of Niconil, all 16 sales people would present the new brand during their calls for six weeks after launch.

Critical Decisions

With just three months to go before the launch of Niconil, Dixon felt he had to comply with the international division's suggestion to include a 14-day supply of patches in each Niconil package, but he debated whether to price the product on a par with or at a premium to cigarettes. Equally important, he had to decide which sales forecast was more accurate so that he could plan production capacity. And finally, he needed to make decisions on the communications program: which advertising concept would be the most effective, what other efforts could be made to enhance product acceptance, and was the current budget adequate to support Warner-Lambert's first national launch of such an innovative product?

Exhibit 1 Cigarette Advertisement from an Irish Magazine

SMOKING CAUSES CANCER
Irish Government Warning

Exhibit 2 Sample Pages from Niconil Support Program

The first step

Fill in the contract in your own words. Write down all the reasons that are most important to you for beating the smoking habit.

Then write down how your life will be better and more enjoyable without the smoking habit.

Finally, write down how you will reward yourself for your courage and hard work. You will deserve something very special.

Choose the day

Decide when to stop and put a ring round that date on your calendar.

Try to find a time when you are not going to be under pressure for a few days. The start of a holiday is good for two reasons. You will not have the stress of work and you will be free to change your routine.

Countdown

1. In the days leading up to your stop date see if you can get your partner or a friend to stop smoking along with you.

2. Ask a local charity to sponsor you or join a non-smoking group. Having other people to talk to who have kicked the habit can be a lifeline when your willpower gets shaky. They will know and understand what you are going through. Your doctor will be able to tell you what groups are running in your area.

3. The evening before your stop date, throw away **all** your cigarettes and get rid of your lighters and ashtrays. You will not need them again.

4. Read over your smoker's diary entries. Know your habit.
- What are the most dangerous times?
- Where are the most dangerous places?
- What are the most dangerous situations?
- Who do I usually smoke with?

CONTRACT

1. I, ...,
HAVE STOPPED SMOKING BECAUSE
I WANT:

2. **MY LIFE WILL BE BETTER WHEN I AM FREE OF SMOKING BECAUSE:**

3. **AFTER BEATING SMOKING FOR A MONTH I WILL CELEBRATE BY:**

SIGNED:

DATE:

WEEK ONE THE WINNER'S DIARY

DAY

1. Today is the greatest challenge. If you succeed today, tomorrow will be easier. You can do it.

2. Well done. The first 24 hours are over. Your lungs have had their first real rest for years.

3. Remember: smoking is for losers. If you find yourself getting tense, use your relaxation tape.

4. Read your contract again. See how much better life is getting now that you are freeing yourself from this unpleasant addiction.

5. Your body says "thank you". It's feeling fitter already.

6. Don't forget to distract yourself at key cigarette times.

7. Well done. You're through your first week. Give yourself a treat. Go out for a meal or buy yourself something you've always wanted.

COUNT DOWN TO D-DAY

DAY 1

Cigarette	Time of day?	Where were you?	Who were you with?	What were you doing?	How did you feel?
1					
2					
3					
4					
5					
6					
7					
8					
9					
10					

Exhibit 3 Niconil First Year Marketing Budget (£'000)

Advertising	
Ad creation	£ 4
Media advertising	28
Total advertising	**32**
Promotion	
Development of support program	3
Production of support programs	35
Training/promotional materials	44
Direct mailing to GPs	2
Total promotion	**84**
Public Relations	
Launch symposium	5
Roundtable meeting	2
Press release/materials	1
Total public relations	**8**
Market research	3
Sales force allocation	23
Product management allocation	50
Total budget	**£ 200**

Exhibit 4 1990 Niconil Media Advertising Schedule

Publication	Frequency	Circulation	Cost/1.000	Placements
Irish Medical Times	Weekly	5,200	£154	13
Irish Medical News	Weekly	5,100	137	11
Modern Medicine	Monthly	3,700	176	5

Exhibit 5 Sample Niconil Logo and Packaging

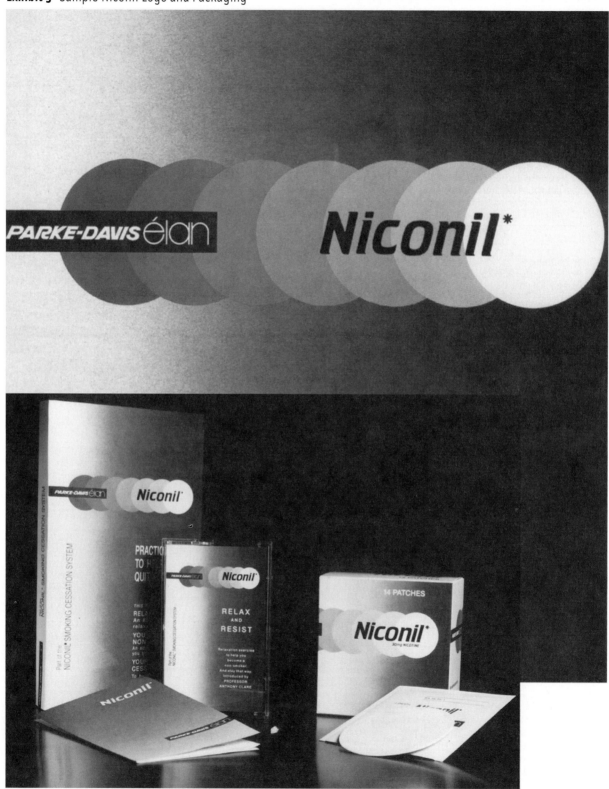

THE ARAVIND EYE HOSPITAL, MADURAI, INDIA: IN SERVICE FOR SIGHT

I (the casewriter) arrived early at 7:00 a.m. at the outpatient department of the Aravind Eye Hospital at Madurai, India. My sponsor, Thulasi (R.D. Thulasiraj, hospital administrator), was expecting me at 8:00, but I came early to observe the patient flow. More than 100 people formed two lines. Two young women, assisted by a third, were briskly registering the patients at the reception counter. They asked a few key questions: "Which village do you come from?" "Where do you live?" "What's your age?" and a few more, but it all took less than two minutes per patient. The women seemed very comfortable with the computer and its data-entry procedures.

Their supervisor, a somewhat elderly man with grey hair, was hunched over, gently nudging and helping them along with the registration process. He looked up and spotted me. I was the only man in that crowd who wore western-style trousers and shoes. The rest wore the traditional South Indian garment ("dhoti" or "veshti"), and many were barefooted because they could not afford "slippers." The old man hobbled from the registration desk and made his way toward me. The 50-foot distance must have taken him 10 minutes to make because he paused every now and then to answer a question here or help a patient there. I took a step forward, introduced myself, and asked to be guided to Thulasi's office. "Yes, we were expecting you," he said with an impish smile and walked me to the right wing of the hospital where all the administrative offices were. He ushered me into his office and pointed me to the couch across from his desk. It was only when I noticed his crippled fingers that I realized this grand old man was Dr. Venkataswamy himself,

the 74-year-old ophthalmic surgeon who had founded the Aravind Eye Hospital and built it from 20 beds in 1976 to one of the biggest hospitals of its kind in the world in 1992, with 1,224 beds.

Dr. V. spoke slowly and with a childlike sense of curiosity and excitement:

Tell me, can cataract surgery be marketed like hamburgers? Don't you call it social marketing or something? See, in America, McDonald's and Dunkin' Donuts and Pizza Hut have all mastered the art of mass marketing. We have to do something like that to clear the backlog of 20 million blind eyes in India. We perform only one million cataract surgeries a year. At this rate we cannot catch up. Modern communication through satellites is reaching every nook and corner of the globe. Even an old man like me from a small village in India knows of Michael Jackson and Magic Johnson. [At this point, Dr. V. knew that he had surprised me. He suppressed a smile and proceeded.]

Why can't we bring eyesight to the masses of poor people in India, Asia, Africa, and all over the world? I would like to do that in my lifetime. How do you think we should do it?

"I'm not sure," I responded, completely swept away and exhausted by the grand vision of this giant human being. But I don't think he wanted an answer that did not match his immense enthusiasm. He wanted a way to further his goal, not a real debate on whether the goal was feasible.

Professor V. Kasturi Rangan prepared this case as the basis for class discussion rather than to illustrate either effective or ineffective handling of an administrative situation.

The Blindness Problem

As of 1992, there were 30 million blind people in the world—6 million in Africa, 20 million in Asia, 2 million in Latin America, and the rest in Europe, the former Soviet Union, Oceania, and North America.[1] The prevalence of blindness in most industrialized countries of Europe and North America varied between 0.15% to 0.25%, compared with blindness rates of nearly 1.5% for the developing countries in Africa, Asia, and Latin America. While age-related macular degeneration, diabetic retinopathy, and glaucoma were the dominant causes in developed countries, cataract was the major cause of blindness in the developing countries, accounting for nearly 75% of all cases in Asia. Of the several types of cataracts, more than 80% were age-related, generally occurring in people over 45 years (and increasing dramatically in the over-65 age group).

Cataract

As illustrated in Figure A, the natural lens of the eye, which is normally clear, helps to focus light on the retina. The lens becomes clouded in a cataract eye and light is not easily transmitted to the retina. The clouding process takes three to ten years to reach maturity and surgical removal of the clouded lens is the only proven treatment. Ophthalmic surgeons in some developing countries usually preferred to remove cataracts only when they were mature (i.e., when they significantly diminished sight.)

Cataract removal was considered a fairly routine operation, usually performed under local anaesthesia, with a higher than 95% chance of improved vision. Two principal surgical techniques were used: intracapsular surgery without intraocular lens (ICCE), and extracapsular surgery with intraocular lens (ECCE). ICCE remained the most widely used procedure in the developing countries. The surgery, almost always performed without an operating microscope, used fairly simple instruments and could be completed in under 20 minutes. Some three to five weeks after surgery, after the eyeball returned to its original shape, the patient was fitted with aphakic spectacles (rather thick lenses that improved vision to an acceptable level). In contrast, the ECCE technique was always performed under an operating microscope. This surgery often required close to 30 minutes, because the surgeon left the posterior capsule intact when removing the natural lens, and then inserted a tiny transparent plastic intraocular lens (IOL) in the posterior chamber. Patients often therefore did not require corrective spectacles to restore vision. Moreover,

the quality of the restored sight was near-natural and free of distortion or magnification. Unlike ICCE patients, ECCE patients usually experienced significant improvement in sight within days of the operation. ICCE patients, on the other hand, usually experienced gradual improvement over a three- to five-week period.

India

India's population of 850 million in 1991 was the second-highest in the world, after China. Although there were nearly 20 million blind eyes in India, with another two million being added annually, only 12 million people were classified as blind because the rest had better than 20/200 or 6/60 vision in one eye. Cataract was the main cause in 75% to 80% of the cases. The annual per-capita income of an Indian citizen was Rs. 6,800 ($275), with over 70% below the Rs. 2,500 ($100) poverty line; the incidence of cataract blindness, however, was fairly uniformly distributed across the various socioeconomic groups. Although India's 8,000 ophthalmologists[2] (eye doctors) performed nearly 1.2 million cataract operations a year, the medical infrastructure to clear the backlog of cataract cases was woefully inadequate in making maximal use of existing resources. The United States, for instance, had twice as many ophthalmologists for a population of only about 250 million. India had about 42,000 eye hospital beds,[3] and the medical resources and infrastructure were two-thirds skewed to the urban areas where less than one-third of the nation's population lived. The government, through its Ministry of Health and Family Welfare, took an active role in blindness prevention programs. Its 425 district hospitals (about one for every two million people) offered free eye care and cataract surgery to people who could not afford private treatment. About 30% of all cataract surgeries in India were performed in the government sector (both central and state), free of cost to the patients. Another 40% were performed in the private sector for a fee, and the remaining 30% were performed free of cost by volunteer groups and NGOs (nongovernment organizations). The government currently allocated about Rs. 60 million ($2

---

[1]A distance of 20 feet (or 6 meters) is used as a minimum standard in measuring the eye's ability to recognize certain sizes/profiles/shapes of objects. A less-than-normal eye would only be able to recognize objects at this minimum distance, which a normal eye could distinguish at a further distance (e.g., 40 feet or 12 meters). Such a vision, 20/40 or 6/12, would then have to be corrected with glasses. According to the World Health Organization, sight worse than 20/400 or 3/60 (even after correction with glasses) is considered blind.

[2]Ophthalmologists are trained eye doctors with medical degrees. They examined patients and prescribed treatment; if the treatment involved corrective glasses, the patients could get them from an optician. Unlike in the United States, there were very few optometrists (professionals who measured eyesight and prescribed glasses) in the Indian medical system.

[3]These were located in government hospitals, medical college hospitals, mobile hospitals, eye hospitals, and private nursing homes.

Figure A

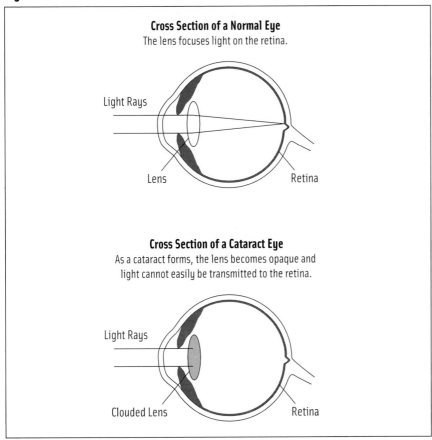

Cross Section of a Normal Eye
The lens focuses light on the retina.

Light Rays

Lens

Retina

Cross Section of a Cataract Eye
As a cataract forms, the lens becomes opaque and
light cannot easily be transmitted to the retina.

Light Rays

Clouded Lens

Retina

million) annually for blindness prevention programs. A recent report to the World Bank estimated that nearly $200 million (Rs. 6,000 million) would be required immediately to build the infrastructure for training personnel, purchasing equipment, and building facilities to overcome the country's blindness problem.

Dr. V. and the Aravind Eye Hospital

The eldest son of a well-to-do farmer, Dr. Govindappa Venkataswamy was born in 1918 in a small village near Madurai in South India. After his education in local schools and colleges, Dr. V. graduated with a bachelor's degree in medicine from Madras University in 1944. During his university years, and immediately thereafter, he was deeply influenced by Mahatma (meaning "great man") Gandhi, who united the country in a nonviolent movement to seek independence from British rule. Dr. V.

reasoned that the best way to serve his country in the struggle for freedom would be in the capacity he was best trained for—as a doctor. So he joined the Indian Army Medical Corps in 1945, but was discharged in 1948 because of severe rheumatoid arthritis. Dr. V. recalled,

> I developed severe rheumatoid arthritis and almost all the joints were severely swollen and painful. I was bedridden in a Madras hospital for over a year. The arthritis crippled me badly and for years I could not walk long distances, which I was accustomed to doing as a village boy. In the acute stage, for several months I could not stand on my feet and I was confined to bed for over a year. I still remember the day I was able to stand on my feet. A relative of mine had come to see me in the hospital ward and I struggled hard to keep my feet on the ground and stand close to the bed without holding it. When I did, it felt as though I was on top of the Himalayas. Then, for several years, I used to struggle to walk a few yards or squat down on

the floor. Even now in villages we normally squat on the floor when we eat, and I find it difficult. I could not hold a pen with my fingers to write in the acute stage of arthritis. We normally eat food with our fingers. I found it difficult to handle the food with my swollen fingers. Later I trained slowly to hold the surgeon's scalpel and cut the eye for cataract operations. After some years, I could stand for a whole day and perform 50 operations or more at a stretch. Then I learned to use the operating microscope and do good, high-quality cataract and other eye surgeries.

By the time of his retirement in 1976, Dr. V. had risen to head the Department of Ophthalmology at the Government Madurai Medical College and also to head Eye Surgery at the Government Erskine Hospital, Madurai. After retirement, in order to fulfill a long-cherished dream—the creation of a private, nonprofit eye hospital that would provide quality eye care—Dr. V. founded the Aravind Eye Hospital, named after an Indian philosopher and saint, Sri Aurobindo. Dr. V. noted:

> What I learnt from Mahatma Gandhi and Swami [saint] Aurobindo was that all of us through dedication in our professional lives can serve humanity and God. Achieving a sense of spirituality or higher consciousness is a slow, gradual process. It is wrong to think that unless you are a mendicant or a martyr you can't be a spiritual person. When I go to the meditation room at the hospital every morning, I ask God that I be a better tool, a receptacle for the divine force. We can all serve humanity in our normal professional lives by being more generous and less selfish in what we do. You don't have to be a "religious" person to serve God. You serve God by serving humanity.

History

The 20-bed Aravind Eye Hospital opened in 1976 and performed all types of eye surgery; its goal was to offer quality eye care at reasonable cost. The first three surgeons were Dr. V.; his sister, Dr. G. Natchiar; and her husband, Dr. P. Namperumalswamy (Dr. Nam). A 30-bed annex was opened in 1977 to accommodate patients convalescing after surgery. It was not until 1978 that a 70-bed free hospital was opened to provide the poor with free eye care. It had a four-table operating theater with rooms for scrubbing, changing, and sterilization of instruments.

A main hospital (for paying patients), commenced in 1977 and completed in 1981, had 250 beds with 80,000 square feet of space in five floors, four major operating theaters (two tables per theater), and a minor one for septic care. There were specialty clinics in the areas of retina and vitreous diseases, cornea, glaucoma, and squint corrections, diabetic retinopathy, and pediatric ophthalmology; the heads of all but one of these clinics were family members of Dr. V., and all had received training in the United States. The Main Hospital was well-equipped with modern, often imported, equipment to provide the best possible eye care for its patients. (In 1992, there were about 240 people on the hospital's staff, including about 30 doctors, 120 nurses, 60 administrative personnel, and 30 housekeeping and maintenance workers.)

In 1984 a new 350-bed free hospital was opened. A "bed" here was equivalent to a 6' x 3' mattress spread out on the floor. This five-story hospital had nearly 36,000 square feet of space and its top story accommodated the nurses' quarters for the entire Aravind group of hospitals. The hospital had two major operating theaters and a minor theater for septic cases. On the ground floor were facilities for treating outpatients; in-patients were housed in large wards on the upper floors. The Free Hospital was largely staffed with medical personnel from the Main Hospital. Doctors and nurses were posted in rotation so that they served both facilities, thereby ensuring that nonpaying and paying patients all received the same quality of eye care.

Until 1989, all the patients in the Free Hospital were attracted from eye camps. In 1990, Aravind opened its Free Hospital to walk-in patients. Every Saturday and Sunday, teams of doctors and support staff with diagnostic equipment fanned out to several rural sites to screen the local population. Eye camps were sponsored events, where a local businessman or a social service organization mobilized resources to inform the local public within about a 25- to 50-mile radius of the forthcoming screening camp. Camps were usually held in towns that served as the commercial hub for a number of neighboring villages. Local schools, colleges, or marriage halls often served as campsites. Patients from surrounding villages who traveled by bus to the central (downtown) bus stand were transported to the campsite by the sponsors. Several patients from the local area came directly to the campsite. The Aravind team screened patients at the camp, and those selected for surgery were transported the same afternoon by bus to the Free Hospital at Madurai. They were returned three days later, after surgery and recuperation, back to the campsite where their family members picked them up. Patients who came from nearby villages were taken to the central bus stand and provided return tickets to their appropriate destinations. A clinical team from Aravind went back to the campsite after three months for a follow-up evaluation of the discharged patients. Patients were informed of the dates for the follow-up camps well in advance—in many cases, at the time of the initial discharge after surgery. Aravind provided the services of its clinical staff and free treatment for the patients selected for surgery; the camp sponsors bore all other administrative, logistical, and food costs associated with the camp. (Exhibit 1 shows the location of the various Aravind hospitals; Exhibits 2 and 3 show the inpatient ward at the Aravind Main Hospital, Free Hospital, and some typical eye camp activities.)

As the Aravind Eye Hospital grew from a 20-bed to a 600-bed hospital, many members of Dr. V.'s family joined in support of his ideals. His brother, G. Srinivasan, a civil engineering contractor, constructed all the hospital buildings at cost and later became the hospital's finance manager. A nephew, R.D. Thulasiraj (Thulasi), gave up a management job in private sector to join as the hospital's administrator. Thulasi, at Dr. V.'s insistence, trained at the University of Michigan in public health management before assuming administrative duties at Aravind. Thirteen ophthalmologists on the hospital's staff were related to Dr. V. In order to provide continuous training to its ophthalmic personnel, Aravind had research and training collaborations with St. Vincent's Hospital in New York City and the University of Illinois' Eye and Ear Infirmary in Chicago; both institutions also regularly sent their own ophthalmologists for residency training to Aravind. Aravind was also actively involved in training ophthalmic personnel in charge of administering blindness prevention projects in other parts of Asia and Africa. Explaining the unfailing support of his family members, Dr. V. recalled:

> We have always been a joint family through thick and thin. I was 32 when my father died. I was the eldest in the family, and in a family system like ours, I was responsible for educating my two younger brothers and two younger sisters, for organizing and fixing their marriages—that is the usual custom we have—for finding suitable partners for them. I was the head of the family and looked after all of them. But that was not a problem. I was not married, because of my arthritis trouble. Now it has become a boon. My brother takes care of me, and I stay with him all the time. His children are as much attached to me as they are to him.

Dr. Natchiar, Dr. V.'s sister and now the hospital's senior medical officer, elaborated:

> When Brother retired from government service, he seemed awfully impatient to serve society in a big way. He asked me and my husband [Dr. Nam] if we would give up our government jobs to join him. Usually in India, when one leaves government service to enter private practice, incomes go up threefold. In this case, we were told that our salaries would be about Rs. 24,000 a year (approximately $1,500 in 1980). And worse still, Brother always believed in pushing the mind and body to its highest effort levels. So we would have to work twice as hard for half the salary. My husband and I talked it over and said yes. We did not have the heart to say no. But what we lost in earnings was made up by the tremendous professional support that Brother gave us. We were encouraged to attend conferences, publish papers, buy books, and do anything to advance our professional standing in the field. It is only in the last five years that our senior surgeons' salaries are reasonably consistent with their reputation in the field.

On his insistence that the hospital staff be totally committed and dedicated to the mission of the Aravind Hospital, Dr. V. expressed his philosophy:

> We have a lot of very capable and intelligent people, all very well trained in theoretical knowledge. But knowledge by itself is not going to save the world. Look at Christ; you cannot call him a scholar, he was a spiritual man. What we need is dedication and devotion to the practice. When doctors join us for residencies, we gradually condition them physically for long hours of concentrated work. Most believe they need work only for a few hours and that, too, for four days a week. In government hospitals, rarely do surgeons work for more than 30 hours a week; we normally expect our doctors to go 60 hours. Moreover, in the government hospitals there is a lot of bureaucracy and corruption. Patients feel obliged to tip the support staff to get even routine things done. Worse still, poor villagers feel totally intimidated. We want to make all sorts of people feel at ease, and this can only come if the clinical staff and their support staff view the entire exercise as a spiritual experience.

Aravind Eye Hospital: 1992

By 1988, in addition to the 600 beds at Madurai, a 400-bed hospital at Tirunelveli, a bustling rural town 75 miles south of Madurai, and a 100-bed hospital at Theni, a small town 50 miles west of Madurai, were also started (see Exhibit 1). There were plans afoot to set up a 400-bed (Rs. 10 million) hospital at Coimbatore, a city 125 miles north of Madurai. Coimbatore, like Madurai, was the hub of its district and was bigger than Madurai in population and commerce. Dr. Ravindran, a family member who currently headed the Tirunelveli Hospital was slated to run the Coimbatore Hospital. Succession plans for the Tirunelveli Hospital would then have to be worked out. Managing the Theni Hospital, which was located in Dr. Nam's home town, was not a big problem: first, because the facility was small, and second, because of the informal supervision it received whenever Dr. Nam visited his home town. In fact, Dr. Nam had been instrumental in setting up this facility to serve his community.

In Madurai, by adding a block of 50,000 square feet to the Main Hospital and some reorganization in the Free Hospital, another 124 beds were added in 1991—74 in the Main Hospital and 50 in the Free Hospital, respectively.

By 1992, the Aravind group of hospitals had screened 3.65 million patients and performed some 335,000 cataract operations—nearly 70% of them free of cost for the poorest of India's blind population. (See Exhibit 4 for a performance summary since the hospital's inception in 1976, Exhibit 5 for details of its 1991 performance.) All this was achieved with very little outside aid or donations. According to Dr. V.:

> When we first started in 1976, we went around asking for donations, but we didn't have the credibility. A few friends promised to help us, but even they preferred to avoid monetary assistance. It was simple: we had to get started. So I mortgaged my house and raised enough money to start. Then one thing led to another and suddenly we were able to plan the ground floor of the Main Hospital. From the revenue generated from operations there, we built the next floor, and so on until we had a nice five-story facility. And then with the money generated there, we built the Free Hospital. Almost 90% of our annual budget is self-generated. The other 10% comes from sources around the world, such as the Royal Commonwealth Society for the Blind [U.K.] and the SEVA Foundation [USA]. We expend all our surplus on modernizing and updating our equipment and facilities. We have enough credibility now to raise a lot of money, but we don't plan to. We have always accepted the generosity of the local business community, but by and large, our spiritual approach has sustained us.

(See Exhibit 6 for a 1991–1992 statement of income and expenses, and Exhibit 7 for a historical financial summary.)

Having grown from strength to strength, Aravind in 1991 made a bold move to set up a facility for manufacturing intraocular lenses (IOLs).

IOL Factory. IOLs, which were an integral part of ECCE surgery, cost about $30 (Rs. 800) apiece to import from the United States. At a cost of Rs. 8 million, in 1991, Aravind had therefore set up a modern IOL manufacturing facility. Called the Auro Lab, it could produce up to 60,000 IOLs a year. Currently, Auro Lab production yielded about 50% defect-free lenses, quality rated on par with imported lenses. Mr. Balakrishnan, a family member with extensive engineering experience and doctoral education in the United States, had returned to manage Auro Lab. Dr. V. reasoned that within a year or two when the factory yield improved, it would be possible to bring down the manufacturing costs from approximately Rs. 200 per lens to approximately Rs. 100:

> People come for cataract surgery very late in life, because the quality of regained vision after intra-cap surgery is so-so, but not excellent. With extra-cap surgery and IOL implants, the situation is dramatically different. People would opt for surgery earlier, because they can go back to their professions and be productive right away. My aim is to offer 100% IOL surgeries for all our patients, paying and free. That is the better-quality solution, and we should provide it to all our patients.

Thulasi, Aravind's hospital's administrator, explained the challenges ahead (see Exhibit 8 for occupancy statistics):

> Yes, our expansion projects are all very exciting but we cannot take our eye off the ball. We have to concentrate on the things that made us good in the first place. For instance, my biggest concern is the occupancy rate in the free hospital. On Monday, Tuesday, and Wednesday we are choked and overflowing with patients. Our systems have all got to work at peak efficiency to get by. But on Thursday and Friday, we suddenly have a slack. We need some continuity to keep our staff motivated and systems tuned.

Dr. Ravindran, head of the Tirunelveli hospital, concurred:

> We have some fundamental management problems to sort out. While our cash flows and margins look all

right at Tirunelveli, I am unable to repay the cost-of-capital. Thank God, Madurai buys all the equipment on our behalf. We started the Tirunelveli hospital with a lot of hope and experience. Even the physical design was an improvement over our Madurai facility. We have integrated the paying and free hospitals for economies of scale. The wards and patient examination rooms in the free section are far more spacious than at Madurai. Moreover, in order to better utilize operating room capacity, we have a central surgical facility which the free and paying sections of the hospital jointly utilize. Yet, after four years, we are not yet financially self-sufficient at Tirunelveli.

Thulasi mentioned another issue:

When we expand so fast, we have to keep in mind that we need to attract quality people. Fortunately our salary scales are now reasonable in comparison with the private sector, but we are still not there. For example, an ophthalmologist at Aravind would today, on an average, make Rs. 80,000 annually. Not bad, compared to government sector salaries of about Rs. 60,000. Of course, in private practice, some ophthalmologists can make Rs. 300,000. But not everyone has the up-front capital to get top-notch equipment to facilitate such practice. Our nurses are paid Rs. 12,000 a year on average, which is not bad at all given that our staff is recruited and trained from scratch by us. They don't come from nursing school; we provide the training for them. It is like getting a prestigious degree and job training all in one.

A Visit to the Aravind Eye Hospital

The Main Hospital

Located one block from the Free Hospital, the Main Hospital functioned very much independently. Complicated cases from the Free Hospital were brought in when necessary for diagnosis and treatment, but by and large all patients at this hospital paid for the hospital's services. Patients came to this hospital from all over Madurai district (i.e., towns and villages surrounding the city). The cost of a normal cataract surgery (ICCE), inclusive of three to four days' post-operative recovery, was about Rs. 500 to Rs. 1,000. If the patient required an IOL implant (ECCE), the total cost of the surgery was Rs. 1,500 to Rs. 2,500. The hospital provided A, B, and C class rooms,

each with somewhat different levels of privacy and facilities and appropriately different price levels.

The morning rush was usually very heavy, and by early afternoon, most people divided into two groups for a sequential series of evaluations. First, ophthalmic assistants recorded each person's vision. The patient then moved to the next room for a preliminary eye examination by an eye doctor. There were several eye doctors on duty, and ophthalmic assistants noted the preliminary diagnosis on the patient's medical record. Ophthalmic assistants then tested patients for ocular tension and tear duct function, followed by refraction tests. The final examination was always conducted by a senior medical officer. Not all patients passed through every step; for example, those referred to specialty clinics (such as retina and vitreous diseases) would directly move to the specialty section of the hospital on the first floor. Similarly, patients diagnosed as needing only corrective lenses would move to the optometry room for measurement and prescription of glasses. Those diagnosed as requiring cataract surgery would be advised in-patient admission, usually within three days. Most such patients followed up on the advice.

On the day of the surgery, the patient was usually awakened early, and after a light breakfast, was readied for surgery. On a visit to the operating theater, I noticed about 20 patients seated in the hallway, all appropriately prepared by the medical staff to enter into surgery, and another 20 in the adjacent room in the process of being readied by the nursing staff. The procedure involved cleaning and sterilizing the eye and injecting a local anaesthetic. The operating theater had two active operating tables and a third bed for the patient to be prepared prior to surgery.

I (the casewriter) watched several operations performed by Dr. Natchiar. She and her assistants took no more than 15 minutes for each ECCE cataract surgery. She generously offered me the east port of the operating microscope to observe the surgical procedure. She operated from the north port, directly behind the patient's head. A resident in training from the University of Illinois occupied the west port. I had never seen a cataract surgery before, but was amazed at the dexterity of her fingers as she made the incision and gently removed the clouded lens, leaving the posterior chamber in place. Then she inserted the IOL [intraocular lens], and carefully sutured the incision. Even while she was operating, she explained to me in a methodical step-by-step fashion the seven critical things she had to do to ensure a successful operation and recovery. When she was done, she simply moved on to the adjacent operating table, where the next patient and a second supporting team were all ready to go. Meanwhile, the previous surgical team helped the patient off the operating table to walk to the recovery room and prepared the next patient, who was already waiting in the third bed for the next surgery. Dr. Natchiar had started that day at about 7:30 a.m., and when I left at about 10:30 a.m., was still going strong in a smooth, steady, uninterrupted fashion. The whole team carried on about their tasks in a well-paced, routine way. There was none of the drama I had expected to encounter in an operating theater.

In contrast, Dr. Nam was performing a retina detachment repair in the adjoining operating theater. Without looking up from his task, Dr. Nam told me that he was in the midst of a particularly difficult procedure and it would probably be another hour before he could comfortably converse. His surgical team bent over the operating table in deep concentration, reflecting the nonroutine nature of their task.

The Free Hospital

The outpatient facilities at the Free Hospital were not as organized as the Main Hospital's. There was a temporary shelter at the Free Hospital's entrance where patients waited to register. Those who came for a return visit were directed to a different line from those who came for the first time. The patient flow inside also seemed somewhat crowded. The sequence, however, remained the same: registration; vision recording; preliminary examination; testing of tension and tear duct function; refraction test; and final examination.

The people in the hallways and waiting rooms appeared significantly poorer than those I had seen at the Main Hospital. A handful of administrative assistants in blue uniforms moved around in the crowd, helping patients and guiding them along in the sequential flow. As I walked up to the operating theaters on the next floor, patients from the previous day's "eye camp" were awaiting their turn to be prepared for surgery. Some older patients, clearly tired, had spread themselves out on the floor and against the walls. There was a lot more commotion here than at the Main Hospital.

Almost all the surgeries at the Free Hospital were of the intracapsular (ICCE) type. An extracapsular (ECCE) procedure with IOL was performed only when medical reasons dictated against an intracapsular surgery.

The operating theaters also appeared more crowded and cramped. The uniforms of the supporting staff here were green, whereas they were blue at the Main Hospital, and only one of the other operating tables was equipped with an operating microscope. The patient preparation for surgery and flow was similar to that at the Main Hospital. Two surgeons operated in the same theater, and each had two operating tables and one staging bed to organize the workflow. Historically, at Aravind, a team of five surgeons and 15 nurses could operate on about 150 cases in about five hours.

Dr. Narendran, who was in the midst of a cataract operation, invited me to the operating table. The critical steps in surgery here were essentially the same as I had seen in the Main Hospital except that the intact clouded lens, along with its supporting membrane capsule, was removed here with a cryogenic device and the incision was sutured. An IOL was not inserted. These patients would be fitted with aphakic glasses three days later. Dr. Narendran had the following conversation with his patient:

Doctor: Old man, what do you do for a living?

Patient: I don't do anything. I just sit at home.

Doctor: Does your wife provide you with food?

Patient: No, my wife died long ago. My daughter-in-law takes care of me.

Doctor: Does she take good care of you?

Patient: No, but she does the best she can. Once a day she gives me "kanji" [boiled rice and salt]. That, with some water, takes care of my needs.

Doctor: What will you do after you regain your eyesight?

Patient: I will go back to tending a herd of sheep. I used to know the owner [rancher]. He used to pay me a small fee.

Doctor: What will you do with that money?

Patient: Oh, I can then buy some meat once in a while. And I can also take my grand-daughter to the temple fair next year.

Unlike the Main Hospital, patients in the Free Hospital did not have "beds" in which to recuperate and recover, but rather were taken to big rooms on the upper floors and each was provided with a 6' x 3' bamboo/coir mat, which was spread out on the floor as a bed, and a small-sized pillow. There were several such rooms, each accommodating 20 to 30 patients. Each room had self-contained bathroom facilities. People from the same or nearby villages were usually accommodated in the same room. They moved together as a cohort, both before and after surgery. The post-operative recovery period was usually three days, when the bandage was removed, patients' eyes checked and, if all was well, aphakic glasses fitted. Patients were advised to come back in three months for follow-up evaluation.

At the Free Hospital, detailed records were kept of all post-operative complications (see Exhibit 9). Some complications, such as iritis, were considered minor and easily treatable, while others required extra care and additional hospital stay. Such complications were directly traced to the operating team, even to the level of the individual surgeon. Senior medical officers reviewed the data with the individuals concerned and offered coaching and advice to rectify operating techniques, if necessary.

At the records room in the Free Hospital, I pulled out six patient records at random to get a sense of the improvement in sight after surgery. A summary is provided below.

	Preoperative Sight Recording	Post-operative Sight Recording
Patient 1	No vision. Can register hand movements	6/12 [20/40]
Patient 2	No vision. Can register hand movements	6/12 [20/40]
Patient 3	No vision. Cannot register hand movements Can perceive light	6/36 [20/120]
Patient 4	No vision. Can register hand movements	6/06 [20/20]
Patient 5	No vision. Can register hand movements	6/18 [20/60]
Patient 6	6/60 [20/200]	6/12 [20/40]

The Eye Camp

I visited a typical eye camp, at Dindigul, a semi-urban town about 100 miles east of Madurai. These screening camps were almost always conducted with the help of local community support, with either a local business enterprise or a social service organization taking the lead role in organizing them.

The local sponsors provided information regarding the eye camp to all the neighboring communities (about a 25-mile radius). Public announcements in marketplaces, newspaper advertisements, information pamphlets, and other publicity material were prepared and distributed one to three weeks in advance of the camp. The camp was usually promoted under the sponsor's name, with the Aravind service playing only a supporting role. The sponsor not only paid all the publicity costs but also the direct costs associated with organizing the camp—patient transportation, food, and aphakic glasses. In addition, the sponsors also paid for the costs of transporting, feeding, and bringing back the patients selected for surgery. This portion was estimated at Rs. 200 per patient. Aravind bore the costs of surgery and medicines.

The camp at Dindigul was sponsored by a local textile mill owner. There were three other Aravind-associated camps in other parts of the Tamil-Nadu state that day. One was sponsored by a religious charity (Sathya Sai Baba Devotee's Association), one by a popular movie actor fan club (Rajni Kanth Appreciation Club), and the third by the Lion's Club. According to Dr. V.:

> The concept of eye camp is not new. As the head of the government hospital, I used to go out with a team of doctors and support staff several times a year to screen patients in their own villages. Many of my colleagues in other parts of India also use this idea as part of their outreach programs. We were somewhat fortunate in the sense that we invested in the infrastructure, such as the vans and the equipment and committed doctors to support the demand we got from philanthropic individuals and organizations.

In the formative years of Aravind, patients attending the screening camps were examined and those needing surgery were appropriately advised. Even though surgery was free, the patients had to come to Aravind at their own expense. The response rate was less than 15%. Concerned by the low turnout, a research team from Aravind conducted in-depth home interviews with a randomly selected group of 65 patients for whom surgery was recommended but who didn't respond for over six months. The study revealed the following constraints:

- Still have vision, however diminished   26%
- Cannot afford food and transportation   25
- Cannot leave family   13
- Fear of surgery   11
- No one to accompany   10
- Family opposition   5
- Others   10

As a consequence, Aravind requested and the camp sponsors readily agreed to bear the costs of food, transportation and, in many cases, the cost of aphakic glasses to be worn by the patient after surgery. In order to reduce the fear of surgery, as well as to encourage a support group, patients were transported to Madurai as a group by buses. Patients were asked to bring a small travel bag in case it was necessary to go to Madurai. The sequence of screening steps matched those at the base hospitals:

1. Registration
2. Vision recording
3. Preliminary examination
4. Testing of tension and tear duct function
5. Refraction
6. Final examination by a senior medical officer
7. Optical shop (for those that needed it)

In addition, those selected for surgery had to undergo tests for blood pressure and urine sugar and, if qualified, their surgery papers were prepared on the campsite. In addition, Aravind camp organizers, as well as local community elders, explained and reassured the patients regarding the importance of the surgery and the other logistics involved. Bus trips were so organized that individuals from the same or nearby villages were always clustered in the same bus trip, which reduced the need for anyone to accompany the patients. They were all returned together after three or four days. This established a support group during their recovery phase. A team from Aravind returned for follow-up after three months.

The Dindigul camp was very well run. Soundararaja Mills (the sponsors) had organized bus shuttles from the central town bus stand to transport passengers to the campsite. About 1,000 people came from villages within a 25-mile radius of the town. The mill owner had sought the cooperation of a local college, of which he was a trustee and a significant donor, for providing the physical facilities. At the campsite, the college principal was actively supervising the arrangements. He brought me a chart of the historical performance of the Soundararaja camp for the last five years. Many volunteer students were helping the Aravind staff organize the patient flow. The mill owner's son, also its finance manager, walked around the camp constantly inquiring about the arrangements. There was a sense of festivity in the air, as recorded "nadaswaram"[4] music was being played over the public address system. A packed lunch was provided for those selected for surgery, and refreshments and a sit-in lunch for all the doctors and support staff participating in the camp. One of the school teachers who had organized the marketing of the camp explained:

> My students simply worked flat out in the last one week. Soundararaja Mills provided us transportation to cover over 1,000 driving miles. Our "propaganda" was effected through handbills, wall posters, and traveling megaphone announcements. Last Thursday night, they were mounting publicity posters on every public bus. We could not do it earlier because buses in this town are all scrubbed and cleaned every Wednesday night.

The camp had commenced on a Sunday morning at 8:00 a.m., and when I left at about 2:00 p.m., about 800 people had been screened and nearly 150 selected for surgery. The first group of patients were ready to leave for Madurai. Dr. Nam and his team were working away at a steady pace. He explained to me that nearly two-thirds of the work was done, but the turnout was a little lower than expected, because just two months prior to this camp, another organization had conducted an eye camp in the same area. (Exhibit 10 provides a history of Aravind's "eye camp" performance. Exhibit 11 provides further detail by type of sponsor for the 1991 eye camps.)

In the past, Aravind had also conducted several surgical camps. That is, patients identified as needing surgery would be provided the requisite treatment on-site. Recently, however, there was a conscious effort to move away from surgery camps because of the higher cost as well as lower quality of service they provided. For example, the makeshift operating theaters were not air-conditioned, cleanliness and hygiene were often not up to hospital standards, patient amenities were inferior, and post-operative complications were difficult to monitor.

The Aravind organization included a 10-person team of camp organizers. These individuals reported to Meenakshisunadaram (Sundar), the camp manager. Camp organizers were responsible for working closely with the camp sponsors, helping and guiding them with directions for mounting publicity, organizing the logistics, and arranging physical facilities for the eye camp. In addition to working closely with the sponsors who needed help, camp organizers also guided new sponsors

---

[4]Nadaswaram, a wind instrument much like a clarinet, was often played at auspicious occasions such as weddings in South India.

who approached Aravind for their expertise and help in bringing eye-care to certain targeted communities. Camp organizers were aligned by district as shown in the territory map (Exhibit 12) and traveled extensively within their assigned territories. They all met at Aravind's headquarters at Madurai, once a week under the chairmanship of Dr. V. At one such meeting which I attended, Dr. V. went around the table from person to person asking for territory plans and every once in a while urged a camp organizer, "Why was the camp yield so poor in your territory? We could get only 14 surgery cases from a catchment population of nearly 100,000! Something is not right. Brother, find out what is going on! Work with the sponsor to improve propaganda." (See Exhibit 13 for districtwide camp particulars.)

According to Sundar, the camp manager:

We really don't have to sell the idea of an eye camp to anyone. There are far more individuals, businesses, and social organizations that need our services than what we can effectively offer. The prestige and goodwill that our sponsors earn, in their communities, far outweighs the financial burden. What they really need help on is how to organize the camp, how to create propaganda, and how to organize the logistics. That is where we are trying to put together a consistent set of procedures and a common set of principles.

Conclusion

I asked Dr. V. what his biggest challenge for the next three years was. His reply:

My goal is to spread the Aravind model to every nook and corner of India, Asia, Africa; wherever there is blindness, we want to offer hope. Tell me, what is this concept of franchising? Can't we do what McDonald's and Burger King have done in the United States?

Exhibit 1 Aravind Eye Hospital Locations

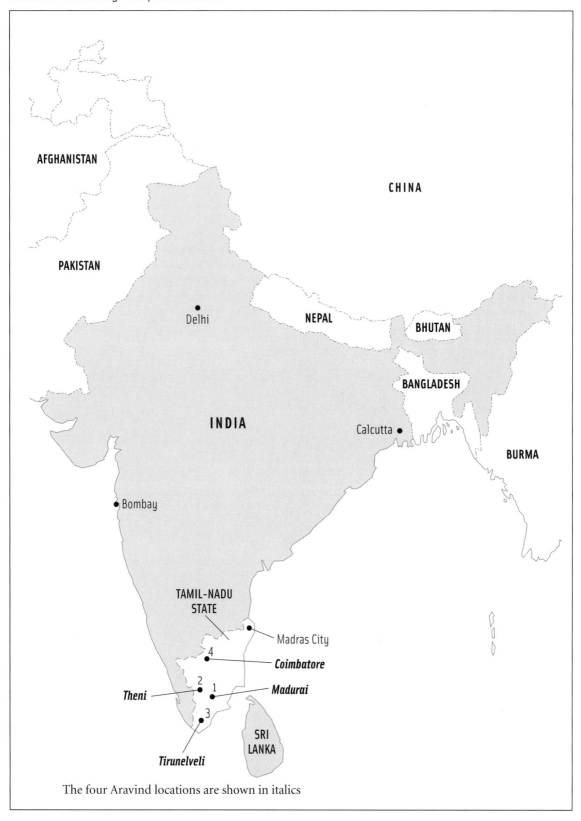

The four Aravind locations are shown in italics

Exhibit 2 The Aravind Hospitals

In-patient ward at the Free Hospital

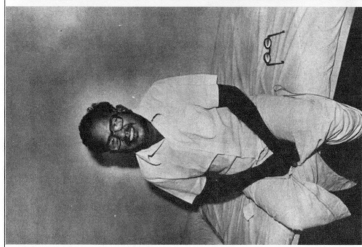

A private room in the main hospital

Exhibit 3 Eye Camp Activities

From top, clockwise:
a) Patients arriving by bus to the campsite.
b) Patients registering at the campsite.
c) Testing and preparing patients selected for surgery.

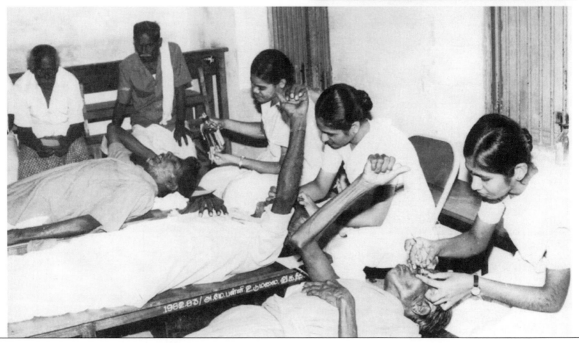

Exhibit 4 Historical Patient Statistics (Consolidated)

Year	Paying		Free and Camp[a]	
	Outpatient Visits	Surgery	Outpatient Visits	Surgery
1976	–	248	–	–
1977	15,381	980	2,366	–
1978	15,781	1,320	18,251	1,045
1979	19,687	1,612	47,351	2,430
1980	31,334	2,511	65,344	5,427
1981	39,470	3,139	75,727	8,172
1982	46,435	4,216	79,367	8,747
1983	56,540	4,889	101,469	11,220
1984	69,419	5,796	103,177	11,954
1985	89,441	7,194	153,037	17,586
1986	111,546	8,202	164,977	19,623
1987	121,828	9,971	180,181	21,562
1988	182,274	12,702	232,838	23,635
1989	203,907	15,103	290,859	25,867
1990	227,243	17,896	338,407	31,162
1991	241,643	19,511	327,692	31,979
Total	1,471,929	115,290	2,184,043	220,409

Source: Aravind Eye Hospital

[a]The 1990 and 1991 outpatient visits data includes camp patients as well as walk-in patients. See Exhibit 10 for camp details.

Exhibit 5 Patient Statistics: 1991

	Madurai	Tirunelveli	Theni	Total
Outpatient visits – Paying – Free	167,884 212,809	50,802 91,482	22,957 23,401	241,643 327,692
Surgery – Paying – Free	16,447 23,110	2,572 7,339	492 1,530	19,511 31,979
Hospital outpatient visits	263,518	84,360	30,457	378,335
Eye camp outpatient visits	117,175	57,924	15,901	191,000
Total outpatient visits	380,693	142,284	46,358	569,335
Screening camps	331	293	83	707
Surgery Details				
Cataract and other lens removal procedures (without IOL)	23,321	6,618	1,535	31,474
Intraocular lens (IOL)	7,846	1,466	227	9,539
Trabeculectomy	359	80	13	452
Retinal detachment	401	1	–	402
Vitreous surgery	331	–	–	331
Membranectomy	61	2	–	63
Squint correction	262	–	–	262
Keratoplasty and therapeutic grafting	65	–	–	65
Ptosis	27	–	–	27
DCR, DCT and other septic operations	1,347	669	158	2,174
Pterygium	297	181	14	492
Laser and xenon photocoagulation	1,467	–	–	1,467
Nd Yag iridotomy	787	133	–	920
Nd Yag capsulotomy	806	201	–	1,007
Argon laser trabeculoplasty	43	–	–	43
Other surgical procedures	2,137	560	75	2,772
Total Surgery	39,557	9,911	2,022	51,490

Source: Aravind Eye Hospital

Exhibit 6 Income and Expenditures for 1991–1992 (Rupees)

Revenue		
1. Medical services	3,380,985.00	9.57%
2. Operation charges	23,235,389.00	65.77
3. Treatment charges	2,225,609.25	6.30
4. Consulting fees	3,424,728.35	9.69
5. Laboratory charges	857,265.49	2.43
6. X-ray charges	206,890.00	0.59
7. Donations	771,474.80	2.18
8. Interest	1,062,889.50	3.01
9. Miscellaneous, course and others	129,666.65	0.37
10. Sale of ophthalmology books	33,835.00	0.10
Total Revenue	35,328,733.04	100.00%
Operating Expenses		
1. Medicine and cotton	1,307,968.00	3.70%
2. Hospital linen	148,848.30	0.42
3. Library and subscription	66,519.40	0.19
4. Building maintenance	1,117,550.04	3.16
5. Electricity charges	1,667,964.01	4.72
6. Installation and equipment maintenance	774,129.46	2.19
7. Electric items and bulbs	196,195.55	0.56
8. Printing and stationery	564,841.48	1.60
9. Postage and telephone charges	447,750.30	1.27
10. Building rent	7,980.00	0.02
11. Cleaning and sanitation	356,515.70	1.01
12. Stipends and staff salaries	4,285,017.70	12.13
13. Employer's PF contribution	190,208.50	0.54
14. Bank commission	9,748.08	0.03
15. Traveling expenses	758,876.91	2.15
16. Miscellaneous expenses	236,508.18	0.67
17. Photography	181,316.90	0.51
18. Resident doctors' hostel expenses	54,338.10	0.15
19. Camp expenses	1,347,457.90	3.81
20. Vehicle maintenance	459,361.43	1.30
21. IOL	2,926,520.00	8.28
Expenditure Total	17,105,615.94	48.41%
Costs Offset by		
1. W.H.O., Ford Foundation and Jain Hospital	96,246.00	
Actual Expenditure Total	17,009,369.94	48.41%
Percentage		
Net Surplus	18,319,363.10	51.59%

Source: Aravind Eye Hospital

Exhibit 7 Historical Financial Summary (Rupees)

Year	Income	Expenditure	Percentage of Expenditure Over Income
1979–1980	933,306.62	131,641.80	14.10
1980–1981	979,991.18	242,968.70	24.80
1981–1982	2,936,440.45	1,385,642.50	47.20
1982–1983	3,546,240.27	2,142,939.20	60.36
1983–1984	4,334,257.49	2,688,550.23	62.03
1984–1985	5,971,711.49	3,526,423.49	59.05
1985–1986	6,614,342.74	5,018,583.94	75.87
1986–1987	9,325,540.79	5,349,419.00	57.36
1987–1988	12,694,531.22	9,268,150.96	73.00
1988–1989	17,840,116.84	10,987,700.44	61.58
1989–1990	21,054,621.30	12,669,999.79	60.18
1990–1991	29,320,202.61	15,837,644.93	54.02

Source: Aravind Eye Hospital

Note: One U.S. dollar was convertible to Rs. 12–Rs. 15 during 1979 to 1984; Rs. 18–Rs. 20 during 1985 to 1989; and Rs. 25–Rs. 28 during 1990 and 1991.

Exhibit 8 January–July 1992 Performance Summary

| | Paying | | | | Free | | | | | | | | | Grand Total |
| | | | | | Madurai | | Tirunelveli | | Theni | | Total | | | |
	Madurai	Tirunelveli	Theni	Total	Direct	Camp	Direct	Camp	Direct	Camp	Direct	Camp		
Outpatients														
New cases	50,498	14,710	5,669	70,877	30,662	65,669	8,900	30,863	3,662	7,312	43,224	103,844		217,945
Review cases	57,428	16,831	4,196	78,455	28,912	0	11,215	0	2,797	0	42,924	0		121,379
Total Patients	107,926	31,541	9,865	149,332	59,574	65,669	20,115	30,863	6,459	7,312	86,148	103,844		339,324
Cataract operations	7,382	1,211	228	8,821	5,192	8,290	1,195	2,739	402	551	6,726	11,580		27,127
Other major surgery	905	55	1	961	278	15	23	9	0	0	301	24		1,286
Other minor surgery	3,171	761	75	4,007	1,236	319	378	318	83	30	1,697	667		6,371
Total Surgery	11,458	2,027	304	13,789	6,706	8,624	1,596	3,066	485	581	8,724	12,271		34,784
Bed capacity	324	200	40	564	400		200		60		660			1,224
Beds occupied per day (six-month average)	265	51	10	326	167	229	62	92	14	14	243	335		903

Source: Aravind Eye Hospital

Exhibit 9 Free Section Complication Details for the Patients Operated on in the Month of October 1992

Complications	Pre-operative		Post-operative		Total	
	(#)	(%)	(#)	(%)	(#)	(%)
A/C shallow	0	0.0	39	2.7	39	2.7
Accidental extra	2	0.1	0	0.0	2	0.1
Blood clot	1	0.0	113	7.8	114	7.9
Cornea oedema	0	0.0	55	3.8	55	3.8
Cortex	2	0.1	36	2.4	38	2.6
Endophthalmitis	0	0.0	1	0.0	1	0.0
Exudate in pupil area	0	0.0	8	0.5	8	0.5
Flap turn	0	0.0	6	0.4	6	0.4
Hyphema	2	0.1	34	2.3	36	2.4
Hypopyon	0	0.0	10	0.6	10	0.6
Hypotony	0	0.0	1	0.0	1	0.0
Iridodialysis	1	0.0	1	0.0	2	0.1
Iris prolapse	0	0.0	1	0.0	1	0.0
Iritis	0	0.0	226	15.6	226	15.6
P.A.S.	1	0.0	0	0.0	1	0.0
Posterior synechiae	1	0.0	0	0.0	1	0.0
Pupillary block (air in PC)	0	0.0	2	0.1	2	0.1
S.K. (straight keratitis)	0	0.0	55	3.8	55	3.8
Vitreous bulge	0	0.0	1	0.0	1	0.0
Vitreous disturbance	5	0.3	0	0.0	5	0.3
Vitreous loss	2	0.1	0	0.0	2	0.1
Wound leak	0	0.0	1	0.0	1	0.0

Source: Aravind Eye Hospital

Exhibit 10 Eye Camp Performance

Year	Screening Camps	Operating Camps	Outpatients Seen	Operations
1978	118	–	18,251	1,045
1979	215	–	47,351	2,430
1980	198	10	65,344	5,427
1981	140	13	75,727	8,172
1982	205	9	79,367	8,747
1983	204	9	101,469	10,975
1984	247	21	103,177	11,796
1985	475	18	153,037	17,586
1986	516	13	164,977	19,623
1987	506	12	180,181	21,562
1988	536	9	232,838	23,635
1989	818	2	290,859	25,867
1990	884	3	203,805	20,852
1991	707	3	191,000	20,818
Total	5,769	122	1,907,383	198,535

Exhibit 11 1991 Eye Camps[a]

Name or Organization	No. of Camps	Total Outpatients	Surgery		
			Cataract	Others	Total
Lions Clubs	105	42,439	5,071	139	5,210
Rotary Clubs	42	17,629	1,941	69	2,010
Vivekananda Kendra	190	30,899	2,657	240	2,897
Bhagavan Sri Sathya Sai Seva Org.	20	7,114	1,472	47	1,519
Jaycees	18	3,823	309	10	319
Banks	27	4,854	371	18	389
Mills and factories	28	10,543	966	53	1,019
ASSEFA	6	900	104	5	109
Schools and colleges	50	8,577	475	17	492
Hospitals	12	4,291	974	57	1,031
Trusts	16	6,329	1,224	34	1,258
Youth and fans associations	37	6,291	365	27	392
Other religious organizations	41	12,696	1,315	47	1,362
Other voluntary service organizations	75	23,356	1,913	68	1,981
Others	40	11,259	791	39	830
Total	707	191,000	19,948	870	20,818

Source: Aravind Eye Hospital
[a]These statistics include the work of all three hospitals. For example, in 1991, the breakdown by hospital was as follows:

	Total Camps	Outpatients	Operations
Madurai	331	117,175	14,951
Tirunelveli	293	57,924	4,922
Theni	83	15,901	945
Total	707	191,000	20,818

Exhibit 12 Camp Organizer Territories

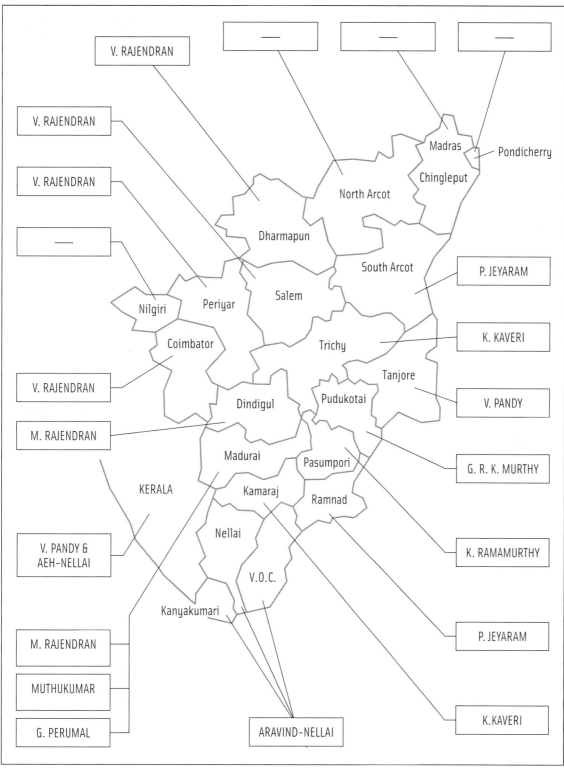

Exhibit 13 Districtwise Camp Particulars—1991

	District	Population (millions)	of Camps	of Cases Screened	Advised Surgery	Accepting Surgery
1.	Madras City	3.795	–	–	–	–
2.	Chingleput	4.621	–	–	–	–
3.	North Arcot	3.000	–	–	–	–
4.	South Arcot	4.871	4	4,491	1,058	1,009
5.	Dharmapuri	2.396	5	4,495	657	609
6.	Salem	3.914	17	14,026	3,333	3,179
7.	Periyar	2.323	21	12,760	2,145	2,064
8.	Nilgiris	0.705	2	465	22	19
9.	Coimbatore	3.531	19	11,836	2,114	2,002
10.	Trichy	4.114	12	7,029	654	592
11.	Tanjore	4.527	23	9,264	1,208	1,095
12.	Pudukottai	1.322	12	2,432	231	201
13.	Madurai	3.448	119	19,992	1,693	1,184
14.	Dindigul	1.769	45	9,399	991	828
15.	Pasumpon	1.075	32	5,514	583	427
16.	Kamaraj	1.554	44	8,800	1,185	1,004
17.	Ramnad	1.136	46	6,402	769	647
18.	Nellai	2.493	123	18,031	2,680	1,795
19.	Kanyakumari	1.591	60	8,994	796	529
20.	VOC	1.156	75	11,066	1,678	1,174
21.	Pondicherry	0.500	4	2,893	288	258
22.	Kerala State[a]	12.000	44	33,111	2,912	2,202
Total			707	191,000	24,997	20,818

Source: Aravind Eye Hospital

[a]The first 21 districts listed in the above exhibit are part of the Tamil-Nadu state. Kerala is a neighboring state. Statistics for Kerala have been aggregated for its 10 districts.

THE BLACK & DECKER CORPORATION (A): POWER TOOLS DIVISION

Joe, I like you guys. But, look, I give Makita 10 feet of space. I give you 10 feet of space. They outsell you 8 to 1. What are we going to do about that?

In January 1991, statements like this no longer surprise Joseph Galli. Black & Decker's (B&D) vice president of sales and marketing for power tools had heard similar sentiments expressed by many trade accounts. Makita Electric of Japan had practically taken over the professional power tools for tradesmen business since it entered the United States market a decade ago. "Tradesmen" was one of the three major segments of the power tools business—the others being "Consumer" and "Industrial." "Consumer" represented "at home" use, while both "Tradesmen" and "Industrial" covered professional users. The distinguishing characteristic of the "Tradesmen" segment was that these buyers, such as a carpenter, bought tools for their own use on a job site. In "Industrial," the buyer was generally a corporation purchasing tools for use by employees. By late 1990, Makita's success in the Professional-Tradesmen segment was such that it held an 80% share in cordless drills, the single largest product category, and a 50% segment share overall. B&D had virtually created the portable power tools business in the United States beginning in the early 1900's. While it maintained the #1 market share position in the Consumer and Professional-Industrial segments, its entry in the relatively new Professional-Tradesmen segment held only about a 9% share.

The trade was asking for advertising allowances and rebate money on B&D's Tradesmen products and profitability in this segment was near zero. B&D's senior management resolved to put an end to this "no win" game, and

Galli set about developing and gaining corporate support for a viable program to challenge Makita for leadership in this segment. He could not help but see the irony of a 9% Tradesmen segment share and no profitability against the results of two recent research studies; one showing B&D to be among the powerful brand names in the world; and, the second establishing B&D's professional tools to be the highest quality in the industry.

Black & Decker

In 1910, Duncan Black and Alonzo Decker, Sr. started a machine shop and, in 1917, received a patent on the world's first portable power drill with pistol grip and trigger switch; 73 years after receiving its first patent, B&D was the world's largest producer of power tools, power tool accessories, electric lawn and garden tools, and residential security hardware. Headquartered in Towson, Maryland, B&D's sales reached $4.8 billion in 1990, with nearly 50% of product revenues from outside the United States. Alonzo G. Decker, Jr. was Honorary Chairman of the Company and a member of the Board of Directors. He had been Chairman of the Board and Chief Executive Officer from 1968 to 1975. Prior to his becoming CEO, the CEO post had always been held by his father or co-founder Black. From its roots in power tools, B&D began a move "from the garage to the house" in 1979 with the introduction of the very successful Dustbuster® hand-held vacuum. This "into the house" thrust led to the purchase of General Electric's Housewares Division in 1984 for $212 million. As part of the sale agreement, B&D could use General Electric's name on products only until 1987.

Nolan Archibald, a Harvard Business School graduate and a former group president at Beatrice, became President and CEO in 1986. The early 1980's had been volatile years at B&D. It began the decade with a 19% net revenue increase to $1.2 billion in 1980, but sales stagnated at this level through 1983. In 1985, with net revenues at $1.7 billion, B&D posted a $215.1 million restructuring cost and a $158.4 million loss. For the 5-year period from 1981 through 1985, the company lost money.

Figure 1 Black & Decker Revenues and Operating Income 1986–90

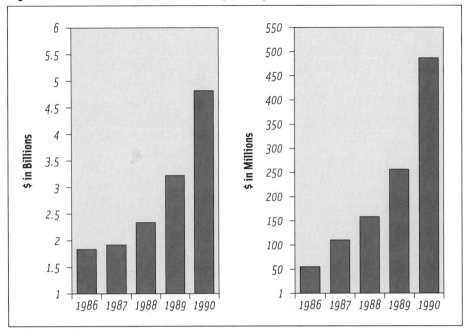

B&D's $2.8 billion acquisition of Emhart Corporation in 1989 more than doubled B&D's revenues and brought new strong brands, including Kwikset® locks and Price Pfister® faucets, but raised the company's long-term debt to $4.2 billion, representing about 84% of total capital. Figure 1 shows the growth in B&D sales and net income since Archibald became CEO.

The five largest product groups and their percentage of B&D's 1990 sales were:

- Power Tools and Accessories 29%
- Household Products 15%
- Information Systems and Services 11%
- Outdoor Products 9%
- Security Hardware 9%

Household products included hand-held vacuums, irons, mixers, food processors and choppers, coffee makers, and toasters and toaster ovens. The well-known Dustbuster and Spacemaker® (under-the-cabinet appliances) brands were part of this group. The B&D franchise was especially strong in cordless vacuums, irons, and toaster ovens, each holding over a 50% market share in the United States. In 1990, 29 new household products were introduced, including the Power Pro™ Dustbuster® heavy duty cordless vacuum. The house-hold products line was heavily supported with media advertising.

The B&D name enjoyed substantial equity in both the United States and Europe. An independent survey of 6,000 brands showed Black & Decker's brand strength ranking to be #7 in the United States and #19 in Europe.[1] This put Black & Decker in the company of Coca-Cola, Campbell's, Walt Disney, Pepsi-Cola, Kodak, NBC, Kellogg's, McDonald's and Hershey, the other firms rounding out the U.S. top ten.

Power Tools Market

In 1990, portable power tools in the United States was a $1.5 billion market. Products ranged from an electric screwdriver for the consumer who might use it once a year at home to heavy-duty miter saws used continually throughout the day at construction sites. Segmentation of the market was as shown in Figure 2.

Non-professional users accounted for $530 million or 35% of the market. In this Consumer segment, consumers bought tools at mass merchants, such as

---

[1]Landor Associates Survey.

Figure 2 Segmentation of the U.S. Power Tools Market

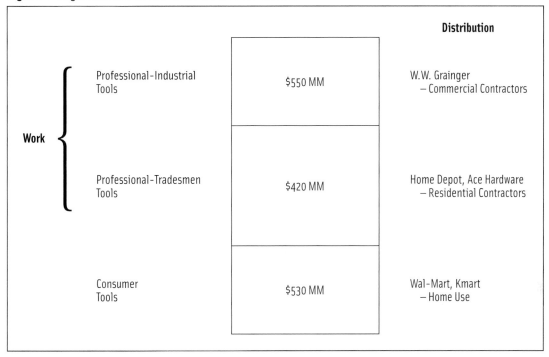

Wal-Mart and Kmart, and hardware stores for their own home use. The "for work" market was divided into a Professional-Industrial segment and a Professional-Tradesmen segment. The $550 million Professional-Industrial segment was made up primarily of commercial contractors working on large projects, e.g., office buildings, bridges, etc. and company assembly lines, e.g., automobile plants. In this segment, distributors (of which W.W. Grainger of Skokie, Illinois, with over 300 branch offices, was by far the largest) played an important role in providing technical expertise and service. For a given job, the distributor could both specify the contractor's tool requirements and recommend specific brands. Grainger stocked more than 32,000 items to provide prompt delivery. In the Professional-Industrial segment, tools were typically purchased and owned by the company rather than the individual users.

The Professional-Tradesmen segment was targeted largely at tradesmen such as electricians, plumbers, carpenters, framers, roofers, and general remodelers working in residential construction. These tradespeople were expected to show up at the job site with their own neces-

sary tools of the trade in working condition. These buyers tended to patronize newly emerging retail distribution channels including home centers such as The Home Depot and Lowe's, in addition to the traditional hardware stores, such as Ace. While the smallest of the three segments in 1990, at $420 million (28%), Professional-Tradesmen was growing fastest at 9% compared to a 7% growth rate for Consumer and no growth for Professional-Industrial. Some "heavy do-it-yourselfers" bought tools in the Professional-Tradesmen segment, but this segment primarily comprised people who made a living with their tools.

B&D participated in all three segments. Black & Decker®-brand power tools held nearly a 30% share of the U.S. market overall.[2] To serve these segments, B&D offered three separate lines and brand designations all under the Black & Decker family name, as follows:

---

[2]In addition, it manufactured some professional power tools under the Craftsman label for Sears, which held an additional 4% of the Professional-Tradesmen segment.

U.S. Market Segment	Brand Logo	Product Color	Approximate	
			B&D Segment Share 1990	B&D Segment Revenues 1990
– Professional-Industrial – Size = $550MM		Charcoal Grey	20%	$110 MM
– Professional-Tradesmen – Size = $420MM		Charcoal Grey	9%	$35 MM
– Consumer – Size = $530MM		Black	45%	$250 MM

In the Professional-Industrial segment, B&D's share was near parity with Milwaukee Electric of Brookfield, Wisconsin. Founded in 1924, Milwaukee was a privately held firm, selling only in the high end of the market at a rate of approximately $200 million per year worldwide. The second tier suppliers in the Professional-Industrial segment were Bosch, Porter Cable, and Makita. The very knowledgeable purchase decision influencers in the Professional-Industrial segment viewed B&D as offering high-quality, differentiated products and excellent service. At the other end of the performance spectrum, in the Consumer segment, B&D's brand recognition and image helped it attain the #1 position in the marketplace with nearly a 50% share over suppliers such as Skil, Craftsman, Wen, and various private label products.

B&D's strengths in the Professional-Industrial and Consumer segments did not transfer to the Professional-Tradesmen segment, where the approximate share positions in 1990 were as shown in Table 1.

Three product types, (i) drills, (ii) saws, and (iii) sanders, represented nearly 80% of the total sales in the Professional-Tradesmen segment. The top three manufacturers offered broad product lines at approximately 175 SKU's each. Since its entry into the market in 1978, Makita had staked out leadership positions in virtually all products and distribution types within the Professional-Tradesmen segment. Exhibit 1 shows approximate shares for Makita, Milwaukee, and B&D for the largest categories in the segment. Exhibit 2 shows shares of Makita and B&D by the five major outlet types: (i) Two-Step (sales through distributors to independent retailers, such as Ace and ServiStar), (ii) Home Centers, (iii) Warehouse Home Centers, (iv) Membership Clubs, and (v) Farm Outlets.

Professional-Tradesmen revenues of approximately $35 million in 1990 for B&D translated into about $3 million in operating income. Gross margins ran about 35%, but SG+A costs were about 25%.

Table 1 Power Tools, Professional-Tradesmen Approximate Segment Shares 1990

Makita	~50%
Milwaukee	~10%
Black & Decker	~9%
Ryobi	~9%
Skil	~5%
Craftsman[a]	~5%
Porter-Cable	~3%
Bosch	~3%

[a]Manufactured in part by B&D and marketed by Sears

These numbers had become even more vivid for Galli in a recent Monday morning conversation with his boss, Gary DiCamillo, B&D's President of Power Tools for the United States, who recounted this story:

- Joe, yesterday, I stopped by that new Home Depot. It was a nice afternoon; lots of people around. They had one of those woodworking guys out on the sidewalk giving demonstrations for a couple of hours. He was using all Skil saws, and he was just packing up to go home when I came by at about 4 o'clock.

I said to him "What do you think of the Skil saws?" "Pretty good," he said. So, I said, "Who else do you like?" He said "Oh, Milwaukee makes a nice reciprocating saw; Ryobi's got some okay things." "What about Makita?", I said. He said, "Oh, they're okay—they're all pretty good really—you just have to stay away from that Black & Decker!"

Black & Decker and the Professional Segment Buyer

While the "just got to stay away from that Black & Decker" view was perhaps extreme, Galli understood that B&D's strength as a consumer brand was not necessarily beneficial for the Professional-Tradesmen segment. Some tradespeople viewed all B&D products as for use at home rather than on the job; and, conversely, there had been instances of a B&D product designed for at home use being subjected to the demands of the job site and failing.

The typical plumber, electrician, or general remodeler working in residential construction had about $3,000 invested in 10 or so "tools-of-the-trade." He or she bought tools when a replacement was needed, spending on average $1,000 per year. Tools and their performance were a constant topic of conversation at the job site. Generally, tradespeople were satisfied with the tools available—the perception being that Makita provided a good baseline option in all major categories, and other suppliers had particular product strengths, e.g., Skil in circular saws.

As noted above in Exhibit 2, this buyer bought most frequently in independently owned stores served by distributors, i.e., the Two-Step in Exhibit 2. However, the Home Centers noted in Exhibit 2 were growing in importance. For example, the largest single outlet of Professional-Tradesmen tool sales in 1990 was The

Home Depot at approximately $5 million; second was Home Club at $3.5 million, compared to the largest of the Two-Steps, Ace and ServiStar, at $2 million each. The Home Depot was the largest of the rapidly growing collection of home improvement chain stores. With 145 stores and $3.8 billion in 1990 sales, The Home Depot's strategy was to stock 30,000 items in a 100,000 square foot location, with prices about 30% less than the traditional hardware store, while also providing superior customer service. Makita's rise to marketplace dominance was aided by the rapid development of this new type of distribution.

B&D's research on tradespeople's perceptions of suppliers' quality showed four tiers in the marketplace, as shown in Figure 3.

Both Milwaukee and Makita priced at premiums over B&D, averaging 10% and 5%, respectively. Despite the price premium over B&D, Makita's prices on some products were less than half of what the product sold for in Makita's home market, Japan, where Makita was #2 in market share to Hitachi.

While Makita's position with tradespeople was strong, retailers were not uniformly positive toward Makita. Some regarded it as "arrogant and dictatorial." Makita offered no channel protection, selling the same products throughout a range of outlets including the discount oriented Membership Clubs, which B&D had decided not to include among its distributors of Professional-Tradesmen tools (see Exhibit 2). Some believed Makita to be "trading-down" its offerings by, among other things, positioning them as appropriate for Father's Day giving.

While no tradesperson would explicitly note "product color" as a key attribute in the purchase decision, color was generally regarded as a significant product differentiator. Consumer tool manufacturers had largely followed B&D's 1981 lead of making consumer tools black or charcoal grey. B&D's policy was to use black as its

Figure 3 Brand Perceptions of Professional-Tradesman Segment Buyers

Highest			➤Lowest
Makita	Bosch	Black & Decker	Wen
Milwaukee	Hitachi	Ryobi	
	Porter Cable	Skil	
	Panasonic	Craftsman (Sears)	

consumer grade color and charcoal grey for its Professional-Industrial and Professional-Tradesmen grades. Competing brands of professional tools were more highly differentiated in color, as shown in Figure 4.

Black & Decker Product Research

Product development had been a B&D focus since 1985 and B&D tools were highly regarded in the demanding Professional-Industrial segment, so Galli believed that the source of B&D's share problem in the Professional-Tradesmen segment was not inherent product quality. This belief was tested in two ways. First, B&D conducted laboratory tests on its own and competitive products to assess performance, reliability, and durability. Figure 5 summarizes the results for the 14 major Professional-Tradesmen products. B&D's offerings were characterized on a scale ranging from weak/undeveloped to competitive to leadership.

Second, B&D did extensive field tests. All identifying marks and colors were removed from products (both B&D and competitors). The products were then used in actual work situations for one month. Users provided comments on product performance and their interest in buying the product when a replacement was needed. This user testing supported the findings of the laboratory tests of Figure 5, i.e., B&D's product quality was very strongly competitive in the large majority of product categories.

Research on Brand Awareness and Perceptions

Telephone surveys and B&D's annual Image Study provided data on brand awareness, relative perceived quality, and ratings on specific attributes. Overall awareness of the major brands among the Professional-Tradesmen segment end users are shown in Table 2.

Table 2 1990 Total Awareness of Power Tool Suppliers Among Tradespeople

Awareness	
Black & Decker–98%	Hitachi–77%
Milwaukee–95%	Hilti–73%
Skil–93%	Porter Cable–67%
Makita–90%	Ryobi–50%
Bosch–87%	

Figure 4 Color Differentiation: Professional End Users

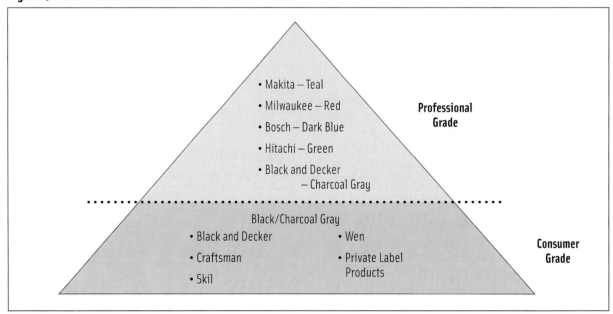

Figure 5 Black & Decker Product Assessment

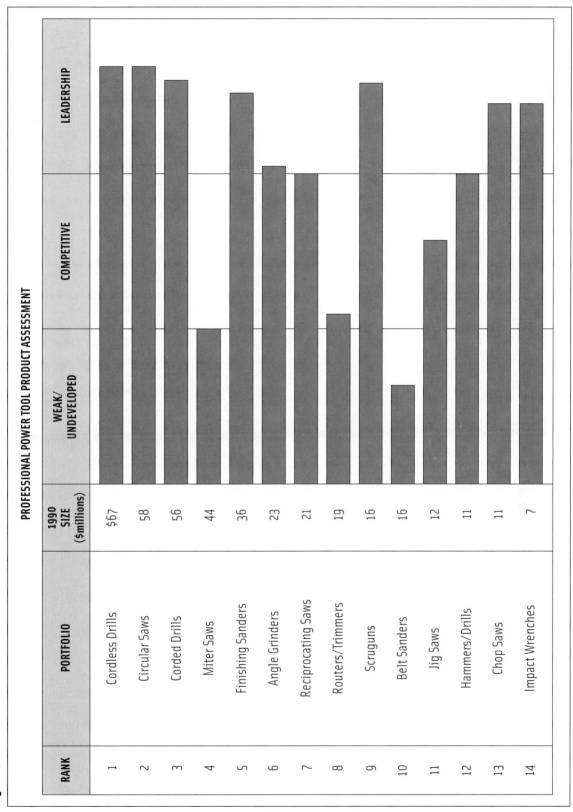

PROFESSIONAL POWER TOOL PRODUCT ASSESSMENT

RANK	PORTFOLIO	1990 SIZE ($millions)	WEAK/ UNDEVELOPED	COMPETITIVE	LEADERSHIP
1	Cordless Drills	$67			
2	Circular Saws	58			
3	Corded Drills	56			
4	Miter Saws	44			
5	Finishing Sanders	36			
6	Angle Grinders	23			
7	Reciprocating Saws	21			
8	Routers/Trimmers	19			
9	Scruguns	16			
10	Belt Sanders	16			
11	Jig Saws	12			
12	Hammers/Drills	11			
13	Chop Saws	11			
14	Impact Wrenches	7			

Respondents were also asked to state their level of agreement with the statement, "*Brand X is one of the Best.*" The data on percentage of respondents "agreeing" or "strongly agreeing" with the statement are in Table 3.

The Image Study provided the same agree/strongly agree data at the level of specific attributes. In particular, Table 4 segregates those expressing a preference for Makita and those expressing a preference for Milwaukee and compares perceptions of those brands to perceptions of B&D.

As Galli reflected on the research data, he recalled some of the comments made to him by two tradesmen during site visits:

> ". . . Black & Decker makes a good popcorn popper, and my wife just loves her Dustbuster, but I'm out here trying to make a living . . ."

> ". . . On the job, people notice what you're working with . . . if I came out here with one of those Black & Decker gray things, I'd be laughed at."

Galli knew that a copycat strategy, e.g., paint it blue and spend some advertising dollars on a "Black & Decker as appropriate for the tradesmen" theme, would not receive internal support. Three options presented themselves:

Table 3 "One of the Best" Agreement Data

Milwaukee	80%
Makita	67%
Black & Decker	44%

Table 4 Percent Agreeing with the Statement

	Those Who Prefer Makita		Those Who Prefer Milwaukee	
	Makita	B&D	Milwaukee	B&D
Makes High-Quality Tools	82%	51%	91%	43%
Makes Durable/ Rugged Tools	71%	48%	91%	42%
Proud to Own	78%	43%	86%	36%
Easy to Get Service	44%	67%	68%	66%
Stands Behind Products	56%	61%	69%	52%

Option 1. Harvest Professional-Tradesmen Channels

In this strategy, B&D would focus on the Consumer and the Professional-Industrial segments. In the Professional-Tradesmen segment, the focus would be on profitability even at the expense of market share.

Option 2. Get Behind Black & Decker Name with Sub-Branding

While there had been several half-hearted attempts to rebuild the B&D name in the Professional-Tradesmen segment, they had not been successful. One new aspect which might offer promise, though, was the sub-branding strategy, which had been so successful with the Spacemaker line and which Galli had used earlier in his career in the accessories business. Specifically, he had transitioned replacement saw blades from "Black & Decker" brand to "Piranha® by Black & Decker." (See Exhibit 3.) In 1990, B&D had introduced the Sawcat™and Super Sawcat™ circular saws with some success. An intense sub-branding program could be developed in an integrated fashion.

Option 3. Drop the Black & Decker Name from the Professional-Tradesmen Segment

Galli imagined what internal reaction would be to such a proposal. Everyone had taken great pride in the #7 "brand power" position of the B&D name. As one of his colleagues commented to him, "Joe, it can't make sense to pull the name of the creator of the power tools industry from a power tool. You'd be saying that B&D can't make it in power tools. Besides, if General Electric can put its name on everything from jet engines to telephones, why can't we?"

If he were to propose dropping the B&D name, he would need an alternative. One possibility was to develop a new brand name free of any negative associations, similar to Toyota's creation of the Lexus brand. The other would be to use some other name already in B&D stable of brands. One of these possibilities was the DeWalt® brand from a line of stationary woodworking equipment. DeWalt was founded in 1918 and bought by Black & Decker in 1960. DeWalt was a leader in sales of large radial arm saws permanently installed at lumber yards. While sales of DeWalt products had reached $70 million annually at one time under B&D, the company had recently deemphasized the line due to the amount of product liability exposure that came with large, stationary workworking equipment. The DeWalt name had never been used on a portable power tool.

The DeWalt name had been included in the awareness research described in Table 2 above. It received a 70% awareness rating, and most of those who knew DeWalt were positively disposed to it. Surprisingly, it had achieved an "Is One of the Best" agreement percent of 63% from tradesmen as compared to B&D's 44% (Table 3). Further research on the DeWalt brand showed that 51% of tradespeople would have some "purchase interest." The "level of endorsement" by B&D impacted the "purchase interest" score. Specifically:

Identified As	% Purchase Interest
DeWalt	51%
DeWalt–Serviced and Distributed by Black & Decker	58%
DeWalt–Manufactured, Serviced and Distributed by Black & Decker	53%

Galli felt that any plan involving investing to build market share—Option 2 or Option 3—would have to provide for a minimal objective of doubling B&D's Professional-Tradesmen segment share from under 10% to nearly 20% within three years, with major share "take-away" from Makita. Operating income would be expected to improve steadily from under 10% to at least 12%. He also knew that the Membership Clubs, which represented about 10% of segment sales for the industry were and would continue to be off-limits. Thus, he would not be able to attack the 85% share Makita held within that channel.

He wondered what type of reaction to expect from Makita if he pursued a "build share" option. Finally, he considered the risk. On the one hand, B&D was not making much money in the Professional-Tradesmen segment anyway, so financial risk was limited. On the other hand, there might be implications for the other two segments and embarrassment in the retail channels.

One of the color options he was considering was a bold "Industrial Yellow"—a familiar job site color associated with safety, but not yet used by any power tool brand. But, if the strategy was not success, Galli could not think of anything good that could come from his product being the same color as a lemon.

Exhibit 1 Market Shares of Professional-Tradesmen Tools by Product Type—1990

Product	Approximate % of Market	Approximate Shares		
		Makita	Milwaukee	B&D
– **Drills** (30%)				
– Cordless Drivers	16%	80%	<5%	<10%
– Corded	13%	50%	20%	25%
– **Saws** (35%)				
– Circular[a]	14%	55%	15%	<10%
– Miter	11%	45%	–	15%
– Reciprocating	<10%	30%	30%	25%
– Jig	<5%	25%	15%	<10%
– Chop	<5%	50%	<5%	20%
– **Sanders** (>15%)				
– Finishing	<10%	60%	<5%	<10%
– Belt[b]	<5%	20%	–	–

[a]Skil held approximately 20% of Circular Saws.
[b]Ryobi held approximately 45% of Belt Sanders.

Exhibit 2 Market Shares of Professional-Tradesmen by Channel Type—1990

	Approximate % of Professional Segment Sales in This Channel	Approximate Shares Within Channel Type	
		Makita Share	B&D Share
Two-Step	40%	55%	<10%
Home Centers	25%	45%	<10%
Warehouse Home Centers	15%	45%	20%
Membership Clubs	10%	85%	0%
Farm Outlets	5%	45%	15%

Exhibit 3 Piranha Sub–Brand

Product Policy

The note "Product Policy" introduces the key issues involved in managing a product program over time. As the note sets out, myriad issues fall under the heading of product policy. The six cases in this module were developed and selected to provide coverage of the key issues.

"Northern Telecom (A): Greenwich Investment Proposal . . ." and "Northern Telecom (B): The Norstar Launch" detail the process by which Northern Telecom designed a new phone system to replace its first-generation product, which was turning in a disappointing performance. In addition to presenting the problem of designing a launch plan for both the Canadian and U.S. markets, the two cases provide the opportunity to analyze the product development process at work. This discussion can lead to a wider analysis of the hallmarks of a "good" process.

"Swatch Group: On Internet Time" presents the problem of analyzing not a replacement product but a product line extension. Swatch is introducing the concept of Swatch Internet Time and a watch suited to the new metric. What is the role of the new watch in the product portfolio? Is this a good idea for the firm or not?

The next two cases take us into the realm of high technology. "net.Genesis, Inc." concentrates on a small start-up poised to take on Microsoft and others in the "e-business intelligence" market. Given the company's limited resources, net.Genesis faces tough questions about market selection and product positioning as the company seeks leadership in an immature market.

Turning the clock forward a few cycles from where net.Genesis finds itself, "Barco Projection Systems (A)" presents questions on how best to evolve a product line over time. In light of competition from strong, global players, what R&D investment strategy is needed to secure a sustainable, profitable position?

"Goodyear: The Aquatread Launch" also presents questions about the evolution of a product line evolution. Goodyear's considerations are complicated by the fact that not only consumer but also dealer response to any plan must be assessed. These intermediaries will be key to the product's performance.

The module closes with a "big," complex case, "L'Oreal of Paris: Bringing 'Class to Mass' with Plénitude." The case presents the most extensive consumer research data encountered thus far in the book. Included is an introduction to an important research technique, "Perceptual Mapping." When analyzed well, these data provide insight into L'Oreal's current position in the market and help resolve key issues of product line emphasis facing this international giant.

PRODUCT POLICY

Firms face a wide variety of critical product policy decisions. For example,

- Northern Telecom had to determine the feature set to include in its new phone system. This required assessing the tradeoff between cost and customer value delivered from inclusion of features such as conference calling, speed dialing, etc.
- Barco had to devise a strategy for evolving its projection systems over time, in light of the stream of innovations in the technologies underlying projectors, and competitors improving their price/performance ratios over time.
- L'Oreal's skin care group had to assess the benefits of expanding its product breadth by adding a group of products aimed at young consumers. A key consideration was whether this would broaden or dilute the brand.
- Merck had to set a strategy for the introduction of an over-the-counter version of Pepcid, its ulcer medication. What timing should be sought and how should the new version of the drug be positioned given its competition, not only with offerings from other firms, but also with the prescription version of Pepcid.
- Eastman Kodak had to decide whether to "trade down" its film product line by offering a new, cheaper version of its film to meet low priced competitors.

A useful way to think about product policy decisions is to start with the concept of a product line. A product line is a group of items which serve a similar function. For example, Callaway Golf offers a line of golf clubs (woods and irons). The line has three entries:

1. HawkEye—made of titanium;
2. Steelhead—made of steel;
3. Little Bertha—a starter set for children beginning to play golf.

Callaway offers other product lines as well. Its full product mix is as follows:

Exhibit 1 Callaway Product Mix

←Product Line Breadth/Width→				
Woods & Irons	**Putters**	**Wedges**	**Golf Balls**	**Accessories**
• HawkEye • Steelhead • Little Bertha	• Odyssey Brand ("White Hot" Putters) • Odyssey Brand ("Dual Force" Putters) • Odyssey Brand ("Triforce" Putters)	• Odyssey ("Dual Force")	• Callaway (Rule 35 Brand)	• Golf Bags • Hats & Visors • Travel Items • Handy Items

(Line Length indicated by vertical arrow at left of Woods & Irons column)

Professor Robert J. Dolan prepared this note as the basis for class discussion rather than to illustrate either effective or ineffective handling of an administrative situation.

Its product mix is made up of five related product lines. These five lines determine the product line breadth or width. In 2000, Callaway increased its line breadth/width by investing $170 million in Research & Development and a manufacturing facility to introduce its first golf ball, the Callaway Rule 35 brand.

It is often useful to describe a product mix in terms of its "consistency," i.e., the extent to which the various product lines "go together"—either in drawing on the same technology or serving the same market. Since all

Callaway products relate to the game of golf, most would describe its product mix as "highly consistent." In contrast, Yamaha offers a less apparently consistent line of products, ranging from golf carts to pianos to helium leak tester systems. A final idea is product mix "depth," i.e., how many variants of a given product are offered. There is no single summary measure of depth of product mix since it varies by product. For example, there is only one Little Bertha set of clubs, but many different Hawk-Eye and Steel Head configurations.

Callaway's golf ball is not as deep as it offers only two variants: Softfeel or Firmfeel. In contrast, the leading golf ball marketer, Titleist, offers twelve different types of balls. Titleist offers a Ball Fit program on its Website to help a customer find "which Titleist golf ball will perform best for you." Callaway's approach has been to simplify things for the consumer by limiting choice. Its Website describes the rule 35 ball and notes: "Finally, choosing a golf ball is easy. Simply select according to feel: Softfeel or Firmfeel. Yes, it's that straightforward."

In summary, product policy decisions exist with respect to the individual cells of the product mix matrix (i.e., the number of variants and features of each variant), the number of columns (i.e., the number of different product lines), and the number of rows in each column (i.e., the number of items in each line). We now describe some of the keys to effective product policy. We begin by considering decision-making related products which are "new" to the firm, e.g., Callaway's introduction of a golf ball line. We then consider issues in managing existing product lines, e.g., the addition of the new type of club to the Callaway equipment offerings.

New Product Decision-Making

Products which are "new" to the firm come in many different varieties, e.g.,

- The Sony Walkman was a technological breakthrough that created a new product category. Consumers had not been expressing a long felt desire for such product, but reacted very positively when exposed to it.
- Cisco's routers, which enabled two previously incompatible computer systems to communicate were also technological breakthroughs. But, in this instance, potential consumers had been explicitly declaring their need for such a product for years.[1]

The majority of "new" products, though, are not products which establish new product categories. Rather, they are entries into an established product category, hoping to achieve success by being "better" than existing competitors—at least in the eyes of some substantial part of the market. For example, both Sony and Cisco attracted competitors into the markets they created. Compaq entered the personal computer market pioneered by IBM; Glaxo and Merck entered the ulcer medication market created by Smith-Kline years earlier with Tagamet. The marketing challenges differ greatly depending upon the context of the introduction. Cisco's situation is the ideal: creating a new market but with a customer need already deeply felt. This made the adoption process relatively quick as sophisticated end-users were actively looking for a solution and were able to evaluate Cisco's. With no direct competitors, Cisco was able to shape the market and gained a market position it has retained over time.[2] Sony had no direct competitors but had to create the market; as did Smith-Kline with its Tagamet, the pioneering ulcer drug.

When entering an existing market, the customer education job is different. One need not educate so much about the category, e.g., why a drug is a better solution than stomach surgery for ulcers, but rather why your offering is better than a competitor's.

There has been extensive academic research on what makes for successful new products. This research clearly shows the importance of the firm having a well-thought-out and practiced *process* behind its product development. Being actually used is the key. Many firms have highly formalized, structured processes which become an impediment rather than stimulus to thinking as managers just go through the motions of the process. Cooper's research shows: "The mere existence of a *formal* product development process has absolutely *no effect* on performance . . . There is no correlation at all between having a formal process and performance result."[3] Processes vary a great deal in their quality. Hallmarks of an effective process are:

1. Involvement of marketing, manufacturing, and engineering in a coordinated way. One of the jobs

---

[1]Cisco's product development process is described in D. Bunnell with A. Brate, *Making the Cisco Connection: The Story behind the Real Internet Superpower,* John Wiley, 2000.

[2]Cisco's market share of routers directing data through the Internet is "some 80 percent" according to Bunnell and Brate, op. cit., p. xviii.

[3]R. G. Cooper, *Product Leadership: Creating and Launching Superior New Products,* Persus Books, Cambridge, MA, 1999, p. 34.

of marketing is to make sure that the voice of the customer is heard throughout the development process. Typically, a variety of research techniques is useful on this. In some cases, the company is anticipating customers' needs and designing something beyond the target user's current experience. In these cases, the voice of the customer cannot usefully be heard explicitly through quantitative surveys for example; but, rather, must be "sensed." A useful route is the technique of "empathic design" wherein the user's preferences are sensed through empathy with their situation rather than through explicit inquiry.[4]

2. This coordinated process between marketing, manufacturing, and engineering involves substantial work before the actual product design begins. Many firms push products into design to create a tangible sign that the process is moving quickly. Often, however, this is at the cost of later, costly redesigns.

3. The process has real go/no-go decision points. The proper new product development process is often described as a sequential process, or "funnel." Ideas are generated; some are rejected after initial consideration and others pass the test and continue on. At each stage, the "funnel" of still serving product ideas becomes narrower and narrower. However, as Cooper puts it, the reality in many companies is that, "the process is more like a *tunnel* than a *funnel*."[5] Products take on a life of their own. No one really gives serious consideration to actually killing the product idea once it is on the track. The initial check was only on whether the idea was worth considering formally; but once it passed this weak test, there really was no way to get it out of the process. Incremental changes could be made through the process, but the product continues to consume resources and is never really subjected to a tough test before launch. Cooper found the lack of tough go/kill decision points to weed out marginal products is, "The weakest ingredient of all process factors studied . . ."[6] The objective of the

process is, of course, a product that delivers superior value to the target customers. Recall that it is the customer's definition of value that counts. In new markets, there is no direct competition initially; so, the customer defines valued by comparison to the old way of doing things: either the old way of solving the problem (e.g., stomach surgery for ulcers) or continuing to live with the problem (e.g., continuing to live with incompatible computer networks). When entering existing markets, the comparison is more direct and the new product's degree of differentiation (in a valuable way) is key. The power of useful, valued differentiation has been documented by Cooper. He finds the following new product success rates:[7]

Me-Too Products	Products with Moderate Advantage	Truly Superior, Differentiated Products
18.4%	58%	98%

A key in developing truly superior, differentiated products is to draw on the distinctive competencies of the firm. Thus, in addition to assess into the product-market fit of new products, the process should assess the product-company fit, i.e., how well it fits the company's capabilities.

Managing Existing Product Lines

More often than not, a product introduction fits into an already existing product line. Diet Coke was an expansion of the Coca-Cola product line. Snapple introduces new flavors as consumer tastes evolve. Established high-technology firms such as EMC, Cisco, and Oracle offer new versions of storage, network routers, and database and application servers. Compaq offers new personal computers for home use for each of the three main selling seasons each year.

Product lines can stretch out on a horizontal and/or vertical dimensions. Coca-Cola's offering of Coke, Diet Coke, and caffeine-free versions of each is a horizontal product line. The products do not differ in inherent quality, e.g., in no objective sense is one better than the other. It is a matter of consumer taste whether Coke is "better" than Diet Coke or vice-versa. Coke is attempting to serve various segments of the market with the array of offerings.

In a vertical product line, products are more clearly delineated on a price/performance basis. For example, in October 2000, eMachines offered three different PCs on its Website:

---

[4]See for example, D. Leonard-Barton, E. Wilson and J. Doyle, "Commercializing Technology: Understanding User Needs," in Morgan, Shapiro, and Moriarity, *Business Marketing Strategy*, Irwin, 1995.

[5]R. Cooper, op. cit. p. 49.

[6]Ibid. p. 49.

[7]Ibid. p. 65.

Price	Processor Speed	Hard Drive Size
$799	700 Mhz	30GB
$599	633 Mhz	20GB
$399	566 Mhz	7.5GB

The situation was simply the higher the price, the greater the functionality. Unlike the Coke situation, there is a clear ordering of performance regardless of who the customer is. While there could be great variation in the *extent* to which different people preferred the 700 Mhz, 30GB model over the other two, each would in fact prefer the 700 Mhz, 30GB model (all other factors, including price, bring equal) because it runs faster and holds more information.

McGrath[8] defines a product-line strategy as, "a time-phase conditional plan for the sequence of developing products within a product line." The key point here is that the unit of analysis is the sequence of products to be offered. Thus, the firm should be looking ahead with a vision of where it wants to be over time. As suggested by McGrath's use of the adjective "conditional," the plan can change over time as events unfold (such as competitors' new product introductions) but there needs to be a guiding philosophy on the desired extent of product proliferation, and how products will be added/deleted over time.

The key reason to have a product line rather than a single product is to serve various market segments better. A particularly important strategy is the development of a product platform from which customized products can be developed at low incremental cost. For example, Boeing has a number of what it calls "product families."

The 777 is one of these families. The 777 is the product platform for the 777-200 plane, introduced in May 1995. The 200 had a range of 5,925 miles for up to 440 passengers. In 1997, the 777-200ER (extended range) was introduced to fly the same number of passengers as the 200, but up to 8,861 miles. The 777-300 was introduced in May 1998 to fly up to 500 passengers. A longer-range version of 300 is also available. Boeing terms these models "derivatives" and notes that their introductions "fulfill the original vision of the 777 family plan" as a platform to fill the size gap between its own 767 and 747 platforms.[9]

Given the multimillion dollar investment required to bring a new plane to market, it is easy to see why Boeing looks years ahead and develops a "vision of the family plan." A danger in less R&D intensive situations is that little forward planning takes place and product lines evolve opportunistically. The lack of a vision frequently results in a proliferated product line with poor coverage of the market segments and too much competition between the company's own product offerings.

Different products in the line should clearly map to different target market segments. A key problem in managing an introduction into a new product line differentiated on the vertical dimensions is cannibalization, i.e. the new product eating into the sales of an existing product. Product planning should consider the extent to which demand for a new product will be truly incremental or represent merely a shift of customers from one of the firm's existing products to the new one. Obviously, the relative profitability of the new and cannibalized items is a key factor. If the unit margin of the new product is better than that of the item which will be cannibalized (as is often the case when a company discovers a lower-cost way to bring the same level of functionality to market), this is not as serious an issue. However, the overall economics of the enterprise are still impacted by the level of incremental vs. cannibalization. If the economics of the new item are not as favorable as items it threatens to cannibalize, (as is often the case when a company "trades down" its product line to reach more of the mass-market), then careful consideration must be given to programs to limit the rate of cannibalization.

Over time, lines typically proliferate; it is harder to delete an item from a line than to add one. Recent purchasers of the product may feel abandoned or poorly served by the company since a salesperson allowed them to buy a product on the "to be discontinued" list. The trade reaction will likely be to force its inventories of the discontinued items back on the firm. However, a strong product line planning process includes systematic investigation of a line for deletion opportunities which will ease customers' decision making and improve the overall economics of the line.

Summary

Product decisions come in many shapes and forms. The changing nature of the marketplace requires constant attention to customers' and competitors' actions to adapt current offerings and drive new product development efforts.

[8]M. E. McGrath, *Product Strategies for High-Technology Companies,* McGraw-Hill, 1995, p. 61.
[9]Source: Boeing Website, www.boeing.com.

NORTHERN TELECOM (A):
GREENWICH INVESTMENT PROPOSAL (CONDENSED)

Proposing significant new investment in Northern Telecom's Business Products Division (BPD) had not been part of Mike Ennis's mandate. Installed as the general manager of this Northern Telecom division in February 1985, his assignment was clear: to "stop the bleeding." The Calgary, Canada-based division had generated negative cash flow of $61 million over the past three years manufacturing and marketing the Vantage[1] key system, a telephone system targeted to small businesses. Vantage had achieved the number one share position in Canada but it was eroding, and the product had failed to achieve any significant sales in the United States, holding less than 1% share.

Now, in November 1985, Ennis had prepared a proposal entailing an additional $54 million investment by Northern to develop a completely new key system product line to replace Vantage. Ennis's business plan for this new product line, code-named Greenwich, included arresting the decline and modestly improving Canadian market share, achieving a 15% share in the United States by 1991, lowering production costs, and greatly improving product reliability. The North American key systems market had over 100 suppliers. Ennis's proposal was for Greenwich to become the product of choice for resellers and end-users by virtue of its simplicity.

Background

Connecting all the world's telephone sets to one another involved a variety of equipment. Each terminal had to be "switched" to connect to any other terminal (see Figure 1).

Professor Robert J. Dolan prepared this case as the basis for class discussion rather than to illustrate either effective or ineffective handling of an administrative situation. Certain non-public data have been disguised.

A major city may have had several central office switches, and each significant population center usually had one switch. For each terminal to reach any other terminal, the central office switches must be connected to each other. This was accomplished with wire and cable or electronic equipment (see Figure 2).

Many telephone or terminal users were associated with each other in an office environment (e.g., in a business, hospital, etc.), with most of the communication needs being between fellow employees rather than with the outside world. Under these circumstances, it was often uneconomical to connect each telephone or terminal to a central office which might be several miles away. Instead, switching equipment was placed on the business subscriber's premises. This type of switching equipment was called a private branch exchange (PBX).

The equipment needed to provide this overall networking capability is grouped under the heading of **Business Communications and Networks** (see Figure 3).

Northern's 1984 sales revenue of $3.4 billion was largely divided among these three product lines:

1. Central office switches (50% of sales revenue).

2. Business communication systems (30% of sales revenue): This product line was made up of private branch exchanges, commonly known as PBXs, and key systems. PBXs were targeted to organizations with 100 or more employees, and were typically sold through and installed by local telephone companies. A PBX system investment could range up to $15 million for a large organization. (Northern was one of the leaders in the PBX market in North America, along with AT&T, Rolm, and MITEL.)

   Key systems were designed for small businesses with between 2 and 100 employees and, unlike the PBX business, were a highly fragmented business with over 100 different suppliers. (Only Northern and AT&T had manufacturing operations in North America. All other suppliers produced product in the Pacific Rim.) A key system

---

[1]Vantage is a registered trademark of Northern Telecom.

Figure 1

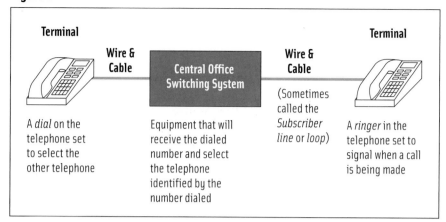

Terminal

Wire & Cable

Central Office Switching System

Wire & Cable

(Sometimes called the *Subscriber line* or *loop*)

Terminal

A *dial* on the telephone set to select the other telephone

Equipment that will receive the dialed number and select the telephone identified by the number dialed

A *ringer* in the telephone set to signal when a call is being made

consisting of a set of telephone stations and a central control unit, called a key system unit (KSU) needed access either to a Central Office Switch or PBX for "outside calls." It offered small firms an advantage over Centrex: the ability to handle calls within the organization without access fees; in addition, multiple stations (i.e., telephone sets) could be linked to the system. The key system business was not as technologically demanding for suppliers as the Centrex or PBX business, and entry barriers were low.

3. Transmission equipment (12% of sales revenue).

Through its participation in the Central Office and PBX markets, Northern had good relationships with local telephone companies (telcos) throughout North America. These firms were Northern's major customers for Central Office systems and major resellers or distribution networks for PBXs. In the 1980s, the U.S. market had undergone a drastic change when AT&T was forced to divest its 23 local companies. These 23 companies were reorganized into seven Regional Bell Operating Companies (RBOCs): Ameritech, Bell Atlantic, Bell South, NYNEX, Pacific Telesis, Southwestern Bell, and U.S. West. As part of the legal process creating the RBOCs, they were forbidden from manufacturing telephone equipment. AT&T kept its long-distance network and maintained the right to manufacture equipment thus, being a competitor of Northern.

Figure 2

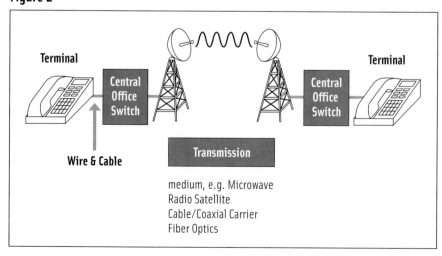

Terminal

Central Office Switch

Central Office Switch

Terminal

Wire & Cable

Transmission

medium, e.g. Microwave
Radio Satellite
Cable/Coaxial Carrier
Fiber Optics

Figure 3

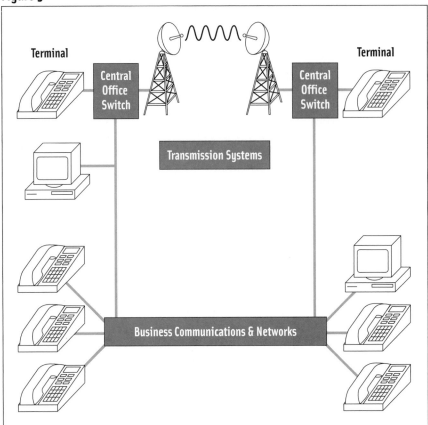

Business Products Division

The Vantage System was designed to be state-of-the-art in electronic key systems. Vantage, AT&T's Merlin system, and the systems of many Pac-Rim suppliers represented significant advances over the "plain old telephone set." They offered the small-business user features such as speed dialing, call forwarding, conferencing, intercom, and volume controls. Vantage was targeted at the business user needing between 2 and 50 stations within the organization. However, the Vantage product line had difficulty from the beginning. A Northern document written to capture the "Learning from Vantage" chronicled the product's history as follows:

> Ultimately a good system, the Vantage key system came too slowly and too late. . . . Launched in 1977 in London, Ontario, and moved out to Calgary when the Business Products Division (BPD) was created, Vantage took a glacial seven years to cover the small-business market. During that time, its technological

superiority vanished; what remained was a potentially attractive system with severe cost and quality problems. Deregulation aggravated the cost problem. Once a multitude of offshore products became available from telcos and interconnect dealers (the sales channels),[2] consumers began to make their own choices. All else being roughly equal, they chose overwhelmingly on the basis of price. Vantage was expensive all across the size range, and particularly in the sensitive lower end. The first Vantage had been a mid-size system, and the small system bore many of its expensive characteristics. To price-sensitive buyers, these superior features meant nothing. The absence of a full-

---

[2]The regional telephone companies (telcos) were important resellers in the North American market, particularly in Canada, where they handled 70% of key systems sales. Independent dealers sold the other 30%. The distribution channels in the United States were more complex since AT&T sold its own brand (Merlin) directly to end users accounting for 42% of sales. Telcos accounted for 25% (18% by RBOCs and 7% by independents). Dealers sold the other 33%.

range product (and particularly the lack of a viable entry-level system that could grow with a new company), then the crushing blow of deregulation hobbled the business; a division staffed and equipped to handle the North American market was actually handling only a shrinking portion of the Canadian market. Economies forced by the division's perilous financial position slowed the redesign work that was essential to improve the quality and lower the cost. Suppliers' efforts to improve their quality were hampered by traditional supplier/customer attitudes compounded by distance and the division's siege mentality. An unhelpful attitude to the sales channels' problems further tarnished a lackluster reputation. All key systems were plagued by a variety of technical problems, plus the unanticipated complexity of training technicians and users. Effective resolution of these problems was important to the telcos, because just two service calls a year to a customer site will eliminate their margins. The division, however, disavowed responsibility for non-technical issues; telcos and dealers were effectively forced to demonstrate a genuine technical issue before a problem would be addressed.

While the strong reputation of Northern Telecom in Canada propelled Vantage to be the best-selling key system in the Canadian market at one time, it failed to achieve even 1% share in the United States. The Calgary operation had been set up in anticipation of this appreciable U.S. market penetration. This, plus all the "fix up" problems in Canada, led to continuing losses.

	Vantage Sales	Net Income
1982	$29MM	($23MM)
1983	$50MM	($20MM)
1984	$72MM	($18MM)

Thus, when Ennis took over in February 1985, he was asked to analyze four options:

1. Abandon key systems;
2. Maintain status quo with better controls;
3. Shut down Calgary and consolidate key systems into another division;
4. Keep Calgary operating but as a cost center, subordinated to another division's P&L.

Ennis explained his philosophy:

I am an old banker. I knew that if you are into a bank for $70 million as we were, they would like to find a way to work with you to turn it around rather than just walk away from it. None of these options I was supposed to look at had a chance of turning it around. So, that's why I decided to look at the "Expand" option even though nobody asked me to. What would it cost to do key systems right, and what kind of impact could we expect if we did it right? It was obvious we needed a new product. I figured it would cost $35 million to get a first release to market and $50 million to deliver a full product line. Six million dollars of this was to revamp internal processes. With this kind of investment, you would have to get 20%–25% market share in the United States in the longer term. Then, to have a really important business, you'd have to build off the North American market and compete globally. Could we do it?

Key statistics on the market in 1985 and projected changes by 1991 are given in Table B.

A variety of market research procedures delivered the same conclusion: the Key Systems industry had failed to deliver *useable* functionality to the desktop. A Northern study concluded: "Simplicity has not been adequately

Table B Comparison of Key Market Statistics for 1985 and 1991 Projection

	1985	1991 Projection
U.S. market (units sold per year)	5.5 million	5.5 million
Canadian market (units sold per year)	455 thousand	539 thousand
Total dollar market value	1.6 billion	1.1 billion
Manufacturer's average net revenue received per station	$268.00	$182.00

Source: Company records

addressed by any competitor. Lack of simplicity is the greatest source of end-user dissatisfaction and a significant source of cost to the channel. Simplicity is focused on self-evident feature usage and system administration via terminal displays."[3]

The net of the consumer research was that Ennis and his team perceived an opportunity with consumers if Northern provided a product with an "appropriate price, absolute simplicity, and useable functionality."

Reseller Analysis

End users were not particularly knowledgeable about the key systems. While price sensitive, the typical buyer's search-and-acquisition process for a key system was: "I called the telephone company and they came out and put one in." This made achieving distribution and reseller support key for manufacturers. The reseller situation was dramatically different in the Canadian and U.S. markets. In Canada, the regional telephone companies sold 70% of units, while independent dealers sold the remaining 30%. As shown in Exhibit 1, the dominant channel in the United States was AT&T selling its own product direct to end users. AT&T was a fully integrated supplier offering its own branded product (Merlin) supported by an AT&T sales and service organization. With divestiture in 1984, AT&T chose not to sell its PBX or key system equipment to the Regional Bell Operating Companies. Regulations precluded the RBOCs from manufacturing their own equipment. The other 58% of the market was sold through dealers (33%), independent telecommunications companies such as GTE (7%), and the RBOCs (18%). While there were about 100 manufacturers of key systems worldwide, 40 suppliers actively vied for the business of these resellers. With the exception of Northern Telecom, all of these manufactured in the Pacific Rim. The two dominant ones in 1984 were TIE (with 19% share of the total U.S. key systems market) and MITEL (with 16%).

While the key systems market had grown rapidly in the early 1980s, resellers had not been able to make satisfactory profits. The lack of simplicity in useability with respect to the end user resulted in many calls to resellers for additional training. Many "repair requests" turned out to be for properly functioning equipment just not being used properly. Since the products were typically under warranty, "repairs" were a cost, not a source of revenue, for resellers. Although the number of potential vendors and lack of significant product differentiation led to continual price wars, this did not translate into satisfactory levels of reseller profit, due to these "repair" and other costs. Resupply from the Pac-Rim was unreliable. The Pac-Rim manufacturers operated on a four-month replenishment cycle. Market growth patterns were irregular, making the resellers' forecasting task difficult. In most cases, inventory was badly managed. In 1985, many resellers were in heavily overbought positions. The mentality was that large levels of inventory were one's only protection against demand uncertainty and the long replenishment cycle from the Pac-Rim. New vendors and new products also obsoleted resellers' inventory. In general, Northern's research showed widespread reseller dissatisfaction, centering around the complexity of running a key systems business. The question was whether Northern could convert this reseller dissatisfaction into a viable key systems business throughout North America.

Ennis developed the financial projections for the Investment Option shown in Exhibit 2. This plan represented an early 1988 launch of Greenwich and 1990 market shares of 53% and 15% in the Canadian and U.S. markets respectively. Ennis believed that a $54 million R&D investment could deliver a full Greenwich product line starting with an entry-level system with the right cost level and then modular additions to this basic architecture to reach more performance-oriented, larger customers. In 1986 and 1987 some of the R&D allocation would be to the Vantage line to reduce its cost and improve its quality. Ennis believed it was crucial for the launch of Greenwich to be preceded by satisfactory performance of the Vantage line, which would continue to be sold in 1986 and 1987 as the Greenwich system was being developed.

---

[3]Self-evident feature usage: making a feature work like a user would intuitively think it would without reference to a manual. System administration via terminal displays: having liquid crystal display on the phone set which could walk a user through how to access a particular feature. (This would obviate the need for reference to a manual.)

Exhibit 1 Key System Distribution Channels in the United States, 1984

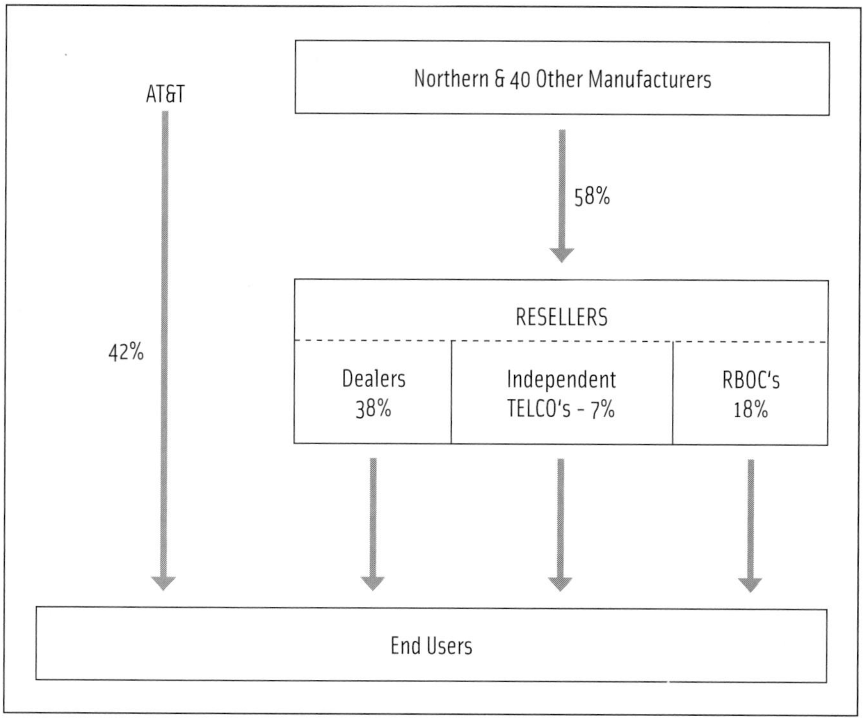

```
                    ┌─────────────────────────────────────────┐
     AT&T           │  Northern & 40 Other Manufacturers       │
                    └─────────────────────────────────────────┘
                                      │
                                     58%
                                      ↓
                    ┌─────────────────────────────────────────┐
                    │               RESELLERS                  │
     42%            ├──────────┬───────────────┬───────────────┤
                    │ Dealers  │ Independent   │  RBOC's        │
                    │  38%     │ TELCO's – 7%  │   18%          │
                    └──────────┴───────────────┴───────────────┘
                         │          │               │
      ↓                  ↓          ↓               ↓
┌──────────────────────────────────────────────────────────────┐
│                        End Users                               │
└──────────────────────────────────────────────────────────────┘
```

Exhibit 2 Key Financial Projections for Expand Option (US$ millions)

	Plan Year				
	1986	**1987**	**1988**	**1989**	**1990**
Total Sales ($):	68.3	74.7	108.1	186.1	240.2
Canada	39.1	35.8	39.4	50.5	59.8
United States	27.6	37.5	67.3	124.3	159.2
International	1.6	1.4	1.4	11.3	21.2
Cost of sales (% sales)	75	70	65	61	61
Sales and marketing (% sales)	12	15	13	13	12
R&D ($)	8.7	12.4	11.0	11.2	10.9
EBT	(4.9)	(2.9)	6.2	22.6	32.7
Cash flow	(3.7)	(2.3)	(.7)	(2.4)	12.7

NORTHERN TELECOM (B): THE NORSTAR LAUNCH

In March 1988, Mike Ennis, general manager of Northern Telecom's Business Products Division (BPD), prepared the final details for the launch of the first product in the Norstar Key Systems family.[1] Two and a half years earlier, Ennis's plan to develop the Norstar line, then code-named Greenwich, had been accepted by Northern Telecom's Executive Commitee, though some members regarded it as a high-risk proposition. It was strategically important for Northern to be in the key systems business. However, the $70 million in losses incurred by the Vantage, Norstar's predecessor, created some concerns within the corporation about the wisdom of investing $50 million in the development of another key system product family.[2]

As the outlines of Northern's plans came to be known, some security analysts expressed their surprise at the investment and Northern's goal of challenging AT&T for leadership in the U.S. market. In an article headlined "Setting skyhigh goals for Meridian Norstar," the *Financial Times of Canada* noted one analyst's concern about Northern's lack of a distribution channel in the United States, referring to Northern as a "tiny, inconsequential player in key systems for years. And then last year we heard rumors that they were spending millions of dollars on key system development. Frankly, we thought they were crazy."[3] Roy Merrills, president of Northern's U.S. operations in Richardson, Texas, reiterated Northern's goals for Norstar: "It's the right product at the right time. We are firmly committed to success in the key system market. We're in it for one reason and one reason only—to be number 1. Our goal is leadership."

Ennis had directed the product development activities aimed at making Norstar the "right product at the right time" and the vehicle for both global leadership and profitability in key systems. The Norstar Compact System for users with need of up to 16 stations was now ready for market. Ennis had to be sure BPD's marketing strategy supporting Norstar would achieve sales in an intensely competitive marketplace. The proposal to invest $50 million in Norstar development had been justified on the basis of attaining 55% share in Canada and 15%–20% in the United States. He recognized enormous differences between the Canadian and U.S. markets. While he believed the Norstar product fit the needs of both, there would have to be some customization of the supporting elements of the marketing mix to the individual markets. In Canada, Northern held the leading market share in virtually every telephone-related product category, was well-known to consumers, and had strong relationships with the telephone companies. These telcos held 70% of the Key System business and would be the prime resellers of the Norstar line. In contrast, Northern was virtually unknown to small-business customers in the United States. The Vantage System held only 1% share, placing it No. 18 in market share ranking. In addition, the Regional Bell Operating Companies (RBOCs), whom Northern was targeting to be prime resellers, held only 20% of the U.S. Key System market.

Since 70% of the demand for key systems was outside of North America, Canada and the United States would be only the first challenges for Ennis. However, he knew that success here was a necessary platform to approach markets worldwide. Similarly, he had recognized two years earlier that, like it or not, the Vantage product line was the platform off which he had to stage his Norstar effort.

---

[1]Meridian, Norstar, and Vantage are registered trademarks of Northern Telecom.

[2]Key Systems were telephone sets designed for the small-business market, that is, organizations needing between 2 and 100 telephone sets or stations. Those with requirements for more sets would typically be better served by purchasing a Private Branch Exchange (PBX). Details on the key systems market and Northern's considerations to develop the Norstar line are given in "Northern Telecom (A)," HBS No. 9-593-103.

[3]*Financial Times of Canada,* March 21, 1988, p. 3.

Vantage Product Line

The financial impact documented in black and white on BPD's profit and loss statements since 1982 was only one of the negative effects of the Vantage product line. Northern people associated with the line were dispirited and feared for their jobs; resellers were disgruntled with it, and end users favored less-expensive models. Once the decision was made for Northern to continue in the key systems business, Ennis appointed two key managers to rectify the Vantage problems. Fouad Aziz, director of Customer Service, and Alan Stewart, director of Quality, were responsible for turning the Vantage experience into a positive position from which to launch the Norstar line.

Aziz explained: "There was a major learning cycle for everybody with Vantage—users, resellers, and us. It was one of the first pure electronic key systems in the marketplace. There was a general lack of understanding about how to make, sell, install, and maintain these systems. Vantage had some problems initially, no doubt about it. From 1985 to 1987, when everybody else around here was working on Norstar, my job was to focus on Vantage: get costs down, fix it in the field, and figure out what Vantage was telling us about how to do it better for the next generation product. While development of Norstar was a big investment, we knew we also had to invest in fixing Vantage."

Figure 1 documents the results of investment in Vantage research and development to "get the costs down." It shows the manufacturing cost per station for Vantage for 1984–1987.

The success of the cost-reduction program had a parallel with respect to customers. In 1985, Alan Stewart, director of Quality, instituted BPD's first systematic measurement of customer satisfaction. The survey, distributed to a variety of people within resellers' organizations, asked for an overall rating on Northern's performance and specific ratings in the areas of hardware, documentation, services, sales and marketing, and software. Previously, the "quality" effort had been focused on the inspection of incoming parts from suppliers. The customer satisfaction survey represented the redefinition of quality to a customer-based concept. This formal interaction with resellers and Stewart's personal follow-up on any problem areas served to improve Northern's understanding of the resellers' business situation and their perceptions of Northern. It also changed the customers' attitude toward Northern.

Stewart related the importance of this change: "Vantage gained market share back in Canada and together with the cost-reduction program, this got us more support for Norstar from corporate; but, more important, all our activities with Vantage during this time got us our customer credibility back. When Vantage first started to have problems in the field, we adopted the attitude that

Figure 1 Vantage Cost per Station

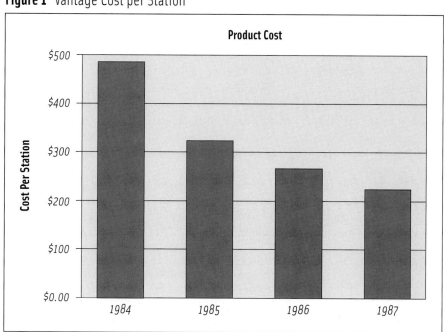

the product was fine and the resellers just were not installing it right or training end users well. This really hurt us and we had to rebuild those relationships if the next product we offered was going to have any chance with these customers."

In addition to the customer credibility, Aziz emphasized the significant learning about the resellers from this development of a closer association: "We really came to understand how they work, how they are organized, how they communicate or don't communicate within the organization, what was their attitude toward training courses, how the installation and repair group worked. . . . It also helped us to establish the right links in the organization. We learned a lot which will help us with marketing Norstar."

The Norstar Development Program

Ross Matthews, BPD's manager of Manufacturing Engineering during both the development of Vantage and Norstar, explained how the development program for Norstar was a direct result of the Vantage experience.

Vantage was the outcome of a product-development program based on a serial delivery concept. First, the product group develops a commercial specification. This basically says what the product is supposed to do. Then, the designers come in. At Northern, our design house is Bell Northern Research [BNR], an organization which is 70% owned by Northern and 30% by Bell Canada. The design group takes the commercial specification and goes off and develops the product specification. In this case, the design group is located two time zones and 2,000 miles away from the product group. They get together again with the product group, iterate through it and ultimately hash it out. The design group sometimes adds some neat features they think would be good, something that's real differentiating based on the latest technology they have developed. Finally, after lots of discussion usually, the product group accepts the product specification and signs off on it. Now here we are in manufacturing. The first involvement we have in this thing is as the design document flies over the wall. Vantage's problems were evidence of the deficiencies in this system of product development. It had cost problems; it had quality problems; and was in the middle of the pack on MTBF.[4] There was just no way the product as designed could be manufactured in Canada at competitive cost and quality levels.

Norstar's development process was designed to overcome this situation by a team effort of the product/marketing group, design, and manufacturing to fulfill the basic business proposition of "appropriate price, absolute simplicity, and useable functionality." Ennis and Howie Bender, vice president of BNR, became co-chairs of monthly program reviews. As the client of BNR, Ennis insisted that all members of the BNR team assigned to Norstar work in the same location and only on Norstar.[5] The design team was to understand the entire Norstar business plan. Second, the specific client of the design team within Northern's BPD was redefined to include not just the product group but also manufacturing. The design job was conceived of as the co-design of both the product and the manufacturing process. The team was told to zero-base the manufacturing operation, forgetting about how the factory currently operated, the people skills on hand, and the available equipment. The mandate was to find the optimal combination of product and manufacturing process to achieve the business objective.

Matthews commented on the change in philosophy:

This was a very new role for us in manufacturing. Manufacturing was now being pulled into the product development process well ahead of the product definition stage. Being in on the conceptual stage of things was not anything we had done before. At first, it sounds great—you will be able to voice your concerns earlier and get people to think about your issues. But it's a big change too. For the first time, we had to understand the whole business process because we had to figure out what manufacturing should be. What cycle time targets, overhead levels should we have? Having "ease of manufacture" become a design criterion of the people at BNR wasn't easy either. Many of the BNR designers had never been in a factory. You can't design something for "ease of manufacturing" if you don't really understand how manufacturing works. So, we brought them all here to see what goes on; first the lead designers, then the rest. It cost about $1500 in expenses for each of the 30 of them and two days of their time and ours, but it was well worth it to have them just look at an assembly operation. They then quickly understood the implications of the various design actions on us.

---

[4]MTBF: an acronym for "Mean Time Between Failure"—(a measure of a product's reliability).
[5]BNR's policy was to have development spread over multiple locations and a designer simultaneously assigned to multiple projects.

Exhibit 4 Example of Proposed Advertising Copy for Canadian Market

Exhibit 5 Example of Proposed Advertising Copy for Canadian Market

APPENDIX

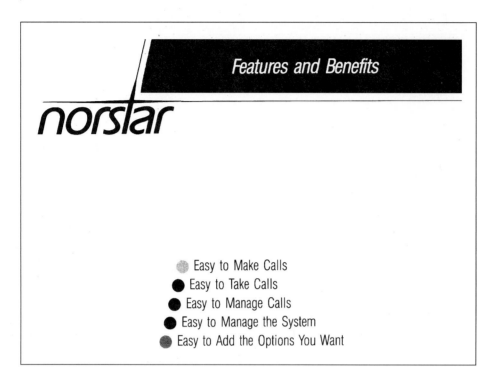

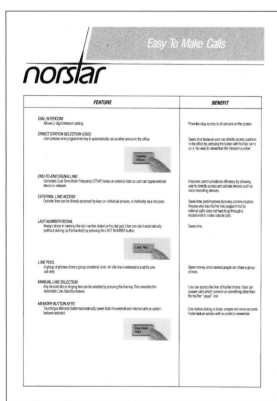

Easy To Make Calls

FEATURE	BENEFIT
ON-HOOK DIALING A user can activate the set and dial digits on an external or internal line without lifting the handset or pressing the Handsfree key. On hearing the party answer, the user lifts the hand-set or presses Handsfree to converse.	No need to pick up the handset. Saves time and increases productivity.
PAGING Norstar sets can make paging announcements three ways: *Internally,* through the set speakers. *Externally,* through a customer-supplied amplifier and speaker. Both *internally* and *externally* at the same time.	Saves time, makes it easier for the user to find the needed party.
PAUSE Allows the user to insert a 1.5 second waiting period between digits being dialed. Used when programming Speed Dial numbers.	Easier programmed dialing.
PRIME LINE SELECTION For outgoing or incoming calls, the user lifts the receiver or presses the Handsfree key. The set will automatically select an open line. As an inside call is made, the display shows whether the phone being called is busy, using *Do Not Disturb,* or on *Call Forward.* The name of the party being called is also displayed.	For incoming calls, the user doesn't have to decide which line is ringing. It's second nature to just pick up the phone. For outgoing calls, the user doesn't have to select a line, it is done for him automatically. Provides information to help the caller assess the telephone status of the called party, personalizes and improves office communications.
RING AGAIN ON BUSY Ring Again on Busy Set alerts a user when a busy internal set becomes available. Ring Again on Busy Line Pool alerts a user when a line in a line pool becomes available.	Saves time. Increases productivity because the user doesn't have to keep checking to determine if a set or line is available.
RING AGAIN ON NO ANSWER Alerts a user when the next activity occurs at an internal set that previously failed to answer a call from the user.	Saves time. Increases productivity since the caller doesn't have to keep trying to reach the person who didn't answer his phone.
SPEED DIAL – SET Allows user to program and dial up to 24 Speed Dial numbers of their own choice. An outside line is selected automatically and the number dialed is displayed.	Saves time, prevents misdialing. Every user can have his/her own private speed dial numbers.
SPEED DIAL – SYSTEM Any set can access 30 Speed Dial numbers shared by the system, and the number dialed is displayed.	Provides fast access to numbers frequently used by everyone in the office.

Easy To Take Calls

norstar

FEATURE	BENEFIT
CALL IDENTIFICATION On an inside call, the name of the calling party is displayed.	Personalizes office communications. Allows the called party to prepare himself/herself for the call. Increases office efficiency. On call forward, allows professional answering of colleagues' phones.
CALL PICKUP (GROUP) Any user in a pickup group can answer external or internal calls ringing at another telephone without leaving their work station. The user either presses the pre-programmed CALL-PICKUP button on a set so equipped, or presses FEATURE 75.	Better customer service, less irritation from the sound of unanswered ringing phones.
CALL TIMING The display shows the length of the current or most recent call in minutes and seconds when queried by the user.	Can be used to record time charges.
DISCRIMINATING RINGING Internal and external calls have different ringing cadences.	the user can distinguish internal from external calls
DISTINCTIVE RINGING The set can be programmed to ring with one of four distinct tone combinations, so that the user can distinguish the ringing of the user's set from that of other sets nearby.	Eliminates confusion. Useful in open office environments
DO NOT DISTURB If the user activates this feature while a call is ringing his or her phone, the call will ring at the Prime phone. This is a selective form of *Call Forward.* Activating DND puts the user in DND mode, which suppresses: voice calls, ringing, paging announcements, and *Ring Again* offers. It stops all tones and ringing, except *Next Line Reminders* to DND mode, incoming calls still appear on the line indicators, but *Call Identification* for incoming inside calls is not displayed.	User can work uninterrupted without worrying about calls going unanswered. Because all visual signals still appear on the set, user can decide to answer any call. User can still make outside calls.
TIME-DATE DISPLAY The time and date appear on the display when the user is not on a call.	Provides extra convenience; saves space on user's desk.
VOICE CALL DENY User can prevent the set from receiving Voice Calls. All internal calls to that set will then be received as ringing calls.	User can prevent interruptions from voice calls, while still being alerted to the fact that there is an incoming internal call

norstar

FEATURE	BENEFIT
AMPLIFYING HANDSET Amplifying handset allows users who have hearing impairments or who are in a noisy environment it to boost volume.	Ensures communications effectiveness.
AUTOMATIC HOLD A busy line will automatically be placed on hold it the user, without pressing the HOLD button or hook switch, presses a second line button, an INTERCOM button, or the CONF/TRANS button.	Prevents internal and external calls from being accidentally cut off during a transfer or when the user inadvertently presses another button.
CALL FORWARD - ALL CALLS The user can forward internal and external calls to another set.	Ensures user's calls will be answered if he/she wants to leave the workstation or work uninterrupted. Improves customer service.
CALL FORWARD OVERRIDE When one set is forwarded to another, this feature allows the forward destination to call the forwarding set. Also called *Secretarial Filtering*; this feature lets a secretary take calls for a supervisor and call him or her periodically to give messages.	Allows the secretary to convey important messages, even when the phone is forwarded to the secretary.
CALL STATUS DISPLAY The line lamp on a telephone shows the line status in one of these ways:	Allows the user to effectively manage a flow of calls by being able to tell at a glance the status of lines/calls.
LAMP OUT The line is idle. STEADILY LIT The line is in use. SLOW FLASH An incoming call is ringing on the line FAST FLASH A call is on hold on the user's station. SLOW FLICKER A call is on hold on the line at another station.	
CALL PROGRESS TONES Audible indication of telephone numbers dialed.	Allows user to discern whether button depression was recorded by the set
CONFERENCING This feature lets the user establish a three-party conference by connecting two calls to the user's set	Saves time and avoids miscommunication by having three parties privy to the same conversation.
To create a conference, the user: (1) Makes the first call. (2) Presses the CONF/TRANS button. (3) Makes the second call. (4) Presses the CONF/TRANS button. (5) Presses the line button of the first held call. Alternatively, the user can call up step-by-step instruction on the display panel.	User does not have to remember codes or sequence of operations. The phone guides the user through each step.

Once a conference call is established, any of the following operations can be carried out:

FEATURE	BENEFIT
Split the conference: The conference originator can talk privately with either of the two parties involved, while the second party is on hold. The originator can also put the other parties on hold independently, preventing them from talking to each other. *Force release a conference party:* Lets the user disconnect one party. *Transfer from the conference:* Lets the user drop out of the conference, leaving the other two parties connected. If the other Parties are both outside the office, the user must put the Conference on hold, and disconnect only after both parties have hung up. *Consultation:* User can put a conference call on hold to make or answer another call. User presses another line button; conference call is automatically put on hold.	Allows user to temporarily interrupt a conference to deal with another matter, then easily reactivate the conference.
EXCLUSIVE HOLD When the user places an external call on exclusive hold, it cannot be picked up on any other set.	Allows total system-wide privacy and confidentiality.
HANDSFREE ANSWERBACK ON INTERCOM This feature allows the user to respond to a voice call without physically answering the call.	User can answer the phone without touching it and continue working, if desired.
HANDSFREE/MUTE CAPABILITY Handsfree operation allows the user to participate in a telephone call with the receiver on the hook by speaking to the telephone set in a normal voice and listening to the other party over the telephone set loudspeaker. The user may confer privately with people near the telephone by depressing the Hands-free/Mute button, which suppresses voice transmission to the other party.	Handsfree operation lets the user answer calls hands-free, so the user can continue working. Handsfree also allows one or several people near the set to converse with the party on the line. Pressing the mute button lets the user conduct in-office conversations privately from the caller.
HEARING AID COMPATIBLE The receivers on all Meridian Norstar sets are compatible with hearing aids.	Allows users with hearing aids to use any Norstar phone in the system comfortably and effectively.
HELD LINE REMINDER When the user places an external call on hold, this feature generates periodic reminder tones until the call is removed from hold.	Reminds the user that he/she has a caller on hold. Improves customer service.
HELD CALL REMINDER TRANSFER TO PRIME After two minutes, a held call will signal the prime set.	Improves customer service.
I-HOLD/U-HOLD INDICATION The set that places a line on hold flashes at a faster rate. Other sets will flash at the regular rate for that line.	Set user can easily differentiate the call he or she has put on hold from calls put on hold by other set users sharing the same group of external lines.
LEAVE MESSAGE/LIST The user can send a personalized display message requesting another person in the office to call back. The user can display up to four sent messages, and cancel any if desired. When leaving a message, the user is guided by the display.	Saves time, since the user doesn't have to keep calling back.

Easy To Manage Calls

FEATURE	BENEFIT
LINK KEY The user can have the system generate a timed hookswitch flash to communicate with a host PBX or Centrex by pressing the link key or dial pad code.	Allows the system to interface behind a larger telephone switch. Individual departments/locations can have all the features of a Meridian Norstar system, yet still easily access the features of the larger system.
LISTEN ON HOLD If the user has been placed on hold by the other party, the user can depress the HANDSFREE button and place the handset on hook while waiting for the other party to return. When the other party announces his or her return, the user hears the announcement through the loudspeaker and can then pick up the handset and resume the conversation.	The user can continue working, with both hands free, if placed on hold, and can easily resume the call when the other party returns.
MESSAGE WAITING LIST The set display tells the user when a message has been received. The set can automatically place an internal call to the party that sent the message, or can cancel the message without calling back.	Improved internal communications.
NIGHT SERVICE This feature permits incoming calls, normally directed to the attendant/Prime set, to be routed to a preselected Night Service set. Any set can be the night phone.	Better customer service; better staff communications.
PRE-SELECTION/CALL SCREENING The user can select a ringing line on the set by pressing the ringing line key. Then the identifier "<name> calling" (for internal calls) and "Line <n>" (for external calls) is displayed.	Allows the user to determine who is calling or which line is being used.
PRIME LINE Administration can assign a prime line to a set. If a set has a prime line, Automatic Outgoing Line Selection occurs and external dialing features (Autodial, Speed Dial, Last Number Redial) will select an outgoing line automatically. Automatic Incoming Line Selection will automatically select a prime line call before calls ringing on other lines.	The user does not need to select a line when making a call.
PRIVACY When the user is on a line, no other set can access the call. This feature is automatic on all calls.	Security and confidentiality.
RELEASE The release key disconnects an active call.	Allows the user to disconnect a call without lifting/replacing the handset. Saves time.
TRANSFER To transfer a call to an internal local, the user calls the internal local, touches the Conf/Trans button, and the first party button after the call is answered. The user touches the disconnect button to disconnect from the call.	Makes it very difficult to lose a party being transferred. Better customer service; more professional image.
USER PROGRAMMABLE FEATURE KEYS Each user of each set can assign many desired features to programmable keys. On Meridian M7310, each of the larger "Memory" buttons (non-indicator programmable keys) can store two phone numbers or features. The triangular button shifts between the two.	Each user can customize a set to his/her needs, and change the programming as those needs change.
VOLUME CONTROL The individual user has complete volume control of handset receiver, handsfree speaker, headset, ringing, incoming background music, and set paging.	User can adjust volume for his/her own personal preference. Improves comfort and efficiency.

Easy To Manage The System

norstar

FEATURE	BENEFIT
AUTOMATIC SET RELOCATION User can move phones from jack to jack. Phone number and individual programming moves with the phone.	Saves time since no features have to be reprogrammed. Saves money since there is no need to call an installer for move phones.
CENTREX/PBX REACHTHROUGH When behind Centrex or BPX, users can access features which require tone signals in addition to dialing. These features include: Timed Release: A code signals Centrex or the PBX (longer duration than a flash) to disconnect the call and then give a dial tone. The code can be included in an autodial sequence, speed dial bin, or the last number redial buffer. Run/Stop: A code allows the user to store two or more sequences in the same key, with successive depressions of the key sending out successive sections of the stored sequence.	Allows Centrex features to be accessed in a convenient fashion.
CUSTOMER TEMPLATES Button overlays which the System Coordinator places on individual sets when programming system features. The overlays identify buttons which take on the functions named on the overlay when used in conjunction with an administration code. A programming sheet supplied by the installer is used to record phone numbers and features assigned to each phone.	Simplifies programming tasks done by the System Coordinator.
DEFAULT ADMINISTRATION Defaults are features programmed into buttons before delivery. They make the system operational immediately upon installation. The System Coordinator can reprogram any button setting except for inside and outside line buttons and Handsfree/Mute.	Makes the phone system operational immediately upon installation.
DELAYED RING TRANSFER After three full ring cycles, an external call will transfer to the prime set.	Improves customer service since unanswered calls transfer automatically to the prime set.
EXECUTIVE FLEXIBLE CALL RESTRICTION OVERRIDE The user can override any call restriction on any phone by entering a 3-digit password.	Improves convenience and efficiency for selected personnel by allowing them to bypass Call Restrictions on any phone.
EMERGENCY TRANSFER/POWER FAIL CUT-THROUGH If there is a commercial power failure, this feature provides basic telephone service via a single-line phone acting independently from the system.	Ensures continued basic telephone service will be available in the event of a power loss.
FLEXIBLE CALL RESTRICTIONS The user can prevent any phone or line from accessing specific numbers (eg. long distance).	Improves cost control.
FLEXIBLE CALL RESTRICTION OVERRIDE The user can establish specific numbers which are exceptions to the restrictions.	Maintains general call restrictions cost control, yet provides system-wide access to selected numbers within the restricted categories.
MULTIPLE LINE KEYS Each call is accessed on a separate line key. Multiple line keys allow the user to manipulate calls easily. By allowing calls to provide visual alerting and be answered easily when the user is active on another call, these line keys also serve a "call waiting" function.	Allows the user to handle calls easily, as each telephone may have up to 6 lines on it.

FEATURE	BENEFIT
MUSIC-TONE/SILENCE ON HOLD This feature allows held external calls to be presented with music or a periodic tone.	By presenting the party on hold with music or a periodic tone, the user can re-assure customers that they have not been forgotten.
PAGE ORIGINATION/RECEPTION – INTERNAL Through the set speakers, the user can make a page or be paged internally.	A paging announcement can be easily sent to all phone sets.
PAGE ORIGINATION – EXTERNAL Through set speakers connected to a user-supplied amplifier and speaker, the user can make external paging announcements.	A paging announcement can easily be sent to all phone sets and to staff in rooms or areas without phone sets.
PRIME SET A prime set is a set which receives unanswered calls. A prime phone supports these call management features: *Delayed Ring Transfer* transfers external calls to the Prime Phone if they go unanswered after the third ring. *Held Line Reminder* begins at the Prime Phone two minutes after an outside call is put on hold, if the Prime Phone has the outside line. *Do Not Disturb* transfers incoming external calls to the Prime set.	More efficient call handling because one set gets all unanswered calls.
PRIVATE LINES An external line can be assigned to one set as a private line. It can appear only on that set and the Prime Set. Calls that are put on hold or left unanswered on this line cannot be picked up by any other phone.	Provides extra privacy, as well as better access (since only one person has the line, that user will always have access to one outside line).
PROGRAMMABLE USER NAMES The System Coordinator can program user names to appear on the LCD Display during inside calls. The display shows the name of the person calling or the name of the person the user is calling.	Professional handling of calls forwarded by colleagues. Enhanced message waiting.
PULSE/TONE DIALING Dialing numbers are automatically sent as pulse or tone signals, whichever is most appropriate for the trunk lines receiving the transmission.	Allows the system to operate regardless of the type of signaling used by the user's telephone exchange.
RINGING LINE PREFERENCE When a person picks up the handset to answer a call, if two or more lines are ringing, he will automatically be connected to the first call.	Allow the user to answer calls without first selecting a line.
SET BASED ADMINISTRATION General administration (programming activities normally done by the user's System Coordinator) include time and date, system speed dial entries, night service set designation, name assignment to sets, call restrictions and overrides, executive password.	Allows fast, accurate administration set-up and changes by remote access.
SHOULDER REST The shoulder rest holds the receiver comfortably and securely on either shoulder.	Improves comfort and efficiency for users who are on the phone a lot and who prefer hand-held operation.
SIMULTANEOUS VOICE/DATA CAPABILITY Facsimile, answering machines, credit card terminals and other services can be accommodated on the same line that handles voice calls.	No separate dedicated line required to accommodate phone-linked equipment.
SQUARE/NON-SQUARE/HYBRID CONFIGURATION The system can be configured as a square, non-square or hybrid system. In a square system, all sets have direct access to all external lines (up to six). In a non-square system, fewer programmable keys are used for line access, so not all external lines can be directly accessed by each set.	Square system configuration can provide tariff advantages, satisfy a user need for direct control of external lines, or conform to traditional user expectations. Other configurations make more programmable keys available for direct feature access.

norstar

FEATURE	BENEFIT
ANALOG TERMINAL ADAPTOR This device allows the user to accommodate analog equipment including answering machines, credit card readers, modems, fax machines, and other standard analog tip-and-ring devices without the need for a separate dedicated line. In addition to providing analog terminal connectivity, the ATA will enable off-premises extensions. Whether on or off-site, the ATA will allow the analog terminal to access many of the Meridian Norstar features. These features include: C.O. and intercom lines (prime is programmable), Hold, System speed dial, Conference, Call Forward, Paging, Call restrictions. The ATA can be connected to any Meridian Norstar digital station port. The number of ATAs which may be connected to a Meridian Norstar system is limited only by the number of available ports.	Maximizes efficiency while keeping hardware costs as low as possible.
AUXILIARY LOUD BELLS An auxiliary ringer supplied by the user can be connected to ring on internal and/or external calls.	Ensures that a ringing phone will be heard in noisy areas.
BACKGROUND MUSIC Background music can be connected to the KSU to play through Meridian Norstar telephone speakers. Music automatically disconnects when the set is in use. User can program background music on or off.	Can improve the general office working environment.
BUSY LAMP FIELD UNIT This module attaches to the Meridian M7310 set. It allows the user to see the busy/not busy status of other sets on an ongoing basis.	Helps to ensure that calls are handled efficiently and that no calls are missed.
CONFIDENCER For noisy locations, this unit replaces the standard handset and filters out excessive background noise.	Makes it easy to hear calls in noisy locations.
HEADSET An approved headset can be plugged into the special jack built into every Meridian Norstar phone. No additional wiring or power is required. The Handsfree/Mute button controls the headset in the same way that it controls Handsfree calls. Volume is adjusted using the Volume button.	Plug-in headset makes it easy to provide handsfree privacy and convenience at any phone.
LANGUAGE CHOICE ON DISPLAY LCD Display panel contains built-in bilingual message capability. Display language can be changed in seconds on a per set basis.	Saves money when people speaking the alternate language are employed (no need to keep changing sets to accommodate new employees).
NIGHT SERVICE BELLS Any set can be the night phone. This phone can also be programmed to ring the Auxiliary Ringer for all ringing calls at the Night Service phone while active.	Ensures night calls from customers will be heard in noisy locations.
OFF-PREMISE EXTENSION The OPX capability of the system allows the user to have a single line set operational at other than the main system location.	Better customer service.

THE SWATCH GROUP: ON INTERNET TIME

[Swatch Internet Time is a] great idea! We are living in one world so we should use one time . . . I'm just wondering when this will become our official time? Darn, I'll have to buy a new watch!

I really would like to put Internet Time on my homepage, but I can't have banners all over my site saying "Swatch" and linking back to your site. Dump the banners. Okay, it was your idea. So what? If you want this idea to really break through, it can't be connected with a company.

—Comments from visitors to the Swatch Web site

Swatch is a triumph of engineering, but even more so one of fantasy and imagination. If you combine powerful technology with fantasy, you can create miracles. The secret is to keep the creativity, the dreams, and the imagination of a child. My wife refers to me as a six-year-old boy with the experience of a 66-year-old man.

—Nicolas G. Hayek, Chairman and CEO,
The Swatch Group

In November 1998, 90 children from 54 countries attended the Massachusetts Institute of Technology's (MIT) Junior Summit. Another 3,000 participated online. The purpose of the summit was to promote international dialogue about advanced technology among children worldwide. Attendees of the 1998 summit were the first to test a new universal unit of time called Swatch Internet Time (SIT). Their week-long schedule was driven by SIT and each participant was given a Swatch Beat, the newest Swatch watch model that

kept both Internet and local time, and also counted down days until the new millennium (see Exhibit 1).

Pioneered by The Swatch Group, makers of the Swatch watch, SIT divided every day into 1,000 "beats" equivalent to 86.4 seconds each. Each day began @000 (@ was the abbreviation for beats) and noon was @500. A new day in Tokyo, for instance, began at @667 BMT. A new meridian line was created that passed over Swatch headquarters in Biel, Switzerland, making Biel Mean Time (BMT) the official reference for Internet time. "Internet time is absolute time for everybody," explained Nicholas Negroponte, founder and director of the MIT's Media Laboratory and a proponent of SIT. "Now is now and the same time for all people and places. Later is the same subsequent period for everybody. The numbers are the same for all."[1]

SIT was the latest entrepreneurial move by The Swatch Group, led by Chairman and CEO Nicholas G. Hayek. "The Greenwich people told us this is blasphemous," Swatch CFO Edgar Geiser recounted. "They asked, 'How is this scientific?' We told them that it was not but we went ahead anyway."[2] "Since we basically reinvented the concept of time with Swatch in the early 1980s," added Yann Gamard, president of Swatch USA, "it is only natural that Swatch comes up with a concept of time that addresses cyberspace in the digital era. Since you can download it for free, there are no direct dollars *per se,* but in terms of brand enhancement and brand awareness, it's exactly in line."

Many nevertheless questioned the motive behind SIT. In 1991, the company initiated a series of telecommunications joint ventures (JVs), and an ecologically friendly car was in conception by 1994. None of these ventures, however, had met expectations. Some believed that launching SIT was merely a way to reenergize the Swatch brand in markets such as the United States where sales and the Swatch image were suffering. Others questioned whether the concept of SIT would catch on.

Research Associate Cate Reavis prepared this case under the supervision of Carin-Isabel Knoop, Director, Research and Development, Executive Education and Assistant Professor Luc Wathieu as the basis for class discussion rather than to illustrate either effective or ineffective handling of an administrative situation.

---

[1] Mark Gibbs, "Internet time: Old wine, new bottles," *Network World* (November 16, 1998).

[2] For SIT to be accepted as an official time measurement, Swatch needed endorsement from the worldwide body of standards and keepers coordinated by France's Bureau International des Poids et Mesures.

"Controlled Chaos"[3]

In 1998, The Swatch Group was the world's largest watch company. With total production of 119 million watches and watch components, it accounted, in value terms, for 20% to 25% of worldwide watch sales (and 37% of the Swiss watch industry). Europe accounted for 35% of sales, followed by Asia with 32%, North America with 25%, and 8% for the rest of the world. In volume terms, The Swatch Group's worldwide market share was 14% (see Exhibit 2). In addition to watch production, the company's activities included microelectronics (67% of revenues from the production of 1.5 volt chips came from markets outside the watch industry),[4] production services, automobile, R&D, telecommunications, and JVs (see Exhibit 3). In 1998, company revenues totaled $2.2 billion (a 9% increase in local currencies) with profits of $230 million (see Exhibit 4). On the 1998 *Business Week* Global 1000 list, The Swatch Group ranked 713 in market value ($5.82 billion).

In addition to the Swatch brand, ranked globally as the 30th most well-known brand overall and 6th in fashion, the company owned luxury brands Blancpain, Omega, Rado, and Longines, plus medium- and low-end brands Tissot, Certina, Mido, Pierre Balmain, Calvin Klein, Hamilton, Flik Flak, Lanco, and Endura. (See Exhibit 5 for sales breakdown by brand.) All brands were managed (and housed) separately, and were responsible for their own design, marketing, communications, and distribution. Hayek explained that each watch brand was promoted with its own message: "We are not just offering people a style. We are offering them a message that tells people who you are and why you do what you do. Ultimately we are not just offering watches. We are offering our personal culture."[5] For example, according to Hayek, Omega watches were for "people who are somebody because they make themselves somebody, not because their grandfather left them a trust fund or because they made money from insider trading."[6] In the case of Swatch, the message was high quality, low cost, joy of life, and challenging society.

Along with the standard Swatch that retailed for $40 (the same price as in 1983), Swatch retailers carried the Swatch Chrono ($70 plastic, $110 metal); the Swatch Beep, the world's first pager in a wrist watch that retailed for $99; the Swatch Access, a $50 watch that included an integrated microchip that enabled wearers to enter concerts, museums, or ski lifts, to order meals in restaurants, or to ride public transportation; the Swatch Skin, the world's thinnest plastic watch, that sold for $70; the Swatch Talk, a cellphone/wristwatch that retailed for $350;[7] and finally the $80 Swatch Beat, which, along with its utilitarian features also included one of three animation scenes designed by world-renowned cartoonists: Switzerland's Gerald Poisson, J. Otto from the United States, and KM 7 from Japan. One animated scene depicted a dog jumping around the dial, playing with a bone until it became tired, concluding its routine by relieving itself against a lamppost. The company also developed Irony Beat and Skin Beat models. The company predicted that by 2001, 10% of watch revenues would come from Swatch Beat.

Culture

"Impatient," "convincing," "confrontational" and "dedicated" were a few of the adjectives colleagues used to describe Hayek. Top management saw him as a challenging and demanding boss. "Hayek has ideas and then people have to implement them," Geiser explained:

> Sometimes he needs to be reminded that "it is an excellent idea but. . . ." He is a teacher of unique and special skill. He always checks things from different angles. He has not changed at all, perhaps gotten better with age. His weak points are that he is very impatient, and is always three steps ahead while the rest of the company tries to follow. He cannot understand that the battleship that is the company cannot move as fast as he can.

Born in 1928 in Beirut of a Lebanese mother and an American father, Hayek went on to study mathematics, physics, and chemistry at the University of Lyon, France. He then worked as an actuary and, soon after, a mathematician trainee. After a brief stint directing his father-in-law's foundry in Switzerland, he worked as a consultant in Zurich in 1957, and in 1963 founded Hayek

---

[3]Background for this section was drawn from Nicholas G. Hayek, HBS case No. 495-005.

[4]"Swatch: Cash is what you make of it," *Dresdner Kleinwort Benson* (February 22, 1999).

[5]William Taylor, "An interview with Swatch titan Nicholas Hayek," *Harvard Business Review* (March/April 1993).

[6]Ibid.

---

[7]The Swatch Talk would not be available in the United States until after the millennium due to incompatible telecom frequencies.

Engineering AG[8] to consult on product and marketing development strategies.

Through his consulting experience, Hayek developed a management philosophy around which he eventually built The Swatch Group. "I learned that you should never think that people cannot change, because there is always a chance to start over," he stated. "You should also never think that things are cut in stone. Keep your mind open."

Hayek attributed his success to his even-handed skills as an entrepreneur and manager:

> An entrepreneur is like a composer: he builds and creates things. He hears and sees things that other people don't hear or see. A manager is like a conductor: he executes and implements music. He can make a vision come true. Very rarely do you find people who can do both successfully. People usually excel in one of the two.
>
> As a consultant, I saw that management and leadership cultures were extremely important. Positive targets and easy-to-understand messages draw people to your company and into your stores. Previously successful companies stopped being successful because they forgot that a company has to have an emotional message. If ambitious goals are sought persistently as well as with heart and emotion, you motivate people.

Being fiscally conservative was also important. "It is said that our management is obsessed with productivity," Hayek stated. "We're not obsessed. But we do keep our eye on what matters. We don't spend a penny that we don't have to spend. My mother hated debts, and I promised myself never to have debts. And this is exactly how I run my company today, with virtually no debt."

Hayek believed for creativity and innovation to thrive, a company had to be lean and hierarchy flat. "Multilayer hierarchies don't guarantee innovation; they stifle it," he stated. "Look at any hierarchical company: every time an idea has to move one step up the corporate ladder of hierarchies, chances are that it won't advance, or only in a scaled-down version. This takes away dynamism, innovation, and speed to change." The Swatch Group, comprised of 211 profit centers, had 450 managers and a 21-member extended Management Board (two of whom were female), for some 18,000 employees worldwide. The majority were Swiss.

Finally, Hayek sought to hire resourceful people. He often asked candidates what they would do if he asked them to get a book in a neighboring town but their car broke down on the way. "If the candidate answers, 'I go home and try tomorrow,'" Hayek explained, "they don't get the job."

If they say, "What should I do?" and run through options, then they may be idea-rich individuals but I still would not hire them. If the person says, "I leave the car in traffic, take the train, get the book and come back," that is the person I need. But there are very few such people.

"Among four people that we hire, two understand our culture, two don't," Gamard added. "One of the two who understood our culture will not like it, and one of the two who did not will stay. Out of the two who are left after three or four years, one will use the experience and will go somewhere else. With success comes turnover." Gamard continued:

> Our company culture is "controlled chaos." We are in an ever-changing environment that forces us to challenge ourselves every six months. At Swatch, the same rhythm of the collection exists as in the fashion industry and every time we are on our knees because we come up with a new collection from scratch each time. The spirit of the people has to be the same: *"Toujours se remettre en question,"* constantly putting oneself in question. That is why Swatch is a very young brand even though it's 16 years old. As a company we always have to remain young.

The Birth of Swatch

The Swatch Group was established in the midst of crisis in the Swiss watch industry. In the late 1970s, Japanese and Hong Kong manufacturers, with access to cheap labor, mass production, and quartz technology (developed—but not used—in Switzerland), penetrated the world watch market with low cost watches that eroded the market share of Swiss-made watches.

By the end of the 1970s, the Swiss had no presence in the low-end/high-volume market segment where watches were priced up to $75 and comprised 90% of world unit sales. The Swiss held just 3% of the mid-market segment of $75 to $400 watches that accounted for 8.5% of world unit sales. Only in the over $400 luxury market did the Swiss retain 97% share, though these accounted for just 1.5% of world unit sales.

---

[8]Hayek Engineering consulted to a wide variety of clients, ranging from U.S. Steel and Dow Chemical to Krupp, Siemens, the Chinese and the Swiss governments, Olivetti, Nestlé, BMW, and Daimler-Benz.

Despite rapid world market growth, Swiss exports fell from 91 million watches and movements in 1974 to 43 million in 1983 (from a market share of 43% to less than 15%). This poor performance was attributed to an inability to adapt to the changing market conditions, a reluctance to focus on building innovative and competitive new products, as well as poor R&D and brand management. Watch companies attempted to restore profitability by raising prices, restructuring, and laying off workers. In the 1970s, almost 1,000 of the 1,600 Swiss watch companies closed and the watch labor market contracted by two-thirds.

Hayek's Diagnosis

In 1981, three major Swiss banks—Swiss Bank Corporation, Union Bank of Switzerland, and Credit Suisse—retained Hayek Engineering to conduct a worldwide market and consumer psychology study of the watch industry. At the time, the banks were ready to write off their losses, selling off all assets of SSIH (Société Suisse de l'Industrie Horlogère), and ASUAG (Allgemeine Schweizerische Uhrenindustrie AG), two of Switzerland's most prestigious watch manufacturers. A Japanese company had offered CHF 400 million to buy Omega from SSIH, which also owned the Tissot and Hamilton brands. A number of Omega managers believed that the brand, which had proliferated to more than 2,000 different models, should be taken down market to compete with Japan's Seiko and Citizen. Hayek believed there was another answer.

His study led to two proposals. One was to merge SSIH with ASUAG, the owner of Rado, Longines, and Ebauches (ETA), a clock workings and movement manufacturer. The merger was approved in 1984 with the stipulation that Hayek would buy the majority of the shares. Hayek convinced a few Swiss investors to join him in the so-called Hayek Pool and together they bought 51% of the new company's shares. The combined companies were renamed SMH (Swiss Corporation of Microelectronics and Watchmaking Industries, Ltd.) in 1986.[9] Before joining forces, the two companies had combined revenues of CHF 1.5 billion and losses of CHF 173 million.[10]

The other proposal was to develop a low-cost, high-quality plastic watch brand. Hayek's study revealed that the same watch model would sell substantially better if it carried the "Made in Switzerland" label; he determined that 75% to 95% of European consumers and 51% to 75% of U.S. consumers were willing to pay a 7% to 10% premium for a Swiss watch over one made in Japan, and a 20% premium over one made in Hong Kong. The majority of Japanese consumers preferred Japanese to Swiss-made watches. Hayek concluded that Switzerland was uniquely positioned to win back the low-margin, high-volume market. He believed a low-cost, high-quality plastic watch was the answer. "There were four reasons for my believing this," he recalled:

> One, if you sell high volumes, you can automate and keep improving on productivity. Second, young people, the future consumers, are most likely to buy low-priced watches. Third, the biggest communication for a brand is the consumer himself and a mass-market brand allows that. And lastly, if you occupy a large part of the lower end, you keep your competitors fighting there instead of moving up. In emotional products like watches, the lower end is very important.[11]

A prototype of such a watch already existed. In the fall of 1979, the executive team of ASUAG had granted ETA engineers permission to develop a low-cost watch from synthetic material. At this time, no manufacturer thought of manufacturing or selling this watch as a proprietary brand. Racing with the Japanese to develop the world's thinnest analog watch in the late 1970s, Swiss engineers reduced a watch's thickness from over 4mm to .98mm. They also discovered that by placing part of the movement into the lower part of the watch case they could design a watch with 51 parts, compared to traditional watches that had 151 parts.

In 1982, after three years of research, ETA presented a waterproof, shock-resistant, accurate timepiece in synthetic material, one that could be mass-produced at low cost in an attractive range of colors. They called it Swatch. The question remained, though, whether there really was demand for a Swiss watch made of plastic. Furthermore, many in the industry questioned whether low-cost production was possible in Western Europe, and whether this new watch would hurt sales of high-end, Swiss-made watches. Hayek was nevertheless given the go-ahead to carry out his recovery plan.

Hayek, charged with launching the watch according to his master plan, suggested to test market the new

---

[9]SMH was renamed The Swatch Group in 1998.
[10]Exchange rate, 1993: US$1.00 = CHF 1.50.

[11]Iqbal Singh, "A time to Swatch," *The Strategist* (April 6, 1999).

watch first in the United States because of the market potential. The JV with a Texan businessman, however, did not generate anticipated demand. In the fall of 1982, SSIH/ASUAG was ready to cancel the project, and sell everything to potential buyers in the United States (Timex, Duracell, and Armitron). They nevertheless decided to test the new watch domestically.

Introducing the Swatch

On March 1, 1983, Swatch was presented to the public in Switzerland at a press conference. Hayek was adamant that from the very beginning consumers be exposed to the Swatch "high quality, low cost, joy of life, and challenging society" message. In launching Swatch, the company relied on an unconventional marketing strategy that echoed this message. When Swatch was launched in Germany the company did not rely on TV advertisements for promotion. Instead, a 500-foot-high (working) Swatch was suspended from the tallest skyscraper in Frankfurt along with the words Swatch, Swiss, DM60 to indicate the price. The same strategy was followed in Tokyo, Japan, while in the United States the brand was promoted through department stores and advertisements.

Swatch turned timekeeping into fashion. When asked by a journalist how many Swatches one person could own and whether the market would soon put a cap on Swatch sales, a Swatch manager replied: "How many ties hang in your closet? Do you stop buying new ones just because you already have 100 of them?" There were Swatch models for various occasions and personalities: the beach and the office, athletes and music freaks, elegant dinner parties and Pop Art exhibitions. There were even scratch and sniff Swatches. In addition, every Swatch was given a name such as "Don't be too late," "Tutti Frutti," and "Hollywood Dream."

Hayek, however, believed Swatch was much more than a fashion icon. "I understood that we were not just selling a consumer product, or even a branded product," he explained. "We were selling an emotional product. You wear a watch on your wrist, right against your skin. It shouldn't be a commodity. I knew that if we could add genuine emotion to the product, and attack the low end with a strong message, we could succeed."[12] Hayek noted:

> Every person who is wearing a Swatch is showing it to at least 5,000 to 7,000 people a year. There is an

absolute certainty that at least 0.2% out of these 6,000 would say "he is a nice guy, he has got good taste and I like his Swatch or his car and want to buy the same one, too."

Furthermore, young people at the beginning of their career do not want to pay a very high price for a watch or a car. But they might buy a Swatch. They get used to buying your products; they get used to the good quality. They will stay with you when they become president of a large company, 20 years after, and then they will want to buy a very expensive watch.[13]

Apart from the regularly employed 20 Swatch designers, who created up to 500 different models each season (of which 140 were chosen), renowned guest artists designed limited-edition watches for special events such as Christmas, Easter, the United States Bicentenary, and Switzerland's 700th anniversary as an independent democracy. Watches designed by Keith Haring, Kiki Picasso, Sam Francis, and Jean Michel Folon, which Swatch sold for a limited time, became highly sought-after collectors' items. The highest price ever paid was CHF 68,200 for a limited-edition Swatch (140 releases), designed by Kiki Picasso in 1985 and sold through Christie's auction house. The watch's retail price was CHF 100.

ETA handled production for all Swatch Group watches, as well as those for most other Swiss watchmakers. The company also produced watches in Brazil and China, and was establishing operations in India. Assembling a Swatch took 67 seconds, and ETA's fully automated assembly line cranked out a new Swatch every 2.5 seconds, producing up to 35,000 watches a day. From midnight to 8:00 a.m., the assembly line moved without human intervention. "The goal," explained Hayek:

> was to be able to compete with low-wage countries through capital-intensive investments, which would allow labor cost to go down to less than 10% of total costs. If labor is less than 10% of costs, there is nothing to stop us from building any product in the most expensive country in the world. Volume sales are as important as dollar revenues.

Managing the Brand

By 1990, worldwide demand exceeded supply, and people started to trade, sell, and speculate with Swatches. A Swatch collectors' club was founded that published a

---

[12]Taylor.

[13]Ibid.

quarterly journal informing members of new releases, special editions, and special events. Every year, the company released a special Swatch as a badge of membership. Membership fees were $80 plus shipping and handling charges. In early 1999, the club had 80,000 to 100,000 paying members. While Swatch relied on limited time only schemes to create consumer frenzy, the company's philosophy was to produce as many watches as the market could absorb. "Everybody should be given the opportunity to buy any Swatch model at the official retail price," Hayek explained.

By the early 1990s, rising demand required expansion of Swatch's distribution channels. The company operated wholesaler organizations (Swatch divisions within Swatch Group subsidiaries around the world) in all countries that were structured in a product-country matrix. Local division managers reported to country managers, who were responsible for the country's total profit and loss, as well as to brand headquarters in Switzerland. Distribution strategies were developed in accordance with the team in charge of the brand at headquarters and with the brand country manager in the country in question.

Initially sold through special stores and department stores, Swatch moved into regular watch stores in the mid- to late-1980s (depending on the country). During the late 1980s and early 1990s, several individual investors and entrepreneurs began opening Swatch stores that sold anything that carried the Swatch brand name. By 1999, there were 250 Swatch retail stores worldwide—20 in the United States. The company planned to have 500 retail stores, 50 flagships, and at least 2,000 kiosks in operation by 2000. While the Swatch website profiled all Swatch models, only the Swatch Beat could be purchased over the Internet; only three Beat watches were allowed per sale.

While the Swatch message seemed to capture global attention early on, by the mid-1990s, sales in the United States were faltering (see Exhibit 6). A number of department stores stopped carrying the Swatch brand. "Swatch came out with more product than the market could bear, and the consumers seemed to back off," offered one U.S. watch retailer. "I guess if you use the word 'fad' for anything, it could be used for Swatch."[14] Gamard took a different position: "It's less known in the United States than it is in Europe that Swatch has 21 product lines. In the

United States, people still think of Swatch as being a youthful plastic, colorful watch. Our marketing is now communicating that we have Chrono, Skin, Access, and Beat watches."

Hayek believed that Swatch's U.S. operations, led primarily by Swiss managers and marketers, did not clearly communicate the Swatch message to the American consumer: "We were stupid to continue letting department stores sell the product as a fashion item alone. We forgot to market Swatch not only as an emotional product, but also a technically advanced product."[15] Timex held 30.6% of the U.S. watch market in 1998, compared to Swatch's 1.6%. Other Swatch Group brands held less than 1%—Hamilton (0.7%), Tissot (0.7%), Omega (0.5%), and Rado (0.2%). According to Gamard, quality was less important to U.S. consumers than it was to Europeans:

> Americans go for the function more than for the quality of a timepiece. The fact that it doesn't hold water is less important. So long as the price is very cheap, Americans will dress up with fashion items even if the quality is not very good. They put price first, then fashion, and then quality.

The Swatch Group spent $40 million to be the official timekeeper for the 1996 Summer Olympics in Atlanta, and was chosen to be the timekeeper for the 2000 Summer Olympics in Sydney.

Beyond Watches

Hayek always believed that The Swatch Group would eventually be about more than just watches. Nevertheless, the company moved with caution. He explained during a speech in 1994:

> The Swatch Group will go into manufacturing of products only where it can add significant value, thanks to our core competencies, which lie in first-rate manufacturing of watches. Thanks to this expertise, we are also strong in microtechnology, micromechanics, and microelectronics. We get many brand licensing requests. But we want to make things that are visible. Mass brings mass. The consumer is the best advertiser. We want to use our brand for emotional consumer products.

[14]Keith Flamer, "Can Swatch bring back the good times?," *Jewelers' Circular Keystone* (December 1998).

[15]Joshua Levine, "Swatch out! (A new marketing strategy of Swatch USA)," *Forbes* (June 15, 1995).

Aside from technological know-how, The Swatch Group seemed to rely on its brand reputation to help it succeed in its nonwatch ventures. "When you talk to anybody about Swatch they automatically have a definition," Gamard explained. "It's going to be something innovative, high-tech, high quality, and very, very different. Whatever we get involved with it has to be very intimate to people."

Telecom

In the late 1980s, The Swatch Group recognized analog telephones as an opportunity. Geiser explained that telecom did not require too much capital and that it was a new way to enhance the Swatch brand. "It was also close to what we understood—the micromechanical product," he explained. Furthermore, Hayek believed the telecom industry needed new brands and a new marketing approach: "How many worldwide brands can you name for telecom products sold directly to the end customer? Alcatel or Siemens understand how to sell to governments and big companies. We understand how to sell to people."[16]

In 1991, shortly after JV talks between The Swatch Group and Finland-based Nokia fell through, the company entered into a JV with German-based Siemens to manufacture analog cordless phones. Siemens provided telecom technology while Swatch contributed its expertise in manufacturing "things that are tiny" as well as a strong brand name. Product design and communication were decided in agreement with the Swatch Group marketing team in Switzerland.

The telecom venture, however, proved to be a challenge. According to Hayek, the company did not understand the distribution channels for telecom products. It also underestimated the regulatory hurdles to getting telecom products licensed and approved in different countries. Furthermore, issues arose between the JV partners. "We had some controversy regarding the multicolor concept to be adopted," recalled Geiser. The company wanted to make phones in unusual colors to make them more than a commodity. In the end, market pressures put an end to the partnership. "A price/commodity war erupted between Philips and Siemens," Gamard explained:

Philips strongly attacked Siemens in its core country with low-price products. Having to defend itself,

Siemens was in no position to exploit the marketing synergies and the marketing multiplication effect of the Swatch brand. We felt we were losing an opportunity there. Swatch does not become involved in commodity or price wars. We parted in good friendship.

Siemens' share of the JV was taken over by The Swatch Group in 1996. "Looking back," Hayek said, "we should have taken the time to find the right people to do it and not rush into it ourselves." In 1999, The Swatch Group marketed a number of its own telecom products, with the same message as Swatch watches. The Twin phone, a dual-handset phone that enabled two people to place or answer calls together, came in blue moon, limelite, and tequila sunset colors, and retailed for US$40. The Swatch Cordless phone came as Toxic Rosella, Frozen Kakadoo, and Loro Azul, was only sold in Europe, and retailed for DM279. The Swatch Digital Cordless phone with answering machine, retailed for DM349, and was only available in Europe. The company also marketed cellular phones and pagers. According to one Swatch executive, of the company's telecom products that were marketed worldwide, the European and U.S. markets had first priority.

Cars

In 1994, The Swatch Group announced the formation of MCC, a JV with German automaker Mercedes-Benz to design and manufacture a two-seat, "ecological" city car that later became known as the Smart car. Using its knowledge of microelectronics, Swatch handled the car's design and marketing strategy, while Mercedes covered mechanics, comfort, safety, and quality. Geiser recalled the context for the original negotiations with Mercedes-Benz:[17]

For [Mercedes] it was fantastic to see what we had achieved in technology and organization. They said, "We have the outside shape of the car, but you have the inside. So let's join forces. We need to get younger customers and cannot do it with the Mercedes brand. We need someone from outside to give input to culture, way of thinking and projects." Who else than Mr. Hayek to join them and bring in such ideas? We had a lot of enthusiasm and a lot of ideas. Everyone was totally excited.

---

[16]Taylor.

[17]The Swatch Group and Volkswagen had already been in negotiations but Volkswagen's new CEO Ferdinand Piech had shelved the deal when he took over in 1991.

When observers questioned the sensibility of the Smart car and the JV with Mercedes-Benz, Hayek's standard response was as follows:

> People like to underestimate other people. Therefore, it comes as no surprise to me that I get criticized for my car. People believe only what they can see, and as long as they don't see the car and its success in the market, they won't believe me and will continue to reprove me.

On December 18, 1997, the JV's board met to discuss the start of production. The project was late and over-budget. "Everyone realized that the product was wonderful but could not be put on the market," Geiser stated. "Technical changes were necessary, they cost a lot but, in the final analysis, it is totally another product." In November 1998, just weeks after launching SIT, The Swatch Group sold its 19% interest in the JV to Mercedes.[18] Nonetheless, Swatch profiled the $10,000 Smart car at the Swatch Exhibition in Malaysia in early 1999. Between October 1998, when the Smart was launched, and the end of March 1999, DaimlerChrysler sold 30,000 Smart cars in Europe; the company estimated that 80,000 units would be sold by the end of 1999. Nicholas Hayek Jr., president of Swatch International, underlined that "the automotive section of our group remains committed to future-oriented mobility solutions."[19] The company was still interested in finding a partner to develop the hybrid electric Swatchmobile.

Geiser felt the management team learned several lessons from the telecom and car JVs:

> First, we must be able to pilot the venture. Second, because we are very lean, we need to be aware every day of what is going on and work around the clock. We cannot survive budget overruns or massive losses the way a larger player can. We do not want to be associated with a venture that asks for money because of losses all the time. Third, we want to have decision-making power in certain areas; we need the ability to change management if we think they do not work or do not surface problems rapidly. Finally, we need to control what is being done and control the two sides of production and distribution, as well as marketing.

Swatch Internet Time

SIT was promoted through a variety of media including PR events, international alliances, traditional print advertisements, and the Internet. "All these activities," explained one executive, "were coordinated and carried out on an international level. The launch and promotion of SIT always went 'hand in hand' with the product. Therefore the communication had a 'double focus': SIT Evangelization and Swatch .beat promotion."

On October 23, 1998 the "Three Nicks" (Hayek Sr., Hayek Jr., and Negroponte) officially launched SIT to the international press. One month later, Swatch began offering free Internet time clock software for PCs on its website (www.swatch.com). One of the site's hyperlinks named the *Dog Award* stated the following:

> If you have an excellent nose for cool innovations, join the *Dog Award* and win a Swatch .beat every 7,000 beats. You only have to put the Internet time on your home page. Every week, a special jury will pick out the coolest site. The winner will receive the *Dog Award* to show on his own home page and a Swatch .beat to show on his wrist. There will be also a "Hall of Fame" with pictures and links to all *Dog Award* participants.

Every participant who entered the contest agreed that SIT could be downloaded onto their Internet site. Winners would be selected by Swatch (company employees were not permitted to participate) and would be informed by email if they won. By the end of April 1999, SIT had been downloaded to 480,000 Internet home pages, 350,000 desktops, and 10,000 personal digital assistants.

The company had also reached agreements to display SIT on the CNN news channel, CNN's website, Sony's computer games, and Apple's iMac PCs (see Exhibit 7). Neither Sony nor Apple was paid by Swatch for using SIT. CNN, however, had a long-time advertising contract with the company.[20] According to one Swatch executive, CNN's endorsement, "created an amazing wave of coverage in the press and all media. The use of an international TV chain, always working across different time zones, provided an ideal medium to quickly spread the word on SIT and support and credibility to the concept."

The company used the traffic it drew to its website to promote SIT to the greater public. Website visitors were asked to post messages that included the word "beat."

---

[18]Originally Daimler-Benz owned 51% and The Swatch Group owned 49% of MCC. A capital infusion in August 1997, financed solely by Daimler-Benz, increased the German conglomerate's share in MCC to 81%.

[19]Lam Seng Fatt, "Staying ahead of time," *New Straits Times* (Malaysia) (February 12, 1999).

[20]"Swatch Group," an analyst report by Auerbach Grayson (March 5, 1999).

Swatch stored those messages in the memory of a Russian Sputnik satellite replica called the Beatnik that was launched from the Mir space station during a space walk on April 16, 1999.[21]

On April 23, 1999 at @ 375 BMT, Swatch presented a live broadcast on its website of a Russian cosmonaut reading the stored messages. The company originally planned to use the ham radio band, intended for sole use by amateur operators, to broadcast messages over one of the hammers' frequencies. A number of people, however, protested the company's plan to use airtime for commercial purposes.

Since Swatch's launch of SIT and its new line of Beat watches, hits to the Swatch homepage had increased from 13 million per month in October 1998 to over 50 million in April 1999. Hayek believed that Internet time was the "perfect measuring stick for the era." "The Internet has made human beings more globally conscious of being on a small planet where we are all really equal," he explained. But public opinion on Swatch's latest venture varied. Comments on the Swatch website included:

- .beat is the right measurement for the next millennium. The world will shrink to a village. Internet and ecommerce will explode. .beat is the right answer in the right moment. It's a revolution.

- Sorry to be against all the favorable comments you've got to the Internet time idea. I guess you have invented it [to] increase your sales. A measure of time independent of borders and places was invented [a] long time ago. It's used everyday in Aviation (civil & military) and naval business around the world. It's called UTC (Universal Time Coordinated). Be serious, please.

- I have just installed the Swatch Internet clock on my PC. Currently its 21:19 here in Melbourne, yet the swatch beat shows @513. This is 1 hour ahead of actual time! Is this due to the Swiss having daylight savings? If I turn back my PC clock 1 hour then the Swatch Beat shows @471. Maybe Swatch has forgotten to [consider] the daylight savings issue?

- Time that's dancing to a new "BEAT" . . . awesome idea. Internet time is absolutely ingenious. I also like the fashionable designs on these new Swatch watches. I've just bought the Net-time watch and absolutely love it.

- Great idea, your netbeat. But I think it's ridiculous to call it "Biel Median Time." Just call it "Central European Time." Sorry, but I will never use the expression "bmt" . . . sounds too silly.

- Marketing knows no pompous, arrogant, self-important, conceited barrier, does it? I would advocate that it is best buried quickly, quietly.

Others questioned the logic. As one journalist wrote:

The idea is that you can arrange to talk to someone at the other side of the world by saying: "I'll call you at 500 Swatch beats." Whatever time zone you're in, Internet time is the same all over the world. What Swatch neglects to mention is that you'll still have to do the same calculation for Internet time (let's see, it's 237 beats now, so 500 beats will be in, er . . .) as when you allow 11 hours difference when calling Australia. I have a hunch that it won't catch on.[22]

What Is Swatch?

"One of the problems is that Swatch doesn't have an overall brand look," explained one U.K.-based watch designer:

The different stores, the various materials, colors and finishes don't give a coherent message. When Swatch first came along and put a Swiss time movement in a plastic watch, it was unheard of. But other manufacturers have caught up. No one really understands what Swatch is about. Some of its ideas are great, but so what? I don't think people will buy into these niche ideas.[23]

Hayek Jr. volunteered this answer:

Swatch is a hi-tech brand. Product development at Swatch continuously introduces exciting new innovation and state-of-the-art technology. The Smart car and Swatch telecom products (cordless phones and pagers) are good examples of this, but they are by no means the only ones. Our core business has and will

---

[21]The Beatnik provided emergency support to the MIR communications team and was being used by both the Russian Space Program and NASA to measure ballistic movements.

[22]David Phelan, "Object lesson: Swatch beat watch," *The Independent* (January 17, 1999).
[23]Paul Edwards, "Can Swatch keep up with the changing times?" *Marketing Week* (July 15, 1999).

remain "time" in all its forms, meeting the demands of the times.[24]

"People forget that Swatch is time," Gamard echoed:

Time is in our blood. We have found new creative ways to enhance time. The point is to illustrate the relativity of time, not just the scientific way. I hope it catches on. Anyway, it is a fun concept. Whatever we do that lasts more than two weeks will be a success. We do not know where Swatch will go tomorrow.

---

[24]Lam Seng Fatt, "Staying ahead of time," *New Straits Times* (Malaysia) (February 12, 1999).

Exhibit 1 A Swatch Beat Ad

Source: Swatch.

Exhibit 2 Market Shares in the 1998 Worldwide Watch Market (in Volume)

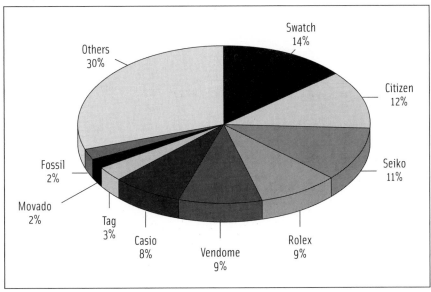

Source: Swatch.

Exhibit 3 Overview of The Swatch Group

Watches	Watches and Components Manufacturing	Electronic Systems	General Services

– *Luxury*
  – Blancpain
  – Omega
  – Rado
  – Longines
	ETA
	Piguet
	Habillage
	SMH Assembly
	Camadur
	Nivarox-Far
		EM Marin
		Micro Crystal
		Oscilloquartz
		Renata
		Lasag
			R&D
			SMH automobile
			Swiss timing
			Finance
			Real Estate

– *Middle Range*
  – Tissot
  – Certina
  – Mido
  – Pierre Balmain
  – Calvin Klein
	Omega Electronics		

– *Basic Range*
  – Swatch
  – Flik Flak
  – Lanco			

Millions of CHF 1998	Watches	Watches and Components Manufacturing	Electronic Systems	General Services	Adjustment	Total
Total Gross Sales	2,261	1,228	312	14	(762)	3,053
Operating profit —in %	292 12.9%	32 2.6%	84 26.9%	(7) –	7 –	408 13.4%
Operational cash flow —in %	307 13.6%	176 14.3%	105 33.7%	1 7.1%	7 –	596 19.5%
Total assets	1,585	1,054	127	1,006	(139)	3,633
Assets net of liabilities	1,158	926	104	689	(64)	2,813

Source: Dresdner Kleinwort Benson estimates.

Exhibit 4 Financial Information

Income Statement (CHF in millions)	1996	1997	1998	1999E	2000E
Sales (CHFmio)	2,770	3,053	3,241	3,445	3,705
EBDITA (CHFmio)	616	596	605	663	745
Margin (%)	22.2	19.5	18.7	19.2	20.1
Operating profit (CHFmio)	267	408	415	463	527
Margin (%)	9.6	13.4	12.8	13.4	14.2
Pretax profit (CHFmio)	346	395	413	463	533
Recurrent net profit (CHFmio)	280	329	341	380	437
Tax rate (%)	17.1	15.9	17.5	18.0	18.0
Net profit (CHFmio)	280	329	341	380	437
Margin (%)	10.1	10.8	10.5	11.0	11.8
Dividend (CHFmio)	60	66	66	72	77
Key Ratios	**1996**	**1997**	**1998**	**1999E**	**2000E**
Net debt/Equity (%)	-28.5	-24.5	-13.7	-18.0	-22.5
Equity/Total assets (%)	66.5	77.2	76.0	77.5	78.6
Interest cover (x)	n/a	n/a	n/a	n/a	n/a
Dividend cover (x)	n/a	5.0	5.3	5.6	6.0
ROE (%)	25.1	12.3	12.3	13.1	13.5
ROCE (%)	29.7	18.7	17.0	17.9	19.2
Sales/Employee (CHFmio)	18.9	17.7	18.7	19.7	21.2
OPPft/Employee (CHFmio)	3.4	2.4	2.5	2.7	3.1
WCR/Sales (%)	31.8	43.1	43.4	43.7	43.7
Cash flow/Capex (x)	3.4	2.8	2.8	2.4	2.6
EV/Sales (x)	2.2	1.7	1.9	1.7	1.5
EV/EBDITA (x)	10.0	8.6	9.8	8.7	7.4
EV/Operating profit (x)	16.5	12.5	14.3	12.4	10.5

Source: Dresdner Kleinwort Benson estimates.

Exhibit 5 The Swatch Group's Watch Sales

End December in CHFmio	1995	1996	1997	1998E	1999E	2000E
SALES						
– *A Brands*	826	909	1,005	1,061	1,125	1,202
– Blancpain	40	45	50	56	63	72
– Omega	336	420	525	593	638	689
– Rado	260	260	250	238	242	247
– Longines	190	184	180	175	182	194
– *B Brands*	290	290	290	356	372	392
– Tissot	90	90	95	114	121	126
– CK Watch	0	0	15	70	88	105
– Certina	70	70	65	63	59	57
– Mido	70	70	60	58	56	55
– Hamilton	40	40	40	38	36	35
– Pierre Balmain	20	20	15	13	13	13
– *C Brands*	880	833	966	1,024	1,070	1,137
– Swatch	770	703	808	861	899	958
– Flik Flak	60	70	88	90	93	98
– Lanco/Private label	50	60	70	74	77	81
Movements and components	453	523	540	486	486	486
Electronic systems	185	220	248	310	388	484
General service	4	4	4	4	4	4
Adjustments	0	0	0	0	0	0
Total Sales	2,638	2,779	3,052	3,241	3,445	3,705
IN % OF SALES						
– *A Brands*	31	33	33	33	33	32
– Blancpain	2	2	2	2	2	2
– Omega	13	15	17	18	19	19
– Rado	10	9	8	7	7	7
– Longines	7	7	6	5	5	5
– *B Brands*	11	10	9	11	11	11
– Tisso	3	3	3	4	4	3
– CK Watch	0	0	0	2	3	3
– Certina	3	3	2	2	2	2
– Mido	3	3	2	2	2	1
– Hamilton	2	1	1	1	1	1
– Pierre Balmain	1	1	0	0	0	0
– *C Brands*	33	30	32	32	31	31
– Swatch	29	25	26	27	26	26
– Flik Flak	2	3	3	3	3	3
– Lanco	2	2	2	2	2	2
Watch and components	17	19	18	15	14	13
Electronic systems	7	8	8	10	11	13
General service	0	0	0	0	0	0
Adjustments	0	0	0	0	0	0
Total Sales	100	100	100	100	100	100

Exhibit 6 U.S. Watch Market and The Swatch Group's Market Share, 1998

	Units	%	Value	%	Swatch Market Share
Mass (under $50)	124,653	78%	2,056	34%	9%
Middle market ($50–$299)	31,840	20%	2,219	37%	4%
Upper/luxury ($300+)	2,705	2%	1,771	29%	21%
Total	159,198	100%	6,046	100%	11%

Source: Dresdner Kleinwort Benson estimates.

Exhibit 7 Apple Website Promoting the PowerBook G3 and SIT

Source: Swatch.

Swatch Internet Time

NET.GENESIS, INC.

In March 1999, Larry Bohn picked up a pencil. This was somewhat unusual for Bohn. As President and CEO of net.Genesis, his fingers were more often on a keyboard. But as he celebrated his first anniversary with the company, he decided to take stock on what the company had accomplished since his arrival and the best course for the future. So he grabbed a legal pad to sketch out some thoughts for himself. After an hour, the sheet of paper looked as shown below:

The triangle at bottom right side of the page summarized the challenges Bohn saw for the company. Goals were at the top to create the category of e-business intelligence and make net.Genesis the leading brand in it. net.Genesis sold software and associated services which enabled companies doing business on the Internet to track visitor/customer behavior. As the Internet ex-

ploded, so had net.Genesis' opportunity. Not only had the number of sites increased beyond most expectations,[1] but the investments made in individual sites increased substantially as the Web became a more integral piece of many firms' business activities. Web site activity became a senior management concern. Integration of Web activity information with other business activity data was also important in supporting firms' decision making about Web strategy and tactics.

Bohn felt Cambridge, Mass.–based net.Genesis was in a great position in 1999. It was an early Internet player, offering consulting on how to build a Web site. It evolved into a software company and now could become what he wrote at the top of the page—"the Nike of e-business intelligence" if it met the two challenges denoted at the top of the triangle: B^2 and C^2. With respect to C^2,

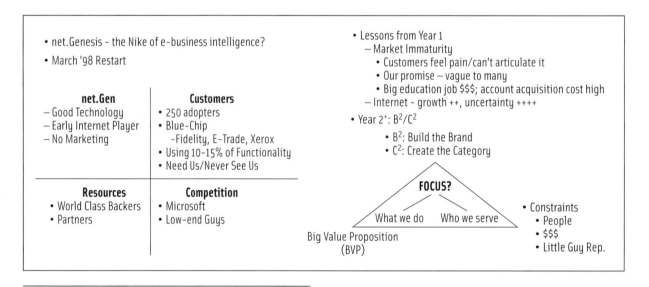

Professor Robert Dolan, Professor Rajiv Lal and Senior Research Associate Perry L. Fagan prepared this case as the basis for class discussion rather than to illustrate either effective or ineffective handling of an administrative situation.

[1]The number of Web sites detected by the Net Craft Web Server Survey increased from 1.6 million in November 1997 to 3.5 million in November 1998.

net.Genesis had coined the term "e-business intelligence" and other suppliers had copied it, using the term in their product positioning. Still, in the nascent market, it was not clear to many customers exactly what "e-business intelligence" meant.

The B^2 and C^2 goals were to be accomplished within the context of net.Genesis having migrated to a Big Value Proposition (BVP) as shown at the bottom left of the triangle. Many suppliers offered a means of rudimentary Web site analysis. Software to capture the number of "hits" on a page was already a commodity, being practically given away in many instances. To get out of the "traffic ghetto" (as Bohn called it), net.Genesis had repositioned itself to high functionality software plus services. The complexity of the resulting net.Genesis product/service offering made the potential revenue from an account greater but also increased account acquisition cost. But the BVP was a key part of company strategy.

Finally, the bottom right of the triangle showed key constraints. As an entrepreneur, Bohn knew he was supposed to see opportunity not constraints; but, still it was foolish to proceed without recognizing that his organization had 65 people, only 10 of whom were actually marketing to customers. The company's relationship with its venture backers was very good (investing $15 million in the firm to date) but, like many affiliated with the Internet, the company was not yet profitable, creating its own source of funds for marketing activities and R&D. Revenues for 1998 were somewhat less than $5 million. Also, while the company had a good reputation for technology with those who knew it, he realized net.Genesis was still a "little guy" with Microsoft, Oracle, and many other traditional software companies on the scene. Bohn summarized all this with a FOCUS? in the middle of the triangle. Should the company focus its business activities and/or its target markets? If so, how? What marketing strategy would achieve B^2 and C^2 to position the firm long-term as a Nike not a Puma, while helping achieve the planned 250%–300% sales growth in the next year? And, as Bohn joked, grow losses at something less than the 250% rate.

net.Genesis

net.Genesis was founded by four MIT students as a corporate Web site construction consulting firm in 1994, the same year Netscape came into being. Early construction projects revealed a related opportunity in monitoring Web site visitor activity. With $5 million in venture capital from investors intent on participating in the Internet revolu-

tion, net.Genesis developed and launched its first software product, net.Analysis, in January 1996. Its two main competitors were Interse and WebTrends of Portland, Oregon.

The typical way to analyze Web site traffic data was Log File Analysis. Each time a visitor requested a page from a Web server, the server inserted a record of it in the Log File. Basic statistics which firms reviewed were, for example:

- "hits"—a request for a page.
- "clickstreams"—the path of mouse clicks and keystrokes a visitor makes in navigating through a Web site.
- "referrers"—the site user last visited before coming to the firm's site.

Managers could review the site's most active pages and times and some descriptors of who (e.g., country of origin, state) was accessing the site.

During 1996–1997, competition in Web site analysis software intensified. WebTrends achieved considerable success with its WebTrends Log Analyzer, selling a low price/minimal functionality package (price: $200–$300) to Webmasters and other technical people building corporate websites. This product sold well because it was easy to get sufficient value out of it to justify the cost and it was targeted at the technical people, rather than managers such as people in the marketing group. In March 1997 Microsoft, as part of its overall Web strategy, bought Interse. Two other competitors, Andromedia and Accrue, entered at the high end of the market.

In 1997, net.Genesis attempted to cover both the high performance/high price and low performance/low price ends of the spectrum. While revenues were about $1 million ("a big deal at that time" according to a company spokesperson), the breadth of the product offering was proving to be a problem, leading to the decision to focus on the high end only.

net.Genesis Restart

In March 1998, net.Genesis' board brought in Bohn as new CEO. Bohn had been president of PC DOCS, Inc., a document management software firm, with revenues of almost $50 million. Bohn's thumbnail sketch of the situation at the time of his arrival was shown [on page 148] under the heading March '98 Restart. He recalled his perception of the situation:

> My thesis was that as companies migrated to the Internet, they would need a whole range of supporting

products and services. The same way you need to know your customers in the real world, you need to know them in the Web world—even though you are seeing only faint shadows of them on your Web site. I went and visited our 12 biggest accounts, companies like Fidelity, E-Trade, Motley Fool and Xerox and it was real clear there was a business here.

In fact, just about everyone was dying for help. People were saying "let us spend money with you." We said, "we don't do services." We had good technology out there in the software but it was clear that many people were accessing only 10–15% of the functionality we were providing them. But we did not have a marketing group or customer service organization—so their feeling was "we need you, but we never see you."

This was the beginning of the idea to migrate to a BVP, i.e., from selling a product to selling a product/service bundle. This would also entail a shift from targeting the technical people at the account to targeting the business managers as the key decision makers. As shown under "Lessons from Year 1" [on page 148], the move to a BVP was impacted by the immaturity of the market. Customers felt a pain, signaling a need for "something" but, due to inexperience in the category, customers could not articulate desired features or their decision-making criteria. As a result, net.Genesis faced a big market education job.

Anne Estabrook joined the company as Vice President of Marketing from Firefly, a leader in personalization software which was acquired by Microsoft. She began to specify how the company could "step up the value proposition." She described the Web business market as having firms at three levels of development:

Stage 1: brochures on the Web

Stage 2: income generation via posting other firm's ads

Stage 3: true e-business

While a Stage 1 firm may have invested $25,000 to get its site up, those at Stage 3 were spending $500,000 for "little" sites and over $1MM for larger sites, and in some cases spending millions more to drive people to those sites.

The company focused on Stage 3 firms providing them with "e-business intelligence." Three key words in the positioning of its net.Analysis product for these customers were "understand," "optimize," and "accelerate."

The net.Genesis Website (netgenesis.com) presented the value proposition in the form of questions to potential adopters:

- How much do you *understand* about your Web site visitor?

- What information would enable you to make decisions that *optimize* your e-business process?

- How much easier would it be to *accelerate* your e-business if you had answers to key questions about site visitors?

A company brochure on its net.Analysis software is reproduced as Exhibit 1.[2]

While Bohn and his team prepared their strategy, they mapped out the Web Support Business into eight categories. As shown in Exhibit 2, they viewed "e-business intelligence" as a distinct category within the overall market. Bohn described the situation portrayed:

This is what makes things a little complicated. We see "e-business intelligence" as a separate area, but they are lots of related things. For example, there are firms that help you with "Targeted Marketing." Especially in an early developing market, the distinctions among the categories are not all that clear to customers. Some firms want to blur the distinction so they can play in multiple categories. You might be partnering with somebody in the morning at an account—you as the E-Business Intelligence piece and them as the "Targeted Marketing" piece—then, in the afternoon, at another account, you are competing with them as they position themselves as providing the e-business intelligence piece as well. Our strategy is to "create the category" of e-business intelligence and be the leaders in it.

To pursue this vision, the company doubled the size of its R&D group to develop the net.Analysis software to its current release 4.0 level of functionality. In addition, to maximize the "intelligence" delivered and its ability to impact management decision making, three other pieces were added to the product/service portfolio:

1. *Design for Analysis (DFA) Methodology.* This methodology led to a Web site design which max-

---

[2]As of April 1999, the net.Genesis Web site (www.netgenesis.com) provided a demonstration of net.Analysis. The demonstration at net.Tour describes a hypothetical use of net.Analysis in an on-line trading company. This gives a more in-depth understanding of the product and its functionality.

imized its analyzability. A DFA engagement began with a needs analysis, during which net.Genesis consulted with this client to identify its business requirements and marketing goals, the current systems architecture and configuration, and organizational standards and processes. Results were presented in a written report, which outlined a site design strategy to meet business goals, and made practical recommendations on system optimization. As Suzie Frank, the East Coast account manager explained:

It's the standardized way we work with companies to make sure that the information they need gets captured at their sites. If the server doesn't record it, it won't be in the logs, and therefore we can't help them analyze it. DFA is our way of making sure sites are "net.Analysis friendly." For example, if someone wants to know how many people reached the point of wanting to place an order, you have to set up the order form on a separate page where you can count the number of specific requests for it.

2. *net.Instruments* was the tool integrating Web generated data with information from other sources. For example, if the client wanted to look at cost per site visitor generated by various portals, it needed to know the number of site visitors coming via the portal, which net.Analysis would trap. But, it also needed to know the cost of the posting on the portal, which had to be imported from an internal budget file.

3. *net.Dashboard*—a graphic user interface (GUI) extension of net.Analysis reports, it formatted reports from the analysis to have the appearance of reports commonly used by managers in decision making. (This feature is part of the tour of net.Analysis given on the net.Genesis Web site.)

net.Genesis also offered a variety of product implementation consulting services. These services helped clients learn the net.Analysis software to maximize the value they derived from it. "Fast Start Product Implementation" was a basic two-day introductory course on net.Analysis. More extensive help was also available. "Project Integration" was a broad category of consulting services that included application deployment, net.Analysis customization, architecture configuration, and enterprise-wide systems integration.

Selling E-Business Solutions

Process

The implication of net.Genesis' migration to a BVP was described by an account manager: "A year and a half ago, I sold software for $10,000. Now I try to sell a product/service bundle for $60,000 initially, followed by a stream of added service revenues. The entry price for net.Analysis is only $12,500 but the follow-on value-added services are the big deal now both in terms of our value to the customer and our revenues. That has made the selling task a bit different, to say the least."

net.Genesis had an "Integrated Sales Model" with four direct selling teams in the United States at the core. A typical team consisted of:

1. *Salesperson*—focused on customers' problems to be solved

2. *Systems Engineer*—a technical person who knows the net.Genesis products in detail

3. *Consultant*—works with the implementation team; stays with account post-installation to provide customized services.

The sales cycle was usually between three and six months, depending on the customer. "Each sale is different," Roger Hodskins, V.P. of sales explained, "some happen as fast as one month; others can take as long as six to nine months. If the company only wants to use the product for its technical features, it's going to be a long selling process. Typically, we get an entry-level solution and offer a proof-of-concept, and then we expand. For example, with E*Trade, we started with a $10,000 sale and have since billed between $400–500K."

For sales outside the U.S., one team was being set up, primarily to work with channel partners rather than in a direct selling mode. In addition, while the focus was on "big" accounts, an internal sales team sold to some small accounts through telemarketing.

In the U.S., net.Genesis had a number of partnership agreements in place. Market Alliance Partners engaged in lead exchange and joint marketing. Net.Genesis followed a "best in breed" approach affiliating only with those it viewed as the best in their respective domains. Among net.Genesis' partners were Allaire Corporation, Engage Technologies, IBM, Netscape, and Sun Microsystems. The November 1998 Press Release describing the agreement between net.Genesis and Allaire typified the approach. It described Allaire as a "leading provider of Internet application development and server software" with the objective of the partnership being to "extend the Allaire development platform by integrating net.Genesis' industry leading net.Analysis e-business intelligence solutions."

Target Market Selection

Hodskins addressed the issue of the accounts net.Genesis pursued:

> Our ideal customer is a company with a clear ability to enunciate an Internet strategy integrated with its overall corporate strategy. It is an organization that is pursuing a business objective and that is trying to use the web to solve it. That is where we get our biggest traction, and hopefully a deep, long-lasting relationship.

Suzy Frank, East Coast account manager, agreed:

> We pursue those companies that have made a serious commitment to their web sites; spent a few hundred thousand dollars. For them, it's worth investing $30,000–50,000 in net.Analysis to manage their web site. In practice this means we target the Fortune 1000 and what we call the "Web 500." These latter companies are smaller, but are more sophisticated in their use of the web.

To date, six vertical markets were key for net.Genesis: financial services, telecommunications, publishing, high technology, pharmaceuticals, and retail. net.Genesis had a top-down sales approach. Frank recalled: "It used to be that we talked to technical people in the IT support department. But with our Big Value Proposition approach, we have found that it is very hard to make the sale happen bottom-up. The commitment to the kind of e-business intelligence we advocate must come from the top down. Until senior management decides to do it, it's really hard to make it happen."

Hodskins elaborated:

> We used to sell to Webmasters and technical people. Generally, we've found that selling to techies lower in the organization was not good for us. Usually they are focused on having the site work without any glitches and they try to give the marketing department as little as is necessary to shut them up. Now we tend to qualify those customers out as quickly as we can. What we really like to see is both the technical and marketing departments involved. That way, they can share the cost of our systems across two departments. That makes the sale easier. But often that's not the case.

Most companies have very limited experience with tools like ours. For that reason we have to do a lot of end-user education, sometimes across multiple departments in the account.

Hodskins estimated that half of the sales leads were buyer-initiated; the other half were generated by net.Genesis sales reps. Trade publications, word-of-mouth, and web referrals were important sales generators. To reduce sales costs, the firm sometimes sent net.Analysis demonstration software to a potential account via the web. But due to market immaturity and lack of customer experience with the level of e-business intelligence net.Genesis was promoting, it was generally hard to communicate the value proposition other than in person.

Key Account Experiences

net.Genesis had developed an extensive client list Key Accounts, shown on its Web site in March 1999, were:

Hardware/software	
Bay Banks	Software.com
Bay Networks	Sun Microsystems
Ericsson Software Technology	3Com
Lotus	Tektronix
Lucent	Wind River
Siemens AG	Xerox
Telecommunications	
Ameritech	Radio Television Italy
AT&T	SNET
Bell Atlantic	US West Dex
Consumer & business products	
Allied Signal	Kinkos
Bose	Nabisco Foods
DuPont	Sherwin Williams
Education	
Princeton University	Southern Illinois University
Finance & e-commerce	
Ameritrade	Fidelity Investments
Australian Stock Exchange	Meadows Credit Union
Barclay's Bank	Morningstar
Bear Stearns	Price WaterhouseCoopers
Dun & Bradstreet	Sallie Mae
E*Trade	Strong Funds

Internet development & internet service providers	
Bonnier Online	Miller Systems
EarthWeb	Nocom
Compuserve UK	Pixelpark GmbH
MCI Systemhouse	Renaissance Virtual Software Ltd.

Pharmaceutical & medicine	
Astra	Pfizer
Bristol-Myers Squibb	University of Kansas
Eli Lilly	Medical Center

Media & publishing	
BBC News	Simon & Schuster
CBS	Paramount Pictures
Gallop & Gallop	Random House
Mainspring	RR Donnelley & Sons
Mecker Media	Sony Music Australia
National Geographic	The Monster Board

Government agencies & municipalities	
Didax	South Dakota World
National Weather Service	Wide Web

A description of its experience with two key accounts follows:

CBS Television and Radio (cbs.com)

The CBS.com Web site, launched in February 1998, was a network of nearly 160 sites, which belonged to CBS and its network television affiliates. The site was a hybrid of national and local information. For example, a site visitor who identified himself as from the Boston area by typing a zip code and selecting "Sports" from a menu was transferred to the web site of the local affiliate, wbz.com, for information on the Bruins, Celtics, and Red Sox. Jaan Vaino, director of business development and administration, CBS New Media, described the situation CBS faced in creating the site:

We set up the sites as a service to the affiliates. We have all of the difficulties of doing business with nearly 160 partners; some of whom are generally inactive; others marginally active; and some are very active. These local sites are generally templated sites; that is, we have a template based on our national site, into which we invite affiliates to build affiliate programmable elements. They provide local news and other information. As such CBS.com is a hybrid site, with both national and local information.

We don't serve flat pages, but dynamically created pages that are updated constantly out of a database. So a visitor to our site calls dozens of elements out of the database which have gone together to build the page and to serve it out. So it's a complex architecture, especially at 30 million page-views a month.

Webmaster John LeBlanc of CBS Boston (WBZ) described one particular use of Web site activity data. "Monitoring your Web site is extremely important to determine what our visitors are interested in. If 80% of our early morning traffic goes directly to the weather page, I need to update that content first. News of an award one of our staff received may only draw a few hits a day, so it can wait to be posted later."

CBS had used a low-end Web Log File Analyzer that tracked page hits, but found the solution wasn't robust enough. "There's no getting around getting your hands dirty with the nuts and bolts of traffic analysis, but hit counts just don't cut it," said Vaino. So Vaino and CBS began looking for a more powerful solution that would do the basic work, but also provide the e-business intelligence they needed on an enterprise-wide level. Vaino described the CBS decision to purchase net.Analysis:

We looked at Accrue's Web site, and at I-Pro, which turned out to cost over $200,000 annually; well out of our ballpark. We talked to a Webmaster within our company about WebTrends, and he raised concerns about its flexibility. Then we called net.Genesis. net.Genesis seemed, at first glance, to provide a richer set of reports. They came in and we were immediately impressed with them because they quickly understood our architecture. We saw that there was no off-the-shelf product that fit our architecture and our needs very well. After debating it for a week and comparing the costs, on the order of $35,000 or so, plus hardware and hosting, we decided to go with them.

net.Genesis committed to having the implementation finished within a couple of months. They assigned their Chief Technology Officer to our project, and we got a lot of his time up front. He wrote scripts that imported the log files from our several servers, sewed them together, imported them into our databases, split them apart into 160 affiliate buckets, so that each affiliate could get reports from their own information, and access their own information only.

net.Analysis enabled CBS to determine from where visitors entered the site, where they clicked on the site, how many page views were recorded during the visit, how long they stayed, their domain and browser, among other variables. net.Analysis through net.Instruments pulled data from each of CBS' servers—an ad server, a commerce server, a database server, etc.—and cross-correlated the information so that CBS could draw an accurate picture of its online customer. The software then produced reports directly over a CBS intranet, so affiliate Web sites across the country received the information per their own customized needs, at the time they needed, regardless of the time zone or schedule they worked.

The implementation was not without difficulty, however, as Vaino described:

> We quickly found that our hardware was pretty inadequate, and within a short time it was taking 14, 16, 18 hours to import one day's data for reporting. There were also operational problems at our hosting company. The log files weren't there at the right time, or they were deficient, they were truncated, and the script would bomb. And then we'd try to take remedial action. That could take most of the day . . . with that kind of schedule we could never catch up.

> So we attempted to get some more of the Chief Technology Officer's time. But he was understandably busy tending to global issues and net.Genesis' small size wouldn't permit that kind of attention immediately. At some point, we screamed loudly enough and finally Larry Bohn proposed that net.Genesis take direct responsibility for rebuilding the architecture of the reporting mechanism and for delivering reports to affiliates' desktops. We got a much larger server with four processors this time. And net.Genesis assigned a-not-quite-dedicated, but largely dedicated engineer to our case who also was very good. Now it takes four to six hours to run reports on the affiliate side. We have reports the next morning.

The net.Genesis perspective on the account was provided by Suzy Frank: "We really cut our teeth on CBS. It was a test of our capabilities. We invested far more time and effort than we billed for. It was too important a client to lose."

CBS Television and Radio is now listed on net.Genesis' Web site in the "Success Stories" section. On the site, Vaino offers the testimonial "net.Genesis has been extremely attentive, giving us lots of their CTO's time."

Bell Atlantic (bellatlantic.com)

Bell Atlantic's Web site challenges reflected those of a large decentralized organization. It sought a Web analy-sis solution that was scalable and provided flexible, drill-down reporting which could be easily shared within the company.

The company believed that analyzing online business visitation information and maximizing the online customer relationship was crucial to its marketing efforts. There were thousands of pages on the Bell Atlantic Web site to monitor, and with an exponentially rising number of visitors, a lot of customers to keep track of. To achieve this goal, Web site management at Bell Atlantic was a cooperative effort between the marketing, information services and creative services groups. Internet Marketing Services, in charge of the site's strategic direction, led a multi-disciplined Web Core team composed of the information services and creative services groups that provide development, infrastructure and publishing support. The Web Core team worked with the dozens of individual Web content area managers from Bell Atlantic enterprises.

Web Core ran over 300 reports on a monthly basis, most of them representing different lines of business and product areas. Designers and marketers needed to know how people traversed their Web sites, where they liked to enter, where they came from, where they spent their time and where they left to. Bell Atlantic also used customized reports to help determine the success of targeted promotions, which drove traffic to the site. "Bell Atlantic is concerned with understanding the Web activity of multiple businesses on the company Web site," said Karen Pettinelli, the company's Internet Marketing Manager. "Sharing this business intelligence across the enterprise helps management determine the effectiveness of its Web marketing strategy, plan future strategies, and perform return-on-investment calculations."

Phil Kemelor, Bell Atlantic's Visitation Analyst, was responsible for the management of the software and for developing report specifications. He also helped various Bell Atlantic business units interpret their net.Analysis reports. Kemelor believed that with net.Analysis a critical link had been forged between Bell Atlantic's Internet Marketing, Information Services and Creative Services, enabling Bell Atlantic to address issues of uniformity and define a Web strategy based on hard customer data, as opposed to guess-work. net.Analysis was used to analyze click-throughs, downloads, length of visits, origin and next destination sites of visitors and visitor travel mapping.

"Bell Atlantic chose us," recalled Frank, East Coast account manager, "because we were willing to work closely with them early on, to design a customized solution for their needs. Bell Atlantic was the first site at which we implemented Design for Analysis. We sent a consultant down there for three days. In Karen Pettinelli we have a great contact. She's trusted us from the beginning, and I believe our success is due to strong communication. Bell Atlantic has been the model I've used for all our large, complex accounts."

Bell Atlantic was also listed as a "Success Story" on net.Genesis' Web site where Phil Kemelor offered the testimonial "We can find exactly the information we need to analyze the effectiveness of our individual pages. . . ." Both Pettinelli and Kemelor were scheduled to speak at net.Genesis' first annual "Worldwide User and Partner Conference" in late April 1999 on the topic "Enabling Results: Meeting the Challenge of Enterprise Wide Traffic Analysis."

Other Customer Comments

Other customer comments on net.Genesis and its products included:

- At the time net.Analysis was significantly cheaper than Accrue. But what attracted us most to net.Analysis was its Windows-friendly interface. The graphing was relatively sophisticated and it gave us the ability to drill down into data and to set up custom filters on data that were definable by me or somebody with a little MBA training. It really seemed like a strong marketing tool.

- I'm very satisfied, but I know that the Web is moving very quickly and the next generation net.Analysis should more tightly integrate with other databases. Right now, the way they talk to one another is in my Excel spread sheet. It would be nifty if you could pull information from disparate sources.

  Right now, net.Analysis also costs us a lot of time to make sure all the files are going in properly. That's another difference between net.Genesis and Accrue. Accrue does it when you're sleeping. With net.Analysis I have to thump my hand on the desk and get the systems guys to make sure that it's no more than a day or two behind in putting these log files in. It works for us but I think that it could be more of a problem if you were doing business on a scale of a search engine or something with real traffic. Our traffic is small compared to some of the bigger sites.

The Competitive Landscape[3]

Exhibit 3 provides a comparison of the key competitors in the Web Analysis software market. In targeting high-end applications, net.Genesis was joined by Accrue and Andromedia. Marketwave targeted the mid-range market and down, while Microsoft's bundled Usage Analyst product and WebTrends targeted the low-end.

Accrue

Founded in 1996, Accrue was similar in size (measured by number of employees) to net.Genesis. It was privately held with cumulative venture backing of $13 million. It proclaimed itself as "the leading supplier of enterprise Internet software."

It focused on five target vertical segments:

1. online publishing (Christian Science Monitor)
2. financial services (T. Rowe Price)
3. retail (Travelocity)
4. entertainment (Dream Works SKG)
5. high technology (Sun Microsystems)

Representative accounts are shown in parentheses. In March 1999, its Web site reported "over 65 industry—leading customers."

Accrue particularly highlighted its "packet sniffer" technology. There were two major ways to collect data about a Web site:

1. Network Collection: Watching the data come and go from a Web server. This allows one to capture, e.g. the amount of time it took to deliver the entire request to the client and the incidence of users hitting the "stop" button.
2. Server Log Files.

Accrue collected both types of data. The network data were collected by "packet sniffers" which tracked the movement of "packets" of information. These data could be reported "live" because there was no need to wait for log files to be fed into the system. This "live" analysis was sometimes called "on-the-wire" analysis.

---

[3]Material in this section was obtained from the individual companies' web sites.

Its Insight 2.5 product supported traffic volume of over 10 million hits per day and was particularly well-suited to complex, multi-site, multi-server configurations. The base product cost ranged from $10,000–$15,000, while its typical development price ran between $60,000–$100,000. It was rumored that the company heavily discounted Insight in order to seed the market.

Andromedia

Andromedia's Web site (www.andromedia.com) claimed its Aria product "unobtrusively tracks, records and reports on customer behavior in real time, and provides . . . the most comprehensive Web site analysis available. ARIA delivers the high-value data you need to meet your online business objectives. Market to the most qualified buyers, refine your campaign strategies, increase ROI, and keep your customers coming back and buying."

Key features of Aria 3.0 were real time reports through packet sniffing, "Live Drill-down Capability" which showed daily, weekly and monthly traffic trends, and "PersonalARIA," which offered custom reporting for individual end-users. Aria was also described as fully automatic: it collected all site activity data and automatically streamed it to the Aria Recorder, a high performance, real-time data processing engine. Each hit was processed as it came in, which meant no nightly batch runs to process large, backlogged log files. Aria was also scalable for large enterprises.

In fall 1998, Andromedia acquired LikeMinds, a personalization software company. Thus, it began to span multiple slices of the pie shown in Exhibit 2. It also developed a partnership with Broadvision, a 1-to-1 marketing firm and promoted itself as a supplier of a "Smart eMarketing" platform.

Aria's base product cost was roughly $10,000, while its typical deployment price ran approximately $100,000. Substantial time and effort were required to set up Aria's database for individual customers. Customers included a wide variety of firms, e.g. 3Com, Audi, Barclays Global Investors, Bell South, The Boston Herald, Broderbund, Cinemax, Colgate Palmolive, Columbia House, Computer Associates, CyberShop, First Chicago Bank, Forrester Research, HBO, Honeywell, Internet Gift Registry, Intuit, iVillage, Levi Strauss, Sandia National Laboratory, Sony Online, Sun Microsystems, Sunburst, Sybase, The Motley Fool, The Weather Channel, and The United States Postal Service.

Marketwave

Marketwave was founded in 1996 and claimed it offered the "ultimate eBusiness intelligence" through its Hit List family of four products. Hit List Professional and Hit List Commerce were basic packages for log file analysis for small to medium web sites. Hit List Enterprise was geared to monitoring high traffic e-commerce sites, and offered extensive web mining, integration, and customization capabilities. Hit List Live offered real time traffic monitoring through packet sniffing. Marketware targeted the Hit List line at Web marketers, Webmasters, and systems administrators.

Marketware's base product cost ranged from $295 for Hit List Professional (which could be ordered at their Web site) to $16,000 for Hit List Live. Figures for typical deployment prices were not available. Marketware's installed base was believed to be largely at the low end of the market. The company claimed more than 40,000 customers for Hit List, including iVillage, Dell Europe, Lehman Brothers, Hewlett Packard, UUNet, Apple, Unisys, Intel, Lotus, Computer Associates, Rockwell, IBM, DEC, Spring, Bell Atlantic, AT&T, Lego, IKEA, House of Blues, Subway, Guinness, Siemens, Motorola, Bell South, Clorox, Mattel, KB Toys, Merck, Liberty Mutual, Compuserve, and AltaVista.

Other Competitors

Microsoft and WebTrends dominated the low end of the site analysis software market. Microsoft bundled its Usage Analyst with its Site Server software, targeted at e-commerce managers. WebTrends offered a family of modular products targeted at Webmasters, Intranet administrators, ISPs, and marketing managers.

While Usage Analyst came conveniently bundled, some felt it was hard to use, had an awkward user interface, and was buggy. WebTrends' modular design made it relatively easy to use—the program produced reports in one easy step. It was also fast, processing 10–28MB of log file per minute. However, WebTrends only stored the results of analysis in its database, not the data itself; which meant that to make changes users had to start from scratch. Neither product offered real time analysis.

Microsoft's Site Server 3.0 cost roughly $5,000, while WebTrends base product price ranged from $299–$1,499. Microsoft counted Barnes and Noble, United Airlines, and The Gap among its customers. WebTrends customers included Kraft, Honeywell, and Polaroid. WebTrends went public in February 1999, trading for most of that month at about $25 per share. On April 1, the stock hit $58.50. With earnings at $.03 per share, that made for a P/E ratio of 1950. For the twelve months ending 12/31/98, WebTrends reported revenues were $8MM. Market capitalization on April 1 was $656 million.

net.Genesis Year 2 + Decisions

As Bohn looked at his notes on the legal pad, he thought about year 2+ and the decisions he saw as critical for net.Genesis. In his mind, while he recognized the difficulty of communicating his value proposition broadly and easily, he felt migration to BVP had been the right move and the path the company should continue on.

As he saw it, there were plenty of potential customers for net.Genesis product/service bundle. In fact, maybe there were too many and more focus on specific target markets was required. Accrue was, for example, staking claim to five key vertical segments. But, was the concept of target markets really relevant for a firm with less than $5MM in sales and zero profitability, serving a nascent market? He recalled some discussion within the company on whether to focus on the Fortune 1000 or the Web 500. Suzy Frank had answered in nanosecond "Fortune 1000 or Web 500? That's easy. Both." Certainly, on a tactical level, the firm had worked especially hard to secure and satisfy potential opinion leader accounts such as Bell Atlantic and CBS. Implicitly, it seemed that serving accounts that would help establish net.Genesis' reputation had been a criterion for resource allocation. As one account rep put it: "If it's a strategic account, we fly there no matter who is involved in the purchase decision." What selection criteria were most appropriate now—reputation enhancement of net.Genesis overall or as a provider to certain vertical markets, potential account profitability, potential value of net.Genesis products to the account or what? Anne Estabrook, the V.P. of Marketing, felt that more opportunity was on its way as the Web moved from being "B2C" (business-to-consumer) dominant to more "B2B." She felt the web offered more value in applications involving e-commerce with businesses as the end user as opposed to consumers as end users. "We need to position ourselves for that emerging market" she felt.

Bohn recalled the marketing maxim that you should be able to identify who it is you *don't* want as a customer. But, he could hardly imagine his upcoming "road show" presentation to raise additional capital containing a color slide entitled: "Customers net.Genesis Does not Want."

Second, Bohn thought about efforts in the Build the Brand/Create the Category vein. The company had been carefully and consistently using the term "e-business intelligence" in its work. He and others in the company were very active in speaking at industry conferences, having exhibits at trade shows and fostering publicity generally. For example, he had recently written an article "Training Your E-Dog" for *The Industry Standard: The Newsmagazine of the Internet Economy* and was also quoted in the *Wall Street Journal*'s article on "The (New) Hidden Persuaders: What Marketers Have Learned About How Consumers Buy on the Web." (*WSJ*, December 7, 1998.) Its own First Annual Worldwide User and Partner Conference was upcoming in a few weeks. Called "Results '99," it was described on the company's Web site and offered attendees the opportunity to "attend net.Genesis tutorials, hear customer success stories, and participate in special interest group roundtable discussions." A number of company people would speak at the event as would some customers and Internet economy luminaries.

Net.Genesis had placed some banner ads on Web sites such as Red Herring and eMarketer. These ads were designed to drive people to the company's Web site where the company and its products were described in detail in an impactful way. These efforts seemed to be efficient but were they enough to have the dual effect of both "Creating the Category" of e-business intelligence and "Building the Brand"? The company had done no print advertising and only a minimal amount of direct mail communication to potential customers. Would now be a good time to add such efforts to its portfolio of communication vehicles? The company had not systematically collected data on consumers' understanding of the term "e-business intelligence" or their perceptions of the net.Genesis "brand" if indeed they saw net.Genesis as a brand. Bohn recalled Anne Estabrook's comments on the idea of market research to establish baseline measures on the category and brand issues. "For now, our market research is being in the field talking to potential customers. Sure, it would be useful. But, there are 50 things I would like to be doing. We have to find the two or three that will give us the most traction, because that's all we can afford to do."

Bohn looked at the top of his page—"The Nike of e-business intelligence" and thought, "well, at least this won't be boring."

Exhibit 1 net.Genesis' net.Analysis Company Brochure

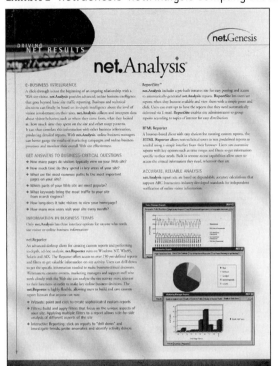

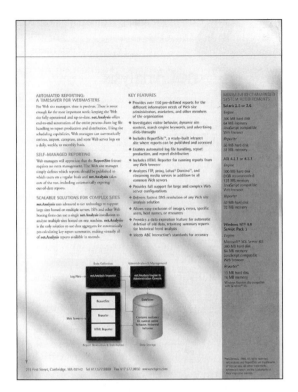

Exhibit 2 Web Analysis Business Segments

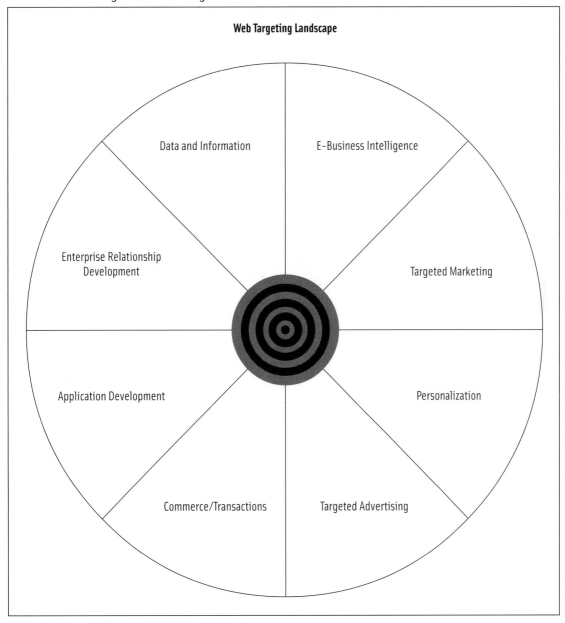

Exhibit 3 Comparision of Leading Web Analysis Software

	net.Genesis	Accrue	Andromedia	Marketwave	Microsoft	WebTrends
Value Proposition	We're the most powerful solution for analyzing and reporting on your enterprise	The choice for "on-the-wire" analysis for large-scale enterprises	We'll enable you to understand your site and to provide real-time personalization across your enterprise	Marketwave's mission is to provide the software and services that make it easy for businesses to maximize their Internet opportunity	The choice for the "all-in-one" package for deploying and analyzing your e-commerce solution	We're the easy-to-use solution for analyzing your Web site—we can get you started and take you to the enterprise level
Target Market	High End	High End	High End	Mid Range	Low End	Low End
Target End Users	Marketing executives, CIOs, managers and Webmasters across the enterprise	Marketing/ad professionals, Webmasters, IS/sys admin Web site content editors	Marketing/IT professionals	Web marketers, Webmasters, systems administrators	E-Commerce managers	Webmasters, intranet administrators, ISPs, marketing managers, executives
Products	Net.Analysis 4.0	Insight 2.0	Aria Reporter V2.5	Hit List Pro V4.0 Hit List Commerce V4.0 Hit List Enterprise V4.0 Hit List Live V4.0	Usage Analyst, bundled with Site Server 3.0	Log Analyzer V4.1a Pro Suite V2.0a Suite for Lotus Domino V1.0 Enterprise Suite V2.0a WT to Firewalls + VPNs V1.0
Base Product Price	$7,500–14,000	$10–15K	~$10K	$295–15,995	$4.5–5.6K (Commerce Edition)	$299–1,499
Typical Deployment Price	$30–50K	$60–100K	$100K+	N/A	N/A	N/A
Method of Data Access	Log File Analyzer, Web Server Plug-ins, Packet Sniffer (to be released—Q2, 1999)	Network Monitoring Packet Sniffer	Web Server Plug-ins/Packet Sniffer	Log File Analyzer/Network Packet Sniffer/Web Server Plug-ins	Log File Analyzer	Log File Reader
Sample Customers	E*Trade, Fidelity, Bell Atlantic, CBS	Qualcomm, Motorola, Knight Ridder	The Boston Herald, First Chicago, Computer Associates	iVillage, Dell Europe, Lehman Brothers	Barnes and Noble, United Airlines, The Gap	Kraft, Honeywell, Polaroid

Source: Company Information

BARCO PROJECTION SYSTEMS (A)

Worldwide Niche Marketing

On Saturday morning, September 23, 1989, Erik Dejonghe, Frans Claerbout, and Bernard Dursin were drafting a crucial presentation that Dejonghe was scheduled to make to the Barco N.V. board of directors on Monday. As senior vice president and chief operating officer (COO) of Barco N.V., with responsibility for Barco's Projection Systems Division (BPS), Dejonghe had to respond to a competitor's recent move that threatened the heart of the division's sales. Claerbout, the general manager of BPS, and Dursin, in charge of managing Barco's distribution subsidiaries and coordinating worldwide marketing of projectors, had both worked closely with Dejonghe to formulate the company's options.

One month earlier, the Sony Corporation surprised BPS and the rest of the industry by unveiling its 1270 "superdata" projector at the Siggraph trade show in Boston. At Siggraph, Sony's product seized first place as the industry's highest performing projector from BPS's BG400. More damaging, the 1270 was rumored to be priced 20% to 40% below the established market price in its performance class. The industry saw the 1270's positioning as an attempt to widen the market through lower prices. For BPS—a small, batch manufacturer—the 1270's combination of low price and high performance threatened both to collapse its traditional market segmentation and drop prices to untenable levels. Dejonghe estimated that BPS stood to lose as much as 75% of its forecast 1990 profits.

Research Associate Krista McQuade prepared this case under the supervision of Professor Rowland T. Moriarty as the basis for class discussion rather than to illustrate either effective or ineffective handling of an administrative situation. The data contained in this case have been adapted and are not useful for research purposes. Historical information has been condensed. This version of the case was revised by Professor Benson P. Shapiro.

The 1270 introduction had been timed to prevent competitive response; the industry's most important trade show, Infocomm, was scheduled to take place in the United States in January 1990. Major customers, industry analysts, and dealers would be there, and BPS's performance would determine its sales for the rest of the year.

Barco's Projection Systems Division

Barco Projection Systems (BPS) was the second largest division of Barco N.V., with 350 employees, and turnover of 1.39 billion Bfr ($35 million)[1] in 1988 (Exhibit 1). Headquartered in Belgium, the division had been formed in the early 1980s to pursue the emerging technology of video projection. The division had grown rapidly throughout the 1980s. In 1988 it represented 23% of Barco N.V.'s turnover

Background: Barco N.V.

Barco N.V. began in 1934 as a producer of radio broadcast receivers. In 1948, it built its first television receiver, and from then on consumer TV formed the bulk of its sales. As a small company, Barco competed successfully by carving out a market on the basis of its R&D strength and product quality. From 1955 to 1975, the company grew rapidly, expanding into broadcast monitors and professional video equipment. At the end of the 1970s, however, during the global recession that followed the 1977 oil supply shock, demand for Barco's consumer products sagged. In response, the company redefined its focus from consumer to industrial markets. In 1989, Hugo Vandamme, Barco's president and CEO, recalled that period:

> We knew that as a small, batch manufacturer we could not have continued to survive in markets for consumer products. Instead, we redrew our strategy to focus on top-of-the-line products in niche mar-

---

[1]For this case, one U.S. dollar is equal to 40 Belgian francs (Bfr). The actual value of the dollar was extremely volatile during the period covered.

kets. In one instance, in 1983, we went as far as to say "no" to a customer asking for 15,000 computer monitors. We were able to turn that order down because we had spread our operations out and become involved in other markets. We had a clear vision of who we wanted to be, how we wanted to operate, and where we wanted to compete. Vision is what counts.

The company's strategy throughout the 1980s comprised three main elements. First, Barco committed itself to becoming a leader in a variety of distinct, but complementary, niche markets. The company entered a new activity only if it had an in-depth knowledge of the market and the technology involved, and if it could be among the top three manufacturers. Second, was a strong commitment to research and development; throughout the 1980s, between 8% and 10% of its annual turnover, and 15% of the company's employees were dedicated to R&D. And third, in addition to growth in its businesses, the company sought to expand its international presence in sales, product development, and production. In 1988, Barco launched a global expansion campaign for acquisitions and joint ventures abroad. Three major acquisitions in the first half of 1989 totalled 4.4 billion Bfr ($110 million). In that same year, Barco reorganized its operations into seven, autonomous divisions, each with its own research, product development, production, marketing, and sales.

In 1989, with 2,400 employees, Barco N.V. was one of the top three worldwide manufacturers in each of its product lines: automated production control systems, graphic arts, computer-aided design, and industrial projection. As a result of the company's early 1989 acquisitions and expanding sales in several key markets, turnover was expected to grow 50% in 1989. A number of international awards testified to Barco's technological lead in several fields. In 1988, for example, the company received the international Emmy Award for its studio monitors. The year after, BPS won the Hi-Vi Silver Award in Japan, given for the product contributing the most to electronic visualization technology.

BPS Organization Within Barco N.V.

As part of the divisionalization of Barco N.V.'s operations in 1989, President Hugo Vandamme and Senior Vice President Erik Dejonghe divided responsibility for products between them; BPS reported to the latter. Dejonghe, who assumed his current position at the time of reorganization, was part of the team that propelled

Barco's industrial projection activities throughout the 1980s. Joining Barco in the early 1980s, he was promoted in 1983 to president of the division that fabricated TVs and large screen projectors. Frans Claerbout was head of the division's R&D department, while Bernard Dursin was in charge of marketing and sales. Dejonghe, Claerbout, and Dursin worked closely together on projectors throughout the decade.

In 1989, Claerbout was promoted to vice president of Barco N.V. and named general manager of BPS. Dursin, also named a Barco N.V. vice president, became general manager of Barco International, a group that managed the marketing of certain Barco product lines worldwide, including projectors. Claerbout's and Dursin's offices remained within shouting distance of each other, however, and they continued to collaborate on projectors. Dursin managed relations with the division's distributors, and, in addition, played a leading role in setting prices for projectors worldwide. Three regional marketing managers, who reported directly to Claerbout, were responsible for sales support to all of the division's distributors. (See Exhibit 2 for BPS's organization chart.)

BPS Products

BPS designed, manufactured, and marketed sophisticated video projectors for industrial applications. Video projectors recreated an image electronically, and Barco's offerings could be connected to TVs, VCRs, and most recently to computers. They were used to project images and information onto large screens, for large-audience viewing (see Exhibit 3 for a diagram of the unit). BPS did not invent video projection, but throughout the 1980s, it played a key role in the development of niche market applications for the technology. By 1989, BPS had developed three lines of projectors: video, data, and graphics.

All based on the same design, BPS's projectors comprised three major components—tubes (3), lenses (3), and electronics. The division's product line was built primarily around a 7″ tube. BPS's traditional strength was in electronics; given the same lens and tube combination, BPS could achieve measurably better performance than its competition in each of the main areas of evaluation. In 1989, the most important considerations for evaluating an industrial projector's performance were brightness (measured in lumens), image quality, and resolution. A projector's three components worked together to provide particular results. In general, the tubes, lenses, and electronics represented 15%, 20%, and 50% of the projector's cost structure, respectively. The housing and mechanics constituted an additional 15%.

What differentiated BPS's product lines was *scan rate,* which measured the speed at which a projector was able to read and process incoming electronic signals. BPS used scan rate to segment its markets; as the sophistication of the application for BPS projectors increased, so did scan rate. BPS's *video* projectors were designed for compatibility with standard video sources, such as broadcast TV and VCR, and scanned at 16 kilohertz (kHz), or 16,000 lines per second.[2] Its *data* projectors scanned at 16 kHz to 45 kHz, and could display input from personal computers as well as video sources. Its *graphics* projectors, BPS's most sophisticated products, scanned from 16 kHz to well above 64 kHz, and accepted input from powerful computer-aided design and manufacturing (CAD/CAM) systems, as well as from video and data sources. A projector needed to match the scan rate of its source to produce a clear picture; Barco's graphics projectors would not be compatible with any computer scanning higher than 64 kHz. BPS was continually upgrading the scan rates of its most sophisticated projector line to match advances in computer technology.

In 1989, BPS was well established in a variety of entertainment, training, and presentation markets. Board rooms, training centers, discotheques, classrooms, airplanes, and betting shops around the world had installed Barco projectors. The monthly sales log of one of BPS's European distributors, for example, listed the sale of four data projectors to the Commission of the European Economic Community (E.E.C.) for video conferencing, five video projectors to a chain of resorts for entertainment rooms, and five data projectors to Groupe Bull, a large French computer company, for training centers. IBM had been one of BPS's best customers throughout the 1980s, having decided in 1984 to equip all its U.S. training centers with Barco projectors.

In addition, BPS was pursuing a number of more specialized markets such as process control and simulation, which used data and graphics projectors. In 1989, BPS installed a series of projectors in the process control room of the U.S. Union Pacific Railroad, which displayed more than 23,000 km of track on a 200-foot-wide screen. Barco projectors were also found at the process control centers for the English Channel Chunnel project, in factories, and in flight simulation rooms for military and aerospace applications.

Evolution of BPS's Product Lines and Markets

Barco N.V.'s involvement in projection systems began in 1981, when it developed a video projector for showing motion pictures in airplanes. The projector, called the BarcoVision 1 (BV1), was priced at 450,000 Bfr ($11,250), and sold strongly in the U.S. and European markets. As the company began to investigate other applications for its technology, Dejonghe, Claerbout, and Dursin presented their views on the future of projection to Barco's board of directors. They believed the company could pursue one of three directions: (1) it could downgrade its technology to suit consumer video applications; (2) it could upgrade its technology for long-distance, high-performance video projection; (3) or, it could enter the untested market for computer applications.

In their presentation, Dejonghe, Claerbout, and Dursin related their discussions of a possible computer-compatible projector with IBM. Developing the computer application, they learned, was feasible, but scan rates would have to be increased to match a computer's faster electronics. Moreover, the projector would have to be designed with enough flexibility so that computer companies with different standard scanning frequencies could use it. But Dejonghe and the others felt that the complexity of the application would work to Barco's advantage by keeping larger firms out of the market. They also thought the application could expand projection markets significantly. The board voted to follow their suggestion and made Dejonghe the new president of the TV and projector division.

In 1983, the division's sales were split 80%/20% between TV and projectors. Dejonghe set out to reverse that ratio. By the end of 1983, BPS had introduced the BarcoData 1 (BD1)—the first computer-compatible projector in the marketplace. Priced at 540,000 Bfr ($13,500) and able to scan to 18 kHz, the BD1 was immediately successful in corporate presentation markets and elsewhere. In 1984, BPS introduced two more projectors—the BV2 (395,000 Bfr, $9,875) and the BD2 (590,000 Bfr, $14,750), which incorporated engineering advances permitting higher scan rates and, thus, broader compatibility. From 1984 on, BPS's video and data lines continued to evolve, keeping pace with breakthroughs in

---

[2]16 kHz = 30 frames of information per second x 533.3 lines per frame.

design, improved components, and, in the case of data projectors, with ever-changing computer technology. In 1986, BPS began work on a graphics application for its technology.

BPS developed its graphics projectors to handle input from CAD/CAM sources, which required upgrading a data projector's scanning frequency to 64 kHz and above. (BPS's most powerful data projector at that time, the BD3, scanned up to 32 kHz.) Dejonghe recalled how the division's market segmentation scheme was formalized:

> I remember when we decided to create a graphics segment with a machine scanning at 64 kHz and above. Limiting the scan rate on our data projectors would frustrate some end-users. Our plan was to respond to that frustration by offering a graphics projector. We could have made it one machine, but not sold it for the highest price.

Dejonghe, Claerbout, and Dursin decided to limit video-only projectors to a scan rate of 16 kHz; data projectors to a scan range of 16 kHz to 45 kHz; and graphics projectors, their newest line, to a scan range of 16 kHz to 64 kHz and above. In June 1987, BPS introduced its first graphics projector, the BarcoGraphics 400 (BG400), for 1 million Bfr ($25,000). The BG400 was the industry's most sophisticated projector, scanning at up to 72 kHz. By 1989, the price of the BG400 had come down to 960,000 Bfr ($24,000). (Exhibit 4 displays a time chart of BPS's product evolution.)

By September 1989, BPS was looking toward its next generation of products—digitally controlled projectors. Currently, all adjustments to BPS projector settings were carried out manually. The new projectors would incorporate digital technology to allow a projector's mecha-nisms to be controlled by a hand-held remote. BPS planned to first introduce the technology in the data segment, and then into the graphics and video segments. BPS engineers had field-tested its first digital data projector, to be called the BD700, and were completing all modifications. The BD700, to be priced at 640,000 Bfr ($16,000), was scheduled for full production and delivery in October 1989.

Frans Claerbout summed up the forces driving the evolution of Barco's projection product line throughout the 1980s as (1) the constant search for the best possible image; (2) flexibility towards inputs; and (3) increasing user-friendliness. Product evolution, he explained, was "more a result of engineering solutions to problems that arose than of a specific development plan." Barco's competition in industrial projection had adopted its practice of segmenting markets by scan rate. Video, data, and graphics had become the standard definition for each market by 1989.

Projector Markets

Through 1994, the worldwide market for projectors was expected to grow 8.5% per year. Growth rates for the product and geographic segments of the market, however, varied widely (see Table A and Table B).

BPS in 1989

In September 1989, the data segment represented the heart of BPS's sales for both units and revenues (see Table C). Because the video segment was moving toward commod-

Table A Product Segment Growth, 1988

	1988 (% units)	Predicted Annual Growth, 1989–1994	Price Range
Video	63%	.8%	200,000–280,000 Bfr. ($5,000–$7,000)
Data	33%	12.3%	320,000–600,000 Bfr. ($8,000–$15,000)
Graphics	4%	40.2%	800,000–960,000 Bfr. ($20,000–$24,000)
Total	100.0%	8.5%	200,000–960,000 Bfr. ($5,000–$24,000)

Table B Geographic Segment Growth

	1988 (% units)	Predicted Annual Growth, 1989–1994
United States	50%	9.0%
Western Europe	36%	11.5%
Asia	12%	18.0%

ity, BPS was concentrating less and less effort there. BPS was the acknowledged technological leader in the high end.

BPS anticipated that the worldwide market for industrial projection would continue to expand for at least five more years before being superseded by new technologies. In 1989, the division's principal products were the BD600, which scanned to 45 kHz, and the BG400, which scanned to 72 kHz. The two projectors sold in 1989 for 480,000 Bfr ($12,000) and 960,000 Bfr ($24,000), respectively (Exhibit 5). BPS's main line of video projectors sold for 280,000 Bfr ($7,000). BPS sold 4,400 units in all three categories in 1988.

Distribution

In 1989, BPS had a two-step distribution system, with 45 distributors and approximately 400 dealers worldwide.[3] The division owned four of its distributors—in Belgium,

France, the United Kingdom, and the United States; the other 41 operated independently but were Barco-exclusive for projectors. Fully-owned distributors represented 61% of BPS's total unit sales, 61% of its revenues, and 59% of its margins. By individual product, they represented 57% of video unit sales; 61% of data units; and 75% of graphics units.

BPS established a distributor price in Belgian francs for each product. The distributors, in turn, set their own price to dealers. On average, prices in the United States were 15% lower than in Europe. The typical pricing relation appears in Table D.

Dealers carrying Barco projectors ranged from "box" dealers to systems dealers. The box dealers, normally found in large cities, sold projectors on the basis of cost alone, providing no service or expertise. Twenty percent of BPS's dealers were "box," and 90% of box sales were video projectors. Systems dealers, at the other extreme,

Table C BPS Sales by Segment, 1988

	% units	% revenues	% margins	BPS Market Share (%)	BPS Projected Annual Unit Growth Rate 1989–1994 (%)
Video	35	23	20	8	1.4
Data	53	54	51	23	12.3
% BD600 of BPS total data	79	67			
Graphics	12	23	29	55	25.0
% BG400 of BPS total graphics	85	80			
Total	100	100	100		

---

[3]BPS could only estimate the number of dealers carrying its products worldwide, since most independent distributors were reluctant to disclose exact figures.

Table D BPS's Pricing Index

	List Price	Actual Price	Comments
BPS	100	100	41% direct cost, 59% gross margin
Distributor	142	142	30% margin, 12% import duties and freight
Dealer	204	173–184	List price calculated with 30% margin Street price incorporates discounts of 10%–15%

had the know-how to integrate and install equipment packages according to the end-user's individual needs. Often these systems involved more than one brand of equipment. Given the complexity of Barco projectors—particularly its data and graphics models—80% of the company's dealers were the systems type.

Projector dealers typically carried three manufacturers' projectors, selecting a line for the low, middle, and high ends of the market—although these could overlap. These dealers also rounded out their sales with other audio-visual equipment such as overhead projectors, lighting, screens, and consumer electronics. A typical dealer in the United States had turnover ranging from 120 million Bfr ($3 million) to 800 million Bfr ($20 million). About 8% to 10% of revenue came from after-sales service.

Although a dealer's ideal margin on projectors was 30%, fierce competition resulted more often in margins of 15% to 20%; occasionally a dealer might go as low as 5% to preserve a customer. Dealer overhead, however, averaged greater than 5%. Margins on service were higher, typically 25% to 35%, and sometimes as high as 70%. Dealers processed information from manufacturers, held vendor fairs and training sessions, and sent out mailings. Barco's dealers were required to attend sales and technical courses given by the distributor, and to hire a certain number of Barco-approved technicians. In return, BPS promised price protection for unsold units when prices dropped, and stable pricing between the time of first customer contact and final order, generally three to six months.

Barco projectors had a dealer reputation for the highest quality final image and excellent reliability once fully installed. Dealers complained, however, that the machines were unnecessarily complex—designed to win awards, not be end-user friendly. Dealers frequently encountered complications in installing equipment. End users, too, often found BPS's control panels and instructions too complex. BPS's engineers contended that many of the problems arose when the instruction manual was disregarded.

The typical end user purchased a new projector every five years. With an eye to ever-increasing computer scan rates, customers tended to purchase more performance in a projector than they needed.

Competition

In 1989, three companies competed with Barco in the data and graphics segments of the market for industrial projection: Sony, Electrohome, and NEC. Several other firms, including Panasonic, Mitsubishi, and General Electric, competed primarily in the video and low-scanning data segments, and were not considered major competitors to BPS. In data projection, Sony held the largest percentage of the marketplace, followed by Barco, Electrohome, and NEC. In graphics, BPS was in first place with 55% of the market. BPS's only major competition in the graphics segment was Electrohome, with 44% (see Table E). Exhibit 6 lists the products of each major competitor.

The Sony Corporation, headquartered in Tokyo, Japan, was a diverse manufacturer of consumer electronics, with 1988 turnover of 460 billion Bfr ($11.5 billion). Industrial projectors, manufactured at the Sony Projectors division, were estimated to represent 1% of the total company's turnover. Sony was the main player in the video segment of the projection marketplace, with 50% of all units sold. In data, Sony held 49% of total units sold; however, its most powerful projector in 1989, the 1031, scanned at only 35 kHz. In 1988, the company's product mix was 66% video and 34% data, on a total of 15,000 units.

Typically, Sony projectors were positioned below Barco's in terms of performance (scan rate, brightness, image quality, and resolution), and were, on average, 15% lower in price. BPS guessed, in addition, that Sony had fewer engineers dedicated to projection than BPS. BPS expected Sony's next product introduction to be a higher-performance data projector, to be unveiled in the fall of 1989, with an upper scanning limit between

Table E Market Share of the Major Competitors, 1988 (as % of total units sold)[a]

	Barco	Sony	E.H.	NEC	Other
Europe					
Data	35	35	8	6	16
Graphics	55	–	43	–	2
North America					
Data	16	62	14	8	–
Graphics	60	–	40	–	–
Far East					
Data	15	30	7	23	25
Graphics	15	–	80	–	5
General Total					
Data	23	49	11	9	8
Graphics	55	–	44	–	1
Total[b]	25	45	14	8	8

[a]To be read horizontally: "Barco held 35% of the market for data projectors in Europe, versus Sony's 35%, Electrohome's 8%," etc.
[b]Omits video

46 kHz and 50 kHz. The division also expected Sony to enter the market with a graphics projector in late 1990.

Sony sold projectors through its worldwide network of captive commercial video distributors. In turn, these distributors worked with more than 1,500 dealers across the globe. It was estimated that 50% of Sony's dealers were box dealers. Its extensive dealer coverage—Sony had 500 dealers in the U.S. market versus BPS's 100—resulted in a low street price for Sony projectors. Although dealers used 30% margins to figure list prices for both Sony and Barco projectors, Sony units were typically discounted 15% for the final sale, while Barco units were discounted 10%. Dealers tended to prefer to sell Barco because they received not only a higher price, but a higher percentage of that price. In general, however, dealers did a higher volume with Sony. In 1989, few dealers could survive without the Sony volume; an estimated 80% to 90% of professional audiovisual dealers worldwide carried Sony video equipment. Sony had a reputation for reliability and low price among dealers.

Sony Components and BPS. Sony entered industrial projection in 1985 with its 1020 video projector. Although the 1020 was slower than Barco's video projectors at that time, it had a sharper focus, indicating a better quality tube. Upon closer examination, BPS engineers found the tube, manufactured in-house at Sony Components (a Sony division), to be far superior in quality to Clinton's, BPS's U.S.-based supplier.

In late 1985, Frans Claerbout traveled to Japan to investigate buying from Sony Components. The division, which remained independent from Sony Projectors up to the chairman's level, agreed to supply Barco, and six months later the first Sony tube was introduced in the Barco Data 3 (BD3). Measured by lumens, Barco was able to achieve better brightness with Sony's tube than Sony itself. Barco terminated its supply relationship with Clinton, and Sony became its sole supplier. Claerbout commented on the relationship:

> Our relationship with Sony is a strange one. We are competitors with Sony projectors yet we source from their in-house supplier. To obtain tubes that suit our needs, we share a certain amount of technical and developmental information with Sony Components, while they keep us abreast of their latest developments. The fact that we rely on them for an important component makes us vulnerable, but at the same time we think that they value our business because we bring their manufacturing costs down. I would say that over the course of our relationship, Sony Components has treated us fairly.

In one instance in 1987, however, Sony introduced a video projector with a tube that Barco had not seen; BPS subsequently purchased the tube, which appeared in its BD600.

By 1989, BPS was actively seeking other tube suppliers. All other tubes available on the market were either inferior to Sony's, more expensive, or both. Many firms manufactured tubes suited to consumer video applications, including Hitachi, Toshiba, Thomson, and Philips, but only the Sony tube had the quality necessary for high-end video projection. Sony, Barco, and Electrohome all sourced tubes from Sony Components. To protect itself against a sudden supply freeze, BPS kept a three-month supply of tubes in-house, and two months of orders in transit from Sony.

BPS spent 90-100 million Bfr ($2.25 million to $2.5 million) annually for approximately 20,000 Sony tubes, which represented around one-fifth of Sony Component's projector tube business. One tube cost between 5,000 Bfr ($125) and 18,000 Bfr ($450), depending on size and quality, and BPS negotiated continuously with Sony to get the prices down. Altogether, perhaps 35% of Sony Component's business was non-captive. BPS's operations manager observed: "Any time Sony wanted to squeeze us out, they could raise the price of their tubes. We would be dead in the water six months before finding another source. But I don't think they will. When we discuss other suppliers, we are taken seriously." Erik Dejonghe agreed:

> Sony has told me that their ultimate goal is to be 50% an industrial supplier, and 50% a consumer supplier—not to beat Barco in projection. I am making a bet that they continue to supply us reliably. They need competition to survive, and we are the only competition with whom they make substantial money.

In February 1989, Sony Components contacted BPS about a new 8″ tube it was developing. BPS received its first sample of the product in June, and its engineers were running tests on the product's performance capabilities. The face of the tube was square, rather than the conventional rectangular shape, and the product was significantly more costly than the 7″ tubes BPS was currently sourcing from Sony. BPS engineers had considered incorporating the new tube in the BD700 data projector, but decided against the idea because to do so would involve redesigning the shape of the projector's chassis and sourcing a new lens to match.

Other Competitors

Electrohome.
Electrohome was a privately held Canadian electronics manufacturer, with 1988 turnover of 5.6 billion Bfr ($139.8 million). Industrial projectors were the most successful group in its Electronics division, which had turnover of 2.5 billion Bfr ($62.5 million) in 1988.

Electrohome operated in the data and graphics segments of the marketplace only, and was BPS's largest competitor in graphics. Electrohome was the third largest player in unit sales behind Sony and Barco, with 1,585 units sold in 1988. Its product mix was 73% data and 27% graphics. Worldwide, the company had an estimated 11% of total data units sold, and 44% of graphics units.

Electrohome was estimated to have distribution strength comparable to BPS's, with nearly 100 dealers in the U.S. market; 80% of Electrohome's dealers were systems specialists. Given the intense competition between BPS and Electrohome in graphics, it was rare to find the two manufacturers' products sold by the same dealer. In general, Electrohome's products were priced just below BPS's. Together with BPS, it was viewed as having higher quality projectors than Sony.

NEC.
A major Japanese electronics manufacturer with 1988 turnover of 876 billion Bfr ($21.9 billion), NEC sold video and data projectors, with a product mix divided 48% and 52% between the two. NEC had pioneered digital convergence technology in the marketplace, introducing a digital data projector in 1987 that became the market standard. The company had not captured as much market share as expected, however, in part due to its inefficient distribution network. Originally, NEC projectors had been sold through the company's well-established network of computer dealers. When sales proved disappointing, NEC granted an OEM agreement to the U.S.-based General Electric Corporation (GE). In 1988, the company sold 1,799 units through its own network, and another 1,200 through GE. The company was estimated to hold 4% (units) of the video market worldwide, and 9% of the data market.

The Sony 1270 Introduction

In August 1989, at the Siggraph trade show in Boston, Sony previewed a projector whose performance shocked Barco and the rest of the industry. Introduced as a "superdata" projector, Sony's new model—the 1270— had the power to scan to 75 kHz, placing it in the market for high-performance graphics applications that BPS could not enter. In addition, the 1270 featured the new 8″ Sony tube, which gave it higher marks than the BG400 in brightness, image quality, and resolution. Price rumors at Siggraph, however, placed the unit in BPS's data range, at 600,000 Bfr to 800,000 Bfr ($15,000 to $20,000). If these rumors proved true, such performance had never been available on the market for such a low price. Erik Dejonghe, Bernard Dursin, and the U.S. regional marketing manager were the Barco representatives at Siggraph that afternoon. The regional manager described the scene:

Sony had chosen the U.S. market for its kick-off preview. They had one pre-production unit set up in a very small booth, and their presentation was quite low-key. But the 1270 was a show-stealer. It was a magnificent product. I spent two days at the booth, in a crowd of people, trying to find out as much as I could.

Dejonghe and the others were not surprised as much by a Sony introduction as by the type of projector the 1270 turned out to be. There had been rumors, spread mostly by dealers, about an impending Sony introduction earlier in 1989. He explained:

Barco had a pretty good idea that Sony was bringing out a new product, but we had expected it to be a direct competitor for the BD600. We thought it would be a 46-50 kHz machine, priced 10% to 15% lower than ours. In response, we planned to introduce a 64 kHz digital upgrade of the BD600 (the BD700) by October. We planned to maintain the 960,000 Bfr ($24,000) price tag on our BG400 until we introduced a digital version (the BG800) in late 1990. Then, we expected Sony to introduce a 75 kHz graphics projector in 1990, priced somewhere near 800,000 Bfr ($20,000). All our projections, however, were based on the assumption that Sony would respect our "vision" of the marketplace. The 1270 did just the opposite. Its positioning threatened to take a great deal of money out of the industry.

Sony announced that it would roll out the 1270 in its major markets in November. The company planned the largest-ever publicity campaign in industrial projection history; for example, 15,000 customers, dealers, and distributors had been invited to the 1270's preview in France, and 5,000 to the preview in Belgium. BPS's regional marketing manager commented:

It is obvious that Sony is not interested in competing with Barco and Electrohome for a few hundred projectors per year in the graphics segment. Instead, their aim is to reconquer our data and graphics markets, and, to do so, they need to break their market image as a mass producer of low-end products.

Although the price reports on the projector could not be confirmed, confusion reigned in the marketplace. Dealers were panicked about the possibility of a low

priced graphics projector from Sony, while Barco distributors were anxious to know how Barco planned to react. In early September, in an effort to calm the market, Barco had spread the word that it did not believe the rumors about the low price of the 1270. Privately, however, BPS management was worried about the potential for significant erosion of its market share. On the plane ride home from the Siggraph show, Dejonghe calculated that BPS stood to lose as much as 75% of its forecast 1990 profits.

Saturday, September 23, 1989

As Saturday morning turned into afternoon, Dejonghe, Claerbout, and Dursin continued to weigh options. Mindful of what BPS risked losing, they had yet to reach agreement.

Pricing Options

Sony's 1270 targeted the U.S. and European markets—markets that represented 83% of BPS graphics revenues and 91% of its data revenues. In the month since Siggraph, Dejonghe, Claerbout, and Dursin had given considerable thought to the potential impact of the 1270 for the rest of 1989 (October, November, and December) and 1990. By their estimations, if the BG400's price remained unchanged and the 1270 was priced at 800,000 Bfr ($20,000), the BG400 could lose 30% of its market share, or 153.8 million Bfr ($3.85 million).[4] At 600,000 Bfr ($15,000), the Sony 1270 threatened to capture 60% of the BG400's market share, or 307.5 million Bfr ($7.69 million). In addition, at this lower price point, Dejonghe and the others were concerned that the 1270 would cause significant share erosion of the BD600, priced at 480,000 ($12,000).

How should the BG400 and the BD600 be priced in response to the Sony 1270? For each machine, there were the questions of how much, if any, of a price change to implement, which markets to lower prices in, and over what time frame. Dursin reported that BPS's German

---

[4]BPS estimated that graphics sales for the last three months of 1989 would reach 106.7 million Bfr ($2.67 million), making the total for the year 426.8 million Bfr ($10.67 million). Assuming 25% growth for the following year, the 1990 graphics revenue estimate was 533.5 million Bfr ($13.34 million). The 15-month revenue estimate was thus 640.7 Bfr ($16.02 million), of which 80%, or 512.56 million Bfr ($12.8 million), could be assumed to be sales of the BG400. A 30% loss in sales of the BG400 would total 153.8 million Bfr ($3.85 million), while a 60% loss would total 307.5 million Bfr ($7.69 million).

distributor was feeling the pressure of the 1270 most severely, and had been calling for a significant price decrease since Siggraph. In early September, the president of the distributorship had declared:

> Germany is the second largest BG400 market in the world. Our dealers inform us that Sony is taking advance orders on its 1270 in Germany. We need to protect this market by dropping the price on the projectors drastically and immediately.

The French distributor, too, was experiencing market pressure to announce a price decrease on the BG400. In the U.S. market, however, the distributor was adamantly opposed to lowering the price. The BPS regional marketing manager described the reasoning behind this opposition:

> It goes without saying that Barco can not win a price war against Sony. Lowering our price might drive Sony to lower theirs further, and we could not follow. We might never be able to recover our price positioning on graphics machines. In addition, a drastic price drop would damage our reputation among recent, and hopefully repeat, BPS customers. Our only option is to develop a competitive projector.

Frans Claerbout was concerned about moving too quickly to lower the BG400 price—in markets where Sony was not coming out strongly, it would be the equivalent of giving away profit. He wanted to wait for confirmation of the Sony price before making any pricing decisions. In direct contrast, Dursin felt strongly that BPS should preempt the pricing of the 1270.

Product Development Options

The three men also had a series of product development options to consider in light of the 1270. Early in 1989, BPS's development plan had been sketched out according to expectations of increased competition in the data segment of the market. The plan called for the introduction of the digital BD700 by October, followed by the development of the digital BG800 for a late 1990 introduction. Twenty-seven person-months were required to complete the BD700 project, while 180 person-months had already gone into the project. In addition, BPS engineers were working concurrently on four other projector-related projects.

BPS could continue its development schedule as planned, introducing the BD700 on time in October for immediate production and delivery. BPS's first digital model, the projector, also incorporated an improved

generator and a scanning frequency of 64 kHz. BD700 sales in 1990 were expected to increase 25% in incremental sales over the forecast revenue of the BD600, representing some 171.7 million Bfr ($4.3 million)[5]. By September, BPS's German distributor and several others already had orders for the BD700, priced at 640,000 Bfr ($16,000), on their books. Claerbout understood how important it was to complete the BD700 project on time for both his engineers' and his customers' morale. At the same time, the BD700 would not beat the 1270's performance at the Infocomm show in January 1990.

Alternatively, BPS could use the advances made in the BD700 development as a springboard to a digital graphics projector, the BG700. Dejonghe estimated that BPS engineers could develop a graphics version in two to three months, working from the BD700's chassis, tubes, and lenses, with the sole addition of higher scanning frequency to match that of the 1270. If this option were pursued, the introduction of the BD700 would need to be postponed until December, causing delay in its delivery to advance-order customers. Also, with BPS's standard 7″ tube, the digital graphics projector would still be inferior to the 1270 in terms of light output, picture quality, and resolution.

BPS's third option was to turn immediately to the development of the BG800. As originally planned, it was to be a digital upgrade of the BG400. Faced with the threat from Sony, however, the BG800 now had to be designed to surpass the 1270's performance. This would require a scanning frequency well above that of the 1270's—at least 90 kHz—as well as the incorporation of the Sony 8″ tube for the best possible performance. Dejonghe had received confirmation from Sony Components that it could begin supplying the tube immediately. The 8″ tube required a special lens, however, and BPS's traditional lens supplier, U.S. Precision Lens of Cincinnati (USPL), had no compatible product. Although in the past Barco and Sony sourced lenses from the same supplier, Sony worked with a Japanese firm, Fujinon, to develop the lens in the 1270. Dejonghe was not sure that Fujinon would supply Barco as well.

Claerbout estimated that developing the BG800 with at least 90 kHz of scanning frequency and new tubes would require at least 80 person-months. In addition, he

---

[5]Data revenues were predicted to reach 912.7 million Bfr ($22.8 million) in 1989, and, assuming 12.3% growth for the next year, 1,025 million Bfr ($25.6 million) in 1990. Sixty-seven percent or 686.8 million Bfr ($17.2 million) in 1990, could be assumed to be sales of the BD600. The BD700 was expected to increase data sales 25% over the BD600, representing 171.7 million Bfr ($4.3 million).

felt strongly that the projector would have to be ready in time for Infocomm if it was to be effective against the 1270. Meeting that deadline would require stopping all other BPS development projects from October 1 on, including the BD700. He voiced a number of concerns about such a drastic move:

> My engineers have been working overtime on the development of the BD700 since mid-summer. Now, we're considering a move that would require the indefinite postponement of the BD700 project, and an even greater commitment on their part. Overtime would be a given, but they'd also need to give up vacation days until Infocomm at least. We have the capability to produce a great machine, one that is superior to the 1270. But the compression of its development could have repercussions on the quality of the final product. In addition, we don't know yet when the 1270 will actually hit the marketplace, how it will be priced, or how the customers will respond to it.

In addition to these considerations, Claerbout gave the BG800 only a 40% chance of making the Infocomm deadline.

Exhibit 1 Key BPS Financial Data, 1988-1989 (in millions of Bfr)

	1988 (Bfr)	$U.S.	1989E (Bfr)	$U.S.
Turnover[a]	1,387	34.7	1,983	49.6
Direct production costs	772	19.3	815	20.4
Total production overhead	40	1.0	45	1.1
Marketing and R&D	130	3.3	170	4.3
Depreciation and charges	138	3.5	329	8.2
Income before taxes	307	7.7	624	15.6

Source: BPS

[a]In addition to sales of video, data, and graphics projectors, BPS turnover recorded sales of projector accessories. In 1988, this category amounted to 168.5 million Bfr ($4.2 million); in 1989 it was 239.3 million Bfr ($6 million)

Exhibit 2 The Management of Barco Projection Systems, 1989

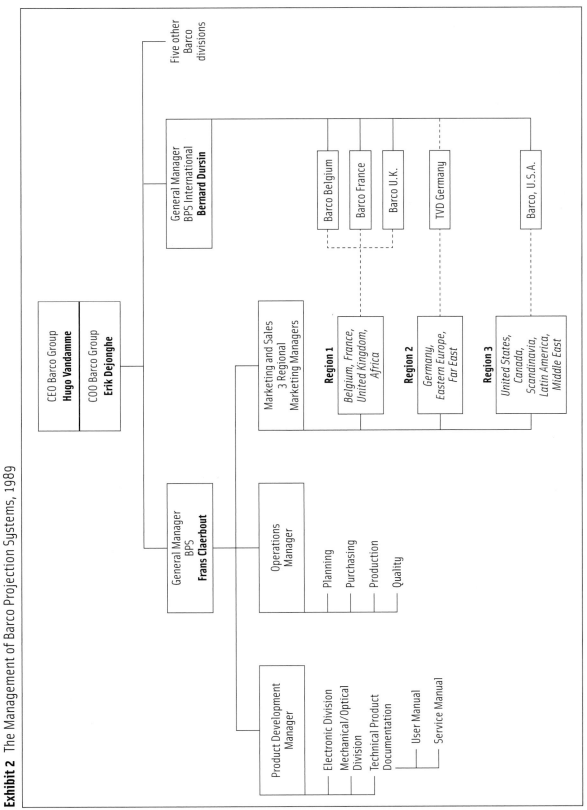

Note: Non-wholly-owned distributors not shown here reported jointly to Barco International and the appropriate regional marketing manager.

Exhibit 3 Projector Diagram

Projector Side View

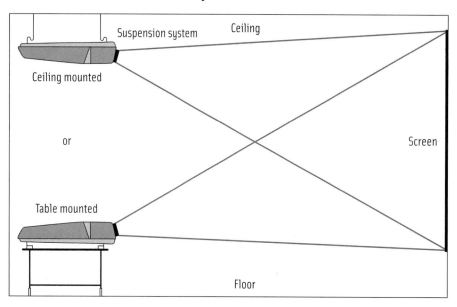

Projector Top View

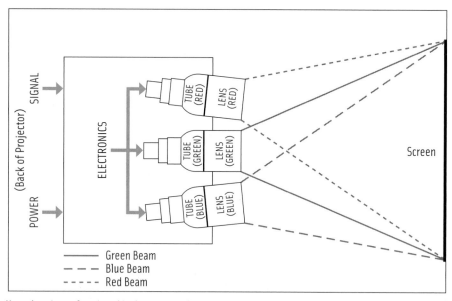

Note: A projector functioned in three stages. First, the information contained in an electronic signal was split into its color (red, green, blue) content. Then, each color's information was redrawn by the electrons of the projector's tubes, one for each color. Finally, the three resulting images were passed through magnifying lenses and projected in sync onto the screen for a full-color image.

Exhibit 4 BPS Product Evolution, 1982–1989

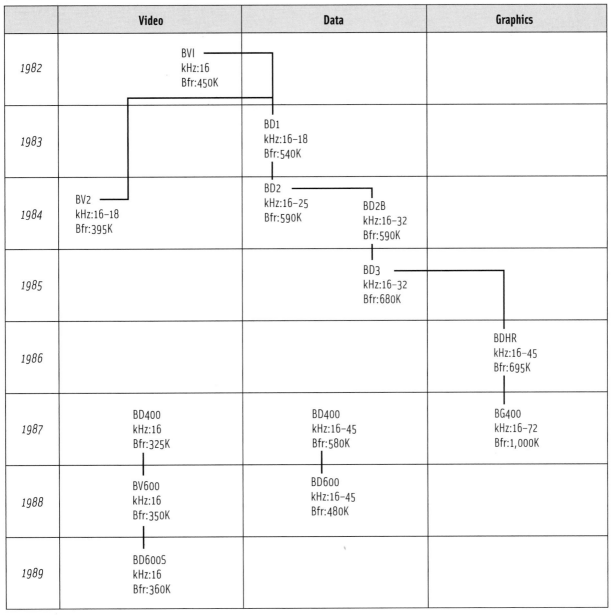

	Video	Data	Graphics
1982	BVI kHz:16 Bfr:450K		
1983		BD1 kHz:16–18 Bfr:540K	
1984	BV2 kHz:16–18 Bfr:395K	BD2 kHz:16–25 Bfr:590K BD2B kHz:16–32 Bfr:590K	
1985		BD3 kHz:16–32 Bfr:680K	
1986			BDHR kHz:16–45 Bfr:695K
1987	BD400 kHz:16 Bfr:325K	BD400 kHz:16–45 Bfr:580K	BG400 kHz:16–72 Bfr:1,000K
1988	BV600 kHz:16 Bfr:350K	BD600 kHz:16–45 Bfr:480K	
1989	BD600S kHz:16 Bfr:360K		

Source: BPS
Note: This diagram contains principal 7# projector introductions only; modifications and special-application projectors are not included.

Exhibit 5 Barco's Product Positioning, August 1989 (pre-Siggraph)

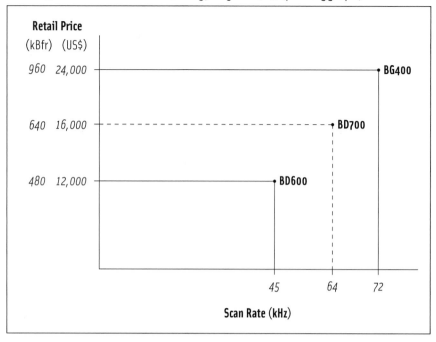

Exhibit 6 Products of the Major Manufacturers, August 1989

Manufacturer	Model	Scan Rate (kHz)	Light Output (lumens)	Resolution (# lines)	Retail Price (Bfr)	(US$)
Barco	BD600	16–45	600	1,600	480,000	12,000
	BG400	16–72	400	2,000	960,000	24,000
Sony	VPH1031	16–35	300	1,100	420,000	10,500
Electrohome	ECP2000	16–36	400	1,280	344,000	8,600
	ECP3000	16–50	650	1,280	580,000	14,500
	ECP4000	16–70	650	1,280	960,000	24,000
NEC	DP1200	16–35	475	800	420,000	10,500
	GP3000	16–54	600	1,100	640,000	16,000

Source: BPS

Note: Light output and resolution were used in addition to scan rate to measure a projector's performance on the world marketplace. Brightness increased with the number of lumens; however, the human eye could discern only large increases. For example, the eye perceived a 1,000 lumen projector as 50% brighter than a 100 lumen projector. With resolution, the larger the number of lines, the better the quality of our final image. Barco believed that its projectors had the highest light output of all the competitors; however, due to differences in the standards used to calculate lumens, light output was difficult to compare between companies.

GOODYEAR: THE AQUATRED LAUNCH

In January 1992, Barry Robbins, Goodyear's vice president of marketing for North American Tires, was contemplating the upcoming launch of the Aquatred, a new tire providing improved driving traction under wet conditions. The Aquatred would be positioned in the U.S. market as a replacement tire for passenger cars. Over recent years, the replacement tire market had matured and new channels had gained share, so Robbins needed to make sure Goodyear had the right product and the right timing to generate support from the company's traditional base of independent dealers. Despite a long and close relationship with those independent dealers, Goodyear was also weighing the risks and benefits of expanding the company's distribution channels. If new outlets were added, Robbins would also have to assess whether the new channel would sell the Aquatred.

The Tire Industry in the United States

From the early 1900s through the early 1970s, the U.S. tire industry was dominated by five companies: Goodyear, Firestone, Uniroyal, BF Goodrich, and General Tire. All five were based in Akron, Ohio, and were run by executives who socialized together at the same country club. The five companies had competed in a U.S. market characterized by not only consistent growth in revenues and profits but also a complete absence of foreign competition. In the 1970s and 1980s, the U.S. tire industry experienced three important changes. The first was the emergence of the radial tire to replace the older "bias" and "bias-belted" tire constructions.[1] Compared with the older constructions, radials offered superior

tread-wear, handling, and gas mileage, but had a stiffer ride. While bias and bias-belted tires lasted under 20,000 miles, by the early 1980s radials lasted over 40,000 miles. Between 1975 and 1991, radials' share of unit sales in the U.S. passenger tire market increased from 32% to over 95%, and virtually all new cars were equipped with radial tires. Converting factories to produce radials required major investments, but many U.S. tire manufacturers had hesitated, hoping that consumers would continue to prefer the softer ride of bias-belted tires.

The second major change was increased foreign competition. Some companies, such as Michelin of France, used expertise in radial production as a lever into the U.S. market. Other tire manufacturers gained access by equipping new cars that were then exported from their home country. Imported passenger tires represented 8% of unit sales in the U.S. passenger tire market (both original equipment and replacement) in 1972, 12% in 1982, and 22% in 1990.

The third major change was in the nature of demand from consumers and car makers. In the 1970s, the price of oil had risen, causing consumers to drive less. Producing one tire typically required seven gallons of oil or derivative products, so the cost of manufacturing tires also increased. Automobile sales shifted towards cars that were smaller, lighter, and had front-wheel drive; these cars placed less wear on tires. Coupled with the radial's longer life, this meant that consumers replaced tires less frequently.

These changes had four major impacts. First, demand for passenger tires grew sluggishly during the 1980s (see Table A). While the average life of a new tire rose from 28,600 miles in 1980 to 37,300 miles in 1990, annual miles traveled per passenger car in the United States grew only slowly, rising from 9,100 miles in 1980 to 10,600 miles in 1990.

Second, new tire prices in the U.S. market declined. The median retail price of a typical passenger tire (size P195/75R14) in the United States dropped more than

Doctoral Candidate Bruce Isaacson prepared this case under the supervision of Professor John Quelch as the basis for class discussion rather than to illustrate either effective or ineffective handling of an administrative situation.

[1]In the radial tire, layers of rubberized material extended from side to side across the tire, perpendicular to the direction of travel. An additional layer or "belt," typically steel, was placed underneath the tread.

Table A Trends in Passenger Tire Sales, 1975–1991 (in millions of tires)

	1991	1986	1981	1976
Replacement	152	144	123	137
OEM	43	54	37	50
Total	195	198	160	187

Source: *Modern Tire Dealer*

25% from 1980 to 1990. By 1991, the average retail price of all passenger tires was $75.00. Third, tire-producing capacity outstripped demand. U.S. tire-making capacity rose 12% between 1987 and 1990; capacity utilization fell from 87% to 76% during the same period. Despite plant closings and layoffs, analysts expected the overcapacity to last through the mid-1990s.

Fourth, the industry's difficult economic conditions, coupled with the tire manufacturers' slow response, resulted in a number of mergers and acquisitions. In 1986, Goodrich and Uniroyal spun off their tire divisions to form the Uniroyal-Goodrich Tire Company, which was sold to Michelin in 1990. In 1987, General Tire was sold to Continental, a German tire manufacturer, while Pirelli, an Italian company, bought the Armstrong Tire Company, and Sumimoto Rubber Industries of Japan acquired Dunlop. In 1988, Firestone was sold to Bridgestone, a Japanese company. By 1991, Goodyear was the only major U.S. tire manufacturer that had not been acquired.

Company Background

Since the early days of the tire industry, The Goodyear Rubber and Tire Company had been known as "The Gorilla" for its dominance of the world tire industry. In 1991, Goodyear operated 41 plants in the United States, 43 plants in 25 other countries, six rubber plantations, and more than 2,000 distribution outlets worldwide. In fiscal year 1991, Goodyear earned net income of less than one percent on total revenues of $10.91 billion; the company had approximately 105,000 employees. Goodyear ranked third in worldwide sales of new tires (see Table B).

Exhibit 1 lists the brand shares of U.S. retail sales for the largest tire manufacturers from 1975 to 1990. During this period, Michelin achieved large share gains in both the replacement and OEM markets. Unlike other U.S. tire manufacturers, Goodyear had made large investments (over $1.5 billion) during the late 1970s to convert its factories to produce radials. The company also had a strong track record in launching innovative products. In 1977, Goodyear introduced the Tiempo, the first all-season radial. All-season radials did not have to be replaced with snow tires during winter months; their unit sales grew from 2% of U.S. replacement passenger tires in 1978 to 71% in 1991. In 1981, Goodyear successfully launched the Eagle, the first radial tire offering high-speed traction for sports cars. On a typical radial, the cost of goods sold was 60% of the manufacturer's selling price, but the Eagle provided Goodyear and its dealers with higher percentage profit margins than standard radials.

Table B World Leaders in New Tire Sales, 1991 (in billions of U.S. dollars)

Michelin/Uniroyal/Goodrich	$10.4
Bridgestone/Firestone	9.8
Goodyear/Kelly-Springfield	8.5
Continental/General	3.9
Pirelli/Armstrong	3.7
Sumimoto/Dunlop	3.5

Source: *Modern Tire Dealer*

Table C Sales and Income for Goodyear and Subsidiaries, 1987–1991

	1987	1988	1989	1990	1991
Net sales (in millions)	$9,905.2	$10,810.4	$10,869.3	$11,272.5	$10,906.8
Net income (loss)	770.9	350.1	206.8	(38.3)	96.6
Net income (loss) per share	12.73[a]	6.11	3.58	(0.66)	1.61

Source: Annual reports
[a]Includes income of $257.0 million, or $4.24 per share, for discontinued operations.

In the early and mid-1980s, Goodyear diversified, making large investments in pipelines for natural gas and oil transmission. In 1986, Sir James Goldsmith attempted to take over Goodyear and was bought out by management after a highly emotional takeover battle which greatly increased Goodyear's debt. Although 13% of the company's work force was furloughed between 1987 and 1991, in 1991 Goodyear was still spending $1 million per day on interest payments, and earnings were sluggish (see Table C).

In June of 1991, Stanley G. Gault, retired chairman of Rubbermaid, became chairman of Goodyear. Gault had been a member of Goodyear's board of directors, and many hoped that he would bring the same marketing flair and new product skills that he had shown at Rubbermaid. Gault stated his goal at Goodyear:

> . . . to create a market-driven organization. That means to serve the customer and the ultimate user. People are wrong to think of tires as a commodity—that a tire is a tire is a tire. . . . Customers want safety—they want that car to stop. They want reliability.[2]

Gault installed his own management team, sold off assets that were not directly related to the tire business, and placed an increased priority on new product development.

The Market for Passenger Tires

The market for passenger tires could be segmented three ways. One segmentation was based on the distinction between performance and broad-line tires. Performance tires were wider than broad-line tires, were more expensive, and provided better traction. Although performance tires could be replaced with broad-line tires, consumers rarely made this substitution because of the resulting decrease in handling and performance. Exhibit 2 shows Goodyear's tire lines for both segments, demonstrating the substantial price differential between them. Exhibit 3 shows the differences among Goodyear's broad-line tires. In the U.S. passenger tire market, performance tires represented 25% of Goodyear's unit sales, 30% of dollar sales, and an even higher percentage of profits.

The market could also be segmented based on replacement and OEM tires. Replacement tires were sold to individual consumers, while OEM tires were sold to car manufacturers. Car makers used volume purchases to negotiate substantial discounts on tires. In 1991, U.S. replacement tire sales were estimated at $8.6 billion (see Table D). In the United States, Goodyear's passenger tire division derived 65% of its revenues from replacement

Table D The U.S. Market for Passenger Tires, 1991

	Dollars (in millions)			Units (in millions)		
	Replacement	OEM	Total	Replacement	OEM	Total
Industry	$8,600	N/A[a]	N/A	152.0	43.0	195.0
Goodyear	1,290	$695	$1,985	22.8	16.3	39.1

Source: *Modern Tire Dealer*
[a]Indicates data were not available.

---

[2]Source: *Fortune*, July 15, 1991.

tires and 35% from OEM tires. Division revenues were $1.98 billion on sales of 39.1 million tires.

A third segmentation scheme was along brand classifications, which included major brands, minor brands, and private label. Major brands, which carried the name of a major tire manufacturer, accounted for 36% of unit sales in the replacement passenger tire market. Major brands had the highest recognition among consumers and included Goodyear, Firestone, Michelin, Bridgestone, Pirelli, and Goodrich. Minor brands represented 24% of unit sales and included tires made by smaller manufacturers as well as tires made by major manufacturers but sold under a different name. Minor brands included Sears, Dunlop, General, Kelly (a Goodyear subsidiary), Uniroyal, Cooper, Yokohama, and Toyo. Although minor, these brands were often well-recognized by consumers and included high-priced niche brands.

Sales of private label tires constituted the remaining 40% of the market. Many small manufacturers specialized in private label tires, while some larger manufacturers used excess capacity to service the private label market. Most private label tires carried names exclusive to a particular retailer, but others were available to any retailer. Private label manufacturers typically had only one distributor per territory, which gave the distributor some flexibility in pricing. In 1991, private label tires constituted 80% of the sales of Goodyear's wholly owned Kelly-Springfield subsidiary; the remaining 20% were sold under the Kelly brand.

The average retail selling price of a private label tire was 18% lower than the price of a comparable branded tire. Although sales of private label tires had grown, their average life remained lower than the life of a branded tire (see Table E).

Many of the attributes important to consumers when purchasing a tire were not apparent upon visual inspection. To certify product quality, some retailers added warranties to their tires. These warranties were paid for by the retailer and would typically guarantee the tire for 60,000 miles, with the value of the guarantee decreasing on a pro-rata basis over the life of the tire. Retailer warranties were particularly common on sales of private label tires.

In past years, Goodyear had produced two lines of private label tires: the All American and the Concorde. The Goodyear brand was not placed on these tires, providing Goodyear's independent dealers with low-priced lines to compete with other types of outlets. In 1991, Robbins replaced the All American and the Concorde with Goodyear-branded tires at comparable prices because market research showed that the nonbranded lines cannibalized sales of branded tires. Although the sales of these two lines were relatively small, some analysts felt that discontinuing the All American and Concorde increased incentives for Goodyear's independent dealers to sell tires made by other manufacturers. Some independent dealers believed that consumers wanted to choose from a range of tires, and favored offering private brands to provide consumers with a reference point, which they argued would increase the sales of Goodyear tires.

Consumers in the Replacement Passenger Tire Market

Consumer Behavior

Most consumers viewed tires as a "grudge purchase"—an expensive necessity to keep a vehicle in driving condition. The average time between purchases of tires was 2.5 years, but over half of all tire-buying consumers made their purchase the same day they became aware of their need for tires. Most tires were bought in pairs: 42% of consumer purchases involved two tires, 40% involved four tires, 16% involved one tire, and only 2% involved three tires. Purchases of sets of four tires accounted for 60% of all units sold.

Table E Average Tire Life (miles)

	All Tires	Branded Tires	Private Label
1991	38,600	39,700	37,000
1986	33,100	34,500	30,900
1981	28,600	29,100	28,500

Source: Company records

Goodyear regularly surveyed car owners, asking about performance attributes considered when purchasing tires. The five most important tire attributes, in order from higher to lesser importance, were tread life, wet traction, handling, snow traction, and dry traction. Goodyear also regularly surveyed car owners concerning the criteria they used to select a tire retailer. The seven most important criteria, again in order from higher to lesser importance, were as follows:

1. Price
2. Offers fast service
3. Can trust personnel
4. Store is attractive
5. Offers mileage warranty
6. Brand selection
7. Maintains convenient hours

A 1989 Goodyear survey had shown that with no other information available, consumers expected Goodyear's broad-line tires to be priced within a six-dollar range from the most expensive to the least expensive. The research also demonstrated that Goodyear's point-of-sale displays did little to alter consumers' expectations of retail prices.

Consumer Segments

Goodyear used research about consumers' shopping behavior to segment tire buyers into four categories (see Exhibit 4):

1. Price-constrained buyers.
Price-constrained buyers bought the best brand they could afford within their budget. They had little loyalty to any specific outlet or brand and tended to shop around for tires before purchasing.

2. Value-oriented buyers.
Value-oriented buyers searched for their preferred brand at the best price. They were predisposed to major brands, shopped around extensively, and had little loyalty to any specific outlet.

3. Quality buyers.
Consumers in this segment were loyal to outlet and brand, tended to be upscale, and shopped for only a brief time before purchasing. The segment could be divided into two subsegments. *Prestige buyers* wanted to own the best tires on the market, while *comfortable conservatives* tended to develop a strong, lasting relationship with a specific outlet. Comfortable conservatives would often buy the brand recommended by their favorite outlet; major brands accounted for 38% of their purchases, versus 65% of purchases made by prestige buyers.

4. Commodity buyers.
Commodity buyers valued price and outlet and could be divided into two sub-segments. Typically, *bargain hunters* were young, with little brand preference, low retailer loyalty, and a tendency to shop around extensively. *Trusting patrons* viewed brand as unimportant and tended to buy lower-priced tires at a preferred retailer. Trusting patrons made their purchase decision relatively quickly, without extensive shopping.

In 1992, 45% of tire buyers were price oriented when shopping for tires; 22% were brand oriented, and 33% believed the outlet was most important. By contrast, in 1985, 48% were price oriented, 26% were brand oriented, and 26% were outlet oriented. Over the past four years, the percent of consumers classified as quality oriented declined by four percent, while commodity buyers increased four percent.

Wholesale and Retail Channels for Replacement Tires

Tire manufacturers sold replacement tires to wholesalers. Wholesalers resold the tires to a variety of retailers and dealers, who then sold the tires to consumers. This section describes both wholesale and retail distribution channels for replacement passenger tires.

Wholesale Distribution Channels

The U.S. replacement passenger tire market depended on the four wholesale channels listed in Table F.

The majority of tires wholesaled to oil companies were resold through franchised or company-owned gas stations or service stations. Wholesaling by oil companies had declined in recent years, reflecting increased competition at the retail level.

Large retailers, including mass merchandisers and warehouse clubs, bought tires directly from the manufacturers to resell in their stores. Independent dealers had increased their share of distribution in recent years. Like other tire makers, Goodyear sold passenger tires to

Table F Distribution Channels (percent of U.S. passenger tire replacement sales in units)

Type of Outlet	1976	1981	1986	1991
Oil companies	9%	5%	3%	2%
Large retailers	24	20	16	19
Manufacturer-owned outlets	11	10	13	12
Independent dealers	56	65	68	67

Source: *Modern Tire Dealer*

three kinds of independent dealers. Dealers who were strictly wholesalers, with no retail operations, accounted for 10% of Goodyear's factory sales to independent dealers and resold their tires to car dealers, service stations, small independent dealers, and other secondary outlets. Another 40% went to dealers who both sold tires at retail and resold tires to other dealers or to secondary outlets. The remaining 50% went to dealers who bought tires to resell in their own retail outlets and did not resell to other outlets. This breakdown was typical of the industry.

Retail Distribution Channels

Six major retail channels competed for market share in the U.S. replacement passenger tire market. (Exhibit 5 shows each channel's market share, relative prices, and reliance on private label tires.) The six channels can be described as follows:

1. *Garages/service stations:* These were typically small, neighborhood outlets offering gasoline, tires, and auto services. Their share of the tire market had declined in recent years in favor of lower-cost, higher-volume outlets. Garages and service stations sold private label tires as well as branded tires to combat price pressure from larger outlets.

2. *Warehouse clubs:* Warehouse clubs operated large stores carrying categories as diverse as food, clothing, electronics, tires, and hardware. Sam's, the largest of the warehouse clubs, had 208 outlets, while PACE had 87 outlets, Price Club had 77 outlets, and Costco had 75 outlets. Warehouse clubs offered a limited brand selection, with the selection changing according to the deals their buyers could strike with vendors. Also, warehouse clubs offered minimal in-store service

other than installation. For example, in some warehouse clubs, consumers had to select tires from sales floor racks, cart the tires to the cash register, and bring the tires around the outside of the store to service bays for installation. Although warehouse clubs were a relatively new retail format, they were growing quickly due to their low prices. Some independent dealers felt that warehouse clubs offered tires at cost to increase store traffic, generating profits from tire installation and sales of other merchandise.

3. *Mass merchandisers:* Mass merchandisers were retail chains that sold tires, performed auto services, and carried other types of merchandise. The largest mass merchandisers had many outlets. Kmart sold tires in 990 outlets, Sears in 850 outlets, Wal-Mart in 425 outlets, and Montgomery Ward in 335 outlets. Mass merchandisers typically maintained a very wide brand selection. For example, Sears sold Michelin, Goodrich, Pirelli, Bridgestone, Yokohama, and its own Roadhandler brand; while Montgomery Ward sold Kelly, Goodrich, Michelin, Bridgestone, General, and its own RoadTamer brand.

4. *Manufacturer-owned outlets:* These outlets, owned and operated by the tire manufacturers, typically sold only one brand of tires and offered a range of auto services.

5. *Small independent tire dealers:* Small independent tire dealers operated one or two outlets, where they sold and installed tires and also offered auto services. Many small independent tire dealers started as single-brand outlets but over time added additional brands. Both small dealers and large independent tire chains derived an increasing portion of their revenues from private label tires.

6. *Large independent tire chains:* Also known as "multibrand discounters," large independent tire chains typically had 30-100 outlets concentrated within a geographic region. Examples of this type of outlet included Tire America, National Tire Warehouse, and Discount Tire. These chains carried major brands of tires as well as private label, and tended to be low-priced, high-volume operations. In recent years, large independent tire chains gained share, often by acquiring smaller independent dealers.

7. *Other:* Half the sales in the "other" category were accounted for by full-service auto supply stores such as Western Auto, Auto Palace, or Pep Boys. These stores sold tires at low prices as traffic builders and were resented by independent dealers as a consistent source of low-priced competition.

In most markets, consumers could choose among these types of channels. As one independent dealer noted, "The tire manufacturer is not only our supplier but also our competitor through manufacturer-owned outlets. On top of that, we compete with the warehouse clubs, mass merchandisers, corner station, and who knows who else."

Goodyear's Distribution Structure

Goodyear did not sell tires in garages/service stations, warehouse clubs, or mass merchandisers; instead, the company relied on three types of outlets. Goodyear's 4,400 *independent dealers* accounted for 50% of sales revenues, while the 1,047 *manufacturer-owned outlets* generated 27% of sales, and the 600 *franchised dealers* accounted for another 8% of sales. (The remaining 15% of sales were primarily to government agencies.) Goodyear was also testing a new retail format, *Just Tires.*

Manufacturer-owned outlets could be opened or closed at the discretion of the manufacturer. During the 1970s, Goodyear opened as many as 200 outlets per year. By 1983, the company owned 1,300 outlets in the United States, but became concerned about the associated demands for capital and management attention. Despite Goodyear's efforts to site company-owned outlets in locations that would minimize competition with its independent dealers, complaints were common. Over time, Goodyear placed increasing emphasis on franchising new outlets and also converted some company-owned outlets into franchised and independent dealerships.

New owners were franchised by Goodyear for three years and then became independent. During the three years, Goodyear provided training in operations, finance, and other aspects of the business. The number of franchised dealers was kept at 600 by adding new outlets as older franchisees became independent.

Goodyear had 4,400 independent dealers, but only about 2,500 were considered active dealers in that they generated a consistent level of sales, maintained the major Goodyear retail displays, and offered the full line of Goodyear tires. A typical independent outlet required the owner to invest $100,000 and generated annual revenues of $1,000,000. Goodyear's independent outlets sold an average of 15.5 tires/day, including both Goodyear and other brands of tires, although most Goodyear dealers derived the majority of their sales from Goodyear tires. The average selling price of all tires sold by Goodyear's independent dealers was $75 per tire. Retail margins for independent dealers averaged 28% on Goodyear tires, 25% for dealers carrying other major brands, and 20% for private label tires. Average wholesale margins were 18% for private label tires and 14% for Goodyear tires.[3]

Although Goodyear claimed not to want its tires sold in low-priced outlets such as warehouse clubs, mass merchandisers, and auto supply stores, those outlets sporadically obtained Goodyear tires. The price-based ads and frequent discounting from those outlets angered Goodyear's independent dealers. One owner of two independent tire outlets said, "The mass merchandisers are eating up the distribution of our product. It could drive me out of the tire business."[4] Industry observers felt that tires were diverted to those outlets by the large independent dealers who acted solely as wholesalers. As one analyst said, "There's a lot of big wholesalers who will sell to anybody."

Goodyear's options to stop the diversion were limited by legal restrictions which prohibited manufacturers from dictating either retail selling prices or to whom their tires could be resold. However, in December 1990, Goodyear sued two automotive chains: Tire America and Western Auto Supply. Both were owned by Sears, and neither was an authorized Goodyear dealer. The suits charged that the Sears units were advertising Goodyear tires without maintaining enough inventory to meet demand. Consumers drawn to the store were allegedly

---

[3]These margins are estimated from several sources and may vary by region or time period.
[4]*Wall Street Journal,* June 24, 1991, p. B1.

switched to other brands in a "bait and switch" tactic. Goodyear also maintained that the chains were not authorized to use the Goodyear trademark in their advertising.

Just Tires was a new retail format under test by Goodyear. Modeled after "quick lube" stores which offered fast oil changes without an appointment, *Just Tires* stores sold and installed tires but did not offer any other products or services. *Just Tires* stores provided consumers with guarantees covering speed and quality of installation.

Although there was some overlap, most outlets that sold Goodyear tires did not sell Kelly-Springfield tires. Kelly-Springfield had no company-owned outlets and sold primarily through mass merchandisers, independent tire dealers, and gas/service stations.

Promotions

It was estimated that three-fourths of all Goodyear tires sold in independent or company-owned outlets were sold on promotion, at an average discount of 25%. This discount was offered to the consumer in a number of ways, such as one free tire with the purchase of three tires, one tire for half price with the purchase of another tire at full price, or 25% off the price of selected tires. For both independent and company-owned dealers, promotions were organized around "core events"—six 3-week periods spread throughout the year during which Goodyear dealers could buy merchandise at a discount. Goodyear supported core events with radio, television, and print advertising announcing special prices on specific tire lines. Every spring, Goodyear offered dealers "spring dating," which provided extended financing on tire orders. Experiments with everyday low pricing in the tire industry had been unsuccessful because price competition among dealers undermined attempts to set consistently low but fair prices. As one dealer explained, "Consumers expect to buy their tires on sale. We have created a price-conscious monster."

Goodyear's Independent Dealers

Goodyear operated separate sales organizations to service company-owned outlets and independent dealers. The company-owned outlets were grouped into 42 districts, each with 20 to 23 stores. There was one district manager per district, plus one store manager per store. Another sales organization called on independent deal-

ers and was organized into 28 districts, each with a district manager and an average of three area sales managers.

Besides providing tires, Goodyear supported its independent dealers with a variety of services, including the following:

Expertise and training on issues such as financing, architecture, wholesaling, operations, and merchandising.

Certified Auto Service, which allowed dealers to attend training classes and become certified in auto services.

The Goodyear Business Management System, a computer system to help dealers with inventory and accounting.

National and regional advertising to support dealer sales.

Research on market trends, such as information on the popularity of each tire, by size, in a given market.

Goodyear serviced independent dealers through the area sales manager, who made sure that dealer orders were placed properly, provided information about market trends, offered advice on operations, and handled complaints. Visits from area sales managers were very important to dealers. As one area sales manager noted, "You never get to the dealer enough. You could spend all day there and then the next day the guy would say, 'Gee, I have this problem today. Too bad you weren't around.'"

Most dealer complaints involved relatively minor billing problems, although complaints about competition from other channels or the location of company-owned outlets were also common. Issues that could not be handled by the area sales manager were referred to the district manager. Complaints common to many dealers were taken up by the dealer council.

Goodyear had established ten regional councils to represent the views of Goodyear's independent dealers. Each regional council elected one dealer to Goodyear's national dealer council for passenger tires. Goodyear's top marketing and sales executives attended council meetings to answer questions, address complaints, or hear suggestions. Council meetings typically covered issues such as market trends in a region or city, new product development, advertising schedules, the availability of particular tires, or Goodyear's overall strategy. Due to antitrust laws, the council could not discuss the selling practices of specific dealers, the brands sold by specific dealers, competition from Goodyear-owned outlets, or retail prices.

The services Goodyear provided its dealers were not free. The cost of these services was built into Goodyear's prices. Discounts were available for dealers who paid upon receipt of merchandise, ordered in full trailer loads, or purchased under occasional promotional programs. Also, various allowances applied. A *wholesale allowance* applied on all approved wholesale sales to any authorized Goodyear dealer within a specific territory. (The wholesale allowance helped Goodyear limit competition among wholesalers.) A *merchandising allowance* of 1.5% was credited on all dealer sales; these credits could be used to obtain point-of-sale materials such as brochures, signs, and displays. Independent dealers also earned *advertising accruals* equal to 4% of tire purchases. The accruals could be used for local advertising, which Goodyear split evenly with the dealers provided no other brands were mentioned in the ad and the ad focused on tires rather than auto services.

Not all of these services were popular with every dealer. For example, some of Goodyear's largest dealers would have preferred to buy their tires at the lowest possible "net" price and develop their own advertising and promotion programs. However, smaller dealers had neither the staff nor the expertise to develop their own programs, and Goodyear was concerned that, without coordinated programs, some dealers would stop advertising and simply reap the benefits of other dealers' efforts.

Independent Dealers in the Tire Industry

In the 1970s, most major tire companies had maintained networks of company-owned dealers. By 1991, tire manufacturers owned fewer of their distribution outlets, as independent dealers typically offered more choice than the single-brand selection offered at most company-owned stores and required less capital and attention from the manufacturer. Some tire companies believed that expanding independent dealer networks would grow sales faster than company-owned outlets. The expectation was that increasing the number of independent dealers would expand brand availability and increase market share. During the 1980s, both Uniroyal and General Tire sold or closed all of their company-owned outlets.

In 1992, Michelin had fewer than 125 company-owned outlets, but Michelin tires were available through 7,000 independent dealers. Most of Michelin's independent dealers were multibrand outlets and sold Michelin as the prestige brand in their product offerings. Michelin tires were also available in 95% of the 600 warehouse clubs in the United States, mass merchandisers such as Montgomery Ward and Sears, and a variety of gas and service stations. Michelin, Uniroyal, and Goodrich had recently combined their sales forces to allow their salespeople to sell all three brands.

Firestone was an exception to the trend toward independent distribution. During the mid-1980s, many of Firestone's independent dealers switched to other manufacturers; some felt that the company had stopped supporting its dealers and its products in order to maximize short-term financial results. In 1991, there were 1,550 company-owned Firestone outlets, which also carried Bridgestone tires. Firestone's presence in independent dealers, mass merchandisers, and warehouse clubs was minimal. Also in 1991, General Tire decided to exit the retail store business entirely and instead rely on independent dealers.

While manufacturer-owned outlets were part of the manufacturer's management hierarchy, independent dealers had more autonomy. For example, tire manufacturers could suggest retail prices, but by law independent dealers were free to set their own prices. Some manufacturers felt that independent dealers' focus on price had contributed to the decline in retail tire prices.

Independent dealers also set their own inventory policies. For many years Goodyear had protected its dealers by not selling Goodyear-branded tires in other outlets; in exchange, Goodyear dealers did not carry other brands. In 1989, 70% of Goodyear's independent dealers carried only Goodyear tires, while 30% stocked other brands. Typically, the other brands were not aggressively merchandised but used only as lower-priced alternatives to Goodyear. By 1991, estimates suggested that 50% of Goodyear's independent dealers sold only Goodyear tires, while the other 50% stocked at least one other brand. Among the latter, some aggressively merchandised other brands but Goodyear tires still generated 90% of the revenues for most independent dealers.

Independent dealers' concern for protecting their interests led the National Tire Dealers and Retreaders Association (NTDRA) to pass a bill of rights in 1992 (see Exhibit 6). NTDRA president Robert Gatzke said, "[T]his bill of rights clearly identifies certain rights which independent tire dealers have a right to expect from their tire suppliers."[5] The bill demanded that

---

[5] Source: *Tire Business*, June 1992.

manufacturers respect the independent dealers' importance, consult independent dealers on key decisions, avoid placing company-owned outlets in competition with independent dealers, supply tires to independent dealers in a timely manner, and grant dealers the same pricing and programs given to high-volume outlets such as wholesale clubs and multibrand discounters.

Auto Services

Auto services were a $50 billion market in 1991. Auto services included jobs such as oil changes, tune-ups, and front-end alignments, as well as repairs to parts such as brakes or transmissions. Revenues from auto services included parts and labor and were differentiated from tire sales. The price of services varied by outlet and job, but $60 was typical. Garages and service stations had a 40% share of auto service revenues, while new car dealers had a 29% share. Specialty outlets focusing on parts such as mufflers or brakes had a 15% share, followed by tire dealers with an 8% share, and mass merchandisers with an 8% share.

Monthly auto service sales for independent tire dealers averaged $38,100 per outlet. Most tire dealers changed oil, performed alignments, replaced shocks, fixed exhaust systems, and did minor engine work. Independent dealers derived, on average, 48% of their revenues from auto services in 1991, up from 26% in 1980. On average, 20% of service revenues came from tire-related work. Margins for independent dealers were 50% on service labor and 20%–25% on parts installed; 70% of service revenues were earned from labor, with the remaining 30% earned from parts. Revenues from tire installation were considered auto services and averaged the following:

Mount and balance new tires:	$8.00 per tire
Place a valve on new tires:	$2.50 per tire
Scrap charge to dispose of old tires:	$2.00 per tire

The average number of tires installed per day at a typical independent dealer increased 13% from 1983 to 1991, but the average service dollars per outlet grew 92% during the same period. Not all dealers were pleased with their reliance on service revenues. As one dealer said, "To me it's an indictment of the industry that we cannot support ourselves on tire sales. We have to have that service to survive." Tires were an expensive purchase for most consumers, and independent dealers worried about the "sticker shock" resulting from service charges increasing the bill to the consumer.

Competition

Goodyear regularly surveyed car owners to monitor their image of the major tire brands (see Exhibit 7). In 1991, Goodyear and Michelin were virtually even, but Michelin's image was stronger among value-oriented and quality buyers, while Goodyear had a stronger image among price-constrained buyers and commodity buyers. The percentage of consumers who did not know what brand of tire they planned to buy next rose to 53% in 1992 from 36% in 1982.

Exhibit 8 presents a brand-switching matrix, showing loyalty by brand among consumers replacing passenger tires. Michelin owners were the most loyal, followed by Goodyear owners, but significant proportions of consumers who owned major brands replaced their tires with private label brands. Goodyear typically spent 9%–11% of sales on advertising and promotion, with 60% being spent on promotion. Among U.S. tire marketers, Goodyear's share of voice in television and magazine advertising was about 60%.

Goodyear's competitors were planning a wide range of campaigns for 1992. Both Bridgestone and Michelin were planning to introduce new tires with 80,000-mile warranties, while Uniroyal was introducing a new tire for light trucks. Under Michelin's ownership, BF Goodrich was focusing on the high performance market, while Goodyear's Kelly-Springfield subsidiary used advertising primarily to announce the low price of its tires.

The Aquatred Tire

In 1989, Goodyear started the NEWEX project, to develop a new and exciting replacement market tire that would have a tangible, perceptible difference over existing models. Howard MacDonald, marketing manager for Passenger Tires, said, "We were looking for something that appearancewise was different—something that a customer would walk into a showroom and tell from a distance that it was different."[6] The Aquatred was developed after comparing 10 different designs on performance and consumer preference. The deep groove down the center of the tire was dubbed the "Aquachannel." According to Goodyear, the Aquatred's tread design channeled water out from under the tire, reducing

---

[6]Source: *Modern Tire Dealer,* March 1992.

hydroplaning and improving traction in wet conditions.[7] Performance tests showed that in wet conditions, cars equipped with Aquatreds traveling at 55 miles per hour stopped in as much as two-car-lengths-less distance than similar cars equipped with conventional all-season radials. When 50% worn, the Aquatred maintained the same wet traction as a new all-season tire.

Goodyear planned to sell the Aquatred with a 60,000-mile warranty and to position the tire at the top of the broad-line segment. The last tire to promise increased wet traction to the broad-line segment was the Uniroyal Rain Tire, introduced in the early 1970s. The Aquatred was patented, but patent protection on tread designs was difficult to enforce. Continental Tire was known to be working on its own antihydroplaning tire, to be called the Aqua Contact, which could be launched in early 1993.

The Aquatred was test-marketed in a large, representative, metropolitan area. A Goodyear survey from the test market compared purchase behavior for Aquatred buyers with purchase behavior for buyers of the Invicta GS, Goodyear's most expensive broad-line tire (see Exhibit 9). Compared with buyers of the Invicta GS, Aquatred buyers were more likely to replace competitors' tires, searched more extensively for information prior to purchase, were more likely to drive imported cars, and more often came to Goodyear outlets specifically for the Aquatred. Exhibit 10 presents data gathered by a "mystery shopper," a Goodyear employee who shopped for tires at independent dealers without identifying his or her affiliation with Goodyear. Despite the uniformity of the company's literature and policies, there was variation in the presentation and pricing of the Aquatred by dealers in the test market.

In another survey, Goodyear asked drivers of cars equipped with either the Aquatred or the Invicta GS to rate their tires' traction on wet roads. Owners of each tire responded as follows:

Response	Aquatred Drivers	Invicta GS Drivers
1 (Poor traction)	5	3
2	5	5
3 (Average)	30	27
4	80	81
5 (Excellent)	180	184
Total responses	300	300

The Launch of the Aquatred

A storyboard for a proposed Aquatred television advertisement is presented in Exhibit 11. Due to the long buying cycles of auto manufacturers, the Aquatred would not be available as original equipment, so all sales of the Aquatred would come through the replacement market. It was estimated that a full-scale launch would cost Goodyear about $21 million.

Managers at Goodyear still had two concerns about the launch. First, did Goodyear have the right product for the dealers and for the consumer? Michelin and Bridgestone both planned to launch new tires with 80,000-mile warranties in 1992 backed by heavy advertising. Would Goodyear's dealers be receptive to a high-priced tire when the industry seemed to be turning toward long-life warranties and low-cost private labels? One dealer had said,

> I would be much more interested in a tire that went 80,000 miles than one that channels the rain out of the way. Even a 35,000-mile tire at a decent price point would be better. The Aquatred is a boutique tire, but where do we make our money as a dealer? Middle-of-the-road products.

Second was the channel itself. Goodyear management debated whether distribution should be expanded, and if so, what specific channels or retailers should be added. Expanding distribution could boost sales and prevent Goodyear OEM tires from being replaced by other brands in the replacement market. However, selling tires in lower-service outlets could erode the value of the Goodyear brand, cannibalize sales of existing outlets, and might cause dealers to take on additional lines of tires. Stanley Gault, Goodyear's new chairman, had expanded distribution at Rubbermaid, and many Goodyear dealers were concerned that he would do the same at Goodyear. As one dealer said, "Today, you can go to any store and get a Rubbermaid product, and the prices on Rubbermaid have dropped accordingly. We feel that Goodyear tires should not be that way."

If the decision was made to launch the Aquatred, there would be a variety of launch-related issues to settle. For example, Robbins was concerned about the timing. Goodyear had made commitments for commercial time

---

[7]Hydroplaning occurs in wet conditions due to a layer of water forming between the tire and road, causing a momentary loss of traction.

during the Winter Olympics in January of 1992 and could use this time to introduce the Aquatred. Launching during the Olympics might spark sales of the Aquatred, but the initial inventory of Aquatreds had been made to fit domestic cars, as opposed to the smaller sizes for imported cars. Molds to produce other sizes would not be available until several months after the Olympics.

Given the wide range of tires sold by Goodyear, dealers would need advice regarding which customers would be likely to switch to Aquatreds. In the test markets, some dealers had tried to sell Aquatreds only to customers who drove newer cars or looked affluent. And if distribution was expanded, Goodyear would need to decide whether the new channel would receive the Aquatred.

In addition, Goodyear had to finalize pricing and promotional policies for the Aquatred. Goodyear hoped to price the Aquatred at a 10% premium over the Invicta GS, but the successful launch of the Tiempo in 1977 was partly attributed to a low retail price. Independent dealers in test markets had consistently asked for price promotions on the Aquatred. Robbins had turned down all such requests, but given the growing problem of tires diverted to unauthorized dealers, it was not clear that the tire could be kept out of channels that were prone to discounting and promotions.

Plans for the national launch were proceeding during an important period in Goodyear's history. Any change in distribution strategy would affect the launch, but the launch and the associated marketing programs would affect Goodyear's dealers. Stanley Gault was upbeat and saw the Aquatred as a product to revitalize Goodyear. Robbins, armed with consumer research, wanted to be sure that the consumer and the channel would agree.

Exhibit 1 Brand Shares of Unit Sales in the U.S. Passenger Tire Market

	1975	1980	1985	1990	1991
– *Replacement Market* *(includes larger* *brands only)*					
– Goodyear	14.0%	14.0%	15.5%	15.0%	15.0%
– Michelin	2.5	7.0	8.0	8.5	8.5
– Firestone	10.5	10.0	9.5	8.0	7.5
– Sears	10.0	10.0	9.0	6.5	5.5
– General	2.0	3.0	2.5	4.0	4.5
– BF Goodrich	4.0	5.0	4.5	4.0	3.5
– Bridgestone	0.0	2.0	2.0	3.0	3.5
– Cooper	1.0	1.5	2.5	3.0	3.5
– Kelly	3.0[a]	4.0	3.0	3.0	3.0
– Uniroyal	3.5	3.5	3.0	3.0	2.5
– Dunlop	2.5	2.5	2.5	2.5	2.0
– Pirelli	0.0	0.0	1.0	2.0	2.0
– Montgomery Ward	4.5	3.5	2.0	2.0	1.5
– Other[b]	42.5	34.0	35.0	35.5	37.5
– *OEM Market*					
– Goodyear	35%	28%	32%	36%	38%
– Michelin	2	5	11	16	16
– Firestone	24	22	22	17	17
– General	11	11	13	12	11
– Uniroyal	20	24	22	17	13
– BF Goodrich[c]	8	0	0	0	0
– Dunlop	0	10	0	1	3
– Bridgestone	0	0	0	1	2

Source: *Modern Tire Dealer*
[a]Estimates
[b]Other included a variety of smaller brands, some of which were exclusively private label.

Exhibit 2 Goodyear Tire Lines With Typical Suggested Per-Tire Retail Prices

Performance Radials		All Season Radials		Light Truck Tires	
Eagle GS-C	$280	Aquatred	$90[a]	Wrangler	$120
Eagle VR/ZR	255	Invicta GS	80	Workhorse RIB	70
Eagle GT+4	140	Invicta GL	65	Workhorse M&S	80
Eagle GA	120	Arriva	60		
Eagle ST	100	Tiempo	50		
Eagle M&S	215	Corsa GT	40		

Source: Company records
[a]Suggested retail price in Aquatred test market.
Note: All tires varied in price according to tire size.

Exhibit 3 Goodyear's Broad-Line Tires

AQUATRED

Improved Wet Road Stopping, Quiet All-Season Performance.

Aquachannel, deep connecting grooves pump water out of the way fast

Exclusive new compound gives road-hugging traction and longer life

Careful tread placement offers a smoother, quieter ride

Sleek sidewall design to complement today's automotive designs

INVICTA GS

Luxury Handling, Smooth, Quiet Ride, All-Season Performance

A smooth, quiet ride enhances the pleasure of driving a vehicle

Unique crisscross tread elements plus deep, effective shoulder grooves produce outstanding year-round traction

A noticeable dexterity in cornering, braking, and handling, the result of carefully selected tread rubber compounds

Impressive long term mileage capability for both front and rear wheel drive vehicles

ARRIVA

Great Traction In Any Weather

All season tread design for year round traction

Aggressive tread design features more gripping edges for improved snow traction

Easy rolling, long wearing tread compound

Dependable wet/dry traction for year-round performance

INVICTA GL

Advanced Rib, All Season Tread Design

All season traction from segmented tread lugs and open shoulder grooves

Long, even wear, quiet ride, excellent fuel economy from advanced tread rib pattern

Precision handling from natural molded shape

TIEMPO

Steel Belted Strength, All Season Traction

Flexible sidewalls deliver a smooth, comfortable ride

Steel belted radial construction delivers strength, tread wear, and fuel efficiency

Tread designed to dissipate heat for tire durability

CORSA GT

Great Handling And Mileage For Small Cars

All season traction designed tread

Center rib tread design and special tread rubber compound deliver long, even tread wear

Wraparound shoulder and tread lug design produce outstanding year-round traction

Exhibit 4 Major Consumer Segments for Replacement Passenger Tires

	Percent of Consumers	Percent of Sales Represented by		
		Major Brands	Minor Brands	Private Brands
Price-constrained buyers	22%	30%	35%	35%
Value-oriented buyers	18	54	29	17
Quality buyers	23	51	28	21
Commodity buyers	37	18	37	45
All tire buyers	100	33	33	34

Source: Company records

Exhibit 5 Share of Retail Sales of Replacement Passenger Tires by Channel (U.S. market only)

Channel Share of Retail Sales	1976	1981	1986	1991
Garages/service stations	18%	11%	8%	6%
Warehouse clubs	0	0	2	6
Mass merchandisers	28	24	16	12
Manufacturer-owned outlets	11	10	11	9
Small independent tire dealers	36	47	46	40
Large independent tire chains	4	2	12	23
Other	3	6	5	4
Total	100%	100%	100%	100%

	Relative Price Index, 1991	Sales of Private Label Tires as a Percent of Retail Sales Dollars, 1991
Garages/service stations	110%	57%
Warehouse clubs	80	8
Mass merchandisers	97	34
Manufacturer-owned outlets	107	16
Small independent tire dealers	100	36
Large independent tire chains	90	54
Other	N/A	59

Source: Company records
Note: Relative price index indicates typical retail prices for the same tire in each channel. Retail prices in "other" category varied according to the specific outlet.

Exhibit 6 Tire Dealers' Bill of Rights

"Tire dealers as independent business people have earned the right to the respect of all other facets of the tire, retreading, and auto service industries since it has long been established that they fulfill the role as the most important channel of tire distribution. . . .

Tire dealers expect to give loyalty to, and receive loyalty from their manufacturers; to be treated like valued customers; and to be encouraged to sell to end users without direct competition from their manufacturers. Independent tire dealers have a right to the uninhibited exercise of their ability to increase their market share with the cooperation of their manufacturers. . . .

Tire dealers have a right to expect reasonable and timely communications from, and where appropriate, consultation with their manufacturers on actions taken by the manufacturers which directly affect independent tire dealers and their customers. . . .

Independent tire dealers have the right to expect their manufacturers to pay careful attention to supply and demand, pursuing neither to excess, and to keep the dealer supplied in a timely fashion with high quality products which will allow the dealer to sell and serve the customer properly. . . .

Independent dealers have a right to a level playing field including the availability of tire lines, pricing, terms, and programs equal to those offered to wholesale clubs, discounters, company-owned stores, mass merchandisers, chains, and other forms of competition. . . .

Tire manufacturers should recognize the need for profits, not only for themselves, but also for the independent tire dealer who performs the major distribution function for them. . . .

Independent tire dealers have a right to the timely, proper, and uniform issuance of credits for advertising, national account sales, return goods, adjustments, and any other money due. . . .

Independent tire dealers . . . have a right to expect that the manufacturer will use the network of independent tire dealers as the first step for expansion, increasing the dealers' market share; and that commitments made are commitments kept."

Source: Adapted from *Tire Business*.

Exhibit 7 Brand Image of Major Tire Manufacturers, 1991

A survey of broad-line tire owners asked what brand of tires the owners intended to buy the next time they needed tires. Results are reported below for the five major brands and for the four major consumer segments.

	Intent to Buy for Major Consumer Segments				
	All Buyers	**Price Constrained Buyers**	**Value-Oriented Buyers**	**Quality Buyers**	**Commodity Buyers**
Goodyear	13%	16%	17%	18%	10%
Michelin	13	9	24	22	6
Other	19	18	20	25	16
Uncommitted	55	57	39	35	68

Source: *Company records*

Exhibit 8 Switching Among Tire Brands, 1991

	Brand Bought						
Brand Replaced	**Bridgestone**	**Firestone**	**Goodyear**	**Michelin**	**Minor Brands**	**Private Label**	**Total**
Bridgestone	29%	4%	8%	8%	7%	43%	100%
Firestone	2	27	11	6	7	45	100
Goodyear	2	5	39	5	9	38	100
Michelin	3	3	7	44	6	36	100
Minor brands	2	4	10	7	32	42	100
Private label	2	5	8	5	7	70	100

Source: Company records
Note: The above chart can be read as follows: Four percent of car owners with Bridgestone tires bought Firestone tires to replace the Bridgestone.

Exhibit 9 Aquatred Test Market Data

	Buyers of the....	
	Aquatred	**Invicta GS**
– *What brand of tire was replaced?*		
– Goodyear	38%	51%
– Michelin	17	15
– Other	25	16
– Don't know	20	18
– *Steps in information search:*		
– Checked newspaper ads	33%	23%
– Telephoned outlets	21	14
– Shopped other dealers	20	12
– *Primary shopping orientation:*		
– Store	36%	44%
– Brand	56	47
– Price	8	9
– *Purchase decision segments*		
– Price-constrained Buyers	6%	6%
– Value-oriented Buyers	23	13
– Quality Buyers	61	64
– Commodity Buyers	10	17
– *Bought four tires*	*91%*	*54%*
– *Reasons for buying tires at Goodyear (multiple answers allowed)*		
– Past experience	36%	49%
– Want Goodyear brand	33	33
– Want Aquatreds	25	N/A
– Convenience	11	18
– Familiar with personnel	11	12
– Advertising	9	N/A
– On sale/good price	8	13
– Recommended by a friend	4	4
– Always go to that dealer	4	9
– Other	26	20
– *Vehicle make:*		
– Domestic	74%	94%
– Import	26	6
– *What features or benefits did the salesperson tell you about the Aquatred? (multiple answers allowed)*		
– Has 60,000 mile warranty	41%	10%
– Great wet traction	33	38
– Didn't tell me about them	13	42
– Won't hydroplane	16	9
– Other	29	18

Source: Company records

Exhibit 10 Results of Mystery Shopping in Aquatred Test Market

A male mystery shopper visited nine independent Goodyear outlets in the Aquatred test market during October 1991. The mystery shopper told the staff in each outlet that his wife needed tires for her Plymouth Voyager. In the sales presentations that followed:

Eight of the nine salespersons mentioned the Aquatred during their presentations. Of those eight, five began their presentation with the Aquatred and three finished with the Aquatred.

Three salespeople made specific claims concerning the Aquatred's superior performance in wet traction. One claimed the Aquatred was 15% better than other tires; another claimed 20%-25%; and a third claimed up to 35% better traction with the Aquatred.

Goodyear's suggested retail prices for the Aquatred were $89.95 with a black sidewall, and $93.95 with a white sidewall. Prices quoted by six outlets were as follows:

Store Number	Price with Black Sidewall	Price with White Sidewall
1	$79.95	$79.95
2	81.95	81.95
3	80.00	83.00
4	85.00	85.00
5	85.00	88.00
6	100.00	100.00

Source: Company records

Exhibit 11 Proposed Aquatred Advertisement

GOOD YEAR

"TIRES OF THE FUTURE" :30

AQUATRED

GTBM 8863

(MUSIC UNDER)
ANNCR: (VO) You're about to see

how Goodyear is changing all-season driving

right before your eyes.

Introducing Aquatred...

only from Goodyear.

(MUSIC)

 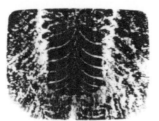 

Aquatred's advanced design

channels water out of your way

for dependable

all-season traction,

especially in the rain

when you may need it most.

Aquatred.

The newest reason why we say the

have Goodyear written all over them.

L'ORÉAL OF PARIS: BRINGING "CLASS TO MASS" WITH PLÉNITUDE

L'Oréal was born in Clichy, France in 1907, the offspring of technological innovation. Nearly 90 years later, the spirit behind answering the needs of a Parisian hairdresser in search of more subtle and lasting hair color for his clientele, was at work in the Health and Beauty Aids aisles of K-Marts, Wal-Marts, drugstores, and grocery stores throughout the United States as L'Oréal sought to bring "class to mass" in the skincare market.

From his office overlooking Fifth Avenue in New York City, Joseph Campinell, President of L'Oréal's U.S. Retail Division explained L'Oréal's strategy for the mass market: "We sell product in the department store and specialty store channels. The research and development we do in support of those brands like Lancôme and Biotherm can be leveraged into mass market outlets as well. We call this 'trickle down and fire up.' We trickle the technology down to the mass markets where the high volumes are and that fires up our next generation of products by funding the research and development. In the retail division we do what the company always does: drive sales with product technology. But, since the drugstores, mass merchants and grocery stores we sell through are 'self-service' types of outlets, we have to support that technology with strong advertising, merchandising and promotions. We have been very successful with this in hair colorings. Our Preference by L'Oréal brand, with the famous advertising tag-line 'Because I'm worth it,' has become the market leader. I'm sure we will get there with the Plénitude skincare line as well, though we clearly have some things to work out there."

Carol Hamilton, Senior Vice President of Marketing for the L'Oréal Retail Division had assumed responsibility for Plénitude in early 1996. The Plénitude line, which included cleansers and moisturizers, had been a smashing success in the French skincare market following its 1982 introduction and was introduced to the U.S. market in 1988. In April 1996, Hamilton commented:

Plénitude has gone through a couple phases here. It had a very strong introduction in the United States, quickly becoming the #2 brand in the market, only behind Oil of Olay. And, the trade loved us. We were upscaling the skincare business and bringing new people into these mass channels from department stores. Plénitude sales grew pretty well through 1991 and we were achieving what we set out to do. We had told the trade we would spend big supporting the brand and we did; we were building a consumer franchise, brand equity, and good trade relations. We weren't making any money. But, we didn't worry about that too much since we knew from the beginning that we would have to invest in the market given the position Procter had with Oil of Olay. But then we just hit a four-year sales plateau. We had lost the #2 position to Pond's. When I took on the brand, we had just regained our position as the #2 brand in moisturizers. However, it was still 8 or 9 years after the U.S. introduction and we still were not making any money here.

Four keys for us now are:

1. Improve the top-line—we need to break through the sales plateau and get more product moving off the shelf to maintain a strong position with the trade.

2. Get the bottom-line moving in the right direction quickly. We lost $12.5 million on the brand in 1995. We don't necessarily have to make money in 1996, but we have to turn it positive soon without harvesting the brand's long-term position.

3. Get the United States in a position to be a major contributor to the brand's position globally. Until 1994, we in the U.S. were only an exclusive licensee of L'Oréal. Now, we are an owned

subsidiary, a true member of the L'Oréal family, so our potential for a real role in the global management of the brand has changed.

4. Make sure that we have suitable skincare products for the U.S. customer; but also that they fit within L'Oréal's technology portfolio.

We have some strong new products but they alone can't carry us to where we want to be. Our new organizational structure combining cosmetics, skincare and haircare in the retail division will be a help and we have done some good research on consumers' shopping and usage behavior, our brand and the competition. So, like Joe said, we will get there, but we have to rethink all aspects of our business—

- do we have too many different types of products?
- is our premium pricing strategy appropriate for all of our products? For any of them?
- is our "star" system of putting almost all our media dollars behind our newest and most technologically advanced product still the best way to go?
- are aspects of our strategy "too French" for the U.S. market?
- how do we best utilize an asset which our consumer research shows is very powerful and no one else in this business has—the L'Oréal brand name?

What makes all this very interesting is the business we are in. We sell beauty products. They are very personal products. Plus, it is very high tech. We spent $300 million on research last year and L'Oréal worldwide registered 300 new patents. People don't realize this but, technology is as critical to us here on Fifth Avenue as it is to those firms in Silicon Valley. But then we sell beauty and that brings a special set of marketing challenges to all of us here.

L'Oréal

L'Oréal was founded by the French chemist Eugene Schueller to develop and market his new process for haircoloring. The "Aureole" process meaning "aura of light" in French, gave name to the company. Ninety years after its founding, L'Oréal was still substantially controlled by Schueller's family. His daughter, Madame Liliane Bettencourt, was a member of L'Oréal's Board of Directors and held 51% of the holding company Gesparal (the other 49% being held by Nestlé) which held a

controlling interest in L'Oréal. The firm's consistent strategy of "quality, innovation and geographic expansion" resulted in sales of 53.4 billion French Francs in 1995 from over 2,000 products, sold under 500 brand names in over 150 countries.[1] Cosmetics represented 81% of revenues with the geographic distribution:

France—23%

Rest of Europe Excluding France—40%

USA and Canada—20%

Latin America—6%

Asia—6%

Rest of World—5%

The firm's innovations were sold to and through a number of different types of outlets. Some haircare lines, for example, were sold exclusively to beauty salons and others direct to consumers in mass outlets. In skincare, brands such as Lancôme and Biotherm were sold to department and specialty stores competing against the likes of Estee Lauder, Clinique, Christian Dior and Chanel while Plénitude was sold through mass channels competing against Nivea (the strongest competitor throughout Europe), Procter and Gamble's Oil of Olay (the U.S. market leader) and others. L'Oréal's 1995 Annual Report noted: "As a result of its worldwide presence and the extent and variety of its cosmetic ranges, L'Oréal's activities are harmoniously divided across all types of distribution channels."

Lindsay Owen-Jones, Chairman and Chief Executive Officer of L'Oréal saw the "trickle down and fire up" philosophy as vital: viz. "Will luxury companies in the next century, which do not have mass market bases, have the resources necessary to do the research to compete? I think the answer is no."[2]

Exhibit 1 shows an organization chart for the company as of March, 1996. Owen-Jones had assumed his Chairman and Chief Executive Officer post in 1988. He joined L'Oréal in 1969 upon graduation from INSEAD. He held a number of international posts for L'Oréal including managing director of the United States operations in the early 1980's. Since 1987, Guy Peyrelongue headed L'Oréal USA activities as President and CEO. At that time, Cosmair, the U.S. licensee of L'Oréal, had Nestlé as its majority shareholder. In 1994, L'Oréal

---

[1]At the end of 1995, one French Franc was equivalent to .2039 U.S. dollars.

[2]S. Roper and P. Born, "OJ: On The Record," *Women's Wear Daily,* May 13, 1994.

bought out Nestlé's interest in Cosmair making it a wholly owned subsidiary of L'Oréal though retaining the Cosmair name. For 1995, U.S. sales were approximately $1.5 billion. Three Cosmair divisions primarily served beauty salons: L'Oréal Technique Professionelle, L'Oréal Salon Classics and Redken, which was acquired in 1993. In 1996, L'Oréal broadened its participation in the mass market by acquiring Maybelline, a leader in the color cosmetics business. Maybelline was given worldwide responsibility for developing a global, popularly-priced color cosmetics business for L'Oréal. The company reorganized in February 1996 combining the formerly separate L'Oréal Haircare Division and L'Oréal Cosmetic and Fragrance Division to form the L'Oréal Retail Division under the leadership of Joseph Campinell.

Plénitude

Plénitude by L'Oréal was one of L'Oréal's first ventures beyond the haircare and cosmetics arena. Its 1982 launch in France positioned the brand as "high end, superior performance but accessible." French women were relatively sophisticated in their use of skin care products and many brands competed in the high end of the market. In the mass market, there were only a few significant brands. The leaders were both Germany-based: Beiersdorf Corporation's Nivea in the "big blue jar" and Henkel's Diadermine. Procter and Gamble's Oil of Olay, the U.S. market leader, trailed these two.

Plénitude was introduced under a "class of the mass" strategy with a single product developed specifically for the French market. "Créme Quotidienne de Soin," a general purpose moisturizer, was introduced at a 30% price premium over incumbents. Exhibit 2 shows the introductory print ad with the brand benefit "Retarde les Effects du Vieillissement" i.e. Delays Signs of Aging. The creative positioning, developed in concert with the Publicis/Bloom Agency, was "I am a modern women, who uses only premium quality, technologically advanced products." Initially, print was the predominant advertising medium to match the practice of the prestige brands. Supported by upscale packaging and merchandising, the product was an early success, achieving sales of one million units in 1983.

From 1984 to 1987, the Plénitude line in France was filled out with special purpose products, e.g. Dry Skin Night Creme, and Anti-Wrinkle Creme. Exhibit 3 shows a print ad for the Plénitude line. The skincare market had two different product types: moisturizers and cleansers. Initially, the Plénitude line consisted of only moisturizers. In 1986, a cleanser product was added and

advertising shifted more to television to reach the mass audience with a "modern woman" message. Cleansers did not offer as much opportunity for product differentiation through technology as moisturizers, and thus L'Oréal had delayed their introduction until the moisturizers had helped establish the Plénitude by L'Oréal "technologically advanced" image. By 1987, the line was still being sold only in France where it took over unit share leadership in moisturizers despite its price premium. For 1987, its dollar share of the French mass moisturizer market was a leading 19.6% vs. Henkel's Diadermine 13.0% and Nivea's 8.8%.

The success of Plénitude in France validated the "class to mass" strategy in the minds of L'Oréal executives in France and L'Oréal began to seek geographic expansion of both Plénitude products and the marketing approach. In France, Plénitude's success continued as L'Oréal introduced a new technologically advanced "Action Liposomes" product three times the price of a basic moisturizer. This patented technology had been introduced to the French market in L'Oréal's prestige Lancôme line under the name Niôsome. L'Oréal used massive advertising to support "Action Liposomes" as a "star product" (capturing 25% "share-of-voice" in the category) to foster not only product sales but also to boost the equity of the entire "Plénitude by L'Oréal" brand umbrella.

Over time, the success in France led L'Oréal to more precise specification of and deeper belief in the formula for success in mass skin care, viz.

1. Have Technologically Superior Products
2. Concentrate Resources and Support on newest "Star Product" to pull the entire line.
3. Follow the "Golden Rules" of Advertising:

   - feature star product
   - provide technological superiority evidence
   - depict an executive woman who is up-to-date and assertive ("I live with the times")

Could the French "class to mass" formula for success be exported to the United States and other countries around the world?

The United States Launch and Early Results

Plénitude was first test marketed in Atlanta and Dallas in 1988. While seeking to maintain the basic French success formula, advertising research showed that a change in the advertising positioning from "Delays the Signs of Aging" to "Reduces the Signs of Aging" would be beneficial for the U.S. market. With moisturizer market shares reaching as high as 14% in the test markets and good supporting, diagnostic data, L'Oréal decided to launch the brand nationwide.

Whereas the French launch had been a single moisturizer product, followed sequentially by introduction of special purpose moisturizers and then a cleanser, the U.S. strategy was to introduce the entire line as it had been developed in France. Specially, 14 SKU's were introduced covering three categories:

- basic moisturizers
  - treatment moisturizers
- cleansers

A print ad for the U.S. introduction is shown in Exhibit 4.

Marianne Coll, then a director of sales described the introduction:

We had a cosmetics salesforce but it was clear that in the mass channels, the skincare action was in the Health and Beauty Aids (HBA) section over on aisles 2 and 3 not the pegged board cosmetics section on the far wall. There were a few skincare players in cosmetics like Revlon and Almay, but 80% of the business was with Olay, Pond's, Neutrogena and Nivea over in the HBA section. So, even though we were in the accounts with L'Oréal lipsticks and nail polish and hair coloring products, we had to establish new relationships with different buyers and what we were asking for had never been heard of before. We were not selling a product so much as trying to create a department store environment at mass accounts. We knew that American consumers really did not know much about skin care compared to European women—so we were proposing to educate them at the point-of-purchase. Different women had different needs so we needed to be able to map products to people in the store based on the skin type and problems. In department stores, this is what the salesperson does. In mass, we had to do it without a person there to help the users. So, we said to these HBA buyers whom we did not know: "You have to take our entire product line, all 14 SKU's, and you have to take this one-linear-foot merchandising unit; and put this on your shelf. (Exhibit 5A shows the desired presentation of the L'Oréal Plénitude Skincare Center at retail locations and Exhibit 5B shows a close-up of the packaging and merchandising unit information for repre-

sentative products.) Oh, and incidentally, we want to be at eye-level right next to Oil of Olay." Naturally, we got some push back on this but we would not negotiate on the 14 SKU's—we couldn't if we were going to recreate the department store experience in a self-service format. You had to take all the products and you had to merchandise them the way we said.

The L'Oréal name was absolutely critical to us in selling this concept. L'Oréal had a reputation with everyone in the trade—we were known for living up to our commitments. If we said we were going to spend $30MM behind a product we did; and, our products historically were good profit generators for the trade. By the time of the Plénitude launch in August 1988, all of our existing customers were signed up. Some of them said "we don't agree" but even they said "we'll give it a shot." Year 1 we spent $32.5 million on advertising and did 10,000 store events with demonstrators, samples—all the kinds of things you see in department stores. And, we hit our sales targets.

While some of the products were adjusted to U.S. consumers' preference for a lighter in texture, less heavily perfumed product than sold in France, the core elements of the French success formula were followed. French advertising executions were basically translated into English and the "I live with the times" image sought. Advertising resource allocation followed the "star system" with the bulk of dollars spent on the newest, most technologically advanced product. Ad spending focused on:

1989: Full Plénitude product line.

1990: Action Liposomes introduction (see Exhibit 6 for print ad.)

1991: Eye Defense Creme introduction.

1992–93: Hydra Renewal introduction. Wrinkle De-fense Creme upgrade to "Advanced"

1994: Excell-A3 introduction

1995: Revitalift Face introduction

Exhibit 7 presents 1991 to 1995 statistics on the size of the market and dollar shares by manufacturer for both moisturizers and cleansers.

In 1990, its first full calendar year on the U.S. market, Plénitude sales were $31.7MM; total advertising and promotion costs $35.5MM; and $25.4MM pre-tax loss. By 1995, net sales doubled. However, advertising and promotion spending had increased (in nominal terms) from $35.5MM in 1990 to $38.3MM in 1995 as Plénitude regularly introduced new products which required support in a highly competitive environment. With cost-of-goods sold at 25% of gross revenues, the brand lost $12.5MM pre-tax for 1995.

Researching the Market and Plénitude's Position

Carol Hamilton's skincare team was well aware of Plénitude's historical financial performance and the recent success of its latest new product, Revitalift. As part of the planning process for accomplishing Hamilton's three goals of: top-line growth, bottom line improvement, and influence on the global brand strategy, they gathered together the marketplace data to understand Plénitude situation fully.

The brand team had data it tracked through its market research information sources such as ACNielsen which reported market size, unit and dollar share by specific product, distribution levels, average prices, and trade feature advertising. Dollar shares of mass channels and ad spending for 1995 were as follows:

1995 Dollar Shares (ACNielsen data)			
	Moisturizers	Cleansers	1995 Ad Spending[3]
Plénitude	14.0	3.4	$29.2MM
Olay	28.2	7.9	48.1MM
Pond's	15.1	11.2	18.1MM
Alpha Hydrox	5.4	–	11.9MM
Nivea	6.2	–	12.8MM
Neutrogena	5.2	6.2	13.3MM
Revlon	4.3	–	
Almay	4.6	4.1	
Noxzema	–	21.6	11.5MM
Sea Breeze	–	8.9	
Clean & Clear	–	6.7	10.0MM
$ Size Category (Retail)	$471MM	$328MM	

Moisturizers were of two basic types: daily care and treatment care. Manufacturers differed as to the proportion of the unit sales from daily and treatment, e.g. for 1995.

Moisturizer Units Sold		
	% Daily	% Treatment
1. Alpha Hydrox	11%	89%
2. Plénitude	35%	65%
3. Pond's	51%	49%
4. Nivea	73%	27%
5. Neutrogena	78%	22%
6. Olay	88%	12%

Exhibit 8 gives Plénitude and competitive pricing information in late 1995. The exhibit shows the size of the product, its cost to the trade, and approximate everyday retail price (i.e. the price when not on sale) in a typical chain drug store. Other outlets such as mass merchants took generally smaller margins on products than drug stores but the relative margins across manufacturers were similar for all outlet types. Part A of Exhibit 8 presents data for the entire Plénitude line, i.e. its 5 daily moisturizers, 8 treatment moisturizers and 6 cleansers.[4] Part B is for all competitors' cleansers; part C for competitors' daily moisturizers; and part D for their treatment moisturizers.

The group also commissioned a number of custom market research studies, the most important of which were:

- Facial Skin Care Market Study
  - a large scale quantitative telephone and mail survey of over 3500 women age 16–69 who used one or more moisturizers or treatment creams at least once a week.
- Qualitative Research Among "Acceptors and Rejectors" of Plénitude. This was followed by a similar study among Oil of Olay and Pond's Acceptors and Rejectors.
- A Plénitude Shelf Shopping Study.

Major findings from each follow.

[3]As estimated by Publicis/Bloom, Ad Agency.

[4]Costs of goods approximated 25% of the trade price across the Plénitude line. For case calculations, use 25% of the trade prices in exhibit 8A as Plénitude's item costs.

Facial Skin Care Market Study—September 1995

This study found that consumers could be divided into five "benefit" segments as follows:

1. "Unconcerned" (25% of respondents)
   - basically buy on price.
2. "Ingredient Apathetic" (17%)
   - concerned with reducing signs of aging; but not so concerned about gentleness or specific ingredients.
3. "Price Conscious Socializers" (17%)
   - worried about looking better but price/value is a concern.
4. "Stressed Out" (22%)
   - not concerned about price; want effective product that reinvigorates skin and reduces signs of aging.
5. "Age Focused" (18%)
   - similar to "Stressed Out" group but with more attention to price and natural ingredients.

The survey showed Plénitude was disproportionately used by the last two groups, viz. 54% of Plénitude users fell into groups 4 or 5 as opposed to 36% of Olay users. Alpha Hydrox with 62% was the other brand whose users fell heavily into the "Stressed Out" and "Aged Focused" groups.

The study included a perceptual mapping exercise; the results of which are in Exhibits 9 and 10. (Appendix 1 describes the perceptual mapping procedure and how to interpret results for those not familiar with the technique.) Results in exhibits 9 and 10 are both from ratings provided by those respondents who were aware of the brand. Exhibit 9 maps their perceptions of the brands while exhibit 10 maps their perceptions of users of the brands. Brands close together in the space compete closely with one another; whereas those farther apart are seen as quite different by consumers.

The study also assessed brand awareness, trial, and current use rates with results as reported in Exhibit 11. The market research company conducting the study summarized the research as showing that "Plénitude has room to grow but must establish a more secure place among skin care consumers."

Acceptor/Rejector Studies (April and May 1996)

Two qualitative acceptor/rejector studies were done. The first was with people who had used Plénitude with Acceptors being those still using the brand and Rejectors those who had stopped. A second study was with acceptors/rejectors of key competitors, Oil of Olay and Pond's. The Plénitude acceptor/rejector study consisted of four 2-hour long focus groups—two in Boston and two in Dallas. For each area discussed, the research company's summary "bullet point" is provided along with selected verbatims from respondents. Each comment under a given "bullet point" is from a different person.

1. *Motivation for Trial of Plénitude*
   - L'Oréal brand name cited by many as primary motivator for trial

     You think because it's L'Oréal it will be a little more expensive, but also be better quality. You just get that feeling from L'Oréal.

     It comes under the umbrella of L'Oréal, so it must be a good product.

     I know about L'Oréal. I buy their mascara and I know that's really good quality.

   - Plénitude as a brand name meant little to people

     The L'Oréal name is what you think of. I didn't know Plénitude was the name of the brand.

     This is L'Oréal. "Plénitude" doesn't really mean anything—that could be gone and it wouldn't make a difference.

     I tell people I use L'Oréal. I didn't know Plénitude was the brand name.

     Plénitude is just there—it's just part of L'Oréal, I guess. I was thinking Plénitude was the name of that particular lotion, rather than the line.

   - L'Oréal by Plénitude seen as department store quality in mass outlets

     I had been buying Estee Lauder, but I just didn't feel like spending that kind of money anymore. This was practically the same thing, at a supermarket price.

     You used to have to pay fifty dollars to get something that did the same things as this. I think it took a while for the technology to get to the supermarket level.

When you go to the department store, they try to sell you everything. When I approach something like this on my own, I can just pick out the things I want.

2. *Response to Product Formulas*

- Young rejectors of the brand found it too heavy or greasy

  It really has a greasy feeling to me; I don't like it. You feel like you're putting Crisco on your face. It doesn't sink in or something.

  It was oily. It was gross.

  It just didn't absorb into my skin. It was way too greasy.

3. *Perception of Plénitude as Full Product Line*

- Uniformly people saw the Plénitude line as having a large number of products; for some this was a plus, for others a minus

  It's really more like a department store line. You go to CVS and you see they have a whole shelf of just different creams. They really offer a lot.

  It does have a big product line with a lot of choice, so you think of it as being more researched, more top of the line.

  There are so many products it's confusing. It's so extensive. You really have to study what you want to get.

  It's kind of confusing to me because they have a lot of products—I don't always have time to read each one and decide which is the best one.

  Some of the other product lines have less of a choice. Rather than get confused by a huge selection, a lot of times I'll pass that by and get something where there's only three products I have to chose from, as opposed to twenty.

  Plénitude seems complicated. You spend an hour in the store, trying to prescribe something for yourself—reading them all.

- Names of individual products could be more helpful in sorting through the line

  If they call it moisturizer, I like that, but when they start getting into Excell A—what is that? What are they trying to tell me? I can't determine that just by reading it.

  I find the names confusing. I want a moisturizer and I want it to say it's a moisturizer. I

don't want to have to read the whole box to figure out what it is.

The name should say succinctly what they take three paragraphs to say on the box.

I think the Eye Defense was the first one I bought—I bought it because it said that. I had decided that I probably should use an eye cream. It said right on the box that this was specifically for your eyes.

I saw this stuff that said "Eye Defense." I thought, "it's been a rough day, maybe I need some defense." That word captured my attention, so I took it home.

4. *Response to Plénitude Packaging*

- Packaging, while generally attractive, seemed overworked to some

  This is very attractive packaging. I think it's feminine looking.

  It has an expensive look to it, too.

  The Plénitude sometimes confuses me; it's a lot to read.

  I find reading all their different packages confusing. Hydro this, hydro that. I don't know what to do with my skin in terms of all that.

  All of this wording stresses me out. I think, "do I need this, or this, or this?" I don't want to read the whole of every package.

5. *Perceived Target Consumer*

- Some felt Plénitude was specifically targeted to older women.

  If it reduces the signs of aging, I think that it would be talking to someone over 50. I think the kids don't need this.

  I don't think this is for 20s, maybe not even 30s.

  I get the impression that it's geared to older people. . . . worried about wrinkles and aging and stuff.

The second acceptor/rejector study was of Oil of Olay and Pond's acceptors and rejectors. It consisted of six focus groups—three in Chicago and three in Baltimore. All participants in the interviews were screened for feeling facial skin care was very important and shopping for these products in self-service outlets.

1. *Motivation for Trial*

- Oil of Olay trial was generated by many mechanisms:

My grandmother told me about it because my skin was getting much drier.

I had a friend turn me on to it because it was light and soaked in well.

It was always advertised in *Seventeen* magazine.

I received mine in a welcome box in college.

- Pond's was seen as a staple of life

  My best friend's mother said, 'When you get older use this.'

  I remember seeing commercials, 10 or 20 years ago.

  Everybody used Pond's when I was a kid.

  I liked to stick my finger in my mother's jar of it when I was a kid.

  It was inexpensive and the shelves were stocked with it; everybody was using it.

2. *Product Satisfaction Sources*

  - Acceptors saw Oil of Olay as light and reasonably priced

    It went right into my skin and feels like my skin was still clean.

    I needed something that was light so I wouldn't feel it under my makeup.

    The price always was very reasonable and different from department store items.

  - Acceptors saw Pond's as reliable, accessible and reasonably priced

    It has a clean scent that's fresh and not overpowering.

    It doesn't irritate my skin and it's very reasonably priced.

    It does what it says it's going to do, and I pick it up at Walgreen's.

    They've been around a long time; you can trust the product.

3. *Brand Imagery*

  - Oil of Olay was seen as the traditional, generational brand

    It's mothers and daughters lounging together in pink robes.

    It's a natural thing, Evian water, deep blue ocean, white sand, laid back.

    Museum setting, mothers and daughters talking about issues that relate to women.

- Pond's brand imagery was older, down-to-earth

  I don't see glamour and glitz; I see everyday people, school teachers and bankers.

  Pond's is women from the forties in house dresses listening to the radio.

4. *Perceptions of the Plénitude Line and Packaging* (When Respondent was Shown a Picture of Plénitude Line)

  - Respondents generally saw the Plénitude line as overwhelming.

    It's like repetitive; do they think one person's going to use all that stuff?

    It's very busy and confusing; they all look the same; too much writing and reading.

    To figure out what product you need takes a lot of work; I don't have time to read those.

    It would take five minutes to read the front to see what it's going to do for me.

    I'd want someone to tell me what it's for; you're diagnosing your own situation here.

    All that stuff that's probably not necessary; it's for somebody who's a lot older than me.

    I don't want to deal with that; they look too complicated.

    Make the boxes so you don't have to have a chemistry degree to read them.

Shelf Shopping Study—May 1996

In this research, an actual mock-up of a typical in-store shelf arrangement was created with Plénitude and competitive products shown. Ten groups of five people each were exposed to this shelving and asked to evaluate the Plénitude line and packaging on its "shopability." Each respondent was interviewed individually and then a group discussion followed. Key findings were:

1. *Overall Category Shopping Experience*

  - Positive Aspects

    I've always found it to be fun. I like to look at all the products and see what's new.

    These products are like my toys. I love to look and see if there are any new products, or just things I haven't seen before.

I really find it to be fun. Most shopping is a drudgery, but this is more like a treat.

I enjoy it most when I don't have the kids with me; then I can really take my time and look at the different products to see what's best for me. I don't always have that kind of time, but when I do, it's great.

There are always new things coming out, new research or whatever. Practically every time you look you see something you didn't see before.

- Negative Aspects

When I get in to this aisle, I get overwhelmed. There are so many, I wonder which is what, what's the difference?

Sometimes there seems to be so much stuff— do I need all of this? Which do I use, which do I not use? It would be helpful if they had some kind of regimen or guideline.

It's very confusing because there are so many different things coming at you. It's mind boggling. You really have to be an educated person to do this. It's a challenge.

I wouldn't say it was fun, I'd say it was frustrating and very confusing. You're looking at all these products and you have no idea what to use and when to use it.

2. *Brand Images of Major Competitors*
   - Oil of Olay

Oil of Olay has just always been the same pink glop. I haven't looked at it in years, but I imagine it's still the same.

When I see that bottle of Oil of Olay I can just picture it on my mother's vanity all these years ago, so I think of it as being a pretty old fashioned kind of product.

I'm amazed they still make Oil of Olay. There are so many new products out, and they're just sort of the same old same old.

I think Oil of Olay is one of the best, really. It's been around a long time and it's always had that sophisticated look to it.

I've just always heard of Oil of Olay, so that was why I started with that. I really like it; it really works for me and I think the packaging looks really nice.

   - Pond's

I see that Pond's and I think, "Oh, no, no, no." Cold cream was what my grandmother used. You think it's going to be really heavy and greasy.

Pond's has just been around forever. I think of it as something my mother used, before all this other stuff was available.

Basically you think of the Pond's as being for old ladies, something really heavy and unpleasant to use. No thanks!

   - L'Oréal

L'Oréal is a step up. I really think that. Just the name L'Oréal has kind of a French twist to it, so it seems more exotic. But that means a step up in price too, which is why I don't go for it.

In my head I just think of the L'Oréal Plénitude as really expensive. I don't even usually look at it when I'm shopping.

The L'Oréal is going to be more expensive because it's coming from the big French company with all the advertising that they do.

When I go in to the drugstore and see the Plénitude, it seems like it's going to be a lot more expensive than the other products. That's the main reason I haven't tried it.

3. *L'Oréal Product Line Presentation* (See Exhibit 12 for example of Plénitude packaging; Exhibit 12A shows the front of the Revitalift box; Exhibit 12B the back.)
   - Negative

The package is just chaos. You have to look at it and look at it. There are too many words.

The product looks really complicated. It's a lot to read, and there's probably a lot of stuff on there that I wouldn't even understand.

You have to pick up the box and read five or six lines before you can see anything.

The L'Oréal packaging is so wordy. I read all this and get confused. The way the L'Oréal is packaged makes me feel like I'm getting confused because I have to read a lot more to decide what I want.

The front of the box looks like it should be the back of the box.

   - Positive

I think the reason I get L'Oréal is because they tell you a lot. They really tell you more than the others about what they do for you.

I like all that information.

With the L'Oréal you get a really good summary of it right on the front. I like that because it will tell me exactly what I'm getting. I know what I'm looking for and I can seen what I want.

The front of the L'Oréal package has a lot of information—it's very helpful. They give you a lot more information than Estee Lauder.

Developing the Plénitude Plan

As Carol Hamilton prepared her plan for revitalizing the Plénitude line and bringing it to profitability, the most recent new product launch in the Plénitude line continued to perform extremely well. Revitalift, known within L'Oréal as a "facelift in a jar," had been introduced in September, 1995. The print ad for Revitalift noting its "double performance" as both anti-wrinkle and firming care is shown in Exhibit 13. Revitalift quickly came to represent 20% of Plénitude sales. It was supported by $5MM in TV advertising in the fourth quarter of 1995 and heavy support had continued through 1996 to date. Plénitude's dollar and unit sales for the first quarter of 1996 by product are shown in Exhibit 14.

Revitalift was an important innovation incorporating Pro-Retinol A and E. L'Oréal's tracking studies showed that the product had brought many new users to the Plénitude franchise as 40% of Revitalift buyers had not previously purchased any Plénitude products. The success of Revitalift, however, complicated decision making on the Plénitude strategy, as Hamilton explained:

The research had just about convinced me that we had to hit a home run with younger customers. Our "Reduces Signs of Aging" message was getting through but it was tagging Plénitude as an older person's brand. Now, I get a great new product that is really moving off the shelf and helping our relations with the trade and I have to worry about what it is doing to the consumer's perceptions of the brand. Revitalift is a treatment product for people who have a problem.

Our research and development people have a new special purpose product coming which does around your eyes what Revitalift generally does for your face. One option for us is to follow up on the Revitalift success, get the new eye product to market as quickly as possible as a Revitalift extension, called something like "Revitalift-Eye." If we follow our "star product" philosophy we would put lots of ad support behind it.

On the other hand, we might want to bring out the product but not make it our "star." Olay is definitely preparing to attack our treatment franchise. Maybe we should be going after the traditional daily moisturizer segment they have. The problem though is that our current products there and in cleansers are really only parity products. The treatment segment is where our technological skills stand out and that helps establish the "class" part of our proposition and the technological superiority of L'Oréal. So, this is a big decision for us:

Do we continue with our "star" product system, putting all our marketing support behind Revitalift for the next few months and then switching everything to Revitalift-Eye or whatever we call it when it's ready? Or, do we try to develop the younger franchise through improving our value-proposition in cleansers and daily moisturizers? If we do try to develop the daily user, do we need to adjust the tonality of our message?

Advocates of the strategy of developing the younger franchise proposed a change in L'Oréal's pricing philosophy. The philosophy had always been premium pricing across the line. For example, the "Plénitude 1995 Pricing Rationale" stated in the 1995 Marketing Plan was: "Maintain premium pricing to reinforce quality and performance." L'Oréal had taken price increases in cleansers in 1994 and 1995 and the clarifying line of cleansers was introduced at $6.25 to the trade in 1995. (See Exhibit 8A)

Some argued for an overall product line pricing adjustment to reflect the degree of differentiation L'Oréal held. Specifically, they advocated across-the-board price cuts in cleansers and daily moisturizers. Deep discounts would be required to bring the L'Oréal cleansers in line with competitive cleanser products, as leading brand Noxema sold to the trade for $2.68 for a 10 ounce jar. L'Oréal's new daily moisturizers for 1995 were priced at $5.85 to the trade at introduction, but had been cut to $4.84 on February 1, 1996 given the dominance and pricing of Oil of Olay.

While all members of the team supported the premium pricing philosophy for treatment products, some felt the pricing structure had become unnecessarily cumbersome. As shown in exhibit 8, there were 2 trade price points in cleansers, 3 in daily moisturizers, and 3 in treatment moisturizers. Simplifying the pricing structure by collapsing to a smaller number of price points might help to make the line easier to shop. But, all realized that it would be difficult to sell in any appreciable price increases to the trade and thus a simplification of the pricing structure probably entailed price cuts on average.

Also, the research indicated that while some consumers liked all the information L'Oréal gave on Plénitude boxes and displays, the majority of customers found the information overwhelming. Hamilton wondered how L'Oréal should address the problem. A broad line of specialty products with lots of information on the technical superiority had been a hallmark of the Plénitude line. Was there advantage in reducing the number of SKU's offered? Or the amount of information provided?

As Hamilton considered her options, she thought about the criticality of success and profits from mass products in the "trickle down and fire up" philosophy of L'Oréal. As she and Joe Campinell were now regular participants in L'Oréal International Development Committee, she knew that Lindsay Owen-Jones was pushing steadily in his effort to move L'Oréal from being a "French Cathedral" as he warmly referred to L'Oréal to a global beauty company. Success in the U.S., if found, could now be effectively leveraged worldwide. Plénitude was now being sold throughout the world. In most markets, it faced tough competition from global players who brought information from many markets to bear. Thus, effective leveraging was not a luxury but a necessity.

Exhibit 1 Organizational Chart—March 1996

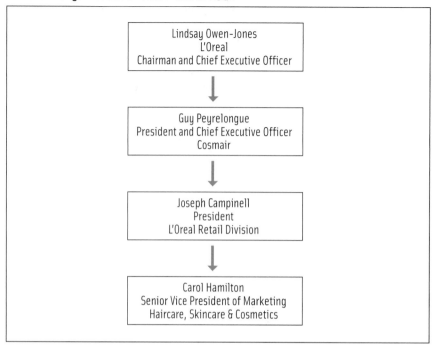

Exhibit 2 Print Ad for French Market for Plénitude Lead Product

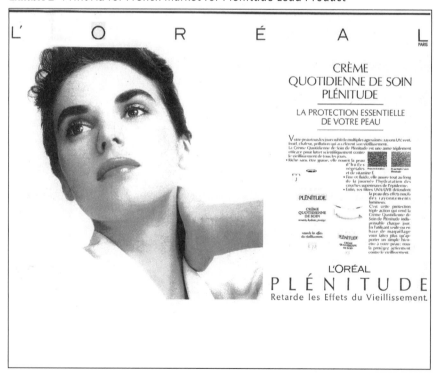

Exhibit 3 Print Ad for French Market for Plénitude Product Line

Exhibit 4 1988 Plénitude Launch Ad for United States

Exhibit 5A Desired Retail Presentation of Plénitude Line at Launch

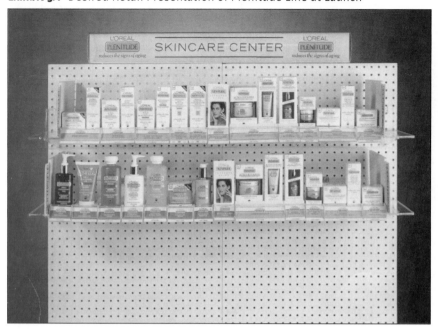

Exhibit 5B Representative Package and Merchandising Unit Information

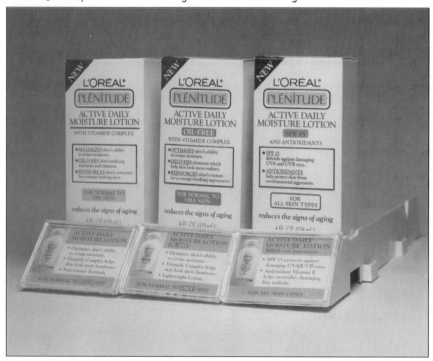

Exhibit 6 1990 Print Ad for New Action Liposomes "Skincare of the Future"

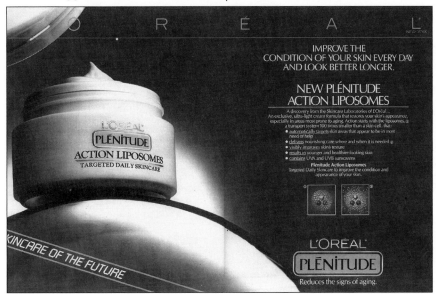

Exhibit 7 Market Size and Brand Shares on Dollar Basis 1991–95

Moisturizers—Market Size and Brand Shares (Dollar Basis—All Mass Outlets)					
	1991	**1992**	**1993**	**1994**	**1995**
Dollar Volume (Retail $)	$309MM	$338MM	$375MM	$440MM	$471MM
Plénitude	11.7	13.6	14.1	13.8	14.0
Olay	38.3	36.1	32.3	29.7	28.2
Almay	5.4	6.0	5.6	4.4	4.6
Nivea	4.8	5.5	6.0	6.2	6.2
Pond's	5.0	4.6	9.1	13.9	15.1
Alpha Hydrox	–	1.0	3.8	5.7	5.4
Neutrogena	7.0	6.5	5.7	4.8	5.2
Cleansers—Market Size and Brand Shares (Dollar Basis—All Mass Outlets)					
	1991	**1992**	**1993**	**1994**	**1995**
Dollar Volume (Retail $)	$252MM	$288MM	$308MM	$308MM	$328MM
Plénitude	3.2	3.2	3.1	3.1	3.4
Olay	11.0	9.9	7.6	6.4	7.9
Almay	4.8	4.8	4.9	4.4	4.1
Noxzema	22.9	24.4	23.8	22.9	21.6
Pond's	11.7	12.6	11.6	12.2	11.2
Neutrogena	4.9	4.9	6.0	6.3	6.2
Sea Breeze	–	–	–	9.4	8.9
Clean and Clear	–	–	–	4.9	6.7

Source: ACNielsen
Note: ACNielsen Reports Results by Four Outlet Types: Drug Stores, Mass Merchandisers, Food and Food/Drug Combination. These Results are averaged over all types of Mass Outlets.

Exhibit 8A Plénitude Product Line Pricing—Trade and Everyday Average Retail of Chain Drug Stores—early 1995

	Size (oz)	Trade Price	Everyday Average Retail[a]
Moisturizers—Daily			
Active Daily Moisturizer—Regular	4.0	4.72	7.11
Active Daily Moisturizer—Oil-Free	4.0	4.72	7.17
Active Daily Moisturizer—SPF15	4.0	4.72	7.21
Hydra—Renewal Jar	1.7	6.83	10.17
Hydra—Renewal Tube	1.6	6.09	9.13
Moisturizers—Treatment			
Advanced Wrinkle Defense Creme—Jar	1.7	8.87	12.15
Advanced Wrinkle Defense Creme—Tube	1.2	7.07	10.30
Advanced Overnight	1.4	8.87	12.26
Eye Defense	.5	8.87	12.07
Excell Cream	1.4	8.42	11.36
Excell Lotion	4.0	8.42	11.51
Serum	1.0	10.43	15.19
Revitalift—Face	1.7	8.87	12.31
Cleansers			
Deep Cleansing Gel	5.0	5.50	6.97
Hydrating Cleansing Cream	6.0	5.50	7.07
Hydrating Floral Toner	8.5	5.50	6.94
Clarifying Foaming Gel	4.0	6.25	8.06
Clarifying Mask	2.8	6.25	8.09
Clarifying Toner	8.5	6.25	8.26

[a]Source: ACNielsen

Exhibit 8B Competitive Cleansers Pricing: Trade and Everyday Average Retail Drug Stores

	Size (oz)	Trade Price	Everyday Average Retail[a]
Cleansers			
Procter & Gamble—Olay			
Foaming Face Wash	6.78	2.12	3.17
Facial Cleansing Lotion	6.78	3.09	4.56
Refreshing Toner	7.2	2.69	3.98
Age Defying Daily Renewal	6.78	N/A	4.76
Pond's			
Cold Cream	3.5	2.78	4.09
Self Foaming Cleanser	4.0	5.03	7.44
2 in 1 Cleanser—Tube	4.0	2.79	4.22
2 in 1 Cleanser—Pump	7.0	3.88	5.60
Neutrogena			
Facial Cleanser	8.0	5.91	8.33
Deep Clean	6.0	4.10	6.07
Deep Pore	2.0	5.50	8.06
Noxzema			
Medicated Skin Care	10.0	2.68	3.71

[a]Source: ACNielsen

Exhibit 8C Competitive Daily Moisturizer Pricing: Trade and Everyday Average Retail of Chain Drug Stores

	Size (oz)	Trade Price	Everyday Average Retail[a]
Daily Moisturizers			
Procter & Gamble—Oil of Olay			
Original Beauty Fluid	4.0	5.86	6.59
Oil Free Beauty Fluid	4.0	5.86	6.65
Sensitive Skin Beauty Fluid	4.0	5.86	6.66
U/V Protectant Beauty Fluid	3.5	5.86	6.74
Original Beauty Fluid (Larger Size)	6.0	7.53	8.76
U/V Protectant Fluid (Larger Size)	5.25	7.53	9.60
Pond's			
Dry Skin Cream	11.0	5.50	8.19
Nivea			
Shine Control Mattifying Fluid	3.0	4.84	7.15
Facial Nourishing Lotion	3.0	4.58	6.87
Neutrogena			
Combination Skin	4.0	7.50	10.43

[a]Source: ACNielsen

Exhibit 8D Competitive Treatment Moisturizer Pricing: Trade and Everyday Average Retail of Chain Drug Stores

	Size (oz)	Trade Price	Everyday Average Retail[a]
Treatment Moisturizers			
Procter & Gamble—Oil of Olay			
Night of Olay	2.0	4.49	6.45
Replenishing Cream (4 SKU's by type)	2.0	4.58	8.73
Age Defying Protective Renewal Cream	2.0	N/A	7.31
Age Defying Protective Renewal Lotion	4.0	N/A	7.36
Pond's			
Age Defying Lotion (Regular or Delicate Skin)	3.0	7.80	10.99
Age Defying Lotion (Regular or Delicate Skin)	2.0	7.80	11.23
Prevent and Correct Lotion	4.25	10.80	14.94
Prevent and Correct Cream	2.5	10.80	15.20
Nivea			
Anti-Wrinkle Cream	1.7	6.13	9.22
Optimale	1.7	7.12	10.52
Neutrogena			
Healthy Skin Oil-Free Bottle	2.5	7.50	10.55

[a]Source: ACNielsen

Exhibit 9 Perceptual Map of Brand Imagery–Among Aware of Brand/Those Who Are

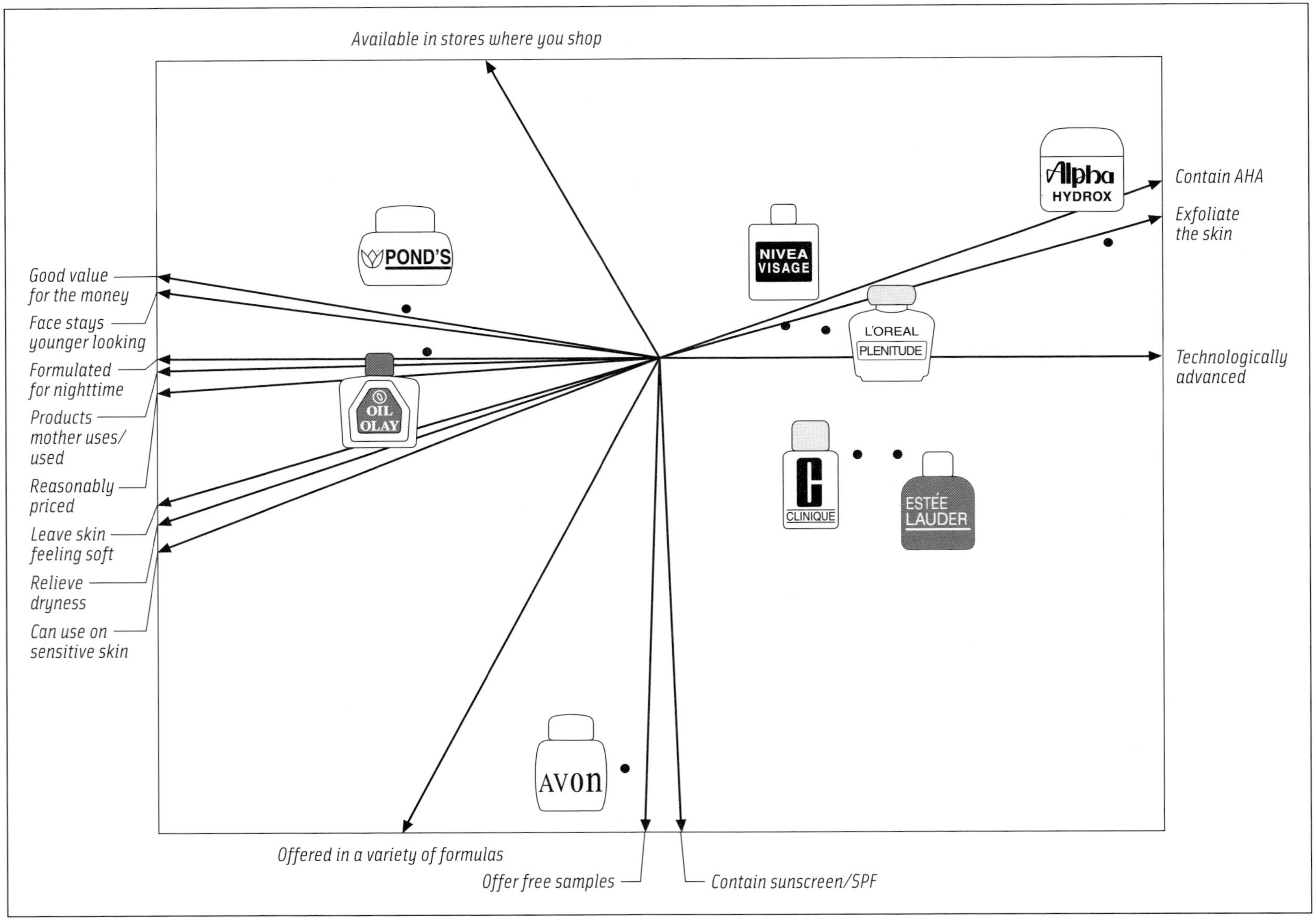
Available in stores where you shop
Contain AHA
Exfoliate the skin
Technologically advanced
Good value for the money
Face stays younger looking
Formulated for nighttime
Products mother uses/ used
Reasonably priced
Leave skin feeling soft
Relieve dryness
Can use on sensitive skin
Offered in a variety of formulas
Offer free samples
Contain sunscreen/SPF
POND'S
NIVEA VISAGE
Alpha HYDROX
L'OREAL PLENITUDE
OIL OLAY
CLINIQUE
ESTÉE LAUDER
AVON

Exhibit 10 Perceptual Map of Brand Imagery–Among Aware of Brand/Those Who Are

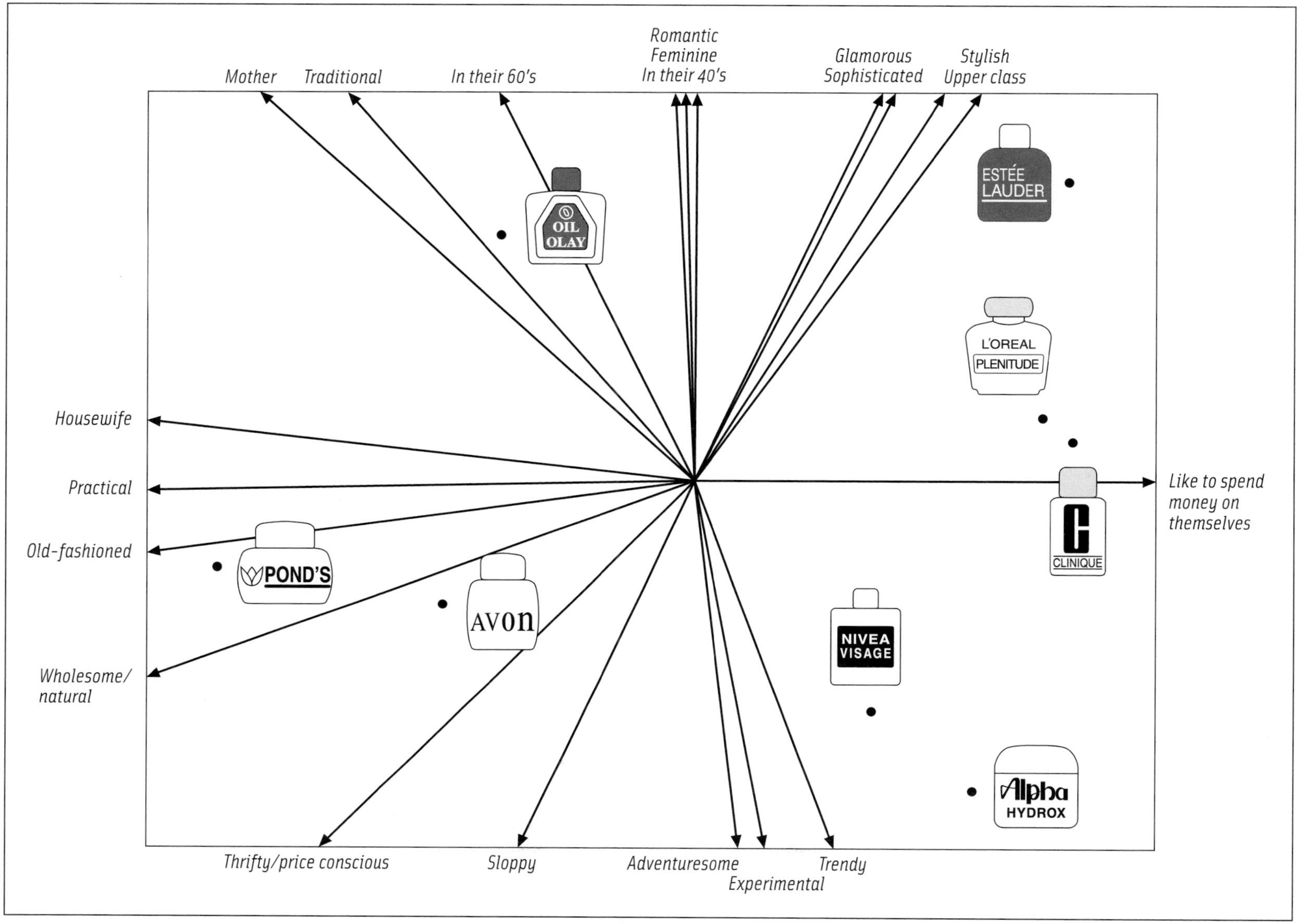

Exhibit 11 Brand Development: Familiarity and Experience with L'Oréal Plénitude versus Competition

Base: Total Respondents (3506)	% Aware %	% Ever Tried %	Conversion Ratio—Awareness to Trial	% Currently Used %	Retention Ratio—Triers to Current Users
Oil of Olay	96	77	80	34	44
Pond's	93	52	56	16	31
Estée Lauder	92	35	38	11	31
Mary Kay	92	48	52	16	33
Avon	91	68	75	23	34
Revlon	90	35	39	10	29
Clinique	82	38	46	13	34
L'Oréal Plénitude	78	23	29	7	30
Nivea/Nivea Visage	76	26	34	6	23
Lancôme	71	17	24	5	29
Alpha Hydrox	66	12	18	5	42

Exhibit 12A Front of Revitalift Package

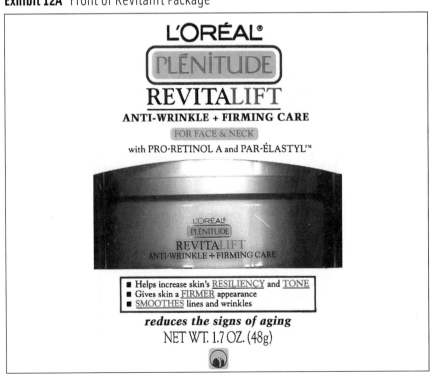

Exhibit 12B Back of Revitalift Package

The Skincare Laboratories of L'Oréal Paris have created an advanced treatment to combat the signs of aging: Plénitude **Revitalift** Anti-Wrinkle + Firming Care for Face and Neck—a multi-performance formula that provides the specific solutions mature skin needs. Plénitude **Revitalift** helps to minimize the look of fine lines and wrinkles while increasing firmness.

1. INCREASES RESILIENCY
   Formulated with Par-Élastyl™, a unique ingredient, **Revitalift** helps increase skin's resiliency, flexibility and tone.

2. FIRMS
   While improving skin's resiliency, **Revitalift** gives skin a firmer and plumper appearance.

3. SMOOTHES
   With Pro-Retinol A, a Vitamin A precursor, and Vitamin E, this cream softens skin's surface texture and visibly smoothes lines and wrinkles.

As a complete treatment, **Revitalift** Anti-Wrinkle + Firming Care reduces noticeable signs of aging, adds firmness and spring to help make skin appear younger looking. With continued use, skin becomes more resilient, smoother and radiant. Contains sunscreen.

APPLICATION This silky, emollient formula is absorbed quickly without a greasy afterfeel. Apply generously to face and neck. Use morning and evening, alone or under makeup.

L'ORÉAL PROMISE Plénitude gentleness has been dermatologically tested in L'Oréal's Skincare Laboratories.

Exhibit 13 Print Ad for Revitalift

Exhibit 14 Plenitude Consumer Sell Through First Quarter 1996

	Size	$ Volume	$ % Change vs. Year Ago	Dollar Share	Unit Volume	Unit % Change vs. Year Ago	Unit Share
Total Plénitude (w/o Makeup Remover)		**$25,807,235**	**32%**	**11.3**	**2,839,909**	**25%**	**6.3**
Revitalift Face	1.7 oz.	5,679,850	+ +	2.5	513,824	+ +	1.1
Eye Defense	.5 oz.	2,297,597	10%	1.0	211,237	10%	0.5
Wrinkle Defense Cream	1.4 oz.	2,193,248	3%	1.0	202,831	3%	0.5
Excell Cream	1.4 oz.	1,580,213	-14%	0.7	151,525	-14%	0.3
Hydra-Renewal Cream Jar	1.7 oz.	1,559,063	-1%	0.7	170,000	0%	0.4
Advanced Overnight Replenisher	1.7 oz.	1,376,694	6%	0.6	125,698	4%	0.3
Excell Lotion	4.0 oz.	1,232,140	+ +	0.5	116,869	+ +	0.3
Acive Daily Moisture Lotion SPF 15	4.0 oz.	1,064,569	354%	0.5	149,734	368%	0.3
Acive Daily Moisture Lotion	4.0 oz.	929,210	217%	0.4	136,079	233%	0.3
Firming Facial Serum	1.0 oz.	760,880	11%	0.3	56,408	8%	0.1
Hydrating Cleansing Cream	5.0 oz.	731,330	43%	0.3	110,573	45%	0.2
Clarify A3–Toner	8.5 oz.	692,416	+ +	0.3	89,226	+ +	0.2
Eye Makeup Remover	4.0 oz.	644,700	N/A	N/A	90,550	N/A	N/A
Clarify A3–Mask	2.8 oz.	638,049	+ +	0.3	83,050	+ +	0.2
Acive Daily Moisture Lotion Oil Free	4.0 oz.	622,619	232%	0.3	90,349	245%	0.2
Hydrating Floral Toner	8.5 oz.	593,784	2%	0.3	85,391	2%	0.2
Wrinkle Defense Cream Tube	1.2 oz.	546,502	2%	0.2	59,106	-3%	0.1
Hydra-Renewal Cream Tube	1.6 oz.	513,212	-18%	0.2	62,397	-18%	0.1
Deep Cleansing Gel Tube	5.0 oz.	467,872	30%	0.2	70,218	30%	0.2
Clarify A3–Cleanser	4.0 oz.	447,221	+ +	0.2	58,051	+ +	0.1

Source: ACNielsen

APPENDIX A:
PERPETUAL MAPPING

A perceptual map, such as shown in exhibits 9 and 10, depicts how consumers "see" brands or users of a brand on various dimensions. For Exhibit 9 for example, consumers were asked to rate each of the 8 brands on 15 dimensions as shown via questions such as: Indicate the extent to which you agree with the statement:

Brand _____ is "technologically advanced" where
　　1 = completely disagree; to
　　10 = completely agree.

Rating 8 brands on 15 dimensions yields 120 numbers. Perceptual mapping finds the best way to show in two dimensions the information content of the 120 numbers. Arrows pointing in the same general direction show attributes that are highly correlated with one another. Brands are plotted in space to capture best where they fall on the attributes. Since the picture is in only two dimensions not 15—it does not perfectly capture the brand's rating on all 15 dimensions but it is as near to it as can be in two dimensions.

To see where a brand falls on a given attribute, one must envision a line from the brand perpendicular to the attribute. For example, consider the attribute "Available in Stores where You Shop" and Pond's from Exhibit 9.

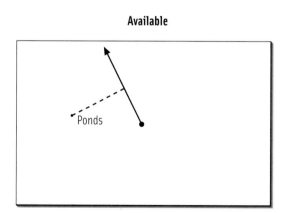

Available

The dotted line projects Pond's back on to the "availability" attribute.

To see where Clinique falls on availability we have to extend the "available" vector back through the origin and then drop the line perpendicular to the vector. Perceptual maps usually extend a vector from the origin in only one direction so the map does not become too cluttered up.

Available

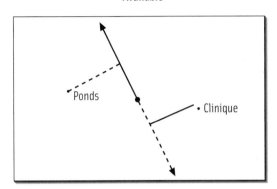

Thus, we see that Pond's is rated higher on the dimension "Available in Stores where You Shop" than Clinique. Plénitude would fall in between these two on availability. Pond's is highest on availability and Avon is lowest.

Perceptual mapping usually assumes that consumers "see" brands in a similar way. One respondent may prefer Pond's over Alpha Hydrox and another the reverse. But both agree that Pond's is high on "good value for the money" and low on "technologically advanced." Thus, generally a map aggregates across respondents and presents a general view of the market.

Basically, perceptual mapping takes the brand by attribute ratings of all respondents and portrays that data in the most faithful way but in just two dimensions so we can "see easily the relationships between brands. For more details, see "Perceptual Mapping: A Manager's Guide," HBS note 9-590-121 by Robert J. Dolan.

Going to Market

Choosing the right way to both generate and fulfill customer demand involves designing a marketing system and managing that system over time. As introduced in the "Going to Market" note, which opens this module, often it is economically efficient for a firm to seek partners to accomplish some going-to-market tasks. However, while partners often have naturally occurring incentives to cooperate in generating sales, there also are possible conflicts that need to be anticipated and managed.

The first three cases in the module set out three different channel structures and management issues. "U.S. Pioneer Electronics Corporation" is a classic case that presents a very simple channel structure: Pioneer distributes its stereo products through a large number of retailers to consumers. However, even a simple channel like this can have struggles for power. The case also shows how going-to-market decisions interact with other marketing decisions, as Pioneer's extensive advertising and resulting brand equity impact how the retail channel operates.

"Rohm and Haas (A): New Product Marketing Strategy" presents a more complex channel situation, typical of one found in an industrial selling situation that requires customer education. A new Rohm and Haas product has not sold well, even though the company thinks it is great. The case allows you to figure out the value of a product to a customer, which in turn helps in diagnosing problem areas. The key question is how to give the right incentives to those you need to work in the system.

The third case, "Pizza Hut, Inc.," presents a different approach to motivation because Pizza Hut is a franchise operation. Here, the rules of partner conduct are specified in a contract—but, as the case illustrates, a contract cannot anticipate all scenarios. As home delivery becomes more important in the pizza industry, Pizza Hut corporate wants to move in that direction but finds mixed reactions from franchisees, who have been granted exclusive rights to defined territories. To implement home delivery effectively, Pizza Hut needs to amend the franchise agreements. How can the company get needed cooperation from powerful franchises that initially are opposed to the idea?

The next two cases address very contemporary channel issues. The issue of whether a company should integrate the Internet into its operation is the focus of "HP Consumer Products Business Organization: Distributing Printers via the Internet"—but with a twist. Hewlett-Packard (HP) has become a leader in the consumer printer business, partly due to its great retail relationships. Using the Internet as a channel, however, could bring HP into conflict with its retail partners. Can the company utilize the new channel efficiently, without destroying its existing channels?

"Priceline.com: Name Your Own Price" presents the operations of a new intermediary in the distribution of airline tickets and other products. The Internet gave birth to Priceline and its novel buyer-driven commerce model. The case allows us to analyze Priceline's underlying economic rationale (or lack of it) in a number of product categories.

These two cases—"HP Consumer Products..." and "Priceline.com: Name Your Own Price"—provide a good understanding of the impact of the Internet on going-to-market decisions.

The final case, "Biopure Corporation," offers a chance to put together all the knowledge developed in Part III to design and set the rules for managing a channel. Biopure is essentially starting with a blank slate. Its first product, artificial blood for dogs, has just been approved for sale. The company has no existing channels and so no constraints on its decisions. Should Biopure develop its own sales force to sell direct to customers, or should it forge partnerships with distributors to help get the new product off the ground?

Part III presents both classic and emerging issues relating to going to market. We see where channel conflicts arise, how power is created and used, and how customer education requirements impact the optimal design. We also see the opportunities afforded by the Internet and the challenges in integrating it with existing channel mechanisms.

GOING TO MARKET

As defined in the Note on Marketing Strategy (598–061), the marketing channel is the set of mechanisms or network via which a firm "goes to market." Figure A shows four major classes of functions this network typically serves. The channel first has to generate demand for a product/service, then fulfill that demand and provide for after-the-sale service. Finally, the channel often serves a useful function in transmitting feedback from the customer base back to the manufacturer.

When we think about "going to market" we have to consider what each of the functions will specifically entail, and who will do them—the manufacturer or a chosen partner such as a distributor or retailer. Very different "go to market" systems can be found in the marketplace. For example:

- Knoll Furniture, a leading maker of high-end office furniture systems, uses its own salesforce to generate demand from large accounts. Demand fulfillment takes place through a dealer network.
- Avon Products generated $5 billion in sales in 1997 selling through 2.6 million sales representatives worldwide. Selling mostly cosmetics and fragrances, these reps are independent agents, not employees of Avon, who work part-time selling to female customers on a door-to-door basis.

Figure A Market Channel Tasks

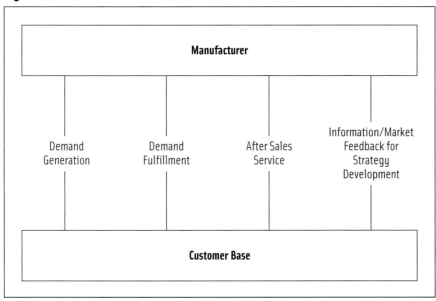

Professor Robert J. Dolan prepared this note as the basis for class discussion rather than to illustrate either effective or ineffective handling of an administrative situation.

- Tupperware follows a similar direct selling model for its food storage containers, utilizing 950,000 independent Tupperware "consultants" worldwide. These consultants sell via the "party plan" in which potential customers gather at the home of a hostess for refreshments, product demonstration, and product ordering.

- The Gap, Inc. designs all its own products which it sells through over 2,000 company-owned retail stores. It recently moved into electronic retailing opening the "Gap Online" store at *www.gap.com.* It outsources manufacturing, purchasing from 1200 suppliers, but manages the "going-to-market" phase entirely itself.

- BMW, on the other hand, goes-to-market through partners, about 300 franchised dealers selling its automobiles in the United States. The dealers and BMW share responsibility for demand generation. BMW designs and implements national advertising. Dealers provide for product display and convenient testing by customers. Dealers fulfill demand, delivering vehicles to customers, and provide local after-the-sale service.

- Compaq Computer sells primarily through third-party resellers. A systems integrator may obtain a Compaq computer and package it with other equipment to sell a system to a customer. Like the Gap, Compaq has recently added a direct on-line selling capability.

Due to differences in the market situation, these manufacturers have seen fit to "go-to-market" in different ways.

The go-to-market approach may vary even within a firm for different customer segments. The firm may choose "multiple channels." The Gap's setup of an electronic store on the Web is an example of this strategy. The not-time-pressured customer who enjoys shopping visits the company store at the mall; while the time-pressured shopper visits the on-line store. A given individual may find a different channel more efficient depending on the buying occasion, e.g. a new sweater meriting a store visit, a simple blue jean replenishment order for a known size and style being best handled "on the Web."

This note expands on the treatment of "Marketing Channels" in the Note on Marketing Strategy. As noted there, and suggested by these examples, the two key issues in "going to market" are (i) designing the network, i.e., who is on the team and what do we want each to do, and (ii) managing the network. In the short term, this means figuring out how do we motivate each team member to do the desired tasks. In the longer term, it means how do we evolve and hold the system together in light of new products, evolution of the customer base (e.g., formation of buying groups) and new communication technologies such as the Internet.

Channel Design

Not too long ago, the most common approach to channel design was a very simple one. It was made simple by two assumptions which are no longer tenable. The first was that you should reach all your customers the same way. The thinking was that "dual distribution" schemes were unworkable, e.g., selling to some customers via a company salesforce and to others via a distributor was asking for trouble; similarly having your own retail store on the streets of Manhattan and relying on retailers for coverage of less densely populated areas was a route to continual conflict. The second assumption was that if you signed up a channel partner between yourself and the end user you basically did a "baton pass" of the entire marketing job to that intermediary. A manufacturer using a distributor shipped product to that distribution and the distributor was responsible for generating leads, qualifying customers, conducting the selling process, closing the sale and delivering the product.

Now, however, the fragmentation of most firms' customer base has ruled out the "one size fits all" channel strategy. For example, the boom in working at home has created a home office furniture business which those traditionally supplying large corporations find too significant to ignore. And, it's obvious you shouldn't sell to American Express and one of its cardholders in the same way. New customers have different information needs from the installed base. At the same time, the options for reaching customers have expanded. Quick delivery of a product in response to a customer used to necessitate a distributor holding stock in local areas. Now, the same can be provided by a single inventory point and a contract with Federal Express.

Instead of a one-size-fits-all, baton-pass mentality we need to break up "the market" into segments and "the marketing job" into its component pieces, having the concept that different mechanisms could be the best way of accomplishing certain tasks for certain segments.

The first step in channel design is to ask: (1a) what segments of the market should be considered and then (1b) *for each segment individually* ask what tasks need to be performed and what are the feasible options for doing them? Moriarty and Moran[1] set out a process for designing "hybrid systems" in which different tasks are accomplished by different players.

In their example, they break demand generation down into four subtasks:

1. Lead generation
2. Lead qualification
3. Pre-sale activity persuading target customer
4. Closing the sale

Their terminology for the two other key channel tasks is:

5. Post-sale service
6. On-going account management

Using these basic tasks as a guide, one should develop a more specific set for each segment. For example, consider an office furniture manufacturer. As step 1a, he elects to serve both the "at home" segment and the large corporate segment. Research shows the following about the tasks needed to be accomplished in "obtaining and maintaining" the "at home" buyer.

- *Preliminary*
  - 1. Attract Attention as Potential Supplier
  - 2. Position Company as Ergonomic Experts and One-Stop Shop for All Needs (desk, chair, files, etc.)

- *Present the Offering*
  - 3. Describe Available Products
  - 4. Demonstrate Products
  - 5. Communicate Prices

- *Sale-to-Install*
  - 6. Accept Order. Provide Means of Tracking Order Status
  - 7. Provide Rapid Delivery ("at home" buyer typically does not pre-plan)
  - 8. Enable Easy Assembly/Installation

- *Post/Sale*
  - 9. Manage Warranty Service Issues
  - 10. Sell Accessories
  - 11. Extend Credit

---

[1]Rowland T. Moriarty and Ursula Moran, "Managing Hybrid Marketing Systems," *Harvard Business Review,* November–December 1990.

Moriarty and Moran suggest using "The Hybrid Grid" to support decision-making on how tasks should be accomplished. The grid, as shown Figure B, is a map of the tasks to be accomplished as the columns and the ways of possibly accomplishing the task as the rows. Each column has one "X" placed in it to show the mechanism via which the task moving the customer through the purchase process may be effected.

At the start of the process, one should think expansively about the possible matrix rows, i.e., the options for providing for specific task accomplishment. For our furniture seller, for example, task #4 "Demonstrate Products" may initially suggest the need for a customer visit to retail outlet. But, with new technology, perhaps an adequate "demonstration" could be done virtually on the Web. Or, if convinced of the power of an in-home demonstration, one could induce it by offering free delivery and return if the product is not satisfactory.

Imagine that the best plan for accomplishing the eleven at home buyer tasks are as follows:

Tasks 1–2: Advertising In Mass Magazines

Tasks 3 and 5: Website Preferred; Catalog For Those Without Web Access

Task 4: Free In-Home Trial

Task 6: Limit Variety Available To Allow Delivery From Inventory And Use Federal Express Or Other Express Shipper

Tasks 7, 8, 9: Company Telemarketing/800 Number

Task 10: Direct Mail (Using Addresses From Shipping Data)

Task 11: MasterCard/Visa

In this model, the firm did not "pass the baton" of its marketing job to another entity. Rather it kept 9 of the 11 functions itself, and outsourced two: task 6 to Federal Express and task 11 to the credit card companies.

Obviously, the approach for our furniture maker to serve a large corporate account moving into a new headquarters building would be quite different. The economics of a large order allow for different selling techniques, but more fundamentally the tasks which need to be accomplished are different, e.g., they might be:

1. Get On Short List For This Job (any account of this size would already be aware of company and its positioning vis-à-vis competitors)

Figure B The Hybrid Grid

Marketing Channel/Method	Tasks to Be Accomplished				
	1	2	3	4	········
A.		X			
B.	X				
C.			X		
D.				X	
.					
.					
.					

2. Present the Product Line

3. Demonstrate Company Ability to Customize a Solution to Client's Needs

4. Work with Client's Architect/Designer to Specify Furniture Solution, including mock-up of Furniture at Customer Location

5. Negotiate Price/Terms

6. Facilitate Disposal of Old Furniture

7. Accept Order

8. Work with Other Vendors to Develop Installation Plan

9. Respond to Changes Made to Order from Time of Order to Delivery

10. Deliver and Install Systems

11. Maintain Systems

12. Sell Accessories and Additional Systems

13. Upgrade as New Products Are Introduced

14. Extend Credit

Again, the Hybrid Grid should be used to specify the possible mechanisms to accomplishing these tasks. This helps to show key handoffs and cooperations. For example, step 2 may be best achieved by a visit to the local dealer showroom. Then steps 3–7 are to be accomplished by the company salesperson without any dealer input.

This example we have worked through is typical in the sense that the different segments have very different marketing systems set up to serve them. In the case here, the at-home buyer and large corporation are so different that the systems are unlikely to come into conflict with one another. They could, if the firm made the mistake of offering a lower price on an item on its Website for the "at home" buyer than it offered to the customer buying large quantities of the same item. But generally, this example's two segments seem to be distinct enough that the manner of servicing one would have little impact on the other. Such is not always the case however. Once the tentative assessments have been made at the segment level, they have to be rolled up into a system view for potential channel conflicts.

As an example, Figure C depicts a marketing system in which the manufacturer has a multiple channel strategy, i.e., it "goes to market" through its own salesforce calling on large accounts and uses distributors to call on smaller accounts. Potential conflict area #1 is that between the company salesforce and distributors. A distributor may regard a potential account as rightfully his to serve and resent the loss in margin opportunity due to the company's serving the large customers directly.

A specific example of this type of conflict in channels was Compaq's November 1998 decision to sell computers directly to small business customers via the Internet. The new Prosigna line was offered via the Compaq DirectPlus on-line service. Compaq was already selling through 44,000 dealers and described the addition of the direct channel for the segment as a melding of traditional sales channels and the Internet, offering customers

Figure C Three Types of Channel Conflict

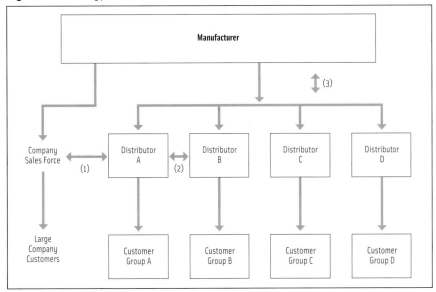

a choice. However, one commentator noted "Customer choice is great, but can they really continue this highwire tension between channel sales and the direct model?"[2]

In the Compaq case, the potential conflict stemmed from a change in the marketing channel. Dealers felt an entitlement to the customers and that Compaq was now bypassing them and reaching customers directly. Conflict issues of type #1 can arise even at the set-up of a marketing channel from scratch. Often a firm perceives two segments in the market: a price sensitive one and a service sensitive one. In an attempt to serve the price sensitive segment, it distributes through "no frills" channels which keep costs low by performing little market education and compete on price. The service-sensitive segment is to be served in a higher cost, more service intensive channel. Conflicts arise when there is "leakage" between the segments. For example, a customer gets his/her education needs met in a specialty store, then goes to buy at a discount outlet or mail-order. Some service customers will not desert their channel, but use the price they come to see in the "no-frills" channel as a negotiating device with the full-service provider.

Conflict area #2 shown in Figure C is between the same type of entities in the channel structure, here two distributors. In the figure, we show the manufacturer has chosen to have four independent distributors. This is the

company's answer to the question of channel breadth, i.e., how intensely to cover the market at a particular stage in the channel. We saw real world examples above.

For example, Tupperware had to figure out how many sales "consultants" it should have running parties. Too few would not generate enough sales for the company; too many would have individuals competing directly for too small a business potential. The Gap set its strategy of owning its own retail stores and then had to decide how many of each type it would have. Even in the same product category, firms can choose different intensity levels. For example, when Nissan set up distribution for its new Infiniti automobile, it chose to limit the number of dealers to just over 100 despite the fact that BMW and Mercedes each had over 350 each in the United States. The basic alternatives with respect to channel breadth or intensity of market coverage are:

1. Exclusive distribution

2. Selective distribution

3. Intensive distribution

In exclusive distribution, the manufacturer establishes only one reseller in each region to carry the product. Yamaha pianos are an example of this policy. Exclusivity is granted by the manufacturer in the hope that it will induce strong selling support by the reseller. The cost is that, with an exclusive policy, the consumer must be willing to seek out the one outlet in his or her area carrying the brand.

[2]R. Guth, "Compaq Goes After Direct-Sales Model," *Infoworld*, November 16, 1998.

The middle ground between exclusivity and seeking the maximum coverage possible is selective distribution. In selective distribution, there is more than one but a limited number of resellers in each market. Selective distribution is practiced by many higher-end clothing manufacturers, such as Perry Ellis and Bally. The purposive limiting of the number of outlets is intended to increase the support the reseller provides the brand over the case of intensive distribution. Having more than one outlet is intended to increase shopping convenience over exclusive distribution.

Finally, many manufacturers try to place their products with as many resellers as possible. For some markets, it is believed that "share of space" (i.e., retail shelf space) delivers "share of market," and, thus, the objective is to be as widely and intensively distributed as possible. Gillette razor blades, Kodak film, and Budweiser beer are examples of intensive distribution at the retail level.

Note that it is not necessarily the case that the more outlets the product is in, the better off the manufacturer is. Moving from exclusive to intensive trades off reseller support in return for easier availability of goods for the consumer.

As is usually the case in marketing, an analysis of consumer behavior is the primary input into the resolution of the channel breadth issue. Consider three examples:

1. *Shaving cream*: Shaving cream is a frequent purchase for the majority of adult males. The acquisition of a new can is a routine and unexciting event. Since the buyer most likely thinks there are a number of acceptable shaving creams, the manufacturer sees convenient availability as critical.

2. *Television set*: A television set is a relatively infrequent purchase of considerably greater expense than shaving cream. When the decision is made to buy a television set, several members of the family get involved—checking *Consumer Reports* and newspaper ads, shopping around, and generally gathering information appropriate to the importance of the decision. Since consumers do shop around, rather than just visit the most convenient outlet and buy there, there is no need for the manufacturer to be in every outlet. In fact, being in every outlet would likely be a mistake if the family relied on the retail clerk for information. Intensive distribution is justified for the shaving cream because the only retail support required is shelf space. However, when strong point-of-purchase personal selling is required,

going beyond selective distribution would jeopardize the required support.

3. *Automobile*: For some makes, the consumer behavior may be like that just described for television sets. However, for a specialty item, such as a Porsche Boxster, it is likely that the purchaser has a very strong brand preference even before the acquisition process begins. Thus, convenience of outlet is not a consideration, and the buyer will go just about anywhere to get the brand he or she insists on. Since the car is purchased infrequently and is an extremely important purchase, the buyer can behave this way. In this event, the permissibility of relatively inconvenient outlets indicates exclusive distribution. (Note that some provision may have to be made for less than exclusively distributed warranty servicing of the car.)

These examples illustrate a categorization of goods frequently used in marketing. Our shaving cream, television, and exotic car represent a "convenience good," a "shopping good," and a "specialty good," respectively. Of course, no item can be definitely classified as any one of these three types for all consumers. However, the following is a useful guideline:

Convenience good $\rightarrow$ Intensive distribution
Shopping good $\rightarrow$ Selective distribution
Specialty good $\rightarrow$ Exclusive distribution

Turning back to the conflicts of Figure C, whereas the first two types of conflict shown are horizontal, the third is vertical, i.e., between successive levels in the marketing system. Channel members are interdependent in the sense that their joint efforts determine the level of sales achieved for the product. Consequently, there is a natural incentive to cooperate. However, there is also an inherent stimulus to conflict. Each party would like to see the other "do more" to improve the sales situation. A distributor wishes the manufacturer would spend more on national advertising to set the stage better for the distributors' salesforce as it calls on customers. The manufacturer wishes that the distributor would invest in better training for the salesforce and outfit them with the state-of-the-art selling tools.

Researchers[3] have identified the major sources of conflict as parties' differences in:

[3]L.W. Stern, A.I. El-Ansary, and A.T. Coughlan, *Marketing Channels*, 5th ed., Prentice-Hall, 1996.

1. Goals
2. Understanding of proper scope of activities
3. Perceptions of reality

An obvious difference in goals between a manufacturer and a distributor is each is focused on its own sales not the other's. The manufacturer may see an opportunity to expand its sales by opening up a new channel like the Internet. The distributor sees this as cannibalizing sales it would otherwise make. A distributor typically incorporates the manufacturer's product with lines from other manufacturers. To suit the distributor's purpose, the line may take on a strategic role that does not serve the best interests of the manufacturer.

These conflicts are natural occurrences between two business entities each trying to serve its stakeholders. Contracts can be set up to mitigate goal incompatibility problems. These might specifically address what each party will contribute to the joint effort, how the effort will be monitored, and the division of the system profits contingent upon inputs each party provided.

The second related major source of conflict is differences in understanding about the scope of activity, viz. (a) the functions which each party will carry out and (b) the target population for whom they will perform these functions. For example, a distributor may see it as the company's job to open new accounts which are then turned over to the distributor for service; meanwhile, the company expects the distributor salesforce to be "cold calling" and can't understand why the customer list is not seeing new additions each month.

A second key scope issue is the population served, defined either geographically or by account type. This is basically the issue of "who owns the account?" If a copier manufacturer serves the City of Boston direct (through its own salesforce) but has a distributor for outlying districts (e.g., Cambridge) whose account is Harvard Business School, physically located in Boston but part of Harvard University based in Cambridge? The hybrid grid model described earlier can be a useful mechanism

for getting all channel partners to understand how the overall system is designed to work and their role in it.

The third source of conflict is simple different perceptions of the reality of a situation. For example, the distributor with its salesforce "on-the-street" every day may see the performance gap that has developed between the manufacturer's product and those of competitors in the eyes of customers. But, the manufacturer still believes it is delivering superior quality. As another example, the manufacturer, tracking unit sales, sees a downward trend while the distributor sees a rapidly declining overall market in which it has more than held market share for the manufacturer.

Effective channel management requires recognition of these potential threats to the system's working as it should. Some issues can be avoided by carefully drawing up a specific understanding about roles, duties, performance measurement, and payoffs. The key is to have all members see the interdependence of system members and to arrange communications and contracts so that each party perceives a "fair" return to their value added to the system.

Summary

Marketing system design issues are critical and can be a source of competitive advantage. Some companies are, in fact, defined more by their marketing system than their products. For example, the innovation and phenomenal success of L'Eggs pantyhose was not so much in the product as in the distribution through supermarkets and drugstores with efficient display racks.

A marketing system also needs to be examined for its adaptability to new market opportunities and new technologies. Tupperware has, for example, banned its "consultants" from using the Internet for sales, seeing no way to integrate the new technology into their system and instead regarding it as a threat to their business model. Because channels involve complex legal relationships, they can be difficult to adjust and flexibility should be a criterion in judging a proposed structure.

U.S. PIONEER ELECTRONICS CORPORATION

In fall 1977 Bernie Mitchell, president of U.S. Pioneer Electronics, placed an ad featuring a portrait of William Shakespeare in several trade magazines. The ad was an open letter from Shakespeare and Mitchell to several dissident dealers franchised to sell Japanese-made Pioneer products in the United States.[1] It alleged that a few dealers had resorted to "disparagement of Pioneer products and 'bait and switch' advertising" and threatened dealer investigations to protect Pioneer's reputation (see Exhibit 1).

Mitchell hoped these "unjustifiable practices" were the sporadic misconduct of only "an unwise few" and could be dealt with individually. If, however, they represented an overall erosion of dealer support for Pioneer products, he was determined (1) to take immediate steps to prevent further erosion, and (2) to establish a new long-run distribution strategy to insure U.S. Pioneer's continued leadership in the hi-fi industry.

Industry Background

The U.S. hi-fi industry was started in the 1960s by a few engineers who, according to industry legend, left their positions (mostly in the aerospace industry) to pursue their hobby of building amplifiers and speakers in their garages and basements. By the late 1960s, larger component manufacturers were beginning to broaden their product lines.[2] For instance, Scott, previously identified solely with electronics, was building its reputation in the speaker business. Sherwood, also an electronics manufacturer, introduced an automatic turntable in 1969. KLH, which had started out making speakers, turned to stereo compacts about the same time.[3]

Japanese hi-fi manufacturers such as Pioneer, Kenwood, Sansui, and Teac also entered the U.S. market in the late 1960s while most original founders of the hi-fi companies, who had operated in a club-like business atmosphere, were leaving the industry.

The 1970s saw a new attitude among hi-fi manufacturers. As Mitchell told one trade magazine reporter:

> Six years ago . . . we only wanted to sell our product to a certain select group of people who had to qualify somehow intellectually and technologically. We didn't want to sell . . . to kids or to ordinary people, only to superpeople. It was a real elitist attitude, and terribly dangerous. We've changed it from an elitist business that didn't really want to grow to an industry that has some pride in itself and its products and says, "These products are so good we won't be happy until we tell everybody." (*Crawdaddy*, July 1976)

Company Background

Pioneer Electronics Corporation was founded in Tokyo in 1938. It started with capital of $235 and by 1977 had expanded to $843 million in worldwide sales. Overseas sales surpassed domestic sales in 1974 and, in 1977, accounted for 65% of the total. Net income (pretax) in 1977 was nearly $61 million.

U.S. Pioneer was established in March 1966 under Ken Kai, vice president, then 26 years old. He had joined the parent company in Tokyo after graduating from col-

---

This case was prepared by Assistant Professor Hirotaka Takeuchi with the assistance of William Falkson (MBA '78) as the basis for class discussion rather than to illustrate either effective or ineffective handling of an administrative situation.

---

[1]The words *retailers* and *dealers* are used interchangeably in this case.

[2]Components were combinations of different audio equipment, which reproduced sound highly faithful (i.e., high-fidelity or hi-fi sound) to the original record or tape. Consumers created component systems of their choice by combining (a) an inlet source, such as a turntable, tape deck, or FM tuner; (b) a control center, such as an amplifier or receiver, which was an amplifier and FM tuner combined into one unit; and (c) an outlet, such as speakers. In audio terminology, receivers and amplifiers were called "electronics."

[3]Compacts were preassembled audio systems, usually consisting of two units—one containing a turntable, receiver, and/or tape player and the other a pair of speakers. A compact system usually cost less and was smaller than a component system. It reproduced stereo sound (i.e., sound reproduced through two separate channels) but not necessarily high-fidelity sound.

lege and was sent to New York a year later as Pioneer's U.S. liaison. In 1966 U.S. Pioneer had less than $200,000 in sales and fewer than 30 dealers.

Bernie Mitchell joined the company in 1970. An economist by training and a music buff, as well as a member of the boards of directors of the New Jersey Symphony and the Metropolitan Opera, he had worked previously with Westinghouse, Toshiba, and Concord Electronics.

To help U.S. Pioneer grow, Mitchell and Kai took on the task of developing the market—making more people aware of and knowledgeable about hi-fi products. U.S. Pioneer sponsored hi-fi shows on college campuses and became the first hi-fi company to advertise in such magazines as *Playboy, National Lampoon,* and the *New Yorker.* These ads featured music, sports, and other celebrities.

The company also strengthened its distribution network. U.S. Pioneer was supplied by its parent in Japan. Commission sales representatives sold to its retail dealers. In 1972 U.S. Pioneer had six independent sales representative offices, which sold only Pioneer products (with the exception of accessories, complementary items, and very high-priced lines of electronics that did not directly compete with Pioneer). Each office served a given region and had from four to seven salespeople, each earning an average annual salary of $20,000. The sales force assisted retailers with merchandising and display, store operations, and sales training. By 1975 U.S. Pioneer had added ten independent sales representative offices and four company-owned offices—in New York, Washington, D.C., Florida, and Missouri. These "captive" offices were paid the same commission as the independents, but were not allowed to carry product lines of direct or indirect competitors.[4]

By 1977 the number of retail outlets carrying Pioneer products had grown to almost 3,600 from approximately 500 in 1970. Retailers had to sign franchise agreements with U.S. Pioneer. Mitchell believed they did so unhesitatingly because the company's strong national and local cooperative advertising created considerable consumer pull. U.S. Pioneer allocated 5% of its sales to local ads featuring its products. In addition, the firm offered dealers attractive gross margins and credit terms.

---

[4]Before 1974, U.S. Pioneer sales representative offices received a 10% commission. In 1974 the rate was reduced to 5%, comparable with that of other manufacturers.

Fair Trade[5] versus Free Market

FTC Action

Just as market expansion and distribution building were starting to generate higher net sales ($80 million in 1974), the Federal Trade Commission (FTC) issued a complaint against U.S. Pioneer and three other competitors. It alleged that Sansui, Sherwood, Teac, and U.S. Pioneer (1) granted dealerships to retailers only if they agreed to maintain suggested retail prices, (2) directed their sales representatives to report on retailers who failed to maintain such prices, and (3) delayed shipments to retailers who cut prices. These practices violated Section 5 of the Federal Trade Commission Act, which prohibited "unfair methods of competition . . . and unfair or deceptive acts or practices in commerce." Their effect, the FTC charged, was to inflate consumer prices.

Consent Decree

In August 1975 the four companies signed consent decrees with the FTC. They did not admit guilt, but did promise not to engage in the alleged practices. Specifically, they were prohibited from fair-trading their products for five years in the 21 states where this practice was still permitted and from using suggested list prices for two years in any part of the country. They also could not ask consumers the price of purchased products on warranty registration forms. Finally, the companies were required to distribute copies of the consent order to all their dealers and to give any dealer whose franchise had been terminated an opportunity to regain it.

---

[5]Fair-trade (or resale price maintenance) laws permitted a manufacturer or distributor of trademarked products to determine their resale prices. Although on the surface such laws seemed to support a manufacturer's desire to influence retail prices, they had initially been advocated by small, independent retailers seeking protection from direct price competition by large chains. The first such state law was passed in 1931, and by 1941 all but three states had such laws. In 13 states a nonsigner clause bound all retailers selling a fair-traded product to the contract if one retailer in the state signed an agreement. The Miller-Tydings Act, passed in 1937, applied resale price maintenance to interstate commerce.

Fair-trade practice and enforcement began to decline steadily in the early 1950s. By 1975 fair trade was being used only for certain brands of hi-fi equipment, television sets, jewelry, bicycles, clothing, cosmetics, and kitchenware. Major efforts to repeal state laws started in 1974. In December 1975, the Consumer Goods Pricing Act terminated interstate fair-trade regulations.

U.S. Pioneer's Response

Asked why U.S. Pioneer decided not to contest the FTC decree, Mitchell replied:

> I don't mind being a crusader. In fact, I kind of enjoy it. But I like to crusade for something that makes some long-term sense.
>
> The FTC is asking us not to violate the law. It has never been our intention to violate the law. They are asking that we no longer fair trade our products. We had already unilaterally made the decision that fair trade wasn't viable anymore anyhow. . . . The third thing they are asking us is that we not conspire to fix prices, either among dealers or among ourselves, and we had no intention of doing that.
>
> We did try to fix retail prices at the dealer level as long as fair trade lasted; that was the purpose of fair trade statutes. When we fair traded, we did it pretty darn well. But when we decided to go off fair trade, we decided we were going to be the best there was at free market practices. (*Electronics Retailing*, October 1975)

To implement this new goal, Pioneer replaced the price sheet in effect during fair trade (see Exhibit 2) with a list that replaced the words "fair trade resale price" with "approximate nationally advertised value" and added optional retail prices under gross margins of 15%, 20%, 25%, 30%, 35%, 40%, and 45% (see Exhibit 3).

According to *Home Furnishings Daily* (August 27, 1975), "Most of the dealers and manufacturers contacted scorned [Pioneer's] list because they felt it was, in the words of one manufacturer, 'an open invitation to cut the hell out of prices.'" Mitchell said in the same article that the initial response was fear and that dealers did not understand the significance of the change from fair-trade to free-market prices.

> Too often, under the fair-trade environment, dealers felt, "If we have a very fine mix of products, and people come in and we tell them wonderful stories about each of those products, they will tell us which products they want. They'll sort of self-sell in an enlightened environment."
>
> I don't really think that's a very good way to run a business. Dealers have to identify what needs the consumer has, acquaint him very quickly with options, suggest an option they think he ought to take, and bear down very hard to lead him to take that option. That's called selling.

Effects of Consent Decree on Sales and Prices

The immediate impact of the consent decree, according to *Home Furnishings Daily,* was a "price war which lowered dealer profit margins to five or six percent in many parts of the country." The newspaper also said that "many retailers began to criticize manufacturers for 'abandoning' them and called for them to control the fluctuating markets." Some softening of the market, according to an FTC spokesperson, was expected as a backlash. But "prices won't stay as low as they are now and higher margins will eventually return. [In the meantime] I expect to see greater sales at discount prices and the good dealers will survive."

In 1976 retail dollar sales jumped 12.6% and unit sales increased 9.4% over the previous year (see Exhibit 4). In 1975, on the other hand, the increases had been 1.6% and 2.2%, respectively. According to Kai, the much smaller percentage increase between 1974 and 1975 probably resulted from the recession and consumer decisions to delay purchases until fair-trade laws were repealed. In New York and New Jersey repeal had been rumored as early as August 1975.

In the meantime, U.S. Pioneer net sales increased from $80 million in 1974 to $87 million in 1975. In addition, its market share increased between 1974 and 1975 in all hi-fi product categories except turntables and speakers (see Exhibit 5). All Pioneer's market share percentages in 1976 were equal to or higher than those of 1974.

Market Growth and Changes

The hi-fi market was growing, and there was evidence that buyer profiles for component parts were changing. As shown in Exhibit 6, there were fewer women, more young adults (ages 18 to 24), more Pacific area residents, more college graduates, and more households with incomes of $25,000 and over purchasing stereo component parts in 1975 than in the previous year.

Realizing a shift in buyer demographics, U.S. Pioneer undertook extensive research to determine (1) the market potential of hi-fi products compared with low-fi products, such as compacts or consoles;[6] and (2) the purchasing behavior of hi-fi component buyers.

---

[6]Consoles were preassembled all-in-one audio systems that were larger, cost more, and had generally poorer sound reproduction than most component systems.

An independent research firm found that sales of components were growing faster than sales of compacts and consoles. In sheer volume, however, compacts outsold components and consoles by a wide margin. In 1975, 3.5 million units of compacts were sold in the United States, compared with 1.5 million component systems and 400,000 consoles. To Mitchell, this meant that 3.9 million U.S. buyers were taken off the hi-fi market. Once they had purchased compacts and consoles, these customers were not expected to consider replacing them with hi-fi components for several years.

"Also, every time a compact or console is sold, you lose the potential of an additional speaker, add-on tape deck, upgraded receiver, tuner, turntable, and more," said Mitchell. The research revealed that this add-on market was larger than expected. In 1975, add-on sales accounted for 55% of total dollars spent on hi-fi components. New system sales made up the remaining 45%.

Buying Influences

Consumer research showed that buyers of different audio systems were influenced by different factors, in order of importance.

Component Buyers

1. Lifelike sound reproduction
2. Superior electronics
3. Add-on capability
4. Status symbol

Console Buyers

1. Esthetics
2. Adequate electronics
3. No involved hookup
4. A lot for the money

Compact Buyers

1. Lower price
2. Small size
3. No involved hookup
4. Ease of operation

The research also found that component buyers:

- depended heavily on advice of family and friends;
- thought they knew just enough about hi-fi components to get by (only 8% thought they knew "a lot");
- shopped around, especially for the initial purchase;
- paid either $350–400 or $650–750 for initial purchase of system;
- replaced or upgraded components approximately one to two years after their initial purchase.

New Marketing Strategy

On the basis of this research, Mitchell established the goal of "doubling the number of people owning and buying *any* brand of hi-fi components next year." He said, "We'd rather see a consumer buy a Marantz, Sansui . . . yes, and even a Technics than a fancy fruitwood console or plastic compact, both of which deliver less than true high fidelity."

To implement this goal, he asked dealers to persuade prospective compact or console buyers to consider lower-priced hi-fi components. He argued that this could be best accomplished by prominently displaying low-end components and explaining their advantages over compacts and consoles. To support this dealer effort, Pioneer introduced lower-priced components. It also allocated $6 million national advertising for 1976. Of this, $2 million was earmarked for persuading consumers that only hi-fi components produced true high-fidelity sound. Head copy for one of the ads read, "BAD SOUND IS AN UNNECESSARY EVIL." The ad referred by name to some of Pioneer's competitors—Marantz, Kenwood, and Sansui—as dedicated companies trying to reproduce high-quality sound.

Mitchell also asked dealers to use direct mail to tap the replacement and add-on markets. Ads were mailed to customers who had purchased audio systems one and two years before.

Results

Mitchell and Kai were very satisfied with their new strategy as Pioneer's sales increased from $87 million in 1975 to $135 million in 1976. Although their goal of doubling the number of hi-fi owners and buyers was not achieved, they felt that more people were buying components than compacts and consoles. The number of compact systems sold in the United States increased from 3.3 million in 1975 to 3.6 million in 1976, whereas component *unit* (not system) sales increased from 8.0 million in 1975 to 8.7 million in 1976 (see Exhibit 7).

They were also impressed by the findings of a Gallup Organization[7] consumer survey for U.S. Pioneer. This survey, conducted in the first half of 1977, measured consumer brand preference for different hi-fi component categories (receiver, FM tuner, amplifier, turntable, speaker, and tape deck). As shown in Exhibit 8, prospective component purchasers preferred Pioneer over all other brands in every category except tape decks.

Retailer Dissidence

Just as Pioneer's "franchise" with consumers was strengthening, Mitchell came across a number of reports suggesting that relationships with its franchised dealers were starting to deteriorate. His particular concern was with sales representatives' reports about dealers (1) disparaging Pioneer products by misrepresenting product specification sheets or manipulating sound demonstrations, and (2) using an illegal and unethical tactic known as "bait and switch."[8]

Pioneer Field Investigation

Disparagement of Pioneer products was spotted in continuous field work by employees (mostly part-time) who, posing as interested shoppers for Pioneer products, visited Pioneer's franchised stores, interacted with store personnel, and then prepared "shopping reports" for the company (see Exhibit 9).

In one report, a U.S. Pioneer employee visited a midwestern hi-fi specialty store and asked for a Pioneer tape deck, but was persuaded by the salesperson to buy a competing brand (see Exhibit 9). The report noted that (1) the store salesperson made a comment on how he "could produce copies of letters that dealers had written

to Pioneer complaining about service"; (2) Pioneer's tape deck (CT-F7272) was missing from its display area; (3) the store salesperson, when asked for a CT-F7272 specification sheet, handed over that of a competing brand but did not have one for Pioneer; and (4) the store salesperson set the playback sound control at maximum volume for the competing brand but at less than maximum for Pioneer.

To counter these objectionable practices, Pioneer placed the Shakespeare ad (Exhibit 1) in major trade publications to appeal to dealers. The company also asked the presidents of all its sales representative offices to identify the offenders in their territories who used the most blatant, most persistent disparagement and bait-and-switch tactics.

Audio Warehouse Suit

In July 1977, U.S. Pioneer filed a suit against Audio Warehouse, a five-store chain with 1977 sales of $10 million, and its advertising agency, both of Akron, Ohio. It charged them with using bait-and-switch tactics, advertising without sufficient inventory, and disparaging Pioneer products to customers. A temporary restraining order barred Audio Warehouse from engaging in these practices.

Ed Radford, the 34-year-old president of Audio Warehouse, told *Retail Home Furnishings* (September 26, 1977):

> Yeah, we're being sued [by U.S. Pioneer] but we're not taking this lying down—we're going to fight it. Pioneer surprised me because they got a temporary restraining order, and within one day, they had it in every newspaper in my state. As far as I'm concerned, Pioneer's trying to make me look bad. The public doesn't understand that a temporary restraining order doesn't mean anything. Anybody who puts up a bond can get one.

To prove his point, Radford (who was called "Fast Eddie" because of his hurried speech and quick rise to fortune)[9] placed a full-page advertisement in two Ohio newspapers (see Exhibit 10). The ad contained Audio Warehouse's version of the suit filed by U.S. Pioneer and offered sharply reduced prices on several Pioneer products.

[7]Gallup Organization was an independent research firm that specialized in survey research and had gained its reputation through political polls.

[8]"Bait and switch" refers to advertising a product at a bargain price to draw customers into the store, then selling them something similar to, but more expensive than, the advertised item. Pioneer products were good baits because of their strong consumer pull—created through national advertising and favorable word-of-mouth communication. In one Pioneer survey, 98% of Pioneer component owners interviewed said they were satisfied and would buy the brand again.

[9]According to the Ohio *Sunday Tribune* (February 12, 1978), Ed Radford, who was orphaned at age five, was planning a "fast" retirement at age 49. He had started his business in 1973 with his life savings of $10,000. In 1978 "Fast Eddie" was a millionaire who still came to work in jeans and an "exploding blond Afro."

Radford contended that "many dealers around the country were having difficulty maintaining margins on Pioneer equipment" and charged that Pioneer didn't "seem to care whether we make a profit or not" *(Retail Home Furnishings)*.

Although Mitchell was confident that the suit would be settled in Pioneer's favor (especially because the attorney general of Ohio became a co-plaintiff), he was concerned about the impact of Audio Warehouse's publicity on Pioneer's dealer outlets. At the same time he wondered whether to initiate legal action against other offenders and/or terminate their franchises.[10]

Dealer Communication Program

Sales representatives suggested that U.S. Pioneer organize an extensive communication program to convince dealers that the company was concerned about their well-being and to demonstrate how effective selling of Pioneer products could improve their profits. The sales reps were increasingly confronted with complaints from dealers such as:

"Most of my customers ask for Pioneer. But I can't make money with Pioneer."

"How can we compete with discounters or mail-order guys who are selling Pioneer for as low as 10% above cost?"

"We'd be better off selling products of smaller manufacturers like Advent and Bose, which still sell at list prices."

"I'm making 50% to 60% margin on house brands; why should I push Pioneer?"

Such comments concerned Mitchell, because he thought dealer support was crucial. Table A shows the results of a consumer survey that asked "What factors had the greatest influence in your most recent purchase of hi-fi products?"

In a sales representatives' meeting, Bob Gundick, president of the company sales office in Florida, displayed a presentation package he had used successfully. A set of flip charts was shown to dealers during regular visits, and handouts (similar in content) were left after the presentations. As shown in Exhibit 12, the package suggested ways the dealers could (a) cope with their competitors, (b) determine their product mixes, (c) creatively sell Pioneer products in combination with other brands, and (d) improve their businesses in general. Gundick offered his package for nationwide use.

Other suggestions during the meeting included (1) direct-mail brochures to all dealers; (2) more salespeople to increase the frequency of dealer visits; (3) cash rebates or other incentive programs (such as a contest for dealers); and (4) organizing a "national dealers' conference" at a resort.

Table A Factors Influencing Purchase of Hi-fi Products

	% of Respondents[a]
Recommendations of friends	29%
Dealers/salespeople	27
Advertising by manufacturers	15
Recommendations of family members	12
Advertising by dealers	8
Store display	7
All others	14
No answer	(n = 1,290)

a. Percentages total over 100 because of multiple answers.

---

[10]Most of these dealer franchise agreements (see Exhibit 11) had been signed during the fair-trade days and did not fully reflect the changes resulting from the FTC consent order.

Although the format of the sales communication program was yet to be determined, Mitchell felt it justified a budget of $3 million. He was uncertain, however, whether the budget should be incremental or whether some funds should be transferred from consumer advertising.

Long-run Strategy Options

Citing the broad changes occurring in the industry, several sales reps argued that the existing situation provided a timely opportunity to reconsider U.S. Pioneer's long-run distribution strategy.

Distribution Shift

One possibility was to shift retail distribution away from specialty stores to department stores and catalog showrooms. In 1977, 75% of U.S. Pioneer's dollar sales were accounted for by hi-fi specialty stores, 5% by department stores, 7% by catalog showrooms, and 13% by appliance/TV/hardware/furniture stores.[11] Department stores and catalog showrooms did not generally offer the extensive customer services provided by specialty stores, including professional sales assistance, demonstration, extended store warranty,[12] on-the-premises repair, home delivery and installation, and loaner component programs. They usually had, however, extensive credit facilities, strong consumer "pull" advertising, and lower prices. Industry sources predicted a substantial increase in the market shares of department stores and catalog showrooms.

Multiple Branding

Some sales reps suggested that one way to take advantage of the trend toward more mass-oriented retail outlets and, at the same time, "keep specialty stores reasonably happy" would be multiple branding. U.S. Pioneer would offer several product lines of varying quality and price points under separate brand names. Different product lines would be carried by different types of retail outlets. The department-store line would presumably be of lower quality and price than a regular line. Supporters pointed out that multiple branding had been used in other industries[13] and that it would enable U.S. Pioneer to adapt most effectively to future changes in retail distribution.[14] Others were more concerned that such a strategy would tarnish Pioneer's reputation for selling only top-of-the-line products.

Company-owned Stores

Another strategic option for U.S. Pioneer was to move toward operating its own retail stores. Some retailers in the low-fi market (such as Radio Shack and Sears) had been selling their own house brands for some time. More recently, house brands were starting to make in-roads in the hi-fi market. For example, house brand sales by Pacific Stereo (a chain of 80 West Coast stores) were estimated to be 25% (unit basis). In other hi-fi specialty stores, house brands accounted for 5% to 10% of unit sales.

Some sales reps felt that house brands would seriously threaten U.S. Pioneer. Because the primary promoters of house brands were large specialty store chains, Pioneer risked being squeezed out of them. One way to counter this prospective threat would be to start Pioneer retail stores by acquiring existing one- or two-unit family-owned stores or converting nonaudio stores into Pioneer shops.

The estimated U.S. Pioneer initial fixed investment for starting up, say, a 5,000-square-foot hi-fi store was about $50,000. Given the operating data for a comparable existing specialty store, shown in Exhibit 13, the initial investment appeared to be recoverable in a short time. (U.S. Pioneer's income statement is provided in Exhibit 14.)

---

[11]In terms of the number of existing U.S. Pioneer retail outlets, 69% were hi-fi specialty stores, 2% department stores, 3% catalog showrooms, and 26% other stores.

[12]Many specialty stores extended the two-year Pioneer guarantee on parts and labor on its electronics to three years.

[13]For example, multiple branding was used in the watch industry. The Bulova Watch Company had three brand names: Bulova (intended for jewelry and department stores), Accutron (for best stores), and Caravelle (for quality drugstores and specialty gift shops). In fact, Bulova had experienced considerable difficulty maintaining discrete channels for these lines.

[14]Should discount stores become a major force in hi-fi components sales, a new line with a new brand name could be added. (Pioneer Electronics of America, a separate, wholly owned subsidiary of Pioneer Electronics Corporation of Japan, currently sold compacts and car stereos to discount stores under the Centrex brand name.)

Exhibit 1 U.S. Pioneer Advertisment

AN IMPORTANT MESSAGE FROM WILLIAM SHAKESPEARE AND PIONEER.

The Granger Collection

"Who steals my purse steals trash . . .
But he that filches from me
    my good name
Robs me of that which not
    enriches him
And makes me poor indeed."

The Immortal Bard said it over three hundred years ago. It's still true today.

It has come to our attention at Pioneer that a few dealers of high fidelity products, acting in what they believe to be their best interest, have taken up the practice of disparagement of Pioneer products and "bait and switch" advertising, often using Pioneer's hard earned reputation in the industry as the "bait."

This tactic hurts Pioneer, hurts the consumer and ultimately hurts all dealers since it will damage the credibility of our high fidelity business in the eyes of consumers. To protect our legitimate dealers, Pioneer will conduct frequent investigations of this practice, and we will take appropriate steps to protect and defend our reputation on behalf of the great majority of our dealers against the unjustifiable practices of an unwise few.

Respectfully,
William Shakespeare, *Stratford-upon-Avon*
Bernie Mitchell, *U.S. Pioneer Electronics*

Source: Trade magazines

Exhibit 2 Price List of Selected Products, April 22, 1975

Stereo Receivers	Description	Fair Trade Resale	1–3 pcs.	4–more	Case	Shipping Weight
SX-1010	AM/FM Stereo Receiver	$699.95	$466.60	$420.00	1	60 lbs.
SX-939	AM/FM Stereo Receiver	599.95	400.00	372.00	1	51 lbs.
SX-838	AM/FM Stereo Receiver	499.95	333.40	310.00	1	44 lbs.
SX-737	AM/FM Stereo Receiver	399.95	266.60	248.00	1	35 lbs.
SX-636	AM/FM Stereo Receiver	349.95	233.30	217.00	1	29 lbs.
SX-535	AM/FM Stereo Receiver	299.95	200.00	186.00	1	27 lbs.
SX-434	AM/FM Stereo Receiver	239.95	160.00	148.80	1	22 lbs.

U.A. Series	Description	Fair Trade Resale	1–3 pcs.	4–more	Case	Shipping Weight
Spec 1	Stereo Pre-Amplifier	$499.95	$333.40	$300.00	1	30 lbs.
Spec 2	Stereo Power Amplifier	899.95	600.00	540.00	1	60 lbs.
SA-9900	Integrated Stereo Amp.	749.85	500.00	450.00	1	50 lbs.
SA-9500	Integrated Stereo Amp.	499.95	333.40	300.00	1	44 lbs.
SA-8500	Integrated Stereo Amp.	399.95	266.60	240.00	1	32 lbs.
SA-7500	Integrated Stereo Amp.	299.95	200.00	180.00	1	30 lbs.
SA-5200	Integrated Stereo Amp.	138.95	93.30	84.00	1	23 lbs.
TX-9500	AM/FM Stereo Tuner	399.95	266.60	240.00	1	24 lbs.
TX-7500	AM/FM Stereo Tuner	249.95	166.70	150.00	1	21 lbs.
TX-6200	AM/FM Stereo Tuner	139.95	93.30	84.00	1	18 lbs.
RG-1	RG Dynamic Expander	179.95	120.00	108.00	1	15 lbs.
SR-202W	Stereo Reverb. Amp.	139.95	93.30	84.00	1	12 lbs.
SF-850	Electronic Crossover	199.95	133.30	120.00	1	16 lbs.
SD-1100	Quad/Stereo Display	599.95	400.00	360.00	1	34 lbs.
WC-UA1	Walnut Cabinet*	34.95**	23.30	21.00	1	11¹/₄ lbs.

*Walnut Cabinet for SA-8500, SA-7500, TX-9500, TX-7500 only.
**Suggested Resale

Turntables	Description	Fair Trade Resale	1–3 pcs.	4–more	Case	Shipping Weight
PL-71	2-Speed, DC Brushless Servo Motor, Anti-skating, Direct-drive	$299.95	$200.00	$180.00	1	33 lbs.
PL-55X	2-Speed, DC Brushless Servo Motor, Anti-skating, Direct-drive Automatic Turntable	249.95	166.60	150.00	1	31 lbs.
PL-A45D	2-Speed, Automatic Turntable 2-motor, Belt-drive, Anti-skating	169.95	113.30	105.40	1	26 lbs.
PL-15D/ᵢᵢ	2-Speed, Automatic Turntable with Hysteresis Synchronous Motor, Belt-drive, Anti-skating	129.95	87.10	83.20	1	20 lbs.
PL-12D & PL-12D/ᵢᵢ	2-Speed, Hysteresis Synchronous Motor, Belt-drive, Anti-skating	99.95	70.00	66.00	1	19 lbs.

Source: Company data

Exhibit 3 Price List of Selected Products, July 1, 1975

		DEALER COST				DEALER'S GROSS MARGINS *AT VARIOUS RETAIL PRICES									
STEREO RECEIVERS	Description	1–3 pcs.	4– more	Case	Shp. Wt.	15% Margin	20% Margin	25% Margin	30% Margin	35% Margin	40% Margin	45% Margin	Approx. Nationally Adv. Value	Your Price	Model Number
SX-1010	AM/FM Stereo Rec.	$466.60	$420.00	1	60 lbs.	$494.00	$525.00	$560.00	$600.00	$646.00	$700.00	$764.00	$700.00	——	SX-1010
SX-939	AM/FM Stereo Rec.	400.00	372.00	1	51 lbs.	438.00	465.00	496.00	531.00	572.00	620.00	676.00	600.00	——	SX-939
SX-838	AM/FM Stereo Rec.	333.40	310.00	1	44 lbs.	365.00	388.00	413.00	443.00	477.00	517.00	564.00	500.00	——	SX-938
SX-737	AM/FM Stereo Rec.	266.60	248.00	1	35 lbs.	292.00	310.00	331.00	354.00	382.00	413.00	451.00	400.00	——	SX-737
SX-636	AM/FM Stereo Rec.	233.30	217.00	1	29 lbs.	255.00	271.00	289.00	310.00	334.00	362.00	395.00	350.00	——	SX-636
SX-535	AM/FM Stereo Rec.	200.00	186.00	1	27 lbs.	219.00	233.00	248.00	266.00	286.00	310.00	338.00	300.00	——	SX-535
SX-434	AM/FM Stereo Rec.	160.00	148.80	1	22 lbs.	175.00	185.00	198.00	213.00	229.00	248.00	271.00	250.00	——	SX-434
U.A. SERIES	Description	1–3 pcs.	4– more	Case	Shp. Wt.	15% Margin	20% Margin	25% Margin	30% Margin	35% Margin	40% Margin	45% Margin	Approx. Nationally Adv. Value	Your Price	Model Number
Spec 1	Stereo Pre-Amplifier	$333.40	$300.00	1	30 lbs.	$353.00	$375.00	$400.00	$429.00	$462.00	$500.00	$545.00	$500.00	——	Spec 1
Spec 2	Stereo Power Amp.	600.00	540.00	1	60 lbs.	635.00	675.00	720.00	771.00	831.00	900.00	982.00	900.00	——	Spec 2
SA-9900	Integ. Stereo Amp.	500.00	450.00	1	50 lbs.	529.00	563.00	600.00	643.00	692.00	750.00	818.00	750.00	——	SA-9900
SA-9500	Integ. Stereo Amp.	333.40	300.00	1	44 lbs.	353.00	375.00	400.00	429.00	462.00	500.00	545.00	500.00	——	SA-9500
SA-8500	Integ. Stereo Amp.	266.60	240.00	1	32 lbs.	282.00	300.00	320.00	343.00	369.00	400.00	436.00	400.00	——	SA-8500
SA-7500	Integ. Stereo Amp.	200.00	180.00	1	30 lbs.	212.00	225.00	240.00	257.00	277.00	300.00	327.00	300.00	——	SA-7500
SA-5200	Integ. Stereo Amp.	93.30	84.00	1	23 lbs.	99.00	105.00	112.00	120.00	129.00	140.00	153.00	140.00	——	SA-5200
TX-9500	AM/FM Stereo Tuner	266.60	240.00	1	24 lbs.	282.00	300.00	320.00	343.00	369.00	400.00	436.00	400.00	——	TX-9500
TX-7500	AM/FM Stereo Tuner	166.70	150.00	1	21 lbs.	176.00	189.00	200.00	214.00	231.00	250.00	273.00	250.00	——	TX-7500
TX-6200	AM/FM Stereo Tuner	93.30	84.00	1	18 lbs.	99.00	105.00	112.00	120.00	129.00	140.00	153.00	140.00	——	TX-6200
RG-1	RG Dyn. Expander	120.00	108.00	1	15 lbs.	127.00	135.00	144.00	154.00	166.00	180.00	196.00	175.00	——	RG-1
SR-202W	Stereo Reverb. Amp.	93.30	84.00	1	12 lbs.	99.00	105.00	112.00	120.00	129.00	140.00	153.00	150.00	——	SR-202W
SF-850	Electronic Crossover	133.30	120.00	1	16 lbs.	141.00	150.00	160.00	171.00	185.00	200.00	218.00	200.00	——	SF-850
SD-1100	Quad/Stereo Display	400.00	360.00	1	31 lbs.	424.00	450.00	480.00	514.00	554.00	600.00	655.00	600.00	——	SD-1100
WC-UA1	Walnut Cabinet†	23.30	21.00	1	11 lbs.	25.00	26.00	28.00	30.00	32.00	35.00	38.00	35.00	——	WC-UA1
WC-UA2	Walnut Cabinet‡	26.70	24.00	1	11 lbs.	28.00	30.00	32.00	34.00	37.00	40.00	44.00	40.00	——	WC-UA2
TURN-TABLES	Description	1–3 pcs.	4– more	Case	Shp. Wt.	15% Margin	20% Margin	25% Margin	30% Margin	35% Margin	40% Margin	45% Margin	Approx. Nationally Adv. Value	Your Price	Model Number
PL-71	2-Sp., DC Brushless Servo Motor, Anti-skating, Direct drive	$200.00	$180.00	1	33 lbs.	$212.00	$225.00	$240.00	$257.00	$277.00	$300.00	$327.00	$300.00	——	PL-71
PL-55X	2-Sp., DC Brushless Servo Motor, Anti-skating, Direct drive, Auto. Turntable	166.60	150.00	1	31 lbs.	176.00	188.00	200.00	214.00	231.00	250.00	273.00	250.00	——	PL-55X
PL-A45D	2-Sp., Auto. Turntable 2-motor, Belt drive, Anti-skating	113.30	105.40	1	26 lbs.	124.00	132.00	141.00	151.00	162.00	176.00	192.00	175.00	——	PL-A45D
PL-15D/ₙ	2-Sp., Auto. Turntable w/Hysteresis Synch. Motor, Belt drive, Anti-skating	87.10	83.20	1	20 lbs.	98.00	104.00	111.00	119.00	128.00	139.00	151.00	125.00	——	PL-15D/ₙ
PL-12D & PL-12D/ₙ	2-Sp., Hysteresis Synch. Motor, Belt drive, Anti-skating	70.00	66.00	1	19 lbs.	78.00	83.00	88.00	94.00	102.00	110.00	120.00	100.00	——	PL-12D PL-12D/ₙ

†Walnut cabinet for SA-8500
‡Walnut cabinet for SA-9900
Source: Company data

Exhibit 4 Retail Unit and Dollar Sales of Hi-fi Components, 1974–1977

	1974	1975	1976	1977
– **Unit Sales** (in thousands)				
– Total components	7,799	7,971	8,719	9,539
– Receivers	960	970	1,050	1,185
– Amps, pre-amps, tuners	231	263	275	320
– Turntables (except OEM)	1,767	1,709	1,866	2,015
– Speakers	2,500	2,550	2,800	3,125
– Tape decks (cassette & open reel)	341	399	428	494
– Headphones	2,000	2,080	2,300	2,400
– **Dollar Sales** (in millions)				
– Total components	$1,056	$1,073	$1,208	$1,390
– Receivers	336	306	341	392
– Amps, pre-amps, tuners	69	76	81	97
– Turntables (except OEM)	168	179	222	252
– Speakers	300	319	350	416
– Tape decks (cassette & open reel)	113	120	133	147
– Headphones	70	73	81	86

Source: *Merchandising*, March 1978, p. 51.

Exhibit 5 U.S. Pioneer Retail Dollar Market Share Data[a]

Hi-fi Product Category	1971	1972	1973	1974	1975	1976
Receivers	7%	15%	23%	22%	25%	25%
Tuners	3	5	25	18	23	18
Amplifiers	3	5	8	9	12	10
Turntables	3	3	3	11	10	11
Speakers	2	1	4	5	3	7
Headphones	10	5	4	7	9	9
Cassette decks	—	—	4	11	26	20
Open reel tape decks	—	—	—	5	9	9

Source: Company data.
[a]Pioneer's overall dollar market share (at retail) was about 19% in 1977, 14% in 1976, and 13% in 1975.

Exhibit 6 Demographic Profile of Buyers of Stereo Component Parts[a]

	1974		1975	
	U.S.	Stereo Components Buyers	U.S.	Stereo Components Buyers
– **Population** (in thousands)	(139,778)	(3,400)	(141,622)	(2,788)
– Men	47.3%	73.4%	49.6%	76.4%
– Women	52.7	26.6	50.4	23.6
– **Age**				
– 18–24	18.1%	42.5%	18.5%	47.6%
– 25–34	20.6	31.8	21.2	26.9
– 35–49	24.6	18.0	24.2	15.0
– 50–64	22.4	6.8	21.7	9.9
– 65 or over	14.2	1.0	14.4	0.5
– **Residence**				
– New England	3.9%	4.4%	5.9%	6.6%
– Mid-Atlantic	22.2	18.6	20.6	18.8
– East Central	13.1	16.9	14.2	15.1
– West Central	16.5	19.8	15.2	16.6
– Southeast	18.0	14.0	19.1	14.9
– Southwest	10.6	10.4	10.1	7.1
– Pacific	15.6	15.9	14.8	20.8
– **Education**				
– Graduated college	11.9%	16.3%	12.5%	25.6%
– Attended college	14.0	30.8	14.7	27.5
– Graduated high school	37.7	39.5	38.0	36.2
– Did not graduate high school	36.4	13.4	34.8	10.7
– **Household Income**				
– $25,000 or more	8.8%	11.5%	11.3%	20.9%
– $20,000–24,999	7.5	9.3	8.4	9.1
– $15,000–19,999	17.1	21.4	18.6	22.7
– $10,000–14,999	24.1	21.5	23.2	21.1
– $ 8,000–9,999	9.2	9.8	8.7	8.5
– $ 5,000–7,999	14.4	10.8	13.3	11.3
– Less than $5,000	18.8	15.7	16.5	6.4
– **Family Life Cycle**				
– Single	16.2%	38.8%	17.3%	41.9%
– Married	69.5	50.4	67.9	52.2
– Widowed/divorced/separated	14.3	10.8	14.9	6.0
– (Parents)	(43.7)	(36.0)	(42.4)	(37.6)

Source: 1975 and 1976 issues of *Target Group Index,* published by Axiom Market Research Bureau, Inc. Sample sizes were approximately 25,000 for 1974 and 30,000 for 1975.
[a]Buyers of stereo component parts within the past year.

Exhibit 7 Unit Sales of Compacts and Components, 1974–1977 (in thousands)

	1974	1975	1976	1977
- **Compact Systems**				
– Cassette tape recorder bimode	32	36	38	44
– Cassette tape recorder trimode	103	190	197	233
– 8-track tape player bimode	652	528	525	527
– 8-track tape player trimode	1,234	798	843	910
– 8-track tape recorder bimode	549	590	555	569
– 8-track tape recorder trimode	480	1,024	1,100	1,183
– Changer bimode	377	325	324	337
– Total	3,427	3,491	3,582	3,803
- **Components Parts (total)**	7,799	7,971	8,719	9,539

Source: Merchandising, March 1978, p. 51.

Exhibit 8 Brand Preference Data for Hi-fi Components, July 12, 1977

	Prospective Purchasers			Prospective Purchasers
Brand of Receiver			**Brand of FM Tuner**	
– Pioneer	26%		– Pioneer	28%
– Marantz	15		– Marantz	18
– Sony	13		– Sansui	14
– Sansui	12		– Fisher	6
– Kenwood	7		– Kenwood	6
– Fisher	2		– Dynaco	3
– Harman-Kardon	2		– Technics	1
– Technics	1		– Sherwin	0
– Sherwood	1		– Rotel	0
– Other	2		– Other	1
– Don't plan to buy	5		– Don't plan to buy	5
– Don't know	14		– Don't know	18
– Total	100%		– Total	100%
Brand of Amplifier			**Brand of Turntable**	
– Pioneer	29%		– Pioneer	24%
– Marantz	17		– Garrard	19
– Sansui	9		– Dual	12
– Kenwood	8		– BSR	8
– Harman-Kardon	5		– Technics	6
– Superscope	3		– Sansui	5
– Crown	1		– Bang & Olufsen	2
– Dynaco	1		– B.I.C.	1
– Technics	1		– JVC	1
– Other	2		– Other	3
– Don't plan to buy	6		– Don't plan to buy	4
– Don't know	18		– Don't know	15
– Total	100%		– Total	100%
Brand of Speaker [a]			**Brand of Tape Deck**	
– Pioneer	32%		– Teac	21%
– Jensen	11		– Pioneer	17
– JBL	11		– Sony/Superscope	15
– AR	5		– Sansui	9
– Infinity	5		– Fisher	6
– KLH	4		– Akai	5
– B.I.C.–Venturi	3		– Bekorder	1
– Technics	3		– Harman-Kardon	1
– Dynaco	1		– Technics	0
– Other	3		– Other	2
– Don't plan to buy	4		– Don't plan to buy	9
– Don't know	18		– Don't know	14
– Total	100%		– Total	100%

Source: Gallup Organization

Note: National probability sample of 196.

[a] Among the different component parts, speakers usually offered the highest gross margin to dealers. One industry source estimated the margin spread between speakers and other components (branded products) to be 10% to 20%. This spread differed by brand and by type of retail outlets.

Exhibit 9 A U.S. Pioneer Employee's Shopping Report

1. Shopper's Name: John Smith

2. Store Visited: ABC Sounds

3. *Salesperson and/or store attitude toward Pioneer:* Store's attitude generally negative. Salesperson was not really negative but went along with negative comment by another salesperson.

4. *Products they tried to get you to buy and discouraged:* Pushed Sankyo STD-1900 (a tape deck on sale for $218) and discouraged Pioneer CT-F7272 (a tape deck on sale for $208).

5. *Unfavorable statements toward Pioneer:* The salesperson made no derogatory remarks about Pioneer to me but became involved in a conversation with another store salesperson and prospective customer in which the other salesperson stated that he could produce copies of letters dealers had written to Pioneer complaining about service.

6. *Favorable statements toward competition:* [Store salesperson claimed that] Sankyo unit had much better frequency response and much cleaner sound. Sankyo was the second largest manufacturer of tape decks and manufactured components for Teac.

7. *How were Pioneer products displayed in comparison to competition?* I did not see any of the Pioneer equipment advertised in the paper displayed in the normal manner. Specifically, CT-F7272 was missing from where all other Pioneer decks were displayed. It was in another room with a Sankyo unit sitting on top of it.

8. *Other comments:* When the salesperson set up to play the tapes back I noted that the Sankyo playback control was set at maximum volume and that he adjusted the Pioneer control to about 6. He began playing the tapes back, switching from one deck to the other and commented on the very audible difference of sound created by the higher frequency response of the Sankyo deck. I made no comment but asked to see the spec sheets on the two units. He came back with the spec sheet on the Sankyo but not the Pioneer.

During the time I spent in the store I overheard no less than six customers ask specifically for one of the Pioneer products advertised in the paper. In each case the customer was told that the particular item had been sold out but that they had lesser or better products in the Pioneer line or comparable products in other lines. I also heard another customer ask if ABC Sounds could order Pioneer's HMP-100s. The salesperson replied, "No, we can't." The customer dropped the idea at that point.

Source: Company data

Exhibit 10 Audio Warehouse Advertisement

Source: Ohio newspaper

Exhibit 11 U.S. Pioneer Dealer Franchise Agreement

𝔇𝔢𝔞𝔩𝔢𝔯 𝔉𝔯𝔞𝔫𝔠𝔥𝔦𝔰𝔢 𝔄𝔤𝔯𝔢𝔢𝔪𝔢𝔫𝔱

AGREEMENT made _____ this _____ day of _____ 19 _____ , by and between
U. S. PIONEER ELECTRONICS CORP. a Delaware Corporation, having its principal place of business in Moonachie, New Jersey (hereinafter called "PIONEER"), and

hereinafter called "Dealer"

Signer's name: _____

Corporate name: _____

dba _____

Address _____

City_____ State _____ Zip _____

Telephone No. (_____) _____

WITNESSETH:

WHEREAS Pioneer is the Distributor of certain quality products which are sold under the Pioneer brand name and trade marks (hereinafter referred to as "Products"); and

WHEREAS, Dealer desires to engage in the sale of Products at retail.

NOW, THEREFORE, Pioneer and Dealer mutually agree as follows:

1. Pioneer hereby appoints Dealer one of its Franchised Dealers in the continental limits of the United States only, and Dealer hereby accepts such appointment and agrees conscientiously and diligently to promote the sales of the above mentioned products.

2. Dealer shall purchase from Pioneer such Products for resale but all sales or agreements by Dealer for the resale of Pioneer Products shall be made by Dealer as principal and not as agent of Pioneer.

3. Prices to Dealer for such Products shall be set forth in the Pioneer Dealer Cost Schedules issued from time to time by Pioneer. Pioneer shall have the right to reduce or increase prices to Dealer at any time without accountability to Dealer in connection with Dealer's stock of unsold products on hand at the time of such change. When a new price schedule is issued by Pioneer it shall automatically supersede all such schedules on and after its effective date.

4. Dealer has represented to Pioneer, as an inducement to Pioneer for entering this agreement, that Dealer is at the time of entering into this agreement solvent and in a good and substantial financial position. Dealer shall from time to time when requested by Pioneer furnish such financial reports and other financial data as may be necessary to enable Pioneer to determine Dealer's financial condition.

5. Pioneer shall have the right to cancel any orders placed by Dealer or to refuse or to delay the shipment thereof if Dealer shall fail to meet payment schedules or other credit or financial requirements established by Pioneer and the cancellation of such orders or the withholding of shipments by Pioneer shall not be construed as a termination or breach of this agreement by Pioneer.

6. Pioneer will use its best efforts to make deliveries with reasonable promptness in accordance with orders accepted from Dealer, but it shall not be liable for any damages, consequential or otherwise, for its failure to fill orders or for delays in delivery or for any error in the filling of orders.

7. No territory is assigned exclusively to Dealer by Pioneer. Pioneer reserves the absolute right, for any reason whatever, to increase or decrease the number of Franchised Dealers in Dealer's locality or elsewhere, at any time without notice to Dealer.

8. Pioneer shall have the right at any time to discontinue the manufacture or sale of any or all of its Products and parts without incurring any liability to Dealer.

9. Pioneer is at liberty to change its service policies, its financial requirements and the design of its Products and parts thereof at any time without notice, and the Dealer shall have no claim on Pioneer for damage by reason of such change or changes.

10. Dealer agrees to forward promptly to Pioneer information concerning all charges, complaints or claims involving Products, by customers or accounts, that may come to its attention.

11. Dealer shall at no time engage in any unfair trade practices and shall make no false or misleading representations with regard to Pioneer or its Products. Dealer shall make no warranties or representations to customers or to the trade with respect to Products except such as may be approved in writing by Pioneer. Dealer shall hold Pioneer harmless from all damages caused by Dealer's violation of this paragraph. Any written representations respecting Pioneer products must first be submitted to Pioneer for its written approval.

12. Dealer will use its best efforts to resell Products purchased from Pioneer.

13. Dealer shall have no rights in the names or marks owned, used, promoted by Pioneer or in the names or marks of Products, except to make reference thereto in selling, advertising and promoting the sale of Products, which right shall be completely terminated upon the termination of this agreement.

14. Nothing herein contained shall be deemed to establish a relationship of principal and agent between Pioneer and Dealer, Dealer being an independent contractor, and neither Dealer nor any of its agents or employees shall be deemed to be an agent of Pioneer for any purpose, whatsoever and shall have no right or authority to assume or create any obligation of any kind, express or implied, on behalf of Pioneer except as specifically provided herein, nor any right or authority to accept service of legal process of any kind on behalf of Pioneer nor authority to bind Pioneer in any respect whatsoever.

15. All negotiations, correspondence and memoranda which have passed between Pioneer and Dealer in relation to this agreement are merged herein and this agreement constitutes the entire agreement between Pioneer and Dealer. No representations not contained herein are authorized by Pioneer and this agreement may not be altered, modified, amended, changed, rescinded or discharged, in whole or in part, except by a written memorandum executed by Pioneer and Dealer in the same manner as is provided for the execution of this agreement, except that the agreement may be terminated by either party as herein provided.

Exhibit 11 U.S. Pioneer Dealer Franchise Agreement (continued)

16. This agreement shall become effective only upon its execution by Pioneer in its executive offices at Moonachie, New Jersey, and no changes, additions or erasure of any printed portion of this agreement shall be valid and binding unless such change, addition or erasure is initialled by both Pioneer and Dealer.

17. This agreement supersedes and terminates any and all prior agreements or contracts, written or oral, if any, entered into between Pioneer and Dealer as of the effective date of this agreement with reference to all matters covered by this agreement.

18. Dealer is appointed a Franchised Pioneer Dealer by reason of Pioneer's confidence in Dealer, which appointment is personal in nature, and consequently this agreement shall not be assignable by Dealer, nor shall any of the rights granted hereunder be assignable or transferable in any manner whatsoever without the consent in writing of Pioneer.

19. This agreement shall be governed and construed in accordance with the laws of the State of Delaware. In the event of the provisions of this agreement, or the application of any such provisions to either Pioneer or Dealer with respect to its obligations hereunder, shall be held by a court of competent jurisdiction to be contrary to any State or Federal Law, the remaining portions of this agreement shall remain in full force and effect.

20. Either Dealer or Pioneer may terminate this agreement at any time by giving five days' written notice to the other and such termination may be made either with or without cause. Neither Dealer nor Pioneer shall be liable to the other for any damages of any kind or character whatsoever on account of such termination. Pioneer, at its option, shall have the right to repurchase from Dealer any or all Products in Dealer's inventory within a reasonable period from said notice of termination, at the net prices at which such Products were originally invoiced to Dealer less any allowances which Pioneer may have given Dealer on account of such Products: If such option to repurchase is exercised by Pioneer, Dealer agrees to deliver the inventory of Products so purchased to Pioneer, Moonachie, New Jersey, immediately after receipt of the exercise of such option.

21. Any notice which is required to be given hereunder shall be given in writing and shall either be delivered in person or sent by registered letter via United States mail to the respective addresses of the parties appearing above. If mailed, the date of the mailing shall be deemed to be the date such notice has been given.

22. Dealer shall not return merchandise without Pioneer's prior written authorization; and Pioneer shall assume no responsibility for returns made without prior written authorization.

IN WITNESS WHEREOF, the parties hereto have caused these presents to be executed the day and year first above written.

DEALER:

BY: _____   **U. S. PIONEER ELECTRONICS CORP.**

Title: _____   BY: _____

Exhibit 12 Sunshine Audio Sales Presentation Program

MOST OF MY CUSTOMERS ASK FOR PIONEER!!!

I CAN'T MAKE MONEY WITH PIONEER!!!

HOW OFTEN HAVE WE HEARD, OR HAVE YOU MADE, THESE VERY STATEMENTS. IF YOU ARE INTERESTED IN INCREASING YOUR OVERALL BUSINESS AND YOU WANT TO INCREASE YOUR OVERALL PROFIT DOLLARS—READ ON.

You and Your Competitor

Your business is really not that different from that of the store down the street. You both sell hi-fi, you both are after the same consumer, you both have to make a profit, you both want your business to grow, and you both are competing against each other. Why?

View your competitor as an ally and see what happens to your perspective of the business. You are both fighting to get consumers' disposable income dollars from the TV dealer, the motorcycle dealer, the travel agent, the car dealer, and any number of places they can spend that extra $300–$700. You and other hi-fi retailers should run ads to make the hi-fi market in your town grow—not to "get the other guy" with a low-ball price. Think about it—how many people in your market know that an RZ105 receiver at $136 is a good buy (cost in fact)? Much less, how many know what a receiver is?

You and Your Sales

Think about this for a minute. Most of your business should be in systems—about 70%. Single-piece sales account for the 30% balance. Fifteen percent are high margin pieces or accessory sales, and 15% are low margin promotional pieces. Now, think about that margin. If you only sell 40% margin products and you are not a "discount" house, how come your balance sheet only shows your gross margin between 28% and 32%? Interesting.

You and Pioneer

Now for the sales pitch. When you put a Pioneer piece in a system you will sell more systems (better brand name recognition) at your usual system margin. Pioneer has plenty of products that sell at full margin all the time—SG-9500, RG-1, turntables with cartridges, component ensembles, RT-2022, and so on. Of course, we have promotional pieces too, CTF 2121, Project 60, 100A, and others. But how low a margin is a CTF 2121 at a cost of $124—with an advertised price of $139—when you sell the deck and its case for $179. This makes the margin 26%; sell tape and your margin is higher. I can't make money on Pioneer. Don't believe it! How about the SX1250 at $595—only a $50 profit. With the $50 rebate recently offered your real profit is $100. Sell an extra three SX1250s each week and we add over 15,000 profit dollars to your bottom line in a year. Even without the $50 rebate, the contribution to profit is $7,500 in one year.

Instead of using your energy not to sell, to down sell, or to sell off Pioneer, what would happen if you put that effort into creatively selling it?

Exhibit 12 Sunshine Audio Sales Presentation Program (continued)

You and Your Business

Some suggestions:

- Put together systems with brand name products that can't be duplicated by any dealer in your market.
- Sell the accessories with the promotional pieces or make them part of a system to increase profitability.
- Sell brand name goods that customers want.
- Think in terms of profit dollars, not always gross profit margin.

You and the Industry

Pioneer will spend close to $7 million in advertising. Take advantage of this tremendous support. Without advertising and without brand names your business will dry up. Most hi-fi dealers have some exclusive lines. But limited distribution can mean limited market and limited growth. Pioneer in a system will help sell more JVC receivers, Bose, JBL or Advent speakers, Technics turntables, or whatever your exclusive is, and your business will grow. Pioneer has a product and a model that will fit almost any system you can design. The quality has never been questioned. Sandy Ruby from Tech HiFi in a recent *Home Furnishings Daily* was quoted as saying, "We're actually not doing as much business in limited distribution lines as we were a few years ago. We've tried to look more toward what the market wants. We see surveys of what people are buying or what they say they plan to buy around the country . . . and then we get that equipment. You can't just look at your sales figures. Sure, you may be selling a lot of private brand equipment, but what about the people who didn't buy from you?" What brand do they want? You've got to have a handle on the customers who walked. Pretty interesting stuff. How many of your customers walked? How many did your salespeople's paranoia scare away?

We can help.

Source: Company document

Exhibit 13 Income Statement of a Hi-fi Specialty Store[a]

	1976
– *Income*	$680,069
– *Cost of Sales*	509,182
– *Expenses*	
– Advertising	34,803
– Sales commissions (4 salespeople)	36,048
– Payroll home office (administration)	12,875
– Payroll home office (clerical)	767
– Payroll taxes	1,770
– Rent	18,780
– Depreciation	1,831
– Insurance	2,937
– Taxes–other	237
– Freight out	2,017
– Store security	1,168
– Outside labor	3,374
– Travel and entertainment	1,336
– Bad debts	3,313
– Repairs and maintenance	579
– Repairs to merchandise	57
– Credit plan service charges	872
– Telephone	5,318
– Heat, light, and power	1,242
– Bad checks	4,108
– Recruiting expenses	889
– Store supplies and expenses	3,055
– Selling and promotion	115
– Cleaning and rubbish removal	45
– Cash over and short	442
– Office supplies and expenses	1,058
– Group insurance	257
– Interest expense	857
– Legal and accounting	3,648
– Auto and truck expense	2,070
– Rental commissions	130
– Computer service expenses	44
– Bank service charges	147
– Officers' life insurance	193
– Miscellaneous	916
– Total expenses	$147,298
– *Operating Income before Federal Taxes*	$ 23,589

[a]One of a four-unit chain on the East Coast

Exhibit 14 Income Statement for U.S. Pioneer ($ thousands)

	1976[a]		1975[a]	
– *Total revenue*		135,094		87,340
– *Cost of goods sold (CGS) (primarily purchases from the parent company)*	91,707		60,470	
– *Selling, general and administrative expenses (SG&A)*	30,608		23,409	
– Income before income taxes		12,779		3,461
– Provision for income taxes		6,530		1,716
– Net income		6,249		1,745

Source: Company data

a. Fiscal year ended September 30

ROHM AND HAAS (A)
NEW PRODUCT MARKETING STRATEGY

On May 15, 1984, Joan Macey, Rohm and Haas market manager for Metalworking Fluid Biocides, was reviewing distributor purchases of Kathon MWX, a new biocide that killed microorganisms in metalworking fluids. She found that total sales to distributors for the first five months were 74 boxes against a first-year target of 1,350 boxes. "I have a super product but I can't sell it," she said. "I am in the process of reviewing our approach of taking this product to market, but at this point I am not convinced we have a better alternative."

Macey was also responsible for the marketing of Kathon 886 MW, a liquid biocide used in large metalworking fluid tanks (above 1,000-gallon capacity). Kathon 886 MW was a powerful biocide, and very small quantities were sufficient to treat large tanks. Because of its low-use level, Kathon 886 MW was not suitable for smaller-capacity tanks, and Kathon MWX was developed specifically for use in tanks with less than 1,000-gallon capacity.

Kathon 886 MW had a sales volume of $5.4 million in 1983; sales for the first five months of 1984 were at the budgeted level of $2.1 million. Kathon MWX had been launched in December 1983, with a targeted sales volume of $0.2 million in 1984; sales in the first five months were about $12,000. Macey estimated the market potential for Kathon 886 MW to be $18 million and Kathon MWX to be $20 million. Explaining the poor sales of Kathon MWX, she said:

> The total usage of Kathon MWX and its substitutes is nowhere near the $20 million potential for this market. Many small users are either unaware or don't see

the need for biocides in their metalworking fluid treatment. We do poorly because we do not have enough competition to build primary demand.

Company Background

In 1906, Otto Rohm and Otto Haas founded the company in Germany to sell chemicals to that country's leather tanning industry. The U.S. branch opened in Philadelphia in 1909. At the end of World War I, Otto Haas incorporated the American branch as an independent company. Over the years it became a leader in chemical technology, especially in acrylic emulsion polymers.[1] In 1983, the American company reported worldwide sales of $2 billion derived from four business segments:

1. *Polymers, resins, and monomers*—for applications in paints, industrial finishes, decorative coatings, and construction products
2. *Plastics*—for applications in signs, skylights, containers, and automotive products
3. *Agricultural chemicals*—herbicides and fungicides for crop diseases
4. *Industrial chemicals*—for lubricants and fuels, water treatment, and the formulation of a wide variety of industrial and consumer products

The company's product lines consisted of over 500 different products. Exhibit 1 gives the trend of sales and profits by business segments.

The Industrial Chemicals business segment consisted of three product groups: Fluid Process Chemicals, Petroleum Chemicals, and Specialty Chemicals. The Kathon microbiocide products with 1983 sales of $25 million were part of the Specialty Chemicals Group. Surface

Professor V. Kasturi Rangan and Susan Lasley, MBA '85, prepared this case as the basis for class discussion rather than to illustrate either effective or ineffective handling of an administrative situation. All quantitative data not publicly available have been disguised.

[1]The technology involves dispersing, or emulsifying, certain monomers in a fluid such as water. Then the monomers are "polymerized"—linked together through a chemical reaction. The resulting emulsion polymer retains the viscosity of water. When exposed to air, the water evaporates and a continuous, tough film remains.

active chemicals (called surfactants) and water-soluble polymers were the other products marketed by the Specialty Chemicals Group (see Exhibit 2 for an organization chart). Joan Macey was market manager for microbiocide applications in the metalworking fluid and latex/adhesives markets. Latex/adhesives biocides (1983 sales of $2 million) were sold directly by the Specialty Chemicals sales force to about 50 compounders for use in emulsions, paints, sealants, and adhesives. The metalworking fluid biocides—Kathon 886 MW and Kathon MWX—were sold through a network of formulator/distributors. All of them manufactured and sold metalworking fluids as well as any auxiliary products such as biocides and corrosion inhibitors. As market manager, Macey was responsible for formulating the marketing strategies for the three products under her charge, all of which were sold by the Specialty Chemicals sales force.

Fourteen of the 40 salespeople employed by the Industrial Chemicals business unit worked for the Specialty Chemicals Group and were responsible for selling all the products of the group (surfactants, biocides, and polymers) to various markets. Salespeople were assigned to exclusive territories and were supervised by three district managers who reported to a national field sales manager based at the Philadelphia headquarters.

All members of the sales force had college degrees in chemistry, chemical engineering, or related fields. The salesperson's role was to offer help and advice to the user in formulation or process design, for example, recommending appropriate chemical levels for cooling tower treatment or detergent formulations. Starting salaries for trainees ranged from $20,000 to $27,000 annually, and the experienced salesperson could earn $50,000 to $70,000. Salespeople were evaluated on several objectives, including new account activity, market penetration, and quantity sold in pounds. Six of the fourteen salespeople had most of the biocide customers in their respective territories. On average, they spent about 20% to 30% of their time on all biocide customers; approximately one-third of this time was spent on metalworking fluid formulators (the primary customers for Kathon 886 MW and Kathon MWX). The rest of the time was spent visiting users. Many of these calls were made jointly with the formulators' salespeople.

Metalworking Fluid Biocides

Metalworking fluid, as the name implies, is used in operations such as turning, milling, grinding, honing, and drilling. The fluid is directed onto the surface of the metal being machined to lubricate and cool the work piece and the machine tool and to remove chips and debris from the work area.

In 1983 about 60 million gallons of metalworking fluid concentrate were produced in the United States. Nearly all of it had to be diluted with water by the user. Water was typically 90% to 95% of the mixture after dilution. The diluted fluid was then placed in a reservoir and pumped to a nozzle that directed the fluid to the machined piece (see Exhibit 3). A tray built into the workstation caught chips, and the used fluid was filtered and returned to the reservoir for reuse.

Microorganisms such as bacteria, fungi, and yeast flourish in the warm aqueous environment of metal machining, and their growth increases with poor shop maintenance. They break down the metalworking fluids, and as the microorganisms develop, they multiply in long chains to clog filters, flow lines, and drains. Their foul-smelling, metabolic by-products stain and corrode work pieces and pollute the work environment.

Biocides are chemicals that kill the microorganisms in water-based metalworking fluids without affecting fluid performance. They have many applications in manufacturing products such as cosmetics, paper detergents, and latex paints. They are used, as well, in water treatment and oil-field drilling.

Chemical companies formulate metalworking-fluid concentrates by mixing emulsified oils and special additives. Formulators often add biocides to the metalworking fluid concentrate to provide some initial protection against contamination. The concentrate is then sent to users who dilute it for their machining operations. Metalworking fluids are depleted by water evaporation and fluid loss and must be replenished each day. As the fluid ages, the concentrate biocide no longer adequately protects it, and a maintenance biocide must be added to extend fluid life. A metalworking system kept free of bacteria, yeast, or fungi uses fluid for a much longer period of time—one or two weeks longer than the three to four weeks for a less well-maintained system. Regular treatment with maintenance biocides and make-up metalworking fluid (every one or two weeks) extends fluid life almost indefinitely and does not require a complete flushing of the fluid tank.

The *concentrate biocide* market was estimated to be $30 million in 1983. Industry sources predicted a downward sales trend, however, because of the growing use of maintenance biocides. The *maintenance biocide* market was estimated to be about $38 million in 1983, but if industry predictions were right, it would replace nearly all of the concentrate biocide market in 10 years.

Kathon Metalworking Fluid Biocides

Kathon 886 MW, a liquid, was the primary maintenance biocide on the market. Too reactive to be used in the metalworking fluid concentrate, it extended the life of diluted fluids in central system reservoirs. Kathon 886 MW was a broad-spectrum biocide generally 10 times more effective than competitive biocides. One gallon of Kathon 886 MW protected 8,000 to 10,000 gallons of metalworking fluid in a central reservoir initially for three weeks. About 10–15 gallons of a competitive product would be required to do the same job. In 1983, Kathon 886 MW had a 30% share of the $18 million maintenance biocide market for large systems. It was distributed by 12 major metalworking fluid formulators, who sold it as part of a fluid maintenance package to their customers. From a practical standpoint, because of its low use level and toxic properties, it could not be used in metalworking fluid reservoirs smaller than 1,000 gallons without creating misuse problems and safety risks.

Customers who were satisfied with the performance of Kathon 886 MW had asked for a convenient, safe-to-use version for their smaller (50- to 100-gallon) reservoirs. A market survey revealed that this was the most common reservoir size for small machines. Rohm and Haas technicians responded with an intense product development effort that led to the development of Kathon MWX.

After attempts to formulate a water-soluble solid product had failed, a unique packaging design to deliver liquid biocide was developed (Exhibit 4). It was a 5.5 x 7.5-inch water-permeable plastic packet containing two ounces of diatomaceous earth[2] soaked with Kathon 886 MW. The packet was designed to hang into the metalworking fluid reservoir by a strap suspended on a plastic hook and could treat 25–75 gallons of metalworking fluid for 2–4 weeks. The customer simply placed the packet in the metalworking fluid; water then flowed through the packet and gradually transferred the biocide from the diatomaceous earth to the fluid. The used packet could be removed from the reservoir for disposal at the first sign of failure (odor) or in one month. No maintenance was required, and the packet was safe to handle and dispense. In expanding the fluid maintenance market to include small machine applications, it was estimated that the potential existed for $20 million in added sales volume.

Although Kathon 886 MW and MWX were maintenance biocides, they could be used in only 70% of the metalworking fluids. Incompatibility with the concentrate biocide in the original formulation rendered them ineffective with the other 30%. By comparison, however, competitive maintenance biocides were compatible in only about 45% of commercial metalworking fluids.

Customers

In 1983, there were about 325 potential customers for Kathon 886 MW or equivalent products, and an estimated 150,000 potential customers for Kathon MWX. Table A breaks down the metalworking industry by machine size. Biocide users worked with either *nonferrous metals* such as aluminum, copper, tungsten, and titanium or *ferrous metals* such as iron and steel.

Nonferrous Metals.
In the domestic market, nonferrous metals were used primarily to make aluminum sheet, foil, and cans in large-scale, fully automated, high-speed manufacturing facilities. Central systems used metalworking fluid in reservoirs as large as 150,000 gallons. Nonferrous operations required the metalworking fluid to be kept completely free of bacteria because of the sensitivity of the metal to staining, and microbiologists and chemists were often employed to develop biocide treatments and monitor systems closely. Kathon 886 MW was the favored biocide of many of these companies and held about 70%–80% of a $3 million–$5 million market.

Ferrous Metals.
The ferrous metal industries ranged broadly from the large-scale automated manufacture of products such as automotive and farm equipment to the smaller-scale production of pumps, instruments, aircraft parts, and nuts and bolts. Customers with large scale manufacturing facilities had central systems similar to those in the nonferrous industries, but bacteria levels in the metalworking fluid were not as critical to ferrous metals as they were to nonferrous metals.[3] Though Kathon 886 MW was adopted by many for its cost effec-

---

[2]An inert solid that when mixed with Kathon had the consistency of moist sand.

[3]The ferrous industry generally accepted up to 50,000 cfu/ml of bacteria (50,000 colony-forming units per milliliter of metalworking fluid).

Table A Metalworking Industry Fluid Systems

Metalworking Fluid System	Reservoir Capacity (gallons)	Number of Metalworking Machines	Number of Plants
Central system	50,000 to 250,000	170	25
Central system	8,000 to 30,000	1,530	300
Individual system	50 to 1,000	1,701,000	150,000

tiveness, its overall share of the $12 million–$16 million ferrous market (only central systems) was only 15%–20%.

Competition

Table B lists the major competitors in the biocide market. In 1983 Rohm and Haas, Lehn and Fink, Dow Chemical, and Angus Chemical each had approximately a 15%–20% share of the maintenance biocide market.

It was assumed that Lehn and Fink and Angus Chemical each employed three salespersons for metalworking biocides. Lehn and Fink sold directly to distributors and end-users, and distributors were supplied at 10% off list price. Angus Chemical sold to distributors and end-users at the same price.

Olin Corporation's Triadine-10, introduced in 1983, was well-received by the market. Two other major chemical companies were planning entries into the maintenance biocide market: Union Carbide with Gluteraldehyde and ICI with Proxel, both for central systems.

Rohm and Haas chemists conducted comparative tests (see Exhibit 5) to demonstrate that Kathon 886 MW was still the most cost-effective biocide for central systems.

The most widely known product for individual systems was Tris Nitro "Sump Saver" tablets, an Angus product. One two-ounce tablet treated 25 gallons of metalworking fluid. Macey estimated that distributors paid $4.00/pound (eight tablets) and sold them to customers for $7.75/pound. Unlike Kathon MWX, these tablets dissolved in the metalworking fluid. They were generally considered less effective against bacteria and ineffective against fungi, and they worked for only about three days.

Another product, Dowicil 75, came in water-soluble packages that were dropped into the reservoir. Each 2.5-pound package treated 500 gallons of fluid. Macey estimated the cost to distributors at $2.34/pound and a resale price of $10/pound. While Dowicil 75 performed well against both bacteria and fungi, it had a heavy ammonia odor, released formaldehyde, and could not be safely used in reservoirs with capacities less than 500 gallons.

Table B Competitors' Products

Company	Concentrate Biocide	Maintenance Biocide	
		Central Systems	Stand-Alone Systems
1. Lehn and Fink	Grotan	Grotan	-
2. Dow Chemical	-	Dowicil 75 DBNPA	Dowicil 75
3. Angus Chemical	Bioban P-1487	Tris Nitro	Tris Nitro
4. Olin Corporation	Triadine-10	Triadine-10	
5. Millmaster Onyx	-	Onyxide 200	-
6. RT Vanderbilt	-	Vancide TH	-
7. Merck	-	Tektamer 38 A.D.	-

Some metalworking operators in small shops, in a makeshift effort to control the odor released by bacteria, poured household bleaches, disinfectants, deodorants, and similar materials into their smaller reservoirs. The odors of these materials usually combined with the bacterial odor to make the working environment even worse for the workers. These substitute materials also interfered with the cooling and lubricating performance of the metalworking fluid.

Distribution Channels

The first level of distributors in this industry were the metalworking fluid formulators. They purchased biocides, both concentrate and maintenance, directly from the manufacturers. The concentrate biocide was incorporated into the metalworking fluid at the time of its formulation. The formulators then sold the metalworking fluid directly to large companies and to other dealers who resold it to smaller accounts. Metalworking fluid generally accounted for more than 90% of a formulator's business. As a service to customers with large central reservoir systems, distributors provided a maintenance package that usually included delivery, fluid preparation, weekly monitoring for microorganisms, and maintenance biocide treatments. Other special-purpose chemicals such as pH adjusters and corrosion inhibitors were provided as needed. Many of these products were sold under the formulators' private brand names. Most formulators engaged in R&D, acceptance testing of manufacturers' additives, and systems monitoring.

In 1983 the total sales of 10 large national formulators were roughly $200 million. Another 20–30 formulators had a combined sales volume of some $100 million. Several hundred small formulators had sales of $0.5 to $1 million each. Because of the number and fragmentation of the ferrous metalworking industries, large formulators distributed their products through a secondary distribution network, consisting primarily of industrial supply houses and machine tool shops.

Industrial supply houses ranged from small, family-managed companies in rural areas to large, professionally managed companies in urban areas. Some specialized in serving particular industry sectors. They were "supermarkets" for their customers. A supply house servicing a ferrous metalworking industry, for example, might carry several brands of biocides, safety accessories, uniforms, small general-purpose tools, shop cleaning and maintenance supplies, worktables, hand trucks, concrete blocks, spill absorbents, and hand soaps.

The 1982 Census of Wholesale Trade listed 14,327 industrial supply houses in the United States. A major metropolitan area might have over 100 supply houses serving a variety of industries. Industrial supply house sales in 1982 amounted to approximately $40 billion. Inside salespeople took telephone orders from regular customers and over-the-counter orders from walk-in customers. Outside salespeople generated new accounts and called on regular customers.

Machine tool shops specialized in distributing and servicing machine tools and items used with them like spare parts, tool bits, metalworking fluids, and biocides. Some also served as sources of metals. There were 3,654 such companies in the United States, and in 1982 their sales were $8.7 billion.

Typically, large industrial companies (e.g., General Motors, Caterpillar Tractor) purchased biocides directly from manufacturers or from their distributors (formulators). They used the secondary network of industrial supply houses and machine tool shops for miscellaneous items (such as safety equipment or paper towels) that were not critical to their line of business. Small companies, however, often relied exclusively on industrial supply houses and machine tool shops for all their needs.

Marketing Strategy for Kathon MWX

Ten of Rohm and Haas's 12 distributors (formulators of metalworking fluid) agreed to distribute Kathon MWX in addition to Kathon 886 MW. The company offered private branding on Kathon 886 MW, but not on Kathon MWX. Though many formulators asked for private branding, only one distributor declined to carry Kathon MWX when turned down on a request for its own-brand product. Explaining the rationale for this policy, a company manager said:

> Kathon MWX is the industrial equivalent of a consumer packaged good; it is a "baggie" product packaged at the factory. We need some uniformity in package design. Moreover, we want the end-user to know it's a Rohm and Haas product. Our end-users hardly see the Kathon 886 MW drum because our formulators include the product as a part of their maintenance service. But Kathon MWX is different; we expect the end-users to do the maintenance themselves.

Kathon MWX was packed in boxes containing 144 packets, each packet weighing two ounces. Quantity prices to distributors per box of 144 packets were as follows:

1–2 boxes	$180.00
3–4 boxes	165.00
5+ boxes	145.00

Joan Macey estimated the manufacturing cost per packet to be about 50 cents. The company did not specify a price to end-users, but most formulators charged end-users and other dealers $2/packet. Some formulators had a strong secondary distribution network consisting of 200–300 industrial supply houses, and in such instances, the secondary level of distribution was known to add a 10% margin. One of the company's distributors with a sales force of 700 commissioned reps claimed that he could sell each packet for $6 to the end-users.

The product launch (December 1983) was accompanied by a press release in 40 metalworking industry journals announcing the availability of Kathon MWX. The announcement included information about characteristics of Kathon MWX and its benefits. Full-page advertisements costing $3,800 each were placed in five issues of *American Machinist* between February and June 1984. Interested readers could get further information and a two-packet sample by filling out a reader service coupon. Over 200 such inquiries were received from the February, March, and April advertisements. All inquiries were forwarded to distributors. Rohm and Haas responded directly with a copy of the very colorful ad, a material safety data sheet, a set of technical notes, and a "how-to-use" booklet (see Exhibit 4). Distributors were expected to follow up on the leads and generate orders.

In spite of all these efforts, the sales in the first five months of the launch period barely touched $12,000.

Joan Macey's Dilemma

Disappointed with Kathon MWX's sales performance, Macey began a review of her marketing plan to take any necessary corrective steps. She also sought opinions from two of her colleagues in the Specialty Chemicals division who had successfully launched and established new products. Her first colleague advised:

You are too hard on yourself, Joan. New products don't succeed overnight. It takes years for the product to get market acceptance and longer still to get dealer support. If you feel comfortable about your original marketing plan, it's worthwhile giving it a chance. We are in the business of specialty chemicals, we offer solutions to customers' problems. We are not in the fashion business!

Her second colleague felt differently; he agreed that Kathon MWX's initial marketing approach was probably not best suited for the product. He encouraged Macey to review the marketing plan, saying, "The only good news on Kathon MWX is that you know there is a problem; therefore you can fix it."

Regardless of what she might ultimately do about her strategy for marketing the product, Macey thought it would be a good idea to contact the 200 prospects who had responded to the reader service coupons. Macey employed a summer trainee who was working toward an MBA to conduct a telephone survey. Explaining her rationale for the survey, she said:

I wish I could thoroughly research the market, but that's not possible. Frankly, what else can I do with the limited budget I have for support activities? Kathon MWX has to show some initial movement before further resources are justified. It is imperative that I make a quick decision. After all, I have other products to manage and my boss has the entire biocide business to manage. One has to place Kathon MWX in its proper perspective. A quick survey should do that.

The survey revealed several major facts:

1. On average, customers discarded used metalworking fluid after three weeks. Rancidity and dermatitis[4] were the primary reasons for this, and most customers believed that bacteria, not metal particles or harsh chemicals, caused the dermatitis.

2. Although most survey participants had their used fluids hauled away, few knew how much this service cost. Those who did know gave figures of $0.29, $0.55, $1.80, and $2.00 per gallon of used fluid.

3. Only about 20% of the participants remembered receiving the Kathon MWX information packet. When asked about the image of the product conveyed by the promotional literature, many said that the product was worth trying. Despite their inclination to use Kathon MWX, they expressed some apprehension about its safety. An explanation of the proper handling technique usually overcame these fears.

---

[4]Dermatitis symptoms are skin eruptions and rashes that last anywhere from a few hours to a few weeks.

4. Users obtained metalworking fluids from tool shops, oil companies, formulators, and industrial supply shops. The majority sourced from two or more small, local tool or supply shops within 30 miles of their businesses, as well as one of the large national formulators. Users occasionally found it necessary to write to a large national distributor for supplies that were not locally available.

5. About 50% of the users used products ranging from household disinfectants to metalworking fluid biocides to kill odor-causing bacteria in their machine sumps. The majority of these products did not seem to work, yet the end-user typically continued to use the product. Only half of the participants who had tried a biocide could remember its name. None had tried Kathon MWX.

From the summer trainee's survey report, Macey extracted the cost information that she thought would be useful in a review of Kathon MWX's marketing strategy (see Exhibit 6). She wondered if raising the price would increase end-user perception of the product's value. She wondered what short-term and long-term sales and market share targets were appropriate for Kathon MWX. Concerned about the appropriateness of the current channels of distribution for Kathon MWX, she considered other options. Finally, of course, she wondered if Kathon 886 MW was a help or hindrance in developing a market for Kathon MWX, especially since marketing plans for Kathon 886 MW projected a healthy growth in distribution and market share.

Exhibit 1 Sales and Profits by Business Segments, 1979–1983 (millions of dollars)

	1983	1982	1981	1980	1979
− *Net Sales*					
− Polymers, resins, and monomers	$745	$707	$753	$665	$626
− Plastics	390	353	376	345	345
− Industrial chemicals	336	331	324	303	265
− Agricultural chemicals	337	336	308	295	243
− Other industries	68	101	124	117	111
− **Total**	$1,876	$1,828	$1,885	$1,725	$1,590
− *Net Earnings*					
− Polymers, resins, and monomers	$79	$47	$45	$53	$50
− Plastics	33	9	14	16	27
− Industrial chemicals	22	12	23	23	20
− Agricultural chemicals	18	24	21	20	16
− Other industries	(11)	2	(6)	(9)	(1)
− Corporate	(3)	(8)	(4)	(9)	(16)
− **Total**	$138	$86	$93	$94	$96
− *RONA[a]*					
− Polymers, resins, and monomers	19.7%	12.9%	11.5%	12.8%	12.1%
− Plastics	13.9	3.7	5.2	7.3	13.2
− Industrial chemicals	12.6	7.4	13.1	13.8	12.0
− Agricultural chemicals	7.2	9.1	7.2	9.8	9.7
− Other industries	(6.3)	1.2	(4.2)	(6.1)	(1.0)
− **Total**	10.5%	7.6%	7.9%	8.9%	9.6%

Source: Company records

Note: Net earnings are from continuing operations (before extraordinary credit in 1979) and are after the allocation of corporate expenses and income taxes. Income taxes are allocated based on the tax effect of transactions included in pretax income. Corporate consists mainly of after-tax interest income and expense.

[a]Return on net assets (RONA) equals net earnings from continuing operations plus after-tax interest expense, divided by year-end total assets.

Exhibit 2 Organization Chart: Specialty Chemicals Group

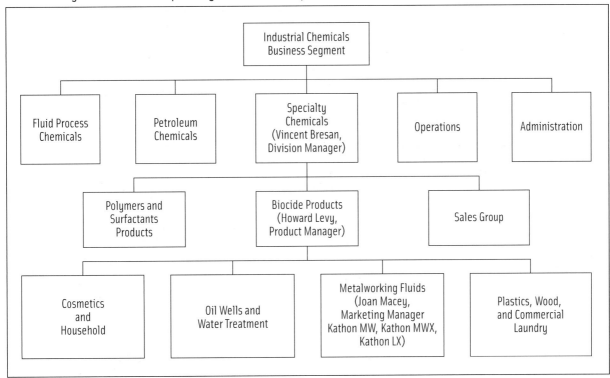

Exhibit 3 Metalworking Fluid

Source: Company material

Exhibit 4 Kathon MWX User Information

Kathon® MWX Biocide Packets
for small machine maintenance

Extends fluid life
Extends fluid life
Extends fluid life
Extends fluid life
Extends fluid life
Extends fluid life
Extends fluid life

- **Extends fluid life**
- **Controls bacteria and fungi**
- **Eliminates odor**
- **Minimizes machine downtime**
- **Effective over a wide pH range**
- **Easy to use, safer to handle**
- **Does not release formaldehyde**
- **Readily disposable**
- **EPA registered for metalworking fluids**

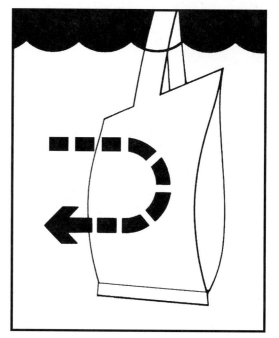

Exhibit 4 Kathon MWX user Information (continued)

What is Kathon MWX?

It is a safer-to-handle plastic packet containing a highly water soluble biocide which controls bacteria and fungi, including the odors they produce.

How should you use Kathon MWX?

Simply attach the packet to the hook provided and suspend it from the edge of the sump into a 50 gallon reservoir of dilute soluble, semi-synthetic or synthetic metalworking fluid.

How many Kathon MWX packets should be used?

For noticeably rancid fluids, use 1-2 unopened 2 ounce packets for every 50 gallons of fluid every 1-2 weeks. Follow this with a maintenance dose of one packet for every 50 gallons every 2-4 weeks.

How does Kathon MWX work?

When the packet is submerged in the fluid, the aqueous fluid enters the packet through the small pores and carries the active ingredient back out into the fluid where it destroys bacteria and fungi, including the odors they produce. This flow action will continue to release active ingredient from the packet to the reservoir until it reaches equilibrium (about 3 days). After this, the active ingredient will gradually be depleted as it continues to prevent the development of rancidity.

How will you know that Kathon MWX is doing the job?

Since the active ingredient in Kathon MWX begins to act immediately, any odor produced by the rancid fluid will be significantly reduced within several hours. Slime and other biological debris will pull away from the sides and bottom of the reservoir and disperse in approximately 3 days.

When should the Kathon MWX packet be removed from the reservoir?

The packet should be left in for a minimum of 3 days to reach equilibrium. At this time, the level of active ingredient in the packet is the same as the level in the fluid. This level – 20 ppm – is non-hazardous and similar to the level used in many consumer products. The packet may be left in place for an additional 2 to 4 weeks since it will continue to provide rancidity control until the active ingredient is essentially gone.

How should you dispose of Kathon MWX?

If the packet is removed in fewer than three days, it should be treated with a deactivating solution (see product literature) before disposal. If the packet is removed after three days, it will consist of the plastic packet, diatomaceous earth and a non-hazardous level of active ingredient. It may be disposed of as trash, unless prohibited by state or local authorities.

Source: Company records

Exhibit 5 Kathon 886 MW Cost Effectiveness

Comparative Cost of Treating a 10,000 Gallon System with Biocide (for one cycle)	
I. With Dowicil 75 10,000 gals.[a] x 8.4 lbs.[b]/gal. x 0.15%[c] x $2.14[d]/lb.	= $269.64
II. With Grotan 10,000 gals. x 8.4 lbs./gal. x 0.15% x $1.20/lb.	= $151.20
III. With Kathon 886 MW 10,000 gals. x 8.4 lbs./gal. x 0.01% x $8.50/lb.	= $71.40

Source: Company records
[a]This corresponds to approximately 400 gallons of metalworking fluid concentrate.
[b]Weight of metalworking fluid per gallon
[c]Biocide concentration required for treatment
[d]Biocide price to end-user

Exhibit 6 Cost Information Gathered from Survey Data

	Average Cost
Metalworking fluid concentrate	$5.68/gallon[a]
Waste disposal	$1.36/gallon[b]
Kathon MWX	$2/packet

- 1 packet of Kathon MWX treats 25–50 gallons of diluted metalworking fluid.
- A typical small machine shop had 22 machines, each with a reservoir capacity of 50 gallons. It discarded fluid every four weeks. By using Kathon MWX they could keep the fluid 2–5 weeks longer.
- Machine downtime, labor, and water costs were negligible for small machines. Costs of other additives (buffers, corrosion inhibitors) were not considered in a differential analysis.

[a]Per gallon of undiluted fluid. A dilution ratio of 1:24 is assumed.
[b]Per gallon of diluted fluid.

PIZZA HUT, INC.

In May 1986, Steve Reinemund, the newly appointed president of Pizza Hut, Inc., announced that he intended to pursue vigorously the "exciting opportunities afforded by our new segment, delivery." Seven months later, the home delivery units had produced mixed results, and Reinemund met with his senior managers to decide how to respond.

Entry into the home delivery market had been a major strategic decision at Pizza Hut, and Reinemund was well aware of the difficulties it presented. Half of the 5,025 Pizza Hut system restaurants were owned by large, powerful franchisees with exclusive rights to the territories they controlled. While some franchisees saw the benefits of home delivery in their markets, others were strongly opposed. Moreover, many franchisees did not agree with the manner in which Pizza Hut would implement delivery. Nevertheless, to be successful, the delivery strategy needed the franchisees' cooperation. Attaining this cooperation in the Pizza Hut franchise system would be, in the words of Jim Baxter, vice president of franchising, "a matter of *sell*, not *tell*."

The Pizza Market

The rapid growth in home delivery in the mid-1980s revitalized the pizza market and was responsible for pizza's position as the fastest-growing part of the $53 billion fast food market. Three main segments comprised the pizza restaurant market: eat-in, carryout, and delivery. The sales for each segment are shown below:

	Eat-In	Carryout	Delivery	Total
1982	$4.3 billion (57%)	$3.1 billion (41%)	$0.1 billion (1%)	$ 7.5 billion
1984	$4.7 billion (48%)	$4.0 billion (41%)	$1.0 billion (10%)	$ 9.7 billion
1986[a]	$5.1 billion (40%)	$5.0 billion (39%)	$2.6 billion (20%)	$12.7 billion
1990[a]	$5.9 billion (27%)	$9.0 billion (41%)	$7.0 billion (32%)	$21.9 billion

Source: GDR/Crest Enterprises, Inc.
[a]Projections based on limited Pizza Hut entry into delivery segment as of third-quarter 1986

Many companies competed in more than one segment; for example, carryout was a significant percentage of most eat-in restaurants' business. At Pizza Hut, carryout accounted for 40% of the dollar volume in 1986, compared with 37% in 1982.

In 1986, while the overall pizza market expanded rapidly (because of home delivery), in-restaurant consumption of pizza was not increasing significantly. Industry observers believed that the restaurant industry was seriously overbuilt; pizza parlors seemed to be on every corner in some towns. They believed that the already intense local competition in the pizza eat-in and carryout segments would soon approach all-out warfare, as evidenced by increased use of couponing, deals, and price competition.

The Pizza Consumer

Pizza was a very popular restaurant food item, second only to hamburgers in frequency of purchase. Pizza was predominantly a dinner food, although many consumers also viewed it as an evening snack. Consumers did not react casually to pizza, unlike their feelings for hamburgers, chicken, and fish. Consumer research had shown that pizza was a personal, almost sensual, experience for many people. Moreover, consumers generally did not believe that great pizza could be made by a fast-food chain.

While pizza consumption was strongest in the northern and eastern parts of the United States, pizza's appeal was broad based, with no areas exhibiting major rejection. However, tastes in pizza varied significantly by region. This presented a challenge for chains attempting to maintain product continuity while expanding into different regions.

By the early 1980s, convenience was crucial to many consumers. Two-career families often found cooking at home or eating in restaurants too time consuming, thereby increasing carryout and home delivery business. In both 1985 and 1986, consumer surveys undertaken by the *National Restaurant Association* identified pizza home delivery as the most important new fast food concept. Another study had shown that consumers generally viewed pizza as eat-at-home food. Many analysts believed that the rapid growth of the in-home video rental market, together with the increasing number of baby-boomers with small children, would further fuel the pizza delivery segment.

Competition in the Pizza Market

Although faced with intense competition from aggressive regional chains and single-unit owner-operated local competitors, Pizza Hut had dominated the eat-in pizza segment nationwide for years (Exhibit 1). Godfather's Pizza, another eat-in/carryout chain, which competed in many of the same local markets as Pizza Hut, traditionally was perceived as Pizza Hut's most significant national competitor.

Before 1984, neither Pizza Hut nor its franchisees thought that Domino's Pizza posed a serious competitive threat to Pizza Hut's leadership position in the overall pizza market. Domino's, however, had grown from sales of $626 million in 1984 to $1.085 billion in 1985, and to $1.55 billion by the end of 1986. In 1985 the chain opened 954 new outlets (bringing the total to 2,839)— the highest one-year total ever recorded by a food service company. Two-thirds of Domino's outlets were franchised; the company used its company-owned stores as sites for required franchisee training. Although there were several large franchisees operating many units all over the United States, most of the 600 franchisees in early 1986 owned only one or two stores. While some of its outlets had carryout windows, Domino's was essentially a delivery-only chain. Domino's management believed the large percentage of carryout business in the industry was especially vulnerable to Domino's delivery strategy.

Pizza Hut first experienced the effects of Domino's expansion in its company-owned stores. While Pizza Hut's franchisees had exclusive rights to most of the smaller markets, Pizza Hut's company-owned stores controlled most of the large, densely populated metropolitan markets. Domino's had initially focused its national expansion on those large metropolitan markets. By late 1985, Pizza Hut senior management was convinced that Domino's dominance of the fast-growing delivery segment was the major threat to Pizza Hut's continued leadership of the overall pizza market. By 1986, Domino's had begun to extend its expansion into the smaller towns generally controlled by Pizza Hut franchisees. Domino's clearly intended to gain total market leadership while maintaining its dominance of the delivery segment.

Pizza Hut, Incorporated

On June 15, 1958, Dan and Frank Carney, two college students from Wichita, Kansas, opened the first Pizza Hut restaurant. It was a startling success. By the following February, the Carney brothers had opened two more restaurants and had begun to develop plans for the first franchised outlet. The chain grew rapidly, with 43 restaurants opened by 1963 and 296 by 1968. Pizza Hut went public in 1969, and in 1977 was acquired by PepsiCo, Inc. In 1981 Pizza Hut became the largest pizza restaurant chain in the world in both sales and number of restaurants. Sales reached $1 billion in 1981; by December 1986, Pizza Hut, still headquartered in Wichita, had a total of 5,025 domestic units and annual sales of almost $2 billion (Exhibit 2).

Since the 1960s, Pizza Hut restaurants were characterized by a distinctive freestanding design and familiar red roof (Exhibit 3). All Pizza Hut restaurants were full-service, eat-in/carryout family-style operations seating about 60 to 90 customers and normally open from 11 a.m. to midnight.

Although the menu had changed over the years, pizza was always the main product in Pizza Hut restaurants. The company paid careful attention to operational efficiency, and continued to offer a high-quality product at a premium price. A constant stream of new product introductions served to invigorate consumer interest, but many franchisees were concerned by the increased cost of operations caused by the expanding menu.

For more than 20 years, the Pizza Hut franchisees had taken the lead in marketing. In the early 1980s, however, the company further strengthened its corporate marketing department and began developing comprehensive national and local market strategies. By 1986, the company was developing and implementing systemwide corporate marketing programs and realizing leverage from national TV advertising.

The Franchise System at Pizza Hut

Franchising was an integral part of the Pizza Hut strategy since the corporation's founding. In 1968, there were 293 franchised restaurants and only seven company-owned restaurants. Over the next seven years, the company built new stores and acquired many more (including the acquisition of the 225 units of a large Pizza Hut franchisee). By the mid-1970s, there were almost as many company-owned as franchised units. In December 1986, 135 individuals, partnerships, and/or corporations operated 2,395 Pizza Hut system restaurants and 96 delivery-only units as franchisees. Meanwhile, the company itself operated 2,173 restaurants and 361 delivery-only units.

Many of the original franchisees, whose holdings had grown with the company, were still part of the system in 1986. Sixty percent of all franchised units were controlled by franchisees whose main offices were still in Wichita. In the Pizza Hut system, exclusive franchises were granted for specified market areas. Unlike franchise systems characterized by single-unit owner/operators, most Pizza Hut franchisees were large companies with diversified holdings, sometimes including other food service franchisor units like Kentucky Fried Chicken and Long John Silver. Of the 135 franchisees, almost two-thirds operated 10 or more Pizza Hut system restaurants in 1986. Except for minority opportunity programs, no new franchise areas had been offered to the public since 1971. When a franchisee chose to sell its holdings, they were purchased by the company or another franchise holder.

Franchisee rights and obligations were specified in formal franchise agreements. Under the agreements, each franchisee was obligated to develop its exclusive market area in accordance with a five-year development schedule. Essentially, the agreement required the franchisee to open an agreed-upon number of new restaurants during the first year of the agreement, an agreed-upon number during the second year, and so on, up to year five. The development schedule represented franchisee commitment to significant continuing investment

in the business. After the five-year period expired, the company could negotiate a secondary development schedule with the franchisee to open additional restaurants in the area, if the company deemed it practicable. Although franchisee failure to comply with either development schedule entitled the company to franchise others or to open company-owned restaurants in the previously exclusive area, this had never been necessary. In no case could there be a restaurant established within two miles of an existing franchisee restaurant.

Franchisees paid Pizza Hut an initial fee of $15,000 for each system restaurant they opened. Franchisees also paid the company an ongoing franchise fee of 4% of monthly gross sales. The company or franchisee invested about $466,000–$816,000 to open each eat-in/carryout restaurant. By contrast, delivery-only units required an estimated $128,500–$198,500 investment. However, by the time one included delivery vehicles, training, additional advertising, and the company's central order-taking computer system, the company's investment in a company-owned delivery unit was about equal to that of a traditional restaurant. Franchisees investing in delivery-only units typically did not buy vehicles and did not always adopt the company's computer-ordering system (see Exhibit 4 for expenses of company-owned delivery units).

The International Pizza Hut Franchise Holders Association

The International Pizza Hut Franchise Holders Association (IPHFHA) was formed in 1967 to "solidify the national image of Pizza Hut and to further product loyalty," and to "devise the most appropriate use of the funds available for national advertising." By 1986, its role had been extended to render many other services to franchisees (e.g., accounting services, group life insurance, workman's compensation insurance, credit union).

Franchisees were required to become members of the IPHFHA. The IPHFHA communicated with the company regularly through the IPHFHA board of directors. The IPHFHA employed a professional staff headed by Gerald Aaron, president, who acted as intermediary between the board and the company. He directed for the association the broad policy areas of marketing, finance, and administration. Joint advisory committees (with franchisee and company members) were formed in 1985 to further enhance communication between the company and the franchisees on the issues of human resources, delivery, products, and buildings and equipment.

The IPHFHA was reorganized in 1975, and the Advertising Committee was formed to "determine and control the amount, kind, and quality of national advertising and sales promotion to be provided . . . for Pizza Hut and its franchisees." (In 1981 the role of the Advertising Committee was continued under the new franchise agreement.) Four marketing professionals made up the Advertising Committee, two representing the company and two representing the franchisees. IPHFHA Members voted on funding for national advertising and other IPHFHA programs. The company, although not a member of IPHFHA, was contractually bound by the franchise agreement to contribute at the same rate as the franchisees. In 1986, the current assessment was 2% of the first $28,000 of monthly sales for each restaurant and 1% of all monthly sales above $28,000. The Advertising Committee controlled the entire advertising budget, and was also responsible for hiring and firing the national advertising agency.

Market area advertising was managed by local co-ops comprising all of those franchisees (and the company if applicable) operating restaurants within a particular market area. All co-op members, franchisees and company alike, were required to make contributions to the co-op for advertising in their area in the amount of 2% of monthly gross sales (in addition to the contributions to the national advertising fund). All disputes arising within co-ops were arbitrated by the Advertising Committee.

In addition to ad hoc interaction between the company and its franchisees at regional store manager meetings, there were two general systemwide meetings each year. Franchisees set the summer meeting agenda and the company set the winter meeting agenda. Company management also regularly met with the board of IPHFHA and with the franchisees on the advisory committees.

Delivery at Pizza Hut, Inc.

For many years, the prospect of entering the delivery market worried Pizza Hut senior managers; delivery units might cannibalize the traditional restaurant business, causing reduced profit margins. In the summer of 1984, however, Pizza Hut began exploring the possibility of such an entry. Because it was believed that the addition of delivery service to traditional eat-in restaurants would create unmanageable operational bottlenecks, the solution for Pizza Hut management was to enter the delivery market with separate delivery-only units (i.e., with no eat-in or carryout facilities). These units would be considerably smaller than the traditional restaurant facilities and would not require parking space or highly visible locations (Exhibit 3); occupancy costs therefore would be about 2.1% of sales rather than 6% for the standard eat-in restaurants.

In 1985 a small delivery task group was formed at Pizza Hut and began opening company-owned delivery units in several markets. Their idea was to open a cluster of delivery-only units in each market and keep their costs as low as possible because of the small expected margins (Exhibit 4). There was considerable resistance to the delivery concept at all levels within the company, and company restaurant managers and supervisors in the markets where delivery units had been opened complained bitterly about the adverse effect on their sales. Nevertheless, Pizza Hut management was becoming increasingly concerned about Domino's rapid expansion, and deemed entry into the delivery segment necessary if the company was to maintain its market leadership position.

By August 1985, eight markets had been opened with a total of 51 company-owned delivery-only units. In the well-developed markets—Atlanta, Georgia, and Norfolk, Virginia—customers called a single phone number. Orders were then sent by facsimile machine to the appropriate delivery unit. Although the system was relatively cheap, as the number of units grew, it became more and more unmanageable, and the "fax" machines presented a significant bottleneck. In late summer 1985, senior Pizza Hut managers visited the Norfolk market and became convinced that, with a number of operational adjustments, the delivery concept was workable, offered tremendous potential growth, and should be pursued. The company postponed further expansion into new markets while it contracted for the development of a computerized central ordering system and perfected other aspects of the delivery concept.

The computerized central ordering system, called the Customer Service Center (CSC), allowed customers in a particular market to call a single number to place an order. The caller first was asked his or her phone number and the system ascertained whether the caller had ordered before. If so, the operator would verify the caller's name and address and ask if the customer would like the same type of pizza previously ordered. The order would then be forwarded automatically to the appropriate delivery unit where a terminal would receive the order information.

The CSC system, although expensive to develop, was designed to be capable of handling the vast number of calls generated in a large market with a large number of delivery units. It was necessary, however, that the system work perfectly. Customers in an eat-in restaurant understood and tolerated waiting a few minutes to be seated. Delivery customers expected their phone call to be answered within seconds, even though 60% of the daily calls for an entire market area might come in during a one-hour period. While there were substantial marketing benefits to having only one phone number for an entire market, there were significant risks in operating such a complex system. In Norfolk, Virginia, initial problems with the installation of the CSC had created serious losses in a once-profitable delivery market.

Although there had been some difficulties during its installation, Pizza Hut management was convinced that the CSC would be a significant competitive advantage. About 70% of Domino's franchisees owned only one store, and Pizza Hut believed that the costs of coordination and management of such a centralized ordering system at Domino's would be prohibitive. In the Pizza Hut system, the concentration of restaurant ownership in the hands of the company and relatively few franchisees would allow for much easier coordination and substantial cost savings. Under the company's delivery concept, the company would invest in the CSC for each market and manage it, coordinating the ordering process and providing service on a fee-per-call basis to participating franchisees and company stores (currently $ .65 per call). Pizza Hut's investment in the CSCs was expected to be large, but management believed that such systems were essential to the delivery strategy. It was expected that eventually the franchisees would purchase the necessary equipment and manage the Customer Service Centers themselves in their own markets.

Another major issue presented in developing a profitable delivery concept was whether there would be a charge for service. Pizza Hut management was convinced that for competitive reasons the company could not charge for delivery (Domino's delivered free with a 30-minute guarantee). The additional cost of providing free delivery was the same, regardless of order size. This meant that, to the extent the average check price could be increased, margins would increase. To help maintain margins when offering free delivery, therefore, it was decided that the size and price of delivered pizzas would be slightly increased over pizza in traditional restaurants (i.e., delivery sizes would be 10-14-16″ versus the 9-13-15″ sizes in the traditional restaurants and Domino's 12-16″ sizes).

Customers would pay approximately 10% more for a small, medium, or large pizza, but would get more as well. This "upsizing" would increase the average check price and gross margin, thereby helping to defray the cost of free delivery and the Customer Service Centers.

In early 1986, Pizza Hut was reorganized to reflect the increasing importance and autonomy of the delivery segment (Exhibit 5). A senior vice president of operations managed all traditional restaurant operations, while Senior Vice President Allan Huston was general manager of delivery. Still another senior vice president led the marketing function for the traditional restaurants. Delivery had its own separate marketing department that reported directly to Allan Huston. Even the regions into which the country was divided were different for delivery and the traditional restaurant business.

Although there was some experimentation with alternative delivery concepts (e.g., no upsizing in some markets) during the spring and summer of 1986, the marketing function for the delivery group was not fully operational until July. Huston concentrated primarily on the operational details surrounding the opening of new delivery units rather than on refining the Pizza Hut delivery concept. In the first half of 1986, Pizza Hut doubled the number of markets where it operated delivery units and had almost quadrupled the total number of units (Exhibit 6). Those delivery units were predominately in metropolitan areas—where most of the company's markets were. The initial units opened were in markets with high levels of traditional restaurant penetration and high "per-store-average" (PSA) sales. A second group, opened later in 1986, were in low penetration and low per-store-average sales markets.

Throughout 1986, Pizza Hut managers on the traditional restaurant side of the business continued to be concerned about competition from the Pizza Hut delivery operation, as well as from Domino's. Huston and other managers in the delivery operation, however, believed that delivery was expanding the market by including people who would not go to a restaurant for pizza. They argued that consumers who ate pizza in restaurants and those who had pizza delivered sought very different benefits, and that delivery did not compete directly with traditional restaurants. Moreover, the adverse effects of Pizza Hut delivery units on traditional restaurant sales growth appeared to be most pronounced in markets where there was weak sales growth already; in strong markets the effect was short lived. As Reinemund noted in early 1986, "We do not yet know how great a factor this overlap will be. But what we do know is that in many cases our restaurant business has actually grown after our delivery units have entered the market." In the words of another senior Pizza Hut manager:

> While it is true that we often are serving the same customers, we are serving them on totally separate dining occasions. When we introduce delivery to a market, we get the business of customers who probably were ordering a competitor's pizza simply for the convenience of home delivery.

As for personnel, it was clear that needs of the delivery business were significantly different from those of the traditional restaurant business. Pizza Hut restaurant managers were trained to manage the "total customer experience" and, because of the isolation from customers, some restaurant managers did not think they would enjoy running a delivery-only unit. While many production and operation functions would overlap, store managers found it hard to see how career paths could cross over from traditional full-service restaurants to delivery units or vice versa. Moreover, moving as quickly as it had into new markets, Pizza Hut found it difficult to manage at the store level. Ninety percent of the people working in the delivery business were new, and delivery presented unfamiliar operational demands in the areas of driver management, trade area definition, and order taking.

The Franchisees' Experience with Delivery

A few Pizza Hut franchisees had been offering delivery unofficially for 20 years. In the early 1980s, the company consistently attempted to dissuade franchisees from offering delivery. Nevertheless, the number of small-town franchisees delivering pizza to college dormitories and military bases from their traditional restaurants had begun to increase. In some isolated cases franchisees faced local competitive environments that they believed necessitated offering delivery. By 1982, about 25 franchisees operated delivery services from a total of about 75 standard eat-in restaurants.

Most franchisees that entered the delivery segment did so by retrofitting existing eat-in restaurants to allow for delivery "out the back door" (Exhibit 6 shows the number of franchisees owning retrofit and delivery-only units from 1984 to 1986). They found, however, that retrofitting significantly increased demands on the restaurant manager and required much greater local management skills. Because of operational bottlenecks,

some franchisees lost money on the delivery business and ceased delivery operations. The company believed this supported its concept of opening separate delivery-only units.

Through 1985, the majority of Pizza Hut franchisees saw no reason for delivery. They faced little or no competition in their market from the major chains offering delivery, and were less interested in overall market share battles than the company seemed to be. Sixty-five percent of all franchised restaurants were in towns with populations under 50,000 people, and delivery in those rural areas was not as easy to justify economically as in more densely populated markets. In late 1985, when the company changed its position completely and began to encourage franchisees to open delivery-only units, most franchisees were not interested in doing so.

In November 1985, the company announced to franchisees that it interpreted franchise agreement development schedules to include delivery and, therefore, the company had the right to require franchisee development of delivery units in their markets. The company announced that it would not exercise that right for one-and-a-half years while it perfected the concept, but urged franchisees to begin developing delivery-only units immediately.

The franchise community's response was quick and clear. Most franchisees saw no reason to risk business in their eat-in restaurants by expanding into the delivery market. They denied that the development schedules allowed Pizza Hut to require them to open delivery units. They openly expressed their disagreement with the company's delivery concept, especially regarding upsizing (referred to by one franchisee as "up-pricing"). They also questioned the necessity of the computerized Customer Service Centers and the delivery-only units (some franchisees wanted to retrofit existing restaurants, and others wanted carryout allowed in the delivery units). Significant tension arose between the company and its franchisees. At a heated IPHFHA board meeting in December 1985, board members and Pizza Hut senior management recognized that they had been concentrating too much on each other and not enough on Domino's. They agreed to operate temporarily under a "yellow flag" plan (an automobile racing term referring to the period when each side continues to operate as before without either side trying to improve its relative position).

The company's upsizing concept continued to be a focal point of disagreement. Although Pizza Hut suggested prices, the franchisees were free to price their products as they pleased. The franchisees argued that, even though they had not increased prices as frequently as the company-owned restaurants had in past years, they were still at a price disadvantage when compared to the competition. This disadvantage was especially acute in the delivery business; franchisees believed that upsizing would exacerbate the problem because customers were conscious only of the absolute price of a small, medium, or large pizza and did not calculate price per square inch of the product.

The franchisees also wanted to know why Pizza Hut needed an expensive CSC system, if Domino's didn't have one. They felt that if delivery was necessary, the costs should be kept as low as possible. This meant simple phone ordering to each local restaurant, and delivery out of existing restaurants where feasible. It was important to franchisees that the system be as flexible as possible so that they could find local solutions to local problems.

The reorganization of Pizza Hut in early 1986, which provided for the delivery business to operate autonomously from the traditional restaurant business, raised another issue in the franchise community. Franchisees were concerned that while the company could afford to run the delivery and eat-in businesses separately, the franchisees did not have the resources for separate marketing and operations departments for the traditional restaurant and delivery business. The mismatch of organizational forms between company and franchisees was expected to create significant management difficulties. To make matters worse, the Pizza Hut national advertising account had been split in two within the advertising agency so that a separate group could begin working only on delivery. Many franchisees viewed the two businesses as one and were concerned that their separation would make coordination between delivery and eat-in even more difficult.

There was little consensus of opinion among the franchisees regarding the various elements of the company's delivery concept. There was, however, virtual unanimous franchisee concurrence that the existing franchise agreement did not cover delivery. In February 1986 Jim Baxter, who had been with Pizza Hut for almost 10 years, was appointed vice president of restaurant franchising and assumed the role of liaison between the company and franchisees. In May, newly appointed president Steve Reinemund accompanied Baxter to a series of regional meetings with the franchisees where Reinemund announced that the company no longer contended that the existing development agreement covered delivery. He also announced the company's intention to negotiate

with the board of the IPHFHA to produce an amendment to the franchise agreement that would provide for systemwide entry into the delivery market. Reinemund suggested that the amendment would include incentives (e.g., reduced or no royalties for a certain time period on new delivery-only units) designed to make franchisee participation in the delivery segment more attractive. These incentives would be retroactive for any franchisee delivery-only units opened in the meantime. The amendment would take effect if franchisees representing 85% of the units approved it within a specified time period.

The August Franchisee Meeting

As the August 1986 franchisee meeting drew near, Pizza Hut management decided it was time to press again for the full involvement of all franchisees in systemwide entry into the delivery market. Pizza Hut operated delivery units in 16 markets, with a total of 284 company-owned units. The company had hired and trained over 10,000 people. The flagship Norfolk market, which had experienced difficulties, was now profitable. The first half-year results from the operating units were impressive, and Delivery General Manager Huston was confident that the company could make a good business case for delivery.

Huston and the delivery group gave an extremely upbeat presentation of the delivery data to franchisees at the August meeting. Their purposes included (1) to convince franchisees that the time had come to give total support to the delivery effort, (2) to "sell" the company's delivery concept to the franchisees, and (3) to successfully launch the amendment negotiation process that was to begin in earnest after the meeting. While many franchisees remained adamantly opposed to delivery, others were becoming convinced that they could, in fact, increase their overall income with delivery even if they would face decreased average margins. While the idea of delivery became more acceptable, however, there was still little support for the particulars of the company's delivery concept.

The Current Situation

As the negotiations for an amendment to the Franchise Agreement continued into the fall of 1986, competition in the delivery market intensified tremendously. Sys-

Exhibit 4 Pro Forma Profit and Loss Statement (based on $8,000/week sales)[a]

	Company-owned Traditional Restaurant	Company-owned Delivery Unit
Gross sales	100.0%	100.0%
Advertising, discounts, promotions, and allowances	16.5%	18.5%
Cost of sales[b] & labor	48.5%	46.2%
Semivariables & premiums[c]	8.7%	5.2%
Vehicles[d]	–	6.1%
Occupancy costs	6.0%	2.1%
General and administrative	7.2%	7.2%
Customer service center costs	–	5.9%
Net field contribution	13.1%	8.8%

[a]Percentages reflect an assumed $8,000/week store. As weekly sales decreased below $8,000, expenses as percent of sales increased significantly. At approximately $7,000/week, Delivery Unit net field contribution was 0.

[b]Cost of sales tended to be lower in the Delivery Units due to a combination of upsizing and higher prices per order. Labor costs for Delivery Units did not include order-taking expenses that were reflected in the Customer Service Center costs.

[c]Semivariables refers to utilities, uniforms, and other operating supplies. Premiums refers to items such as special glassware or toys that were given away or sold below cost to promote the sale of a particular menu item.

[d]Vehicle expenses reflect a mix of driver- and company-owned vehicles. Eighty percent of the delivery vehicles were owned by the drivers, who were reimbursed for their use per trip.

Exhibit 5 Organization Chart

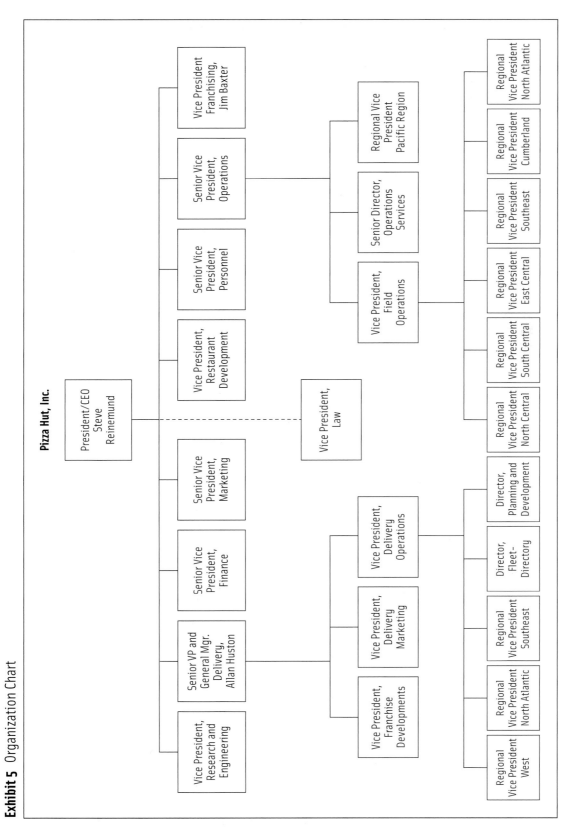

Pizza Hut, Inc.

President/CEO
Steve Reinemund

- Vice President, Research and Engineering
- Senior VP and General Mgr. Delivery, Allan Huston
  - Vice President, Franchise Developments
  - Vice President, Delivery Marketing
  - Vice President, Delivery Operations
    - Regional Vice President West
    - Regional Vice President North Atlantic
    - Regional Vice President Southeast
    - Director, Fleet-Directory
    - Director, Planning and Development
- Senior Vice President, Finance
- Senior Vice President, Marketing
- Vice President, Restaurant Development
- Senior Vice President, Personnel
- Senior Vice President, Operations
  - Vice President, Field Operations
    - Regional Vice President North Central
    - Regional Vice President South Central
    - Regional Vice President East Central
    - Regional Vice President Southeast
    - Regional Vice President Cumberland
    - Regional Vice President North Atlantic
  - Senior Director, Operations Services
  - Regional Vice President Pacific Region
- Vice President, Franchising, Jim Baxter

Vice President, Law

Exhibit 6 Open Pizza Hut System Traditional Restaurants and Delivery Units[a]

	Company-owned		Franchisee-owned		
	Traditional Restaurants	**Delivery-only Units**	**Traditional Restaurants[b]**	**Retrofit**	**Delivery-only Units**
August 1984	2,011	11	2,089	70	15
December 1984	2,025	16	2,137	98	20
August 1985	2,046	51	2,256	131	30
December 1985	2,004	78	2,352	162	46
August 1986	2,208	284	2,277	241	66
December 1986	2,173	361	2,395	292	96

[a]Domestic U.S. restaurants and delivery units only
[b]Totals for franchisee-owned traditional restaurants include those restaurants retrofitted to provide delivery service.

HP CONSUMER PRODUCTS BUSINESS ORGANIZATION: DISTRIBUTING PRINTERS VIA THE INTERNET

In spring 1998, Pradeep Jotwani, vice-president and general manager of the Consumer Products Business Organization of the Hewlett Packard Company (HP), was contemplating the increasing success of eCommerce and its implications for his division. The consumer products group had started selling refurbished printers through an Internet outlet center in December 1997, but Jotwani was now considering a move to sell new printers directly to consumers via this new eChannel. If he were to make such a move, he wondered which products to sell online at what prices, and how to communicate this strategy to the channel partners without damaging the existing distribution structure. Jotwani commented:

> Channel inflections are very challenging. The last time we faced a similar situation was when we had to transform ourselves from being a predominantly business-to-business company that sold printers through value added resellers [VARs] to a consumer products company that had to reach consumers through the retail channel. Even then there were the doubters, but not only did we make the transition successfully, but we also emerged stronger. The challenge today is to decide on the level of strategic emphasis on Internet distribution so that we emerge stronger after the transition, rather than just defending our position.

The decision is complicated by several factors. Companies like Dell have shown that the direct model can work quite well. However, all of our current sales are through retailers and any direct selling efforts may lead to conflict with our retail partners.[1]

HP History

Bill Hewlett and Dave Packard founded HP in 1939 in a Palo Alto garage. One of HP's first clients, Walt Disney Studios, purchased eight audio oscillators to develop a new sound system for the movie "Fantasia." In the 1940s, the needs of WWII created a demand for HP's electronic instruments. HP also began signing with sales representatives to market products throughout the United States. During the 1950s, the company mastered the internal effects of growth, defining corporate objectives and developing a path toward globalization. By 1962, HP was ranked number 460 in the Fortune 500. The company enjoyed growth in the test and measurement segment and introduced itself to related fields, such as medical electronics and analytical instrumentation.

Innovation continued in the 1970s with the release of the first scientific handheld calculator, the HP 35, which made the slide rule obsolete. The 1980s were critical to HP's success, as it became a major force in the computer industry and printer market. Both the ThinkJet (inkjet) and the LaserJet printers were introduced in 1984. In 1985, HP's net revenue was $6.5 billion and the company had 85,000 employees.[2]

With the continuous release of computers, peripherals, and related products in the 1990s, HP became known as one of the few organizations that was able to marry measurement, computing, and communication. This success translated into HP's number 16 ranking on the Fortune 500 list by 1997. Net revenue for HP was then $42.9 billion and employees totaled 121,900, up from

Research Associate Edith D. Prescott prepared this case under the supervision of Professors Kirthi Kalyanam of Santa Clara University and Rajiv Lal as the basis for class discussion rather than to illustrate either effective or ineffective handling of an administrative situation. Parts of this case were based upon the material presented in, "Hewlett Packard Consumer Products Business Organization: Distribution through E*Commerce Channels," by Kirthi Kalyanam and Shelby McIntyre of Santa Clara University, 1998–1999. Shen Li, General Manager of HP Shopping Village, also provided helpful input in the preparation of this case. Some of the information in this case has been disguised for confidentiality.

[1]This section was drawn from "Hewlett Packard Consumer Products Business Organization: Distribution through E*Commerce Channels" by Kirthi Kalyanam and Shelby McIntyre, 1998–1999, p. 1.
[2]*Hewlett Packard Web Site.* August 24, 1999. <http://www.hp. com.>

$38.4 billion and 112,000 in 1996. For the same period, net earnings rose from $2.6 billion to $3.1 billion. Despite these increases, 1997 was the first time since 1992 that revenues increased by less than 20%. Lew Platt, the president and CEO since 1992, blamed HP's inability to control operating expenses, lower demand, and the strength of the dollar as compared to other currencies.[3]

In 1998, HP grouped its products into five general categories: Computer Products, Service & Support; Test & Measurement Products & Service; Medical Electronic Equipment & Service; Electronic Components; and Chemical Analysis & Service.

Computer Products, Service & Support.

In 1997, this segment of operations made up 83% of HP's total revenue and included computers ranging from palmtops to supercomputers, plus peripherals and services.[4] Though HP was well known for its technological innovation and product quality, marketing was the key to HP's success. The company had always considered the needs of its customers and partners; it had not only met their requirements, but had also grown with them as their needs became more demanding and involved. HP knew that the success of its customers and partners was directly correlated with its own.

HP had shown its ability to respond to demanding needs when it introduced its first computer in 1966, which was used to collect and examine data originating from HP electronic instruments. Expansion into business computing occurred in the 1970s with the HP 3000. HP introduced its first personal computer (PC) in 1980 and later released a family of computer systems in 1986 that were based upon RISC architecture. In 1991 HP unveiled the 11-ounce 95LX palmtop PC, the three-pound OmniBook 300 in 1993, and the HP Pavilion PC in 1995.[5] HP was the fastest-growing PC company in the world by 1997, ending the year as the number four PC manufacturer worldwide. The top four companies, Compaq, IBM, Dell, and HP had a combined market share of 38% (and increasing) of the PC market. Compaq held the number one position with a 13.5% market share.[6]

Just as it had been a significant player in the PC market, HP led the printer industry. This was despite the fact that HP was not associated with printers as of the early 1980s. Instead, Epson, Diablo, and Qume led the way with their dot-matrix and daisy-wheel printers. Then, in 1984, HP released its ThinkJet, which was based on the thermal inkjet technology the company had developed in its own labs in the 1970s.[7] Laser printers were also released in 1984 and changed the industry dramatically. These printers generated eight pages per minute (ppm), had 300 dot-per-inch (dpi) resolution, and cost $3,495. The technology later improved to 1200 dpi and 24 ppm. HP released the first network printer, LaserJet IIISi, in 1991, allowing printers to be connected directly to LANs. HP then introduced the first desktop color laser, Color LaserJet, in 1994. Companies were slow to acquire this color technology, however, and vendors had difficulty finding the appropriate price points.[8] In 1997 and 1998, demand for HP products was soaring and the company had leading market shares in both the InkJet and LaserJet segments. HP was also a leader in the printer supply business, which contributed $5 billion to its total sales of $42.9 billion in 1997.[9]

HP management was credited with making two vital decisions that led to the success of the LaserJet series. First was the move to sell via the reseller channel. David Packard said in his 1995 book, *The HP Way*:

> The importance to distribute LaserJets through resellers cannot be overemphasized. It was a critical final piece of the overall strategy. It established a fundamental channel strength for HP that has been a competitive advantage over the past ten years.[10]

The second marketing decision was in the naming of the product. The LaserJet was nearly called the 2686 because the engineers were simply going to use the standard numerical naming sequence. Jim Hall, one of the original engineers on the LaserJet project said:

> There wasn't a jet in it, and we thought we'd be laughed off the street.[11]

[3]*Hewlett Packard 1997 Annual Report*, p. 2.
[4]Ibid., p. 55.
[5]*Hewlett Packard Web Site.* August 24, 1999. <http://www.hp.com.>
[6]Stephen C. Dube, "Computer Industry Commentary," *Wasserstein Perella Securities, Inc. Equity Research*, (May 18, 1998): p. 1.

[7]Kirthi Kalyanam and Shelby McIntyre, "Hewlett Packard Consumer Products Business Organization: Distribution through E*Commerce Channels," 1998–1999, p. 2.
[8]Kelly Damore, "Laser Printers," *Computer Reseller News*, June 1, 1997, p. 80.
[9]Norm Alster, "Is Printer Ink Replacement a License to Print Money?" *Investor's Business Daily*, May 28, 1998, p. 8.
[10]Kelly Damore, "HP LaserJet Milestone," *Computer Reseller News*, May 10, 1997, p. 195.
[11]Ibid.

The Printer Industry

As with all hot new technology, printer prices eventually came down which resulted in lower dollar growth rates for printer manufacturers. Nevertheless, significant enthusiasm remained for new releases of technologically superior printers, fueled partly by the emerging trends in printer usage. One such trend beginning in 1997 was the "distribute-then-print" model for information flow within companies. These models enabled a document created in one location to be distributed electronically to users in multiple locations, where it would be printed out individually.

In 1997, revenues of printer manufacturers were $8 billion for the U.S. and $22 billion worldwide. These numbers included all InkJet, Laser, and multifunction peripherals for personal and home/small office use. As home PCs became more prevalent in the 1990s, printer demand rose dramatically. By 1998, InkJet models accounted for 70% of all units sold.

The printer supply business obviously benefited from this surge in printer sales. Printer supplies, including toner cartridges, were an annuity to the retailer and manufacturer once a printer was purchased. They were very profitable and the strategy was analogous to the razor blade scenario—sell the razor cheap and then charge premium prices for the blades.

InkJet Printers (all speeds).

Most people opted for InkJet printers due to their versatility and low cost. For $150, a consumer could buy even a color InkJet that produced exceptionally good results. In spring 1998, HP had a 55% market share in this segment, up from 49% in December 1997. HP's InkJet sales were expected to improve further with the release of the 2000C in June 1998, which incorporated its new Modular Ink Delivery System (MIDS). Canon's market share was 19% and declining, while Epson's share had increased to 18% due to its aggressive marketing and affordable products. Lexmark's market share, which had nearly doubled to 6% since 1997, was attributed to its low-end $99 ColorJet 1000 and its new $249 model 5700.

Laser Printers (11 ppm and higher).

LaserJet printers could handle high volumes of text documents, had superior quality and speed, and could be used on a network. By 1998 black-and-white laser technology was mature and recent advances had focused on performance and price. A black-and-white laser jet printer giving eight ppm, for example, could be purchased for about $300. Color laser technology was a different story. Although prices had dropped significantly, the price points still began at $3,000.[12] In spring 1998, HP led this segment with an impressive 85% market share, primarily due to the overwhelming adoption of the LaserJet 4000 family. Lexmark was the closest second holding an 8% market share.

Multifunction Printers (MFP).

MFPs, machines that could print, copy, fax, and scan, were introduced in 1993 but did not catch on until 1997. Some units could perform color scanning and copying, and could shrink and enlarge originals. To do all the same tasks with independent machines would cost about twice as much and obviously take up more office space. Another bonus was that they were easier to install than stand-alone machines because separate device drivers were not needed. These machines were criticized, however, for being competent in all functions, but doing none exceptionally well. Because they were slower, they were also unsuitable for high-volume printing. Furthermore, they were not designed to connect to networks—although such connections were technologically possible. And, finally, it was risky to rely on only one device because if one function failed, the whole system went down.[13] The release of new MFPs was directly correlated with the technology updates for InkJets and LaserJets because MFPs had either one or the other capability as its underlying function.

The pace of technology and life cycles of products varied between InkJets and Laser printers. For InkJets, the core technology was the printer cartridge, which affected speed and quality. The life cycle of an InkJet printer was between one and two years and the difference depended on whether the InkJet was targeted to personal or business use. InkJets with longer life cycles were intended for the business customer and were more expensive. For laser printers, key technologies were printer cartridges, toners, photoreceptors, paper handling, optics, and scanners. The life cycle for a Laser printer, which targeted business users, was two-to-three years. The speed of technological change could also be measured by the volume of new SKUs being introduced each year by all manufacturers. By December 1997, for example, 52 Laser and 84 InkJet SKUs were distributed through the reseller channel, the majority of which were introduced during the prior twelve months.

---

[12]Susan Breidenbach, "Printed Matters," *Forbes,* fall 1998, pp. 38–40.
[13]Susan Breidenbach, "The Swiss Army Printer," *Forbes,* fall 1998, pp. 46–48.

Consumer Buying Patterns

The At-Home Market. By February 1997, 91% of people with home computers also owned a printer. Some households had more than one printer with an even split between color and black-and-white models. InkJets were the most common, particularly among color printers. The typical head-of-household in a home with a printer had an average annual income of $60K and children living at home.[14]

The home market could be divided into "first-time" and "repeat" buyers. In general, first-time buyers shopped for about one month, focusing on quality, speed, after-sales service and support, availability, brand, and price. These buyers usually went through the normal phases of awareness, consideration, and purchase behaviors. During the first two phases people visited web sites and physical stores, talked to friends, and read *Consumer Reports*. Most had a preconception of which brand and SKUs to buy before entering a store, but only 65%–70% of the time would a shopper find a particular SKU in a high-volume retailer. Once in the store, shoppers could be influenced by in-store demonstrations of other printer brands. Manufacturer guarantees were an important buying factor because consumers believed that retailers had poor after-sales support and repair services.[15]

First-time buyers also tended to purchase a PC, monitor, and printer as a bundle, which accounted for 20% of all printers sold. Because the PC was the most expensive of these items, it was the focus of the buying decision.

In contrast, repeat buyers tended to buy a printer as a single purchase.[16] Often they were motivated by the need to update previously owned technology (the quality, speed, or color of their printer). Other motivations were the printing needs associated with their growing fascination with digital cameras, scanners, and Internet distribution as well as the emerging needs of their children. For example, a two- or three-PC home might have needed a second printer, or a child off to college might have needed a new and smaller printer for the dorm room. In effect, repeat buyers came in two flavors. When they were simply upgrading their existing technology or buying additional units similar to the original, they had shorter shopping periods and were more likely to buy "sight-unseen." Mail order was a popular channel for these buyers and accounted for 8% of all printer sales. When they were introducing themselves to a new printer category, however, repeat buyers became like first-time buyers, but were more informed. Repeat buyers were also the larger of the two segments.

The Home Office Market. Individuals with home offices became important to the printer market in the 1990s. These individuals were primarily telecommuting, moonlighting, or were self-employed. Their preference for using a home office ranged from a better quality of life to tax deductions and convenience. In 1997, it was estimated that 52 million Americans worked from home and 11 million telecommuted from a home office at least once a month.[17] The changing demands of the work place were expected to sustain this trend.

The all-in-one peripherals, or MFP, were the most popular product for the home office. As previously mentioned, these machines printed, copied, scanned, and faxed, and were particularly useful when minimizing costs and saving space were paramount. Buying patterns for this segment were even more deliberate than in the at-home category because these people tended to know exactly what they needed and had specific price points in mind.

Channels of Distribution

Although HP sold printers to consumers through seven channel types, the first three listed below accounted for bulk of the sales.

1. *Computer Product Superstores.* CompUSA was an example of this type of retailer. It carried a broad and deep assortment of PCs, peripherals, and computer-related products. Store employees were generally knowledgeable enough to respond to customers' questions. This type of superstore was known as a category specialist, focusing on PCs.

2. *Consumer Electronic Superstores.* Circuit City was an example of this type of retailer. Computers and related products were only one of many

---

[14]"1997 Digital Imaging Survey—Printer Ownership & Usage #11073," *Investext*, February 1, 1997, Ch. 5.
[15]Kirthi Kalyanam and Shelby McIntyre, "Hewlett Packard Consumer Products Business Organization: Distribution through E*Commerce Channels," 1998–1999, p. 3.
[16]Ibid.

[17]Debra Cash, "There's No Office Like Home," *Inc. Web Site,* August 26, 1999. <http://www.inc.com.>

types of consumer electronics offered. Salespeople, who often worked on commission, tended to encourage customers to buy more expensive products.

3. *Office Product Superstores.* Staples was an example of this type of retailer. Computers and related products were only one of many types of products offered. The sales mix included printers, copiers, fax machines, telephones, office furniture, and related supplies. Both small offices and home offices (SOHO) were the primary target markets of these stores. Sales help in these stores was as good as in other self-service stores.

The remaining channel types were corporate account dealers, indirect mail-order companies, mass merchants, and department stores.[18] An example of a corporate account dealer was Inacom, which did not have a physical store and derived at least 50% of its revenue from its outbound corporate account sales force. MicroWarehouse was an example of a mail-order company. It generated more than 75% of its revenue from catalogue advertising and/or the Internet. Delivery of goods to consumers was almost always by U.S. mail or UPS. Mass merchants, such as Wal-Mart, and department stores, such as Sears, focused on the at-home market and stocked a limited selection of computers and computer-related products.

Retail Account Management

HP had a solid reputation with its primary retail accounts and was reinforced by all of the services that HP provided. Large retail accounts represented 90% of HP's printer sales (in units). The company used an account team to do business directly with each account. These teams worked with their assigned retailers on many fronts. For example, they helped coordinate co-marketing efforts, which included cooperative advertising and in-store displays, and provided merchandise development funds. These funds, which subsidized retail promotions to consumers, amounted to 2%–3% of sales in computer-related product categories.

Manufacturer's Advertised Price (MAP) policies were common practice in the industry. MAP clauses were typically inserted into the cooperative advertising contracts. These clauses stipulated that the manufacturer would not reimburse the reseller for cooperative ads that involved a price below a specified level. As a result, there was little variation in advertised retail prices across channels for the fast-moving SKUs. Other segments of assistance were category management, which aided the retailer in understanding trends, and detailing. Detailers tended to work for a third party but were paid for and scheduled by HP. They performed functions such as making sure that the appropriate type of paper was being used in the printers displayed on the shop floor and that the signage was adequate. HP teams also helped manage logistics and inventory for its major accounts.[19] The cost of all of these support services to HP was 1.5% of sales, in addition to the cost of cooperative advertising funds. Finally, HP provided price protection for inventory that became obsolete on the retail shelf, and this resulted in a payoff of 1%–2% of sales to the retailer.

HP retailers were responsible for a number of value-added functions. These included breaking bulk orders and shipping merchandise to individual retail stores, sales assistance, advertising, after-sales customer service and support, credit/collections from consumers, and returns processing.[20] Most importantly, retailers enabled shoppers to see the physical products, get a sense for their speed, and judge the quality of their output.

HP also did business with smaller retail chains, such as TOPS. HP, however, used distributors to reach such customers, rather than going direct. These distributors could sell only to HP authorized retailers. The authorization process included an evaluation of the history of the retailer, its operating practices, and the management team.[21]

Retailer Prices & Profitability

Average retail prices for printers had declined steadily and were $299 for the most popular InkJet printer and $999 for the most popular LaserJet printer in 1998. Both retail and manufacturer printer margins had declined over the past five years. On average, printers accounted

[18]This section was drawn from "Hewlett Packard Consumer Products Business Organization: Distribution through E*Commerce Channels" by Kirthi Kalyanam and Shelby McIntyre, 1998–1999.

[19]Ibid.

[20]Kirthi Kalyanam and Shelby McIntyre, "Hewlett Packard Consumer Products Business Organization: Distribution through E*Commerce Channels," 1998–1999, p. 7.

[21]This section was drawn from "Hewlett Packard Consumer Products Business Organization: Distribution through E*Commerce Channels" by Kirthi Kalyanam and Shelby McIntyre, 1998–1999.

for 5%–10% of a retailer's sales volume, with retail margins at 8%–14% and net margins in the low single digits. This was a result of all the services the retailer provided plus the cost of six weeks of inventory in the retail channel and the payment terms to the manufacturer set at 30 days. Moreover, since the popular HP products were advertised frequently by retailers (in the weekly fliers), net margins on HP products were even less than those on competing products.

The printer supply business was profitable for both the retailers and the manufacturer (with net margin in the teens). InkJet cartridges retailed between $22 and $30 and LaserJet cartridges averaged $60 per unit. Office product superstores received the bulk of this business, whereas consumer electronic superstores received a disproportionately lower share of the supply market. Maintaining an adequate selection was challenging because, with so many different SKUs, customers had problems matching their printer models with the corresponding printers' supplies. InkJet cartridges had to be replaced, on average, once or twice a year versus LaserJet cartridges which had to be replaced approximately once a year. Consumers were expected to use about 3–7 cartridges before updating their printers. Together, InkJet and Laser cartridges represented a total U.S. market of $7 billion in sales in 1997.[22]

Retail Disruption and the Internet

The goals of retailing were always to get the right product in the right place at the right price and at the right time. The Internet created the ideal platform for retailers to excel in offering a wide selection of products (more than in any bricks and mortar company), 24 hours a day, at lower prices, and significant time savings. The Internet, in general, was proving to be an unstoppable force and was changing the way everyone worked and played. One hundred years ago British Economist Alfred Marshall said:

> The full importance of an epoch-making idea is often not perceived in the generation in which it is made. A new discovery is seldom fully effective for practical purposes until many minor improvements and subsidiary discoveries have gathered themselves around it.[23]

Who could have imagined, for example, the way the automobile would affect urban design, shopping, and courtship? Or how electricity would enable women to move into the workplace with the creation of the washing machine and vacuum cleaner?

As Irving Wladawsky-Berger, IBM's general manager of the Internet Division, said:

> It's going to be huge. It's going to permeate everything. It's going to be a ubiquitous channel for doing commerce.[24]

eChannels for Computer Products. In spring 1998, two basic types of eChannels existed. First were traditional resellers like CompUSA, Office Depot, and Wal-Mart, which were using their brand leverage from their brick and mortar base and applying it to the web. These companies had existing infrastructure costs and needed to balance strategies between in-store and on-line goals.

Second were the new virtual stores that existed only on the Internet. An example was Value America (VA), which was founded in 1997 and offered a large selection of technology, office, and consumer merchandise. Considered an eTailer mall, VA sold only leading branded products (no private labels or knockoffs) at a discount. VA used a membership structure, just as Costco did, to give customers even deeper discounts—usually 5%. There was no charge for membership, but that was sure to change in the future. One key for VA was the establishment of relationships with over 1,000 brands. VA advertised these brands in exchange for cooperative advertising payments. VA abided by MAP and also received product presentation fees to aid in overhead costs. Another unique aspect was VA's use of non-Internet advertising methods, such as newspapers, to drive sales.

VA kept no inventory and would send product orders directly to distributors or manufacturers. Although VA offered a variety of products, the majority of sales came from computers. As of Q1 1998, the majority of sales were from products supplied by IBM, with the largest other sources from HP, Compaq, and Toshiba. Analysts expected VA to break even by 2002 and to become a major eCommerce destination.[25]

[22]Norm Alster, "Is Printer Ink Replacement a License to Print Money?" *Investor's Business Daily,* May 28, 1998, pp. 8–9.
[23]"When Companies Connect," *Economist,* June 26, 1999, p. 19.

[24]Marc Songini, "IBM's Internet Division Crafts Company Vision," *Network World,* August 18, 1997, pp. 23–24.
[25]Keith E. Benjamin and Laura Cooks Levitan, "Value America–E-Tailing Research," *BankBoston Robertson Stephens Research Report,* May 4, 1999.

Internet Retailing. Convenience shopping dates back to the success of the Sears catalogue mail-order business in 1906, when 2,000 workers were hired to handle the 900 sack-loads of daily orders.[26] These web-retailing roots were transformed into 46 million Internet users in 1997, and this number was expected to grow to 150 million by 2000. Internet use reached this benchmark in only five years, as opposed to radio, TV, and cable which took 38, 13, and 10 years, respectively.[27] Reasons for this rapid adoption included consumers' growing dissatisfaction with the level of service and lack of knowledgeable salespeople offered by the conventional channels. Another reason was the increasing acceptance of the indirect mail-order channel, meaning that shoppers were becoming comfortable purchasing goods "sight-unseen." In fact the mail-order channel accounted for 8% of customers in spring 1998.

One example of Internet retail success was Amazon.com, which achieved a 100% growth rate in every quarter of 1996. Growing at a rate of over 70% in each of the first two quarters of 1997, Amazon sales had reached $148 million by the close of that year. This company, however, did not post a profit—which was standard in this emerging eBusiness category. Based upon this fact, Internet businesses were valued according to their prospect for future growth and their number of new customers, not their profitability.[28] In addition, the most critical aspect of pure-play Internet companies was the expense of acquiring a new customer. This tended to be very high in the early brand-awareness-building stages, but was expected to decrease later as economies of scale came into reach.

The largest wake-up call was by Dell Computer, as it set the standard in the direct-order selling model. As of early 1998, Dell was selling $3 million a day worth of computers, software, and related accessories on the Internet, with the intent to transfer as much as half of its $12 billion revenues to the Internet within three years.[29][30] The Dell model became the standard of industry efficiency because the whole process from order to shipping took 36 hours. Incoming components were pulled through the production process and ordered on a just-in-time (JIT) basis. This allowed Dell to have only about 13 days of inventory, versus 75 to 100 days in an ordinary indirect model.[31] An industry insider remarked:

> While machines from Compaq or IBM can languish on dealer shelves for two months, Dell doesn't start ordering components and assembling computers until an order is booked. That may sound like no biggie, but the price of PC parts can fall rapidly in just a few months. By ordering right before assembly, [Michael] Dell figures his parts, on average, are 60 days newer than those in an IBM or Compaq machine sold at the same time. That can translate into a 6% profit advantage in components alone.[32]

Online retail sales were $600 million in 1996 and over $2 billion in 1997. The most popular products and services in 1997 were computer hardware, travel, brokerage, books, and software (see Exhibit 1). With an estimated 150 million users by 2000, the sales figure was expected to reach $21–$56 billion that year and $115 billion by 2005. As impressive as this seemed, 1997 Internet sales represented approximately a few days of business for Wal-Mart and barely a dent in the $2.5 trillion of overall retail sales. Demographic trends supported these online sales and user predictions. The combination of two-income families and the expanding workweek, for example, had shaved leisure time from 26 hours per week to 19. A 1997 survey by Kurt Salmon Associates also found that 52% of people wanted to reduce their shopping time. In addition, Deloitte & Touche research discovered that 50% of Americans considered shopping an "unpleasant chore" and of this group, 55% under age 34 felt that way.[33]

Potential threats to Internet retailing came from mass merchandisers like Wal-Mart or from manufacturers themselves. Wal-Mart's strong brand awareness, state-of-the-art information technology and distribution systems, and superior channel muscle were expected to pose a formidable challenge to existing web retailers. For manufacturers, it seemed natural to want to eliminate the "middleman" and sell directly to consumers online, but they hesitated for fear of angering their channel partners. K-Swiss, for example, would be hurt by the loss of

---

[26]Robert Gray, "Delivering the Goods," *Marketing,* May 21, 1998, p. 26.
[27]Kirthi Kalyanam and Shelby McIntyre, "Hewlett Packard Consumer Products Business Organization: Distribution through E*Commerce Channels," 1998–1999, p. 7.
[28]Ibid., p. 8.
[29]James Kim, "Dell: Built-to-Order Success Rivals Rush to Imitate Direct Sell," *USA Today,* June 30, 1997, p. 1B.
[30]"Dell Online," HBS No. 598-116, p. 1.

[31]Ibid., p. 4.
[32]Gary McWilliams, "Whirlwind on the Web," *Business Week,* April 7, 1997.
[33]Joel Kotkin, "The Mother of all Malls," *Forbes,* April 6, 1998, pp. 60–65.

its partner Foot Locker, which accounted for about one-fifth of its annual sales.[34] Even some retailers posed a threat as they introduced private label products that competed directly with national brands.

Going direct was not only about increased gross margins. In addition to possible channel disruption, obstacles included: the large investment for developing and maintaining a solid web site; security and bandwidth issues; uncertain return on investment; competitors having easy access to information; higher rates of product return; and customer-incurred shipping charges (which averaged $12–$14 for two-day delivery and $22–$30 for overnight delivery of an HP printer, for example).

Strategic Options

HP believed that its market share neither reflected the company's comparative advantages, nor accounted for consumers' awareness and preferences for its products. The company also believed that the retailers could have provided better in-store support for HP products. This stemmed from high sales personnel turnover and low product knowledge.

HP management was also assessing the position of its Internet outlet center that sold refurbished products at reduced prices, as well as the associated printer supplies and accessories. The outlet store was established for two reasons. One was to enable the company to sell open-box returned products, recovery of which was a significant problem prior to the establishment of the online store. (Previously HP would break down returned products for spare service parts.) The second was to use it to learn the mechanics of Internet direct selling and as a means of recognizing the increasing number of Internet shoppers.[35] HP believed there would be little channel conflict by focusing on refurbished products. Reflecting on this experience, Shen Li, the HP North American channel marketing manager commented:

> We get a continuous stream of information regarding the supply chain (sales, inventory, etc.), advertising response (banner ads and site referrals), and customer behavior (page views, site path, shopping time of the day, day of the week, phone versus Internet orders, shopping basket, etc.). In some ways it is overwhelming to get information with this level of depth

and in a real-time manner. Synthesizing this information is like trying to drink from a fire hose.[36]

HP management considered its options:

1. *Wait and See*—HP could continue selling refurbished printers through its Internet outlet center, which would maintain channel relationships and profits. Competitors were not selling directly on the Internet at this time; thus HP would be taking a risk by being the first to use that channel. If competitors took a direct route, HP could benefit from possible retail retaliation. Alternatively, if competitors became successful on the Internet, HP could join the new channel at a more mature stage.[37]

2. *Participate through Online Retailers*—Some traditional retailers, such as CompUSA, were selling via online stores by mid-1997. HP was already selling to the brick and mortar stores, so it seemed reasonable to expand with them on the web. The problem was that these stores were moving slowly in the eCommerce arena, as opposed to the nimble eTailers like Value America. Also worth noting were computer manufacturers such as Dell and Gateway, who were leaders in direct sales. These companies had had low printer sales in the past, but were beginning to see the advantage as the printer drivers could be preloaded into their machines.[38]

3. *Expand the Offerings Online*—Going direct would enable HP to interact with its customers, build relationships, and strengthen the HP brand. Although there was first-mover risk, there was also potential benefit as evidenced by the success of Amazon.com. If this course were taken, a business plan would have to outline the products and prices to be offered online. A budget would also be needed to allow for development and maintenance of the web site, including marketing and advertising allowances. Amazon, for example, spent $40 million of its $150 million revenue on marketing and advertising expenses in 1997. A general minimum investment was

---

[34]Ibid.

[35]M2 Presswire, "HP Opens Web Outlet Center to Sell Refurbished Consumer Products," January 8, 1998.

[36]This section was drawn from "Hewlett Packard Consumer Products Business Organization: Distribution through E*Commerce Channels" by Kirthi Kalyanam and Shelby McIntyre, 1998–1999.

[37]Ibid.

[38]Ibid.

$500K to develop a web site. A popular advertising method was banner ads, which were priced around $35 per thousand impressions and had a click-through rate of 0.5%–2.5%.[39] Associated with the click-through rate was the visit-to-buy rate of 1%–2%. In addition, the cost of acquiring a new customer had to be considered. This customer acquisition cost was approximately $25 for companies such as Amazon, eBay, and OnSale, whereas it was about $200 for companies such as E*Trade, CDNow, and Preview Travel.

---

[39]Ibid.

Exhibit 1 eTailing Growth by Category (millions)

Category	1997	1998E
Travel	$804	$2,183
Online brokerage	696	1,498
Computer hardware	866	2,432
Computer software	139	385
Books	254	925
Gifts/flowers	77	214
Apparel	53	171
Food/drink	46	120
Music	37	188
Automobile	40	206
Other sales	80	240
Total	$3,092	$8,562

Source: Technology Research, BancBoston Robertson Stephens, February 12, 1999, p. 22.

PRICELINE.COM: NAME YOUR OWN PRICE

Priceline.com flipped a conventional marketing system on its head. Founder Jay Walker explained: "In the traditional model of commerce, a seller advertises a unit of supply in the marketplace at a specified price, and a buyer takes it or leaves it. Priceline turns that model around. We allow a buyer to advertise a unit of demand to a group of sellers. The sellers can then decide whether to fulfill that demand or not. In effect, we provide a mechanism for collecting and forwarding units of demand to interested sellers . . ."[1] Priceline's initial service, launched in April 1998, sold airline tickets. A customer logged onto the company's Web site and through Priceline.com—to adopt Walker's terminology—posted a free "advertisement" that he wanted to go somewhere. The customer specified only the desired days of travel and destination (not carrier or arrival and departure times) and named the price he was willing to pay for the roundtrip tickets. Priceline.com then searched the databases of cooperating airlines with whom it had negotiated availability and prices.

Customers had to be flexible on time of travel and "brand" of supplier. If Priceline.com found a routing, it was assigned to the customer and his credit card was automatically charged the customer's named price. No backing out was allowed even if, for example, the customer's specified Friday to Sunday trip from Boston to Orlando, Florida, turned out to arrive in Orlando at 10 P.M. on Friday evening, leave Sunday morning at 6 A.M., entailed switching planes in Detroit in both directions, and be on one of the customer's least favorite carriers.

Priceline.com thus clearly targeted the budget-minded leisure traveler. About a year after inception, on April 28, 1999, it had its first $1MM day, selling over 5,000 tickets. In this first year of operation, more than 1 million individuals had "named their price" (though not necessarily served at that price). Throughout 1998 and 1999, Priceline.com expanded beyond airlines, introducing "name your own price" services for automobiles, hotel rooms, and home financing. In January 2000, Priceline President and CEO Richard Braddock commented: "It's obvious to everyone that Priceline is working extremely well. Growth is happening before our eyes. We're writing 10 times the ticket volume we did in January '99, and we're rolling out new product areas, and our customer generation has continued at a dramatic pace. We've done a great job at building our brand."[2] While airline tickets still accounted for the vast majority of Priceline's revenues at the end of 1999, Priceline executives were confident about the suitability of the "name your own price" business model for other product categories. Walker saw great opportunity for the model: "You'll see it everywhere. We've already announced that we intend to extend our pricing model to hundreds if not thousands of products and services."[3] Priceline.com termed its business model highly "horizontally scaleable" and the airline service "just the beginning."

While revenues for calendar year 1999 reached $482 million (see Exhibit 1 for financial statements for 1998 and 1999), some observers remained skeptical especially about its performing in a way justifying the company's market capitalization from its March 1999 IPO. For example, a *Fortune* article entitled "The Hype Is Big, Really Big at Priceline" (a take-off on Priceline's own earlier advertising tag-line delivered by celebrity spokesperson William Shatner of Star Trek fame that Priceline was going to be "big, really big") opined:

> The clear-eyed truth is that buyer-driven commerce has so far proven to be more of a marketing gimmick than the centerpiece of a revolution. . . .
>
> Sure, consumers can "name" prices at Priceline, but it remains the airlines that set them. Indeed, because Priceline keeps the prices of its available

Professor Robert Dolan prepared this case from published sources as the basis for class discussion rather than to illustrate either effective or ineffective handling of an administrative situation.

[1]N. Carr, "Redesigning Business," *Harvard Business Review,* November–December, 1999, p. 19.
[2]R. McGarvey, "Is Priceline Vulnerable," *Upside,* January 2000.
[3]N.Carr, op. cit., p. 20.

tickets secret, the company offers consumers what is truly a revolutionary opportunity: the chance to pay more than the asking price.[4]

Others saw the logic of the "name your own price" model for perishable inventories—such as airline tickets, hotel rooms, vacation homes, and car rentals—but questioned the extendibility of the Priceline brand and pricing model to situations where the supplier was not under pressure to sell but could wait for demand to materialize. As one commentator put it: "Hotel rooms, yes: grocery staples, no."[5]

Priceline was also presented with direct competition in the "name your own price" model by Expedia, a leading online travel service spun off by Microsoft in November 1999. (Microsoft maintained an 86% share stake.) Expedia had announced a "Hotel Price Matcher" service similar to Priceline's in September 1999 and followed with "Flight Price Matcher" in December. Priceline believed these services infringed the business process patent granted to it by the Patent Office in August 1999. It filed a complaint in October. Microsoft and Expedia filed for dismissal of the charges in December and it was as yet unclear what the result of the legal process would be. Expedia differentiated itself from Priceline by positioning itself as "the first single Web site to allow customers to specify their own prices for airline tickets and have access to a complete resource of airline and travel planning services."[6] Expedia provided extensive destination information and strong editorial content along with multiple booking options. Whereas Priceline was extending its brand across multiple product categories, Expedia focused on travel: flights, hotels, cars, vacations, and cruises.

The year 1999 had been an exciting year for Priceline.com. Sales had increased more than tenfold; the number of individuals who made at least one "guaranteed offer" reached 3.8 million; research data showed it was the second-most well known e-commerce site, behind only Amazon. Its $16/share public offering closed the first day at $69 and reached $165/share within a month. (See Exhibit 2 for chart of stock price.)

In January 2000, the company bolstered its marketing talent with the appointment of a new Chief Marketing Officer. In the year ahead it sought to continue to enhance the brand, strengthen its position in multiple product categories, expand into new categories, and grow revenues to over $1 billion. Which categories were best suited for the Priceline service? A broader question was, as a player across multiple categories, how could its brand be strong enough to compete against niche players like Expedia in travel, CarsDirect in automobiles, and Lending Tree in home financing?

Building and Extending the Franchise

Services

Priceline.com launched its airline ticket service in April 1998. While not publicized at the time, the cooperating airlines at launch were only America West and TWA. Delta was added as an airline partner shortly thereafter as it received warrants to purchase 18.6 million shares of Priceline stock for .93¢ per share if sales targets were met. Northwest and Continental followed. In November 1999, United (the largest airline in the United States), American (#2) and U.S. Air joined as partners, giving the company broad coverage of the U.S. market as its participating airlines then accounted for over 90% of U.S. domestic capacity. Twenty international airlines also joined. Airline participation agreements did *not* require

- The airlines to make tickets available for any particular route, or to provide any specific number of tickets;
- Particular prices or discount levels;
- Exclusivity in dealing with Priceline to sell discounted tickets.

An airline's ability to exercise its stock options were, however, tied to achieving certain sales levels. Priceline saw its system providing airlines a new channel via which to sell some of the 500,000 empty seats which were being flown each day. While firms in some industries sold perishable goods by price discounting at the last moment, this was not an economically appealing option for the airlines as the "last moment" was when the price-insensitive business traveler showed up. Walker saw Priceline providing value to airlines via brand and price "shields," viz.

> Because the seller is anonymous through the buying process, it gets two clear benefits in addition to incremental sales.

[4]P. Elkind, "The Hype Is Big, Really Big at Priceline," *Fortune,* September 6, 1999.
[5]R. McGarvey, op. cit.
[6]Expedia Press Release, "Customers Can Now Find the Right Flights for Less on Expedia.com," December 9, 1999.

First, it gets a brand shield. If it had publicly advertised a lower price for its product or service, it would have eroded its brand. But since it can accept the unit of demand without letting the buyer know in advance, its suffers no such erosion.

Second, the seller gets a price shield. It can maintain the integrity of its established prices because it never advertises that a lower price is being filled.[7]

While developing its airline supplier base, Priceline also expanded into new product categories introducing services for

- New automobiles (July 1998)
- Hotel rooms (October 1998)
- Home financing (January 1999)

By November 1999, it had also made agreements with (i) Budget Rent A Car and National Car Rental Systems to support a car rental service, and (ii) Net2Phone to support a long distance telephone system. Both systems were to roll out in early 2000. In addition, it entered into a licensing agreement with WebHouse Club to bring "name your own price" to groceries.

Brand Building

Priceline.com described its strategy as an "aggressive brand-enhancement strategy, which includes mass market and multimedia advertising, promotional programs and public relations activities. These activities will involve significant expense."[8] Sales and marketing investments were $24.4 million in 1998 and $79.6 million in 1999. In April 1998, Priceline made a commitment of a large portion of these funds to a radio and newspaper campaign featuring celebrity spokesperson William Shatner. (Shatner was well known as Captain James Tiberius Kirk of the U.S.S. Enterprise in the Star Trek television series and movies.) In late 1999, Walker described this decision undertaken in early 1998:

Two years ago, conventional wisdom was not in favor of celebrity endorsements for Internet products. Internet companies were supposed to focus their advertising online through banner ads and portal deals. Priceline.com believed that the right star power

concentrated in more traditional radio and print advertising would effectively reach both Netizens and non-Internet users alike. Our innovative service and targeted media buying, combined with Bill Shatner, did the trick.[9]

Priceline was the #9 dot.com advertiser in traditional media for the first half of 1999, according to *Advertising Age* estimates. Priceline engaged Opinion Research Corporation to assess the results of its investment in sales and marketing. The company conducted surveys on awareness of "Internet brands" in September 1998 and April 1999. Results for September 1998 placed Priceline in the top five, as shown in Table A.

Brand Institute, a leading brand identity company, referred to the seven brands shown in Table A as "megabrands" as the survey result projected to over 50 million U.S. adults being aware of the brand. Priceline had achieved "mega-brand" status within 150 days of its April 1998 launch. By April 1999, Priceline.com's awareness reached 46.5%, putting it in the company of Amazon.com (51.7%), e-Bay (32.2%), and E-Trade (29.9%) as the four most well known e-commerce sites. This group of four had distinguished itself from other e-commerce sites as eToys was fifth at 21.6% awareness, followed by Autobytel at 17.9%. Priceline competitors such as Cheaptickets, Travelocity, Preview Travel, and Expedia all stood in the 8% to 10% awareness range among U.S. adults.[10] Another mechanism used to drive traffic to the Priceline.com site was the Affiliates Program. Priceline paid operators of the affiliate site $1 each time a visitor coming from that site posted a qualifying offer (over $150 "named price" for a domestic ticket). Special sweepstakes for affiliates were also held.[11]

In December 1999, Priceline signed Shatner to a two-year renewal of his endorsement contract. Hill, Holliday, Connors Cosmopulos, Boston, was selected as the agency to develop a new "image campaign" with heavy planned national television exposure.

---

[7]N. Carr, op. cit., p. 19.

[8]Priceline SEC, Registration Statement, July 1999.

[9]Priceline Press Release, December 16, 1999.

[10]Priceline Press Release, "New Study Shows Top E-Commerce Brands Distancing Themselves from Pack," May 3, 1999.

[11]Affiliate programs are quite common on the Internet. The site Refer-It.com lists and rates over 1,600 programs. An affiliate simply posts a logo/small ad on its site and a link to the sponsor. The affiliate is paid according to a variety of arrangements ranging from cents per click through to commission on sales made at the site on that visit to continuing commission on all future purchases made by the referred person.

Table A Internet Brand Awareness[a] Among All U.S. Adults
(September 1998; Sample Size = 1,013)

Internet Brand	Percentage Aware
1. America On-line	78.8
2. Yahoo	51.4
3. Netscape	48.6
4. Amazon.com	37.4
5. Priceline.com	32.2
6. Infoseek	27.2
7. Excite	26.2

Source: Priceline.com Press Release, "McDonald's, Coke and Nike, Look Out: Here Come the Internet Mega-brands,"
September 21, 1998.
[a]Typically, a brand awareness question is of the form: "which of the following brands are you aware of?" An interviewer
reads list and respondent replies.

Priceline Services

As of January 2000, Priceline offered four services on a broad geographic basis:

1. Airline Tickets
2. Hotel Rooms
3. Home Financing
4. New Cars

Through a license with WebHouse, a grocery service was available in the metropolitan areas of New York, New Jersey, Connecticut, and in Philadelphia. During the first quarter of 2000, the service was to be introduced in Baltimore, Boston, Detroit, Milwaukee, and Washington, D.C. Noted as "Coming Soon" on the Priceline.com web site were Rental Cars and Long Distance Telephone Services. For these services, the site (www.priceline.com) had a picture of spokesperson William Shatner with the caption "This is gonna be bigger than big!"

Airline Services

In 1998, about 600 million passengers enplaned on scheduled U.S. airlines.[12] Scheduled airlines generated over $75 billion in revenues. Frequent business travelers

---
[12]This paragraph is based on information provided by Air Transport Association, the trade group for the principal U.S. Airlines, at its web site www.air-transport.org.

accounted for a large portion of trips, e.g., the 8% of people who flew more than 10 trips per year accounted for 45% of industry business. In 1999, industry "load factors" (i.e., the percentage of seats sold on a flight) ranged from a low of 65% in January to just over 75% during June, July, and August when vacation travelers swelled industry demand. Travel agents were the primary distribution mechanism for airline seats as these 30,000 agents, using airline-owned reservation systems, sold 85% of industry tickets. Pricing in the industry was complex as more than 90% of tickets sold were discounted to some extent and discounts averaged 2/3 off the listed "full fare." Access to highest discount levels typically required booking well in advance of travel dates and staying over a Saturday night. In 1999, the average price for a 1,000-mile economy class flight was $117.30 each way.

The emergence of the Internet provided many alternatives to the travel agent model. Major airlines established their own web sites, sometimes offering special inducements to book direct to bypass travel agents. Many airlines posted special "last-minute" deals on their sites. Sites such as Travelocity and Expedia offered customers online access to a full set of suppliers at published fares. Online bookings were approximated at $4 billion in 1999, with half of these made directly by the airline companies.

Priceline.com's airline service, which accounted for a large portion of company revenues during 1999, offered access to unpublished fares. For nine months ending September 1999, five airline partners accounted for over

90% of airline service revenues.[13] Key elements of the airline service were as follows:

- A logged-in customer specified
  - Dates of travel;
  - Departure and arrival cities;
  - Number of passengers in the party (up to eight).
- The system queried about acceptable airports (if relevant). For example, a customer specifying Boston as the Departure City was asked to indicate which of (i) Logan in Boston, (ii) Manchester, New Hampshire, and (iii) Providence, Rhode Island, airports were acceptable departure locations. Customers were encouraged to "check as many airports as you can to increase your chances." The system provided information on the location of the airports, e.g., "The Providence-TF Green Airport is 47 miles SSW of Boston, Massachusetts."
- Customers were given another opportunity to "increase their chances" by indicating a willingness to fly
  - In off-peak hours (before 6:00 a.m. and after 10:00 p.m.);
  - On non-jet aircraft;
  - Routes with more than one connection.
- The customer was then asked to "Name Your Price" with the notation that price does not include "standard fees/taxes and a $5 per ticket processing charge."
- The customer guaranteed the price to a credit card. Specifically, as noted on the Web site, "If we find tickets at your price, we immediately purchase those tickets and charge your credit card. Because you get to name your own price, tickets purchased through Priceline cannot be changed, transferred, or cancelled."

The service applied only to round trip travel originating in the United States or Puerto Rico. Unless the customer indicated willingness to fly off-peak times, the system guaranteed "you'll always depart between 6:00 a.m. and 10:00 p.m." on a "major full-service U.S. or International airline or its affiliate." Priceline tickets were not eligible for frequent flyer miles.

Given the complete set of customer information and a guarantee of the "named price" to a credit card, Priceline searched airline partner databases containing availability and the prices at which the supplier would provide the seats to Priceline. In some cases, Priceline subsidized sales by supplying tickets even though the charge from the airline partners to Priceline was more than the "Name Your Price." For the first three months after the service was introduced in April 1998, Priceline paid airlines $1.13 for every dollar's worth of tickets sold.[14]

Searching the database showed the supplier and routing fitting the customer's somewhat loose specification (i.e., days of travel only, no brand stipulation) which maximized the spread between the customer's "Named Price" and the necessary payment to airline partner. Within an hour, Priceline either provided a routing to the customer and billed the credit card or rejected the customer's offer. In the event of a rejection, a customer could not just increase the "Named Price" and try again. Only one offer was permitted in a seven-day period—unless the customer changed an aspect of the itinerary, e.g. the travel dates and/or acceptable airports. A revised request could be submitted immediately.

During the first nine months of 1999, Priceline filled 25.8% of customer offers received and 52% of "reasonable" offers, which it defined as no less than 30% below the lowest generally available advance-purchase fare.[15] During the fourth quarter of 1999 (ending December 31, 1999), it sold over 700,000 leisure airline tickets.[16] It also entered into an agreement with Travelocity and Preview Travel on a co-marketing agreement to develop a fully integrated system wherein a customer could have "seamless access" to Travelocity and Preview's published fares and Priceline.com's "Name Your Price" method. Combined, the three sites had a user base exceeding 20 million individuals.

Hotel Rooms

The hotel service operated in a similar fashion. Priceline offered hotel partners the same "brand-shield," telling customers only "you'll always stay in a nationally recognized, name-brand or well-known independent hotel."[17]

---

[13] Priceline.com, Form 10-Q, November 15, 1999.

[14] D. Machan, "An Edison for a New Age?" *Forbes*, May 17, 1999.

[15] Priceline Form 10-Q, November 15, 1999

[16] Priceline Press Release, "Priceline.com Sees Record Customer Growth," January 5, 2000.

[17] Priceline Web site.

Although specific names were not publicized to consumers, more than 12 "leading national hotel chains" were involved, offering space in 1,300 cities, towns, and resorts.[18] The customer specified date(s), acceptable locations, and required level of room from one-star/economy to four-star/luxury. As with airlines, the customer guaranteed the demand to a credit card and received an answer within an hour. On some days, the service booked over 1,000 rooms.

Home Financing

"Name Your Price" financing was available for mortgages, home equity loans, and refinancings. While the information to be submitted was more extensive for this service, it operated under the same general "Name Your Price" principles as airlines and hotels.

For example, in the case of a new home mortgage, the customer specified:

- Type of loan: fixed (term of 10, 15, or 30 years) or adjustable rate (term of 3, 5, 7, or 10 years)
- Amount to be borrowed
- Down payment
- When money was needed (30, 45, 60, 90 days)
- Information about the property
- Information about own credit history
- "Name Your Price" interest rate

Priceline forwarded information to participating lenders. An answer was delivered through Priceline within six hours. If the customer's rate and terms were accepted, the lender charged a $200 "good faith" deposit to be applied to closing costs. Unlike the hotel and airline systems where no counteroffer was made on rejected named prices, lenders could respond with a counteroffer via e-mail if no one was willing to meet the exact rate and terms originally named by the customer.

New Cars

Unlike its policy for other services, Priceline charged a fee ($50) to the customer of the car-buying service if the process resulted in a transaction. The process began with the potential buyer specifying desired make and model.

The system provided both the dealer cost and the Manufacturers Suggested Retail Price (MSRP) of the car plus options selected. Other fees such as destination and advertising were also specified. The buyer then specified acceptable color combinations. Before the customer "named own price," Priceline also provided a "market price" based on previous sales as a guide. The customer then filled in the "Name Your Price" number and specified acceptable locations for pickup. The information, absent any identification of the buyer, was then sent to participating factory-authorized dealers in the acceptable locations. An answer was provided within one business day. If the exact car specified was found and customer's price offer accepted, a $200 penalty was charged if the customer did not show up at the dealership.

Priceline described its competitive positioning in a field populated by many car-buying services such as Autobytel, CarPoint, and CarsDirection.com as follows:

> Priceline.com Auto Services is unique among Internet car buying services in that it enables consumers to research a car or truck and anonymously fill in the price they want to pay for the vehicle. Priceline.com Auto Services distributes the offer to all factory-authorized dealerships in the geographic area specified by the buyer. Because the offers are made anonymously, no car salesman calls to haggle or negotiate a different price. The first dealership to accept the consumer's price gets to sell the car.[19]

Priceline dealers filling the demand pay a fixed fee to Priceline in addition to the $50 collected from the customer. As of January 2000, the service was available in 26 states, with national rollout to be completed in the first half of year 2000.

Grocery Items

Believing in the horizontal extendibility of the pricing model to a large number of product categories, Priceline sought the next category to place under its brand umbrella. According to founder Jay Walker, "When looking for what the next category would be for the horizontal Priceline 'name-your-own-price' model, we were told overwhelmingly by consumers that it should be groceries."[20]

---

[18]Priceline Form 10-Q, November 15, 1999.

[19]Priceline Press Release, "Priceline.com Announces 100% Expansion of Its Name Your Own Price New Car Service," January 12, 2000.
[20]Priceline Press Release, "Priceline's 'Name-Your-Own-Price' Service to Sell 25 Million Items This Year on the Internet in New York Metro Area," January 11, 2000.

To move into groceries, Priceline licensed its business method, affiliated trademark, technology and software to privately held start-up WebHouse Club in return for royalties and warrants to acquire a majority interest in the company. WebHouse Club did not offer home delivery. The process began with a WebHouse Club member (membership was free) accessing the Priceline website where approximately 175 product categories were available, ranging from newborn-baby diapers to cola-cans to ice cream to live lobsters. Selecting a category, the customer was presented with options and was required to specify at least two acceptable brands within each category shopped. For example, in cola-cans, choices were Coca-Cola, Pepsi, and RC Cola and two or all three had to be designated as acceptable. The system provided the "Typical Price Range" (for cola, $2.59 to $3.29 for a 12-pack), and the customer designated one of four prices characterized by Priceline as offering a "Great Chance" (for cola — $2.31), "Good Chance" ($2.15), "Fair Chance" ($2.02) or "Low Chance" ($1.89) of being accepted. (Or, the customer could type in the exactly desired "own price," if desired, rather than select one of the four designated choices.) Multiple categories were shopped with prices named in each. Prices were "locked-in" via a credit card. Within 60 seconds, the "WebHouse Price Machine" indicated which offers had been accepted and charged them to a credit card guarantee. The user printed out a "Prepaid Grocery List" of items and accepted prices. The customer went to a chosen store (selecting from 1,000 participating stores in the New York rollout for example), collected the items on the grocery list from store shelves, proceeded to the checkout counter, and claimed the order with the WebHouse Club Membership card.

During the first two months of the New York rollout, more than 100,000 customers signed up. Priceline projected WebHouse would make groceries "the top selling item on the Internet in New York" with 25 million items sold in 2000.[21] *Consumer Reports,* in its February 2000 issue, tested Priceline in shopping for 20 items and concluded it "offers potential for substantial savings—if you're willing to shop twice: once, filling out an electronic shopping list, and then again cruising the supermarket aisles." A Forrester Research Analyst opined: ". . . this venture is an excellent example of where Priceline should not go. Very few consumers are going to bid on their daily necessities—it's just not worth the time or the effort."[22]

Challenges Ahead

In preparation for the challenges ahead, Priceline added to its marketing expertise by naming Michael McCadden Executive Vice President and Chief Marketing Officer on January 17, 2000. McCadden came to Priceline from a position as Executive Vice President of the Gap, Inc. Direct where he managed all Gap, Inc. non-store businesses. Previously, he had been EVP of Gap Global Marketing. McCadden assumed his position as Priceline rolled out the new major television campaign featuring Shatner, readied further horizontal expansion into car rental and long distance telephone calling, and prepared enhancements to the core airline service, e.g., a Priceline Quick-Answer™ system providing answers in 2 minutes rather than an hour. Priceline's goal for year 2000 was to more than double revenues to over $1 billion.

However, while Priceline had become an Internet "megabrand" with astonishing speed, competition in its core airline business intensified. In December, Microsoft and Expedia filed court documents calling for dismissal of Priceline's suit, calling into question Priceline's ownership of the disputed patent. Expedia's vice president of product development stated ". . . it is clear there are serious questions surrounding Priceline's lawsuit. We remain ready to show that Priceline's claims are without merit and that the Expedia® Price Matcher services do not infringe. . . ."[23] Expedia differentiated its Price Matcher service as follows: "Because these features are deeply ingrained within a broader set of services, customers are better equipped to make educated requests and can feel more confident . . . customers won't overpay with their Flight or Hotel Price Matcher requests because Expedia.com checks those requests against published rates. . . ."[24] If a customer "names a price" higher than the published rate, Expedia charges the lower published rate.

While Priceline had dominated Expedia and other online services in terms of brand awareness among all

---

[21]Ibid.

[22]C.B. Corral, "WebHouse Club puts Priceline in Grocery biz," *Discount Store News,* October 9, 1999.
[23]Expedia Press Release, "Expedia and Microsoft Move to Dismiss Priceline Case."
[24]Ibid.

U.S. adults, Expedia was the most visited online travel site for eight months in a row from April to November 1999 according to Media Metrix.[25] Following its November IPO raising $73 million, Expedia was about to launch its first brand campaign with a budget estimated at $50 million. Both the strength and extendibility of the Priceline brand promised to be tested in the year ahead. How could Priceline best continue to enhance the brand, expand the Priceline franchise, and grow revenues to over $1 billion while keeping to the "commitment to steadily reduce our operating losses and improve our operating margins"[26]—the commitment it had reiterated to analysts as the year began?

---

[25]Ibid.

[26]Priceline.com Press Release, "Priceline.com Reports Record Fourth Quarter Financial Results," January 27, 2000.

Exhibit 1 Priceline Financials 1998, 1999 (all figures in 000s)

	Calendar Year 1998	Calendar Year 1999
– Revenues	$35,933	$482,410

– Cost of Revenues
  – Product Cost
  – Supplier Warrant
	$33,496
	3,029
		$423,056
		1,523

– Gross Profit (Loss)	($1,288)	$57,831

– Expenses
  – Warrant Costs, Net
  – Sales and Marketing
  – G&A
  – Systems & Business Development
	$57,979
	24,388
	18,005
	11,132
		$998,832[a]
		79,577
		27,609
		14,023

– Total Expenses	$111,503	$1,120,041
– Operating Loss	($112,791)	($1,062,210)

Source: Priceline.com Press Release, January 27, 2000.

[a]$910,400 of this is related to issuance of warrants to certain of Priceline's airline partners incurred during Q4 of 1999, e.g., United Airlines was granted 5.5 million shares at an excise price of $52.625 per share.

Exhibit 2 Stock Price Chart

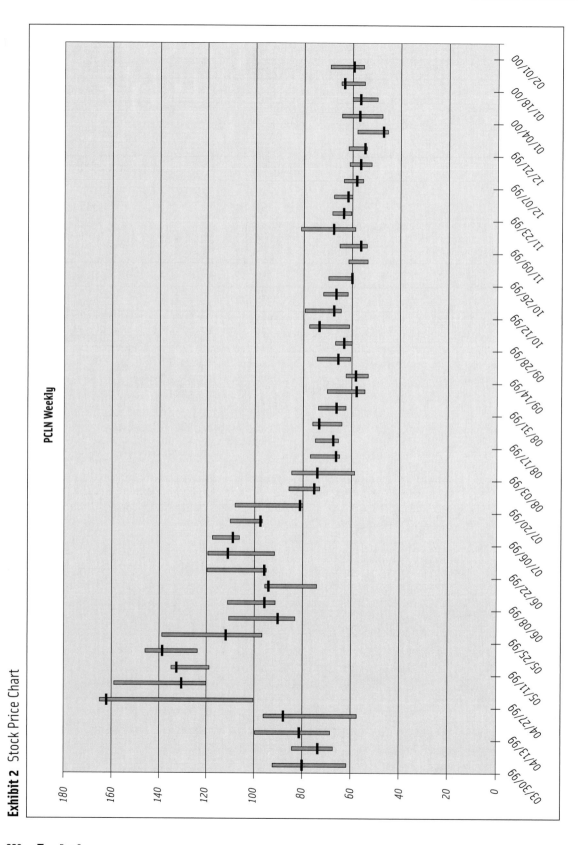

PCLN Weekly

BIOPURE CORPORATION

It was February 5, 1998, as Carl Rausch, president and CEO of Biopure Corporation, opened his *Boston Globe* and read about the U.S. government's final approval of Oxyglobin (see Exhibit 1). Oxyglobin was the first of two new "blood substitutes" on which Biopure's future depended—Oxyglobin for the veterinary market and Hemopure for the human market. While Oxyglobin was ready for launch, Hemopure was still two years away from final government approval. This timing was the source of an ongoing debate within Biopure.

Ted Jacobs, vice president for Human Clinical Trials at Biopure, argued that the release of Oxyglobin should be delayed until *after* Hemopure was approved and had established itself in the marketplace (see Exhibit 2 for an organizational chart of Biopure). Given that the two products were almost identical in physical properties and appearance, he felt that Oxyglobin would create an unrealistic price expectation for Hemopure if released first. As he made clear in a recent management meeting,

> . . . [T]he veterinary market is small and price sensitive. We'll be lucky to get $150 per unit. The human market, on the other hand, is many times larger and we can realistically achieve price points of $600 to $800 per unit. But as soon as we come out with Oxyglobin at $150, we jeopardize our ability to price Hemopure at $800. Hospitals and insurance firms will be all over us to justify a 500% price difference for what they see as the same product. That's a headache we just don't need. We've spent $200 million developing Hemopure—to risk it at this point is crazy. We should just shelve Oxyglobin for now.

Professor John Gourville prepared this case as the basis for class discussion rather than to illustrate either effective or ineffective handling of an administrative situation. Some nonpublic data have been disguised and some business details have been simplified to aid in classroom discussion.

At the same time, Andy Wright, vice president for Veterinary Products, had his sales organization in place and was eager to begin selling Oxyglobin. He argued that the benefits of immediately releasing Oxyglobin outweighed the risks,

> Oxyglobin would generate our first revenues ever—revenues we could use to launch Hemopure. And while the animal market is smaller than the human market, it is still attractive. Finally, I can't stress enough the value of Oxyglobin in learning how to "go to market." Would you rather make the mistakes now, with Oxyglobin, or in two years, with Hemopure?

While Carl Rausch listened to this debate, he also considered his colleagues' growing desire to take Biopure public in the near future. He wondered whether a proven success with Oxyglobin might not have a greater impact on an IPO than the promise of success with Hemopure.

An Overview of Biopure

Biopure Corporation was founded in 1984 by entrepreneurs Carl Rausch and David Judelson as a privately owned biopharmaceutical firm specializing in the ultra-purification of proteins for human and veterinary use. By 1998, this mission had taken Biopure to the point where it was one of three legitimate contenders in the emerging field of "blood substitutes."[1] Blood substitutes were designed to replicate the oxygen-carrying function of actual blood, while eliminating the shortcomings associated with the transfusion of donated blood. Through the end of 1997, no blood substitute had received approval for use anywhere in the world.

Biopure's entries into this field were Hemopure, for the human market, and Oxyglobin, for the animal market. Both products consisted of the oxygen-carrying protein "hemoglobin" which had been removed from red blood cells, purified to eliminate infectious agents, and

---

[1]While the term *blood substitute* has historically been used to describe this class of product, Biopure and the medical community increasingly have used the term *oxygen therapeutic* to describe the latest generation of product. For simplicity, however, we will continue to use the term *blood substitute* in this case.

chemically modified to increase its safety and effectiveness. What distinguished Hemopure and Oxyglobin from other "hemoglobin-based" blood substitutes under development was the fact that they were "bovine-sourced" as opposed to "human-sourced"—they were derived from the blood of cattle. To date, Biopure had spent over $200 million in the development of Oxyglobin and Hemopure and in the construction of a state-of-the-art manufacturing facility.

Both of Biopure's products fell under the approval process of the United States government's Food and Drug Administration (FDA), which required that each product be proven safe and effective for medical use (see Exhibit 3 for an overview of the FDA approval process). In this regard, Oxyglobin had just received final FDA approval for commercial release as a veterinary blood substitute, while Hemopure would soon enter Phase 3 clinical trials and was optimistically expected to see final FDA approval for release as a human blood substitute sometime in 1999.

This recent FDA approval of Oxyglobin brought to a peak a long-simmering debate within Biopure. With its primary goal being the development of a human blood substitute, Biopure's entry into the animal market had been somewhat opportunistic. During Pre-Clinical trials for Hemopure, the benefits of a blood substitute for small animals became apparent. In response, Biopure began a parallel product development process which resulted in Oxyglobin. However, there was little question within Biopure that Oxyglobin was an ancillary product to Hemopure.

As it became apparent that Oxyglobin would gain FDA approval prior to Hemopure, Carl Rausch and his management team discussed how best to manage Oxyglobin. As the first "blood substitute" of any type to receive full government approval, Rausch was eager to get the news out. With this in mind, Andy Wright and a small marketing team had been assembled to bring Oxyglobin to market. However, Ted Jacobs and others questioned whether the immediate release of Oxyglobin might not impinge on Biopure's ability to optimally price Hemopure. After months of debate, it was time to decide on the fate of Oxyglobin.

The Human Blood Market

Blood is essential for life. It performs many functions, the most acutely critical of which is the transportation of oxygen to the organs and tissues of the human body.

Without oxygen, these organs and tissues will die within minutes.

That portion of blood responsible for oxygen transportation are the red blood cells (RBCs). RBCs capture inhaled oxygen from the lungs, carry that oxygen to the cells of the body, release it for use where needed, capture expended carbon dioxide from those cells, and carry that carbon dioxide back to the lungs, where it is released. The key to this process is "hemoglobin," the iron-containing protein found within each RBC to which oxygen and carbon dioxide molecules bind.

The adult human body contains 5,000 milliliters (ml) or about 10 pints of blood. An individual can naturally compensate for the loss of up to 30% of this volume through some combination of increased oxygen intake (i.e., faster breathing), increased flow of the remaining blood (i.e., faster heart rate) and the prioritization of blood delivery to vital organs. In cases of blood loss of greater than 30%, however, outside intervention is typically required—generally in the form of a "blood transfusion."

Human Blood Transfusions

A blood transfusion entails the direct injection of blood into a patient's bloodstream. As of 1998, the most common form of blood transfusion was the intravenous transfusion of donated RBCs.[2] Typically, a healthy individual would donate 1 unit or 500 ml of "whole" blood, which would be tested for various infectious diseases, sorted by blood type, and separated into its usable components (e.g., plasma, platelets, and RBCs). This process would yield 1 unit or 250 ml of RBCs, which then would be stored until needed by a patient.[3]

While potentially lifesaving, the transfusion of donated RBCs has limitations. These include

- The need for exact blood typing and cross-matching between donor and recipient. The RBCs of each human may contain specific blood sugars, or anti-

---

[2]Historically, whole blood transfusions were the norm. Since the 1970s, however, whole blood increasingly had been separated into RBCs, platelets and plasma, allowing for (1) several patients to benefit from a single unit of donated blood and (2) a reduced likelihood of negative reaction for any given patient.

[3]In blood medicine, 1 unit is defined in terms of its therapeutic value. Therefore, "1 unit" or 250 ml of RBCs provides the oxygen-carrying capacity of "1 unit" or 500 ml of whole blood. Similarly, "1 unit" of a blood substitute (i.e., typically 125 ml) provides the same oxygen-carrying capacity of "1 unit" of RBCs or whole blood.

gens. The existence or absence of these antigens creates a complex set of allowable transfusions between donor and recipient, as shown in Exhibit 4. Transfusions outside of those outlined can be fatal to the recipient.

- The reduced oxygen-carrying efficiency of stored RBCs. RBCs stored for 10 days or more are only about 50% efficient at transporting oxygen in the first 8 to 12 hours after transfusion.

- The limited shelf-life for stored RBCs. RBCs can be safely stored for only about 6 weeks, after which time they are typically discarded.

- The need for refrigeration. For optimal shelf-life, RBCs must be stored at 4° Celsius (~40° F).

- The risk of disease transmission. While donated blood is tested for infectious agents, there still exists the risk of disease transmission. For example, the risk of AIDS is 1:500,000, the risk of Hepatitis B is 1:200,000, and the risk of Hepatitis C is 1:100,000.

Autologous Transfusions. In an attempt to overcome some of these limitations, the use of "autologous" or self-donated RBCs has become increasingly common. In an autologous RBC transfusion, a medically stable patient who anticipates the need for RBCs would have his or her own blood drawn weeks in advance, separated into its components, and saved until needed. Research has shown this process to significantly reduce a patient's rate of complication and post-operative infection, thereby hastening recovery and shortening his or her stay in the hospital.

Human Blood Supply and Demand

Human Blood Supply. Fourteen million units of RBCs were donated by 8 million people in 1995 in the United States. Approximately 12.9 million of these units came from individuals who voluntarily donated to one of over 1,000 nonprofit blood collection organizations. By far, the largest of these organizations was the American Red Cross, which collected half of all the blood donated in the United States in 1995 through a network of 44 regional blood collection centers. Typically, the Red Cross and the other blood collection organizations supported "blood mobiles," which traveled to high schools, colleges, and places of employment to reach potential donors. The remaining 1.1 million units of RBCs were autologous donations made directly to a hospital blood center.

Increasingly, blood collection was a struggle. While 75% of all adults qualified as a donor, fewer than 5% actually donated in a given year. Historically, reasons for donating included altruism and peer pressure, while reasons for not donating included fear of needles and lack of time. Since the mid-1980s, an additional reason for not donating involved the misconception that donating put one at risk for contracting AIDS. Public education had failed to counteract this misconception.

Given the low rate of donation and the relatively short shelf-life of RBCs, it was not uncommon for medical facilities and blood banks to experience periodic shortages of RBCs. This was especially true during the winter holidays and the summer months, periods which routinely displayed both increased demand and decreased rates of donation.

Human Blood Demand. Of the 14 million units of RBCs donated in 1995, 2.7 million were discarded due to contamination or expiration (i.e., units older than 6 weeks). Another 3.2 million units were transfused into 1.5 million patients who suffered from chronic anemia, an ongoing deficiency in the oxygen-carrying ability of the blood. The remaining 8.1 million units were transfused into 2.5 million patients who suffered from acute blood loss brought on by elective surgeries, emergency surgeries, or trauma. Exhibit 5 offers a breakdown of RBC transfusions in 1995.

In elective and emergency surgeries, RBCs were routinely transfused in situations where blood loss was greater than two units, as was typical in heart bypass and organ transplant surgeries. In surgeries with blood loss of one to two units, however, RBCs typically were not transfused in spite of their potential benefit. In these "borderline" transfusion surgeries, doctors typically avoided transfusions for fear of disease transmission or negative reaction caused by the transfused RBCs. There were approximately 1 million "borderline transfusion" surgeries in the United States each year.

RBC transfusions were also required in the approximate 500,000 trauma cases which occurred every year in the United States. These cases were characterized by the massive loss of blood due to automobile accidents, gunshot wounds, etc. However, due to the resources required to store, type, and administer RBCs, only 10% of trauma victims received RBCs "in the field" or at the site of the accident. Blood transfusions for the remaining 90% of victims were delayed until the victim arrived at a hospital emergency room. This delay was often cited as a contributing factor to the 30% fatality rate seen in these trauma cases, as evidenced by the 20,000 trauma victims who bled to death each year prior to reaching the hospital. As one doctor put it,

> . . . [T]hose first few minutes after a trauma are known as the "Golden Hour." Life and death often depends on how fast the lost blood is replaced in this period.

Looking forward, while the demand for RBCs to treat chronic anemia was expected to remain stable, the demand for RBCs to treat acute blood loss was expected to rise with the aging U.S. population. Individuals over 65 years of age comprised 15% of the adult population in 1995 and received over 40% of all "acute blood loss" transfusions. By the year 2030, this over-65 segment was expected to double in absolute numbers and to grow to 25% of the adult population.

Human Blood Pricing. Since the AIDS crisis, it has been illegal for an individual to sell his or her blood in the United States. As such, all blood donations are unpaid. In turn, to cover their expense of collection and administration, blood collection organizations sell this donated blood to hospitals and medical centers. Once obtained, hospitals incur additional costs to store, handle, transport, screen, type, cross-match and document the blood. Estimates for these costs are outlined in Exhibit 6. Typically, these costs are passed on to the patient or to the patient's insurance provider.

The Veterinary Blood Market

The role of RBCs for animals is biologically identical to its role for humans: RBCs transport oxygen to an animal's tissues and organs. In practice, however, the availability and transfusion of blood was considerably more constrained in the veterinary market than it was in the human market.

Veterinary Market Structure. There were approximately 15,000 small-animal veterinary practices in the United States in 1995. Of these, about 95% were "primary care" practices which provided preventative care (e.g., shots, checkups), routine treatment of illness (e.g., infections, chronic anemia), and limited emergency care (e.g., simple surgery and trauma). The remaining 5% of practices were "emergency care" or "specialty care" practices. Approximately 75% of primary care practices referred some or all of their major surgery and severe trauma

cases to these emergency care practices. Across both the primary care and emergency care practices, patient volume was concentrated in dogs (~50% of patient volume) and cats (~35% of volume). Exhibit 7 provides a staffing and patient profile of small-animal veterinary clinics in the United States.

Veterinary Blood Demand. In practice, blood transfusions in the veterinary market were infrequent. In 1995, for example, the average veterinary practice was presented with 800 dogs suffering from acute blood loss. About 30% of these dogs would have benefited significantly from a transfusion of blood, but only about 2.5% were deemed "critical cases" and received a transfusion.

The incidence of these acute blood loss cases was relatively concentrated, with 15% of veterinary practices handling 65% of all canine surgeries and 10% of practices handling 55% of all canine trauma cases. Not surprisingly, these "high incident" practices tended to be the larger primary care practices and the emergency care practices. This concentration was also evident in blood transfusions. In 1995, an average of 17 units of canine blood were transfused by each primary care practice, while an average of 150 units were transfused by each emergency care practice.

Veterinary Blood Supply.[4] Historically, the biggest constraint to veterinary transfusions was the lack of an adequate blood supply. In contrast to the human market, there existed few animal blood banks. As a result, the sole source of blood for most veterinary practices were donor animals which were housed at the practice for the expressed purpose of donating blood. When a dog or cat was in need of blood, blood was drawn from a donor dog or cat and then transfused into the animal in need. For primary care practices, donor animals provided 93% of all transfused blood, while blood banks provided the remaining 7%. In emergency practices, these proportions were 78% and 22%.

About 15% of veterinary practices found the "donor animal" system to be administratively or financially prohibitive and did not offer it as a service. Of the 85% of practices that did use a donor system, few had a good sense of its cost. In particular, few practices explicitly tracked the cost of housing the donor animal or the time required to draw the blood. As a proxy for these costs, practices typically looked to the price of a unit of blood

---

[4]Unlike the human market, transfusions in the animal market still tended to be "whole blood" transfusions.

from an animal blood bank. In 1995, that cost was $50 to $100. In turn, a typical primary care practice charged a pet owner $80 to $120 per unit and a typical emergency care practice charged a pet owner $130 to $170 per unit.

Finally, most practices that conducted transfusions lacked the time and resources to properly type both the donor and recipient blood. According to one estimate, only one-tenth of practices reported always typing the blood of both the donor and recipient animal. While complications due to incompatible blood types were not nearly as severe for dogs as they are for humans, this lack of blood typing and cross-matching was shown to prolong the recovery of a patient animal.

These factors resulted in many veterinarians viewing the transfusion of animal blood as the treatment of last resort, with 84% of veterinary doctors reporting overall dissatisfaction with the blood transfusion alternatives currently available in the marketplace.

Human Blood Substitutes

Originally conceived as a vehicle to treat wounded soldiers in battlefield settings, the potential for a human blood substitute for nonmilitary use became increasingly apparent since the 1950s. This period saw a significant rise in auto accidents, the advent of open heart and organ transplant surgeries, and the AIDS crisis, which called into question the safety of the blood supply.

By 1998, several companies appeared to be on the verge of a viable blood substitute with a class of product called "hemoglobin-based blood substitutes." These products attempted to exploit the natural oxygen-carrying capabilities of hemoglobin while eliminating the limitations associated with donated RBCs. Each of these companies was attempting to (1) extract the hemoglobin found within human or animal RBCs, (2) purify that hemoglobin to eliminate infectious agents, and (3) modify the otherwise unstable free hemoglobin molecule to prevent it from breaking down. These purification and modification processes were nontrivial and represented the bulk of blood substitute research conducted over the past 20 years.

Product Benefits. In theory, these hemoglobin-based blood substitutes eliminated many of the limitations associated with donated RBCs. In particular, they were

- "Universal" blood substitutes, eliminating the need for blood typing and cross-matching.

- Free of infectious agents and contamination.
- Increased shelf life. These blood substitutes could be safely stored for up to 2 years.
- Immediately 100% efficient at transporting oxygen. Unlike whole RBCs, modified hemoglobin did not require a period of time to achieve peak oxygen-carrying efficiency.

In addition to these "anticipated" benefits, hemoglobin-based blood substitutes were displaying several "unanticipated" benefits which companies were only just beginning to investigate. In particular, given that hemoglobin molecules were significantly smaller than RBCs, they were able to flow to regions of the body that RBCs might not be able to reach. It was believed that this could lead to improved treatments in cases of stroke and heart attack—cases where RBCs often were slowed or restricted from reaching vital organs either due to artery blockages or decreased blood pressure.

Product Shortcomings. At the same time, these "hemoglobin-based" blood substitutes did have some shortcomings, including:

- A short half-life. While donated RBCs remained in the body for up to two months after transfusion, these blood substitutes were excreted from the body within 2 to 7 days.
- The potential for higher toxicity. While the human body could tolerate the limitless and continuous replacement of one's blood with donated blood, the safety of these blood substitutes had been demonstrated only up to transfusion levels of 5 to 10 units.

In spite of these shortcomings, Dr. C. Everett Koop, the former Surgeon General of the United States, proclaimed,

When the history of 20th-century medicine is written, the development of blood substitutes will be listed among the top ten advances in medicine. . . . [B]ecause of its purity, efficacy and convenience, this product class has the potential to revolutionize the practice of medicine, especially in critical-care situations. . . . [T]he next generation will not know how tough it was for those of us in medical practice before this technology became available.[5]

---

[5]Biopure company website.

Others were less optimistic. One industry analyst presented a less attractive scenario for hemoglobin-based blood substitutes:

> . . . [W]e feel that there is no urgent need for blood substitutes since donated human blood is, for the most part, safe and effective. The expectation that blood substitutes will command vast markets and high price premiums is based on the assumptions that blood substitutes will prove safer and more effective than donated blood. While only time will tell if this is true, it will be an uphill battle given the widespread acceptance of donated blood.

The FDA Approval Process

Human blood substitutes fell under the strict regulation of the U.S. government's Food and Drug Administration (FDA), which required that a product be proven safe and effective for medical use before being approved for commercial release (refer back to Exhibit 3). By early 1998, three companies had products that were in the final stages of this process. These products differed in their source of raw hemoglobin and in the process by which that hemoglobin was purified and modified. The FDA approval process was sensitive to these differences. Short of beginning the FDA approval process anew, each company was limited in its ability to substantially alter either the source of their hemoglobin or the process by which that hemoglobin was purified and modified. In addition, given that most of the companies had patented their purification and modification processes, there was little opportunity for a new entrant to quickly gain FDA approval.

Competitors for a Human Blood Substitute

As of 1998, Baxter International and Northfield Laboratories were the only other companies in late-stage development of a hemoglobin-based blood substitute. All other competitors were either several years behind in their development of a hemoglobin-based product or were pursuing a less promising technology.

In contrast to Biopure's use of cattle as its source of hemoglobin, both Baxter and Northfield relied on human blood as their source of hemoglobin. In particular, both companies had developed a technology to extract raw hemoglobin from "outdated" human RBCs (i.e., RBCs intended for transfusion, but which had been stored for more than 6 weeks). While their production processes and their pending FDA approval did not preclude them from using fresh RBCs, it was the stated intention of both companies to initially rely on outdated human RBCs. Through 1998, Baxter had an agreement with the American Red Cross to obtain outdated RBCs at a cost of $8 per unit. Until recently, Northfield had a similar $8 per unit agreement with Blood Centers of America, another national blood collection agency. However, in early 1997, Blood Centers of America raised their price to Northfield to $26 per unit for outdated RBCs.

In addition to their reliance on human blood, the products of Baxter and Northfield also differed from Biopure's in that they needed to be frozen or refrigerated until used. Biopure's Hemopure was shelf-stable at room temperature.

Baxter International. With over $5.4 billion in sales and $670 million in net income in 1996, Baxter was an acknowledged leader in the development, manufacture and sale of blood-related medical products, ranging from artificial heart valves to blood-collection equipment. In addition, Baxter had a long history of product breakthrough, having developed the first sterile blood collection device in 1939, the first commercially available artificial kidney machine in 1956, and the first Factor VIII blood-clotting factor for the treatment of hemophilia in 1966.

"HemAssist," Baxter's patented blood substitute, was expected to add to this string of breakthroughs. Representing 30 years and $250 million in effort, HemAssist was the first human blood substitute to proceed to Phase 3 clinical trials in June 1996. Initially, these trials were expected to lead to full FDA approval by late 1998. However, in October 1997, Baxter revised its estimate to late 1999 or early 2000—an announcement that was followed by a 10% dip in Baxter's stock price.

Despite this delay, Baxter recently constructed a $100 million facility with a production capacity of 1 million units of HemAssist per year. Aside from its variable cost of source material, Baxter was expected to incur production costs of approximately $50 million per year, independent of production volume. While still just industry speculation, it was anticipated that Baxter would price HemAssist between $600 and $800 per unit.

Northfield Laboratories. Northfield Laboratories of Illinois also had recently entered Phase 3 trials with a hemoglobin-based blood substitute. Northfield's product, "PolyHeme," was very similar to Baxter's HemAssist in its production and usage profile. Based on early positive results from its Phase 3 trials, Northfield anticipated full FDA approval in late 1999.

In contrast to Baxter, Northfield was a small, 45-person firm that was founded in 1985 for the sole purpose of developing a human blood substitute. As such, PolyHeme represented its only product. Analysts expected PolyHeme to be priced comparably to HemAssist upon release.

By early 1998, Northfield had spent $70 million in its development of PolyHeme and in the construction of a pilot production facility with an output capacity of 10,000 units per year. While this facility was sufficient to satisfy demand during clinical trials, Northfield management recognized the need for a full-scale production facility. With this in mind, they hoped to construct a $45 million facility with a capacity of 300,000 units per year. With this factory in place, aside from the cost of raw material, production costs were expected to be about $30 million per year, independent of production volume. By early 1998, selection of a factory site and plant construction had not yet begun.

Animal Blood Substitutes

Through early 1998, Biopure was the only company that was actively engaged in the development of a blood substitute for the small-animal veterinary market. And while there was little to prevent Baxter or Northfield (or anyone else) from attempting to enter the veterinary market, any company wishing to do so would have to initiate an FDA-approval process specific to the veterinary market. By one estimate, assuming a company immediately began such a process, it would take 2 to 5 years to bring a product to market.

Biopure and Its Blood Substitutes

Hemopure and Oxyglobin were nearly identical in terms of physical characteristics and production processes. The only difference between the two products was in the size of the hemoglobin "clusters" that were contained in the final products. In the production of Oxyglobin, both large and small clusters of hemoglobin molecules were naturally formed. However, the small clusters tended to cause minor gastrointestinal problems and discoloration of urine. While considered acceptable in the animal market, these side effects were undesirable in the human market. As a result, Hemopure followed the same production process as used to make Oxyglobin, with a final step added to remove the small hemoglobin clusters.

Biopure had a single manufacturing facility, with an output capacity varying by the production mix of Oxyglobin and Hemopure. The same equipment was used to produce either product, but only one product could be produced at a time. This resulted in an annual capacity of 300,000 units of Oxyglobin or 150,000 units of Hemopure or some linear combination in between. The lower output for Hemopure reflected the facts that (1) the added step to remove the small hemoglobin clusters decreased the rate of production, and (2) the removal of the small hemoglobin clusters decreased yield.

To support these levels of output, aside from the cost of raw material, Biopure anticipated overall production costs of $15 million per year, independent of volume. For raw material, it anticipated a ready supply of bovine blood priced at $1.50 per unit. Biopure paid this money to cattle slaughterhouses to collect and transport the blood of cattle that were being processed for their meat—blood that otherwise would have been discarded. It was estimated that 10,000 cattle could supply enough raw material to support full production in Biopure's existing manufacturing facility.

Status of Hemopure

As of early 1998, Hemopure was in Phase 3 clinical trials in Europe, with FDA approval for Phase 3 trials in the United States appearing imminent. In anticipation of this approval, Biopure had established sites for Phase 3 trials and was ready to proceed immediately upon approval. While acknowledging the potential pitfalls of any clinical trials, Biopure was confident that the Phase 3 trials would be successful and that the FDA would grant full approval sometime in 1999. Biopure expected to commercially release Hemopure sometime in late 1999 or early 2000.

In line with the anticipated price of Baxter's Hem Assist, Biopure planned to price Hemopure at $600 to $800 per unit. However, little systematic testing had been done by Biopure to determine the acceptability of these prices. In particular, little was known of the price sensitivity of medical personnel, insurance providers, or of patients when it came to human blood substitutes.

Status of Oxyglobin

In 1997, Biopure established the Veterinary Products Division and hired Andy Wright to oversee the marketing and sale of Oxyglobin. Working under the assumption that Biopure would begin selling Oxyglobin immediately upon approval, Wright faced a host of decisions, including how to price and how to distribute Oxyglobin. Supporting him in these decisions was a team of seven employees—one director of marketing, one technical service representative (to answer technical questions and complaints), two customer service representatives (to support ordering and billing), and three sales representatives (to make sales calls and generate orders).

The Pricing of Oxyglobin. Some members of Wright's sales team argued for Oxyglobin to be priced at $80 to $100 per unit. These team members pointed to the price sensitivity of the vet market, arguing that few pet owners carried health insurance on their animals. They also noted that the average cost of a visit to the vet was only about $60, with few procedures costing more than $100

(see Exhibit 8). Finally, they noted that vets tended to use a simple "doubling rule" when pricing a medical product to the pet owners, bringing the end-user price of Oxyglobin to $160 to $200 per unit.

Other members of Andy Wright's sales team felt that Oxyglobin should carry a premium price of up to $200 per unit, reflecting the many advantages of Oxyglobin relative to donated animal blood. These team members pointed out that while the average cost of a visit to a primary care practice might be only $60, the cost of a visit to an emergency care practice could easily run from $200 to over $1,000. They also questioned whether veterinary doctors would just blindly double the price of Oxyglobin without regard for its high dollar contribution. Finally, they noted that at a low price, Biopure could never hope to recoup the massive cost of product development.

To better understand the channel's willingness to pay for an animal blood substitute, Biopure conducted two surveys in 1997—one survey of 285 veterinarians and another of 200 dog owners. Table A offers results of the veterinarian survey and Table B offers results of the owner survey.

Table A Veterinarians' Reported Willingness to Trial Oxyglobin

	% of Veterinarians Who Would Trial Product	
Price to Veterinarian	Noncritical Cases	Critical Cases
$50 per unit	95%	100%
$100 per unit	70%	95%
$150 per unit	25%	80%
$200 per unit	5%	60%

Source: Biopure company records

Table B Pet Owners' Willingness to Trial Oxyglobin

	% of Pet Owners Who Would Trial Product	
Price to Pet Owner	Noncritical Cases	Critical Cases
$100 per unit	60%	90%
$200 per unit	40%	85%
$300 per unit	35%	75%
$400 per unit	30%	65%

Source: Biopure company records

In reviewing these surveys, Wright reminded himself that veterinarians often played the role of gatekeeper when it came to potential treatments, recommending less-expensive over more-expensive treatments in an effort to save their clients' money. At the same time, 90% of pet owners reported that they wanted to be made fully aware of all the alternatives available to treat their pets.

The Distribution of Oxyglobin.

Andy Wright also had to decide how best to sell and distribute Oxyglobin and how to educate veterinarians on its use. In approaching this question, he looked to the current distribution practices for medical products in the veterinary market.

In 1997, $1.2 billion worth of product was sold to veterinary practices through a network of 200 independent distributors—each of whom sold and distributed the products of many manufacturers. Two of these independent distributors were national in scope, 18 were regional (e.g., New England), and 180 were local (e.g., metropolitan Boston). Table C provides a sales and staffing profile for these distributors. A manufacturer might contract with one national distributor, several nonoverlapping regional distributors, and many nonoverlapping local distributors. In return for their selling and distribution efforts, a distributor would receive 20% of the manufacturer selling price on a more-established product and 30% of the selling price on a less-established or new product.

A veterinary practice could expect one 15-minute visit per week from the sales representatives of its primary distributor. These 15-minute visits would entail a focused discussion of current promotions on existing products and a more limited discussion of products new to the market. Typically, a sales rep might introduce 100 new products in a given year. To educate a particular distributor's sales reps on a new product, a manufacturer might set up a series of training sessions. These training sessions would be conducted for groups of about 10 sales representatives each and last anywhere from 1 to 4 hours, depending on the complexity of the new product.

Another $300 million worth of products were sold directly to veterinary practices through manufacturer salesforces. Termed "manufacturer direct," this type of distribution often was used by manufacturers with either high-volume, well-established products or products which required a very sophisticated sales pitch. If Biopure chose this route, in addition to the cost of maintaining a salesforce, Andy estimated the cost to physically distribute Oxyglobin to be $10 to $15 per unit.

Andy Wright also considered trade publications and trade shows as another means by which to educate veterinarians about the existence and benefits of Oxyglobin. A quick investigation revealed that five journals had almost universal coverage across veterinarians and tended to be well-read. In addition, six large veterinary trade shows held in the United States each year attracted 2,000 to 10,000 veterinarians each. Typically, these trade shows were taken seriously by attendees and were a valued source of information. Andy wondered if either of these avenues made sense for Biopure.

Biopure's Decisions

While Andy dealt with the question of how best to market Oxyglobin, Carl Rausch wrestled with the larger question of whether and when to launch Oxyglobin. Should he listen to Ted Jacobs and postpone the launch of Oxyglobin until *after* Hemopure had established itself in the marketplace? Or should he listen to Andy and immediately launch Oxyglobin and reap the near-term benefits?

Not lost on Carl was the potential impact of Oxyglobin on a possible initial public offering of Biopure stock. To this point, Biopure had remained a privately held firm with very little debt. And while they currently had no

Table C Profile of Independent Distributors of Veterinary Medicines

Type of Distributor	Number	% of Total Sales	Avg. Number of Sales Reps
National	2	25%	100
Regional	18	60%	40
Local	180	15%	1.5

Source: Biopure company records

revenues, a recent round of capital venture financing had provided them with $50 million—enough money to support operations for another two years. Nevertheless, many stakeholders in Biopure were anxious to take the company public. In this regard, Carl wondered whether a veterinary product with small but steady sales might not prove more attractive to investors than a human product still under development. He was especially sensitive to this issue in light of some recent, high-profile product failures in the Massachusetts biotechnology community (see Exhibit 9).

With all of this in mind, as president and CEO of Biopure, Carl Rausch pondered how best to leverage the opportunity offered by Oxyglobin without jeopardizing the potential of Hemopure.

Exhibit 1 Excerpts from *The Boston Globe* Article, February 5, 1998

Biopure's Blood Substitute for Dogs OK'd

Veterinarians scrambling to find blood for badly injured dogs now have a blood substitute. Biopure Corp. of Cambridge said yesterday it received federal regulatory approval to market oxygen-carrying blood derived from the blood of cows.

Tested in over 250 dogs, the company's blood substitute, called Oxyglobin, is initially aimed at the [canine blood transfusion market], according to Andrew W. Wright, vice president of Biopure's veterinary products.

The US Food and Drug Administration approval makes Oxyglobin the first blood substitutes for dogs, designed for dogs needing blood transfusions because of blood loss from accidents, surgeries, parasite infections, or rare anemia cases.

"This is breakthrough development because it quickly gets oxygen into tissue and organs and buys time for the dog's own regenerative red blood cells to come back," said Dr. Robert Murtaugh, professor of veterinary medicine and section head for emergency and critical care services at the Tufts University School of Veterinary Medicine.

The canine version is designed to largely replace drawing blood from donor dogs some veterinarians use in emergency situations.

Unlike blood that contains red blood cells, Biopure's technology uses a highly purified bovine hemoglobin that does not require blood typing or cross-matching. [Oxyglobin] can be stored in a veterinarian's storage area at room temperature for up to two years. A single bag—equivalent to a pint of whole blood—is sufficient for small to medium-sized dogs; two bags might be needed for larger dogs.

Reprinted with courtesy of *The Boston Globe.*

Exhibit 2 The Organizational Structure at Biopure Corporation

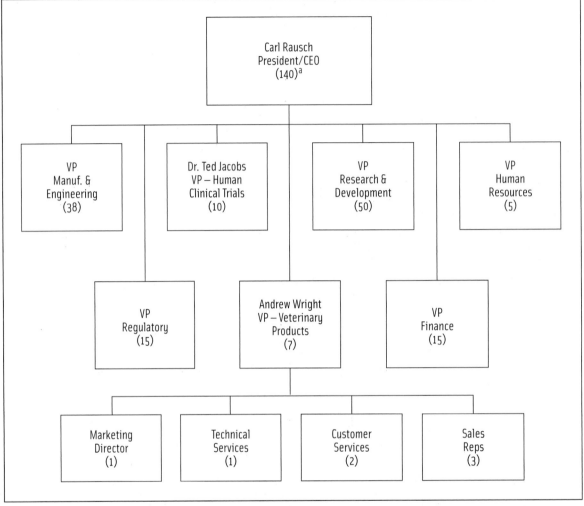

Source: Biopure company records

[a]Numbers in parentheses represents the total number of employees that fall under a particular position's span of control. Thus, 140 employees either directly or indirectly report to Carl Rausch.

Exhibit 3 The United States FDA Approval Process

Phase	Goals	Characteristics
Pre-Clinical Trials	Safety in animals	– Typical length = 5 – 10 years – Need to show safety – Hope to show efficacy – Testing animals include mice, rats, dogs, sheep, etc.
Phase 1 Clinical Trials	Safety in healthy human subjects	– Typical length = 2 – 3 years – 20 – 100 individuals – Single-site testing location
Phase 2A & 2B Clinical Trials	2A – Safety in human patients 2B – Safety & efficacy in human patients	– Typical length = 1 – 2 years – 100 – 200 individuals – Single-site or multi-site testing locations
Phase 3 Clinical Trials	Large-scale safety & efficacy in use	– Typical length = 1 – 2 years – 100 – 500 individuals – Multi-site testing locations – Double-blind testing (i.e., neither patient nor doctor aware of specific product or brand)

Source: Biopure company records

Exhibit 4 Human Blood Typing and Allowable Transfusions[a]

Donor Blood Type	% of Population	Acceptable Recipients
AB	4%	AB[b]
A	40%	A, AB
B	11%	B, AB
O[c]	45%	O, A, B, AB

Source: The American Red Cross
[a]In addition to ABO blood typing, RBCs are either Rh1 or Rh-, further complicating allowable transfusions.
[b]AB is often referred to as the "universal recipient."
[c]O is often referred to as the "universal donor."

Exhibit 5 Red Blood Cell Donations and Transfusions in the United States in 1995

Use of Red Blood Cells	Units (in 000s)
– *Acute Blood Loss*	
– Elective Surgery	
– Anonymous Donations	5,800
– Autologous Donations [a,b]	1,100
– Emergency Surgery (in hospital)	1,000
– Trauma (in field administration)	200
– **Acute Blood Loss Subtotal**	8,100
– *Chronic Anemia*	3,200
– *Not Transfused*	
– Due to Rejection	1,200
– Due to Expiration	1,500
– **Not Transfused Subtotal**	2,700
– **Total**	14,000

Source: Stover & Associates LLC

[a]Autologous donations are in elective surgery only. All other uses of RBCs represent anonymous donations.

[b]Autologous donations include both those units transfused and those unused units discarded.

Exhibit 6 Cost to Patient of Donated Human Blood

	Low Estimate (per Unit)	High Estimate (per Unit)
– *Anonymous Donations*		
– Hospital Acquisition Cost	$75	$150
– Screening/Typing/Crossmatching	25	40
– Transportation/Administration	25	35
– *Final Price of Anonymous*	$125	$225
– *Autologous Donations*		
– Added Administration and Handling	+ 150	+ 200
– *Final Price of Autologous*	$275	$425

Source: Stover & Associates, LLC

Exhibit 7 Profile of the 15,000 Veterinary Practices in the United States (1995)

Class of Practice	Average No. of Doctors	Relative Frequency	Average Monthly Case Load			Average Gross Revenues
			Dogs	Cats	Other	
– *Primary Care*						
– 1 Doctor Practices	1	25%	200	125	80	$265,000
– 2 Doctor Practices	2	30%	300	200	120	$460,000
– 3+ Doctor Practices	4.6	40%	450	300	160	$800,000
– Average Primary Care	2.7	95%	412	265	140	$570,000
– *Emergency Care*						
– Avg. Emergency Care	4.0	5%	400	240	130	$770,000

Source: Biopure Company Records

Exhibit 8 Small-Animal Veterinary Fees for Typical Procedures in Primary Care Practices in 1995

Procedure	Average Fee
– *Average Charge per Visit*	$58
– Office Call–Average Minimum Charge	$25
– Boarding	$10
– Hospitalization	$19
– Anesthesia	$45
– X-rays	$40
– Blood Transfusion	$100
– Hysterectomy	$80
– Heartworm treatment	$250
– Annual Vaccinations	$27
– Rabies Vaccination	$12
– Lab Tests–Average	$23
– Dental Cleaning	$75
– Deworming	$15

Source: *Veterinary Economics,* October, 1996, p. 45

Exhibit 9 Massachusetts Biopharmaceutical Companies' Proposed Drugs Sidelined in the 2nd Quarter, 1997

Firm/location	Date	Problem	Status of company
ImmunoGen Norwood, MA	March 18	Oncolysin B cancer drug halted after Phase 3 trial failure	Significantly downsized operations, extensive layoffs, major restructuring, sold biomanufacturing plant, and relocated corporate offices
OraVax Cambridge, MA	March 19	HNK20, a nosedrop designed to reduce hospitalization for lower respiratory infections caused by respiratory virus in infants, failed in a pivotal overseas clinical trial	Layoff of 20 people in April as part of a corporate reorganization
AutoImmune Lexington, MA	April 21	Myloral, an oral multiple sclerosis drug, did no better than placebo in Phase 3 trial	Major restructuring, now employs 20, down from 90 employees
Genzyme Cambridge, MA	May 5	Sepracoat, a surgical antiadhesion coating, was rejected by FDA advisory committee for lack of sufficient evidence of clinical effectiveness	Company selling Sepracoat in Europe; has FDA approval on related Seprafilm product
Cambridge Neuroscience Cambridge, MA	June 24	Cerestat clinical trial is halted over safety concerns by corporate partner, Boehringer Ingelheim	Six-month investigation begins to find reasons for concern

Source: *The Boston Globe*

Integrated Marketing Communications

Marketing communications encompass a broad array of methods by which the customer is educated, persuaded, and reminded about a product. The Integrated Marketing Communications note leading off this module describes the major communication vehicles and their key characteristics.

Similar to the *Module 3 Going to Market*, Module 4 seeks to present both classic, enduring issues in communication strategy formulation and contemporary ones taking center stage in the Internet age. In "SUAVE (C)," Suave addresses the classic issue of how to devise an advertising strategy. The case "Colgate-Palmolive Company: The Precision Toothbrush," introduces the broader portfolio of communication techniques that typically need to complement one another in a consumer products setting, i.e., advertising, trade promotions, and consumer promotions. "Dendrite International" turns to an industrial situation in which there is a need for consultative selling and ongoing account management. Finally, "Henkel Group: Umbrella Branding and Globalization Decisions" presents the issue of the desired degree of standardization in the way that the brand of the Henkel Group of Germany is presented across world markets.

The final two cases look at contemporary issues arising from the information overload experienced by consumers in this information age. "Launching the BMW Z3 Roadster" explores the way that BMW decided to launch its Z3 roadster not by conventional communications techniques but through a nontraditional campaign—embedding the new product in entertainment, specifically the James Bond film, *GoldenEye*. Is this a sensible approach for the Z3? For other cars? For other products? What is the future of such nontraditional techniques?

The last case in this part is "Alloy.com: Marketing to Generation Y." Alloy.com is a Web company that sells teen clothing by marrying its catalog, its Web ads, and the content of its Web site. The company's goal is to create an "Alloy community." How can Alloy attract and retain teens? How can traditional media like television advertising and catalogs be integrated with Web communications to create the overall desired effect with favorable economics?

Through these cases, Module 4 develops an understanding of the advantages and disadvantages of major alternatives in communications and also develops skill in crafting an integrated package of actions to generate the desired effect efficiently.

INTEGRATED MARKETING COMMUNICATIONS

Introduction

The "Note on Marketing Strategy" (HBS No. 598-061) states "Effective marketing requires an integrated communications plan . . ." because the communication program's role is to foster the consumer's "awareness of the product, knowledge about its features, interest in purchasing, likelihood of trying the product and/or purchasing it." Accomplishing the typically multifaceted communications goals means relying not just on one form of communication, but bringing together a number of different modes in a consistent, complementary way.

For example, when General Motors introduced the Saturn as a "different kind of car company" it hired Hal Riney as its agency to coordinate all communications about the new automobile brand. Riney positioned the brand not only through a national advertising campaign, but also through brochures, the "look" and signage of the retail showrooms, local retailer advertiser, and retailer promotions. GM's idea in having a "single source" of all these materials was to ensure that the program elements worked together to position Saturn in the mind of the consumer in a consistent fashion. As part of the introduction, a local automobile dealer wanted to "give away" a Saturn. This would have been at odds with the message being presented in the rest of the campaign. Riney's involvement in all aspects of the program converted the car "give-away" and the negative associations which could go with that to a promotion in which the prize was a trip to Saturn's manufacturing facility in Spring Hill, Tennessee to meet the committed employees and visit the place where their car was born.[1] This promotion fit with the specialness of the new company.

Similarly, when Southwest Airlines begins service in a new city, a variety of efforts is launched to build consumers' awareness of the new service, to establish Southwest's positioning in their minds, and ultimately induce them to book a flight on Southwest. For example, when Southwest instituted its Baltimore base of operations, the kickoff to the communications program was a joint announcement of the coming event by Southwest's Chairman and Maryland's governor. The announcement event generated wide coverage in the press. As a second public relations event, Southwest took 49 children from Baltimore to Cleveland for a zoo visit—the 49 number being selected to match Southwest's $49 price. Advertising began with direct mail pieces to heavy airline users in the area containing promotional offers and an invitation to join Southwest's frequent-flyer program. Southwest employees then "hit-the-streets" in high traffic areas handing out bags of peanuts to passers-by to emphasize Southwest's "Just Peanut" fares. Traditional newspaper and television advertisements then followed.[2]

As these examples suggest, different types of communications are used for the obvious, simple reason that some types are better than others for specific purposes. For example, television advertising is great for creating awareness of a brand but typically not as powerful as a limited time promotional offer in generating action by the consumer.

In the past, a fair conception of many company's communications strategy was a media advertising program as the core, flanked by other supporting elements such as promotions. However, this primacy of media advertising is no longer a good general description. For a number of reasons, uses of other communication forms have been growing more quickly than media advertising. More pressure for short-term sales results has swung spending to vehicles like sales promotions, which are more capable of producing quick sales results. Also, the rising power of the trade has led to more communications spending directed to them as opposed to end consumers. Today's marketer has the opportunity and challenge of bringing

Professor Robert Dolan prepared this case as the basis for class discussion rather than to illustrate either effective or ineffective handling of an administrative situation.

[1]This is described in D. Aaker, *Building Strong Brands,* Free Press, 1996.
[2]This is described in R. Batra, J. Myers and D. Aaker, *Advertising Management,* Prentice-Hall, 1995.

together a wide variety of possible communication options to achieve the desired consumer impact.

This Note describes major communication vehicles. Section II contrasts personal selling and advertising, discussing media advertising and direct response advertising. Section III covers promotions, of which there are two types: Consumer Promotions and Trade Promotions. A short Section IV describes other communication vehicles rounding out the mix. Section V discusses the process via which elements are brought together to form a cohesive plan. It presents the concept of a "hierarchy-of-effects" model to describe how consumers move through a purchase process and how it can be a useful input to communication program design.

Communication Vehicles

Introduction

Figure A shows two dimensions along which it is useful to contrast communications options.[3] These dimensions are:

1. Broadcast vs. Interactive or One-Way vs. Two Way: The horizontal dimension in Figure A is the distinction between situations in which there is outbound communication only vs. one in which there is an interaction between the initiator and receiver of the initial dialog. When Oldsmobile spent almost $2MM for a 30-second ad during the Super Bowl in January 1999, it sent out a message over the airways to 130 million viewers tuned to Fox TV. Fox TV's technology could not accommodate a reply from the 130 million recipients of the message. It was a simple one way broadcast of a message.

At the other end of the spectrum is communication which is a dialogue, not a monologue. For example, when a prospect visits an Oldsmobile showroom, a salesperson is likely to engage that person. The salesperson delivers a message. The prospect responds. An exchange of some duration typically ensues. If the salesperson's message is persuasive enough, the prospect's ultimate response may well be to buy the Oldsmobile. This type of two-way interaction is instantaneous.

Figure A Characteristics of Communication Options

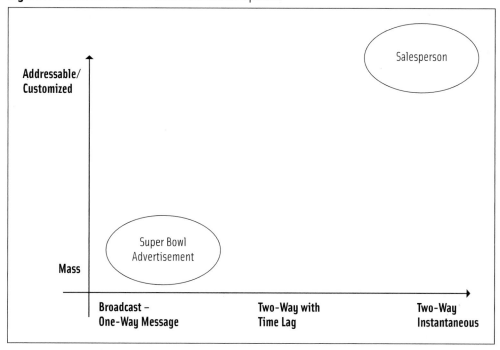

[3]This two dimensional classification was originally suggested by Professor John Deighton.

Figure B Position of Major Communication Vehicles

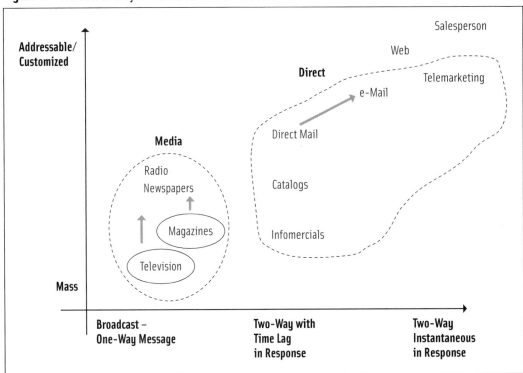

As shown in the middle of the horizontal axis of Figure A, other two-way interactions occur with a time lag. For example, a direct mail piece usually solicits a reply by the receiver. That reply however may await the receiver's attention or next trip to the post office.

2. Mass vs. Addressable/Customized. The vertical dimension of Figure A describes the extent to which the message is able to be varied to meet the particular communication needs of the person receiving it. The Oldsmobile ad on the Super Bowl was not customized, i.e., it was presented to all 130 million people watching in precisely the same way. It is a mass medium.

On the other hand, the salesperson can and should be customizing his or her message to the particular communication needs of the message recipient. A primary advantage and justification for the typically high cost of personal selling is this ability to adjust the message to the situation, e.g. talking about safety features to the family with four children, the cargo carrying capability to the young couple with ski weekends on their minds, and low initial payment leases to the first-time car buyer with no equity in a trade-in.

Figure B fills in this space with some of the more important communication vehicles available. (The positions are generally suggestive rather than absolutes for all situations.) Everything other than Salesperson, anchoring the most northeast position, we can call a form of advertising.

A typical person in the United States is exposed to over 1,500 advertisements per day. Imagine living in a suburb of Boston: your clock radio wakes you with the news that a call to "1-800-54-GIANT" will get your broken windshield fixed; your first sighting of the day as you begin the wake-up routine is the Tom's toothpaste package asserting Tom's "All-Natural" ingredients; the *Boston Globe* snatched from the front doorsteps announces the One-Day Sale at Filene's and tells you it's "Two Thumbs Up!" for a Civil Action; driving to work brings Cindy Crawford and her Omega watch into large view on a billboard; arriving at work and logging on to the Internet to check out the late sports scores on ESPN Sportszone produces the banner that "The New Volvo S80 is here.

Bigger than a BMW 528*i*"; approaching the door into lunch brings the familiar red circle and the reminder "Coke Always"; after work, picking up the mail brings the offer of a 4.9% interest, no-fee credit card if you act now; looking through the program at your kid's Little League baseball game has a reminder that maybe it's not a Volvo but a "Lexington Toyota" for you; watching the evening news shows you can still "Have it Your Way" at Burger King; just before turning out the light, flipping the last page of Stephen Ambrose's *Undaunted Courage* brings information from the publisher about his upcoming sequel to his bestseller, *D-Day*.

Total advertising spending in the United States recently reached $200 billion annually. Two major types of advertising shown in Figure B are media advertising, clustered in the lower left-hand corner, and direct response in the middle. The key distinction is that direct is designed specifically to elicit a purchase action by the consumer whereas media advertising is setting a foundation for that by impacting the consumers' knowledge and attitude.

Characteristics of Leading Media Advertising

Television. Television is largely a national medium with 70% of the expenditures for national (as opposed to local) coverage in the United States. Television's prime advantage is its ability to reach broad segments of the population at a set time with a "sight-and-sound" message. It can be expensive however in both the production of a high impact sight-and-sound message and also in the payment to the media provider, e.g., the average 30-second prime time ad costs about $185,000; a 30-second ad on Seinfeld cost over $500,000 when that show was at its peak; and a 30-second ad on the final Seinfeld show ran $1.7MM.

A common measure used to summarize the cost of a communication option is the "cost-per-thousand." For example, if a prime-time TV show with a 30-second ad cost of $185,000 drew 10 million households as viewers, we would compute the CPM or "cost-per-thousand" household as:

$$\frac{\$185,000}{10,000,000} \times 1000 = \$18.50 \; CPM.$$

A challenge for television advertisers is that multiple advertisers vie for the consumer's attention on a given show. In a typical hour of prime time programming, more than 15 ads will be featured. In addition to competing with these 14 other ads, an advertiser must compete with other activities for viewers' attention. Ads are frequently "zapped" as viewers use their "clickers" (remote controlled channel changers) to switch to another channel temporarily when a commercial break appears.

The upward arrow shown on Television in Figure B is to represent the fact that with the proliferation of cable TV channels, television has increased its addressability/customizability options. Obviously, everyone watching a given show sees the same ad. But, there are now many specialized channels, e.g., The Golf Channel, The Nashville Network (Country Music), which deliver specialized audiences. Ads can be varied by show to match the message to the audience.

Newspapers. In contrast to TV, newspapers are largely a local medium with 90% of dollars in the U.S. placed on local basis. There are about 1,500 daily newspapers in the United States. *The Wall Street Journal* and *USA Today* do attract national advertisers, but most newspaper expenditure is for local presentation of display advertising in the main body of the newspaper or in supplements. A popular type of supplement commonly seen in Sunday papers is the free-standing insert, i.e. a loose sheet, often in color, placed within the paper.

An advantage of newspaper is that most consumers look upon advertising in newspapers positively. Whereas television advertising is deemed an intrusion, newspaper advertising is generally considered informational. Newspapers typically provide broad coverage of the local market as about 70% of adults read a daily newspaper. Newspapers are also flexible in that space need not be reserved far in advance. Noted limitations are: (i) it is a "sight-only" medium with relatively weak reproduction quality (e.g. as compared to magazines) and (ii) the "life" of an ad is typically one day before it is dispatched to the recycling bin or trash with the newspaper.

Radio. Radio is also a largely local medium. Due to the large number of stations available within a market and their distinctive positions, e.g. Rock, Country, Adult Talk, Sports Talk, etc., the audiences are well-segmented. Radio is also relatively low cost and is a good candidate if the marketer is seeking to deliver a message frequently to a well-defined audience.

Limitations are that radio is obviously "sound-only" and ads may easily be tuned out. Also, like television, clutter is an issue as many ads compete for the listener's attention. Most effective radio ads have been creative in capturing the listener's attention and imagination.

Magazines. There has been a sharp increase in the number of magazines published. This has meant a fundamental transformation in the role of magazine advertising. Through the 1950's, leading magazine were similar to television in delivering a broad audience. While some, like *TV Guide,* continue to do this today, a key development has been the emergence of special interest magazines. Magazines like the *Massachusetts Golfer* and *Modern Bride* deliver a very sharply defined audience to the advertiser. This is represented by the upward arrow shown on Figure B. Magazines offer the ability to deliver a visually strong message to a well-defined target audience. Magazine ads also have the longest "life" of any medium and also benefit from pass-along readership.

Direct Marketing

The second major type of advertising shown in Figure B is direct marketing communication. Direct marketing is defined as "an interactive system of marketing which uses one or more advertising media to effect a measurable response and/or transaction."[4] A common characteristic of direct marketing is that a customer file or database records messages sent and whether or not there was a response. Some use the terms "direct marketing" and "database marketing" interchangeably.

A number of direct techniques are used:

(i.) *Infomercials* are basically relatively long video presentations of an information-heavy message. Frequently, the infomercial will combine entertainment and information. While infomercials may conjure up images of late-night cable television placement and heavy selling of "miracle" cooking and cutting devices, they can be delivered in other ways as well and present high quality, detailed marketing messages. For example, Chrysler produced the "Chrysler Showcase" a 30-minute infomercial setting out the positioning for the Chrysler 300M, LHS and Concorde models. The car's designers and engineers explain the new product development process behind the new models. The 30-minute version infomercial was on cable-TV and a shorter version on tape delivered via the mail to prospects requesting information from 1-800-CHRYSLER or the company's Web Site.[5]

Similarly, Valvoline Oil produced a 30-minute infomercial "Inside Valvoline Racing" that provided an in-depth story of two racing teams. The first goal of the production was to deliver entertainment value, which then provided the right context for product and brand messages.

(ii.) *Catalogs,* multi-paged pieces showing merchandise for sale are another common direct technique. Women's apparel and accessories were the largest catalog seller followed by home products, gifts and sporting goods. Many use catalogs to complement a retail presence: e.g., Victoria's Secret, Sharper Image, Brookstone, and J. Crew. A company can have a variety of catalogs, using the customer's purchase history as a guide to which catalogs to send and with what frequency.

Catalogs are a particular form of direct mail which, because of the quality of the production, tend not to be as customized to an individual recipient as a solicitation letter which can be easily and inexpensively customized. *Direct mail* generally includes a letter, a sales brochure, and instructions on how to reply (order) or a reply form. *E-mail,* as shown by its position to the northeast of direct mail in Figure B offers more opportunity for customization and quicker exchange of information.

(iii.) *Telemarketing* is basically selling-by-phone, rather than in-person. Whereas an in-person sales call might average out to $250 per call, telemarketing expenses typically run in the $5 per call range. A big advantage of telemarketing over direct mail, which in some cases justifies its cost premium, is its immediate two-way nature, allowing the caller to customize the message in accord with the message receiver's initial response.

Technology has been a major force fostering the growth of direct marketing. Computers manage lists of customers and sophisticated sta-

---

[4]W. Wells, J. Burnett, and S. Moriarty, *Advertising: Principles and Practice,* Prentice-Hall, 1998.

[5]This is described in "Infomercial Offers Multiple Use," *Direct Marketing,* September 1998.

tistical techniques help find worthwhile solicitation patterns. 800-numbers and fax machines ease the receipt of orders and widespread credit card use facilitates completing the order. Direct mail still accounts for the majority of direct marketing spending. The primary issue with direct mail is the large number of consumers with a "junk mail" attitude.

The most important recent development for direct marketing is the Web. The Web offers the opportunity to exchange customized messages and responses in an instantaneous way. As described in the "Note on Marketing and the World Wide Web," (9-597-037) a distinctive feature of the Web is its "hyper impulsivity" due to its "closer conjunction of desire, transaction and payment than any other environment." That note describes the potential of the Web as "to be as subtle, as flexible, as pertinent and as persuasive as good communication, with a better memory than the most diligent salesperson . . ." The Web can also serve in a less interactive way, via posting of banner ads without the needed supporting Web site development for true interactivity. But, its great potential is as a mechanism for bringing the marketing system all together.

The Role of Promotion in Integrated Marketing Communications

Introduction

Advertising and personal selling generally seek to move a customer through a purchase process by describing reasons to buy. A complementary part of the communications mix is Promotions. In promotions, a specific inducement to generate purchase behavior is offered, e.g., a $1.00 off coupon. Note that a given message to a consumer may include both advertising and promotion components. For example, a page in a magazine may include standard ad copy but then have a coupon at the bottom of the page to be cut out and redeemed at the store. It is important to recognize the two different goals even if the communications are contained in one specific execution.

Promotions can be directed to either the end consumer or the trade. A consumer promotion tries to induce consumer action to "pull" the product through the channel of distribution, while a trade promotion seeks to enlist support to carry an item and/or "push" it through to the end user.

Consumer Promotions

There is a wide variety of consumer promotion executions. Major types include:

(i.) *Free samples* are especially useful in generating a trial of the product. They can be distributed in the mail, passed out at points of purchase or other high traffic areas, or be made available upon request from a potential buyer.

(ii.) Price oriented programs which seek to reduce the consumer's real cost per unit in some way, e.g.: (a) *cents-off coupons* which can be redeemed at the point-of-purchase, (b) *mail-in refunds* or *rebates* in which the consumer receives the specified amount upon submitting proof-of-purchase. Alternatively, special "pacs" can be offered to improve the value consumers receive: e.g., a "*price pac*" offering the normal size but repriced to provide a savings; a "value" pac offering larger quantity at the usual price; or a "*bonus pac*" offering another unit of the good for free if a certain number are purchased at the usual price, e.g. the "buy-one-get-one free" offer.

(iii.) *Premiums*—another item is given away or offered at an attractive price if a certain number of units are purchased, e.g., during Christmas season 1998, Adams offered a free golf bag with the purchase of two of its clubs.

(iv.) *Tie-Ins*—similar to premiums, but involves the joint promotion of two items, e.g. buy a Jeep and get two free season's passes to a local ski resort. Typically, the two parties share in the cost of the promotion.

(v.) *Continuity Programs*—a reward is given in recognition of continuing relationships, e.g. the frequent flyer programs offered by virtually every airline.

(vi.) *Contests/Sweepstakes*—used to generate excitement about product. For example, as part of a large-scale program involving television advertising, free-standing inserts in papers, and point-of-purchase displays, consumers turning in $20 in receipts for Nestle products received certificates for reduced admission to movie theaters and were entered in a drawing for a 5-day "Best of Hollywood Vacation" during the Academy Awards, year 2000.[6] By law, a sweepstakes cannot require the purchase of a product in order to participate, but in many instances participation rates by nonbuyers are low.

The extent of consumer promotions is vast. About 300 billion coupons are distributed annually in the United States. The Sunday newspaper free-standing insert has been the vehicle of distribution for the majority of these coupons. However, as the number of coupons distributed has grown, the percent redeemed has declined, from about 3.5% in the early 1980s to 2.5% in the 1990s. There has been a good deal of research on the impact of coupons on sales and the finding is that while the redemption rates may be low, coupons can have a measurable impact on short-term sales due to their ability to attract new triers and induce brand switching.

Trade Promotions

As with consumer promotions, there is a wide variety of trade promotion executions in practice. The objective of each is generally the same however, i.e. to induce the trade member to "push" the brand and through these efforts induce the consumer to buy. More specifically, a trade promotion can serve to induce the trade to:

- Carry an item
- Increase inventory held
- Display/advertise the item
- Lower the price of the item

Common trade promotion vehicles are:

(i.) *Slotting Allowances*—This is a payment used to induce the trade to take on a new item. As the power of retailers has risen, new products, especially those with less certain sales prospects, effectively have to pay to "rent" shelf space from the retailer.

(ii.) *Cooperative Advertising (Co-op)*—the manufacturer agrees to pay a percentage of the trade's

advertising cost if the product is featured in advertising in a particular way. For example, restrictions might include that the product be the only one of its type in the ad, be the most prominently featured of any product, and not be advertised at a price below a certain level.

(iii.) *Floor Planning*—the manufacturer basically finances the inventory of the retailer for a given period of time. This is common in expensive seasonal items such as snow blowers. If faced with buying and paying for goods in October and given lots of uncertainty about the timing and extent of demand, a retailer would likely take an amount into his store well less than the amount regarded as optimal by the manufacturer. The deferring of payment until after the selling season induces the trade to order more.

(iv.) *Temporary Price Cuts*—the manufacturer cuts its price to the trade for a fixed period of time, e.g. 10%-off-invoice on all items ordered in March. Often, the trade will require the manufacturer to supply its promotion schedule for the year so buying activities can be planned accordingly. Typically, the manufacturer hopes the "deal" (the price cut) is at least partially "passed through" to the end user by the trade.

(v.) *Volume Discounts*—price is reduced for units above a certain level. A quantity discount is a program whereby the same deal schedule is offered to all. Alternatively, some discounts "kick in" when an account exceeds its own last year's sales volume.

(vi.) *Contests*—just as a company may have contests and rewards for its salespeople, e.g. the $1 million club going to Cancun, so too it can generate push by the trade via contests for free gifts or trips.

Rounding Out the Communications Mix

Introduction

As shown on page 323 the five communications options presented to this point are:
Each of these is under the direct control of the company. Many firms round out their mix with programs not wholly under their control, e.g., Event Mar-

[6]S. Thompson, "Nestle musters up 30-plus brands for Hollywood pegged-sweepstakes," *BRANDWEEK*, January 11, 1999.

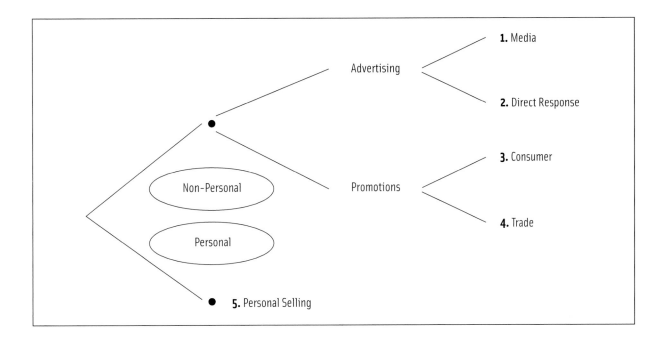

keting/Sponsorships and Publicity and Public Relations. These are not directly under the control of the marketer because another party is involved and to some extent the performance of the other party influences the impact the association will have. For example, if the Boston Celtics and Boston Bruins play poorly, the value of having the Fleet Bank name on the building in which they play decreases. Publicity generally involves a third party who sends its own message about the company.

Event Marketing Sponsorships.
Sponsorship of events can be a mechanism to gain desirable brand associations. The majority of sponsorships revolve around sports: e.g., the naming of athletic arenas such as the Fleet Center in Boston, RCA Dome in Indianapolis, and the Trans World Dome in St. Louis; ties to on-going events like the Nike Golf tour (for professional golfers just failing to qualify for the PGA Tour), the Virginia Slims Tennis tour and the Winston Cup Series of NASCAR (National Association of Stock Car Racing); as well as specific events like the Bob Hope Chrysler Golf Tournament and the AT&T Rose Bowl Football Game.

Many sponsorships are used to enhance the corporate reputation as a responsible, thoughtful member of the community. Philip Morris, the world's largest cigarette manufacturer, affiliates itself with a number of socially desirable activities such as hunger alleviation and the arts.

While many companies see sponsorships as offering a very high return on their investment, these programs are less controllable than advertising and promotion programs. For example, the Olympics has historically been a prime sponsorship opportunity. However, companies affiliated with the Winter Games of 2002 in Salt Lake City have been rocked by the scandal over bribes paid to obtain the award of the games to the city.

Publicity and Public Relations

Communications received from many media sources can influence a consumer's evaluation of a firm and its products. The medium's impact may depend on its perceived impartiality. Advertising is often viewed as biased as compared to the trade press. For example, a favorable review in *Road and Track* or other car enthusiast magazines can be critical in a new car introduction. The manufacturer exerts less control here than in advertising where it specifies the copy, the form and timing of the message's appearance. The marketer can, however, attempt to influence coverage of its product, e.g., by making information available (e.g. Press Releases) or even making the product available for test use to those who would then disseminate information about it to the market.

Formulating the Integrated Marketing Communications (IMC) Program

The "Note on Marketing Strategy" set out the 6M's model for communications planning, i.e.,

1. **Market** — To whom is the communication to be addressed?
2. **Mission** — What is the objective of the communication?
3. **Message** — What are the specific points to be communicated?
4. **Media** — Which vehicles will be used to convey the message?
5. **Money** — How much will be spent in the effort?
6. **Measurement** — How will impact be assessed after the campaign?

The First Three M's and the Hierarchy-of-Effects

The Market/Mission/Message part is basically figuring out the strategic and tactical objectives of the communications campaign, i.e., who is being targeted for impact, the desired impact on the target, and the specific message to be delivered.

A useful approach to resolve the first three of the six M's is to analyze the consumer situation in terms of stages in the purchase and consumption process. While the desired end result of all marketing activities, including communications, is typically an exchange (often of dollars for goods/services), there is typically a sequence of steps a consumer goes through leading up to this. A valid communications goal can be to move the customer from one of these early steps to the next. A general model of the steps that a consumer may go through is called the hierarchy-of-effects model. It specifies the seven steps shown in the figure below.

The seven steps fall into three stages: cognitive, affective and behavioral describing the type of response required from consumers to move along in the hierarchy.

In the cognitive stage, the communications job is to put some facts into the mind of the potential consumer. The first step is to make a consumer *aware* of the existence of the product and then build *knowledge* by conveying some information about it. For example, when Adams Golf introduced its Tight-Lies Golf Clubs, it had to first let potential customers know the club line existed and some of its features: e.g., a lower center of gravity and a shallower club face. This cognitive stage sets the foundation for an affective stage wherein the prospect develops a feeling toward the new product.

Adams moved some potential customers from the cognitive stage of just being aware of club features to understanding of benefits delivered and hence "liking" through infomercials which won awards as the best infomercial in the demonstration category in a national competition.

The remaining steps in the affective stage are to move from *liking* to having a *preference* for the product over others and finally a strong intent or *conviction* to buy it. Finally, the process ends with an action, i.e., advancing to the behavioral stage with a *purchase* of the product.

There is no one universally applicable model of the purchase process. For example, if the product was a non-durable, we might be concerned about another act within the behavioral stage, i.e., "repurchase." In some situations, it may be the case that the cognitive → affective → behavioral process (often called a learn → feel → do sequence) is not even descriptive of what is going on. Some researchers have found that the Learn → Feel →

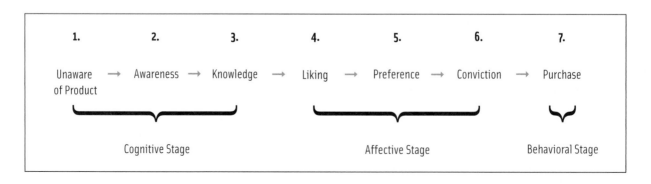

Do sequence may well describe a high-involvement purchase; but, Feel → Do → Learn may be an appropriate description in situations where consumers view the purchase of no great consequence and hence are relatively uninvolved in purchase process.

A first step in developing the Integrated Marketing Communications (IMC) plan is to assess the consumer purchase process relevant to the given situation. Note that it is possible that different segments of the market follow different purchase processes. For example, the entry-level buyer of stereo equipment has a different process than the aficionado/high-end purchaser. Once the right description of the process is developed, the next issue is to obtain at least a general sense of the distribution of potential customers over the states of the process at that point in time. For example, General Motors once developed the following stages for a new car model and distribution of target population.

Unaware →	Aware →	In Buying Class	→	In Consideration Class	→ First Choice
66%	14%	8%		7%	5%

Where:

"In Buying Case" → brand is considered similar to those being actively considered by the person.

"In Consideration Class" → brand is considered favorably by person.

"First Choice" → person would select brand if car purchase were to be made today.

By understanding the distribution of consumers across states, GM had a good understanding of the specific communications job it faced. Additional research showed GM the differences in perceptions/feeling between those in different states and hence what changes had to be brought about in the consumer's mind to move him or her along in the process.[7]

Communications objectives can be stated in terms of altering the distribution of the target market across the states.

---

[7]This is described in R. Batra, J.G. Myers, and D.A. Aaker, *Advertising Management*.

The Fourth M: Media

Sections II-IV of this note set out the many communication vehicle options available. With an understanding of the advantages/disadvantages of each and the communication program objectives, one can determine which mix of vehicles is optimal.

For example, in early 1999 M&M/Mars introduced "M&M Crunchy" to join its existing M&M line-up of plain, peanut, and peanut butter candies. The "hierarchy-of-effects" for a new candy item could be:

$$\text{Unaware} \rightarrow \text{Aware} \rightarrow \text{Positive Attitude} \rightarrow \text{Trial} \rightarrow \text{Repeat}$$

In mid-January 1999, some very small percentage of target customers were aware of the coming of M&M Crunchy. It had been covered in the trade press, like *Advertising Age* which projected $60 million spending on communications to support the launch. As is typical of a new product launch, the first task was to move the concentration of target consumers in the "unaware" state along to awareness and positive attitude. Given the broad target market definition and the awareness task, the spot on the Super Bowl chosen by M&M was an ideal vehicle.

M&M/Mars would be hoping to move a prospect through the hierarchy quickly, so even while the awareness building activities were being carried out on television, programs would be put in place to convert the positive attitude to trial in the store. Retail distribution was gained prior to the advertising and special retail displays and trade promotions could be used to gain desired retail "push."

The Fifth M: Money

The size of the communications budget is frequently a matter of great debate within companies. Many companies use simple rules-of-thumb, e.g. setting budgets as some percentage of expected or previous year's sales. Others adopt a competitively-based benchmark, e.g., "spend to have a share-of-voice (SOV: meaning the percentage of the product category spending attributable to the firm) equal to our share-of-market."

While these guidelines are often used as "reality checks," the right way to approach the budget question is through what is called the "objective and task" method, i.e., figure out what you have to do to attain your objectives and cost it out. Of course, one has to make the business assessment that such expenditures will pay out in the end.

The optimal communications budget is typically a function of:

1. *The Size and Heterogeneity of the Target Audience* to be reached: obviously the larger the audience, the greater the cost typically; but we also have to consider its heterogeneity and accessibility via communication vehicles. For example, it would be less expensive to reach all 1700 MBA students at Harvard Business School than it would be to reach the 100 most technology-oriented students at each of the top 17 MBA programs as identified by *Business Week*.

2. *Nature of Message*: some messages, e.g. the existence of M&M Crunchy in a light blue bag, are easy to get across. Others are more complex; e.g., explaining the details of Tweeter's Automatic Price Protection plan in an impactful way. Many industrial products require intensive communication efforts because new technology must be explained and the user convinced that the new product will interface with his current systems. For this reason, personal selling is often more important in business-to-business situations than in consumer.

3. *Receptivity of the Audience*: if the audience is seeking out information on the product category, the required budget is typically less because there is no need to break through the consumer's mechanism for screening out unwanted messages and then attract attention. For high involvement consumer purchases like automobiles, sporting equipment, and computers, consumers will seek out information in the purchase process. This active information search reduces the burden on the communicator. Alternatively, consider a low interest product category with consumers quite satisfied with current offerings in the category. Here there is the burden of attracting attention and getting a message through when the receiver generally regards such information as unimportant.

4. *Amount of Clutter*: the spending levels of the competition can be a factor in the intensity of the effort needed to get a message through. For example, while a new golf club manufacturer would be aided by consumer search for informa-

tion, the high level of spending by Callaway on its Big Bertha line represents a burden to overcome. At times, spending has to reach a certain threshold before it "breaks through."

Spending levels vary greatly across industries and even across firms within the same category. On average, game and toy manufacturers spend 16% of sales on advertising; candy companies 12%; food companies 6%; household furniture 4%; motor vehicles 3% and airlines 1.5%. Within industries, one can find very different strategies as one firm might have a low price/low spending strategy while another has a strategy of relatively high price but supported by an appreciable communications budget to convince prospects of the value of the product.

The Sixth M: Measurement

An important part of communications planning is to build a mechanism for learning about the effects which the efforts had. This is a critical input to decisions on future spending levels, allocation of the budget across media, and specific communication messages.

Objectives being clearly stated is an important first step. For example, if an objective is to "increase awareness of the three-year warranty on all of our products to 50% of population by June 1," research can be done to see if the goal has been met. Note that "awareness" is not something one can observe in the normal course of business activities. It is a cognitive effect, so we have to do research such as a survey to assess this. As we noted above, another goal may be behavioral, e.g., "get 25% of target population to try the product by June 1." Again, this can be assessed via market research. If a sales goal is specified, e.g. "ship 500,000 cases by June 1" we need only look to company records to assess this.

The trade-off in the type of goals to assess progress against is that behavior/sales is typically the ultimate goal of the enterprise. However, many factors in addition to the communications effort impact sales, e.g., the product quality, price, and activities of competitors. Consequently, separating out the communications program effect is often difficult. Thus, earlier stage measurements of cognitive and affective impacts can be useful adjuncts to the assessment of communications effectiveness and learning about optimal communications methods.

Conclusion

Developing the IMC is a critical part of marketing strategy. A product may in fact offer great value to a target population; but it is that segment's perception of the value that is key. The marketer has a variety of communication vehicles available and the options are expanding with technological developments such as the Internet. A systematic approach in first selecting the target and then understanding the purchase process in detail can lead to an efficient and effective IMC.

SUAVE (C)

We are doing one-third of what we can to aggressively promote this brand. Suave has become the old, reliable brand that has taken a back seat to Finesse. This brand is a marketer's dream. It just needs to get the attention it deserves. The upside for Suave is tremendous.

Tom Kuykendall, group brand manager for Suave, had joined the Consumer Products division of Helene Curtis just one month earlier, in January 1984. His views on the fiscal 1985[1] advertising campaign for Suave shampoo were in sharp contrast to those of Ellen Vallera, who had served for seven years as brand manager:

> Suave is not underadvertised. We cannot afford to spend any more money on advertising because Suave is a price brand. With its low margins we do not have much money to play around with. Any increase in advertising will require an increase in price. That would jeopardize our position as the number one shampoo in unit volume, and we could lose our trade support.

The debate had culminated in two media plans. The original plan was to increase the advertising budget 30%, to $7.8 million; $7.1 million would be divided between daytime and prime-time television, with $700,000 spent on Suave's first print campaign. The more recent proposal placed all television advertising in prime time, resulting in a total budget of $10.2 million.

Bob Thomas, vice president of marketing, was considering these two plans. He felt the brand was "at a watershed." Through October 1983, sales of Suave shampoo had been only 2% ahead of the previous year and 2% below plan. Unit sales share had declined from 12.2% in 1982 to 11.5% in 1983, and operating margin

percentages had fallen. Furthermore, it had been learned that Gillette was test marketing White Rain, a new low-priced shampoo, and that Hazel Bishop Industries would soon introduce a line of three low-priced shampoos. Other major competitors were also planning a flood of new products. Procter & Gamble, according to industry sources, was preparing to introduce a relatively low-priced shampoo under the Ivory brand name that summer. The fight for retail shelf space would be fierce.

Helene Curtis Industries, Inc.

Helene Curtis created, manufactured, and marketed hair-care and other personal-care products, as well as adhesives and sealants. The company had four marketing divisions which generated $10.4 million in net earnings on $330 million in sales in fiscal 1984.

Suave was part of the largest division, Consumer Products. Before 1982, the division sold only the Suave product line. The premium-priced Finesse line was launched with a conditioner in 1982, shampoo in 1983, and hair spray in 1984. By fiscal 1984, Finesse accounted for nearly half of division sales. Finesse was expected to surpass Suave in dollar sales during fiscal 1985.

The division's two brands were marketed through food, drug, and mass merchandise outlets[2] in five large personal-care categories: shampoos, hair conditioners/rinses, hair sprays, deodorants/antiperspirants, and hand and body lotions. Suave and Finesse combined to make Helene Curtis the leading marketer in conditioners and second largest in shampoos (behind Procter & Gamble) in the United States. Suave had become the leading shampoo (in unit sales) and the second largest conditioner; Finesse, the third largest selling conditioner and among the top 10 shampoos.

Finesse had been introduced with $20 million in advertising and continued to be one of the most heavily promoted hair-care brands in the industry. As a result, whereas Finesse had a much higher gross margin than Suave, both had the same projected 1984 operating mar-

Professor Mark S. Albion prepared this case as the basis for class discussion rather than to illustrate either effective or ineffective handling of an administrative situation. All nonpublic data have been disguised.

[1]March 1, 1984–February 28, 1985.
[2]Mass merchandise outlets included discount stores, such as Kmart, Wal-Mart, Zayre, and Caldor.

gin percentage. Nevertheless, because of the price differential, Finesse generated nearly twice the dollar profit per case as Suave.

The Shampoo Market

It is not uncommon for ads and promotion to be the biggest expense. A little bit of money for the cleansing agent, coloring and fragrance, a bit for an agreeably shaped bottle and voila! A shampoo. There are few barriers to entry. You can subcontract out the actual production. All you really need is a good marketing idea and a chemist. And lately, lots of ad money.[3]

Sales in the seasonal $1.2 billion industry had been relatively flat in recent years. Unit sales[4] had grown at only a 2% compound rate since 1978. Industry experts predicted that the next five years would be characterized by continued slow growth, since it was felt that household penetration (90%) and female frequency of use (2.83 times per week) had peaked. The market was considered mature, with most of the forecast growth coming from a predicted slow, steady rate of population growth.

The shampoo market was highly fragmented. Only nine brands held a 3% unit share or greater, and no brand controlled as much as 12% (see Exhibit 1). Firms sought untapped consumer segments to sustain growth. Most shampoo marketers targeted the 18-34 year-old age group, traditionally the heaviest shampoo users. But the Census Bureau estimated that there would be 52.4 million women over 40 by 1990, a 15% increase from 1980. Families were also expected to be smaller.

Competitive Environment

The participants carry on like a heap of insects on a tropical forest floor, swarming all over each other, eating or being eaten with gusto and bringing a variety of ingenious strategies to the fray.[5]

With one point of market share worth over $10 million in sales and gross margins often 40% or more, the shampoo industry was a flurry of new-product activity supported by heavy advertising and promotional expenditures. During the 1970s the number of products had increased dramatically as marketers appealed to specialized needs. Shampoos were introduced to fight dandruff and for use on dry, oily, damaged, or normal hair. A variety of scents was offered as well.

It was expected that 1984 would be reminiscent of these earlier years. Five major competitors (Jergens, Johnson & Johnson, La Maur, Lever Brothers, and Revlon) were each prepared to launch new brands with unprecedented marketing support. In January, for example, Lever Brothers had announced to retailers that it would spend $60 million in 1984 to market its new brand, Dimension. These five brands alone, aimed at a relatively affluent audience, were to be supported by $44.5 million in advertising ($18 million for Dimension), with industry advertising expenditures expected to exceed $145 million. Companies like Procter & Gamble (Head & Shoulders, Pert, Prell) had signaled that increased advertising expenditures would be used to defend share.[6] Historically, nine out of ten new shampoos failed.

Between 1978 and 1983, the industry advertising-to-sales ratio declined from 13.2% to 10.1%. But variation among brands was marked: brands such as Vidal Sassoon, Jhirmack, and Prell averaged 25% ratios in 1983, whereas Flex and Suave maintained 5% to 6% ratios. Similarly, the market could be segmented by price, with Flex (13¢ per ounce) and Suave and private labels (9¢ per ounce, slightly above generics)[7] far cheaper than Vidal Sassoon (38¢), Jhirmack (32¢), and Prell (22¢).

Hazel Bishop's shampoo entries were to sell in 15-ounce bottles for 99¢, and Gillette's White Rain at $1.30 for an 18-ounce bottle, placing these shampoo lines in direct competition in the price/value segment with Suave, private labels, and generics. Private labels had grown to a 5.4% dollar share (6.9% unit share), generics a 1.3% share (2.2% unit share) of the shampoo market

---

[3]*Forbes*, December 6, 1982, "Hair Wars," p. 132.

[4]A unit was defined as a bottle of shampoo, regardless of its size in ounces.

[5]*Forbes*, December 6, 1982, "Hair Wars," p. 132.

[6]For brands after their introductory period, the average industry breakdown of marketing expenditures had been 53% for advertising, 14% for consumer promotions (samples, coupons, contests), and 33% for trade promotions (temporary price cuts to wholesalers and retailers). For Suave, the breakdown in fiscal 1984 had been 25% advertising, 7% consumer promotions, 60% trade promotions, and 8% other (primarily, market research).

[7]Private labels were brands owned by the retail merchants or other intermediaries, as distinct from those owned by manufacturers or producers; they were often called "distributor" or "store" brands. Generics were products that had no brand other than identification of their contents; they were often called "no-name" products.

by 1983. As Bob Thomas acknowledged, "The action in our business is taking place in the high and low end of the price spectrum. The middle is being squeezed."

Retail Channels

"Getting on the shelf is relatively easy; staying there is hard!" exclaimed one exasperated executive. Many manufacturers marketed full lines of hair-care products, often using the same brand names for conditioners or hair sprays, to allow costly television advertising to "carry" the sales of all the products under one brand name. In this way, a fast-selling shampoo could help win shelf space for its less prominent companion products.

With the proliferation of shampoo brands, retail support was critical. Approximately 50% of unit sales were through food stores, 30% through drug stores, and 20% through mass merchandise outlets; for Suave the breakdown was 65%/15%/20%. Retail margins were regularly 30%. The escalating fight for shelf space, however, had caused many manufacturers to augment their trade promotion budgets to satisfy retailers.

The complex consumer buying behavior in the shampoo market had led to increased retail trade importance as well. According to Richard Barrie, senior executive vice president at Faberge:[8] "A big percentage of purchase decisions are made in the store. Some companies spend $15 million to create a 'point of difference.' We fight at the store for shelf position and display."

Brand Loyalty

According to industry experts, perhaps the most important element for achieving success in the shampoo market was establishing brand loyalty. The industry was notorious for fickle consumers. As one manager explained: "Brand loyalty? It changes from the time consumers see an ad on television to when they walk up to the shelf in the supermarket or drug store." To retain their market positions and develop loyalty, companies had accelerated new-product development, appealing to specialized consumer needs. Longer shampoo product lines were marketed to keep consumers "in the family" if they chose to switch among types of shampoos (e.g., herbal versus strawberry scents, dandruff versus regular).

Consumers rarely purchased just one brand of shampoo and commonly kept a number of brands on their shelves at the same time. Users typically got bored with their shampoos easily, tried different types and different brands, and, some believed, developed a perceived physical immunity to specific brands that increased the longer they used them.

Market research by NPD[9] confirmed the low levels of loyalty that bedeviled the industry. According to all measures, Suave had the highest loyalty levels. Suave users satisfied 37% of their shampoo requirements with Suave in 1982–1983, down from nearly 50% in 1981. Private-label brands (35%) and Flex (33%), Suave's main competitors according to Helene Curtis executives, were the only other brands over 30%.

Suave

Originally a men's hairdressing in the 1950s, the first Suave shampoo was introduced in 1962. In fiscal 1984, shampoo still comprised most of Suave sales. Advertising of the Suave brand name began in fiscal 1974. All advertising was recorded under shampoos, although most advertisements included conditioners as well. There was no advertising of other Suave products.

Suave products were used in 16 million homes, with the shampoo alone in 13 to 15 million homes. Suave had become a $100 million brand in fiscal 1984 (see Exhibit 2 for income statement). The brand was commonly sold to retailers at a discount; approximately 60% of the marketing budget was for trade promotions. But with all the new-product activity in the shampoo market, and Suave's history of poor performance in years with many product introductions, the brand appeared to be vulnerable in 1984.

Suave had the longest line of shampoos in the industry, with a total of 40 SKUs[10] and an average of 12 in any one grocery store. New-product variations were constantly introduced to maintain the brand's vitality and to

[9]National Purchase Diary Research, Inc. conducted diary panel survey research on nationally representative samples of households. Households were asked to keep a record of their purchases for a specific period of time. This study was based on a sample of 6,500 households, June 1982–May 1983.

[10]An SKU was a stockkeeping unit, defined as a single item of merchandise for which separate sales and stock records were kept. One brand of shampoo of a particular type in a particular bottle size constituted one SKU.

[8]*Forbes,* December 6, 1982, "Hair Wars," p. 133.

allow Suave customers to switch (or fill more of their household purchases) within the Suave line.

Retail penetration was very good in food stores and mass merchandise outlets. In these stores, Suave was often the merchant's low-priced brand. Drug stores, however, particularly chain drug stores, tended to push their own private labels. They either carried very few (or no) Suave SKUs, or priced Suave higher than did other types of outlets.

Consumer Behavior: The Suave Customer

Helene Curtis conducted a number of market research studies to learn more about the shampoo market in general and the Suave consumer franchise in particular. Past success relied heavily on insight into and repeated research of consumers' usage, habits, preferences, and needs. Extensive large-scale interview data were collected on an ongoing basis from "Awareness, Usage, and Attitude" studies.[11] In addition, independent market research organizations, such as NPD, were commissioned to conduct further studies.

The demographic profile of the Suave user (Exhibit 3) was very similar to that of the heavy shampoo user, since Suave customers tended to be heavy shampoo users (Exhibit 4): female heads of household age 18 to 45, large families with young children, middle income, blue collar occupation. Use by many young children tended to skew the average age downward, and income level varied with the number of household incomes. Psychographic profiles (see "Suave (A)" for a detailed analysis) indicated that Suave users tended to be from heavy German/Dutch neighborhoods in rural, town, and downscale suburban areas, situated in the West Central, West North Central, and Mountain regions.

Concerned that approximately 50% of women who used shampoo had never tried Suave, and that 28% of women who had tried Suave were not current users, management authorized a statistical analysis intended to profile Suave users versus "trier rejectors" (no usage in the last six months) and "never users." The results are shown in Exhibit 5. Suave "trier rejectors" were found to be older women with higher household incomes, smaller families, and shorter, dyed hair. Further focus group interviews[12] uncovered that "trier rejectors" felt there was a difference among shampoos and that Suave was inexpensive and not good enough for their hair. Users stated that all shampoos were basically the same and that Suave was inexpensive and a good value (including benefits). Nonusers had few if any perceptions about Suave beyond "inexpensive" and "old fashioned."

Purchasing Patterns. Exhibit 6 provides a summary of purchasing patterns for shampoos bought in grocery stores. Suave and private-label/generic brands are highlighted. The heavy shampoo usage among Suave buyers (as 21% of total category buyers, they accounted for 38% of category ounces sold) was again evident. But the proportion of shampoo buyers purchasing Suave was smaller than that buying Pert (27%, accounting for 33% of ounces sold) or Head & Shoulders (25%, accounting for 32% of ounces sold). Still, the relatively high loyalty of Suave buyers was impressive.

Combination purchasing profiles were constructed through NPD's diary panel data of household purchases to examine what other brands of shampoo Suave customers purchased. The research indicated that Suave shampoo buyers had an above-average preference for Faberge, Alberto VO5, and private labels/generics. In addition, the research showed that Suave was purchased disproportionately as an alternative brand by Alberto VO5, private label/generic, Faberge, Flex, Prell, Clairol, and Pert customers. Only Suave and Faberge customers purchased private-label/generic brands disproportionately as alternative brands.

Marketing Strategy

Helene Curtis intended to keep Suave as a low-priced, heavily promoted brand. Research on the impact of marketing support had indicated that Suave retail sales, unlike those of other brands, correlated more positively with retail support than with advertising.

Management realized, however, that much of the brand's growth in the past five years had been from the introduction of new Suave shampoos. With less growth

---

[11]These studies were based on national probability samples of female heads of households. Approximately 300 telephone interviews were conducted for each study. Topics included: demographics, hair characteristics, usage patterns, brands purchased, brands ever tried, brand and advertising awareness, advertising recall, and attitudes toward brands and advertisements.

[12]In a focus group interview, a group of consumers was assembled for a free-form discussion on a particular subject. Such groups were led by market research professionals whose job was to encourage free discussion.

	Fiscal 1985 Planned Spending (000)	%	Per Case[a]	Change per Case from Fiscal 1984
Advertising	$7,800	28%	$1.03	+.23
Consumer promotions	1,521	5	.20	−.03
Trade promotions	17,008	60	2.24	+.35
Other marketing	2,018	7	.27	+.04
Total	$28,347	100%	$3.74	+.59

[a]Twelve units in a case; based on forecast volume.

of this type expected, the marketing strategy might have to include changes in the marketing mix to stimulate growth. These changes were most likely to occur, according to management, in direct consumer marketing: advertising and consumer promotions.

For fiscal 1985, as shown above, the marketing support program for Suave was to be increased 18%, to $28.3 million, and the historical Suave 60/40 split between trade and consumer spending maintained:

The rationale behind this initial budget was that the fiscal 1985 marketing support program would rely on price through trade promotions to defend its base volume. Advertising and consumer promotions would enhance the program by generating awareness and incremental volume. Nevertheless, much disagreement remained about the level and composition of advertising expenditures.

Advertising History

Suave had not been a heavily advertised shampoo. Budgets were set on a per-case basis, e.g., $1.00 per forecast case sold. A 5% to 7% advertising-to-sales ratio was typical.

Until July 1981, a price/value-oriented message had been used: "Suave does what theirs does for half the price." However, a new campaign was instituted that summer to stress more of a quality image: "Suave makes you look as if you spent a fortune on your hair." (See Exhibit 7 for a recent advertisement, aired since July 1983.) In addition, prime-time television advertising was used for the first time. Previously, daytime television had been the main media vehicle. An approximate 60/40 division between prime and daytime was scheduled.

With the onset of prime-time television advertising, management began a series of awareness and usage studies. To date, nine "waves" of results had been recorded, for both Suave and other selected brands of shampoos. Exhibit 8 contains the results for Suave, with June 1981 as the base period. The impact of prime time on awareness after Wave II had been called into question.

The Advertising Debate

During the fall of 1983, outside consultants to Helene Curtis delivered a report discussing their fiscal 1985 advertising budget recommendations. Essentially, they agreed with Tom Kuykendall: increase advertising expenditures aggressively and concentrate television dollars in prime time. Their $10.2 million alternative media plan and Ellen Vallera's $7.8 million plan are shown in Exhibit 9. To evaluate different alternatives, data on advertising rates and delivered audiences had been collected for television and selected magazines (Exhibit 10 and 11).

The consultants believed Suave had reached a plateau and there was an opportunity to increase all of the awareness and usage measures. They noted that Suave ranked below several other major brands as follows (June/July 1983 tracking results; Wave VII):

• Total Brand Awareness (88%): Head & Shoulders (96%), Prell (96%), Johnson's Baby (94%), Clairol (90%).

• Unaided Brand Awareness (19%): Prell (52%), Head & Shoulders (37%), Johnson's Baby (28%), Flex (24%).

- Advertising Awareness (29%): Suave ranked below every other brand studied (11 brands); range from Flex (31%) to Jhirmack (60%).
- Ever Used (45%): Prell (59%), Head & Shoulders (53%), Flex (47%).

The consultants argued that daytime advertising would only maintain awareness, whereas prime time would build it. Through prime time, they argued, more current and potential consumers could be reached, particularly working women. Higher expenditure levels, therefore, would be necessary to maintain prime-time *continuity* throughout the year—critical to increasing brand/advertising awareness levels. Data on the demographic categories of viewers and readers were examined to estimate the size and composition of the audiences of the different media vehicles (Exhibit 12).

Vallera admitted that prime time was an effective medium, but felt that the increase in expenditures required for continuity throughout fiscal 1985 could not be justified. In 1982 she had commissioned a one-year BehaviorScan test of higher advertising expenditures in two cities: $8.1 million versus $5.5 million national levels, with split-cable used within each market to regulate the level of advertising viewed by panelists. The results, she maintained, were inconclusive. Whereas a 15% increase in ounce sales of Suave shampoo had resulted, the impact of increased expenditures had lessened over time. She also believed that the number of new customers delivered did not justify additional expenditures. And at a $7.8 million budget level, only daytime television could provide continuity throughout the year.

Vallera argued further that daytime delivered more gross rating points[13] (see Exhibit 13) and had a much lower cost per thousand viewers. Print could be used in the second half of fiscal 1985, when there was no prime time scheduled (Exhibit 9), to supplement daytime and reach working women. Prime time would be used in the first half of fiscal 1985 not only to reach working women, but also to provide tactical support during key promotional periods.

---

[13]Gross rating points (GRPs) were calculated by multiplying reach by frequency, i.e., the total number of people exposed to an advertisement times the average number of exposures per person. GRPs were used as a standard measure of the impact of advertising.

Exhibit 1 Share Trends of Selected Brands of Shampoo

	1980	1981	1982	1983
– *Suave*[a]				
– Unit share[b]	10.3%	11.4%	12.2%	11.5%
– Market share[b]	5.8	6.0	9.4	9.0
– Share of spending[b]	3.0	3.5	5.5	5.1
– *Agree*				
– Unit share	4.8	3.8	3.2	2.6
– Market share	4.3	3.4	2.7	2.2
– Share of spending	4.1	5.3	3.5	4.7
– *Flex*				
– Unit share	7.3	7.2	6.7	6.5
– Market share	7.1	6.8	6.6	6.4
– Share of spending	4.2	3.3	2.6	3.0
– *Head & Shoulders*				
– Unit share	12.0	11.2	10.9	10.4
– Market share	11.7	11.6	9.5	9.1
– Share of spending	17.5	18.3	17.1	14.3
– *Jhirmack*				
– Unit share	1.4	3.0	3.7	4.1
– Market share	NA	NA	NA	3.4
– Share of spending	2.4	4.8	4.2	8.0
– *Pert*				
– Unit share	4.7	6.6	5.3	4.7
– Market share	3.4	5.6	4.5	3.6
– Share of spending	18.3	14.6	9.5	8.0
– *Prell*				
– Unit share	8.6	7.3	7.1	6.8
– Market share	7.3	5.7	5.8	5.6
– Share of spending	11.8	10.3	10.3	13.6
– *Silkience*				
– Unit share	2.8	4.0	3.5	2.6
– Market share	2.1	4.3	3.3	2.6
– Share of spending	7.7	9.2	5.7	4.4
– *Vidal Sassoon*				
– Unit share	3.0	3.5	3.7	3.4
– Market share	3.3	4.6	4.2	4.4
– Share of spending	8.4	8.8	11.1	11.5
– *Total Category (millions)*				
– Unit sales volume	489	504	508	530
– Dollar sales	912	1,016	1,082	1,160
– Ad spending	115	117	100	118

Source: Company records.
[a]Reflects advertising for full line of Suave products; sales data for shampoo only.
[b]Unit (bottles) share, market (retail dollar) share, share of (industry advertising) spending; brand advertising spending included only media costs, not production costs.

Exhibit 2 Suave Income Statements[a] (in thousands)

	FY 1982 (ended 2/28/82)	% Net Sales[b]	FY 1983 (ended 2/28/83)	% Net Sales[b]	FY 1984 (ended 2/29/84)	% Net Sales[b]
Net sales	$73,335	100.0%	$89,755	100.0%	$99,005	100.0%
Variable costs	42,127	57.4	50,689	56.5	56,281	56.8
Gross margin	$31,208	42.6	$39,066	43.5	$42,724	43.2
Marketing expenditures						
– Advertising	4,094	5.6	5,457	6.1	6,054	6.1
– Prime time	2,279	3.1	3,124	3.5	3,539	3.6
– Daytime	1,815	2.5	2,333	2.6	2,515	2.5
– Print	0	–	0	–	0	–
– Consumer promotion	956	1.3	1,175	1.3	1,862	1.9
– Trade promotion	9,830	13.4	12,258	13.7	14,379	14.5
– Other marketing	1,503	2.0	1,540	1.7	1,670	1.7
Total marketing	$16,383	23.3%	$20,430	22.8%	$23,965	24.2%
Operating margin	14,825	20.2	18,636	20.8	18,759	18.9

Source: Company records.
[a]Reflects full line of Suave products.
[b]Numbers may not add precisely to totals because of rounding.

Exhibit 3 Suave Demographic Profile: 1981

Demographics	Total U.S. (000)	Suave Buyers (000)	Composition[a] (%)	Coverage[b] (%)	Buyer Index[c]
Total women	84,137	9,309	100.0	11.0	100
Female homemakers	77,178	8,321	89.4	10.8	98
Employed mothers	16,985	2,635	28.3	15.5	141
18–24	14,653	2,463	26.5	16.8	152
25–34	18,860	2,611	28.0	13.8	125
35–44	13,270	1,504	16.2	11.3	103
45–54	11,647	1,057	11.4	9.1	82
55–64	11,498	824	8.9	7.2	65
65 or older	14,389	850	9.1	5.9	54
18–34	33,513	5,075	54.5	15.1	137
18–49	52,352	7,052	75.8	13.5	122
25–54	43,776	5,172	55.6	11.8	107
35–49	18,839	1,977	21.2	10.5	95
Graduated college	10,781	980	10.5	9.1	82
Attended college	13,592	1,656	17.8	12.2	110
Graduated high school	35,091	4,163	44.7	11.9	107
Did not graduate high school	24,852	2,511	27.0	10.1	92
Employed	41,299	5,167	55.5	12.5	113
Employed full time	32,548	3,888	41.8	11.9	108
Employed part time	8,751	1,279	13.7	14.6	132
Not employed	43,018	4,142	44.5	9.6	87
Professional/manager	11,131	1,130	12.1	10.2	92
Clerical/sales	16,972	2,217	23.8	13.1	118
Craftsmen/foremen	823	102	1.1	12.4	112
Other employed	12,373	1,719	18.5	13.9	126
Single	14,314	1,503	16.1	10.5	95
Married	50,503	6,036	64.8	12.0	108
Divorced/separated/widowed	19,500	1,770	19.0	9.1	82
Parents	32,209	4,938	53.0	15.3	139
White	72,858	8,563	92.0	11.8	106
Black	9,685	623	6.7	6.4	58
Other	1,774	123	1.3	6.9	63
Household income $35,000 or more	8,095	986	10.6	12.2	110
$25,000 or more	19,296	2,271	24.4	11.8	107
$20,000–$24,999	27,398	2,945	31.6	10.7	97
$15,000–$19,999	10,637	1,193	12.8	11.2	102
$10,000–$14,999	10,197	1,284	13.8	12.6	114
$ 5,000–$ 9,999	17,269	1,836	19.7	10.6	96
Under $5,000	18,816	2,051	22.0	10.9	99
Household of 1 or 2 people	37,622	3,198	34.0	8.5	77
3 or 4 people	32,293	3,769	40.5	11.7	106
5 or more people	14,402	2,343	25.2	16.3	147
No child in household	47,610	3,672	39.4	7.7	70
Child(ren) under 2 years	6,638	1,121	12.0	16.9	153
2–5 years	12,590	1,958	21.0	15.6	141
6–11 years	16,251	2,518	27.0	15.5	140
12–17 years	18,905	2,666	28.6	14.1	128
Residence owned	60,513	6,527	70.1	10.8	98
Value: $40,000 or more	27,980	2,757	29.6	9.9	89
Value: Under $40,000	32,533	3,770	40.5	11.6	105

Source: Company records; based on research conducted by Simmons Market Research Bureau, 1981.
[a] 100.0 = 9,309; 89.4 = 8,321/9,309. To be read, "89.4% of Suave female buyers were homemakers."
[b] 11.0 = 9,309/84,137. To be read, "11.0% of all women bought Suave."
[c] 152 = 16.8/11.0 To be read, "Women 18–24 were 52% more likely to buy Suave."

Exhibit 4 Selected Brand Shares of Buyer Categories: 1979

	Total Buyers		Light Buyers [<64 oz.]		Medium Buyers [64–144 oz.]		Heavy Buyers [>144 oz.]	
	% Buyers	% Volume	% Buyers	% Volume	% Buyers	% Volume	% Buyers	% Volume
Total for category	100.0%	100.0%	66.6%	29.8%	24.5%	37.6%	8.9%	32.6%
Suave	23.1[a]	11.9[a]	10.0[b]	6.7[b]	39.3	10.7	76.9	18.2
Agree	16.8	5.0	12.3	5.9	22.6	4.6	34.4	4.7
Breck	9.7	3.3	7.0	3.9	12.6	3.1	21.3	3.0
Clairol Herbal Essence	6.3	2.4	4.6	2.4	8.5	2.0	12.7	2.7
Flex	15.6	8.6	9.8	7.0	24.0	8.5	35.2	10.1
Head & Shoulders	25.6	7.8	22.5	11.2	32.7	8.5	28.9	3.8
Johnson's Baby	11.6	3.9	8.6	4.1	17.6	4.7	16.7	2.7
Prell	17.8	5.0	15.6	6.3	21.3	5.0	26.3	3.9
Selsun Blue	5.5	1.0	4.7	1.4	7.3	1.0	6.2	0.5
Vidal Sassoon	4.7	1.2	2.9	1.3	7.3	1.3	10.7	1.1
Private label	23.0	11.7	14.1	9.1	35.1	11.1	56.9	14.8
Other	-	38.2	-	40.7	-	39.5	-	34.5

Source: Company records; based on research conducted by Golatny & Blattberg, Inc., using National Purchase Diary Research Inc. 1979 results.
[a]To be read, "23.1% of all buyers purchased Suave. Suave accounted for 11.9% of all volume."
[b]To be read, "10.0% of all light buyers (purchased less than 64 ounces of shampoo in a year) purchased Suave. Suave accounted for 6.7% of all volume purchased by light buyers."

Exhibit 5 Summary Overview of Different Suave User Profiles[a]

	Current Suave Users[b]	Suave "Trier Rejectors"[b]	Suave "Never Users"[b]
– *Last brand used*	Suave Flex Johnson's Baby	Silkience	No specific brand(s)
– *Total brand usage (ever)*	Head & Shoulders Pert Prell	Silkience Sassoon	No specific brand(s)

– *Hair characteristics:*
  – *Hair length*
  – *Hair type*
  – *Hair texture*
  – *Colored hair*
	Longer
	Normal
	Normal
	No
		Shorter
		All types
		All textures
		Yes
			Shorter
			Normal/dry
			Fine
			Yes

– *Demographics:*
  – *Age*
  – *Household size*
  – *Children*
  – *Income*
	Younger
	4+
	Yes
	Average
		Older
		2
		No
		Higher
			Older
			2–3
			No
			Average

Source: Awareness, Usage, and Attitude Study, September 1982 (Wave V); company records.

[a]Results determined by assessing directional skews in data across user groups through multivariate, discriminant analysis.

[b]Base of 296 women. "Suave users" (197) were women who had used Suave in last six months. "Trier rejectors" (78) were women who had used Suave at least once more than six months ago, but no longer used it. "Never users" (103) were women who were aware of Suave, but had never used it.

Exhibit 6 1981 Purchasing Patterns: BehaviorScan Markets[a]

	Total Shampoo	Suave		Private Label/Generic	Hi/Lo Range (26 brands)
Ounce share	100%	18.3%	(1)[b]	17.0%	0.3–18.3%
Dollar share	100%	9.3%	(3)	7.4%	0.3–16.0%
Share index (dollar share/ounce share)	100%	51	(25)	44	44–367
Unit share	100%	13.1%	(2)	9.9%	0.1–14.4%
% of shampoo buyers purchasing	100%	21.2%	(3)	21.1%	0.9–26.6%
Ounces/buyer	46.4[c]	40.1[c]	(1)	37.3	5.4–40.1
Ounces/purchase occasion	12.5	17.4	(3)	19.6	3.9–19.6
Units/purchase occasion	1.1	1.1	(2)	1.0	1.0–1.2
Purchase occasions/buyer	3.7	2.3	(1)	1.9	1.1–2.3
Average days between purchases	76	86	(15)	92	45–104
% of total shampoo ounces accounted for by brand buyers	100%	37.8%	(1)	34.3%	1.9–37.8%

Source: Company records; based on research conducted over 52 weeks by Information Resources, Inc., in Pittsfield, Massachusetts and Marion, Indiana grocery stores; stores were equipped with UPC scanners to track sales, and purchase record of 2,956 households in each market were analyzed.

[a]Data were for grocery stores only, which represented 54% of the panel household sales in these two markets. Suave unit and dollar shares reported here are higher than those in Exhibit 1 because these data are for grocery stores only, where Suave is strongest.

[b]Ranking of Suave among 26 brands analyzed.

[c]To be read, "Those who purchased shampoo averaged 46.4 ounces of shampoo bought in grocery stores during the year; those who purchased Suave averaged 40.1 ounces of Suave bought in grocery stores during the year."

Exhibit 7 "ACTRESS"

ACTRESS: I'll never forget my first speaking part. There were only two words to remember.

Money was pretty tight back then.

So I started using Suave.

After I got (SHE GIVES SHEEPISH LAUGH) "discovered"

I tried those expensive shampoos and conditioners.

And I made a little discovery of my own.

They weren't any better than Suave.

They just cost more.

These days, it's not hard to spend a fortune on your hair.

I don't. Suave just makes me look like I do.

(SFX: APPLAUSE)

ANNCR: (VO) Suave makes you look as if you spent a fortune on your hair.

Exhibit 8 Suave Tracking Study Waves I–IX: Key Measures for Suave

	Waves[a]								
	I	II	III	IV	V	VI	VII	VIII	IX
	%	%	%	%	%	%	%	%	%
– Brand awareness									
– Unaided[b]	11	20	25	25	23	17	19	24	18
– Total[c]	77	83	82	87	85	91	88	93	89
– Aided Advertising									
– Awareness[d]	26	34	39	34	42	30	29	33	29
– Ever used	38	44	51	51	50	41	45	50	51
– Used in past six months	15	16	23	23	23	16	16	20	26
– Used in past four weeks	9	11	12	14	12	9	9	NA	NA
– Ever purchased	40	44	50	48	48	52	52	58	52
– Purchased in past six months	18	22	26	26	24	24	19	24	23
– Purchased in past four weeks	10	10	12	18	14	13	9	NA	NA
– Base (all women)	(300)	(299)	(308)	(307)	(296)	(300)	(270)	(270)	(270)
	Change in suppliers and methodology ⟶								
– Date of tracking	6/81	9/81	1/82	6/82	9/82	4/83	6/83	9/83	12/83

Source: Awareness, Usage, and Attitude Studies; company records.

[a]New advertising campaigns were started in 7/81, 8/82, 8/83. Prime-time advertising was used 7/81, 10/81, 5/82, 8/82, 10/82, 5/83, 8/83, 11/83.

[b]The percentage of respondents who mentioned Suave when asked, "What shampoo have you heard of?"

[c]The percentage of respondents with unaided brand awareness plus those with aided brand awareness who replied positively when asked, "Have you heard of Suave shampoo?"

[d]The percentage of respondents who replied positively when asked, "Have you seen an advertisement for Suave shampoo lately?"

Exhibit 9 Alternative Media Plans: Fiscal 1985

FY 1985	1984 MARCH 27 5 12 19 26	APRIL 2 9 16 23 30	MAY 7 14 21 28	JUNE 4 11 18 25	JULY 2 9 16 23 30	AUG 6 13 20 27	SEPT 3 10 17 24	OCT 1 8 15 22 29	NOV 5 12 19 26	DEC 3 10 17 24 31	1985 JAN 7 14 21 28	FEB 4 11 18	Advertising ($)
$7.8 Million Plan													
PRIME NETWORK													
40 W18-49 GRPs/10 Weeks[a]		XXXX	XXX		XXXXXXX	XXX							3,391.5
DAY NETWORK													
45 W18-49 GRPs/21 Weeks	X X	X X		XXXXXXX		X	X X	X X X	X X	X X	X X	X	3,702.9
30 W18-49 GRPs/5 Weeks	X X	X X	XXX	XXXXXXX	XXXXX	X	X X	X X X	X X	X X	X X	X	
PRINT: 10 INSERTIONS							←——3——→	←————→	←—2—→	←—3—X—2—→	←—3—X—2—→705.6		705.6
TOTAL													7,800.0
$10.2 Million Plan													
PRIME NETWORK													
40 W18-49 GRPs/28 Weeks	XXXXXXXX	XXXX XXXX	XXXX	XXXX	XXX	XXXXX	XXXXXXXX	XXXXXXXX		XXXXXXX	XX	XXXXXX	9,520.0
PRINT: 10 INSERTIONS							←——3——→	←————→	←—2—→	←—3—X—2—→705.6			705.6
TOTAL													10,225.6

Source: Company records.

[a] To be read, "Will deliver 40 Gross Rating Points weekly for 10 weeks (400 GRPs) on women 18–49 years old."

Exhibit 10 Television: Costs and Audience Delivery[a]

Prime Time—Network					
	Estimated Audience Delivery (in millions)				
Cost of Average 30-Second Commercial	**Homes**	**Total Female**	**Women 25–54**	**Total Male**	**Men 25–54**
$77,975	12.9	13.3	4.9	12.0	4.5
Daytime—Network					
	Estimated Audience Delivery (in millions)				
Cost of Average 30-Second Commercial	**Homes**	**Total Female**	**Women 25–54**	**Total Male**	
$13,350	5.0	5.1	2.1	4.6	

Source: Company records, 1983/1984
[a]All numbers were averaged and do not reflect seasonal differences.

Exhibit 11 Selected Magazines: Costs and Audience Delivery

Publication	Circulation Rate Base (000s)	4-Color Page Cost	Black and White Page Cost	Average Audience (in thousands)			
				Men 18+	Men 18–49	Women 18+	Women 18–49
General Orientation							
– Fortune	690	$36,020	$23,700	1,860	1,376	897	660
– National Enquirer	5,075	32,780	26,000	6,987	5,434	11,567	7,728
– The New Yorker	480	18,700	11,750	1,311	829	1,238	811
– People	2,600	49,200	38,175	7,871	6,479	13,953	10,931
– Time	4,600	101,825	65,275	12,322	9,181	9,146	6,500
– TV Guide	17,000	85,000	72,000	16,737	12,859	21,100	15,227
Male Orientation							
– Playboy	4,400	53,765	38,395	8,422	7,357	–	–
– Popular Science	1,800	31,280	22,055	3,801	2,685	–	–
– Sports Illustrated	2,425	66,175	42,415	10,786	8,929	–	–
Female Orientation							
– Cosmopolitan	2,500	36,575	27,180	–	–	8,253	7,068
– Family Circle	7,250	68,150	57,275	–	–	16,613	10,443
– Glamour	1,900	31,200	22,100	–	–	5,784	5,145
– McCall's	6,200	64,620	52,560	–	–	14,536	9,124
– Redbook	3,800	46,940	35,495	–	–	7,743	5,631
– Working Mother	500	11,750	8,850	–	–	993	793

Source: Company records, 1983/1984.

Exhibit 12 The Viewership of Television and the Readership of Magazines by Female Demographic Category (in thousands)

Total Base	Demographic Category	Viewership/ Readership[a]	Television Prime Time	Television Daytime	Magazines
33,513	Women 18–34	Heavy Medium Light	11,622 7,576 14,316	11,931 6,301 15,282	16,676 5,984 10,854
52,424	Women 18–49	Heavy Medium Light	19,112 10,926 22,314	16,854 9,277 26,220	24,322 9,128 18,901
20,049	Working Women 18–34	Heavy Medium Light	6,390 4,110 9,549	4,892 3,540 11,618	11,126 3,247 5,680
31,959	Working Women 18–49	Heavy Medium Light	10,630 6,079 15,251	7,048 5,391 19,519	16,505 5,034 10,420
13,465	Nonworking Women 18–34	Heavy Medium Light	5,232 3,466 4,767	7,039 2,761 3,664	5,553 2,737 5,174
20,465	Nonworking Women 18–49	Heavy Medium Light	8,484 4,847 7,063	9,806 3,886 6,701	7,818 4,094 8,481
5,551	Women 18–34 Suave Users	Heavy Medium Light	2,126 924 2,501	1,869 1,048 2,634	2,732 900 1,919
7,746	Women 18–49 Suave Users	Heavy Medium Light	3,113 1,414 3,219	2,455 1,481 3,810	3,661 1,314 2,771
19,346	Women 18–34 Heavy Shampoo Users	Heavy Medium Light	6,706 3,877 8,763	6,516 3,821 9,009	10,056 3,365 5,925
27,147	Women 18–49 Heavy Shampoo Users	Heavy Medium Light	9,820 5,447 11,880	8,549 5,163 13,453	13,304 4,545 9,299

Source: Company records, 1983/1984.

[a]The data provided estimates of how many women were considered to be heavy, medium, or light viewers of television and readers of magazines. To be read, "11,622,000 18–34 year-old women were heavy viewers of prime-time television."

Exhibit 13 Media Mix Analysis: GRPs, Reach, and Frequency[a]

Prime Time	Daytime	GRPs[b]	Reach W18–34 3+[c]	Reach W18–34 6+	Reach W18–49 3+	Reach W18–49 6+
100%	0%	700	74.2%	50.6%	79.1%	53.2%
50	50	800	76.6	50.6	78.5	51.6
0	100	1,420	53.6	43.2	53.6	43.2

Source: Company records, 1983/1984.

[a]These numbers were calculated based on an assumed fixed advertising budget.

[b]Gross rating points (GRPs) were calculated by multiplying reach by frequency, i.e., the total number of people exposed to an advertisement times the average number of exposures per person. GRPs were used as a standard measure of the impact of advertising. Often markets used ERPs (effective rating points) to measure the "real" effectiveness/impact. ERPs were calculated by multiplying GRPs by an index which was based on day-after advertising recall scores. Company records used 1.00 (prime time), 0.71 (daytime), and 0.50 (magazines) as that index.

[c]To be read as the percentage of women 18–34 who would see the commercial three or more times, e.g., a reach of 74.2% if all prime time was used.

COLGATE-PALMOLIVE COMPANY: THE PRECISION TOOTHBRUSH

In August 1992, Colgate-Palmolive (CP) was poised to launch a new toothbrush in the United States, tentatively named Colgate Precision. CP's Oral Care Division had been developing this technologically superior toothbrush for over three years but now faced a highly competitive market with substantial new product activity.

Susan Steinberg, Precision product manager, had managed the entire new product development process and now had to recommend positioning, branding, and communication strategies to division general manager Nigel Burton.

Company Background

With 1991 sales of $6.06 billion and a gross profit of $2.76 billion, CP was a global leader in household and personal care products. Total worldwide research and development expenditures for 1991 were $114 million, and media advertising expenditures totaled $428 million.

CP's five-year plan for 1991 to 1995 emphasized new product launches and entry into new geographic markets, along with improved efficiencies in manufacturing and distribution and a continuing focus on core consumer products. In 1991, $243 million was spent to upgrade 25 of CP's 91 manufacturing plants; 275 new products were introduced worldwide; several strategic acquisitions (e.g., of the Mennen men's toiletries company) were completed; and manufacturing began in China and Eastern Europe. Reuben Mark, CP's C.E.O. since 1984, had been widely praised for his leadership in

Research Associate Nathalie Laidler prepared this case under the supervision of Professor John Quelch as the basis for class discussion rather than to illustrate the effective or ineffective handling of an administrative situation. Proprietary data has been disguised.

transforming a "sleepy and inefficient" company into a lean and profitable one. Since 1985, gross margins had climbed from 39% to 45% while annual volume growth since 1986 had averaged 5%. Although international sales remained CP's strong suit, accounting for 64% of sales and 67% of profits in 1991, the company faced tough competition in international markets from Procter & Gamble, Unilever, Nestle's L'Oreal Division, Henkel of Germany, and Kao of Japan.

Colgate-Palmolive's Oral Care Business

In 1991, CP held 43% of the world toothpaste market and 16% of the world toothbrush market. Other oral care products included dental floss and mouth rinses. A team of 170 CP researchers worked on new technologies for oral care products, and in 1991, new products launched in the U.S. market included Colgate Baking Soda toothpaste and the Colgate Angle and Wild Ones toothbrushes.

In 1991, worldwide sales of CP's oral care products increased 12% to $1.3 billion, accounting for 22% of CP's total sales. CP's U.S. toothbrush sales in 1991 reached $77 million, with operating profits of $9.8 million. Toothbrushes represented 19% of CP's U.S. Oral Care Division sales and profits, and CP held the number one position in the U.S. retail toothbrush market with a 23.3% volume share.

Exhibit 1 presents operating statements for CP's U.S. toothbrush business since 1989. CP offered two lines of toothbrushes in 1991—the Colgate Classic and the Colgate Plus. Colgate Classic was positioned in the "value" segment and was CP's original entry in the toothbrush market, while Colgate Plus was positioned as a higher-quality product in the "professional" segment.

The U.S. Toothbrush Market

As early as 3000 B.C., ancient Egyptians used toothbrushes fashioned from twigs. In the twentieth century, a major design advance occurred in 1938 with the launch of Dr. West's Miracle Tuft Toothbrush, the first nylon-bristle brush. In the late 1940s, Oral-B began selling a soft-bristle brush which was better for the gums, and in 1961 Broxodent launched the first electric toothbrush.[1] Until the late 1970s, toothbrushes were widely viewed by consumers as a commodity and were purchased primarily on price. More recently, new product launches had increased and performance benefits had become increasingly important purchase criteria. (Exhibit 2 summarizes new product introductions in the category since 1980.)

In 1991, the U.S. Oral Care market was $2.9 billion in retail sales and had grown at an annual rate of 6.1% since 1986. Toothpaste accounted for 46% of this market, mouth rinses 24%, toothbrushes 15.5% ($453 million in retail sales), with dental floss and other products making up the remainder. Dollar sales of toothbrushes had grown at an average rate of 9.3% per annum since 1987, but, in 1992 they increased by 21% in value and 18% in volume, due to the introduction of 47 new products and line extensions during 1991–1992. In the same period, media support increased by 49% and consumer coupon circulation by 48%. Consumers took more interest in the category and increased their purchase frequency. The trade, for whom toothbrushes represented a profitable, high-margin business, responded by increasing in-store promotional support and advertising features. Dollar growth exceeded volume growth due to the emergence of a "super-premium" sub-category of toothbrushes partly offset by downward pressure on average retail prices in mass-merchandiser channels and because of growth in the sales of private label toothbrushes. Unit sales growth in 1993, however, was projected to be slower due to a buildup in household inventories of toothbrushes in 1992 as a result of increased sampling of free brushes through dentists and an abnormally high number of "two-for-one" consumer promotions.

Product Segments

In the 1980s, industry executives divided the toothbrush category into two segments: value and professional. Many consumers traded up to professional, higher-priced toothbrushes with a resulting erosion of the value segment despite growth in private-label sales. The late 1980s saw the emergence of super-premium brushes (priced above $2.00). By 1992, super-premium brushes,

with retail prices between $2.29 and $2.89, accounted for 35% of unit volume and 46% of dollar sales. Professional brushes, priced between $1.59 and $2.09, accounted for a corresponding 41% and 42%, and value brushes, priced on average at $1.29, accounted for 24% and 12%.

In 1992, three players dominated the U.S. toothbrush market overall: Colgate-Palmolive and Johnson & Johnson, whose brushes were positioned in the professional segment; and Oral-B, whose brushes were positioned in the super-premium segment. New entrants in the early 1990s included Procter & Gamble and Smithkline Beecham; both had positioned their new product launches in the super-premium segment. Table A profiles the principal new products offered in the super-premium toothbrush segment in 1992.

Toothbrushes differed by bristle type (firm, medium, soft, and extra soft) and by head size (full/adult, compact, and child/youth). Firm-bristle brushes accounted for 8% of toothbrushes sold but were declining at 13% a year. Medium-bristle brushes accounted for 39% and were declining at 4% a year. Soft-bristle brushes held a 48% market share and were growing at 7% per year. Extra-soft-bristle brushes held only a 5% share but were growing even more rapidly. Sixty-nine percent of toothbrushes were sold with adult, full-sized heads, 17% had compact heads, and 13% had child/youth-sized heads.

In the late 1980s, many new toothbrushes were introduced on the basis of aesthetic rather than functional features. The children's segment in particular had seen a variety of new products. For example, in 1988 and 1989 new toothbrushes targeting children featured sparkling handles, Bugs Bunny and other characters, and glow-in-the-dark handles. By 1991, however, new product introductions were again focused on technical performance improvements, such as greater plaque removal and ease of use.

Consumer Behavior

CP's consumer research indicated that consumers of the baby boom generation (adults born in the 1940s, 1950s and early 1960s) were becoming more concerned about the health of their gums as opposed to cavity prevention and were willing to pay a premium for new products addressing this issue. CP estimated that 82% of toothbrush purchases were unplanned, and research showed that consumers were relatively unfamiliar with toothbrush prices. Although consumers were willing to experiment with new toothbrushes, they replaced their brushes on average only once every 7.5 months in 1991

---

[1]As of 1991, electric toothbrushes were used by only 6% of U.S. households.

Table A Major New Products in the Super-Premium Toothbrush Segment

Product/ Manufacturer	Feature	Benefit	Reason	Tag-line	Launch date	# SKUs
Oral-B Indicator ORAL-B (GILLETTE)	Indicator Bristles	Tells you when to change toothbrush	Blue band fades halfway. Dental heritage	The brand more dentists use	7/91	4 adult
Reach Advanced Design JOHNSON & JOHNSON	Angled neck; raised rubber ridges on handle	Cleans in even the hardest-to-reach places	Slimmed down, tapered head	Feel the difference	8/91	3 adult
Crest Complete PROCTER & GAMBLE	Rippled bristle design. Handle with rubber grip	Reaches between teeth like a dental tool	Rippled end-rounded bristles	Only Crest could make a brush this complete	8/91 (test) 9/92 (national)	10 adult
Aquafresh Flex SMITHKLINE BEECHAM	Pressure sensitive, flexible neck linking brush and handle	Prevents gum irritation	Flexes as you brush	For gentle dental care	8/91 (Flex) 9/92 (line extension)	6 adult 1 child

(versus 8.6 months in 1990), while dental professionals recommended replacement every three months. Due to the prevalence of "two-for-one" offers, purchase frequency lagged replacement frequency, with consumers purchasing toothbrushes once every 11.6 months in 1991 (compared to 12.4 months in 1990 and an expected 9.7 months for 1992).[2] Unlike toothpaste, toothbrushes were not typically shared by members of the same household.

Most consumers agreed that toothbrushes were as important as toothpaste to effective oral hygiene and that the primary role of a toothbrush was to remove food particles; plaque removal and gum stimulation were considered secondary. Proper brushing was seen as key to the prevention of most dental problems. According to CP research, 45% of consumers brushed before breakfast, 57% after breakfast, 28% after lunch, 24% after dinner and 71% before bed. Forty-eight percent of consumers claimed to change their brushes at least every three months; the trigger to purchase a new brush for 70% of them was when their toothbrush-bristles became visibly worn. Eleven percent decided to switch to a new brush after seeing their dentists, and only 3% admitted

to purchasing on impulse.[3] Sixty-five percent of consumers had more than one toothbrush, 24% kept a toothbrush at work, and 54% had a special toothbrush for traveling.

Brand choice was based on features, comfort and professional recommendations. Exhibit 3 summarizes the main reasons why consumers used specific brands. Consumers chose a brush to fit their individual needs: size and shape of the mouth, sensitivity of gums, and personal brushing style. The handle, bristles, and head shape were perceived to be the most important physical features of a toothbrush.

Consumers differed in the intensity of their involvement in oral hygiene. Table B summarizes the buying behavior of the three groups. Therapeutic brushers aimed to avoid oral care problems, while cosmetic brushers emphasized preventing bad breath and/or ensuring white teeth. Uninvolved consumers were not motivated by oral care benefits and adjusted their behavior only when confronted by oral hygiene problems.

---

[2]In 1992, consumers purchased toothbrushes more frequently than in 1991.

[3]Dentists played a significant role, both as a source of information on proper brushing techniques and as a distributor of toothbrushes. At any time, one in four consumers was using a toothbrush given to them by a dentist.

Table B Consumer Segmentation of Toothbrush Users

Involved Oral Health Consumers - Therapeutic Brushers (46% of adults)	Involved Oral Health Consumers - Cosmetic Brushers (21% of adults)	Uninvolved Oral Health Consumers (33% of adults)
Differentiate among products. Search out functionally effective products	Search for products that effectively deliver cosmetic benefits	View products as the same. Lack of interest in product category
Buy and use products for themselves	Buy and use products for themselves	Buy and use products for all family members
85% brush at least twice a day, 62% use a professional brush and 54% floss regularly	85% brush twice a day, 81% use mouthwash, 54% use breath fresheners, 69% floss, 54% use a professional brush	20% brush once a day or less, 28% use only regular toothbrushes 54% floss 66% use mouthwash
Major toothbrush brands used are Oral-B Angle and Oral-B Regular followed by Colgate Plus and Reach.	Major toothbrush brands used are Colgate Classic and Oral-B Regular followed by Colgate Plus and Oral-B Angle	Major toothbrush brands used are Colgate Classic and Oral-B Regular followed by Colgate Plus and Reach

Competition

Exhibit 4 lists the major brands and product prices for each of the three toothbrush product segments. Exhibit 5 shows the number and type of stockkeeping units (SKUs) for each major brand, and Exhibits 6 and 7 summarize market shares over time and by class of trade. Major competitor brands in the super-premium segment included Oral-B, Reach Advanced Design, Crest Complete, and Aquafresh Flex.

Oral-B (owned by Gillette) had been the market leader since the 1960s. In 1991, it held a 23.1% volume market share and a 30.7% value share of U.S retail sales, with 27 SKUs. Oral-B relied heavily on professional endorsements and was known as "the dentist's toothbrush." In July 1991, Oral-B launched the Indicator brush, priced at a 15% premium to its other brushes. The Indicator brush had a patch of blue bristles that faded to white when it was time for replacement (usually after two to three months). In 1992, consumer promotions were expected to cost $4.5 million (5% of sales) and include $1.00-off coupons, "buy-one-get-one-free" offers and $2.00 mail-in refunds. Media expenditures for 1992 were estimated at $11.2 million (12.7% of sales). Television commercials would continue to feature "Rob the dentist" using the Oral-B Indicator product. In 1991, Oral-B's operating margin on toothbrushes, after advertising and promotion costs, was estimated to be approximately 20% of factory sales.

In 1992, Oral-B announced that it would restage its dental floss, roll out a new mouthwash, and possibly introduce a specialty toothpaste. Oral-B management stated that "to be a leader in the oral care category, we must compete in all areas of oral care."[4]

Johnson & Johnson (J&J) entered the U.S. toothbrush market in the 1970s with the Reach brand, which, in 1991, comprised 18 SKUs. In 1988, J&J introduced a second product line under the brand name Prevent, a brush with a beveled handle to help consumers brush at a 45% angle—the recommended brushing technique. This product however, was being phased out by 1992. In 1991, J&J ranked third in the U.S. retail toothbrush market with a 19.4% volume share and a 21.8% value share. The Reach line was positioned as the toothbrush that enabled consumers to brush in even the hardest-to-reach places, thereby increasing the efficiency of brushing. New products included Glow Reach (1990) and Advanced Design Reach (1991), which offered tapered heads, angled necks, and unique non-slip handles. Reach Between, scheduled for launch in September of 1992, had an angled neck and rippled bristles that targeted the areas between the teeth. Consumer promotions in 1992 were estimated at $4.6 million (8.6% of sales) and included 604 coupons, $1.00 refunds by mail, and "buy-two-get-one-free" offers.

---

[4]*Brandweek,* October 12, 1992.

Media expenditures were expected to reach $17.1 million (31.7% of sales) with a heavy reliance on television commercials. Johnson & Johnson's expected 1992 operating margin on toothbrushes, after advertising and promotion costs, was 8.4% of factory sales.

Procter & Gamble (P&G) was the most recent entrant in the toothbrush market with Crest Complete, an extension of the company's toothpaste brand name, Crest. Based on successful test markets in Houston and San Antonio from August 1991 to August 1992, P&G was expected to launch Crest Complete nationally in September 1992. The brush had captured a 13% value share in test markets and was expected to reach similar total market share levels in its first year after full launch. The product had long, rippled bristles of different lengths, designed to reach between the teeth. Crest Complete claimed to have "the ability to reach between the teeth up to 37% farther than leading flat brushes." It was expected to be introduced at a manufacturer's list price to retailers of $1.67 and capture a 2.0% volume share and a 2.6% value share of the U.S. retail market by the end of 1992. Consumer promotions already announced included 55 cent coupons and $1.99 refunds on toothbrushes purchased from floor stands. Media expenditures for the last quarter of 1992 were estimated at $6.4 million; television commercials would carry the theme "Teeth aren't flat, so why is your brush."

Smithkline Beecham entered the U.S. toothbrush market in August 1991 with Aquafresh Flex, an extension of the company's toothpaste brand. Aquafresh Flex toothbrushes had flexible handles that allowed for gentle brushing. By the end of 1991, Aquafresh Flex held a 0.9% share by volume and 1.1% by value of the U.S. retail market with six SKUs. In September 1992, the line was expected to expand to include two adult compact heads and one child brush. The 1992 promotion plan, estimated at $4.6 million (25% of sales), included $1.99 mail refunds, "buy-two-get-one-free" offers, toothbrush on-pack with toothpaste, and a self-liquidating premium offer of towels. Media expenditures at $10 million (almost 50% of sales) included television commercials that showed the product brushing a tomato without damaging it, to demonstrate the "flexibility and gentleness" of the brush. Smithkline Beecham was expected to make an operating loss on toothbrushes in 1992.

Other competitors included *Lever, Pfizer,* and *Sunstar.* In 1991, Lever offered three lines of toothbrushes: Aim; Pepsodent Professional with 5 SKUs; and Pepsodent Regular with 4 SKUs. Combined, Lever held a 7.2% volume and 6.6% value share of the U.S. retail market in 1991. Lever's products were sold primarily in the value segment and the company did not have a track record of innovation in the category. Pfizer entered the market in June 1991 with its Plax brush, which had a special groove for the thumb; it had captured 1.8% of the retail market by year end. Sunstar, with its Butler brand, held 2% of the retail market in 1992 and 19% of the $45 million in toothbrushes distributed through dentists.

Advertising and Promotion

In the toothpaste category, it was hard to increase primary demand, so new products tended to steal sales from existing products. In the case of toothbrushes, however, increased advertising and promotion enhanced the category's visibility which, in turn, seemed to fuel consumer demand.

As the pace of new product introductions quickened in the late 1980s, the advertising media expenditures needed to launch a new toothbrush rose: Johnson & Johnson spent $8 million in media support to introduce its new Reach brush; Oral-B spent $10 million to launch its Indicator brush; and Procter & Gamble was expected to support its Crest Complete brush with $15 million in media expenditures. Total media spending for the category, primarily on television advertising, was estimated to total $55 million in 1992 and $70 million in 1993. Exhibit 8 shows media expenditures and shares of voice for the main toothbrush brands. Exhibit 9 summarizes the main message in each brand's commercials, and Exhibit 10 summarizes the copy strategy of Colgate Plus's television commercials over time. Advertising and promotion expenditures for Colgate toothbrushes are given in Exhibit 11.

Growing competition also increased the frequency and value of consumer promotion events. In 1992, 8% of all brushes reached consumers either free with toothpaste (as on-pack or mail-in premiums) or free with another toothbrush (buy-one-get-one-free offers). The number of coupon events for toothbrushes increased from 10 in 1990 to 33 in 1992. In the same period, the average toothbrush coupon value increased from $0.25 to $0.75.

Retail advertising features and in-store displays increased toothbrush sales. A typical CP toothbrush display increased sales by 90% over a normal shelf facing. When Colgate toothbrushes were combined with Colgate toothpaste in a single display, toothbrush sales increased by 170%. The importance of point-of-purchase displays and the variety of items, bristle qualities, and handle colors in each manufacturer's line led each to develop a variety of racks and display units for different classes of trade. CP for example, had four display systems: Counter Tops, containing 24 to 36 brushes; Floor Stands, 72 brushes; Sidekicks (used by mass merchandisers), 144 to 288 brushes; and Waterfall displays, 288 to 576 brushes. Exhibit 12 illustrates these display racks. In 1991, the percentages of special Colgate displays accounted for by each type were 10%, 50%, 25%, and 15% respectively.

The CP toothbrush line held 25% to 40% of the category shelf space in most stores. To maximize retail sales, CP salespeople tried to locate the Colgate line in the middle of the category shelf space, between the Reach and the Oral-B product lines.

Distribution

In 1987, traditional food stores sold 75% of oral care products, but by 1992 they accounted for only 43% of toothbrush sales and 47% of toothpaste sales. Mass merchandisers gained share due to increased in-store promotional support. Partly in response and partly because of the increasing number of SKUs, food stores began to expand shelf space devoted to oral care products. Exhibit 13 summarizes toothbrush retail distribution trends by volume and value.

Though purchased too infrequently to be used as a traffic builder, toothbrushes provided retailers with an average margin between 25% and 35%, twice that for toothpaste. As a result, many retailers were more receptive to adding new toothbrush products than new varieties of toothpaste. In considering which brands to stock and feature, trade buyers evaluated advertising and promotion support and each manufacturer's track record in the category. Between October 1991 and February 1992, the average number of toothbrush SKUs had increased from 31 to 35 for mass merchandisers, from 27 to 34 for drug stores and from 30 to 35 for food outlets. In September 1992, the average number of brands carried by these three classes of trade were 10, 12, and 8 respectively. Shelf space devoted to toothbrushes had also increased. Kmart, for example, had increased per-store shelf space for toothbrushes from 2 to 7.5 feet in two years. Retail sales remained fragmented, with 60% of sales derived from 40% of the SKUs.

In 1992, 22% of all toothbrushes were expected to be distributed to consumers by dentists. With a dedicated sales force, Oral-B dominated this market segment. Manufacturer margins on toothbrush sales through dentists were less than half those achieved through normal retail distribution. Exhibit 14 summarizes competitors' shares in this segment of the market.

The Precision Marketing Mix

Product Design and Testing

The Precision toothbrush was a technical innovation. In laboratory experiments, researchers used infrared motion analysis to track consumers' brushing movements and consequent levels of plaque removal. With this knowledge and through computer aided design, CP developed a unique brush with bristles of three different lengths and orientations (see Exhibit 15). The longer outer bristles cleaned around the gum line, the long inner bristles cleaned between teeth, and the shorter bristles cleaned the teeth surface. The result was a triple-action brushing effect. In initial clinical tests, the brush achieved an average 35% increase in plaque removal, compared with other leading toothbrushes, specifically Reach and Oral-B. At the gum line and between the teeth, the brush was even more effective, achieving double the plaque removal scores of competitor brushes.

In 1989, CP had established a task force comprising executives from R&D and Marketing, dental professionals, and outside consultants. Its mission was to "develop a superior, technical, plaque-removing device." The entire research and development process was managed from start to finish by Steinberg. The task force had five goals:

- Understanding the varying techniques consumers used when brushing their teeth. Researchers later concluded that brushing usually did a good job of removing plaque from teeth surfaces but was often ineffective at removing plaque from the gum line and between the teeth.

- Testing the between-teeth access of different toothbrush designs. The tests revealed that CP's new design was superior to both Oral-B and Reach in accessing front and back teeth, using either horizontal or vertical brushing.

- Establishing an index to score clinical plaque-removal efficacy at the gum line and between teeth. In tests, a disclosing solution was used to reveal the otherwise colorless plaque, and each tooth was divided into nine specific areas. Presence of plaque was measured on each tooth area; the percentages of tooth areas affected by plaque pre- and post-usage of different brushes were then calculated.

- Creating a bristle configuration and handle design offering maximum plaque-removing efficacy. Three similar designs evolved from the above research, all incorporating bristles of different lengths that would allow freer movement of each individual tuft of bristles and thereby enable different bristle tufts to target different areas of the mouth. Clinical trials established that the new product removed an average 35% more plaque than other leading brushes and therefore helped to reduce the probability of gum disease.

- Determining, through clinical and consumer research, the efficacy and acceptance of the new toothbrush design. Extensive consumer research was carried out over a period of 18 months to test product design and characteristics, marketing concept, and competitive strengths. In addition, dental professional focus groups and product usage tests were conducted to determine the overall acceptance of Precision.

In July 1992, CP senior management decided to launch Precision early in 1993. It was decided that Precision would be priced within the super-premium segment and distributed through the same channels as Colgate Plus. However, the decision on how to position the product and the corresponding branding and communications strategies remained to be finalized.

Positioning

Precision was developed with the objective of creating the best brush possible and as such, becoming a top-of-the range, super-premium product. It could be positioned as a niche product to be targeted at consumers concerned about gum disease. As such, it could command a 15% price premium over Oral-B and would be expected to capture 3% of the U.S. toothbrush market by the end of the first year following its launch. Alternatively, Precision could be positioned as a mainstream brush, with the broader appeal of being the most effective brush available on the market. It was estimated that, as a mainstream product, Precision could capture 10% of the market by the end of the first year. Steinberg developed a marketing mix and financial projections for both scenarios, and this information is summarized in Table C. Her assumptions and calculations for the niche and mainstream positioning scenarios were as follows:

Volumes. Steinberg believed that with a niche positioning, Precision retail sales would represent 3% volume share of the toothbrush market in year 1 and 5% in year 2. With a mainstream positioning, these volume shares would be 10% in year 1 and 14.7% in year 2. Total category unit volumes were estimated at 268 million in 1993 and 300 million in 1994. Table C outlines how these unit volumes would reach the consumer.

Capacity and Investment Costs. Three types of equipment were required to manufacture the Precision brush: tufters; handle molds; and packaging machinery. Table D gives the cost, depreciation period, and annual capacity for each class of equipment.

Production Costs and Pricing. Production was subcontracted to Anchor Brush who also manufactured CP's Plus line of toothbrushes. Production costs included warehousing and transport costs. Under a niche positioning strategy, Steinberg decided that CP would establish a factory list price to the trade of $2.13, a premium over Oral-B regular and at parity with Oral-B Indicator. The mainstream strategy price would be $1.85, at parity

Table C How Unit Volumes Reach Consumer

	Niche Positioning Strategy	Mainstream Positioning Strategy
# *Units Retail*	Year 1 = 8 MM, Year 2 = 15 MM.	Year 1 = 27 MM, Year 2 = 44 MM.
# *Units Consumer Promotion Sampling*	Year 1 & 2 = 2 MM.	Year 1 & 2 = 7 MM.
# *Units Through Professionals*	Year 1 & 2 = 3 MM.	Year 1 & 2 = 8 MM.

Table D

	Investment Cost	Annual Capacity	Depreciation Time
Tufters	$500,000	3 MM units	15 years
Handle Molds	$300,000	7 MM units	5 years
Packaging	$150,000	40 MM units	5 years

with Oral-B regular. In practice however, almost all sales to the trade were made at a discount of approximately 5%. Eighty percent of sales through dental professionals would be priced at $0.79 per unit; the remainder would be sold at $0.95.

Positioning Precision as a mainstream toothbrush raised concerns about the possible cannibalization of Colgate Plus and about pressure on production schedules that had been developed for a niche positioning. Production capacity increases required 10 months' lead time, and switching to a mainstream positioning could result in inadequate supply of product. Some executives argued that unsatisfied demand could create the perception of a "hot" product but others felt that the problems associated with allocating limited supplies among trade customers should be avoided if possible. They argued for an initial niche positioning, which could later be broadened to a mainstream positioning as additional capacity came on line.

The positioning decision had important implications for the appropriate shelf location of Precision. Steinberg believed that the best location for Precision on the retail shelves would be between the Colgate Plus and Oral-B product lines, with the Colgate Classic product line on the other side of Colgate Plus. She wondered, however, if mainstream Precision could be located separately from the other Colgate lines, close to competitive super-premium toothbrushes such as Aquafresh Flex and Crest Complete. If Precision was positioned as a niche product, with 4 SKUs, it was unlikely that any existing SKUs would be dropped. However, positioning Precision as a mainstream product, with 7 SKUs, would probably require dropping one or more existing SKUs such as a slow-moving children's brush from the Plus line.

Steinberg also believed that the positioning decision would impact distribution and percentage of sales by class of trade. Specifically, she reasoned that Precision, positioned as a niche product, would be carried primarily by food and drug stores. Under a mainstream launch scenario, a relatively greater proportion of sales would

occur through mass merchandisers and club stores. Steinberg consolidated her best estimate of the cost and price data (see Table E). When combined with the unit volume estimates in Table C, she hoped to develop a pro-forma income statement to compare the profit implications of the niche versus mainstream positioning strategies. She remained uncertain, however, about cannibalization; anywhere from 35% to 60% of the volumes indicated in Table C could come from Colgate Classic and Colgate Plus.

Branding

At the time consumer concept tests were carried out by the task force, name tests were also conducted among those consumers positively disposed towards the concept. Alternative names tested included Colgate Precision, Colgate System III, Colgate Advantage, Colgate 1.2.3, Colgate Contour, Colgate Sensation, and Colgate Probe. The Colgate Precision name was consistently viewed more favorably—it was deemed appropriate by 49% of concept acceptors and appealing by 31%.

CP executives had not yet decided the relative prominence of the Precision and Colgate names on the package and in advertising. They debated whether the brush should be known as "Colgate Precision" or as "Precision by Colgate." Executives who believed that the product represented "big news" in the category argued that the product could stand alone and that the Precision brand name should be emphasized. Stressing *Precision* as opposed to *Colgate* would, it was argued, limit the extent of cannibalization of Colgate Plus. It was estimated, both under the mainstream and niche positioning scenarios, that cannibalization figures for Colgate Plus would increase by 20% if the Colgate brand name was stressed but remain unchanged if the Precision brand name was stressed. On the other hand, CP's stated corporate strategy was to build on the Colgate brand equity.

Table E Alternative Positioning Scenarios for Precision

	Precision as a Niche Product	Precision as a Mainstream Product
Planned capacity unit volume	Year 1 = 13 MM units Year 2 = 20 MM units	Year 1 = 42 MM units Year 2 = 59 MM units
Investment in capacity, where year 2 figures are for additional capacity	Year 1 = $3.250 M Year 2 = $1.300 M	Year 1 = $9.400 MM Year 2 = $3.100 MM
Depreciation costs (Derived from Table D)	Year 1 = $316,667 Year 2 = $450,000	Year 1 = $ 886,667 Year 2 = $1,270,000
Manufacturer per unit cost: Year 1 and 2	$0.66	$0.64
Manufacturer price Suggested retail price	$2.02 $2.89	$1.76 $2.49
Advertising- Year 1 Year 2 Consumer Promotions- Year 1 Year 2 Trade Promotions- Year 1 Year 2	$ 5 Million $ 5 Million $4.6 Million $ 4 Million $1.6 Million $2.7 Million	$15 Million $12 Million $13 Million $10 Million $4.8 Million $ 7 Million
# SKUs Brushes Colors	4 adult 6 colors	6 adult/1 child 6 colors

Communication and Promotion

Once the basic product design was established, four concept tests, conducted among 400 adult professional brush users (Colgate Plus, Reach, and Oral-B users) 18 to 54 years of age, were run during 1990-1991. Consumers were exposed to various product claims in prototype print advertisements and then asked about the likelihood that they would purchase the product (see Exhibit 16 for copies of the advertisements). The results of these tests are summarized in Exhibit 17 and indicate that a claim that the toothbrush would prevent gum disease motivated the greatest purchase intent among test consumers. Additional consumer research, including in-home usage tests, revealed that 55% of test consumers found Precision to be very different from their current toothbrushes, and 77% claimed that Precision was much more effective than their current toothbrush.

Precision's unique design could remove more plaque from teeth than the other leading toothbrushes on the market. However, the brush looked unusual and test participants sometimes had mixed first impressions. A further problem was that the benefit of reduced gum disease from extra plaque removal was difficult to translate into a message with broad consumer appeal, since few consumers acknowledged that they might have gum disease. Steinberg believed that Precision was the best brush for people who cared about what they put in their mouths but was still searching for the right superiority claim.

Consumer research revealed that the more test consumers were told about Precision and how it worked, the greater their enthusiasm for the product. Precision created such a unique feel in the mouth when used that consumers often said, "You can really feel it working." Once tried, consumer intent to purchase rose dramatically, and Steinberg therefore concluded that sampling would be critical to Precision's success.

There was considerable debate over the CP toothbrush advertising and promotion budget, which amounted to $24.1 million in 1992, with $9.6 million in advertising and $14.4 million in consumer and trade promotion. Some executives thought the budget should remain level as a percentage of sales in 1993 and be allocated among Classic, Plus, and Precision. Others believed it should be increased substantially to support the Precision launch with no reduction in planned support for Classic and Plus. One proposal consistent with a niche positioning for Precision was to increase total CP category spending by $11.2 million and to allocate this to the Precision launch. However, Steinberg believed that this was not enough to permit Precision to reach its full sales potential. She argued for an 80% increase in CP category spending in 1993, with fully 75% of all advertising dollars assigned to Precision and 25% to Plus. However, the Colgate Plus product manager, John Phillips, argued that Plus was the bread-and-butter of CP's toothbrush line and claimed that his mainstream brand should receive more rather than less support if Precision was launched. He argued that continued support of Plus was essential to defend its market position against competition.

Consumer promotions were planned to induce trial. Steinberg was considering several consumer promotions to back the launch: a free 5 oz. tube of Colgate toothpaste (retail value of $1.89) with the purchase of a Precision brush in strong competitive markets; and a 50%-off offer on any size of Colgate toothpaste (up to a value of $1.00) in conjunction with a 50¢ coupon on the Precision brush in strong Colgate markets. The cost of this promotion was estimated at $4 million and Steinberg believed it should be used as part of the launch program for a mainstream positioning strategy. The Colgate Plus product manager pressed for trade deals to load the trade in advance of the Precision launch. He believed that the trade would be unlikely to support two Colgate brushes at any one time. However, Steinberg believed that the launch of Precision would enable CP to increase its overall share of trade advertising features and special displays in the toothpaste category.

Another important tactic was to use dentists to sample consumers since professional endorsements were believed important to establishing the credibility of a new toothbrush. Steinberg believed that, under the niche scenario, 3 million Precision brushes could be channeled through dental professionals in the first year after the launch, versus 8 million under the mainstream scenario.

Conclusion

Steinberg believed that Precision was more than a niche product or simple line extension and that the proven benefits to consumers represented a technological breakthrough. She wondered how Precision should be positioned, branded, and communicated to consumers, as well as what the advertising and promotion budget should be and how it should be broken down. Steinberg had to develop a marketing mix and profit-and-loss pro forma that would enable Precision to reach its full potential, yet also be acceptable to Burton and her colleagues, particularly the Colgate Plus product manager.

Exhibit 1 Income Statements for Colgate-Palmolive Toothbrushes: 1989–1992

	1989		1990		1991		1992E	
Unit sales ('000s)	55,296		63,576		70,560		78,336	
Net sales ($'000s)	43,854	(100%)	57,248	(100%)	77,001	(100%)	91,611	(100%)
Cost of sales	23,988	(55%)	28,190	(49%)	36,827	(48%)	44,846	(49%)
Total fixed overhead	4,429	(11%)	6,304	(11%)	10,007	(13%)	11,423	(12%)
Total advertising Media Consumer promotions Trade promotions	 3,667 4,541 3,458	 (8%) (10%) (8%)	 6,988 5,893 4,134	 (12%) (10%) (7%)	 8,761 5,286 6,287	 (11%) (7%) (8%)	 9,623 6,978 7,457	 (11%) (8%) (8%)
Operating profit	3,744	(9%)	5,739	(10%)	9,833	(13%)	11,284	(12%)

Source: Company records

Exhibit 2 Chronology of Toothbrush Innovations in the U.S.

Date	New Product Introductions	Main Feature
1950s	Oral-B Classic	Traditional square head
1977	Johnson & Johnson Reach	First angled handle
1985	Colgate Plus	First diamond-shaped head
1986	Lever Bros. Aim	Slightly longer handle
1988	Johnson & Johnson Prevent Colgate Plus Sensitive Gums	Aids brushing at 45 angle Softer bristles
1989	Pepsodent Oral-B Ultra	"Commodity" brush Improved handle
1990	J&J Neon Reach Oral-B Art Series	Neon-colored handle Cosmetic feature
1991	Colgate Plus Angle Handle Colgate Plus Wild Ones J&J Advanced Reach Design Oral-B Indicator Aquafresh Flex Pfizer Plax	Diamond-shaped & angled handle Cosmetic feature Rubber-ridged, non-slip handle Bristles change color Flexible handle neck Groove for thumb
1992	Crest Complete Colgate Precision	Rippled bristles Triple action bristles

Source: Company records

Exhibit 3 Brand Decision Factors for Consumers

Main Reasons for Using a Brand	Percent of Consumers
Fits most comfortably in my mouth	63%
Best for getting at hard-to-reach places	52%
The bristles are the right softness	46%
The bristles are the right firmness	36%
Toothbrush my dentist recommends	35%
Important part of my oral care regimen	30%

Source: Company records
Note: Respondents could check multiple items.

Exhibit 4 Toothbrush Brand Prices: 1992

	Manufacturer List Price	Manufacturer Net Price	Average Retail Selling Price (Food channel)
– Super-premium			
– Oral-B Indicator	$2.13	$1.92	$2.65
– Oral-B Regular	$1.85	$1.78	$2.51
– Crest Complete	$1.67	$1.67	$2.40
– Reach Advanced	$1.75	$1.66	$2.38
– Aquafresh Flex	$1.85	$1.61	$2.32
– Professional			
– Colgate Plus	$1.42	$1.35	$2.00
– Reach Regular	$1.37	$1.30	$2.01
– Pepsodent Prof.	$1.20	$1.08	$1.88
– Value			
– Colgate Classic	$0.69	$0.69	$1.22
– Pepsodent Regular	$0.91	$0.48	$1.25

Source: Company records
Note: Net price was the effective manufacturer's price to retailers after a variety of discounts.

Exhibit 5 Principal Toothbrush Brand Product Lines : August 1992

Brand	Number of Stockkeeping Units	
	Adult	Child/Teen
Colgate	28	8
Oral-B	16	5
Reach	14	4
Crest Complete	10	0
Aquafresh Flex	6	1
Lever	7	2
Plax	2	1
Total	83	21

Source: Company records

Exhibit 6 Principal Toothbrush Brand Unit and Dollar Market Shares: 1989–1992E

Brand	1989		1990		1991		1992E	
	Vol (%)	$ (%)	Vol (%)	$ (%)	Vol (%)	$ (%)	Vol (%)	$ (%)
– Colgate								
– Plus	12.0	12.6	13.7	15.2	16.9	18.5	17.3	18.5
– Classic	8.5	6.6	8.1	6.2	6.4	4.9	4.9	2.9
– **Total**	20.5	19.2	21.8	21.4	23.3	23.4	22.2	21.4
– Oral-B								
– Oral-B Indicator	0.0	0.0	0.0	0.0	1.0	1.3	3.7	4.9
– **Total**	24.0	31.7	24.5	32.6	23.1	30.7	19.8	26.2
– J & J								
– Reach	18.1	20.5	18.2	20.0	17.8	20.0	15.2	15.8
– Reach Advanced Design	0.0	0.0	0.0	0.0	0.7	0.9	4.0	5.2
– Prevent	2.5	2.7	1.6	1.9	0.7	1.1	0.2	0.1
– **Total**	20.6	23.2	19.8	21.9	19.2	22.0	19.4	21.1
– Lever	10.5	10.4	9.8	9.0	7.2	6.6	5.0	4.0
– Crest	0.0	0.0	0.0	0.0	0.0	0.0	2.0	2.6
– Aqua-Fresh	0.0	0.0	0.0	0.0	0.9	1.1	4.6	5.7
– Butler	N/A	N/A	N/A	N/A	2.0	2.4	2.0	2.2
– Private Label	N/A	N/A	N/A	N/A	11.2	5.9	11.5	6.1

Source: Company records
Note: N/A = not available.

Exhibit 7 Principal Toothbrush Brand Unit and Dollar Market Shares by Class of Trade: 1991

	Food		Drug		Mass	
	Vol (%)	$ (%)	Vol (%)	$ (%)	Vol (%)	$ (%)
– *Colgate*						
– Plus	18.9	21.3	9.6	11.4	29.3	31.4
– Classic	7.0	4.8	4.5	3.7	3.9	3.2
– **Total**	25.9	26.1	14.1	15.1	33.2	34.6
– *Oral-B*						
– Oral-B Indicator	0.9	1.1	1.0	1.5	0.7	0.9
– **Total**	20.5	28.2	25.1	34.1	22.4	27.6
– *J & J*						
– Reach	22.3	23.8	14.3	16.6	18.3	20.7
– Reach Advanced Design	1.2	N/A	.3	0.4	0.3	0.4
– Prevent	0.8	1.2	0.8	0.9	0.5	0.6
– **Total**	23.2	25.0	15.1	17.5	18.8	21.4
– Lever	9.1	8.9	5.8	5.6	6.3	7.4
– Crest (TX test market)	5.1	6.5	0.0	0.0	0.0	N/A
– Aqua-Fresh	4.9	N/A	0.4	0.5	0.3	0.5
– Butler	1.3	2.0	3.5	6.6	0.5	0.9
– Private Label	10.7	5.5	17.4	10.6	4.4	2.4

Source: Company records

Exhibit 8 Principal Toothbrush Media Advertising Expenditures and Shares of Voice: 1991–1992E

	1991		1992E	
	Media $MM	Share Voice(%)	Media $MM	Share Voice(%)
Colgate Plus	7.0	19	8	15
Reach	15.5	42	17.1	31
Oral-B	10.2	27	11.2	20
Crest Complete	0.4	1	6.4	12
Aquafresh Flex	0.4	1	10	18
Pfizer Plax	2.3	6	2.2	4

Source: Company records

Exhibit 9 Television and Advertising Copy Strategies and Executions for Competitor Toothbrush Brands: 1991

Product	Message	Tag-Line	Execution
Crest Complete	Has rippled bristles to reach between teeth (37% further than a flat bristled brush).	"Only Crest could make a brush this complete."	Visual comparison of Crest Complete versus a dental tool.
Aquafresh Flex	Has a flexible neck that is gentle on the gums.	"For gentle dental care"	Spokesperson / demonstration
Advanced Design Reach	Features a new head/handle design.	"Advanced Design Reach"	Visual demonstration of product design with cartoon character.
Oral-B Indicator	Will tell you when to change your toothbrush.	"The brand more dentists use"	Testimonial with demonstration.
Plax	Is especially designed to remove plaque.	"The new Plax, plaque removing toothbrush"	Computer graphic display of product design.

Source: Company records

Exhibit 10 Colgate Plus Television Advertising; Copy Strategies and Execution: 1985–1992

Date	Marketing Situation	Colgate Copy Platform	Execution	Tag-line
1985–1986	First toothbrush with diamond-shaped head. First professional toothbrush from a leading oral care company.	Unique head Scientific/technical tone Comfort and efficacy	Product depicted as a hero.	"Shaped to keep your whole mouth in shape"
1987–1990	Aim enters market, spurring increased competition. Colgate Plus market share suffers.	Diamond-shaped head Evolution of comfort/efficacy Lighter contemporary tone Implied superiority Emphasizes visual differences	"Odd looking" toothbrush character introduced in bathroom setting.	"Odd looking, super-cleaning, comfy feeling toothbrush"
1991	Need to re-energize Colgate advertising copy given long duration of "Odd Looking" campaign.	Diamond shape fits mouth and removes plaque from hard-to-reach places.	The "Odd looking" character in a dental chair. Implied dental recommendation.	"Because your smile was meant to last a lifetime"
1992	Increased competitive activity and consequent need for harder-hitting copy.	Plaque focus Efficacy message	"Armed to the Teeth" execution where the bristles are soldiers.	"In the fight against plaque, it's a Plus"

Source: Company records.

Exhibit 11 Advertising and Promotion Expenditures for Colgate-Palmolive Toothbrushes: 1989–1992E ($ in thousands)

	1989		1990		1991		1992E	
Media[a]	$3,667	(31%)	$6,988	(41%)	$8,761	(43%)	$9,623	(40%)
Consumer Promotions	4,541	(39%)	5,893	(35%)	5,286	(26%)	6,978	(29%)
Trade Promotions	3,485	(30%)	4,134	(24%)	6,287	(31%)	7,457	(31%)
Total Advertising and Promotion	$11,693	(100%)	$17,015	(100%)	$20,334	(100%)	$24,058	(100%)

Source: Company records

[a]Includes: working media expenditures; production and operating costs; and dental professional advertising.

Exhibit 12 Colgate Toothbrush Point-of-Sales Display Racks

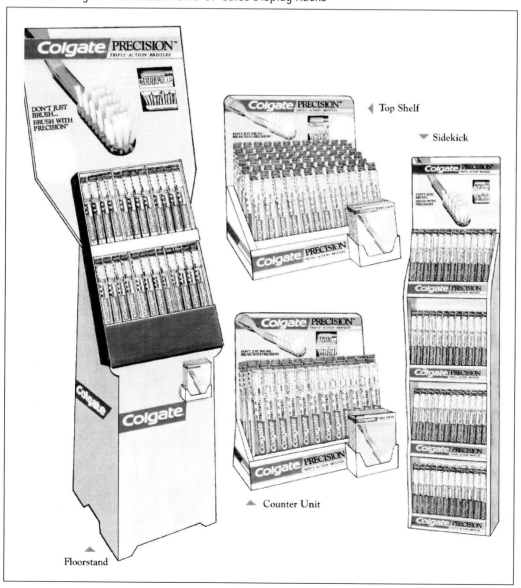

Exhibit 13 Retail Toothbrush Sales: 1989–1992E

	1989		1990		1991		1992E	
	Units MM	$ MM	Units MM	$ MM	Units MM	$ MM	Units MM	$ MM
Food stores	110 (45%)	175 (47%)	107 (44%)	175 (44%)	110 (42%)	192 (42%)	128 (42%)	236 (43%)
Drugstores	77 (32%)	123 (33%)	74 (31%)	131 (33%)	77 (29%)	148 (33%)	88 (29%)	168 (31%)
Mass merchandisers	46 (19%)	61 (17%)	44 (18%)	69 (18%)	54 (21%)	89 (20%)	68 (21%)	114 (21%)
Military	4 (2%)	5 (1%)	5 (2%)	5 (1%)	5 (2%)	5 (1%)	5 (2%)	6 (1%)
Club stores	3 (1%)	4 (1%)	9 (4%)	11 (3%)	12 (5%)	15 (3%)	15 (5%)	19 (3%)
Other	3 (1%)	4 (1%)	3 (1%)	4 (1%)	3 (1%)	4 (1%)	3 (1%)	4 (1%)

Source: Company records

Exhibit 14 U.S. Professional Dental Market for Toothbrushes: Competitor Market Shares: 1991–1992E

	1991		1992E	
Brand (Parent Co)	$ millions	Market Share (%)	$ millions	Market Share (%)
Oral-B (Gillette)	14.3	34.0	14.3	31.8
Butler (Sunstar)	8.5	20.2	8.5	18.9
Colgate (CP)	6.7	16.1	8.3	18.4
Reach (J&J)	4.0	9.5	4.0	8.9
Pycopy (Block)	3.4	8.1	3.4	7.6
Aquafresh Flex (Beecham)	0.0	0.0	0.4	0.9
Crest Complete (P&G)	0.0	0.0	0.8	1.7
Other	5.1	12.1	5.4	11.9
Total	42.0		45.0	

Source: Company records
Note: Aquafresh Flex and Crest Complete were not launched until 1992.

Exhibit 15 Reproductions of the Colgate Precision Toothbrush

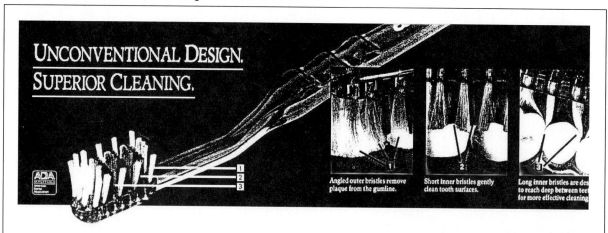

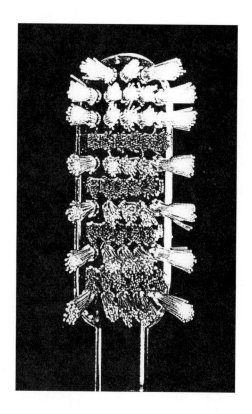

Exhibit 16 Copies of the Advertisements used in the Consumer Concept Tests

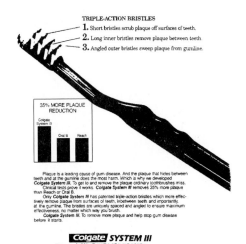
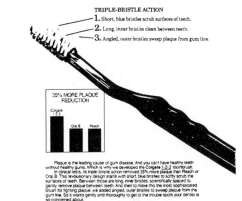

Exhibit 17 Summary of Consumer Concept Test Results

CONCEPT TEST 1.			
	Plaque Remover	**Healthier Gums**	**Trouble Spots**
Probably Would Buy	69%	68%	66%
Definitely Would Buy	15%	15%	10%

CONCEPT TEST 2.			
	35% More Plaque Removal Prevent Gum Disease	**35% More Plaque Removal**	**Prevent Gum Disease**	**Feel the Difference**
Probably Would Buy	80%	71%	74%	68%
Definitely Would Buy	19%	19%	18%	14%

CONCEPT TEST 3.			
	Gum Disease/ Replacement	**Gum Disease Only**	**Replacement Message**	**Trouble Spots**
Probably Would Buy	63%	72%	62%	66%
Definitely Would Buy	13%	16%	11%	14%

CONCEPT TEST 4.	
	No Price Given Prevent Gum Disease	**20% Price Premium to Oral-B Prevent Gum Disease**
Probably Would Buy	87%	61%
Definitely Would Buy	29%	19%

Source: Company records
Note: "Definitely would buy" is a subset of "probably would buy"

DENDRITE INTERNATIONAL

In July 1993, John Bailye, president of Dendrite International, was considering changes affecting Dendrite's customer base. Bailye commented:

> Dendrite is currently a leading sales automation supplier to pharmaceutical firms. We have been unique in this marketplace, offering a global product that is customized to local market needs and backed up with in-depth customer service. But in the United States, 80% of pharmaceutical sales reps are now supported by automation systems of one kind or another. Other developments may reduce the size of pharmaceutical sales forces in the United States, Europe, and Japan.

Among the issues raised by these developments were the best means of ensuring Dendrite's future growth and possible changes in account management procedures.

Company and Industry Background

John Bailye had been a partner of Foresearch, an Australian company that provided market research services to pharmaceutical firms operating in Australia and southeast Asia. During the early 1980s, government regulations in many of these countries affected drug pricing and physicians' incomes. Bailye recalled: "Doctors had less time to see sales reps but reps continued to be measured on the number of calls they made, which is still standard practice in the industry. Meanwhile, the introduction of laptop computers offered a vehicle for improving sales productivity." Bailye established a division called Dendrite,[1] which in 1985 developed software

---

Professor Frank V. Cespedes and Research Associate Marie Bell prepared this case as the basis for class discussion rather than to illustrate either effective or ineffective handling of an administrative situation. Certain company data, while useful for discussion purposes, have been disguised.

to assist with call planning and reporting tasks. After a one-year pilot with an Australian firm, financial support for Dendrite was provided by a chemical company.

In 1987, Bailye and 12 employees moved their families and Dendrite headquarters from Sydney, Australia to Warren, New Jersey. Bailye recalled:

> In trying to sell our product to major pharmaceutical firms, we soon found that they wanted a visible commitment in the United States, the single biggest market in the industry. We chose New Jersey because many pharmaceutical firms are headquartered there and because the Unix system we use on our main computer was developed by AT&T's Bell Labs, which is also in New Jersey. We therefore felt this area would provide well-trained technicians.
>
> But we knew little else about what we were getting into. It probably is hard for most Americans to realize how complex and different this country is. Our early days were tough: we had no credit background, little cash, and our families were adjusting to new ways of doing things. We also learned that, in the United States, it is not the product alone that matters. You must present a credible total organization to be given a real business opportunity.

In the United States, Dendrite was the ninth vendor supplying sales automation software to pharmaceutical firms. "All of these firms were of similar size and financial standing," Bailye noted, "so competition was fierce but relatively even." In 1988, however, Dun & Bradstreet (a $4 billion firm operating in a variety of information services markets) acquired a competitor, Sales Technologies, Inc. (STI), which soon dropped product prices and promoted itself as the only viable long-term option for corporate customers. "Customers started to compare this new 'giant' with other 'start-up' vendors and new business moved to STI," Bailye explained. "Dendrite was too new in the market to have credibility, despite the fact that our technology was better and, unlike STI, focused on the sales tasks of pharmaceutical reps. We also lacked the financial resources to wage a price war. Change was necessary and eventually involved all elements of organizational structure, market positioning, and technology applications."

---

[1]A dendrite conducts impulses from a nerve cell to central nerve fiber.

Management first reassessed its primary target market. It decided that pharmaceutical firms were still the best market for Dendrite. "These firms are large, profitable, driven by sales productivity requirements, and among the earliest to adopt sales automation," noted Bailye. "The industry also comprised the core of our applications knowledge and working relationships." To distinguish itself, Dendrite decided to become a global supplier of both software and service to pharmaceutical firms. Martha Cleary, vice president of Planning, commented:

> This was an audacious decision for a small firm. In this industry, sales automation software had been supplied on a "turnkey" basis, leaving the customer to operate the system after its installation. We decided to introduce and enhance the concept of outsourcing, whereby Dendrite provided continuous support to maintain and operate the technology and service the needs of client sales reps through help line, training, and facilities management services. This strategy required that we provide full-service facilities in countries which, together, represent 75% of pharmaceutical salespeople.
>
> We had to make many changes simultaneously: redesign the software for multinational application; refinance the company to allow for expansion; restructure marketing programs to emphasize recurring service income, which was necessary to attract capital; and adopt new costing methods, since a key issue in running a service business is managing many unpredictable costs.

Management raised funds from venture capital firms and, by 1991, had established subsidiaries in Belgium, England, France, Germany, Italy, Japan, and Spain in addition to its offices in Australia, New Zealand, and the United States. This expansion was aided by Dendrite's product development strategy. About 80% of the programming code was "core code" which Dendrite then customized to local market needs and company specifications. One executive emphasized:

> Developing this core code took four years and over $5 million in funds from a cash-constrained company. But it's the generic engine which allows us to move into new markets more quickly and cost effectively than competitors. For example, we were able to enter Europe with 300,000 lines of core code which meant that we had to write an additional 100,000 lines for each local market. Competitors must start from scratch and each line is a potential "bug."

Dendrite's sales, less than $250,000 in 1987, were more than $23 million in 1992 (Exhibit 1), about 60% from software licensing and product customization fees and 40% from service, maintenance, and facilities management agreements. Projected sales for 1993 were $33 million. In 1993, more than 15,000 sales reps at 40 companies in 11 countries used Dendrite systems. Commenting on the company's growth, Bailye remarked:

> A number of big pharmaceutical firms found that the risks associated with installing sales productivity tools are reduced with a single vendor as opposed to different vendors in each country. And the risks for customers are considerable: when 3,000 reps can't or won't use a system installed at a total cost of $15 million or more, that bends careers in Sales and IS at these firms. We were fortunate that, during this period, our major competition sold standardized systems installed without comprehensive service, and so many of these systems weren't utilized.

Product and Pricing

Vendors providing electronic territory management (ETM) and other sales automation systems multiplied in the 1980s. Productivity gains from such systems varied widely. The biggest impact generally resulted from a reallocation of time from administrative to selling tasks (an average 25% decrease in administrative tasks, according to Dendrite client studies) and from better targeting and territory management (2%-9% sales gains, according to Dendrite client studies). Bailye described "an evolution in field automation during the past decade":

> Product development among vendors has begun to take two distinct paths. Some firms focus on more intensive tools for sales efficiencies, while others seek diversity of functionality—i.e., to provide the means for improving information linkages between Sales and other functions in client companies.

Dendrite's product was a mix of software and services which, in a typical application (see Exhibit 2), could be briefly described as follows. Sales reps carried a laptop or notebook computer (purchased by the client company), which contained a database of a given rep's territory data (physician profiles, call histories, etc.). Each night, reps phoned the host computer and communicated their activities for reporting purposes. In turn, the system allowed reps to:

- Access a database concerning current and potential customers including physicians, hospitals, pharmacies, HMOs, etc. Information included basic data such as names and phone numbers as well as data about drug prescribing patterns which was collected by third parties, processed by Dendrite on its host computer, and "downloaded" through phone lines to the rep's laptop.

- Develop targeted lists of high-potential customers, and integrate these lists into a call plan that could be discussed with field managers.

- Record most sales-related activities such as number and type of sales calls, time spent in training or district meetings, and vacation or sick days.

- Send and receive messages via electronic mail with anyone else on the system, and also produce personalized letters and administrative documents.

- Use programs that provide quantitative tools useful in analyzing customer data and tracking progress against quarterly or annual objectives.

Sales managers received reports (weekly or monthly, depending on client preference) from Dendrite about the data continuously collected by the host computer. Field managers could also query the host database directly and produce their own reports. "They can compare the calling activities of different reps," a Dendrite manager noted, "or telemarket to all physicians to whom presentations on a particular drug were made the day or week before. We find that the capability spurs new marketing ideas at clients." Headquarters managers also received reports and could query the database. "Corporate sales managers," explained a Dendrite executive, "often use the data for redeployment purposes or to cross-reference their data with third-party information."

Dendrite's software was sold in two parts: the Base system (which provided the fundamentals required to manage call reporting) and various Added Value Modules (for advanced applications where territory-planning and optimization models were provided). Service involved a dedicated client team composed of customer service personnel at Help Centers (located in Dendrite offices) as well as technical service personnel who assisted clients in customizing, implementing, and maintaining the system.

Depending upon the configuration purchased, pricing involved a license fee, maintenance and support agreement, and service contract (see Exhibit 3 for examples). The initial license fee was a one-time charge, rang-ing from $250,000 to over $1 million for the use of Dendrite's software. Maintenance and support agreements involved annual fees to maintain and customize the software, and provide a predetermined number of enhancements. Service contracts covered ongoing facilities management and other services provided by Dendrite's client teams. In the United States and Japan, Dendrite's service pricing was based on the number of system users, and ranged from $300 to $2,000 per user annually; in Europe, where pharmaceutical sales forces were smaller, service contracts were often quoted as a fixed annual fee.

Customers incurred other costs for ETM projects, including the purchase or upgrade of computers for salespeople and communications linkages between the host computer and corporate systems. Typical total costs for implementing an ETM project in a large pharmaceutical firm in 1993 might be $8 million, of which 35% was for Dendrite products and services and 65% for other products and services required to operate the system.

Competition

Including the hardware, forecasts indicated a worldwide $900 million market for ETM by 1995. In 1993, the majority of ETM sales were from hundreds of vendors offering generic, stand-alone software packages which retailed for $100-$400 per unit. These systems allowed a diligent user to collect and maintain information on customers, but were not designed for any specific industry or for integration with other parts of a firm's management system.

The latter capability was available from vendors who offered integrated systems that sold for $1 million or more. Some of these vendors (like Dendrite) specialized in an industry or vertical segment, and others sold across industry segments. In 1993, most were serving 5,000 to 10,000 representatives on their systems. In the pharmaceutical industry, Dendrite's major competitors in this category were STI, Walsh International, PharmaSystems, and Cornet. Dendrite's management believed that key success factors in integrated systems were service support and product flexibility (i.e., the ability to modify database structures to accommodate specific client requirements and subsequent ability to integrate with other client information systems). Management believed that Dendrite offered much higher levels of service than its competitors and, with the exception of Cornet, greater product flexibility. In addition, Dendrite was currently the only supplier with an ETM product developed for the Japanese Kanji language.

STI had estimated 1992 sales of $48 million from ETM systems used in industries including consumer packaged goods and petrochemicals. In pharmaceuticals it held a 40% share of installed reps in the United States. D&B also owned IMS, a supplier of market data to the pharmaceutical industry. In 1992 in Europe, STI began offering IMS data on its ETM system. However, STI had encountered lengthy delays in product development and implementation of its systems, some service problems, and had lost two major clients during the past 18 months. In late 1992 a number of top executives at STI were removed by D&B.

Walsh International, based in the United Kingdom, had sales of about $100 million, mainly derived from paper-based call reporting and data services for pharmaceutical firms. In 1990, Walsh launched an ETM system called PRECISE and by 1993 had automated about 5% of pharmaceutical reps worldwide. A Dendrite executive commented that "Walsh grew in the 1980s by acquiring call reporting companies in Europe and Canada, but they also have an office in Japan and claim to be producing a Japanese ETM product. Their main business is the sale and analysis of industry data, and they are a major competitor with IMS. They're in the process of converting their paper-based clients to PRECISE and often position the product as a 'give away' for clients buying their data. However, their ETM system is fairly rigid and does not currently lend itself well to integration with established client communication procedures and systems."

Pharma Systems (PS), based in the United Kingdom, was a newer company with a focus on ETM and management reporting systems. PS had entered the U.S. market in 1991 with venture backing from the British Coal Board. To date, PS had less than $1 million in sales and only one major client. But other firms had expressed interest in the PS system because it was compatible with a database called Express, which was also used in a market information system utilized by many pharmaceutical firms.

Cornet, based in the United States, had an installed base of about 13% of pharmaceutical reps worldwide, mainly derived from two large firms who licensed Cornet's software code for in-house development and customization. A Dendrite executive noted that, "strategically, outright sale of code can get your foot in the door; we did that with a large firm in 1988. But there is no recurring income and the cost of keeping the code current is high. Cornet will need to develop a product-service package in order to remain a player."

Phoenix, based in the United States, had an installed base of about 8% of pharmaceutical reps. The firm also offered direct mail, sample fulfillment, telemarketing, and market research services to pharmaceutical firms. In ETM, Phoenix offered a low-end product which sold for about $1,500 per year per user (including the handheld hardware unit), but had little potential for integration with other client information systems.

Dendrite also faced indirect competition from information services firms such as Andersen Consulting and Electronic Data Systems. These firms managed the design and installation of hardware and software systems, and had recently managed projects that affected sales and marketing information systems at some pharmaceutical companies. Further, some pharmaceutical firms developed their own ETM systems via in-house MIS departments.

Customers

Worldwide in 1993, there were about 200,000 pharmaceutical salespeople (and an additional 20,000 sales managers), 80% of whom sold in the United States, Western Europe, and Japan (Exhibit 4). In nearly all countries, pharmaceutical salespeople did not take orders; their primary task was to persuade doctors to choose their firm's product over that of a competitor.

The selling cycle for Dendrite usually required 18 months or more, during which time Dendrite's salesperson typically maintained daily telephone contact in addition to weekly on-site visits. "Ideally," a Dendrite salesperson noted, "we begin with the V.P. of Sales, who recognizes a productivity problem and delegates the issue to a direct report, usually the head of Sales Administration (responsible for sales reporting systems at the firm). The decision-making unit quickly expands from there, and often includes various users and commentators from Sales, Marketing, and IS." Another salesperson noted: "User groups help to define the business needs to be addressed by the system, while IS translates those needs into technical specs and possible connections with other aspects of the company's information infrastructure."

Following preliminary discussions with a prospect, Dendrite's salesperson arranged for a software demonstration and sought to have key decision makers attend full-day orientations about the system at Dendrite headquarters. The goal was to familiarize the prospect about Dendrite's support capabilities and, as one salesperson commented, "to build necessary trust and credibility":

Eighty-five percent of my time is spent face-to-face with client personnel, ranging from sales reps to VPs of Sales and IS. They're investing millions in hardware and software that is very visible in their organizations. They want to know whom they're dealing with. I have been a pharmaceutical sales rep and field manager, and know what information the client's sales force wants. I also bring client personnel to meet our technical people, business managers, and customer service reps, and have them talk to the people that staff our Help lines.

Clients usually ranked vendors on the basis of ease of use, functionality, connectivity with other company systems, financial strength, and commitment to product development since an installed system involved continual maintenance and new technology applications. The "short list" of potential vendors generally included at least three firms. Also, while most pharmaceutical firms were interested in ETM systems, their goals often varied by geographical market.

In the *United States* (about 30% of worldwide pharmaceutical sales and 60% of Dendrite sales in 1992), pharmaceutical sales forces were among the largest in the world, ranging from 500 to more than 3,000 reps per firm. Sales reps called on medical personnel every four to six weeks to leave product samples and literature, perform service tasks, and (especially in private office segments) build relationships with prescribing physicians. A Dendrite manager explained, "U.S. managers are concerned with customer profile data such as prescribing patterns, medical specializations, and patient volume. In evaluating field productivity, they tend to focus on call frequency as well as sales in the rep's territory for higher-margin products."

In *Western Europe* (32% of pharmaceutical sales), sales forces were generally 100 to 200 reps in size, with the largest being 700. Government funding of health care and large, managed-care organizations were common. Most of these organizations had established "formularies" (lists of approved drugs from which their employee physicians could choose) and also restricted the activities of pharmaceutical reps with prescribing physicians. "In Europe," a Dendrite manager noted, "pharmaceutical reps generally see a given doctor once per year, always by appointment, and can only leave one sample. This places more marketing emphasis on advertising, direct mail, medical meetings and conferences, and on the information flows relevant to linking all people in the vendor organization who have contacts with managed care personnel." Bruce Savage, Dendrite's VP for Europe, commented:

Europe requires more product customization due to language and regulatory differences by country. Also, European clients are more price sensitive. It's often easier for a U.S. pharmaceutical executive to justify a budget request for a 2000-person sales force than it is for the European executive to do this for a 200-person sales force. Postsale, we require about $1,300 per user to cover the personnel costs on our client support teams, and smaller sales forces mean fewer economies of scope in ongoing maintenance and service tasks.

In *Japan* (18% of pharmaceutical sales), sales force sizes were like those in the United States and, with fewer doctors, there was one pharmaceutical salesperson in Japan for every six physicians. Twenty U.S. pharmaceutical firms employed about 6,300 reps in Japan.

In the United States and Europe, physicians prescribed but did not dispense (or sell) drugs to patients. In Japan, physicians had historically combined prescribing and dispensing functions. Sales reps typically negotiated prices with individual physicians, who often received fees from pharmaceutical firms based on the number of prescriptions written. Many Japanese physicians also derived income from using free samples with patients and then submitting the prescription record to the government for reimbursement. Hence, abundant samples (often provided through allied wholesalers) were an accepted part of the selling process. In addition, most Japanese doctors worked in clinics or hospitals which required sales reps to wait outside to see the doctor. One result, a Dendrite executive explained, is that "social selling is very important in Japan. Reps develop face time with doctors by washing their cars, entertaining them, and running all sorts of errands. In turn, tracking these expenses is a key task for Japanese pharmaceutical firms. Daily call reports involve detailed information about the hospital, doctor, samples distributed, and any gifts or other expense-item tasks performed." Bill Magee, Dendrite's VP for Asia, added:

In the United States and Europe, our ratio of support staff to client sales reps is 1:200, but 1:100 in Japan due to the emphasis on personal service. We generally don't make money with a Japanese client until the second or third year. Also, while we're the only vendor with a fully operational Kanji system, there's a bias here toward doing business with Japanese-owned firms.

Market Developments

In 1992, spending on prescription drugs in the United States was about $50 billion and, as a portion of medical spending, had declined from 16% in the 1960s to 7% by 1990. However, U.S. health care costs had grown to over $900 billion by 1992, more than 14% of GNP. President Clinton had made health care a key issue in his campaign and had appointed a task force to draft legislation. The task force had singled out drugs for attention and, in mid-1993, was reviewing various options. While the eventual outcome of any government action was unclear, most observers believed that more managed-care facilities was a likely outcome in the United States.

Managed care referred to institutions such as HMOs that limited a patient's choice of doctor and hospital(s), used centralized buying and formularies to lower product acquisition costs, and eschewed traditional fee-for-service physician compensation in favor of cost controls aimed at diagnosing and treating ailments with fewer tests and visits. By 1993, 56% of Americans in group health plans were enrolled in managed care networks, up from 29% in 1988. Forecasts indicated that, by 1995, 20% of prescription sales in the United States would be from pharmacies in managed care facilities and another 35% via contracts between retail pharmacies and managed care institutions that employ hundreds of staff physicians. One observer commented:

> Admission to the formulary will depend on physicians' input, but will be heavily influenced by administrators interested in price, cost-in-use, and added value services in addition to product safety and efficacy. Also, the many doctors practicing in both managed care and private-office settings are unlikely to sustain different prescribing habits for their patients. So a firm with products on the formulary also has access to another large market.
>
> Many managed-care firms are also developing information systems to track prescribing practices for each patient and physician and to develop therapy guidelines. Physicians who continually prescribe outside the guidelines will be questioned and may suffer economic penalties. Conversely, pharmaceutical firms will face greater demands for comparative data and cost-benefit information as a prerequisite for formulary admission.

In this environment, pharmaceutical sales forces in the United States will be downsized. After R&D, the Sales organization represents the largest fixed asset investment of a pharmaceutical company. The targets for their activities will drop from 250,000–300,000 individual physicians to about 35,000 committees. The optimum size of the field force for a major pharmaceutical firm operating in the United States may be 400 to 700 reps, rather than 1,500 or more.

In Europe, managed care was already more common than in the United States, but pharmaceutical spending was a bigger portion of health care costs than in the United States. In response, many European countries were imposing price controls and other regulations. In early 1993, Germany imposed reimbursement regulations that resulted in a 27% reduction in prescriptions in the first month and a 32% reduction in the second. In the United Kingdom, there was a trend toward more centralized buying of health care products, including drugs. In response, noted one observer, "pharmaceutical firms in Europe may move toward even smaller, more specialized sales forces focused on a given product or therapeutic area."

In Japan in 1992, fixed-invoice pricing for pharmaceuticals was mandated and wholesaler rebating abolished. Under the previous system, wholesalers were reimbursed by manufacturers for supplying products to customers at prices below manufacturers' list price. Under the new system, manufacturers were barred from intervening in wholesaler/customer price negotiations. Japan also instituted caps on health care reimbursement, including drugs, and was moving toward the separation of prescribing and dispensing for pharmaceuticals. One observer commented:

> Sales reps can no longer discuss product prices and discounts with physicians, and more attention must be paid to wholesalers. They must place more emphasis on the therapeutic qualities of their companies' products. Reimbursement caps make Japanese clinics and hospitals more price sensitive, and the separation of dispensing and prescribing by doctors would alter pharmaceutical sales tasks. Samples become a less effective device for building relationships; product and market information becomes more pertinent; and pharmaceutical firms would also need to develop and coordinate distribution to more pharmacies and other drug suppliers. That may mean more reps.

Worldwide, there were fewer "blockbuster" drugs in the product pipelines of many firms. Of the 30 biggest selling drugs in the United States, for instance, 14 would be off-patent by the end of 1996, leaving billions in annual sales vulnerable to lower-priced generic competition. A Dendrite executive commented: "Pharmaceutical sales forces expanded in the 1980s, fueled by patented products whose margins made increased selling resources possible and desirable. But companies without such products are less likely to add to their already sizable distribution costs."

Organization

Exhibit 5 outlines Dendrite's organization in 1993. Reporting to John Bailye were vice presidents for each geographical area as well as controller, planning, and technical services (responsible for new product development and support and maintenance of core code). Client teams in each country reported to their area vice president.

Sales

"We have two types of sales activities," noted one executive, "initial sales to clients and follow-on sales to existing accounts." Initial sales were handled by salespeople, all of whom had previous experience in the pharmaceutical industry, supplemented by the area vice presidents. Salesperson compensation involved a base salary, and a commission based on both the dollar volume of the contract and account profitability; sales commissions were paid only after the annual budget for that client team had been achieved, not when the contract was signed. Incentive compensation in 1992 averaged about 30% of the salesperson's total compensation. One salesperson commented:

In a customized software business, no two client situations are identical. Hence, we must be flexible in pricing, delivery dates, and the array of services and support we offer to clients in order to close a sale. This is especially true for a global supplier. Many corporate pharmaceutical executives want to negotiate pricing on a global basis. And for us, multiyear contracts in several countries are attractive. But their country managers are usually very protective of their autonomy. That means many changes in our system for each country at the same client. So, while we in Sales may negotiate a price that assumes standardized reports across a client's countries, postsale margins may suffer as many changes are required to get and keep the system in a country organization.

I ultimately can't control client demands, and this is a very competitive business where we tend to be the high-service/premium-priced supplier. Also, the sell-

ing process involves working across Sales, IS, and other client functions for a major capital expense which attracts board of director attention. I don't want to see a multimillion dollar agreement killed because of a quarrel about an additional $50,000 worth of applications or support service.

As well as managing client teams, Business Managers (BMs) were responsible for business development at existing accounts. Incremental sales were made by adding users to the system and/or application modules (priced on a per-user basis) as user feedback revealed additional client needs. A Dendrite executive noted: "Facilities management allows us to collect information about clients' changing business demands. The BM's task is to provide, from our range of modules, the applications most pertinent to their evolving concerns. They are in an ideal position to identify ongoing sales-enhancement tools."

Dendrite had 20 BMs in 1993. Most had a technical background and experience in operations or IS project management, usually outside the pharmaceutical industry. Their compensation involved a base salary and a bonus based on achieving financial and customer satisfaction goals (based on quarterly surveys of customers). Each client team was a profit center, and BMs were responsible for managing expenses. One BM noted:

Postsale, my major contacts are with the client's IS managers. I soon know more about their user needs than they do. For example, the field data we collect is very relevant to their Product Management and Market Research functions, and can also help Finance and Procurement manage supplies and other expenses. These areas often don't realize that Dendrite is a data and communications source. IS is very leery about vendor personnel approaching other functions and acts as a strong gatekeeper. A BM must be a good technical analyst in order to identify applications opportunities and then an accomplished diplomat in order to sell any opportunity to and beyond IS.

Meanwhile, my primary job is managing services for clients and account profitability for Dendrite. I'm usually brought in after price negotiations with the client and so "inherit" what Sales has negotiated. In an increasingly cost-conscious environment, Sales often agrees to provide applications, services, and delivery dates with less attention than I'd like to the costs, headcount, and deadlines involved. Most of my postsales time is absorbed by the efforts required to deliver on these agreements and still break even on the project.

Client Teams

Upon an agreement with a client, Dendrite formed a dedicated team responsible for customized applications, hardware connections, pilot testing, roll-out, and then ongoing maintenance and management of the account (Exhibit 6). Team size was related to the number of users and ranged from 3 to 50 members, with an average of 22 people. Each team was headed by a BM and included Customer Support (CS) and Technical Support (TS) managers. Annual fully burdened costs for the BM, one TS rep, and one CS rep were more than $250,000, with additional costs for additional technical and service personnel dedicated to the account.

In the project phase, TS managers defined, customized, and installed the system on the client's hardware and computer network. TS also helped clients in purchasing equipment from vendors and managed Dendrite's leased-equipment program. After rollout, TS managers focused on system maintenance which involved system backups, communications support, data security, ongoing software enhancements, and 24-hour service for any hardware or system problems. In the project phase, CS managers developed system documentation, company-specific training materials and service manuals, and user training programs at client sites. One CS manager noted:

> The field reception of an ETM system is a function of how the client's corporate headquarters has "sold" the system, and we're there to help in this process. When it's been sold well, reps see the system as a tool that can help them, not a big-brother device to micro-manage their activities. Also, it takes about one month for a rep to use the system efficiently, and our role is to accelerate this learning curve.

After rollout, CS managers focused on the telephone Help lines dedicated to that client. Help lines were available to users from 8:00–5:00 P.M. daily (in each time zone) and in the United States averaged 400 calls per month per client. A CS rep explained that "Help line calls range from questions about software or malfunctioning power cords to requests for data. We receive training about the client's product line and, during rollout, quickly become familiar to the client's field reps. They will call to discuss marketing ideas, suggestions about reformatting a report, or other matters." In general, there was one CS rep and one TS rep for every 200 system users at clients.

Exhibit 7 outlines BM responsibilities. Before rollout, BMs worked closely with client IS and Sales Administration managers on system design, installation, and training. After rollout, BMs worked on ongoing customization, new or add-on modules to be incorporated in the system, and (with client IS managers) on evaluating the reception and effectiveness of the system.

One BM noted that "Clients basically want two things from the BM: that you really listen and care; and that you do everything else yesterday." Another noted that "As a rule of thumb, a cost-effective client team needs a minimum of 400 users. That makes European clients especially challenging from a P&L point of view. We have shared client teams, but that limits the levels and types of service you can provide." A third BM commented that "An ongoing issue in account management is guarding against 'service creep': most contracts negotiated with clients stipulate a flat fee per user, and clients have a tendency to ask for more and more services under this flat fee arrangement. If BMs were involved earlier in the sales process, we could identify this and try to price service more appropriately." A Dendrite executive commented:

> There's a shift in the BM's role from consultant during project development and installation, to service provider and account manager after rollout. The service role tends to be focused on daily firefighting tasks across a client's many field locations. These concerns make IS the key contact for BMs; and IS tends to focus on minimizing software bugs and hassles, not on business goals. Their measure of success is our product's technical performance, not productivity improvements or enhancements. In fact, for IS, enhancements run the risk of generating problems (for which they are blamed) and not just more sales calls or revenues (for which Sales or Marketing get credit). That's one reason IS managers don't like BMs talking to other departments.

Current Issues

Commenting on Dendrite in mid-1993, Bailye said: "Technology and customer concerns are dynamic. New programming tools make it possible for six computer jockeys in a garage to reverse-engineer basic software and sell it more cheaply. The pharmaceutical industry is poised for a shift in many countries. Meanwhile, what we can do with our own product-service offering has also changed, and that raises fundamental strategic choices."

Bailye was considering several alternative routes of potential company growth: into other markets besides pharmaceuticals, into other functional areas within pharmaceutical clients, or "deeper" into sales and marketing applications in the current target market.

Most sales automation vendors targeted multiple markets besides pharmaceuticals, including insurance, consumer package goods, and other industries that relied on large field forces to sell products. Some managers believed that Dendrite should also expand into other vertical markets. "We have both offensive and defensive reasons to do this," noted one manager. "On the one hand, our software remains among the best for sales reporting and data dissemination, and specific formats can be customized for various industries. On the other hand, with fewer large pharmaceutical field forces available, the economics of our current market are changing. Also, the entry point for new vendors is typically smaller field forces, and we should expect increasingly heavy competition for pharmaceutical clients."

Estimates indicated that $10 million would be required to adapt core code and facilities management services to another industry's selling tasks, implying some time before a market entry would break even for Dendrite. This investment could be reduced substantially if development focused on stand-alone software with little or no support services provided by Dendrite.

Another possibility was to expand into other functional areas within pharmaceutical firms. One manager noted that "We are now the link between our clients' sales reps and their I.S. and sales administration managers. But the data we collect and disseminate has enormous cross-functional value for clients, and we can be the link between other departments and ongoing field sales and customer activity data. As sales force sizes decrease, we must evolve from a sales planning to a management information tool at clients." Another manager emphasized:

Both technological and customer developments support this strategy. Network technologies, which allow computers to share data, are spreading throughout industry, making cross-functional linkages more accessible. And, for pharmaceutical firms in particular, selling to big managed-care organizations will require better information links between field sales, national account groups, product marketing, finance, and distribution. We are now experts about a critical node in these evolving networks and should capitalize on our position.

Dendrite had under development a managed-care module for its current system, and estimated additional core-code development costs of $2-$5 million depending upon the number of areas covered by a cross-functional approach. However, other managers wondered about the selling and service requirements inherent in this approach, and noted that competition would include multinational information consulting firms that were much larger than Dendrite and already had long-standing relationships beyond IS and Sales departments in clients.

A third option was to continue concentrating on sales applications and product enhancements that increased Dendrite's value to pharmaceutical clients. One manager noted:

The United States may be a mature market for sales automation, but not Europe or Japan. Also, some competitors are beginning to link with industry data providers, and we must continue to add value to our system through module applications and support. Pharmaceutical firms are very protective of their databases and there's a limit to how far they will let *any* vendor into their organization. To be successful, we must link our initiatives to sales automation because that's our base and identity in these firms.

Dendrite could develop many product extensions, including computer-based training modules, additional analysis and performance evaluation systems, multimedia applications that allowed for individualized sales presentations tied to on-line data sources, and use of current software for palm-sized computers expected to be introduced in coming years. Development costs for these enhancements were generally $1 million and often shared with current clients interested in expanding sales force applications.

Another issue facing the company was the coordination of Dendrite's sales and service efforts and possible changes in the role of the Business Manager. Many believed that the current arrangement immersed BMs in daily operations with little time to develop business opportunities. They proposed the addition of an Operations Manager to client teams, responsible for day-to-day technical and customer support issues. Costs of such a position would be comparable to those for the BM position. One executive commented:

Growing an account requires a strategic rather than tactical focus, and contacts beyond IS and sales administration. Ideally, we would want two project teams: one for development/installation phases and one for on-going support. Now, however, the installation phase identifies the BM as the tactician who handles all the details and ties that person closely to IS, who doesn't want the BM "wasting" time with other functional areas. The Operations Manager position would free BMs from daily firefighting and allow them to sell to other areas at the client. It would also create a career path for CS and TS managers to become Operations Managers and subsequently grow into a BM role.

Others were uncertain about the impact of this proposal on service provision during the various phases from initial proposal to installation and ongoing operations. They argued for involving BMs earlier in the process, before contracts are signed. "If involved during the first draft of an agreement," said one manager, "a BM can impact the product configuration and deliverables, recognize the true costs of postsale service, and establish relationships with the other client personnel who get involved before a contract is signed but who tend not to interact with our client teams after the contract is signed." Still others questioned whether BMs had the skills or temperament required for selling new business. One manager commented: "People should do what they do best. BMs' strengths are in project management and fixing problems. Even with sales training, they will remain operations managers. And, given developments in our customer base, they will need to manage ongoing service and support costs even more tightly."

Reflecting on these options, John Bailye commented:

We are financing the business from ongoing operations and our venture backers will eventually look to reap returns on their investments via an IPO. Hence, growth remains important even as we face an environment where there are lots of forecasts but no certainties. Should we grow within the sales function across geographies, into other departments at global clients, or into new vertical markets? What are the implications for BMs and the organization of our account management activities? And how do possible changes at pharmaceutical firms affect current and future strategy? I want Dendrite working on those areas that will yield the best return over the long haul.

Exhibit 1 Consolidated Statements of Operations for Year Ended December 31, 1992
and Period September 1, 1991 (Date of Reorganization) to December 31, 1991 ($'000s)

	1992	1991
– Operating revenues	$23,300	$ 4,853
– Cost and expenses	20,953	5,647
– Operating profit (loss)	2,347	(794)
– Other income (expense):	(8)	(35)
– Interest expense	71	7
– Other	63	(28)
– Income taxes:		
– Reduction of income taxes from net operating loss carryforwards	286	—
– Net income (loss)	$ 1,161	(822)
Consolidated Balance Sheets, December 31, 1992 and 1991 ($'000s)		
Assets		
– Current Assets:		
– Cash and cash equivalents	600	874
– Trade accounts receivable	5,063	1,762
– Prepaid expenses and other current assets	669	479
– Deferred tax assets	80	—
– Total Current Assets	6,412	3,115
– Fixed assets, net of accumulated depreciation	1,699	1,448
– Intangible assets, net of accumulated amortization	2,106	2,688
– Organization costs, net of accumulated amortization	2,106	2,688
– Capitalized software development costs	895	30
	$11,204	$ 7,398
Liabilities and Stockholders' Equity		
– Current Liabilities:		
– Trade accounts payable and other current liabilities	$ 2,825	$ 1,464
– Current installments of lease obligations	65	26
– Current portion of deferred revenues	2,050	120
– Current income taxes payable	270	—
– Total Current Liabilities	5,210	2,710
– Obligations under capital leases	41	31
– Deferred revenues, excluding current portion	110	146
– Deferred tax liabilities	435	—
– Total Liabilities	5,796	2,887
– Stockholders' Equity:		
– Common stock, no par value	3	3
– Retained earnings (accumulated deficit)	339	(822)
– Equity adjustment for foreign currency translation	(445)	(94)
– Less consideration to former stockholder of acquired business in excess of his basis in net assets sold	(1,364)	(1,364)
– Total Stockholders' Equity	5,408	4,511
	$11,204	$ 7,398

Exhibit 2

SaleStar™ is a turn-key system of user-friendly software, hardware and support services that enables you to turn information management into increased productivity. Developed by Dendrite International, Inc., SaleStar™ is backed by the same focus on client service and support that has made Dendrite the leader in state-of-the-art electronic territory management systems for the global pharmaceutical industry.

FEATURES	BENEFITS
Call Planning	Enables sales representatives to improve productivity and performance by providing strategy to the call planning process.
Customer Profiles	Enables sales representatives to increase the productivity of every call by providing easy access to vital information (e.g., demographics, call history, pre- and post-call analysis, prescribing profile) on all their accounts.
Call Reporting	Enables sales representatives to easily and effectively track and communicate information from each sales call.
Customer Targeting	Easy manipulation of customer information enables sales representatives to target customers strategically based on a variety of criteria (e.g., best times to call, hospital department, affiliation, rating, call frequency, etc.)
Sample Tracking	Enables the home office to assess current and future sample needs, adjust marketing plans, determine how well a product is being received, and meet regulatory requirements.
Report Viewing	Provides sales representatives and managers easy and timely access to internal and third-party information such as product pricing, sales data and comprehensive management reports.
Third-Party Information	Provides sales representatives with up-to-date micro-marketing data on customer and industry profiles. (Information may be gained from several sources, including Scriptrac, AMA, SMG, and others.)
Expense Forms/ Weekly Attendance	Enables sales representatives to spend more time on sales by making administrative reporting faster and easier.
Meeting Planning & Recording	Enables sales representatives to easily and effectively plan, record and review information gained from peer programs, focus groups, or multiple customer presentations.
Electronic Mail	Provides managers and sales representatives with daily access to a reliable communication tool that doesn't depend on memos or telephone calls.

CUSTOMER SUPPORT SERVICES ★

	SALESTAR™ SERVICES
Field User/Manager Support	
Help Line	✔
"How to" Instructions	✔
Log-in Advice	✔
Dendrite Log-in Reports	✔
System Disk Request	✔
System Utilities	✔
Profile Q & A	✔
Profile Addition/Deletion/Move	✔
Correct Entry Error	✔
E-mail Support	✔
Rep. Tracking	✔
Call Tracking	✔
Home Office Support	
Reports QC/QA	✔
Reports Distribution	✔
Help Desk	✔
Field Support-Home Office	✔
Realignment Support	✔
Client Meetings	✔
Hardware Services	
Field Hardware Support	✔
Hardware Diagnosis	✔
Hardware Replacement Request	✔
Hardware Tracking	✔

TECHNICAL SUPPORT SERVICES ★

	SALESTAR™ SERVICES
System Administration - Hardware	
Daily, Weekly, Monthly Back-ups	✔
Communications Support	✔
Off-Site Storage	✔
System Security	✔
Laptop Support	✔
System Administration - Software	
Transaction Processing	✔
File Structure /Source Code Maintenance	✔
E-mail Administration	✔
Software Defect Resolution	✔
Help/Screen File Updates	✔
Processing/Dist. of Suite of Reports	✔
Customer Support Services	
Error Correction	✔
Data Issues	✔
Sales and Marketing Support	
Territory Realignments	✔
Third Party Data Updates	✔
Data Extracts	✔
Reports Generation, Processing & Dist.	✔

Exhibit 3 Project Pricing and Costs: Examples (in thousands, for twelve months ended December 1992)

	"Small" = client with < 400 users ; "Large" = client with 1,500+ users	
	Small	Large
– *Sales:*		
– One-time license fees[a]	–	–
– Service fees	–	–
– Customization	–	–
– Implementation	–	–
– Software maintenance	–	–
– Hardware support	–	–
– In-house publishing		–
– Other	–	–
Total Revenue	$891.6	$3,244.0
Cost of Sales	$489.5	$1,753.2
Gross Margin	$402.1	$1,490.8
Gross Margin (%)	45.1%	46.0%
– *Operating Expenses:*		
– Repair/Maintenance	–	–
– Travel	–	–
– Entertainment	–	–
– Supplies/Computer supplies	–	–
– Personnel	–	–
– Hardware support		–
– In-house publishing		–
– Overhead allocation	–	–
Total Expenses	**$370.9**	**$ 962.6**
Project Trading Profit	$ 31.2	$ 528.2
– *Headcount (Dendrite Client Team)*	7.00	20.30

[a]These examples represent established clients. In year one of these projects, software license fees were 50%–60% of revenues.

Exhibit 4 Estimated ETM Market Size (1992)

	United States	Western Europe[a]	Japan	Rest of World	Total
Number of reps	44,000	70,000	42,000	44,000	200,000
Number of reps automated	35,331	5,683	2,760	N/A	43,774
Percent automated	80.3%	8.1%	6.6%	N/A	21.9%
Number automated by Dendrite	7,893	2,467	2,305	0	12,665
Number automated by other firms and internal sources	27,438	3,216	455	N/A	31,109

[a]Western Europe includes England, France, Germany, Italy, Spain and the Benelux countries.

Exhibit 5

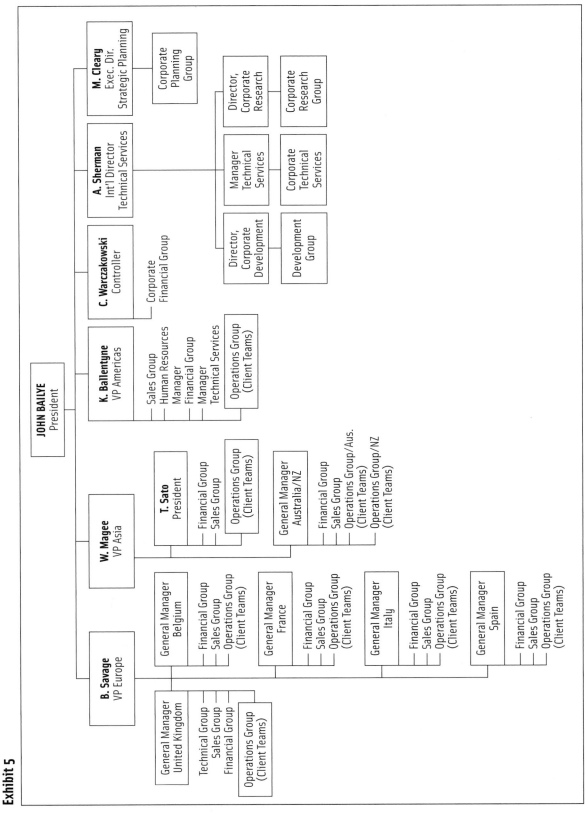

Exhibit 6

Project Life Cycle

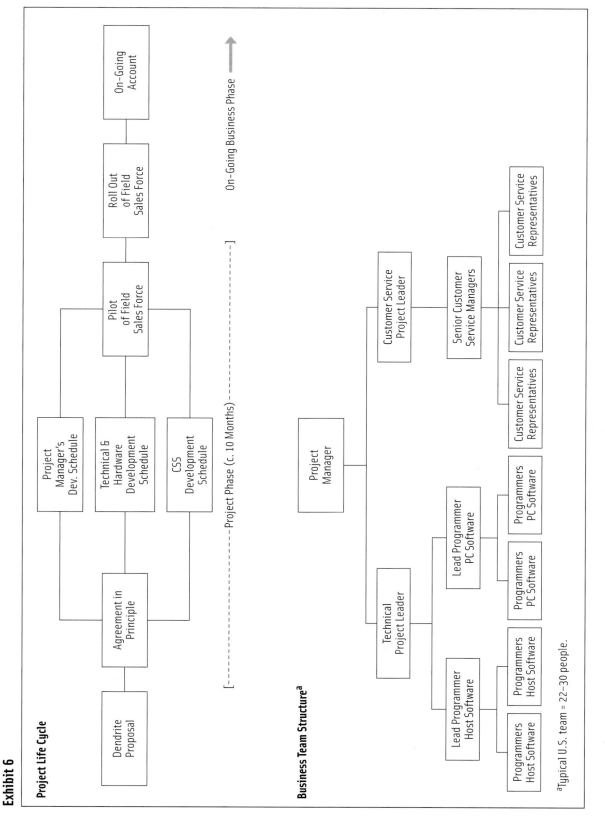

```
Dendrite        Agreement in        Project            Pilot          Roll Out       On-Going
Proposal        Principle           Manager's          of Field       of Field       Account
                                    Dev. Schedule      Sales Force    Sales Force

                                    Technical &
                                    Hardware
                                    Development
                                    Schedule

                                    CSS
                                    Development
                                    Schedule
```

[-------- Project Phase (c. 10 Months) --------]

On-Going Business Phase

Business Team Structure[a]

```
                              Project
                              Manager

        Technical                                    Customer Service
        Project Leader                               Project Leader

Lead Programmer    Lead Programmer                   Senior Customer
Host Software      PC Software                        Service Managers

Programmers        Programmers    Programmers    Customer Service    Customer Service    Customer Service
Host Software      PC Software    PC Software    Representatives     Representatives     Representatives

Programmers
Host Software
```

[a]Typical U.S. team = 22–30 people.

Exhibit 7 Business Manager's Project Responsibilities

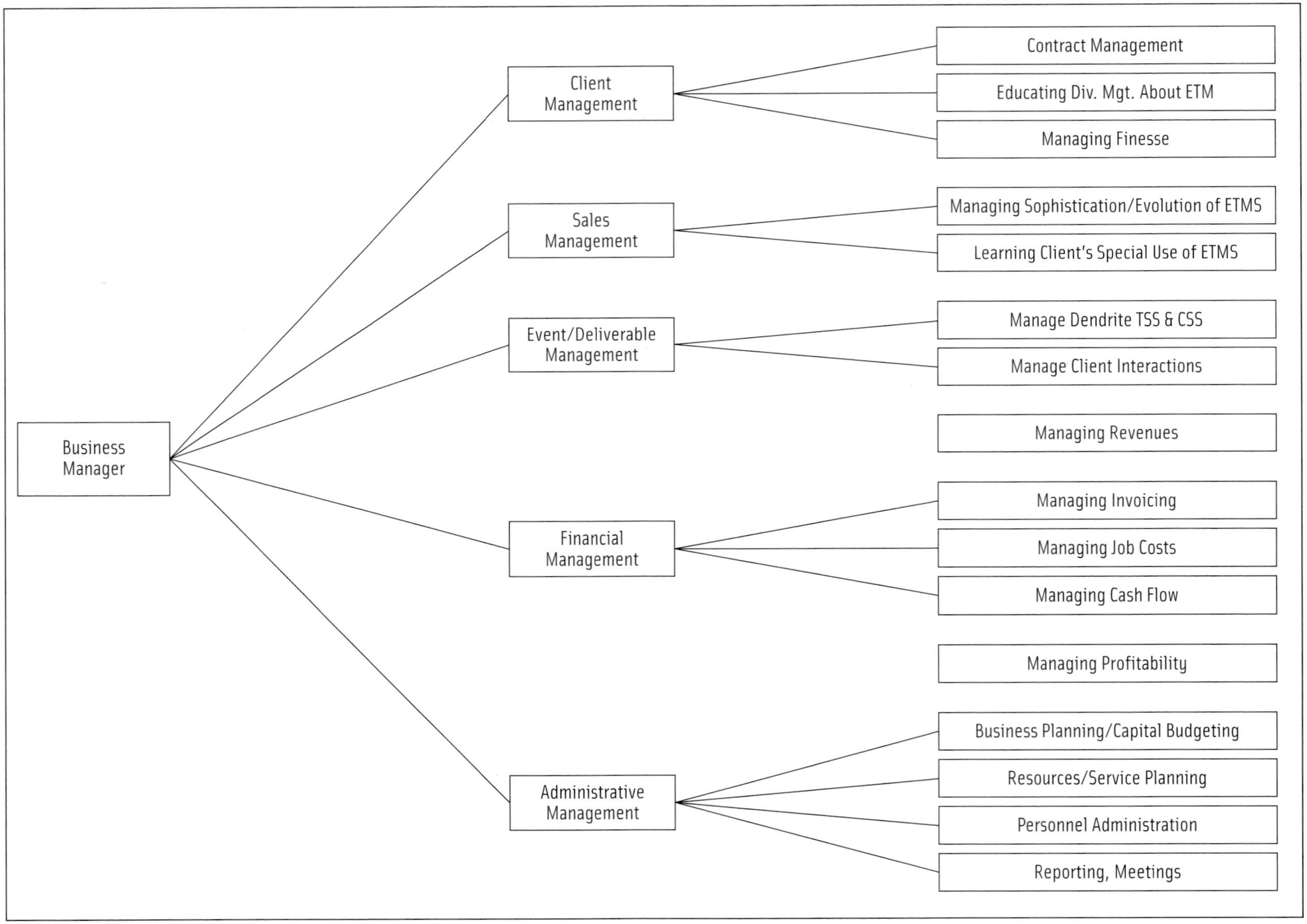

Client Management
- Contract Management
- Educating Div. Mgt. About ETM
- Managing Finesse

Sales Management
- Managing Sophistication/Evolution of ETMS
- Learning Client's Special Use of ETMS

Event/Deliverable Management
- Manage Dendrite TSS & CSS
- Manage Client Interactions

Financial Management
- Managing Revenues
- Managing Invoicing
- Managing Job Costs
- Managing Cash Flow
- Managing Profitability

Administrative Management
- Business Planning/Capital Budgeting
- Resources/Service Planning
- Personnel Administration
- Reporting, Meetings

Business Manager

HENKEL GROUP: UMBRELLA BRANDING AND GLOBALIZATION DECISIONS

At Henkel Group, headquartered in Dusseldorf, West Germany, brand names were a highly valued asset. For example, the company's Persil brand detergent, introduced in 1907, was one of the most widely known and respected brand names in Europe. As marketing director of Henkel's Chemical Technical Products for Craftsmen and Do-It-Yourselfers (HD/BC), Gunther von Briskorn was custodian of two of Henkel's most important brands: Pritt and Pattex. In early 1981, von Briskorn was concerned about the performance of these household adhesives on an international basis. He was considering a radical change in brand strategy. As he discussed with Wolfgang Heck, his group product manager for Craftsman/DIY/Household Adhesives, and Mr. Heck's assistant for Household Adhesives, Herbert Tossing:

> Mr. Heck, if we are to be successful in Germany and the rest of the world, we must find an innovative approach. These adhesive markets are small to begin with and now we are seeing increased fragmentation and specialization. Our friends in the detergent group do not face the same issues. Every country market they go into has a large, not strongly segmented detergent market. They can afford a policy of one brand for one product. The brand philosophy which has been successful for them has not been successful for us—we must develop greater coordination between the individual products we sell and the individual country markets we sell them in. Please get together with Mr. Printz (the HD/BC advertising manager assigned to von Briskorn's group) to develop some ideas on how we can move in the direction of greater coordination across products and markets.

This case was prepared by Associate Professor Robert J. Dolan as the basis for class discussion rather than to illustrate either effective or ineffective handling of an administrative situation.

In July 1981, six months of work researching and thinking about the problem had resulted in a proposed strategy which would fundamentally change HD/BC marketing practices. The strategy embodied two major concepts: umbrella branding (i.e., developing an integrated strategy for the marketing of a variety of products under each of the two brand names) and global standardization of the umbrella. As von Briskorn considered the proposal he had developed, he recognized that both concepts underlying the strategy were counter to the traditional "each product/each country profit center on its own" philosophy of the Henkel Group. Second, Dr. Roman Dohr, head of the Adhesives and Chemical Auxiliaries Division, had expressed concern about the umbrella branding aspects. In his own mind, von Briskorn knew the strategy was not without risk. Both Tossing (who became product manager when Heck was given a U.S. assignment in connection with Henkel's acquisition of Ross Chemical in Detroit) and Printz had raised quite valid concerns in laying out the "pros and cons" of the strategy. In view of the importance of the decision, von Briskorn resolved to consider all the evidence once again in resolving the issues he faced:

- Does the umbrella branding concept make sense for the household adhesives markets?

- Does it make sense specifically for the two brand names? Which products could be put under each umbrella?

- Is it possible to globalize an umbrella strategy?

- How could a global/umbrella strategy be implemented?

- What are the alternatives if we decide not to follow this strategy?

Henkel Group

In 1980, the over 8000 products sold by the Henkel Group yielded sales revenues of DM 6.9 billion. The family-owned company, founded by Fritz Henkel as a bleaching powder company in 1876, had grown to over 100 operating companies in more than 40 countries. The international scope of the company resulted in 60% of sales being outside Germany.

The diverse product line was sold by eight groups:

1. Detergents and Cleaning Agents
2. Personal Care Products and Cosmetics
3. Household Care Products
4. Adhesives
5. Inorganic Chemicals
6. Organic Chemicals
7. Foodstuffs
8. Packaging

The common element through the groups was a reliance on "chemistry in production." Top management considered Henkel to be "specialists in applying chemistry to the needs of the consumer, of institutions, of industry, and of craftsmen."

Adhesives represented a major growth opportunity for Henkel. In 1980, the adhesives product line contained over 800 products and generated sales of approximately DM 1.2 billion. As shown in Exhibit 1, the Adhesives Division had three groups:

1. Industrial Adhesives
2. Leather and Textile Auxiliaries
3. HD/BC: Chemical Technical Products for Craftsmen and Do-It-Yourself Markets/Building Chemical (in German, Handwerk/DIY/Bauchemie, hence the HD/BC abbreviation)

The pattern of new product development in the Adhesives group was typically to develop a product for industrial and craftsman use and then adapt it to the household market if possible. Despite the focus on industrial sectors for new product development, the HD/BC group accounted for 57% of Henkel's adhesives sales. The 15 items in the HD/BC product line are shown in Exhibit 2. These products were targeted to a variety of users, representing very different levels of product performance requirements and product knowledge. Main target groups included (see column 2):

As a consequence, HD/BC employed a broad array of distribution channels (see Exhibit 3) ranging from lumberyards to supermarkets.

Gunther von Briskorn explained the major marketing problems facing HD/BC:

Craftsmen	Households	Other
Painter	DIY-ers	Office
Decorator	Hobbyists	School
Paperhanger	"Moonlighters"	Kindergartens
Carpenter		
Shoemaker		
Floor coverer		
Bricklayer		
Metalworker		
Plumber		

As you can see from the number of products we sell and the channels we use, we face selling into very deeply segmented markets. Some of our users are very sophisticated—the craftsman usually has a very specific need, so we have to have the product out there to meet that need. For example, take our SISTA sealants product line. We have four different types of sealant: bathtub, glass, joints and cracks, and "multipurpose" because of differing needs. Then, you need different colors and package sizes—all told, we have 47 different type/color/package combinations. So, the craftsman coming into the store knows what he's looking for and we have it. But look what this does to our other market—households. This poor fellow probably buys sealants once a year, does not know anything about sealants. He comes into the store knowing he needs something to fix a drafty window—but he doesn't know if he should use tape or an adhesive or what. He may not even know what sealants are. And we give him four different types to choose from! So, first we have to educate him what to buy and then how to apply it—and all this on a small communications budget because it's a low expenditure per capita item.

Of course, our international strategy adds a second dimension to the problem. We sell the Pritt line in 15 European countries and 50 outside Europe. So, the "small markets" problem we see due to the low purchase frequency and deep segmentation in Germany is really compounded when we go into a market like Finland, where there just are not that many people. That's why I think we have to get multiple use out of our own resources—by umbrella branding and global standardization where possible.

We face strong competition from Uhu, now owned by Beecham. Historically, there were two main segments of the craftsman/DIY market: contact adhesives for heavy jobs and "all-purpose" adhesives for jobs not requiring great bonding strength. We dominated the contact adhesive segment with our Pattex brand originally oriented to the craftsman and Uhu dominated the all-purpose segment with its more consumer-oriented products. In 1969, we attacked their light duty market by offering the Pritt Glue Stick. Uhu was not yet offering a contact adhesive although they did come after us in that segment four years later with Uhu Greenit adhesive. Ever since then there has been brand proliferation and greater segmentation of the market.

Pattex Brand

Pattex held the "strength adhesive" positioning within HD/BC. Launched in 1956 as a contact adhesive for the professional, Pattex penetrated the household and DIY segments as well and became the leading contact adhesive in West Germany. The bonding strength required for the professional market, e.g., furniture and leather workers, necessitated a somewhat messy, drippy-with-strings formulation. By 1973, HD/BC was able to serve the DIY market better with a nondripping formulation, which sacrificed bonding strength to convenience. Pattex Compact, as the brand was called, was positioned as "The Clean and Powerful Adhesive." It was supported by an introductory advertising campaign of DM 2 million on television. It proved to be a good extension to the line, allowing Henkel to penetrate new segments rather than cannibalizing the original Pattex.

In 1980, Henkel held 80% of the contact adhesive market in West Germany (with sales split equally between Pattex and Pattex Compact). Brand awareness in West Germany topped 80% and trade support was excellent. Over 65% of Pattex sales came from outside Germany as Pattex was distributed in more than 50 countries worldwide. Total Pattex sales were approximately DM 66 million worldwide.

While worldwide sales increased during the late 1970s, sales in the West German market had stagnated (see

Exhibit 4). Since Pattex was probably the second most important brand name within Henkel (next to Persil), Gunther von Briskorn was concerned about the performance as he assumed the HD/BC marketing director position in April 1979. Von Briskorn explained the situation:

> We were basically experiencing product life cycle problems. We had a pretty traditional technology—while we were holding our share of the contact adhesive market based on the Pattex technology, we were being attacked by alternative technologies. Probably the most important of these was the cyanoacrylates or CAs, the "Superglues" as people called them. In some respects they were super—offering a one-minute curing time as compared to Pattex's ten minutes plus they were being offered by strong companies like Uhu and Loctite. At this time, we were selling lots of CAs to industrial users, but we were really concerned about offering it as a consumer product for health reasons. Anyway, these more modern technologies really hurt us—we had a great brand name in Pattex, but the product/technology attached to it was weakening.

During 1980, Henkel responded to Uhu and Loctite's CA progress by introducing their own CA brand: Stabilit Rasant. However, the brand was given very little advertising support since it was a late entrant and some health concerns still remained within Henkel. Von Briskorn described the situation in early 1981:

> It was pretty clear where the contact adhesive market was going—there were new, innovative growth segments popping up and attacking the "general purpose" contact adhesives like Pattex. First there were the Superglues, then the Two Component Glues. Also, we saw some potential for moving the hot melt technology from the industrial sphere to the consumer end. We already saw this occur in the U.S. and some small companies were offering it in Europe—but with no clear brand profile yet emerging.

Pritt Brand

Through the 1960s, the dominant company in the consumer adhesive market in Germany was Uhu. Introduced in 1932, Uhu's "Alleskleber" (i.e., all-purpose glue), held 80% market share and had easily fended off several competitive "all-purpose" strategies. The Pritt Glue Stick was an innovation developed as a segmentation strategy in the market. In 1969, Henkel introduced the Glue Stick to serve a special purpose: paper-sticking.

This segment represented roughly 40% of the total consumer "all-purpose" adhesive market. The nationwide launch in 1969 (managed by von Briskorn as his first assignment with Henkel Corporation) was supported by a DM 3 million television, print, promotion, and point-of-purchase campaign.

The Pritt Glue Stick was a patentable innovation in formulation and convenience-oriented packaging. The density of the glue stick allowed it to be packaged in a twist-up tube, similar to lipstick. The user simply took off the top, twisted the bottom of the tube to push up the glue stick, and then applied a small amount of glue on the paper—the same way one would write with a crayon. Main user groups were households, offices, and schools. Schools were important because research in the adhesive market had shown that adults tended to use the brand they used as children. Thus, having the "no-mess" Pritt stick in kindergartens was important for future Pritt sales, as well as current revenues.

Henkel licensed the Glue Stick technology to a few selected licensees including Uhu. However, because of cannibalization problems and its commitment to the "general purpose" concept, Uhu did not aggressively pursue the stick market. The introduction of the Glue Stick was not easy for Henkel. Positioned as the "clean, easy-to-use paper glue," the primary markets would be schools and offices. Serving these markets effectively required stationery store distribution rather than the wallpaper and paint stores where Henkel was established selling the contact adhesive. Pelikan was the market share leader in products such as carbon paper, ink, stamps, etc. in the stationery story channel. Henkel and Pelikan reached an agreement for Pelikan to handle Pritt Glue Stick distribution in the paper/office/stationery (PBS) sector in Germany. The price of the Pritt Glue Stick was DM 1.2 for the German introduction. Production capacity for 1969 was strained at this price level.

In 1970, the international expansion of Pritt Glue Stick began. The introduction was standardized globally and by 1980, the Pritt Glue Stick was Henkel's most successful brand internationally. Distributed in 15 countries in Europe and 50 outside of Europe, annual sales totaled more than 50 million units with sales revenue of DM 80 million.

From 1972–1981, five additional products were introduced under the Pritt brand name. As shown in Exhibit 5, these products were:

1. *Pritt Alleskleber:* The Pritt All-Purpose Adhesive was introduced in 1972 with DM 2 million advertising support. Essentially a "me-too" product to Uhu's all-purpose product, it received good sell-in to the trade because of the Pritt name and advertising support, but poor customer takeaway because of lack of any advantage over Uhu. Reformulated to have a "no-drip" feature, the product was relaunched in 1975, but was unable to achieve even sell-in to the trade because of the 1972 failure. These two failures led to adoption of a "no more me-too's" policy within HD/BC.

2. *Pritt Allesklebe Creme:* The Pritt All-Purpose Creme glue was launched in 1976 with a unique selling proposition. Other adhesives were solvent-based, which created health issues and concern about "glue sniffing." The All-Purpose Creme glue was not solvent-based and was therefore harmless. Supported by a DM 3 million advertising budget, the product received good sell-in but, as with the first Pritt all-purpose product, poor takeaway. Reasons for the lackluster performance seemed to be two: (i) the product performance was not very good on paper and cardboard, and (ii) this was the first time an adhesive product used "creme" in the product name. The brand positioning was "strong bonding" and there was some concern about the compatibility of the positioning and the name. "Creme" did not seem to imply strength.

3. *Pritt Hafties:* Pritt Buddies (as they were referred to in English) were introduced in 1976. Small wads of adhesive, these Buddies were to be used to stick notes on a door temporarily, hold an item in place on a desk, hopefully a wide variety of other uses and which consumers would discover. Initially supported by a DM 2 million advertising budget, the Buddies did well but sales dropped quickly as soon as the advertising support was dropped.

4. *Pritt Alleskleber (bottle):* In 1977, the Pritt all-purpose adhesive was put out in bottle form. Sales were poor due to inferiority in dispensing technology as compared to the Uhu bottled adhesive, the Uhu Flinke Flasche, introduced in 1976.

5. *Pritt Klebepads:* Introduced in 1978, Pritt Adhesive Pads (double-sided foam pads) were very similar in concept to the Pritt Buddies; the physical difference was that the adhesive pads were flat and used for permanent sticking. Not given any special support, the product never did very well. Consumers never seemed to figure out the best applications for these pads or Buddies.

Von Briskorn had been product manager for the Pritt Glue Stick launch in 1969, but had not presided over the product line extension activities of the 1970s, having left Dusseldorf for Henkel assignments in Italy and France. In April 1979, he returned to Dusseldorf to assume the role of marketing director HD/BC, responsible for 15 brands including his first assigned brand, Pritt. In early 1981, he addressed Wolfgang Heck, the present group product manager for Craftsman/DIY Products:

> The Pritt Glue Stick has been great. It was a real innovation and allowed us to capture the clean, easy-bonding positioning. It is an international success story. But these flankers, the all-purpose product and the creme product and so on—they have really hurt us. We have created so many flops; we are losing money on them and everybody is mad at us. The retail trade is not giving us the sell-in and Pelikan, our key distributor, is angry too. We jeopardized our relationship with Kokuyo in Japan—the all-purpose products and the Buddies flopped there too. Maybe it's the products, they are really average in performance. There has been no real significant innovation since the Glue Stick. But we have not really developed any coordinated marketing strategy for these products either—the product line has no visual harmony (see Exhibit 5), all advertising has been for a single brand at a time. We face a real challenge in a few years when the Glue Stick formula patent expires. By that time, we have to be executing a coordinated strategy for the Pritt family or have cleared the scenery of these products which are pulling us down.

Umbrella Branding Possibilities

With Wolfgang Heck's departure from Dusseldorf to a Henkel assignment in the United States, Herbert Tossing assumed the position of product manager Household Adhesives. Along with Joachim Printz, advertising manager, Tossing had the primary responsibility of developing the marketing strategy responsive to von Briskorn's declaration that "if we are to be successful in Germany and the rest of the world, we must find an innovative approach." Exhibit 6 gives the HD/BC organizational structure through which Herbert Tossing would have to work in developing and implementing the strategy. Basically, HD/BC integrated sales and product management in the same organization. As shown in Exhibit 6, profit center responsibility was given to the three sales organizations serving Germany, and the affiliated companies in Europe and the affiliated companies overseas. Product

management had no regional profit center responsibility, but rather global consolidated responsibility. It had an international role developing the central brand strategy, coordinating the individual market strategies and monitoring progress. The advertising function was similar in its international orientation. Printz would be responsible for developing the basic advertising concept and then coordinating with advertising agencies across the markets to ensure international implementation of the advertising strategy. Regional autonomy and profit center responsibility for affiliated companies was a strong part of the Henkel culture. Tossing began his strategy formulation with the Pattex brand.

Pattex Umbrella Potential

In the case of Pattex, the umbrella question was easy to state: could a very highly regarded brand name (Pattex) tied to a product in a no-growth segment (contact adhesives) be transferred to new products to be positioned in higher growth segments of the market? In particular, Tossing saw three possibilities:

1. Remarket Stabilit Rasant, Henkel's recent but unsupported entry into the fast-growing CA market, under the name Pattex Super Glue.
2. Develop a Pattex entry into the emerging "hot melt" market.
3. Market a Pattex No-Mix product which would be a new generation two component glue, a special purpose item.

The first step in assessing the viability of these steps was to determine consumers' current perception of the Pattex brand name. Research in West Germany, Benelux and Austria showed the Pattex name to be associated with "strong bonding" and "technical uses." Researching the potential for stretching the Pattex name in the three directions noted above, Tossing found that:

1. CAs had a very popular, not at all technical image. Consequently, the fit with Pattex's image on this dimension was not strong. However, Stabilit Rasant was not doing well because of its late entry into the market after Uhu and Loctite.
2. The *Hot Melt* market (with the dispensing guns) had a technical image. This could enhance the Pattex name. Henkel possessed the production know-how from industrial experience. Consequently, Henkel could probably produce a high

quality product for most applications. Consumer research showed that DIY-ers viewed Henkel as a credible source for hot melt products. Unlike other Pattex products, it would be a seasonal, gift-oriented item because of the cost of the dispensing gun. It was also felt that the market may be a price-oriented one.

3. Serving the *Two Compound Glue* segment with Pattex No Mix would definitely enhance the Pattex technical image as it required no dosing or mixing. The product would, however, be a niche product generating low turnover for the trade. Historically, Pattex had been viewed as a "fast mover" by the trade. A second problem with No Mix was consumers perceived it to smell very bad—would this "bad smell" perception hurt other Pattex brands if No Mix were brought under the Pattex umbrella?

In general, the research finding was that a line extension would not degrade consumers' perception of the Pattex name as long as the umbrella products were compatible with Pattex's high-bonding strength image. The research results in Exhibit 7 show the mean score on a 1–10 scale of 100 respondents exposed to just the Pattex name (control group) and a test group exposed to the line extension through seeing product package mock-ups and product descriptions. The second research finding was that the new brands would benefit greatly from the power and authority of the Pattex name.

Pritt Umbrella Potential

The Pritt situation was quite different from Pattex. The Pattex name was currently positioned in a no-growth category and the extension under consideration was to new products or to a very recent introduction (Stabilit Rasant). The question for the Pattex situation was can the new products save the brand? In Pritt, the question was can the brand save the products (i.e., the flankers to the Glue Stick) if more actively promoted? Printz played a key role in reviewing packaging design, proposing a new line design, and testing the consumers' reaction to the new line.

The first step was to review the Glue Stick design for consumer acceptance and conveyance of a "modern image." Based on research in Benelux and West Germany, the red, white and black Pritt stick design was deemed acceptable and "modern." Based on this, Printz proposed a visual harmonization of the line, all oriented toward the leader product. The proposed design is shown in Exhibit 8. This design introduced the chevron to all packages and extended the red background, black lettering on white color scheme of the Glue Stick to all elements in the line.

Printz proposed a similar visual harmonization as recently created for Pattex line where the chevron was used but with yellow as the primary background color. Tests of the nonharmonized vs. harmonized design for the Pritt product line were conducted. Results are shown in Exhibit 9. Respondents were exposed to either the harmonized or nonharmonized lines and asked to rate both Pritt and Uhu on the dimensions shown.

Decisions and Implementation

Whatever strategy decisions he made, von Briskorn had to be concerned about how he could get the strategy sold within Henkel. He knew that Dr. Roman Dohr, head of Adhesives and Chemical auxiliaries, would have questions on all aspects of the strategy. He had previously expressed concerns about the risks inherent in an umbrella strategy. The recent problems with the Pritt flankers and the declining fortunes of Pattex had made these two products highly visible in the Adhesives group. Von Briskorn and his product management team would also have to convince those with profit center responsibility in the affiliated foreign companies to implement the plan. His problems only began with the decision of which products to put under the umbrellas. He would have to make suggestions as well on Henkel advertising strategy, e.g., should they advertise the whole umbrella as a group, concentrate on one brand and hope others got pulled along somehow, or divide dollars and advertise each on its own? What should be the timing of the expansion of the strategy to worldwide markets—what kind of markets should be tried first? Should he advocate standardization of the strategy across markets or be yielding on individual adaptation? Last, he had to consider how to sell the ideas to the trade. Distributors and retailers were vital to Henkel success; however, with the recent record of HD/BC, trade receptivity to another HD/BC venture was not overwhelming.

Von Briskorn believed very strongly in the brand philosophy he had developed over the past few years— "Concentrate on a few, but really strong umbrellas and, as far as possible, have an internationally standardized strategy." In the abstract, the philosophy seemed to fit the adhesives market well, but now was the time to implement rather than philosophize.

Exhibit 1 Henkel Group: Umbrella Branding and Globalization Decisions

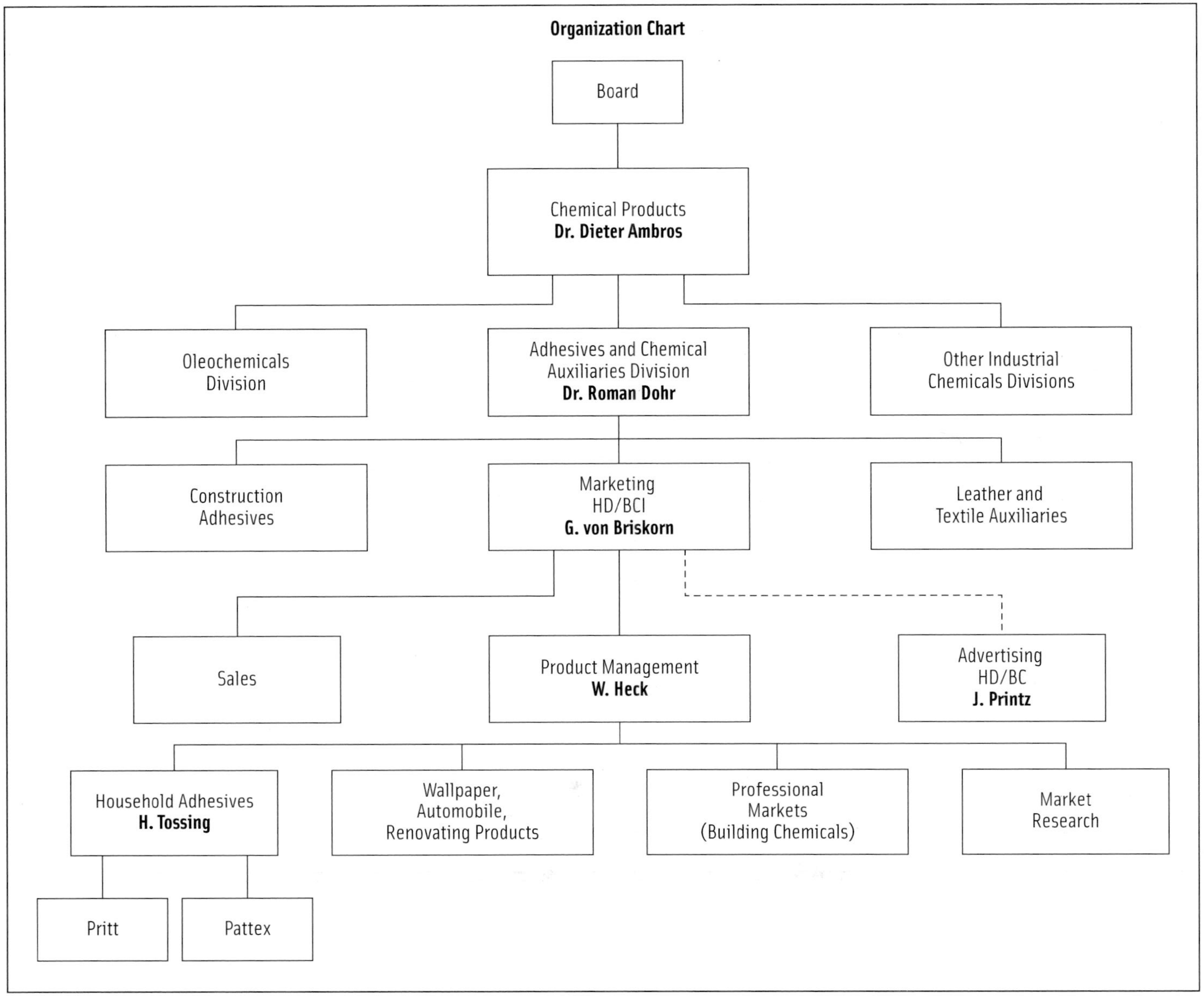

Organization Chart

```
                                    Board
                                      |
                         Chemical Products
                         Dr. Dieter Ambros
        ┌────────────────┬────────────┼────────────────┬────────────────┐
   Oleochemicals    Adhesives and   Other Industrial
   Division         Chemical        Chemicals Divisions
                    Auxiliaries Division
                    Dr. Roman Dohr
        ┌────────────────┬────────────┼────────────────┬────────────────┐
   Construction     Marketing         Leather and
   Adhesives        HD/BCI            Textile Auxiliaries
                    G. von Briskorn
        ┌────────────────┬────────────┼─ ─ ─ ─ ─ ─ ─ ─ ─┐
     Sales       Product Management              Advertising
                 W. Heck                         HD/BC
                                                 J. Printz
   ┌──────────┬──────────────┬──────────────┬──────────────┐
Household    Wallpaper,     Professional    Market
Adhesives    Automobile,    Markets         Research
H. Tossing   Renovating     (Building
             Products       Chemicals)
   ┌────┬────┐
 Pritt  Pattex
```

Exhibit 2 Henkel Group: Umbrella Branding and Globalization Decisions *HD/BC Product Line*

HD/BC Product Line	
Pattex contact cement	Thomsit floorlaying adhesives
Ponal wood glue	Ovalit wallcovering adhesives
Metylan wallpaper paste	Tanglt pvc pipe adhesives
Pritt stick/all purpose glue	Duflx home decorating products
Saxit tile adhesives	Gorl wood preservatives
Polifac car care products	Sista sealants + PU foam (Insulating Foam)
Assil structural adhesives	Kleselit silicate paints
	Randamit construction products

Exhibit 3 Henkel Group: Umbrella Branding and Globalization Decisions *HD/BC Distribution Channels*

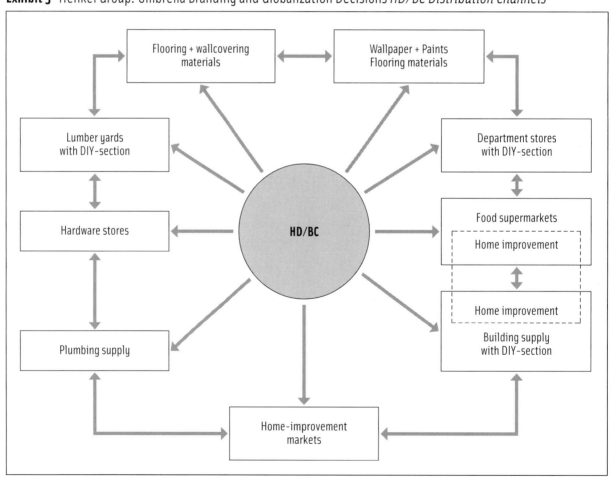

Exhibit 4 Henkel Group: Umbrella Branding and Globalization Decisions

	Sales and Advertising in Germany			
	PRITT		PATTEX	
Year	Sales (DM millions)	Advertising (DM millions)	Sales (DM millions)	Advertising (DM millions)
1970	4.0	1.0	16.0	.3
1973	7.0	0.5	22.0	2.0
1976	9.0	2.0	22.0	1.0
1980	8.5	.5	21.0	1.5
1981 (est.)	8.0	.5	24.0	1.5

Exhibit 5 Henkel Group: Umbrella Branding and Globalization Decisions *The Pritt Product Line*

Exhibit 6 Henkel Group: Umbrella Branding and Globalization Decisions *HD/BC Organization Structure*

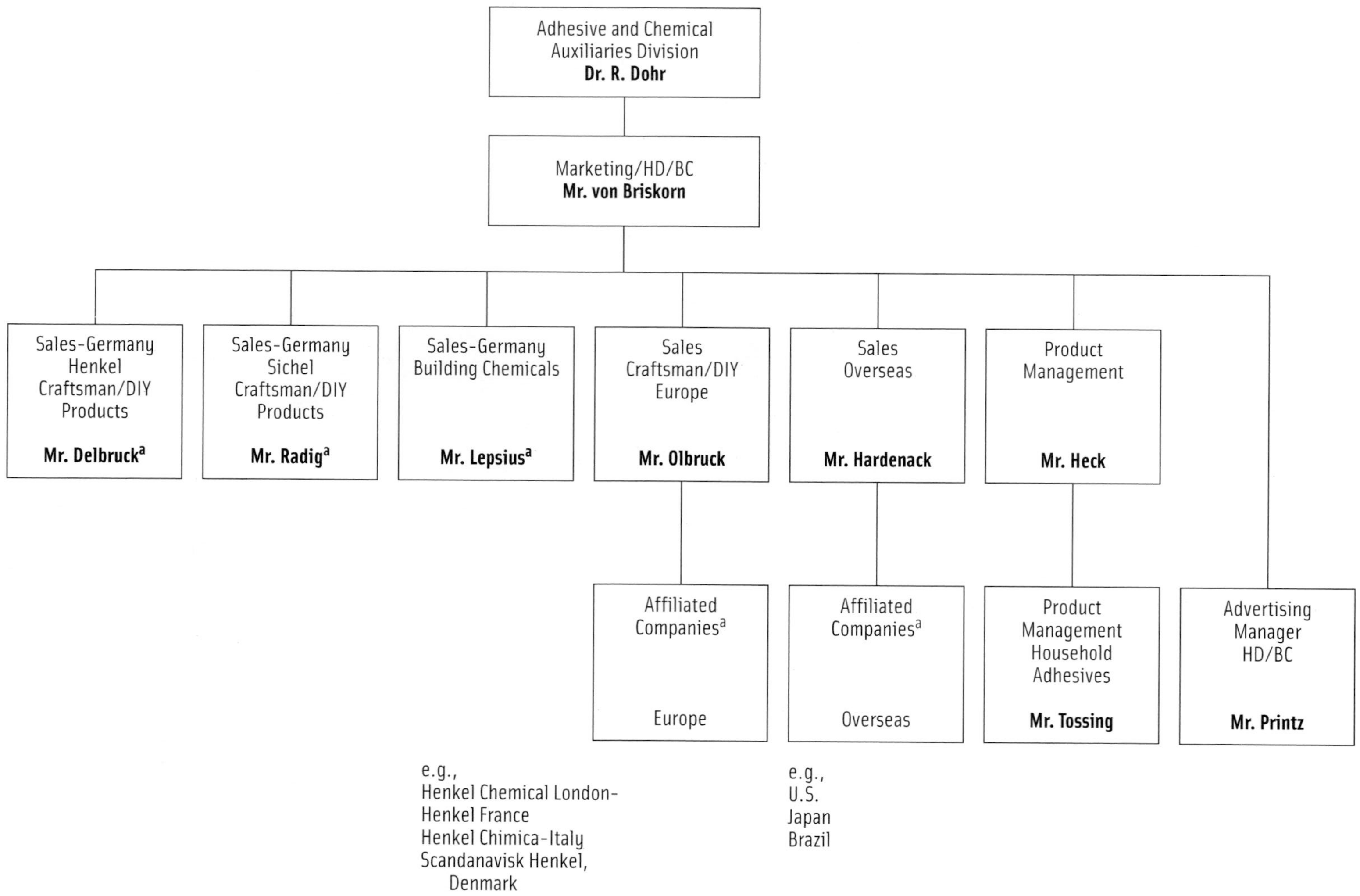

Adhesive and Chemical Auxiliaries Division
Dr. R. Dohr

Marketing/HD/BC
Mr. von Briskorn

Sales–Germany Henkel Craftsman/DIY Products
Mr. Delbruck[a]

Sales–Germany Sichel Craftsman/DIY Products
Mr. Radig[a]

Sales–Germany Building Chemicals
Mr. Lepsius[a]

Sales Craftsman/DIY Europe
Mr. Olbruck

Sales Overseas
Mr. Hardenack

Product Management
Mr. Heck

Advertising Manager HD/BC
Mr. Printz

Affiliated Companies[a]

Europe

Affiliated Companies[a]

Overseas

Product Management Household Adhesives
Mr. Tossing

e.g.,
Henkel Chemical London–
Henkel France
Henkel Chimica–Italy
Scandanavisk Henkel,
Denmark

e.g.,
U.S.
Japan
Brazil

[a]Designates regional profit center responsibility.

Exhibit 7 Henkel Group: Umbrella Branding and Globalization Decisions *Research Results—Pattex Brand*

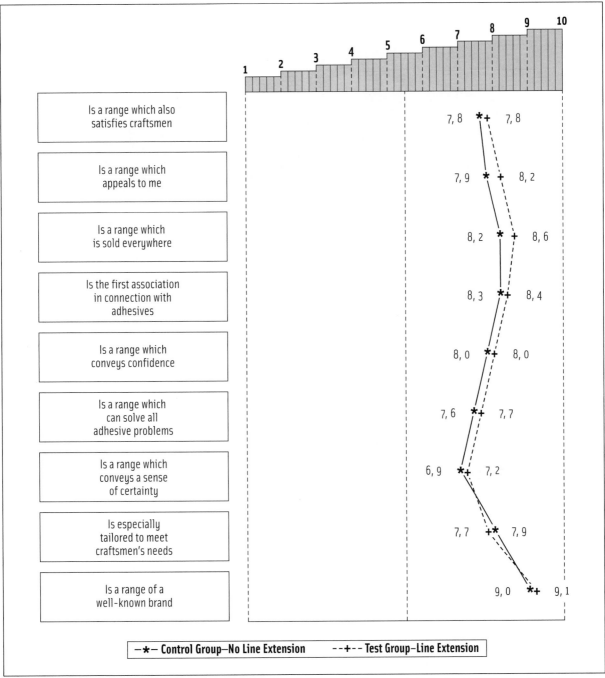

Note: One hundred people in each of the test and control groups were asked to indicate agreement/disagreement with the statement "Pattex is . . ." 1 indicates "strongly disagree" and 10 indicates "strongly agree."

Exhibit 8 Henkel Group: Umbrella Branding and Globalization Decisions
Proposed Visual Harmonization of the Pritt Product Line

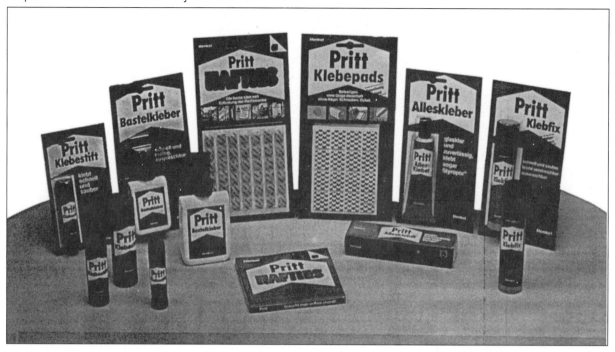

Exhibit 9 Henkel Group: Umbrella Branding and Globalization Decisions
Research Results on Perceptions of Pritt Current Line, Pritt Harmonized Line, and Uhu

	Pritt Current (see exhibit 5) N = 100		Pritt Harmonized (see exhibit 8) N = 100	
	PRITT	**UHU**	**PRITT**	**UHU**
conveys confidence	6,8	8,5	7,5	8,3
is of high quality	7,2	8,4	7,5	8,4
is for special uses only	6,5	5,5	5,6	5,6
is only for sticking paper	5,7	4,3	4,8	3,9
is somehow likeable	6,4	7,2	6,6	7,2
glues reliably	7,1	8,4	7,5	8,5
is of great strength	6,9	8,3	7,1	8,4
is a well-known brand	7,9	9,7	8,0	9,6
is for general purposes	6,5	8,1	7,0	8,1
is usually reasonably priced	6,5	6,7	5,9	6,4
is sold everywhere	7,4	8,9	7,9	9,0
offers all adhesives you need	7,1	8,3	7,2	7,9
is more for children	4,9	4,5	4,9	4,6
is more known from the office	6,3	5,6	5,9	5,5
offers useful adhesives	8,0	8,7	8,1	8,7
has a well-structured range	6,9	7,9	7,8	8,1
is something for experts	2,4	3,0	3,3	3,5
is clean in use	7,6	7,7	8,0	7,7

Note: One hundred people in each group were exposed to simulated store setting showing either the current Pritt or proposed harmonized packaging design. They were then asked to indicate agreement/disagreement with the statements shown for Pritt and Uhu (1 = strongly disagree, 10 = strongly agree).

LAUNCHING THE BMW Z3 ROADSTER

January, 1996 marked the beginning of Phase II of BMW of North America Inc.'s Z3 roadster introduction. Phase I had centered around the placement of the new $28,750 two-seat convertible in the James Bond hit movie, *GoldenEye*, which premiered several months earlier. While not yet critically evaluated, results of the "out-of-the-box" pre-launch campaign appeared very positive: word-of-mouth concerning the Z3 and the James Bond cross-promotion were favorable, and product orders far exceeded BMW's initial expectations. The challenge now was to design a marketing program that would sustain product excitement until dealer product availability beginning in March. Phase II planning had to be undertaken within the context of other important events in the BMW product family: (1) the April launch of the redesigned 5-Series; and (2) the company's role as "official international automotive sponsor" of the 1996 Atlanta Summer Games, which would begin in earnest with the Olympic-Torch Relay 5-Series event in June.

While these other elements of the BMW product family clearly impacted the Z3, the marketing approach and ultimate results for the Z3 would influence the whole BMW operation in the United States. Dr. Helmut Panke, Chairman and CEO of BMW (U.S.) Holding Corp. since 1993, noted that the Z3 was destined to be "the first BMW not made by mythical little creatures in the Bavarian woods. This car will be made in Spartanburg, South Carolina. Some people think BMW means German-made. With the Z3, we must show we can be successful as a global company, manufacturing at strategic locations—even if not in Bavaria. Assembling of cars in the United States requires BMW to replace 'Made in Germany' as a symbol of quality with 'Made by BMW'." As *Brandweek* put it, Panke was "saddled with the task of exporting BMW's mystique from the Bavarian hills to the fields of South Carolina." Industry commentators characterized the Z3 as "the new standard bearer for a line that had relied on German engineering as its point of difference," and wondered whether "the mystique of the BMW brand, so closely interwoven with its Munich parentage, could survive and even thrive after a surgical transplant to South Carolina." Panke and his team were aware of the new era BMW was entering and of the "new and unique" challenges this presented. Meeting the unique challenges was the prime responsibility of Victor Doolan, President of BMW North America.

Project leadership for the Z3 launch in the United States was the job of James McDowell, BMW's Marketing Vice President. The objectives of the roadster launch were two-fold: (1) to use the roadster to motivate and stimulate the dealer network to meet higher standards to qualify for the roadster; and (2) to build an order bank to enable the new Spartanburg plant to build to the specifications of BMW customers. To this point in the Z3 launch, BMW had been quite innovative in addressing their marketing goals, using for example the Bond film placement as a centerpiece of the marketing plan. Now Doolan and McDowell had to put the rest of the program in place to make sure the new "Made in the USA" Z3 was successful, in its own right and for the BMW franchise as a whole.

Background

BMW Business Strategy

BMW was a global company with a significant position in the luxury/performance segment of the U.S. automotive market, having rebounded considerably from setbacks imposed by Lexus, Acura, and Infiniti in the mid- to late-1980s (see Exhibit 1). The company reversed the sales decline beginning in 1992 with a program which included a repositioning of the brand from "Yuppie Status Symbol" to the more quality-oriented "Ultimate Driving Machine." At the same time, BMW adjusted model prices as necessary in light of the new competitive situation, improved the dealer network to bring the consumer buying experience in line with evolved expectations for service, and made significant improvements to the product line. All the while, the company's overall business strategy remained the same: To provide the world market with luxury/performance vehicles that were each "the best in its class, with a unique and definitive positioning in the marketplace." While focused on being "the best" rather than the "biggest," BMW wanted to position itself to attain an annual unit sales volume near 100,000 units in the United States as this was a mark that identified major players in the global automotive marketplace and permitted operation at an efficient scale.

Franchise expansion into more youthful targets seemed the most promising way to add incremental sales to the brand. Related recommendations included an updating of the corporate image and a new product development program capable of sustaining that image. As *Adweek*[1] put it: "BMW needs to be perceived as a little less serious and tradition-bound . . . they need to preserve their reputation for driving performance but reposition their German-made cars as being stylish and fun to drive as well."

The BMW Z3 Roadster New Product Initiative

As related by Bert Holland, BMW's Series Manager of the Special Projects Group, the development process that led to the identification of the roadster concept all started in 1992 with the decline of the worldwide motorcycle market. This sparked an internal effort to identify product concepts that were capable of addressing the same feelings, emotions, and fantasies that motorcycles had satisfied. Several alternative platforms on which to execute the "emotional fantasy theme" were developed: race cars, dune buggies, sport utility vehicles, roadsters. The roadster sportscar concept was adopted because it fit best with the overall BMW positioning of driving excitement, evoked BMW's heritage as a producer of roadsters in years past, embodied the spirit of the company, and captured the essence of the BMW brand. Also, while the concept reflected a niche opportunity, it fit the corporate goal of being the best, not the biggest. No products on the market at the time delivered against this positioning. However, other luxury car import manufacturers (e.g., Porsche, Mercedes) were rumored to have similar concepts under development, so BMW had to move quickly to secure competitive advantage.

The roadster product concept was refined over the next two years. The two-seater convertible Z3 would use the same 1.9 liter 4-cylinder engine as currently used in some 3-series models. The base model would include a six-speaker sound system, power windows and seats, fog lights, cruise control, and air conditioning. Leatherette upholstery would be standard, with upgrades to leather available.

Concept tests revealed high interest across a number of lifestage-defined segment, e.g. Generation Xers interested in unique image statements, men and women in their 40s who expressed a desire "to have that roadster I've been dreaming of all my life," and nostalgic late-Baby Boomers yearning for roadsters of yesteryear. Common across these diverse demographic groups was a "lover of life" mindset and a propensity to seek unique expressions of individuality indicating a target market defined in psychographic versus demographic terms.

Being the first BMW vehicle from the company's new Spartanburg, South Carolina manufacturing plant, and its first 100% "Made in America" offering from the German engineering leader, the Z3 roadster project assumed strategic importance beyond its franchise-expanding mission. Other German manufacturers were already trying to promote skepticism among consumers regarding BMW's impending U.S.-manufactured cars. Helmut Panke explained the strategic significance of the Z3:

> Spartanburg is much more than simply escaping Germany's high cost environment. Yes, the plant will cushion BMW against international monetary fluctuations. More importantly, though, Spartanburg demonstrates that we are firmly committed to the U.S. market and re-dedicated to the performance values that made BMW a cult here in the 1980s. The investment tally at Spartanburg is $600 million dollars and growing. The plant can build 250 to 300 cars a day and production is set up to be flexible so that it can produce several models on the same line in random sequence. The plant currently employs 1,500 people and the plan is to grow to 2,000 by the end of this decade. This is our first auto plant outside Europe. This is a chance for BMW to take a step away from being a German car manufacturer towards its long-term goal of becoming a truly global brand. Spartanburg can really change what BMW stands for.

Victor Doolan commented on the system-wide implications of the Z3 launch:

---

[1]Source: *Adweek Eastern Edition;* September 11, 1995; p. 7

Spartanburg offers us the opportunity to develop a new set of relationships in North America. With news of our commitment in Spartanburg, our dealers have gotten serious about this franchise again, and have begun to reinvest in facilities, equipment, and manpower. You can see a complete rejuvenation in enthusiasm for the brand and our products. Dealers are ecstatic about this plant. And that enthusiasm carries into the marketplace.

The Roadster Introductory Marketing Plan

Setting the Preliminary Marketing Platform

In early Spring 1994, the launch team led by James McDowell, Vice President of Marketing, articulated a preliminary marketing platform for the Z3 introduction. As one BMW manager put it, the central goal of the launch was "to expand the BMW franchise and further the rejuvenation of the BMW brand by positioning the Z3 squarely in American culture and settling into the hearts and minds of the American public." Managers talked of "weaving the car into the fabric of the American experience," "putting it in the American landscape," "aligning it with everyday experience," and "establishing the vehicle as a cultural icon." According to James McDowell:

> The intent was get people to talk about the roadster in the course of normal daily events: in essence, to get the car on people's conversational agenda. The plan was to leverage the excitement and enthusiasm of the core customer base in a way that would draw broader attention and interest to the brand. Management referred to this as "leveraging the buzz."

Given this intent, the launch team focused on "non-traditional" marketing methods believing them more effective than the standard fare of television and print advertising.

> The strategic import of the launch dictated the need for something quite different, attention getting. (Bert Holland, Product Advocate)

> It's a unique vehicle, so we were looking for unconventional ways to introduce it. (Tom McGurn, Corporate Communications Manager)

By their very nature, non-traditional media are inherently more capable of leveraging the buzz. (James McDowell, Vice President Marketing)

Non-traditional media give you more exposure. (Carol Burrows, Advertising Manager)

Given our psychographic segmentation, non-traditional media are more cost efficient per dollar spent. Traditional media are sold more on demographics. Non-traditional delivers a broader base, something we found especially valuable in light of our goal of getting into the hearts and minds of a large group of publics. (George Neill, Consumer Communications Manager)

BMW also wished to be "multi-media" in its communications strategy. As one executive put it:

> We wanted consumers to experience the message in many media, to hear it in many voices. This was a philosophy directly opposed to the repetition philosophy governing traditional advertising thought. This idea operated more along the lines of a 'choir' but we recognized that literal ties and threads must be evident across the disparate message elements and that all elements must strengthen and reinforce each other. This would require agencies willing to integrate across each other in an atypical team environment.

In June 1994, requests for proposals were sent to a broad collection of 30 advertising, public relations, and promotional agencies believed capable of mounting an unconventional campaign to achieve company goals. BMW pursued serious discussions with ten of those agencies based on mutual interests and relevant prior experience. Agencies were prepped with a stock footage video expressing the basic concept of the car. They also received input concerning BMW's view of what types of elements qualified as "non-traditional," and preliminary opinions regarding non-traditional marketing tools that might be especially effective. Ideas for a product placement in a premier film, a TV show sponsorship, and a fashion world tie-in ranked among BMW's top choices though agencies were encouraged to come up with their own recommendations.

Based on a review of solicited proposals, seven agencies were invited to make presentations at BMW. Many elements were selected from a proposal by Dick Clark Corporate Productions, a leading Hollywood-based promotional agency known for its experiences in the entertainment industry. These were added to a framework of core events and programs that BMW had developed internally including an aggressive program of dealer facility upgrading, staff training, and the production of 150 pre-production cars for use in pre-selling promotions at the time of the product launch.

A corporate switch from Mullen Advertising to Fallon McElligott was also instituted at this time. Mullen, a small creative shop in Wenham Massachusetts, had been retained in February 1993 to reposition BMW beyond its Yuppie image. Fallon was selected based on their proven experience in integrated and electronic marketing—key skills for a non-traditional launch.

Fixing the First Marketing Element: The *GoldenEye* Product Placement

BMW's predisposition toward movie placements in fact reflected a broader industry trend toward the addition of product placements into the marketing mix.[2] For film producers, manufacturers' branded products added authenticity and realism to settings and aided in character development through the provision of instantly-recognized symbols. Payments and free merchandise also helped defray costs in an increasingly expensive production and marketing environment.[3] Manufacturers who offered their brands for placement sought many rewards beyond exposure and visibility through their Hollywood alliances. The trade press commented on these benefits to corporate partners:

> It's a great way to build brand equity.[4]

> In this increasingly fragmented world, advertisers are forced to go to great lengths to reach their audiences. When we [the viewers] can zap a commercial out and move on, they have to find new ways to reach us. This is a more subtle way for advertisers to reach us.[5]

> In addition to a dollop of glamour, movies give marketers access to two audiences that are hard-to-reach through network TV or print: foreign viewers and young people.[6]

In general, fees for movie placement deals ranged from nothing to several million dollars, with an average fee of $40,000[7] for a highly-visible placement in which the star actor actually used the product (an "impact placement," in industry terms).[8] Many placements were conducted on a quid pro quo basis, however, with manufacturers receiving product visibility in exchange for providing movie producers with product-related cost savings.[9] BMW, as a matter of policy, does not pay for movie placements.

In a newspaper interview, Norm Marshall, a longstanding consultant to BMW, commented on the uncertainty of movie product placement effects:

> Why don't companies have to pay big bucks to get their goods in a picture? In some cases we do. But the counter balance against that is that they can't guarantee anything as they can when you buy an ad. And you never know if it is going to be in the movie or not. And even if it is, you don't know if the movie is going to bomb or not. The reality is, the vast majority of movies are not successful at the box office. So we make choices. Hopefully we are right more than we are wrong.[10]

Exhibit 2 contains examples of some noteworthy movie product placements from 1983 to the present.

BMW entered into deal negotiations with MGM/United Artists on the James Bond *GoldenEye* film in Fall 1994. Immediately upon reviewing the script, BMW pegged the opportunity as "a perfect fit" for both parties: MGM sought a partner that could help them revive their 33-year old Bond franchise; BMW sought a premier movie placement capable of reinforcing its brand image. Other firms that contracted with MGM for the *GoldenEye* film included Omega, Perrier, Sharper Image, Yves St. Laurent, and IBM.

Karen Sortito, MGM's Senior Vice President of Promotions, described her first encounter with the Z3:

> We had seen spy photos of the car and it looked great. We all snuck out to BMW's production facility one morning to see the car. It was like an episode of *Get Smart:* we were going through all these doors and they were slamming behind us. They pulled the cover

---

[2]Source: "Planning for a Market Fall?," *Brandweek,* July 22, 1996, p. 32–39.

[3]Source: "Now It's the Cars that Make the Characters Go," *The New York Times,* April 21, 1996, section 2, p. 13.

[4]Source: "Casting Call Goes Out: Products Play Major Roles in Movies," *Marketing News,* July 31, 1995, p. 1.

[5]Source: "Movie 4 Sale!," *The Courier-Journal,* May 30, 1996, p.1C.

[6]Source: "Cue the Soda Can," *Business Week,* June 24, 1996, p. 64, 66.

[7]Source: "It's a Wrap (But Not Plain): From Budweiser to BMW, Brand Names Are Popping Up More and More On Screen," *The Los Angeles Times,* September 3, 1995, p. 4.

[8]Source: "Junior Mints: I'm Gonna Make You A Star," *Forbes,* November 6, 1995, p. 90

[9]Source: "Product Placement: How It Began, How It's Grown," *St. Louis Post Dispatch,* April 8, 1995, p. 4D.

[10]Source: "We Ought to Be in Pictures: That's the Rallying Cry as Companies Vie to Get their Products in Movies and TV," *St. Louis Post Dispatch,* April 8, 1995, p. 1D.

off the car and we all "ooh'ed and aah'ed." Then we took turns sitting in it, just to make sure it was cool enough for Pierce Brosnan, our newest James Bond.[11]

McDowell elaborated on the perceived fit between Bond and the Z3 brand personality:

BMW was looking for a hero, and a glamorous one at that. The Bond character fit the bill perfectly. He was handsome, sexy, wealthy, resourceful, and adventurous. He was perceived as a man who loves life and is in control of his destiny. He was known for the technology he used. Heck, he was even recognized as a man with a penchant for good, fast cars! The quintessential hero for a quintessential car!

BMW was excited by the strategic significance of the film for MGM and the dollar investment MGM was willing to put behind the re-launch of its cultural icon. Management believed that this level of support and commitment would play well with the dealers. MGM was also talking of the possibility for a multi-movie deal, a prospect that offered continuing leverage potential.

The BMW/MGM agreement was orally sealed in January 1995, and formally signed in July 1995. The basic exchange was simple: MGM got the use of several prototype vehicles for their movie; BMW got placement of the Z3 in *GoldenEye* and obtained worldwide rights to reference that placement in corporate communications through March 1996.

To movie industry insiders, the BMW/MGM deal qualified more as a "co-launch" than a traditional movie product placement. The basic marketing agreement between MGM and BMW was that from September through December 1995, the two marketers would jointly promote the Bond actor (Pierce Brosnan), the *GoldenEye* film, and the BMW Z3 roadster. In addition to covering product costs for prototype vehicles, BMW agreed to invest in advertising to support the Z3 as James Bond's new car. MGM, in turn, agreed to support the Z3 in *GoldenEye* movie previews and film trailers.

The Z3 appeared in the movie for only 90 seconds, but was prominent in that it replaced the Aston-Martin, Bond's signature car. "That Aston Martin is such an engrained part of Bond. It's his trademark, really. This marked a first-ever use of the car category in the film series' history," noted Marshall.[12] Bond is presented the Z3

by Q, the legendary R&D engineer at Britain's M5 Secret Service Agency who says: "Now, pay attention Bond. First your new car. A BMW . . ."[13] The Z3 placement was noted in the marketing press for its "seamless integration" into the storyline, as explained by Entertainment Resources Marketing Association President, Dean Ayers:

A word that comes up a lot in our work is seamless. Subtly rendered. A blurring of the lines between advertising and entertainment. That's the way placements have to function to be successful. People prefer to see a can of Pepsi or some other familiar brand rather than one that just says 'Soda.' But nobody wants to pay to see a commercial. You have to pay just the right amount of attention to the product to get this effect.[14]

Acclaim for the seamlessness of the roadster product placement was considered ironic by some in light of the product's limited exposure in the film, as McDowell described:

A lot of people were surprised that the car was not in the movie for a great amount of time. The car shows up in two segments for a total airtime of 1.5 minutes. It really was intended only as a preview, a teaser. We much rather wanted the car to fit naturally into the film than to look as though someone had forced it into the scene and it was there so long it wore out its welcome.

The *GoldenEye* box office opening was scheduled for November 17, 1995. While the six-month gap between the film launch and Z3 dealership availability presented obvious tactical challenges, the timing fit well with other planned BMW product events and gave the factory the opportunity to build cars to exact customer specifications. The early launch also gave BMW a leg up on the forthcoming Mercedes introduction. By virtue of its timing, the Bond connection became the foundational element around which the remaining Z3 launch plans were formulated.

The Final Pre-Launch Marketing Plan

With the *GoldenEye* placement agreed to in January 1995, the launch team sought to build the other comple-

---

[11]Source: *Brandweek;* March 11, 1996; p. 21

[12]Source: "It's a Wrap (But Not Plain): From Budweiser to BMW, Brand Names Are Popping Up More and More On Screen," The *Los Angeles Times,* September 3, 1995, p. 4.

[13]Q is the research and development engineer responsible for design of Bond's state-of-the-art weaponry.

[14]Source: Ibid.

mentary elements of the program which would both presell the Z3 and generate dealer traffic, stimulating interest in other models in the BMW product line. Among the additional elements which would form the launch program for the Z3 were:

1. Neiman Marcus Christmas Catalog offer of a Special Bond Edition Roadster.
2. Featuring the Z3 on BMW's site on the World Wide Web.
3. A large scale public relations event "unveiling" the car in New York's Central Park.
4. An appearance on Jay Leno's *Tonight Show.*
5. The Radio DJ Program.
6. "Go: An American Road Story" Video.

Along with these elements, BMW planned some television and print advertising as well as dealer activities. Each of these programs is described in turn below. A timeline of key program decisions and events is provided in Exhibit 3.

1. Neiman Marcus Catalog Offer

BMW put together a promotion in which a Special Limited Edition Bond Roadster would be available in the Neiman Marcus Christmas Catalog (see Exhibit 4), a publication renowned for its unusual product offerings. On September 11, the catalog insertion and vehicle were featured on the *Today Show.* Originally BMW and Neiman Marcus had set a 20-unit sales goal over the $3\frac{1}{2}$ month Christmas selling period: "the 20-unit number seemed right in light of past experience of the catalog," according to McDowell. In two days, 100 Z3 orders were placed, so BMW agreed to increase the total production to 100 units. By Christmas, Neiman's had received 6000 customers orders or waiting list applications for the 100 cars.

2. BMW Internet Site

In October, BMW unveiled its new Website. Among the items on the site were *GoldenEye* film segments and the *Today Show* clip featuring the catalog offer. A module developed by the Fallon Agency proved impactful in generating "hits" on the site. This "Build Your Own Roadster" module allowed the site visitor to select exterior, interior, and top colors as well as various options for a

Z3. The module then displayed the user "his/her car" from a variety of perspectives, e.g. top up and top down. It also provided the MSRP for the car with options as selected by the user. Hit rates tripled with the addition of this module, from an average of 35,000 hits per day to 125,000. Apple Computer, whose technology was employed to build the module, approached BMW in December for rights to reference the "Build-Your-Own-Roadster" module in their own corporate advertising (see Exhibit 5). Apple's TV spot aired during the Academy Awards in March 1996. "And we got a full 25 of those 30 seconds," noted McDowell.

3. Press Launch in Central Park

The most prominent PR event was the Central Park Launch in which the Z3 was formally introduced to the public. Over 200 media representatives were on hand as *GoldenEye* character Q detailed the specifications of BMW's "latest invention." The Z3 was revealed amid a splash of special effects precipitated by CEO Panke's entry of "the secret code" that exploded the crate shielding the car. To cap the event, Bond actor Brosnan drove onto the scene in his Atlanta Blue Roadster after completing a circuit through Central Park with a motorcade escort.

On the morning of the press launch the Z3 was also showcased in a segment of the *Today Show* that included an interview with CEO Helmut Panke and test drives with the show's host.

The Central Park event generated extensive coverage in both broadcast and print, including mention on *Hard Copy, This Morning's Business, The Money Wheel,* and all major network news programs. McDowell added: "There were even cartoons published in the newspapers about how Brosnan was being upstaged by a car!" Exhibit 6 contains a sample press clipping from the event. Exhibit 7 contains the cartoon from *Automotive News.*

4. Jay Leno *Tonight Show*

In early November, prior to the *GoldenEye* premier, the Z3 appeared on the *Tonight Show.* BMW had offered Jay Leno the use of a Z3 on his show "should he find it useful in anyway." NBC accepted for Leno without specifying his intent. Leno's writers incorporated the Z3 in a skit where Bond dodged all approaches from NBC Security in crossing the studio lots. In the end, it was a case of mistaken identity since Pierce Brosnan was already in the studio. McDowell commented:

"The unpredictability of the message content was almost unbearable: It was a carefully calculated gamble. We did not know what Leno would say or do, and we would basically not know until the rest of the country knew it as well. We sent one of our guys to sit in the studio audience during filming, and he called us on his cellular to tell us what was going on. But it all worked out very well."

5. Radio DJ Program

Timed coincident with the beginning of TV advertising in early November, the Radio DJ Program featured DJs from leading radio stations in 13 major metro markets. DJs were screened on the basis of disc jockey personality, show content and listener demographics. Qualifying DJs were approached with the opportunity to design a program segment that would somehow incorporate the Z3 into their radio shows or scheduled personal appearances. DJs were encouraged to be innovative in their proposals and to adopt creative license in whatever they did. They were informed that while BMW would suggest potential copy points, they would not censor accepted programs in any way.

Twenty-five radio stations participated with some interesting programs. A DJ in Atlanta, for example, dressed up in a Santa suit and drove his borrowed Z3 roadster onto the Atlanta Falcon's playing field at half-time of a National Football League game. Another gave away a Z3 roadster during a live radio broadcast in L.A. Baba Shetty, BMW's Media Communications Manager commented on the overall effect:

> The DJ Program was considered the most 'at-risk' element of the plan. It was not until the 11th hour . . . only 1 and a half weeks before d-day . . . that management finally committed to go with it. But it was great. The DJs granted amazing credibility to our product message. The event was very successful in getting the brand into the conversational milieu. We think it had three times the word-of-mouth effect of other programs. We got over 6,000 spots from the event and we were only promised 3,800.

6. "Go: An American Road Story" Video

The BMW Communications Group, in conjunction with Dick Clark Productions, created this story of Faber, an overworked architect who decides to relive a cross-country road trip he took with his Aunt Edna Rose when he was 10 years old. Faber drives his Z3 from Savannah to Oregon, retracing his Aunt's steps along the way. The story provides a "celebration of the road focused on the emotional character of the driving experience." The story's original song title, "Feel the Wind in your Soul," captures this theme. The video was made available through BMW's 1-800 number in December, with references to the tape made in corporate advertising.

TV and Print Advertising

In concert with these "non-traditional" activities, BMW considered a possible complementary role for advertising to be produced by their new agency Fallon McElligott. The extent of advertising and the most appropriate media were issues to be considered in light of the "non-traditional" platform. Fallon developed TV and print advertising which, it was ultimately decided, would break nationally on November 1. While the advertising used "traditional" media of print and television, the launch team felt the non-traditional spirit was maintained. "Even traditional media can be executed in non-traditional ways," noted one BMW executive.

The advertising message was a simple one: James Bond traded in his car on a new BMW. "In essence it was a new Bond in a new world in a new car. Life had evolved and so had Bond," explained Carol Burrows, BMW's Advertising Manager. The tonality of the advertising was bold, witty, and entertaining. The new campaign with its central elements of humor and fantasy provided a sharp departure from traditional BMW advertising, which tended to emphasize performance capabilities in a no-nonsense manner.

The multi-million dollar campaign included two television spots scheduled for placement in popular network shows (*Seinfeld, ER,* and *90210*) and lifestyle cable programming. National print advertising (see Exhibit 8) was placed in business and lifestyle books (*Business Week, Forbes, Fortune, Traveler, Vanity Fair*) as well as auto buff magazines (*Car and Driver, Auto Week, Auto World*). Advertising was scheduled through December, with heavier weight in the initial period to prime excitement for the Bond film. (See Exhibit 9 for comparative launch advertising expenditures in the industry).

The resulting advertising was impactful, according to Market Research and Information Manager, William Pettit:

We attained more mentions of advertising content than ever before. A full 15% of TV viewers demonstrated proven advertising recall. We have not seen a number this high in 10 years. This was 50% higher than the 10% proven recall Mercedes was able to generate for their similarly-timed E-class launch advertising, with an estimated launch budget three times as great. This type of data is great because it provides a sort of controlled experiment of a traditional versus non-traditional launch of an entirely new product line.

Dealer Advertising and Promotions

As with all new car launches, generating dealer motivation and cooperation behind the program was critical to success. BMW wanted its dealers to be integrated into the promotion from the outset. Baba Shetty, Media Communications Manager, commented:

> They were not overly enthusiastic when we first told them we wanted them to spend their scarce resources promoting a brand new car that would not be ready for delivery until March of the following year. The Z3 situation provided an important test of BMW's renewed dealer relations. We had to get it right.

Shetty began dealer visits in June 1995 with a presentation emphasizing the strategic value of the launch to BMW, the marketing support levels both BMW and MGM were putting behind the Bond campaign, and the positives of the launch timing vis-à-vis other planned BMW activities. Shetty commented on his dealer road show experience:

> Plan execution was complicated. We had 345 dealers and only 150 cars available for them to display in their showrooms during the promotional period. We had to run the program in three waves, with the vehicles circulating among dealers. Now, that would have been enough in and of itself, but the presentations were about as tough as they get. Some of the dealers just sat there, looking at me in disbelief as I explained this phenomenal opportunity that would not come to fruition until.... March of 1996. I basically told them, "Look. You can go with this and make the most of the opportunity, or you can ignore it. It is your choice. But we are behind it, and MGM is behind it, and we are both behind it 150%." The quality of the promotional materials did the rest.

The dealer promotional package showcased a private screening of the Bond film and car before the box office film opening. Dealers compiled a guest list of 200–400 of their best customers and mailed personalized invitations to the film screening. Dealership owners were on-hand at opening night to greet customers and deliver motivating introductory speeches. Some dealers hosted cocktail receptions before or after the show. "007: Licensed to Sell" kits (see Exhibit 10) were also created. These included multi-media kiosk videos, a film canister of "spy films" of the product in action, and a mock "BOND 007" license plate. Car toppers, showroom display cars (for a limited loan period), and database-building ideas were also made available to participating dealers. The theater arrangements for the screening events were made courtesy of MGM studios, at the participating dealer's expense. These events attracted great local publicity, appearing in local newspapers, and often reported on metropolitan television and radio.

Frederick Tierney, General Manager of Foreign Motors West, Boston's largest BMW dealership, commented further on dealer reactions to the overall launch plan:

> I had no problems with the overall program or the advertising. It was innovative. It seemed impactful. To be honest, I thought that they were *over*doing it. The Z3 was a special interest niche car, it was only shown in the Bond film for a minuscule amount of time, and BMW was going to such elaborate lengths to publicize it. What if they sold too many roadsters with all the hype? How were we going to maintain all this momentum and keep the customers patient? It seemed like a big job ahead for the dealerships.

Success of the Phase I Launch Plan

The final launch plan budget was split 40/60 between what might be labeled "traditional" and "non-traditional" elements. Internally and externally, the MGM/BMW co-launch was declared a success. The Bond film had the largest opening weekend in MGM's history, grossing $26.2 million in ticket sales (see Exhibit 11 for box office performance data of other notable film placement examples). Marshall estimated that "the advertising, promotion, and associated publicity from the BMW tie-in added millions to *GoldenEye's* earnings."[15] Z3 product reviews were favorable (see Exhibit 12). Over

---

[15]Source: "Now It's the Cars that Make the Characters Go," *The New York Times,* April 21, 1996, section 2, p. 13.

9,000 Z3 product orders were pre-booked by December 1995, as compared with 5,000 projected. The product's unavailability, once viewed as a potential liability, was retrospectively viewed as a great asset. According to James McDowell: "It heightened the excitement value of the message and made people ripe with anticipation for the experience." Dealers agreed, as reflected in comments by Sales Manager Joe Santamaria of Boston's Foreign Motors West BMW dealership:

> It was a real shot in the arm for us. Traffic in the dealership was up, and lots of people came in saying, "Hey! That's the car that Bond drives!" Or "I saw that in the movie!" They were placing orders for the car sight unseen. The hype in the movie was excellent.

The net result was that the dealers upgraded to meet the challenge, BMW developed an order bank, the roadster was successfully launched, and a niche was created. Management also noted cost efficiencies gained with the non-traditional launch plan. Management was left with the feeling that the dollars spent were more impactful than they would have been if placed in traditional programs.

> We spent about 50% less than the Share-of-Voice/ Share-of-Market rule dictates.[16] (Baba Shetty) (see Exhibit 13).
>
> We definitely got higher impact per dollar spent. (George Neill)

---

[16]Share of voice (SOV) refers to a company's share of total advertising expenditures for all products in a given category. The Share-of-Voice/ Share-of-Market rule for ad budget setting declares that all things being equal, the advertising share of voice should be set equal to the company's share of market.

Bill Pettit added a more sober summary: "Bottom line, how do we measure the success of the program? Nothing blew up."

Phase II Launch Strategy

Phase I of the Z3 launch created "a sort of paradigm shift" at BMW. McDowell explained:

> We will probably never return to traditional programs after getting a taste of the power of a plan like this. Sure there are negatives but the impact simply cannot be matched using traditional elements. Usually the risks of new product introduction are so great you find yourself relying on traditional marketing elements for the false sense of security they provide. But that's what it is: a false sense of security. It would have cost at least three times more to do what we did relying solely on traditional media.

This change in philosophy colored January planning meetings in which Phase II Z3 strategies and tactics were to be set. The whole process had been invigorating for the managers involved. But as the January planning progressed, fond memories of Hollywood premiers and rendezvous in Central Park with celebrities were mixed with recognition of the $600 million investment in Spartanburg and the strategic significance of the Z3. As one manager put it, "This is fun. But we better get it right."

Exhibit 1 BMW Unit Sales History (U.S. and Worldwide)

	U.S. Unit Sales[a] (in thousands)	Worldwide Unit Sales[b] (in thousands)
1984	70.9	434.0
1985	87.9	440.7
1986	96.8	446.1
1987	87.8	461.3
1988	73.3	484.1
1989	64.9	523.0
1990	63.6	525.9
1991	53.3	552.7
1992	66.0	588.7
1993	78.0	534.4
1994	83.8	573.9
1995	94.5	590.1

[a]Source: Ward's Automotive Yearbook.
[b]Source: Bayerische Moteren Werke AG BMW, various years.

Exhibit 2 Notable Movie Product Placement Examples

Movie	Product/Brand	Placement Fee	Placement Detail	Media Comments
E.T. The Extraterrestrial	Reeses Pieces	N/A	Candy trail used to coax E.T. out of hiding place	M&Ms' decline of original deal cited as "marketing blunder that ranks with Ford Edsel and New Coke." A Reeses sales increase 66%.
Risky Business	Rayban	N/A	Tom Cruise sports Raybans in his new role as pimp	Rayban sales triple.
License to Kill	Lark cigarettes	$350,000	Lark as Bond's cigarette brand of choice	"Cigarette placements are tricky. Most companies don't want any part of it anymore because they hear too much negative feedback."
Grand Canyon	Lexus	N/A	Lexus breaks down in seedy L.A. neighborhood	N/A
Silence of the Lambs	Arby's Roast Beef	N/A	Crumbled Arby's wrappers and cups included among decrepit decor of serial murderer's house	"Focus group participants very outspoken about how they would never eat at that restaurant because every time they saw the logo they thought of the killer. I think we can count that as a bad placement."[b]
Forrest Gump	Dr Pepper	N/A	Dr Pepper portrayed as Gump's beverage of choice	"If that's not the best placement of '94, I don't know what is."
Dumb and Dumber	Hawaiian Tropic Suntan Lotion	Products and ads for filming	Last 5 minutes of movie show Hawaiian Tropic Girls in Hawaiian Tropic Tour Bus	"Hawaiian Tropic received over 100 placements last year. It's the best kind of advertising there is for a small brand like us."
Natural Born Killers	Coca-Cola	"Polar bears" ad licensing rights	Coke commercial aired as backdrop to violent crime scene	N/A
Get Shorty	Oldsmobile Silhouette minivan	Products for filming	Silhouette, touted as "Cadillac of Minivans," becomes one of film's running gags.	Vehicle selected over Ford for side door that opens automatically. Sales down, though dealers like traffic and word-of-mouth that movie generated.
Waiting to Exhale	Mercedes Benz	N/A	Disgruntled wife burns husband's Mercedes	Company was looking for "nice upscale place ment," not pleased with the way vehicle depicted.
Twister	Dodge Ram Pickup Truck	5 $25,000 trucks; 20 windshields	Investigative team chases tornadoes in Ram trucks	Ford battled over this "perfect script for a truck" but lost.
Mission Impossible	Apple PowerBook	$15 million tie-in ad campaign	Laptops prove integral to solving intrigue plot	Apple sales continue long-term sales.
Flipper	Pepsi	$40,000	Shot of crunched-up soda can on dock	Pepsi label digitally added after scene shot with Coke can in response to marketing deal with parent.

aSource: "We Ought to Be In Pictures," *St. Louis Dispatch*, April 8, 1995, p. 1D

bSource: "Movies: It's a Wrap," *L.A. Times*, September 3, 1995

cSource: "Now It's the Cars that make the Characters Go," *New York Times*, April 21, 1996, section 2, p. 13.

dSource: "We Ought to Be In Pictures," *St. Louis Dispatch*, April 8, 1995, p. 1D.

eSource: "Casting Call Goes Out; Products Needed to Play Major Roles in Movies," *Marketing News*, July 31, 1995, p. 1

f"It's A Wrap (But Not Plain): From Budweiser to BMW, Brand Names Are Popping Up More and More on Screen," *L.A. Times*, September 3, 1995, Calendar Section, p. 4.

Exhibit 3 Timeline of Key Events

Date	Event
1992	Special Project Group founded to lead new product development initiative
1993	Beginning of product clinics to develop roadster concept
May 1993	Spartanburg facility announced. Car(s) to be produced there not specified to public
Spring 1994	Z3 launch team specifies "Non-Traditional" Launch
June 1994	RFP's to 30 agencies for "non-traditional, innovative launch plan"
September 1994	First U.S. made BMWs roll off Spartanburg production line
Fall 1994	Negotiations with MGM begin for *GoldenEye* film
January 1995	BMW/MGM oral agreement (signed 6 months later)
June 1995	Dealer visits begin
September 11, 1995	Neiman's catalog promotion announced on the *Today Show*
November 1995	Central Park Launch Event, *Tonight Show* appearance, Radio DJ Program, Go: An American Road Story Video, and *GoldenEye* Premier
March 1996	First cars available at dealers

Exhibit 4 Z3 Roadster Neiman Marcus Christmas Catalog Offer[a]

[a]Copyright 1995, NM Direct. Reprinted with permission.

Exhibit 5 1996 Apple Corporate Print Advertising Referencing BMW Website[a]

Exhibit 6 Sample Press Clipping from the Central Park Z3 Roadster Launch Event[a]

BMW Roadster meets Bond, James Bond

By Melanie Wells
USA TODAY

NEW YORK — BMW of North America is hitching a ride with Hollywood for the introduction of its new two-seat roadster: Brace yourself for BMW 007.

In *GoldenEye*, the latest James Bond flick from MGM/United Artists, Hollywood's favorite spy exchanges his $135,000 Aston Martin for a BMW Z3 Roadster. The BMW is expected to sell for under $30,000 when it rolls out in the first quarter of 1996.

The link offers the kind of highbrow panache that a low-priced luxury sports car could only find in movieland. David Stolkos of Automotive Marketing Consultants calls the deal a "marketing coup" for the carmaker.

BMW was able to approve the *GoldenEye* script for the studio's use of its car. It's also able to feature the movie's latest Bond, actor Pierce Brosnan, in two TV spots without having to pay a customarily steep celebrity endorsement fee. Why? The actor appears as part of the movie's promotion.

TV commercials break tonight from BMW's new ad agency, Fallon McElligott. Print ads will also feature cuts from *GoldenEye*.

Among the other advertising and promotional plans for the Roadster:

▶ BMW's first-ever cinema commercial — a two-minute spot that will run closer to the time of the Roadster's launch — and an airplane in-

'GOLDENEYE': Ads for BMW Z3 Roadster feature images from new James Bond movie.

flight video, both coordinated by Dick Clark Corporate Productions in Burbank.

▶ A promotional appearance for the car during late night NBC programming, probably on *The Tonight Show*.

▶ Prominent placement during the Olympic Torch Relay, of which BMW is the official "mobility" sponsor. The color of the BMW featured in *GoldenEye* is a new cerulean shade the carmaker calls Atlanta Blue.

BMW vice president of marketing James McDowell says the Roadster's launch will comprise about 15% of the carmaker's 1996 ad budget.

The German automaker spent $64.9 million on all advertising during the first seven months of '95, according to Competitive Media Reporting. The total for 1994: $102.6 million.

Exhibit 7 *Automotive News* Cartoon[a]

[a]©Arkie G. Hudkins, Jr. As seen in *Automotive News,* November 20, 1995. For T. A. Brooks. Reprinted with permission.

Exhibit 8 Introductory Print Advertising for the BMW Z3 Roadster

Exhibit 9 Comparative Launch Advertising Campaign Expenditures[a] and Introductory Year Sales

Product/Brand	Launch Date	Introductory Year Sales[d] (units)	Launch Advertising Support (millions)
– *Sport Utility Vehicles*			
– Kia Sportage	January 1995	8,015	30.0
– Toyota RAV-4	January 1995	29,815	30.0
– Ford Expedition	January 1996	N/A	35.0
– Acura SLX	November 1995	1,657	40.0
– *Sedans/Minivans*			
– Dodge Neon	January 1994	93,300	88.7
– Plymouth Breeze	January 1996	N/A	45.0
– Hyundai Accent	February 1995	50,658	99.9
– Ford Contour	September 1994	140,987	55.3
– Ford Windstar	March 1994	62,317	57.0
– Mazda Millenia	April 1994	29,096	30.0
– Nissan Altima	September 1992	69,489	70.9
– Oldsmobile Aurora	May 1994	33,206	42.7
– *Luxury/Performance*			
– Land Rover Discovery	October 1994	14,085	9.4
– Acura RL	January 1996	N/A	40.0
– Infiniti I-30	May 1995	15,194	35.0
– Lexus LX 450	January 1996	N/A	20.0
– Mercedes C-Class	November 1993	19,351	
Average Launch Budget			$20 million
Average Launch Reach[b] Goal			75–90%
Average Launch Frequency[c] Goal			2.5

[a]Source: Competitive Media Reporting and Media Week *SuperBrands 1995*.

[b]Note: Reach defined as percent of target audience exposed at least once to advertising in a given period.

[c]Note: Frequency defined as average number of times target audience member is exposed to advertising in a given period.

[d]Note: Sales figures reflect first twelve months after launch date.

Exhibit 10 "007: Licensed to Sell" Dealer Promotional Kits

Exhibit 11 Box Office Draws for Noteworthy Product Placement Movies[a]

Film	Introductory Year	Opening Week Ticket Sales (in millions of dollars)
Twister	1996	$41.1
Mission: Impossible	1996	56.8
Flipper	1996	4.5
Waiting to Exhale	1995	14.1
GoldenEye	1995	26.2
Get Shorty	1995	12.7
Natural Born Killers	1994	11.2
Dumb and Dumber	1994	16.4
Forrest Gump	1994	24.5
Silence of the Lambs	1991	13.8
Grand Canyon	1991	0.3
License to Kill	1989	8.8
Risky Business	1983	4.3
E.T. The Extra Terrestrial	1982	13.0

[a]Source: *Variety,* various dates

Exhibit 12 Sample Product Reviews from Major Automotive Magazines

It's movie star looks notwithstanding, the Z3 is at its best on sun-blurred country lanes, when the engine is in full, reedy song and your hair is buffeted into bug-laced dreadlocks. This is a great sports car, an enthusiasts driver's first wish from the genie. Sexual dynamite on the outside, as intimate as a shared cigarette on the inside, perfectly constructed and effortless fun to drive, the Z3 leaves one wounded with desire. Not bad for a car made in Spartanburg, S.C. (*New York Times*, Automobiles section)

At the start of the day-long press event, I wasn't quite sure that the world really needed another roadster, but by noon I was convinced the BMW Z3 is a vehicle that mankind can't do without. And with the announcement of a $28,750 base price, it's certain that great hordes of Americans will find the Z3 just as irresistible. Z3 fans wishing for more romp in their roadsters will have to wait for the release of versions with the new 2.8 in-line six, which will deliver about another 60 horsepower. But, before you gripe about this machine's lack of tire-burning power, consider this: the 1.9 liter four makes the $28,750 price, putting the Z3 in reach of many more buyers than would a six-powered version, which will be closer to $40,000. (*Motor Trend Magazine*)

I wanted to drive the Z3 to see for myself what all the shouting was about. But I probably would have wanted to put the car through some paces even if it hadn't been the star of the latest Bond movie. There were at least three good reasons for being curious about the Z3. First because it is a Beemer. We all know that the Bavarian factories don't design any junk. The BMW—any BMW—has that good, unmistakable solid feeling of careful German engineering that everyone likes and responds to in a car. The second reason was that it is built in Spartanburg, S.C. The third reason has to do with money. Everyone likes a deal, and the Z3 was priced at just under $30,000 which seemed like a bargain. Word was that Mercedes and Porsche were floored by the price, since they are scheduled to bring out competitive cars in the next year or so but hadn't been planning on giving them away. Maybe, people said, BMW was going to sell the car as a kit . . . you do the final assembly and paint the thing. Well, I got to drive the Z3 and I am here to report, straight out, that BMW isn't selling any kits, and that the car is as exciting as the price. Is the car fun to drive? The answer is: yeah, man. I kept thinking that this was a car that fills a particular niche and fills it just about perfectly. It'll be worth it, believe me. (*Forbes*)

Exhibit 13 1995 Unit Sales and Advertising Spending within the U.S. Luxury/Performance Segment

Manufacturer	Total Sales[a] (units)	Media Expenditures[b] (millions)
Acura	112,137	$197.2
Audi	12,575	25.8
BMW	84,501	87.5
Cadillac	162,672	227.4
Ford/Lincoln	120,191	30.6
Infiniti	51,449	106.7
Jaguar	15,195	34.5
Land Rover	12,045	18.9
Lexus	87,419	202.8
Mercedes	73,002	88.4
Porsche	5,838	10.9
Saab	21,679	31.2
Volvo	81,788	56.5
Average Advertising Expense Per Luxury Car Sold		$982
Average Advertising Eexpense For All Cars Sold		$372

[a]Source: 1995 J.D. Power & Associates
[b]Source: 1995 LNA Competitive Media Reporting
Note: Spending includes local dealer and dealer association dollars.

ALLOY.COM:
MARKETING TO GENERATION Y

On May 12, 1999, Matt Diamond, James Johnson and Sam Gradess were visiting San Francisco for a last round of meetings with West Coast investment analysts. They were just days from the initial public offering (IPO) of shares in Alloy.com, the catalog and Internet merchant of teen-oriented clothing that they had founded on Diamond's graduation from Harvard Business School in 1996. Snarled in freeway gridlock, Diamond was on his cellphone discussing the IPO's pricing with analysts back in New York City.

An analyst urged Diamond to respond to an invitation by the world's largest Website and portal, America Online (AOL), to make Alloy an anchor tenant on its teen shopping site. AOL wanted $2 million per year for the rights. "Matt, if you say yes, that will be big. If you announce tomorrow that AOL's partner in the Generation Y market is Alloy, it will put Alloy on the map. It will definitely affect the IPO price."

Diamond sighed. A headline deal with AOL today could be worth perhaps 10% on the stock price. But AOL was asking rich terms. It was widely rumored that AOL preyed on startup companies in the weeks before they went public, tempting them with star billing on its portal at the very moment when the publicity was most valuable. He estimated that he'd be paying a $45 cpm (cost per thousand exposures) to anchor the AOL teen shopping site. Nobody paid more than $30 for Web eyeballs. In the three years that he had been running Alloy, Diamond had prided himself on doing deals that made sense. If he could not anticipate a profit to Alloy from a promotional deal, he reasoned that Wall Street would not anticipate a profit either.

"It won't pay out," he told the analyst firmly. "We only do deals that produce value." To his colleagues in the limousine, he wondered out loud, "Am I right?"

The Generation Y Market

Termed the "hottest demographic of the moment," Generation Y came to the attention of marketers in the late 1990s. This "echo of the baby boom" was made up of children and teenagers born in the United States between 1975 and 1989 and therefore aged between 10 and 24. They were estimated to be a 56 million strong group of actual and potential consumers, some three times the size of their immediate predecessor, Generation X.[1] The U.S. Census Bureau projected that the 10 to 24 age group would grow from 56.3 million to 63.1 million by 2010, growing faster than the general population.

Although Generation Y matched its parent's generation in size, in almost every other way it was very different. One in three was not Caucasian. One in four lived in a single-parent household. Three in four had working mothers.[2] "Body glittered, tattooed, pierced, they're a highly fragmented, unpredictable group of teenagers who, while tottering around on five inch soles, voice conservative opinions about sexuality,

Professor John Deighton and Visiting Scholar Gil McWilliams prepared this case as the basis for class discussion rather than to illustrate either effective or ineffective handling of an administrative situation. The contribution of Ann Leamon, Manager, Center for Case Development, is gratefully acknowledged. Certain sensitive information in this case has been disguised and should not be regarded as informative as to the prospects of the company.

[1]Neuborne, Ellen and Kathleen Kerwin. "Generation Y," *Business Week*, February 15, 1999, Cover story.
[2]Neuborne, Ellen and Kathleen Kerwin. "Generation Y," *Business Week*, February 15, 1999, Cover story.

government, the American dream and an end-of-century commitment to spirituality."[3] They were computer literate: 81% of teens used the Internet, according to Chicago-based Teenage Research International (TRI), which also noted that over a 3 month period on AOL, they posted more than 2 million Leonardo Di Caprio related messages.[4]

According to Lester Rand, Director of the Rand Youth Poll, they had money to spend and an appetite for spending it.

> They have a higher incremental allowance from their parents, and with the growth in our service economy, they are able to secure jobs easily and at rising minimum wages. They're exposed to so many different products on TV, in the mall and through their friends. It's a generation who grew up with excess as a norm.[5]

In 1999 Jupiter reported that 67% of on-line teens and 37% of on-line kids said they made use of on-line shopping sites, either buying or gathering information about products.[6] Generation Y was expected to spend approximately $136 billion in 1999, before accounting for the group's influence on purchases made by parents and other adults. (See Exhibits 1 and 2 for this and other estimates.)

On-line Competition for Generation Y Spending

Generation Y's size and spending power had not gone unnoticed. Many conventional and on-line retailers courted them. Alloy viewed its most significant competitors as dELiAs and the on-line magalog mXg. The neighborhood mall was also a threat.

dELiAs Inc.[7]

The largest on-line and catalog merchant serving Generation Y was New York-based dELiAs, with 1998 sales of $158 million. Founded in 1995 by two 33-year-old former Yale roommates, Stephen Kahn and Christopher Edgar, dELiAs sold through print catalogs mailed to more than 10 million recipients, of whom 6 million had bought within the past year. It managed its own order fulfillment from a warehouse complex, and operated twenty conventional retail stores. Most of dELiAs' 1,500 employees were under 30. Its phone representatives were often high school and college students, and they frequently offered fashion advice as well as taking orders. In November 1998 dELiAs Inc. paid $4.75 million for the trademarks and mailing lists of bankrupt Fulcrum's 5 catalogs (Zoe for teenage girls, Storybook Heirlooms, Playclothes, After the Stork, and Just for Kids), giving them 5 million names which nearly doubled their database. It also paid $2.4 million for merchandise from Zoe and Storybook.

By 1999, dELiAs went to market with a complex set of brands and marketing methods:

- The dELiAs brand marketed to teenage girls as a catalog through the mail and as dELiAs*cOm on the Web.

- The gURL.com Website was an on-line magazine for girls and young women, carrying articles as well as free e-mail, free homepage hosting and publishing tools, and links to a network of third-party sites for girls and women. gURL was the only property that was not engaged in commerce.

- The droog brand marketed apparel to 12-to 20-year-old males through the mail and on-line.

- The TSI Soccer catalog sold soccer gear by mail and on-line.

- Storybook Heirlooms retailed apparel and accessories for girls under 13 by mail and Web catalog.

- Dotdotdash sold apparel, footwear and accessories for girls aged 7 to 12 by mail and Web catalog.

- Discountdomain.com was a subscription Website selling discounted close-out merchandise.

- Contentsonline.com offered unusual home furnishings, light furniture and household articles to females aged 13–24. While predominantly a Web catalog, the property appeared intermittently as a print insert in dELiAs' print catalog.

[3]O'Leary, Noreen. "Marketing: The Boom Tube," *Adweek,* Vol. 39, No. 20, May 18, 1999, pp. S44-S52.

[4]Brown, Eryn. "Loving Leo Online," *Fortune,* April 12, 1999, p. 152.

[5]BAXExpress, July/August 1999, http:baxworld.com/baxexpress/0799/consumers.html.

[6]Sacharow, Anya. "Shadow of On-line Commerce Falls on Postmodern Kids," Jupiter Communications report, June 7, 1999.

[7]Information drawn from company website: www.dELiAs.com

In April 1999, dELiAs Inc. spun off its Internet properties in an IPO, selling shares in a company called iTurF which earned revenues from all of the above on-line elements. In terms of the deal, these on-line businesses could advertise in dELiAs' print catalogs at a rate of $40 per 1,000 catalogs. The dELiAs catalog, 60 million of which were printed in 1998, had the largest domestic circulation of any publication directed at Generation Y. The on-line magazines also shared the parent company's 354,000 square foot distribution center in Hanover, PA. Because iTurF did not take ownership of inventory until a customer's order was placed, the risk of obsolescence and markdowns remained with the parent company. ITurF shared offices with the parent company, enjoying a sub-market rent for New York metropolitan space.

In May 1999, iTurF announced record quarterly sales of $2.6 million (up from $0.69 million in the first quarter of 1998). Gross profit was $1.3 million, or 49.1% of revenues, up from $0.34 million or 49.3% of revenues 1998 (see Exhibit 3). However, dELiAs reported that it expected its iTurF unit to report a loss for the fiscal year. By April 1999, the number of people who had ever bought at the iTurF Websites was 66,000 (up from 35,000 at the end of December 1998), and the number of unique visitors was 731,000 in April 1999 alone. Analysts estimated that each customer cost $26 to acquire.[8] Private label merchandise accounted for 40% of iTurF's sales, in line with dELiA's ratio.

iTurf entered into agreements with RocketCash Corp. and DoughNET, companies that had been established to let parents control the on-line spending of their children. For example, RocketCash let parents establish a credit card account and set each child's access to specific merchant sites, times of operation, and the option to set up an auto-allowance to periodically replenish the account. DoughNet was a virtual debit card that parents could set up for their children. Parents could customize DoughNET's site to guide teens through all aspects of managing their money.

In April 1999, dELiAs' decision to spin off iTurF seemed shrewd. The market capitalization of dELiAs Inc. was $90 million, on sales of $200 million annually. ITurF was capitalized at $200 million on a sales run rate of $12 million annually.

mXg Media Inc.[9]

Hunter Heaney and Stuart MacFarlane graduated from the Harvard Business School in 1996. MacFarlane joined Bain & Co. and Heaney joined BancBoston Robertson Stephens. Heaney told how he got the idea for mXg while Christmas shopping at Nordstrom's for his then girlfriend. A saleswoman had told him that the "Y" necklace featured on the "Friends" sitcom was in style. "I knew there had to be a more direct way to find out about fashion trends influenced by entertainment," Heaney said.[10]

In 1997, Heaney and MacFarlane quit their jobs and moved to Manhattan Beach, CA, to be close to Hollywood and surfers and skaters. Using the pay phone while staying at a local motel they raised $250,000 in increments of $5,000, and launched mXg, styling it a "magalog," a hybrid of catalog and magazine,  aimed at teenage girls. Unlike a conventional magazine, mXg reported exactly where to go to buy the fashion items that it featured on its pages. MacFarlane recalled their early lean times: "Typically, retailers order inventory in sixes (one small, two medium, two large, one extra large). But instead of saying 'We'll take 2,000 sixes' we said 'We'll take six'—literally one of each." They could fund a circulation of only 20,000 for the magazine's launch in the fall of 1997, but it did well. Some 5% of the recipients bought from it. The numbers were good enough to induce Urban Outfitters, a retail fashion chain, to invest $5 million for 40% of the company, incorporated as mXg Media, Inc.

Merchandise accounted for most of mXg Media's revenues, but advertising revenue was doubling each issue. The company used newsstand distribution (150,000 issues per quarter at $2.95 each, refunded with a purchase), as well as distribution in bookstores like Barnes & Noble, and B Dalton Booksellers. The magazine had a pass-along rate of almost six readers per copy.

Sensitive to the tastes of their target audience of female teenagers, they hired teens, paying them $7 per hour to work after school answering letters, doing interviews, and writing copy to make it sound authentic. "No printed word goes out without a teen girl checking it . . . being

[8]CIBC World Markets, Equity Research, June 2, 1999.

[9]Information drawn from company website: www.mXgonline.com
[10]Waxler, Caroline. "Guys with moxie," *Forbes*, May 31, 1999, pp. 130–131.

uncool is the kiss of death in this business."[11] At the start of each fashion season mXg recruited 30 "Moxie girls" to spend a hypothetical $150 each. Their virtual purchases determined which items appeared in the next issue. The magazine paid staffers to model clothes and invited would-be teen celebrities to pose free to gain recognition.

A Website, mXgonline.com, was established in the summer of 1997. It comprised a magazine, chat rooms, and community sites, and sold clothes and accessories. mXg Media pursued other access points for their on-line magalog, featuring it in on-line fashion malls such as fashionwindow.com. In 1999, mXg sponsored concerts featuring acts like Gus Gus which were favored by Generation Y. Yahoo produced a series of Webcasts of the concerts for teens. The company described its mission as cross-media publishing, targeted exclusively at teen girls. It planned to add mXgtv, an Internet video site, to its media portfolio later in the year.

A Crowded Marketplace?

Other companies vied for the attention of Generation Y. Bolt.com was a content-based magazine-type site skewed towards a market slightly older than that of the Generation Y market, but into which the older end of the Y market might eventually fall. Bolt.com included sections titled jobs, money, movie reviews, music, news and issues, sex and dating, and sports. It had a chat room and free e-mail, and sold branded merchandise. It boasted that 5,000 people joined it every day.

The magazine *Seventeen* had an on-line version, offering chat rooms and message boards, as well as its regular articles, quizzes and features. Indeed many magazines were now launching on-line versions of their magazines, and new print publications like *Twist* and *Jump* had appeared to compete for generation Y advertising revenues.

Broader on-line retailers served this market, such as bluefly.com selling discounted brands on-line. Strong competition came from mall-based stores such as The Buckle, Gadzooks, Abercrombie & Fitch, The Gap, American Eagle Outfitters, and Guess, all of whom sold merchandise on- and off-line. Apparel and sportswear manufacturers were developing on-line sales sites. Nike and Tommy Hilfiger planned to launch e-commerce sites with broad product offerings.

---

[11]Waxler, Caroline. "Guys with moxie," *Forbes*, May 31, 1999, pp. 130–131.

Alloy.com

As a Harvard MBA student in 1996, Matt Diamond wrote a business plan proposing the idea of marketing 'extreme sports' clothing by catalog to young people in Japan. The premise was that the popularity of this style of clothing among American youth might generate demand abroad, and that catalogs would be able to tap that demand faster than would store distribution. On graduation, Diamond implemented the plan. He and a friend, Jim Johnson, used seed money from friends and family to design and print a Japanese-language catalog, which they branded Durango Expedition. They mailed it in January 1997, and at the same time they went live with Japanese and English Websites, as alternative channels.

The venture flopped. The mailing generated no significant sales. However, they discovered to their surprise that they were receiving hits on the English Website from American youths. Within a month they had reconceptualized the business to serve American teen girls through catalog and on-line channels, under the name Alloy. Diamond and Johnson each contributed $60,000 in cash and another friend, Sam Gradess, added $150,000 in cash when he joined six months later from Goldman Sachs. In November 1997, the first issue of the Alloy catalog, 48 pages in length, was mailed to a purchased mailing list of 150,000 teen names. At the same time Alloy's Website became active. The intention at that time was to reduce the number of catalogs mailed as on-line sales grew.

Organization

Diamond became president and CEO of the fledgling company. Johnson took the title of chief operating officer. Gradess was chief financial officer. Neil Vogel joined from Ladenburg Thalman & Co., a consumer and Internet investment banking group to be the chief corporate development officer. Fellow Harvard sectionmate Andrew Roberts left PricewaterhouseCoopers to join Alloy in January 1999 as VP of business development. Another Harvard MBA, Joan Rosenstock, was hired as marketing director, having held positions in marketing at the National Basketball Association as well as in advertising account management. Erstwhile music editor of teenage magazine *Seventeen*, Susan Kaplow, became executive editor and Karen Ngo, who had been a feature editor and fashion stylist at *Seventeen*, was hired as creative director.

Alloy outsourced as many of its operations as it could. Working with mostly domestic vendors who could produce and ship within a 2–8 week timeframe, Alloy purchased only 50% of its featured products and relied on a quick order and re-order ability so as to control inventory levels. Telephone orders and order-processing were outsourced to Harrison Fulfillment Services, based in Chattanooga, TN. OneSoft Corp., based in Virginia, handled on-line ordering and fed its orders to Chattanooga for fulfillment. Alloy personnel concentrated on marketing and merchandising issues.

Target Market

Unlike dELiAs, Alloy opted for a single-brand strategy targeted at both genders. "Rather than dividing our marketing resources across multiple brands and Websites, we seek to maximize the impact of our marketing efforts by promoting a single brand. We believe this allows us to attract visitors to our Website and build customer loyalty rapidly and efficiently."[12] Indeed Diamond considered that Alloy's key differentiator lay in being gender neutral, believing that a successful Generation Y community depended on dynamic boy-girl interaction. He thought of their community site as an MTV-like interactive distribution channel. "It's an opportunity for girls to talk to boys, boys to talk to girls, to deliver music, to deliver fashion, to deliver lifestyle." Diamond conceded that the majority of the visitors to its Website were girls, and the print catalog was even more skewed towards girls. However, it was the intention to attract boys to the Website by other means. There was some evidence that this strategy was working, as the percentage of female Website visitors declined from 70% in early 1999[13] towards a desired 60/40 ratio. Boys tended to be drawn by music, extreme sports, and games, while girls appeared to be more responsive to chat and browsing. Diamond felt, however, that just as both teen boys and girls hang out in shopping malls, watching each other as well as chatting, the on-line presence of both boys and girls was important.

Alloy's target was teens making buying decisions with parents "somewhere in the background." The target group ranged from 12-20, but the median age was 15. Alloy was careful not to aim too young, partly for regulatory reasons, but also because they felt that by targeting 15-year-olds they reached a group at an important buying point in their lives. About 35–40% of teenage purchasing was on apparel and accessories, and Alloy monitored what else this group bought. As owners of a "piece of real estate" they did not see themselves as limited to selling apparel and accessories, and had moved into soft furnishings.

The Offering

It was standard practice among catalog retailers, such as Land's End and L.L. Bean, to sell products under the catalog's brand. Even at dELiAs, private-label sales accounted for about 40% of the mix. Alloy, however, emphasized recognized teen brands such as Vans, Diesel, and O'Neill, both to attract buyers and to offer reassurance of quality. Only 20–25% of Alloy's sales came from labels that were exclusive to Alloy, such as Stationwagon and Local 212. Diamond was philosophical about the pros and cons of private label, "There's no denying you get better margins on own-label goods. But running with your own labels leaves you vulnerable to ending up as a skateboard brand."

The Alloy site aimed to build what Diamond termed the 3 Cs of on-line retailing to this generation: Community, Content, and Commerce. He noted that constant communication was key to understanding this generation. They had a strong need to chat about movies, television, music and what was happening at school, and to seek advice from one another, sound off about pet hates, and occasionally shop.

A small team of in-house editors created editorial content on the site, supplemented by syndicated content. The audience also contributed content, receiving in exchange a sense of community, in chat-rooms and message boards, and by submitting their own letters, poems, drawings and articles. Poems and drawings would be voted upon interactively. Chat rooms in particular were popular and frequently full (in contrast to some of the chat rooms of competitors). The chat rooms were moderated from end of school-time until midnight on a daily basis, with software employed to spot offensive or obscene language. Advice columns were a dependable magnet. (See Exhibit 7 for a sample of user-generated content.)

Andrew Roberts remembered vividly the moment when he knew that Alloy was really "onto something." In the aftermath of the Columbine High School shooting tragedy, one of the editors knew that Alloy had to respond and fast. She worked all night creating the appropriate spaces in chatrooms, and editorial content.

---

[12]IPO Offer Document May 1999.
[13]Chervitz, Darren. "IPO First Words: Alloy Online CEO Matt Diamond." Interview at CBS MarketWatch.com, June 14, 1999. http://cbs.marketwatch.com/archive/19990614/news/current/ipo_word.htx?source=htx/http2_mw&dist=na

By 8:30 a.m. the day after, 15 hours after news of the tragedy broke, Alloy had received 7,311 postings related to the events at Columbine. Roberts explained that it wasn't so much the number that impressed him, but the content of the postings. "These kids were really anxious. We had kids who followed the goth fashion who were really scared about how others would treat them. Other kids were reassuring them and saying "Don't worry, we know it wasn't you or the goths who made these guys do what they did." They just had a desperate need to talk with each other, and be reassured by each other."

Building the Brand

Alloy built its brand, and with it traffic to the Alloy site, in several ways. It undertook traditional advertising in print media (*Seventeen Magazine, YM, Rolling Stone,* and *Snowboarder*). It used hot-links from sites such as seventeen.com to advertise promotional deals. It had special co-promotional deals with, for example, MGM Entertainment, Sony Music, Burton Snowboards, MCI and EarthLink/Sprint, who provided free products and services that were used as special promotions for the Alloy community (such as private movie screenings, exclusive music give-aways, and celebrity on-line chats). Finally, it bought banner advertising on gateway sites such as Yahoo Shopping, Fashionmall.com, CatalogCity.com and CatalogLink.com.

The Business Model

There were two revenue streams: merchandise sales, and advertising and sponsorship. An agent had been retained to sell advertising on the Website, and the longer-term intention was to build an in-house sales force to sell sponsorships, banner-ads, targeted advertising (segmented by Website area, time of day, user location, or age), and combination print and Website advertising. To this end, Samantha Skey, who had been responsible for commerce, advertising and sponsorship for Disney Online and Family.com and had worked for Buena Vista Internet group, was hired in 1999 as VP of e-commerce and sponsorships. In 1999, about 10% of revenues were generated by sponsorship and advertising deals, and the proportion was expected to rise to 20% in year 2000. Alloy was aware that it would never meet all of its customers' requirements. It was happy to offer links to other sites that could be seen as competitive, such as Gap's on-line site. "Look, we figure they're going to go there anyway," noted Roberts. "If they go via us, we at least get something for it. We're happy to have such complementary deals. Probably not with dELiAs, though," he grinned.

Exhibits 4 and 5 report annual fiscal year performance 1996–1998, and quarterly performance between last quarter 1997 and first quarter 1999.

To hear Diamond describe it, running Alloy was, at least day-to-day, like running a production plant. "We know what it costs to get a customer, and we know what a customer will spend. We just have to keep the two numbers in balance. We could make a profit today, but in this investment climate there's no reward for beating your loss numbers."

By April 1999, Alloy had a database of 2.6 million names and addresses, comprising 1.7 million previous buyers and 900,000 visitors to the Website who had registered their names and addresses but had not yet made a purchase. It was mailing monthly to the most responsive of the names on this list, supplemented by purchases of new names, and it hoped to mail 20 million catalogs over the course of 1999.

Alloy's catalogs cost $450 per thousand to design, print and mail. If Alloy mailed catalogs to names from the database who had bought from it before, it received an order from about 3% of the names each time it mailed. If Alloy bought a list of new names, for example a list of American girls who owned personal computers, at a cost that was typically $100 per thousand names, the response rate on the new names[14] was about 1.5%. Alloy would often exchange some of the names of its customers for the names of customers of similar firms, if it could count on a response rate on the swapped names of close to its own 3%. By blending names from these three sources, Alloy could choose whether a particular mailing would yield a high rate of orders or expand its customer base. Over the year, Alloy's mailings comprised 10% swapped names, 70% past customers and 20% new names. Diamond found that some people in the private investment community were not well informed on the ease with which response rates could be manipulated. "Analysts ask me, why is your response rate down last month? I say 'you want a 10% response rate, I'll give you one. I'll just mail to my very best customers.'"

---

[14]List brokers typically sold names on a 'deduplicated' basis, meaning that the buyer had the right to delete and not pay for any names that it already owned.

Most orders were received by telephone, and orders from all lists ranged from $65 per customer in spring to $85 in winter. The gross margin on an order was about 50%. Alloy paid its fulfillment company $6.00 to handle each telephone order. Customers paid the shipping charges.

Traffic to the Website, as measured by Media Metrix in the quarter ending March 1999, comprised 263,000 unique visitors[15] per month. While about half of the visitors eventually registered themselves with the site by entering a name, address and e-mail information, the proportion of unique visitors in a month who registered in that month was about 8%. In addition to catalogs and Web visits, Alloy interacted with Generation Y by means of a weekly broadcast e-mail, Alloy E-Zine, sent to 850,000 site visitors who had asked to receive it.

When a visitor to the Alloy Website registered, the name was added to the print catalog mailing list. Names gathered in this way, although they had not previously bought from Alloy, tended to respond to the catalog at a rate close to the past-buyer rate of 3%. Calculating the cost of attracting someone to become a registered visitor was difficult, because Web traffic resulted from many actions: banner advertising, listings on search engines, and Alloy's print advertising in media like *Seventeen Magazine*. The catalog was a significant driver of traffic to the Web. On the day that the catalog reached its audience, traffic to the site would jump 40%. It would continue to rise to about 180% of pre-mailing levels for a week, and slowly fall back. Possessing a copy of the latest Alloy catalog conferred significant prestige in a junior high school lunchroom. And then there was word-of-mouth. Many visitors to the Website, and many who decided to register, came at no cost to Alloy because a friend had mentioned the site, had e-mailed a chat room story, or had asked for an opinion on an item of clothing shown on the site.

Less than 5% of Alloy's revenues came from orders placed on the Website. When an order was submitted on-line instead of by phone, Alloy paid its fulfillment company $3.00 instead of $6.00 to reflect the saving of telephone handling charges. Alloy's e-mailed catalog, termed Alloy E-Zine, was another small element of the business. Because Alloy had no way of knowing whether a recipient's e-mail system was able to view graphic displays or color, it used only text in the E-Zine. Only 25% of those who indicated willingness to receive it ever opened it, and of those 1% placed an order in the course of a year. These orders were fulfilled at $3.00 each if they were placed by return e-mail.

Sponsorships and banner advertising were a small but rapidly growing source of revenue. As Alloy's base of registered visitors and catalog recipients grew, both became assets that interested advertisers.

The AOL Deal

Diamond reflected on the AOL deal. It was not a question of finding $2 million. If the IPO went ahead at the planned price of $15, it would generate $55.5 million and Alloy would be awash in cash. Diamond tried not to be annoyed at the idea that AOL would offer this deal on the eve of his IPO. "I've been talking to AOL for a year about opening a teen shopping area, showing them what a big revenue opportunity it could be. Now suddenly they get it, and they think it's worth $2 million."

He thought to himself, "What else can I do with $2 million? That's over 4 million catalogs, which means more sales, more site visits, more registrations, and more E-Zine registrations. Alternatively, it could buy us exposure on television, and that would build a stronger brand." Alloy's budget for 1999 included a line item of $2.5 million for production of two television spots and $2.5 million for air time. Then again, he could buy banners on other portals and Websites at prices in the range of $20 to $30 per thousand exposures. Industry norms suggested that he could expect about 0.5% of these exposures to 'click through' to the Alloy site.

Yet AOL was Alloy's most important source of traffic to the Website. More than a third of visitors to the Alloy site used AOL as their Internet service provider. Would a competitor on the AOL site be able to intercept them? Would the announcement of a competitor's deal with AOL on the eve of the IPO be as bad for Alloy's share price as an Alloy deal would be good?

The cellphone rang again. It was his partner, Neil Vogel. "Matt, Wall Street would like it if you would do that deal. They don't want iTurF to pick it up. This is valuable real estate on a really important teen property."

---

[15]Many of the visitors to a site came more than once a month. Media Metrix used the term "unique visitors" to emphasize that they were counting visitors, not visits.

Exhibit 1 Total Teen Spending in 1996

	$ billions	%
Apparel	36.7	34
Entertainment	23.4	22
Food	16.7	15
Personal Care	9.2	9
Sporting Goods	6.7	6
Other	15.3	14
Total	108.0	100

Source: Packaged Facts via InterRep Research, in MSDW Equity Research: "Fashions of the Third Millennium," June 1999.

Exhibit 2 Estimates of Teen Spending

	Rand Youth (Adweek May 18, 1998)	Morgan Stanley Dean Witter's report "Fashions of the Third Millennium," June 1999	Teen Research Unlimited (quoted in Alloy press handout)
1996		$108 billion	
1997	$91.5 billion		
1998			$141 billion
1999		$136 billion	

Exhibit 3 Consolidated iTurf Income (in $ thousands)

	1st Quarter Ending 1 May 1999	1st Quarter Ending 30 April 1998
Net revenues	2615	69
Cost of goods	1332	35
Gross profit	1283	34
Selling, general and admin.	1753	109
Interest income (expense)	(112)	11
Loss before tax	(358)	(86)
Income tax (benefit)	(161)	(33)
Net loss	(197)	(53)
No. of unique visitors	Apr 99 = 731,000	Feb 99 = 635,000
No. of page views in April	50 million	4 million
Size of mailing database	11 million names	

Source: IPO Filing

Exhibit 4 Alloy Online Annual Fiscal Performance

Fiscal year	1996 (thousands)	1997 (thousands)	1998 (thousands)
Net merchandise revenues	$25	$1,800	$10,100
Of which on-line order placement accounted for:	-	$40	$710
Sponsorship and other revenue	-		$125
Gross profit %	32.5%	41.7%	46.3%
Selling & Marketing expenses	$98	$2,000	$9,200
Web pages views (Month of March)		1,500	25,000
Weekly e-zine registrations			480

Source: Company records

Exhibit 5 Alloy Online Quarterly Performance ($'000)

	1997 Oct 31	1998 Jan 31	1998 Apr 30	1998 Jul 31	1998 Oct 31	1999 Jan 31	1999 Apr 30
Net merchandise revenues	401	1396	1353	2082	3215	3436	2391
Sponsorship, etc.	–	–	1	5	46	73	163
Total revenues	401	1396	1354	2087	3261	3509	2544
COGS	263	783	906	1200	1665	1715	1249
Gross profit	138	613	448	887	1596	1794	1305
Gross profit % of revenue	34%	44%	33	42.5%	49%	51%	51%
Operating expenses	903	1437	1782	2992	3396	2679	3529
Net loss	(749)	(806)	(1312)	(2165)	(1901)	(985)	(2302)
Number of registered users						400,000	800,000

Source: Company records

Exhibit 6 Circulation of Leading Teen Magazines

Publication	Publisher	Circulation as of 1998/99
Seventeen (monthly)	Primedia Consumer Magazine Group	2,400,000
Teen (monthly)	EMAP	2,400,000
YM (10 x year)	Gruner & Jahr	2,200,000
Teen People (monthly)	Time Inc.	1,300,000
Jump (10 x year)	Weider Publications	350,000
Twist (monthly)	Bauer Publishing	265,650
Girl	Lewitt & LaWinter/Freedom	250,000

Source: Various

Exhibit 7 Examples of consumer-generated content on Alloy Website

ASK TUCKER

today's advice:

Q. Here's the deal. I have a crush. I really want to ask her out, but, if she says no, my social life will be totaled. She's pretty popular and if she says no, she'll tell someone and it will all go down the drain. I live in a small town and whover gets dumped (for some reason) loses their popularity. What do I do????

more ask tucker...

DATING
CRUSHING
FRIENDS
FAMILY
SEX
SCHOOL
FASHION
OTHER RANDOM STUFF

dizzy

Perfection and bliss riding on a dizzy
cloud of euphoria and joy
Blissfully falling into your strong arms
You sweep me up and clutch me close
I can't breathe and I can't think anything but you
Choking from the pure ecstasy of unconsciousness I awaken in a breathless
wonder
I am alive in a whirlwind of color
And I am floating
In your arms breathing
In your scent laughing
In your soul living
In your mind crying
In your emptiness and then gone

Source: Alloy Website

Pricing Policy

Inevitably, pricing issues have arisen in the cases in the first four parts of this book. It is inevitable because of the complementary nature of (1) the three Ps of "value creation"—product, place, and promotion—and (2) "value capture" through pricing. One cannot isolate a pricing decision from decisions about the rest of the marketing mix. The cases in Part V were selected because the pricing decision was of prominent concern in the situation but the context in which the pricing decision arises was still clearly set out.

Like previous parts, Part V addresses both classic and contemporary issues, which are supported by two notes. The first, "Pricing: A Value-Based Approach," supports the first three cases and their presentation of classic pricing issues. "Cumberland Metal Industries: Engineered Products Division, 1980" focuses on the role of manufacturing costs, value to the customer, and marketing costs when making a pricing decision. The case also raises the question of how a pricing strategy should evolve over time. Cumberland has a real innovation to market, but what about pricing in later stages of the life cycle?

Pricing in the later stages is the subject of the next two cases. In "Eastman Kodak Company," Eastman Kodak faces a decline in perceived product differentiation, and the strategy it puts in place helps to flesh out the options the company faces: using a pricing solution to a lost market share problem as opposed to an advertising or new production introductions solution.

"Becton Dickinson & Company: VACUTAINER Systems Division (Condensed)" presents the related problems of increased buyer power and a buyer who tries to wield that power in a negotiation process. What should Becton give on price? On other marketing issues?

The second note, "Pricing and Market Making on the Internet," provides a structure for analyzing the last two cases, both of which investigate the ways that the Internet enables new ways of transacting business. The Internet's impact on speed and communications cost makes it feasible for companies to incorporate auctions, dynamic pricing, and new marketing schemes, as illustrated in the Priceline case in the Part III: Going-to-Market. Here, the introductory note supports two cases: Onsale, Inc. which looks at the operations of an early Internet auction house, and "Coca-Cola's New Vending Machine (A): Pricing to Capture Value, or Not?" which explores the possibility of dynamic pricing where prices change regularly with demand or supply conditions. Is this a good idea for Coke? For other marketers? For consumers?

Building on the pricing knowledge developed in earlier parts, the material here advances your skill in developing pricing plans that are consistent with value creation activities and that deliver dollars to the bottom line.

PRICING: A VALUE-BASED APPROACH

As described in the Note on Marketing Strategy (598-061), a firm's marketing program is directed to creating value for its customers. Understanding customers' wants is the foundation for building the marketing mix consisting of:

- A product meeting the wants;
- An information program conveying the value of the product to customers;
- A distribution program making the product readily available.

Each part of this value creation process obviously costs money. Pricing's role in the marketing mix is to tap into the value created and generate revenues to: (i) fund the current value creation activities, (ii) support research activities for future products and, for most organizations, (iii) generate a profit from the firm's activities.

A complete pricing program has many components. For example, consider U.S. Pioneer's pricing of its DVD player, model DV-525:

- A unit price to dealers/distributors had to be set
- Accompanying terms and conditions specified, e.g.
  - any quantity discounts
  - when payment was due
  - any discounts for payment in that time interval
  - whether price included shipping or not
- The Manufacturer's Suggested Retail Price (MSRP) was set at $425.00
- For Christmas season 1999, a $50 consumer rebate was offered for this model
- Terms and conditions set for the rebate.[1]

Thus, in addition to setting the unit price to dealers for the DV-525, Pioneer's pricing policy also included decisions on: (i) terms and conditions governing the sale, (ii) how to "position" the product in its DVD line via the $425 MSRP, (iii) a "sale" offered to consumers for a limited time, (iv) the form that "sale" would take (a direct-to-customer mail-in rebate), (v) restrictions on where the "sale" would be available.

Pricing decisions have a broad scope and a highly levered effect on net income. Consider the impact of being able to increase average price received from customers by 1% while still holding unit sales volume. This could be done for example by finding 10% of customers for whom the product was "underpriced" by 10%, or 20% for whom it was "underpriced" by 5%, and raising prices accordingly. How much would that impact net income? Given a cost structure typical of a large corporation, a 1% boost in price realization yields a net income gain of 12%.[2] Thus, "getting pricing right" is a big deal. However, pricing is often an afterthought in corporate strategy. If:

$$\text{Profits} = [\text{Price} - \text{Cost}] \times \text{Unit Sales}$$

there is often more emphasis on the Cost and Unit Sales parts of the profit equation than Price. Price is seen as "determined by the market" or "something we really don't have much control over." Marketers with this reactive attitude typically miss great profit opportunities.

This note covers some of the important fundamentals behind "pricing right." It builds on The Note on Low Tech Marketing Math (9-599-011) which presents the margin and break-even analysis useful in pricing decision making. The three major sections of this note address:

- Determining Customer Value and Sensitivity to Pricing
- Customizing Price to the Value Delivered
- Integrating Price with the Other Mix Elements

Professor Robert J. Dolan prepared this note as the basis for class discussion.

---

[1] The rebate only applied to bricks-and-mortar retail purchases and at the two Pioneer authorized Internet sellers (Crutchfield and Circuit City).

[2] See R.J. Dolan and H. Simon, *Power Pricing*, Free Press, 1997, p. 4 for specific firm examples and discussion.

The note closes by consideration of important legal and ethical issues.

Determining Customer Value and Sensitivity to Pricing

Pricing should be driven primarily by the value of the product to the customer. There are a number of ways in which this value can be estimated. This value analysis should be complemented by an analysis of just how important price is in the customer's decision making process. This price sensitivity varies markedly across situations.

Consider, for example, an interventional cardiologist preparing to do surgery on a heart patient with an artery blockage. The best solution is to insert a "stent" into the artery to hold back the plaque against the artery walls allowing blood to flow freely again through the artery. There are three major stent suppliers in the market—how important is the price of the stent to the doctor in choosing which one to insert?

Not very. Because this is a life-or-death situation for the patient, product performance is the key. Second, the doctor is a very knowledgeable, sophisticated decision maker, aware of stent features and the advantages/disadvantages of each for various types of blockages. Third, he or she may have more experience inserting one type of stent or another and would prefer not to shift away from the "usual brand" if it is appropriate for the situation. Finally, perhaps the fact that the doctor is not the one paying for the stent would be an added factor in depressing the sensitivity to price.

Much of this may seem pretty intuitive or common sense. But, a systematic approach can be helpful in judging price sensitivity and seeing how it may even be influenced by marketing efforts. Five major areas to be considered are now discussed in turn.

1. Product Category Factors

Price sensitivity tends to be lower in low cost product categories, e.g. a 10% price differential may not be a big deal when the issue is choosing among hammers in the $5 price range, but a bigger deal when considering $1500 personal computers. Three factors should be considered:

A. Absolute Dollar Cost

B. Dollar Cost to be a "regular user" of the product. This accounts for purchase frequency. For example, a "no-name" golf ball may cost $2.00 and a Titleist $3.00. But a retired individual playing golf 200 times per year on a water-hazard-filled course may see it as a decision on a yearly supply of three balls per day making it a $1200 versus $1800 decision not a $2.00 versus $3.00 decision.

C. Dollar Cost of item as a percentage of total cost. Particularly in business-to-business situations, it is important to understand the proportion of the total cost represented by the item. The lower the percentage, the lower will be the price sensitivity. Dolan and Simon[3] give the example of a chemical whose use accounted for 50% of the cost of producing heat insulation and 5% of the cost of producing polyesters. A 10% price increase for the chemical would increase the heating insulation manufacturer's total cost by 5%; polyester producer's by only .5%. The polyester producer was less sensitive to any price increases.

2. Who Pays?

Some things the user of the product pays for; sometimes not (as demonstrated by the interventional cardiologist example). Situations vary from ones wherein the decision maker pays no portion to the cost, to shared-cost situations (e.g. the decider pays some percentage of the cost), to cases where the decision maker bears full responsibility. To the extent that the decider is responsible for the costs, the greater is the price sensitivity.

3. Competitive Factors

A number of competitive factors influence price sensitivity. Price sensitivity is higher to the extent that:

A. The decision maker does not perceive significant differences in alternative products

B. (A slight variation of #1)—the more knowledge a decision maker has about alternative products and their prices (a corollary of this is that price sensitivity is higher when such information is easy to obtain).

---

[3] R.J. Dolan and H. Simon, *Power Pricing,* Free Press, 1997, p. 130.

C. It is easy to compare products and their price schedules. Some comparisons are apples-to-apples, e.g. two life insurance policies paying $1 million if the holder dies. Easy comparison on product features highlights price. Price sensitivity is dampened when products are not easily compared (e.g. two disability policies varying in number of days after disability that payments begin, maximum number of days of coverage, and type of injury/certification required to qualify.) Price sensitivity is also dampened when price is hard to compare, viz. price schedules are stated differently, e.g. one vendor is 10¢ per unit consumed in the month, another is 8¢ per unit plus a $10 per month fee.

D. It is easy for the decision maker to switch products. Difficulty in switching can arise for psychological reasons (e.g. a perception of risk and the desire to stick with the familiar brand) or functional ones (e.g. other systems have been set up anticipating being used in tandem with this particular item, loyalty programs such as frequent flyer miles, or investments in training).

4. Reference Prices

In some situations, the consumer develops a "reference price" which forms the foundation from which the suitability of actual prices is judged. The reference price may be function of: (i) what is seen as "fair" (based perhaps on some estimate of the cost of production), (ii) a competitor's price for a similar item, (iii) the price last paid for the item, and (iv) what others are paying for the item. Reference prices are subjective formulations in the consumer's mind and thus are possibly influenced by many factors including the firm's marketing program. Price sensitivity is greater to the extent that price moves above this "reference" value.

5. Price/Quality Relationships

In some categories, particularly ones in which product quality is difficult to judge by inspection before purchase (e.g. perfume, consulting services), price can be used as cue to product quality. Price being used in this way dampens price sensitivity.

There is no formula to blend these various considerations together but a systematic consideration of these,

which may individually point in different directions, helps assess overall sensitivity.

Assessing a Product's Value to Customers

Once price sensitivity is understood, regardless of the summary judgment on how great or small it is, it is important to develop an understanding of the product's value to customers. The major methods of assessing this value, whose applicability varies by situation, are:

- Judgments based on an understanding of the buyer's cost structure
- Surveys in which customers are asked either directly or indirectly about value.

1. Cost Structure Studies

In a cost structure study, one assesses the "true economic value" (TEV) of a product to a customer by understanding the competitive alternatives, the price and performance of those alternatives, and the buyer's costs.

TEV has two major components:

$$TEV = \text{Cost of the Alternative} + \text{Value of Performance Differential}$$

If the buyer has several alternatives, the calculation has to be relative to the "best" alternative. For example, what is the value of a flight on the Delta Shuttle to a busy advertising agency executive needing to get from Boston to New York? One could calculate the TEV relative to going on the bus; but, this leads to an irrelevant number, as the "best" alternative is the U.S. Air Shuttle, flying essentially the same departure every hour schedule as Delta from the same airport. In this case, the "Value of the Performance Differential" is likely to be very small, as there is little product differentiation. Hence, in this situation, the executive's TEV for Delta would be very close to U.S. Air's price.

This approach is more useful when there is a performance differential to be considered. A product may be superior to the reference alternative in some dimensions, but inferior in others. For example, consider a "reference product" and "new product" with the following characteristics:

	Reference	New
Operating Cost/Hour	$10	$15
Probability of System Crash	20% over one year	1% over one year
Price	$75,000	To be determined

The "New" product has higher operating cost per hour but a significantly lower probability of System Crash.

Consider a customer obtaining a one-year useful life of the system and operating it 2500 hours over that time. To assess the TEV of "New" to this potential customer one needs to estimate the cost of a system crash. If this was $100,000 (and both "Reference" and "New" agree to bear the cost of any crash after the first one in the year):

TEV = Price of Reference + System Crash Savings − Added Operating Cost

= $75,000 + [.2(100,000) − .01(100,000)] − {[2500 hours × $15/hour] − [2500 hours × $10/hour]}

= $75,000 + $19,000 − $12,500

= $81,500

While this is the *true* economic value, it may not be the economic value the customer *perceives*. For example, if the customer perceived the cost of a system crash to be only $50,000, the perceived value of "New" would be seen to be $72,000. In many situations, marketing's job is to make the perceived value approach true economic value. This is done by customer education. For example, in this case, "New" would have established the cost of a system crash in the customer's mind and also provide compelling evidence that its probability of failure was only 1% as compared to Reference's 20%. TEV's is important because it usually sets an upper bound to what a customer will pay. It can be the case that the customer perceived the value to be greater than the TEV, e.g. if in the above example the customer perceived the cost of the system crash to be $250,000. The common case though is that marketing's task is to educate the customer to push perceived value up to TEV.

2. Customer Surveys

A second way to assess customer value relies on survey methods. Two fundamentally different methods are commonly used to obtain price response data from customers:

A. Directly ask for reaction to certain prices, price changes, or price differentials.

B. Infer the response from an analysis of data on customers' expressed preference for one product over another.

Direct Price Response Surveys. In a direct response survey, the respondent is typically asked a question such as:

- What is the likelihood you would buy this product at a price of $25?
- At what price would you definitely buy this product?
- How much would you be willing to pay for this product?
- How much of this product would you buy at a price of 99¢?
- At which price difference would you switch from product A to product B?

Eastman Kodak Company used this method to set prices for a new line of cameras. Respondents were provided a description of a new generation of cameras, presented prices of $150, $80, and $40 and asked to indicate their purchase intention on a seven-point scale, from "Definitely Not Buy" to "Definitely Would Buy." Results were:

	Stated Price of Camera		
	$150	$80	$40
1. Definitely Would Buy	4%	5%	15%
2.	–	–	2%
3. Probably Would Buy	7%	14%	30%
4.	1%	2%	4%
5. Probably Not Buy	22%	34%	18%
6.	2%	2%	1%
7. Definitely Not Buy	65%	54%	30%

Purchase Intention for Camera. The fact that 47% of people responded at the "probably would buy" level or higher for the $40 price (as opposed to only 19% for the $80 price) was instrumental in Kodak's introducing the line at a suggested retail price of $39.95.

The direct questioning method is simple, easily understood, and inexpensive, but has important limitations for some situations. It can:

- Induce unrealistically high price consciousness in respondents.
- Suffer from bias in that respondents may be reluctant to admit that they cannot afford a premium product or that they "buy cheap." Under these circumstances, they would overstate their willingness to pay.

Preference-Based Inference: Conjoint Measurement. Conjoint measurement is a relatively new but powerful procedure which has been widely applied for both consumer and industrial products and services to overcome some of the limitations of the direct questioning method. It has been used in the pricing and design of many products ranging from computer hardware and software to hotels, clothing, automobiles, and information services.

Its superiority stems from the fact that the questions posed to respondents replicate the realistic scenario of a customer facing an array of competitive alternatives with different features and prices and having to choose among them. For example, in the camera situation a consumer might be asked which is preferred "A" or "B" where features were:

	Camera A	Camera B
Image Size	3 × 5 inch	4 × 6 inch
Camera Weight	1.2 lbs.	1.8 lbs.
Built-In Flash	No	Yes
Price	$75	$100

A series of this type of preference questions for different product profiles yields the input data to a statistical method whose output is the customer's tradeoff of price versus product features. The procedure is discussed in detail in the note "Analyzing Consumer Preferences" (9-599-112).

Customizing Price to Value Delivered

Upon adopting the perspective of pricing-to-value, one quickly realizes that in many cases the value varies markedly across individuals. For example, the value of the latest innovation in golf club technology is more highly valued by someone trying to make a living on the professional tour than it is by even the serious amateur. A number of factors cause value variation across potential customers, e.g.

- *The simple matter of taste*—some people think Godiva Chocolates are the greatest; others would just as soon have a Hershey bar.
- *Knowledge/availability of substitutes*—those with access to and knowledge of the availability of the *Boston Globe* newspaper "on-line" may value home delivery of the "hard copy" less.
- *Prices/"deals" made available by substitute providers*—one hotel's "50% off for senior citizens" rate on weekends creates value variation by age group for rooms at the hotel adjacent to it. If generally viewed as substitutes, the adjacent hotel's value will be less for those able to access the "special deal" of the competitor.
- *Importance of performance differentials to the user*—the experienced computer user values speed and storage capacity more than the novice user.
- *Ability-to-pay*—the executive, retiring after an Internet IPO, simply has more capacity to pay for a high-definition television set than a true television fan of lesser economic means.
- *Intensity of use*—convenience features on a cell phone are more highly valued by a person using the device regularly as compared to those in "emergency use only" mode.

Since value can vary greatly across customers, part of the pricing program must consider the advisability of customizing prices to the values, i.e., getting those who value the product more highly to pay more for it.

The four primary methods of customizing prices are:

A. **Product line sorting:** This entails offering "high-end" products with many features for the high value customer and more basic models for lower value. For example, most new automobiles come from "stripped" to "loaded" and customers placing high value on the options simply select that option. Generally, the higher featured items yield greater margins.

B. **Controlled availability:** This involves making different prices available only to certain groups.

For example, a direct mail operation can vary the prices in the catalog sent into a home depending on past purchasing history. Online sellers have the same ability to "address" prices to individuals. Delivering money-off coupons to selected households for redemption at the point-of-purchase is another method for selective pricing.

C. **Price based on buyer characteristics:** Here, one looks for some characteristic of buyers which correlates with willingness-to-pay. For example, common buyer characteristics observed are:

- Age—children and "senior citizens" discounts
- Institution type—end user versus reseller

D. **Price based on transaction characteristics:** Price is tied to the particular features of the transaction, e.g., when the airline ticket was bought, quantity discounts schemes in which the number of units of material bought impacts price.

Integrating Price with Other Mix Elements

A key to effective pricing is to have pricing's value *extraction* "in synch" with the value *creation* process of the other elements of the marketing mix. For example, when Glaxo introduced its ulcer medication Zantac at a substantial price premium to market incumbent Tagamet, it was still able to become the market leader because the product was superior and Glaxo invested in the marketing effort necessary to communicate that superiority to consumers. In other words, the core product itself established a TEV and Glaxo's marketing effort pushed the customers' perceived value up to TEV. In turn, the high margins generated by the premium pricing funded that marketing effort.

The pricing/marketing spending choices can often be captured in the following 2X2 matrix:

		Low	High
Price	**High**	No Unit Sales	Feasible
	Low	Feasible	No Unit Contribution

Marketing Expenditure

As shown, two strategies are feasible. The company can follow a low marketing expenditure and low price (relative to TEV) strategy. The product must speak for itself in establishing value; but, because of the low price, the hurdle to purchase is not high. Similarly, it can follow the Zantac "high/high" strategy: investing in marketing to boost perceived value but pricing to capture the perceived value thereby created, attaining the margins necessary to fund marketing effort.

Conversely, the other price/expenditure combinations are not feasible in the long term. High price/low marketing fails because the perceived values do not get pushed high enough to justify the price; consequently, unit sales are low. Low price/high marketing, on the other hand, generates sales but at unattractive margins.

Legal/Ethical Issues

Pricing is an area which can raise a number of legal and ethical issues whose resolution requires full consideration of the specific context.[4] Only several can be covered in this brief note. Since consideration of price customization has been advocated in this note, it is important to state that it is not illegal to charge different prices for the same product. Some, however, view the practice as "unfair" or "unethical." Some studies have, for example, shown that poor people, lacking mobility and access to alternative sources, pay higher prices for groceries in local supermarkets. Others have criticized the pricing of pharmaceuticals particularly of life-saving variety, such as AIDS-drugs. In some cases, the criticism has been about how high prices are in a market (e.g. United States) versus a neighboring region (e.g. Canada). In others, the criticism has been about too much price similarity across markets, advocating instead very low prices in countries with low per capita incomes and overall low ability to pay.

Legal questions arise whenever pricing actions including price customization are seen as potentially having the impact of reducing competition. Pricing actions with potentially anti-competitive effects include:

- *Predatory pricing*—price "low" for a time to drive a competitor from the marketplace

---

[4]See "Ethical Issues in Pricing" by G.K. Ortmeyer in C. Smith and J. Quelch, *Ethics in Marketing,* Irwin, 1993 and Chapter 14, "The Law and Ethics" in T. Nagle and R. Holden, *The Strategy and Tactics of Pricing,* Prentice-Hall, 1995.

- *Pricing fixing*—setting prices in a cooperative agreement with competitors
- *Price maintenance*—requiring that distributors/retailers of goods sell only at a specified price level. One may *suggest* reseller prices (as noted for Pioneer at the beginning of this note), but may not *require* that such prices be maintained.
- *Price customization*—charging competing resellers of a product different amounts so as to reduce one's ability to compete (this has been alleged by mom-and-pop pharmacies as drugs are sold to big chains at lower prices).

A company can be charged by the government and/or sued by customers or competitors for anti-competitive acts. The situation is not easy to navigate, e.g. one observer noted ". . . when pricing tactics are illegal is not always clear. The laws themselves are vague."[5] This means that pricing practices need to be subjected to both investigation from an ethical perspective and informed legal review within the company before being implemented.

---

[5] T. Nagle and R. Holden, ibid., p. 386.

PRICING AND MARKET MAKING ON THE INTERNET

Introduction

The emergence of the Internet raises important price management issues. Many observers see the Internet creating downward pressure on price levels. Potential buyers can speedily search the Net, perhaps employing shopping agents to check prices. These low consumer search costs will lead to greater price competition and ultimately lower prices and better value for customers. Some have proclaimed that the Internet economy means "inflation is dead—dead as a doornail" or even "an era of negative inflation."[1]

The specter of price pressure and resulting slashing of margins has cooled many's enthusiasm for e-commerce. They perceive doing business on the Internet to be a necessary evil. Thus, an important question is whether lower prices and margins are the inevitable conclusion of doing business on the Internet—in all situations, in some, and can the seller do anything about it? In addition, there is a second, more general issue. The same technology behind customer search power enables other important phenomena driving how the e-commerce market operates, e.g., the Internet:

- Facilitates a buyer's acquisition of quality information for various goods.

- Enables suppliers to update prices dynamically in response to observed demand.

- Allows a seller to create a meaningful market of potential buyers with price being the outcome of an auction process rather than prespecified by the seller.

- Permits a prospective buyer to specify in detail the product's requirements and put fulfillment out to bid to an organized market of potential sellers.

These impacts may be more fundamental than any effect of more customer price information. They change how exchanges between buyers and sellers take place. The how of a transaction, i.e., the connecting a buyer and a seller has many forms.

For example, consider a couple buying a new home:

- During a break in the home hunting trip, they walk into a McDonald's, see 99¢ as the *posted price* for a hamburger and decide whether to buy it or not.

- Finally finding a desirable house, they hear the seller's $695,000 "asking price" and begin to *negotiate* downward from that price.

- Having bought the house, they go off to an Estate *Auction* to bid on needed furniture.

- Needing to move some personal belongings to the new home, they contact several moving companies *requesting proposals*. The companies submit *bids* for meeting the couple's requirements.

- Needing to come up with a down-payment for the house, they instruct their broker to sell 500 of their shares of IBM stock on the New York Stock *Exchange.*

The couple has thus transacted through five different market mechanisms. These same five market mechanisms can be found in business-to-business situation in the real world and also on the Internet. The Internet makes certain ways of transacting more broadly feasible. As shown in Figure 1, the mechanisms are of three fundamentally different types. Type I is the set price mechanism. Within this, there are two subclasses. First is the I(a) situation shown where prices are updated only periodically, like at McDonald's. A second subclass is shown as I(b) wherein the set of "take it or leave it prices" is updated continually,

Professor Robert J. Dolan and Professor Youngme Moon prepared this note as the basis for class discussion rather than to illustrate either effective or ineffective handling of an administrative situation.

[1]W.A. Sahlman, "The New Economy Is Stronger Than You Think," *Harvard Business Review,* November–December 1999, p. 99–107 and J.N. Sheth and R.S. Sisodia, "Consumer Behavior in the Future," in *Electronic Marketing and the Consumer,* R.A. Peterson, ed., SAGE Publications, 1997.

e.g., as the airlines do. Type II is the negotiated price mechanism. In a negotiated price situation, there can be either: II(a) a specified starting point for the negotiation (e.g., the seller's asking price on a house, the dealer's "list price" on a new car) or not, II(b). Type III is a class of mechanism which relies on competition across buyers and sellers to produce prices. Here there are three subclasses.

In an auction system, III(a), the seller does not specify a price; but, rather provides an item which buyers compete for the right to buy in a bidding process. III(b) is "reverse buying" where the customer takes the lead in organizing the pricing process. An example of this is when the buyer develops a Request for Proposal on an item or service and price is determined via a competition involving a bidding process among potential sellers. This is termed a "Reverse Auction." Finally, in III(c), there is a coming together of multiple buyers and multiple sellers and a price determined by the interaction on an exchange to "clear the market."

One impact of the interactive nature of the Internet is that market mechanisms of type III can be very effi-

ciently organized. For example, the owner of a 1955 Coca-Cola sign could not really conduct a nationwide auction for that single item pre-Internet. The Internet, and sites such as eBay, make this possible. Generally, the Internet makes the choice of market mechanism a salient question in many situations. The challenge of managing price on the Internet is not only how to set price in an era wherein the consumer has more information; but also, how to select the most advantageous combination of market making mechanisms via which to transact exchanges.

This note describes the operation of each of the three market mechanisms on the Internet. We describe the rationale for each, examine the determinants of economic efficiency, and assess pressure—upward or downward—on prices. The goal is to provide insight to guide price management, not only in a set price situation but also to illuminate when an alternative market mechanism is desirable. Throughout the note, reference will be made to currently operating sites of interest.

Figure 1 Three Types of Marketing Making Mechanisms

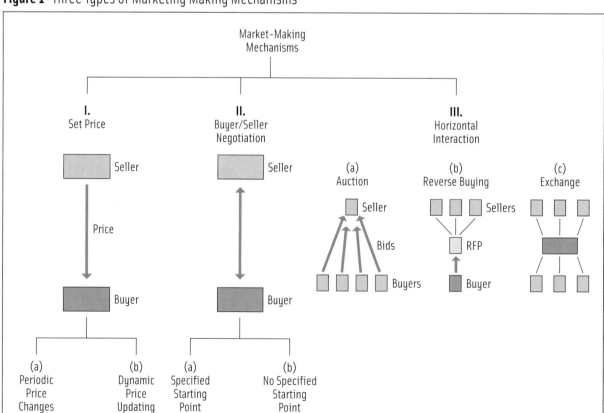

Type I: The Set Price Mechanism

Are Set Prices Lower on the Internet?

In the "set price" scenario (see Figure 1, Type I), the seller simply sets a fixed price, and the buyer is expected to either accept or reject that price. Negotiation is not an option; the seller's attitude is "take it or leave it." This mechanism has some advantages, viz. (i) low transaction costs (no haggling, for example), and (ii) perception of fairness (since every buyer must pay the same price).

Numerous Internet retailers, including Amazon.com and eToys.com, have adopted fixed pricing mechanisms. These leading Internet retailers are often perceived as having *lower* fixed prices than their real-world counterparts. Indeed, as mentioned above, the conventional wisdom is that the Internet tends to drive prices down, primarily because online consumers have easier access to accurate information about the market.

In traditional retail markets, buyer ignorance is often a source of profit for companies. Firms set prices with reasonable confidence that the majority of buyers is unlikely to spend a large amount of time and effort comparison shopping. But on the Internet, several factors have begun to bite into this "ignorance premium." For one thing, potential buyers no longer have to physically travel from store to store in search of the best deal; rather, they can comparison shop a number of websites from the comfort of their own computer. In addition, a number of Internet search tools have made online comparison shopping even more efficient. These search agents (also called "bots" or "spiders") can theoretically compare prices and features across every available retailer on the Internet. Of course, none of the existing tools are currently capable of searching the entire Web universe, and several online merchants have even succeeded in "blocking" search agents from mining their sites for data. Nonetheless, these search agents are becoming increasingly sophisticated. Some of the more popular tools include:

- *Third-Party Price Comparison Sites.* Price comparison sites like MySimon.com, Compare.Net, and DealTime.com perform automatic price and feature comparisons in a matter of seconds. Potential buyers simply visit the site, indicate the item of interest, and the search agent scans product and pricing information from a list of hundreds of online sellers stocking the item. Many of these sites charge merchants a fee to be part of their searches. Other sites, such as MySimon.com, earn a commission every time a buyer accesses a merchant site and ultimately buys an item, through the search.

- *Third-Party Price Comparison Agents.* Imagine someone infiltrating the checkout line at an Office-Max, peeking into people's shopping baskets, and telling them exactly how much money they could be saving on the same products at Staples. Several companies including ClickTheButton, DealPilot, and R U Sure have developed a new breed of online search agents that do exactly that: Offer shoppers better deals on whatever merchandise they happen to be viewing on a Web page. Once a user has downloaded software from one of these agent services, the software is activated anytime the user's Web browser is open. A consumer viewing a book on, say, Amazon.com, is then automatically given price comparison information on the same book from competing retailers.

- *Retailer Price Comparison Agents.* Some online merchants have become so resigned to the prospect of comparison shopping that they offer their customers a comparative pricing feature *within* their own websites, as a means of building customer trust. Online computer merchant NECX, for example, offers buyers a "Price Comparison" feature. Click on the price comparison, and the buyer finds the competitors' price of the item being considered at NECX. In some cases, these competitive prices are lower than NECX's and for those shoppers wishing to take their business to one of these competitors, NECX even provides a direct link.

Classic economic theory predicts that if electronic tools allow consumers to comparison shop more easily, the end result will be greater price competition and ultimately, downward price pressure. A number of high-profile, "zero margin" Internet businesses seem to be bearing this prediction out. For example, Buy.com pioneered the strategy of selling products at or below cost to lure customers, aiming to make money eventually by selling advertising on its website. Its proprietary software works 24 hours a day to gather millions of prices for books, CDs, computer hardware and software, and other products from hundreds of competitors. In order to circumvent attempts to "block" its gathering of price information from competitors' sites, Buy.com enlists hundreds of individual, anonymous accounts from Internet Service Providers to conduct its price comparison searches. All of this technology is designed to sniff out the cheapest bargains online and help the company deliver on its advertising promise to have "the lowest prices on earth."

Critics have described Buy.com's business model as "selling dollar bills for 99 cents," and in one year, the cost to Buy.com of the products it sold actually *exceeded* the amount of sales it generated by several million dollars. But the company's phenomenal growth spawned a host of zero-margin imitators. Onsale.com, the Internet auction company, recently launched an AtCost model built around a similar pricing strategy. Free-PC made a splash in 1998 by "giving away" computers to consumers who agreed to view advertisements every time they used their computer.

But despite these rather conspicuous examples, there is to date no conclusive evidence that prices on the Internet are lower per se than prices in conventional outlets. In fact, the results of studies conducted on Internet pricing have yielded mixed results.[2] In addition, the long-term sustainability of zero-margin Internet businesses remains to be seen. For example, on the verge of going public, Buy.com recently announced that it was moving to a more conventional pricing strategy of offering certain items at a loss to draw traffic and promote the sale of higher-margin items. Onsale.com, which recently merged with Egghead.com, also appears to be moving toward a more conventional "loss leader" pricing strategy, lowering prices on some items while keeping prices high on others.

Perhaps most tellingly, some of the most popular online retailers do *not* offer the lowest prices. Amazon.com is a good example; it continues to grow marketshare despite dozens of competitors offering lower prices. Clearly, merchants are able to leverage other dynamics—such as branding and trust, the shopping "experience," and lock-in—to maintain healthy margins on products.

Branding and Trust. Branding and trust may take on added importance in electronic markets for several reasons. First, buyers are often purchasing from sellers they have not seen and whose physical location is either unknown to the buyer or quite distant. Second, most online transactions are not instantaneous; they typically involve a delayed exchange of money and goods. Buyers usually have to submit their payment and then trust that they will receive their goods in a timely fashion. Third, a significant percentage of buyers may be purchasing goods online for the first time; this may lead to heightened concerns about being "ripped off." Assurances from credit card companies about protection offered to buyers may reduce some of these concerns. However, for all of these reasons, online consumers may still be willing to pay a premium to purchase a product from a retailer they are familiar with, rather than risk dealing with an unknown seller.

Conversations with managers from price comparison sites support this view. These managers point out that many of the shoppers using their sites to compare prices end up purchasing items from branded retailers such as Amazon.com, even when they are given information about dozens of other retailers offering lower prices.[3] In fact, Amazon.com reportedly gets two-thirds of its business from returning shoppers. And some online companies feel so strongly about the importance of building consumer confidence, they are refusing to compete on price alone. For example, although NECX raised eyebrows when it began offering the built-in price comparison tool that seemed to encourage its customers to shop elsewhere, it argues that the feature reinforces consumer trust. As proof, it claims a 30% *increase* in business since launching the feature.

The Shopping Experience. As in the brick-and-mortar world, online retailers offering similar products and prices may differ significantly across a variety of other dimensions. Some websites are simply easier to navigate than others, for example. The most sophisticated shopping sites offer a number of features that contribute to the shopping experience, such as:

- superior product information;
- sophisticated search tools;
- extensive product reviews from experts and other customers;
- product samples (e.g., music clips, book chapters)
- product recommendation tools;
- convenient check-out services.

All of these features contribute to the creation of a particular shopping environment that affects the likeli-

---

[2]Smith, M.D., Bailer, J., and Brynjolfsson, E., "Understanding Digital Markets: Review and Assessment," forthcoming in *Understanding the Digital Economy* (E. Brynjolfsson and B. Kahin, eds.), MIT Press.

[3]"Call your agent for online shopping," *Information Week*, December 7, 1998.

hood that customers will enjoy shopping at the site. Firms that successfully leverage these features may be able to charge a price premium.

Lock-In. Lock-in refers to mechanisms that increase customers' switching costs. Sometimes lock-in occurs simply as a result of familiarity with a particular website. Rather than incur the switching costs associated with learning how to navigate a new website, customers may choose to pay a higher price to avoid this inconvenience. In other cases, firms explicitly attempt to increase lock-in by creating additional incentives for repeat customers. Frequent buyer programs, such as that marketed by Netcentives, are a good example of this. Other, less obvious, mechanisms include personalization features such as individualized shopping lists, customized interfaces, and "one-click" ordering accounts.

One company that has managed lock-in particularly well is Dell Online. While first-time visitors are greeted with Dell's standard website, for its most valuable corporate customers Dell has developed hundreds of *customer-specific* webpages. These Dell Premier Pages not only display specific computer configurations that have been pre-approved by the customer's firm, but they display prices that reflect negotiated discounts. Detailed account purchasing reports and inventory analyses are also customized for these customers. As a result, Dell's Premier Pages have become management control tools for its customers, who use the customized webpages as a means of enforcing product standards and increasing internal efficiencies. Dell's prices may not be the lowest in the industry, but the company has succeeded in creating extremely high switching costs for its most valuable customers.

Dynamic Pricing

Figure 1 describes another set price mechanism in which posted prices are continually updated (Type Ib). Of course, dynamic pricing is not new. Airlines, for example, often have dozens of different fares paid by passengers on a given flight. These fares depend on a number of variables, including how early customers booked their flights, inventory of available seats at the time of booking, what restrictions they were willing to accept, their travel history, etc. The hotel and car rental industries have followed suit, adopting the airline industry's yield management principles. Grocery stores also employ dynamic pricing using "smart" cash registers. These cash registers automatically offer customers discounts (e.g., cents-off coupons) depending on their purchases. Even soft drink

companies are experimenting with vending machines that charge different prices depending on the weather (the hotter the temperature, the higher the price).[4]

On the Internet, the opportunities for dynamic pricing are even greater, for at least two reasons:

- *Customer Information.* While the Internet has made it easier for customers to collect information about products and prices, it has also made it easier for *sellers* to gather information about *customers.* This information can be used to more accurately determine how much individual customers are willing to pay for certain goods.
- *Lower Menu Costs.* Menu costs refer to the costs associated with making price changes. For example, every time a traditional catalog retailer decides to change prices, it must incur the costs associated with reprinting its catalog. On the Internet, lower menu costs increase the likelihood that retailers will change prices more frequently.

Add to these factors the fact that technology has made it easier for online retailers to check the prices of their competitors, and the end result is that online prices tend to be more dynamic than prices in conventional settings. As one online computer merchant has advertised:

> When you shop at eCOST.com, you don't have to wonder if you're getting a great value on what you need . . . To make sure we are offering you the best price at all times, we update our prices at least once a day, and more often as needed . . . When you visit eCOST.com, you can be sure you are getting the latest information available.
>
> —eCOST.com website

Dynamic pricing can be implemented in a variety of ways. Firms can simply update prices frequently, as in the eCOST.com example. Firms can also engage in various forms of price customization, where different customers are charged different prices, as in the airline example.

On the Internet, price customization has many forms:

- Some online retailers track the clickstreams of customers, instantaneously making special offers based on their online activity.

---

[4] *Revenue Management*, R.G. Cross, Broadway Books, 1997 discusses the broad applicability of yield management/dynamic pricing techniques across industries.

- Other retailers rely on their extensive customer databases to "micromarket" customized offers to customers based on their past purchase behavior, often using personalized e-mail.
- Dell's Premier Pages allow for a relatively novel price customization mechanism, in that the company is essentially establishing different "storefronts" that reflect variable pricing schemes.
- Some online merchants are using price comparison technology to develop instantaneous "price-matching" systems. When a customer visits the website directly, the posted prices are fixed. However, if the customer uses a third-party search tool to compare prices among a number of competitors, the prices automatically drop. As a result, customers that access the website via the price comparison tool get a lower price than customers who access the website directly.

This movement to price customization is pursued widely and when well implemented can offset the added customer information on prices. The ultimate form of price customization is customization directly to the buyer's willingness-to-pay. That is pursued on the Internet via auctions which will be addressed fully later in this note.

Type II: The Buyer/Seller Negotiated Price Mechanism

Negotiations, big and small, are commonplace in the real world. Agents negotiate the price of star athletes' services with teams. A buyer haggles over the $2.00 asking price for a set of six chipped saucers at a Saturday morning yardsale. Some buyers like the negotiation or bargaining process, perceiving it as a route to a "good deal." Others detest it. This latter segment has grown large enough that it has prompted the institution of the option of "no haggle" pricing in some historically negotiation situations. For example, General Motors institutionalized "no haggling" for its Saturn model and many dealers of other vehicles have adopted "Saturn pricing" either on a full-time basis or for special sales events.

However, a supplier's expressing a willingness to negotiate can attract certain customer groups. It can also offer an additional way in which the seller can customize the price to the individual buyer.

Historically, the negotiation mechanism has had some disadvantages compared to Type I: Set Price. For example, in a negotiation situation:

(i)   it typically takes longer to complete the transaction;

(ii) the price aspect of the transaction can become highlighted dominating the buyer-seller interaction and squeezing out presentation of the product features and value;

(iii) for negotiation to be effective, the customer contact person must have some degree of pricing authority.

The Internet provides an efficient mechanism for buyer/seller(s) interaction alleviating each of these problems. For instance, to overcome disadvantage (iii), the seller can develop an intelligent agent to simulate the process of person-to-person negotiation. Several general purpose and many special purpose negotiation sites have operated on the Internet.

NexTag.com is a site of market mechanism type II(a)—negotiation with a specified starting price. To illustrate the process, consider a customer wishing to buy a Palm V. To start, NexTag produces the "seller price" from a number of vendors. In one buying experience at the site, there were ten potential sellers sorted by "seller price" ranging from $288.98 to $437.12. Entering a ship-to zip code adds the supplier's shipping and tax to yield a comparison of out-of-pocket or "Total Price." If the price from any seller is acceptable, the customer can just purchase the item and we have just reverted to a Type I mechanism. However, if no price is acceptable, Step 2 is to "Enter Your Own Total Price" and select the suppliers to whom this information or counteroffer is conveyed. At this point, the buyer is under no obligation; e.g., the buyer could enter $275.00 but is not obligated to buy the product if a supplier accepts that price. The process follows the real world negotiation process. Sellers respond to the "total price" offered by the buyer. Some seller responses were automated, viz. as the NexTag site put it, "If a seller's systems has been fully integrated with Nex-Tag.com, you may see an immediate response to your offer. . . ." Sellers can send a message along with their price counteroffer. As in the real world, the seller's response can be more complex than just a price offer; it could be for a substitute item (e.g., a Palm III not a V) or include other goods (e.g., hold on price but throw in software). NexTag notes that "most sellers respond within minutes." NexTag provides a "price history" of completed transactions for the item to help the buyer in the negotiation. This "price history" also serves to indicate to the buyer what a reasonable offer might be, which helps keep the system from being clogged with bargain hunting that will prove fruitless.

This transition of the negotiation process to the Internet overcomes many of the disadvantages of negotiations in the real world. From a customer's point of view, negotiation can be done with multiple suppliers at once. Because response is immediate in many cases, the transaction can still close quickly even with multi-supplier negotiation. The customer is always in control and not subject to unwanted persuasion attempts such as many have encountered trying to end a real world negotiation about a car purchase. The advantage to the seller is that the dialog about price provides information about the buyer which can be used to customize prices.

Other sites offered variations on the theme. For example, Make Us An Offer offered "Real-Time Online Haggling" hosted by an animated "artificially intelligent sales agent" named Chester. It positioned itself as a solution to the delayed respond time of other sites such as the auction site eBay, as bid responses are delivered "within seconds." Hagglezone "where everything is negotiable" featured six hagglers with "unique personalities, moods and tendencies." A buyer chose the haggler to deal with. Hagglezone emphasized the fun/entertainment aspects of buying. Its television ad campaign humorously showed a woman attempting to haggle in a traditionally set price format (a supermarket) as the customer behind her became upset given the time involved in completing the transaction.

Special purpose sites, such as Adoutlet.com, simulate face-to-face negotiations for a particular product category. Adoutlet brings together media buyers and sellers. Adoutlet displays available inventory, e.g., a one-page ad for a particular issue of *Mac World* at its "rate card" price. The buyer then makes an offer which the seller responds to with "accept, reject, or hold" (hold meaning the seller wants to wait and see if other offers come in or not). If not accepted, the potential buyer is free to make another offer.

Buying-Power Based "Negotiations"

A common negotiation tactic in the real world is to stress the size of the order at issue or even increase the quantity of goods to be purchased as a mechanism to get the price down, e.g., "I'll take both the white and blue set of chipped dishes if you give them to me for $1.50 each." Even this "buying power" tactic has an analog on the Internet. Sites such as Accompany and Mercata aggregate the demand from different customers, who are unknown to one another, to use in "negotiating" lower prices. Accompany called itself the "Get It Together Network."

Rather than truly negotiating lower prices as buyers come together, Accompany had pre-determined a set of quantity discount schedules with its "Supplier Partners." These discount schedules were provided to buyers at the site. For example, for the Palm V on December 1, 1999 at 1:40 p.m., the price schedule off the Manufacturer's Suggested Retail Price of $399.00 was:

Number of Buyers	Price
0–5	$304.95
6–10	$297.95
11–20	$290.95
21–50	$279.95
51–126	$267.95

At that point in time, 74 buyers had already signed up so that "tier 5," the last price tier of $267.95, was already hit. Consequently, a new buyer arriving at the site could join the 74 already committed to the item knowing that $267.95 would be the price paid. In contrast, when buyer #8 signed on, only "tier 2" had been reached; so he or she agreed to pay up to $297.95 but with the prospect of the price declining as more users signed on for the deal. This is precisely what happened, driving the price for all buyers down to $267.95 per unit (in contrast to a $299.99 price the same day at Egghead.com).

It is not clear at this point in time how important these negotiation sites will be in the long run. Clearly, the Internet creates situations in which this Type II mechanism is feasible. Some buyers prefer the option to "haggle." Sellers have the ability to automate the process on their side via intelligent agents, yielding more price customization opportunity. Thus, for at least some segment of the market, this mechanism will likely be operative as the market mechanism itself provides value to buyers.

Type III: Auctions and Exchanges

Figure 1 displays three types of pricing mechanisms involving *horizontal* interactions between buyers and sellers. In Type II, negotiations, it was one-on-one vertical negotiation between entities at different levels of the marketing system that drove prices. In these three cases, competition across buyers and/or sellers produces prices that can be highly variable across transactions. In the case of the "classic auction" model (Type IIIa), competition across buyers leads to a price. In the case of the "reverse buying" model (Type IIIb), competition across sellers leads to a price. And in the case of "exchanges" (Type IIIc), multiple buyers and multiple sellers interact to set prices.

III(a): Classic Auctions

In the classic auction a vendor puts items up for sale and would-be buyers are invited to bid in competition with each other. Bidding can take a number of forms, e.g., Sealed bid or open. Most common is the ascending price format wherein the highest bidder "wins" the item. As more potential buyers become involved, there is upward pressure on prices.

Classic auctions differ from other pricing mechanisms in several fundamental ways. In contrast to "take it or leave it" pricing, classic auctions involve a flexible pricing scheme in which prices are *tailor-made for each transaction*. Moreover, in a fixed price system, the item can sit unsold. In an auction the price moves to a level where the item is sold. And in contrast to negotiated selling in which a seller bargains with an individual buyer, classic auctions bring buyers together in *competition* with one another. They are basically demand aggregation models that function to deliver the best price for the seller, given the market demand the seller has been able to assemble.

Classic auctions have existed for hundreds of years, typically in situations where the value of the product is (i) difficult to determine, (ii) a matter of private taste and opinion, or (iii) highly variable depending on market conditions. For example, the world-famous auction houses of Sotheby's and Christie's both date back to the 1700s and specialize in the sale of antiques, artwork, and other fine collectibles—products whose value is almost impossible to determine prior to the actual sale.

Until a few years ago, classic auctions—while the predominant mode in certain industries (e.g., the famous Dutch Fresh Flower Auctions, the Thoroughbred Horse Auctions in Kentucky)—tended to be a niche phenomenon. They also tended to be concentrated in highly specialized agricultural and commodities markets. The interactive nature of the Internet has changed all of that; indeed, auctions constitute some of the most popular sites on the Web. Their popularity has largely been driven by the fact that the Internet increases the economic efficiencies associated with auction models. More specifically, for suppliers the Internet has not only lowered the search costs associated with finding a critical mass of buyers in the market, but it has also lowered the costs associated with making inventory available to buyers on an immediate basis. For buyers, the Internet has lowered the costs associated with accessing hard-to-find items, and finding other buyers who share common interests.

The Internet Lowers the Search Costs for Sellers Looking for Buyers.
In traditional markets, sellers face significant hurdles associated with "finding" a critical mass of buyers in a large, unorganized open market. In order to access these potential buyers, they often have no choice but to incur significant marketing costs. In some cases, geographical dispersion precludes the efficient organization of potential buyers altogether. An auction can be risky because it is not clear that at any one time the market of potential buyers can be brought together.

The Internet, however, has produced a number of "market-makers" that have been able to pool together significant numbers of potential buyers without having to deal with physical search and travel costs. These market makers set up the infrastructure which individual sellers can plug into.

Indeed, in the Web universe, several factors make it easy to transform "niche" market segments into "mainstream" market segments. First, the global reach of the network provides a much greater pool of potential buyers to draw from. Second, reduced search costs make it easier to identify small pockets of people with highly specialized needs. Finally, reduced communication costs make it easier to establish and sustain relationships with these segments.

The end result is a situation in which firms are discovering that there is significant value associated with simply aggregating demand among these market segments. Some of the busiest sites on the Web are those fulfilling this market-making function, in three settings: the consumer-to-consumer, business-to-consumer, or business-to-business context.

The Internet Lowers the Costs Associated with Making Inventory Available to Buyers Immediately.
When it comes to excess merchandise—such as surplus, refurbished, or closeout computer merchandise—the need to liquidate inventory has traditionally been a problem for suppliers. Internet auctions, however, allow suppliers to make this inventory available to buyers on an immediate, and continually updated, basis. When sellers make errors forecasting demand for perishable inventory, instantaneous auctions mitigate the costs associated with such errors.

Of course, sellers who choose to dispose of surplus goods via auction must accept the uncertainty associated with dynamic pricing. However, for many sellers, this uncertainty is easily worth the cost-savings associated with quick inventory turnover: online auctions generally move goods much more quickly than direct sales, catalogs, or off-line auctions. In addition, firms that use auction mechanisms to liquidate surplus goods are able to bypass liquidation brokers who tend to pay fire sale prices. As a result, auctions—particularly business-to-consumer auctions—are becoming an increasingly common mechanism by which firms adjust inventory levels.

For Buyers, the Internet Lowers the Costs Associated with Accessing Hard-to-Find Items.
In the past, buyers searching for hard-to-find items had very restricted choices, regardless of whether those items consisted of collectibles and memorabilia, or closeout computer hardware. In the former case, hobbyists were left to either scan local classified listings or make the rounds among a few, scattered dealers who specialized in such merchandise. In the latter case, bargain-hunters typically had to choose from the limited supply of surplus goods carried by their local computer retailer. In both cases, even when buyers were able to find what they were looking for, prices tended to be non-negotiable.

Internet auctions have significantly increased the options available to buyers in the market for hard-to-find items. Indeed, the online classic auction houses not only aggregate demand for sellers, they aggregate *supply* for buyers. In this sense, they have become convenient "one-stop shopping" sources for buyers in this market. A collector looking for a rare Beanie Baby now has a myriad of online auction choices; similarly, a home-office worker looking for a deal on a 17″ computer monitor can now bid on dozens of such monitors online. Moreover, buyer choices are not limited to the big auction firms. Niche auction companies have sprung up all over the Web, covering every product category imaginable.

The Interactive Nature of the Internet Facilitates the Creation of Buying Communities.
While the economic efficiencies afforded by Internet auctions have no doubt played a large role in their popularity, it is impossible to overlook another factor that has contributed to their success: Auctions are "fun." Indeed, online auctions owe at least some of their popularity to the fact that they have become choice destinations for bargain-hunters who derive significant pleasure from the "thrill of the hunt."

In this regard, it is important to reiterate that classic auctions do not necessarily lead to bargain prices; on the contrary, the competitive dynamic tends to push prices upward (the "winner," after all, is typically the individual willing to pay the highest price).

Classic auctions on the Internet also have had a distinctly social component that most successful auction sites not only recognize, but promote. They provide an online forum where buyers and sellers can become acquainted, discuss topics of common interest, and exchange information about one another. A typical example: Members of the eBay community who met while trading in the Elvis category have forged such strong relationships that they now gather to make annual pilgrimages to Graceland together. As Meg Whitman, eBay's CEO explains, this community-building dynamic is impossible to replicate off-line:

> Whereas so many of the Internet companies in existence had borrowed something that existed off-line and translated it into an online version, [eBay] is actually the creation of something that could not be done in the real world.[5]

Types of Classic Auctions

Classic auction firms on the Internet can be roughly categorized into three groups: consumer-to-consumer sites that conduct auctions in which both the sellers and the buyers are individuals; business-to-consumer sites that conduct auctions for businesses wishing to sell products to consumers; and business-to-business sites that conduct auctions in which both the sellers and the buyers are businesses.

Consumer-to-Consumer Auctions.
In 1999, the total consumer-to-consumer auction market on the Internet was estimated to be about $2.3 billion (sales), and expected to grow to $6.4 billion by 2003.[6] And while most activity in this category was in collectibles, antiques, memorabilia, and second-hand goods, the amount of variety was growing.

Typically, firms in this category do not own the goods up for auction; rather, they simply conduct auctions on behalf of a large group of sellers. For this reason, they do not have to deal with the logistics associated with shipping

---

[5]From *eBay, Inc.,* HBS case #700-007.
[6]Source: Forrester Research.

of actual products. They simply act as electronic intermediaries, connecting sellers with a pool of buyers.

For these firms, the bulk of their revenues tends to come from seller fees, although they occasionally collect additional revenues from advertisements and buyer fees. eBay is the runaway leader in this category. It has over 7 million registered users who at any given time can find up to 3 million items at auction, ranging from placemats to cars to homes. eBay collects a modest fee from sellers in exchange for listing an item, ranging from $0.25 to $2. It also collects a seller's fee, i.e., a percentage of the sale ranging from 1.25% to 5%. From the seller perspective, the fees are a bargain compared to the $50 it would typically have cost them to post a traditional classified ad for a week. And from the company perspective, the commissions may seem tiny, but they add up: eBay had net revenues of over $150 million through three quarters of 1999, and net income of almost $6 million over the same period, making it one of the few profitable sites on the Web.

One of the biggest challenges facing consumer-to-consumer auction businesses was fraud. Because firms served only as intermediaries, they exerted little direct control over the sellers posting items. The most common complaint came from buyers who paid for merchandise, only to have the seller disappear without delivering the goods. eBay, however, has implemented some elegant (albeit imperfect) ways to address some of these potential hazards. On its site, regular sellers establish a "reputation" for reliable delivery and quality through a ratings system based on comments from previous buyers who have transacted with the seller. Bidders can not only browse through these comments and ratings, but they can also add their own feedback, based on their experience. Extensive chatboards also let eBay-ers share tips and gossip. In effect, the company relies on the users themselves to establish trust between buyers and sellers. Its fraud rate is subsequently very low: 25 out of every million transactions. Note that this reputation-building system not only promotes "community," but it increases the switching costs for both buyers and sellers.

eBay currently faces competition from a number of competitors, including Yahoo! auctions and Auction Universe. And, recognizing an opportunity to leverage its already existing customer base, Amazon.com jumped into the auction business in the spring of 1999. Traditional, off-line auction houses are also entering the fray. Butterfield's, a high-end auction firm, was recently purchased by eBay, while Sotheby's recently forged an alliance with Amazon. There are also literally hundreds of niche auction sites on the Web, including Mobilia (a place to bid on specialty automotive products), Planet-Bike, Hasbro Collectors, Vintage Surfboard, etc.

Business-to-Consumer Auctions.

In 1999, the total business-to-consumer auction market on the Internet was estimated to be about $0.4 billion (sales), but was expected to grow to $12.6 billion by 2003, overtaking the consumer-to-consumer category.[7] While many sites in this category began by specializing in computer hardware and other technology-related items, a number have since expanded to offer everything from travel packages to sporting goods items.

In some cases, firms in this category do not own the goods up for auction; rather, they conduct auctions on behalf of vendors in exchange for a seller's fee. In other cases, they take title to the goods and handle shipment to customers.

Onsale (recently merged with Egghead.com) was the first business-to-consumer auction site on the Internet and is still one of the largest. Other sites that fall into this category include uBid, BidOnline, and WebAuction. Niche sites are also becoming increasingly popular. Millionaire.com—founded by Robb Report founder Robert White—targets the high-end market by connecting buyers of luxury items such as antiques, fine art, yachts, watches, wine and jewelry with dealers and galleries. The Sharper Image holds auctions at its website that include a range of yuppie gizmos.

Even investment banks got into the on-line auction business. Many initial public offerings display classic signs that shares are being sold too cheaply and to the wrong people (i.e., not to those who value them the most highly). As a result, there is often a sharp rise in price on the first day's trading, and a huge volume of shares changes hands. W. R. Hambrecht instituted OpenIpo, an auction process to sell initial public offerings of shares more efficiently. Investors submitted secret bids; the price was set at the highest level at which all available shares could be sold, and allocated at that price to everybody who bid that amount or more. This extended the buying group from business to individual consumers.

Business-to-Business Auctions.

Business-to-business auctions were expected to eventually make up most of the volume of the online auction market. In fact, many auc-

---

[7]Source: Forrester Research

tion firms that started out as business-to-consumer firms (e.g., Onsale, uBid) found that an increasing percentage of their revenues were being generated by business customers.

In general, business-to-business auctions involve fundamentally different dynamics than consumer auctions. They typically involve larger amounts of money, firms are not seeking entertainment, and firms tend to be wary of jeopardizing long-term strategic relationships.

AdAuction.com was an example of an business-to-business auction site. The company provided a venue for companies to buy and sell advertising space for all sorts of media: online, broadcast, and print. Sellers had to fulfill certain criteria to qualify for participation in the auctions, which provided the opportunity to sell excess ad inventory to over 6,000 registered media buyers. Trade-Out was a business-to-business liquidator auction with products ranging from a lot of 2,000 Duncan Yo-Yo's to 70 tons of Borosilicate Glass Tubing. Its developer was inspired in his design by reading eBay's prospectus. eBay invested in TradeOut in November 1999.

Entering the Classic Auction Market.

In all of the classic auction categories, barriers to entry are relatively low, and competitors can launch new sites at a relatively low cost using commercially available software. However, the biggest hurdles involve building a potential bidder and seller base. Success literally breeds success; the large bidder base draws the suppliers which enhance the site's appeal to bidders. For smaller players seeking to enter the market, breaking this self-reinforcing cycle can pose quite a problem.

But several firms arose to offer smaller players an alternative. These firms focused on helping other firms get into the auction business by using network synergies to quickly build a large bidder and seller base. FairMarket, a leader in this category, created an auction network that connected a number of smaller auction sites hosted by some of the leading portals and vendors on the Web, including Microsoft (MSN), Excite, Lycos, AltaVista, Dell, CompUSA, Cyberian Outpost, MicroWarehouse, and Boston.com. Each individual site was connected to a single massive database of merchandise. A computer listed from Dell at www.dellauction.com, for example, automatically appeared on all the auction sites in the FairMarket network. Besides developing the network, FairMarket provided a number of other services to its members: It hosted the servers, and created the software and user interface for member auction sites. It also provided customer service, including fraud protection and

security features. In 1999, the company had a combined reach of 50 million users (compared to eBay's audience of 7 million).

III(b): Reverse Buying

The term "reverse" buying refers to the fact that in these mechanisms there is a flip in the usual role of buyer and seller. Usually, the seller indicates what is for sale and buyers search around for what they want. In reverse buying, the buyer is more proactive—specifying what it is that will be purchased; then, suppliers' bids indicate the price of fulfilling the specified demand. In some situations, this happens in a true reverse auction process, as sellers perceive themselves in active competition with one another. In other cases, a service will identify potential sellers and their posted prices for buyers, but without anything approximating a bidding process among sellers.

Reverse Auctions.

In a reverse auction, a buyer communicates a need to a set of potential suppliers and suppliers bid on fulfilling that demand. The reverse auction has been a staple of purchasing in business-to-business situations for many years, often under the name of competitive bidding.[8] The process entails the buyer drafting a Request-for-Proposal (RFP) or Request for Quotation (RFQ) specifying what is to be purchased. This request is transmitted to qualified sellers. In some cases, drafting the RFP/RFQ and then identifying and communicating to potential suppliers is easy. For example, when the Tennessee Valley Authority needed electrical generation equipment in the 1950s, it knew only three suppliers, Allis-Chalmers, Westinghouse and General Electric were qualified to supply its needs. The products to be bought were well-known commodities, easy to specify. Similarly, in current times, a U.S. government agency making a bulk buy of PCs would need only contact a few firms and these firms would be well known to them. In other situations, the "making of the market" by bringing in a more complete set of potential suppliers is a major task.

Supplier bidding can be of two general types:

(i) sealed bidding, in which each qualified supplier submits one secret bid and the buyer chooses on the basis of bids submitted in that round

---

[8]See for example, Chapter 9 "Competitive Bidding" in B.C. Ames and J.D. Hlavacek, *Managerial Marketing for Industrial Firms*, Random House, 1984.

(ii) open bidding, in which sellers interact in real time just as buyers do in a classic auction, except the bidding goes down over time and the lowest supplier price wins

The Internet's interactive communication capability broadens the feasibility of economically efficient reverse auctions. The Web expands the scope of sellers participating. This creates an overall downward pressure on prices. Online analogs of business-to-business competitive bidding situations emerged on the Web. Need2Buy, for example, was a special purpose site at which a buyer could engage in a ready-made reverse auction for electronic components. These components were tightly specified by industry standards so the buyer needs were easily expressed, e.g., part number 74L5240AN meant the same thing to everyone in the industry. The process worked as follows: The buyer submits the RFQ to the system and indicates his choice of the Sealed Bid or Open Bidding format. The Need2Buy expert system searches the database to find vendors carrying the requested product. The buyer may delete vendors unacceptable to it. Accepted vendors then receive an e-mail inviting bids on the RFQ. In an open-bid system, vendors are informed of the lowest bid and invited to rebid if not the lowest. The buyer reviews the final bids, which could include quantity available and delivery date in addition to price, and decides how to proceed, following up with sellers via e-mail, fax, or telephone as desired.

FreeMarkets attracted lots of attention as a firm creating effective Competitive Bidding Events for industrial buyers. In contrast to some vendors selling just reverse auction software enabling buyers to construct their own auctions, FreeMarkets' approach was to provide the total package of services necessary for an effective reverse auction process. It recognized that, in many situations, preparation of the RFQ is a non-trivial task. As stated on the company's Website, ". . . products are often technically complex and custom-made. That's why we work with several members of each client's organization to specify their needs in detail and communicate them to buyers." FreeMarkets' staff worked to have auction bidders (suppliers) "present and prepared" at the bidding event. At the bidding event, FreeMarkets' BidWare proprietary software was used by suppliers from many geographic locations to submit real time bids. FreeMarkets online auctions covered over $1.5 billion in purchase orders from January 1998 to June 1999. Major clients included General Motors, Quaker Oats, and AlliedSignal. A November 1999 *Wall Street Journal* ad of FreeMarkets described its work for United Technologies Corporation (UTC) in its acquisition of specialty metals. In one bidding day, 14 bidders submitted 318 bids covering about $20 million in UTC requirements, saving UTC 22% in the process. In general, the company estimated that its process saves individual buyers between 2 and 25%.

The Internet makes possible the more efficient organization of reverse auctions—bringing in the maximum number of qualified suppliers, well-informed on the requirements. The real-time bidding process also helps the buyers. Overall, the net result is downward pressure on prices.

Emerging Business-to-Consumer Reverse Buying Models.
Business-to-Consumer reverse buying services were less well developed as of late 1999, and less truly auctions, but several types of mechanisms were in operation. For example, as described on its website, imandi was the place "Where Customers Rule"—"Connecting You with Thousands of Merchants Competing to Serve You." imandi trademarked the phrase "we're turning shopping on its head." As the site put it, "our aim is to put an end to fixed pricing on the Web." Originally set up for the acquisition of services from a fragmented supplier base of painters, carpenters, etc., the scope expanded to include collectibles. An individual buyer effectively entered an RFQ, i.e., what it wished to purchase. imandi searched its database of merchants (168,000 of them as of December 1999) to provide a list of local and national merchants believed capable of supplying the desired product. The buyer eliminated any undesired suppliers. imandi transmitted the RFQ to the remainder who submitted price quotes. imandi had 40,000 registered users in December 1999 compared to 7 million for eBay.

Similar services were offered by MyGeek and Respond. Basically, these operations functioned as buying services broadcasting a buyer's RFP to potential suppliers who responded via e-mail. The customer could then choose the seller to transact with or not buy at all. Respond was able to accommodate a situation in which the buyer was only able to describe the item sought in generic terms, e.g., "an inexpensive two-bedroom condominium rental on a beach." Buyers remained anonymous to potential sellers and could choose to follow up or not on e-mailed offers sent to Respond.com for their attention.

The Priceline-type Variant.
A particularly high-profile variant in the reverse buying genre was Priceline, with the marketing proposition (as noted on the website and

in advertising) "Name Your Own Price and Save!" It was hyped as the ultimate in consumer-driven commerce.[9] In some respects, however, the service represented the sacrifice of customer power in favor of solving a vendor's problem of selling off excess inventory.

Priceline's initial product category was airline seats. This process had a buyer naming a price he or she was willing to pay for a roundtrip flight between points A and B. The customer specified only the day of departure and day of return. Then, supplier databases were searched to see the minimum revenue an airline cooperating with Priceline was willing to take to fly someone from A to B and back on those days.

Restrictions included the following:

- The buyer could not specify a preferred carrier, nor even exclude a carrier which was undesirable to them;
- The buyer could not specify times of travel and must take anything the system found between 6 a.m. and 10 p.m.;
- When the buyer named an "offer" price, he or she was obligated to pay that price if the departure/return days were met.

Note that the database of vendors' minimum revenue requirement for fulfilling the demand could show numbers significantly lower than the willingness-to-pay expressed by the buyer. (To induce consumers to express high willingness-to-pay, requests could be made only once a week.) The buyer was charged the expressed willingness-to-pay price, generating margin for Priceline.

As described by Priceline on its Website, ". . . we collect consumer demand . . . By requiring customers to be flexible with respect to brands, sellers and/or product features, we enable sellers to generate incremental revenue without disrupting their existing distribution channels or retail pricing structures."

Priceline has extended the service to additional product categories: hotel rooms in 1100 cities, home financing, and new cars. In December 1999, a grocery service was in-test in metro New York and Priceline announced plans to expand to long-distance telephone calls. For the first six months of 1999, Priceline received 1.5 million "guaranteed offers" from consumers representing $486MM in revenue. It fulfilled just over one-third of these offers, generating $135MM in revenue. Total revenue for the nine monthes ending September 30, 1999 was $313MM, 88.4% of which was paid to suppliers. With other expenses at 55% of revenues, like many other Internet companies, Priceline was running at a substantial loss.

Microsoft offers a similar service at Expedia for hotel rooms: "Hotel Price Matcher." Expedia describes the service as "It's all about helping you get the price you want—YOURS! If Hotel Matcher finds a hotel that meets your criteria and price, we'll automatically select that hotel on your behalf and charge a pre-paid, nonrefundable reservation to your credit card."

Rationale for Reverse Buying Models

As an Internet-based analog to familiar real world competitive bidding, reverse auctions on the Internet have the potential to reduce acquisition costs significantly in many situations. For complex products, an integrated approach as proposed by FreeMarkets is necessary. Their work with very sophisticated purchasing organizations has already proven the value of developing the worldwide seller pool and providing the tools for real-time bidding which promotes competition. For commodity products, simple systems can be effective in expanding the seller base to promote lower prices for buyers.

The economic rationale for reverse buying of the Priceline and Expedia variety is less clear. These systems seem less a reverse buying mechanism with great customer power (as these companies have touted) than a way to create a new product—the unbranded, unknown airline seat or hotel room. In an age of increased buyer information, here the buyer works with markedly *less* information and cannot withdraw from the deal when the actual product definition is known. It offers "guaranteed demand" to suppliers and lots of flexibility in exactly how to meet it. It degrades the quality of the product supplied to the consumer and presents downward pressure on price as compared to a regular transaction.

III(c): Exchanges

Exchanges are electronic marketplaces where a group of buyers and a group of sellers interact to trade and set prices for transactions. The familiar exchanges would be the stock exchanges and currency exchanges around the world. The early electronic product exchanges of the Internet were typically organized around a particular industry. For example:

---

[9]This has been noted in the popular press, e.g., see "The hype is big, really big at Priceline," by Peter Elkind, *Fortune,* September 6, 1999.

Metal Site: has 18 sellers of metals interacting with many buyers. It also is designed to be a comprehensive industry resource providing information on factors influencing industry supply and demand.

Fast Parts: an exchange, patterned after the NASDAQ, to serve the electronics manufacturing and assembly industries. The site has also added an auction facility.

ESteel: for the steel industry, facilitates negotiations between buyers and sellers rather than an auction model.

ChemConnect: Internet's largest chemical and plastics exchange. The exchange evolved out of an online suppliers directory.

The general process at an exchange is conceptually that for each item, a dynamically updated list of "offers to buy" and "offers to sell" is maintained. These buys/sells are matched up through a process. The process on ChemConnect's World Chemical Exchange is exemplary. A buyer arriving at the site with a need to procure something began by querying the system to see currently posted Product Offerings. The system showed available offers to sell including price, quantity available, and expiration time of the offers. (Product offering submitters may post an expiration time of between 15 minutes and 7 days when the offer is posted.) The buyer also saw any bids already made for a given Product Offering.

The buyer then selected among the Product Offerings posted and submitted a bid. The exchange member who posted the Product Offer could then negotiate with the buyer on his bid via an e-mail process. An offering firm could accept bids on any terms it wished and the buyer could modify the bid at any time to reflect current market conditions.

If the current list of Product Offerings did not include the item the buyer was seeking or if the offers were in any way undesirable, he could post a Product Request. The system first showed other buyers' Product Requests posted for the same item (if any) and any offers made against those Product Requests. The prospective buyer's Product Request typically included an indication of the price the buyer was willing to pay, quantity desired and any other important terms-and-conditions of sale. Sellers submitted offers against the Product Request which could then be accepted, rejected or negotiated by the buyer.

At ChemConnect, all negotiations had to be anonymous, i.e., neither buyer nor seller could reveal their identity in the negotiation process. The outcome of the negotiation was to be a product of the forces of market supply and demand. A seller coming to the exchange behaved in a mirror-image fashion to buyers—typically first checking Product Requests posted by potential buyers, then perhaps posting Product Offers, interacting with buyers as described above. No access fees were charged to either buyers or sellers. Both the buyer and seller paid a fee for completed transactions.

A major advantage of these organized exchanges is that they bring together buyers and sellers on a global scale. The impact of this on average price paid is not clear. A buyer benefits by having access to all sellers on the exchange—not just those with whom he is familiar or in geographic proximity. For an individual transaction conducted at a given point in time, this expanding of the potential supplier pool should drive the price paid down. On the other hand, the exchange also opens up a host of new potential buyers to sellers. A seller needing to sell quickly will sell at a less distressed price than if his potential set were restricted to local, known buyers. A real benefit to both buyers and sellers is a reduction in the variability of prices across transactions. Prices on the exchanges are the product of marketwide economic forces impacting all buyers and sellers—not specific, highly variable and relatively unpredictable local conditions.

Summary

As the description above shows, the Internet has already changed the way many markets are organized and consequently the mechanisms via which prices are set. Figure 1 set out three distinct market making mechanisms and, for the sake of clarity in exposition, discussed each separately. However, some sites already in effect offer a combination of these market mechanisms, from which the buyer can choose. For example:

Set Price and Negotiation Combination: As noted in the NexTag discussion (under the Negotiation heading above) the process begins by searching sites and bringing back the set prices of alternative suppliers. If any of these set prices is acceptable, the buyer can select one and conduct the transaction in that way without invoking the negotiation capability of NexTag.

Set Price and Auction Combination: Some sites offer a capability wherein a seller conducting an auction can specify a "Quick Buy" price. Any buyer willing to pay the "Quick Buy" price in order to save time can click on it, effectively buying under a set price mechanism.

Negotiation and Exchange Combination: While some exchanges, such as ChemConnect discussed above, require anonymous exchanges between buyers and sellers, others such as e-Steel allow the buyer to restrict the set of sellers to whom requirements are made known. By restricting the seller set to one or two potential vendors, the market mechanism becomes more negotiation than open market exchange.

To summarize the impact of the Internet on pricing by saying that increased price information availability to buyers will drive prices down is like saying "the effect of global warming is that it's hotter at the beach in July." As usual, the answer to seemingly simple question "will prices go up or down?" is the not so simple "it depends." Markets will be more efficient and different forms of market mechanisms will operate. As noted above, different price effects will be found.

A great deal depends on the nature of the product. Certainly, commodity products will experience increased price pressure due to more buyer information about prices. As discussed at the outset of this note, the information of the Internet cuts into the "ignorance premium." However, even for commodities, the Internet can increase some realized prices. In an inefficient information market, some commodities bring a price of zero— unsold advertising time is used for a public service announcement, empty seats fly into the air, and a truck delivering an order in Boston from New York returns to New York empty. While the Internet will not increase airline industry load factors to 100% or put an end to truckers returning to home base empty, it can create a market for the commodities which would have gone unsold even though buyers were willing to pay more than sellers required as a price. National Transportation Exchange (NTE) created such a service for shippers, planning to evolve it into a system where individual drivers will respond to buyer RFPs in real time from the road via wireless Internet access devices.[10]

In contrast to the general price pressure befalling commodity products, the Internet can be a boon to price realization for those with a differentiated product. While the Internet can convey to consumers a more full understanding of competitive products and prices, it can also provide another communication vehicle via which to create the perception of value in the consumer's mind. For example, the Bose site provides detailed information on the Bose Wave Radio/CD including "The Technology Inside" in supporting the premium $499.00 price; the Gap site includes current television commercials and communicates the benefits of Gap's integration of online and real world presence for consumers; and the BMW site lets a buyer build a custom car. More customized information can be delivered in response to either consumers' explicit requests or their observed behavior.

In short, the Internet offers expanded opportunities for avoiding the commodity trap. More consumer information can mean more information about how sellers are the same and increase the emphasis on price. Alternatively, it can mean more appreciation of how sellers and products are different, decreasing the emphasis on price.

The Internet is a disaster for those with a commodity selling mentality. For them, the story of increasing consumer power over sellers resulting in price pressure and margin erosion will come true. The more sophisticated will see the possibility of new market mechanisms for transacting with customers and take advantage of the opportunity to differentiate themselves not only by giving consumers products they want to buy but also by giving them choices about how they can buy them. For these marketers, the Internet will not be a story of buyer triumph over sellers through information but rather a mutually beneficial success story built on taking advantage of more efficient communication and the opportunity for a more intimate, personalized relationship.

---

[10]"The Rise of the Infomediary," *The Economist,* June 26, 1999.

CUMBERLAND METAL INDUSTRIES: ENGINEERED PRODUCTS DIVISION, 1980

Robert Minicucci,[1] vice president of the Engineered Products Division of Cumberland Metal Industries (CMI), and Thomas Simpson, group manager of the Mechanical Products Group, had spent the entire Wednesday (January 2, 1980) reviewing a new product CMI was about to introduce. (See Exhibit 1 for organization charts.) The room was silent, and as he watched the waning rays of the sun filtering through the window, Minicucci pondered all that had been said. Turning toward Simpson, he paused before speaking.

> Curled metal cushion pads seem to have more potential than any product we've ever introduced. A successful market introduction could as much as double the sales of this company, as well as compensate for the decline of some existing lines. It almost looks too good to be true.

> Simpson responded, "The people at Colerick Foundation Company are pressing us to sell to them. Since they did the original test, they've been anxious to buy more. I promised to contact them by the end of the week."

> "Fair enough," Minicucci said, "but talk to me before you call them. The way we price this could have a significant impact on everything else we do with it."

The Company

Cumberland Metal Industries was one of the largest manufacturers of curled metal products in the country,

Jeffrey J. Sherman, research assistant, prepared this case under the supervision of Professor Benson P. Shapiro as a basis for class discussion rather than to illustrate either effective or ineffective handling of an administrative situation. It was made possible by a company that prefers to remain anonymous. All data have been disguised.

having grown from $250,000 in sales in 1963 to over $18,500,000 by 1979. (Exhibit 2 shows CMI's income statement.) It originally custom fabricated components for chemical process filtration and other highly technical applications. Company philosophy soon evolved from selling the metal as a finished product to selling products that used it as a raw material.

The company's big boost came with the introduction of exhaust gas recirculation (EGR) valves on U.S. automobiles. Both the Ford and Chrysler valve designs required a high temperature seal to hold the elements in place and prevent the escape of very hot exhaust gases. Cumberland developed a product that sold under the trademark *Slip-Seal*. Because it could meet the demanding specifications of the automakers, the product captured a very large percentage of the available business, and the company grew quite rapidly through the mid-1970s. Company management was not sanguine about maintaining its 80% market share over the long term, however, and moved to diversify away from a total reliance on the product and industry. Thus, when a sales representative from Houston approached CMI with a new application for curled metal technology, management examined it closely.

The Product

Background

The product that Minicucci and Simpson were talking about was a cushion pad, an integral part of the process for driving piles.[2] Pile driving was generally done with a large crane, to which a diesel or steam hammer inside a set of leads was attached. The leads were suspended over the pile for direction and support. The hammer drove

---

[1]Pronounced Minikuchi.

[2]Piles were heavy beams of wood, concrete, steel, or a composite material which were pushed into the ground as support for a building bridge, or other structure. They were necessary where the geological composition could shift under the weight of an unsupported structure.

the pile from the top of the leads to a sufficient depth in the ground (see Exhibit 3).

The cushion pads prevented the shock of the hammer from damaging hammer or pile. They sat in a circular "helmet" placed over the top of the pile and were stacked to keep air from coming between striker plate and ram, as shown in Exhibit 3. Of equal importance, the pads effectively transmitted energy from the hammer to the pile. A good cushion pad had to be able to transmit force without creating heat, and still remain resilient enough to prevent shock. With an ineffective pad, energy transmitted from the hammer would be given off as heat, and the pile could start to vibrate and possibly crack.

Despite the importance of these pads to the pile-driving process, little attention had been paid to them by most of the industry. Originally hardwood blocks had been used. Although their cushioning was adequate, availability was a problem and performance was poor. Constant pounding quickly destroyed the wood's resiliency, heat built up, and the wood often ignited. The blocks had to be replaced frequently.

Most of the industry had shifted to asbestos pads (normally 1/4-inch thick) which were used most often and seemed to perform adequately, or stacks of alternate layers of 1/2-inch-thick aluminum plate and 1-inch-thick micarta slabs. (These were not fabricated, but simply pieces of micarta and aluminum cut to specific dimensions.) Both pads came in a variety of standard diameters, the most common being 11 1/2 inches. Diameter was determined by the size of the helmet, which varied with the size of the pile.

Curled Metal and the CMI Cushion Pad

Curled metal was a continuous metal wire that had been flattened and then wound into tight, continuous ringlets. These allowed the metal to stretch in both length and width and gave it three-dimensional resiliency. Because it could be made of various metals (such as copper, monel, and stainless steel), curled metal could be made to withstand almost any temperature or chemical. Stacking many layers could produce a shock mount, an airflow corrector or a highly efficient filter. Tightly compressed curled metal could produce the Slip-Seal for exhaust systems applications or, when calendered and wound around an axis, a cushion pad for pile driving.[3]

Cumberland purchased the wire from outside vendors and performed the flattening and curling operations in-house. The CMI pad started with curled metal calendered to about one inch thick and wound tightly around the center of a flat, metallic disk until the desired diameter had been reached. A similar disk was placed on top, with soldered tabs folded down to hold it all together. The entire structure was then coated with polyvinyl chloride to enhance its appearance and disguise the contents (see Exhibit 4).[4]

The advantage of this manufacturing process was that any diameter pad, from the standard minimum of 11 1/2 inches to over 30 inches for a custom-designed application, could be produced from the same band of curled metal.

Comparative Performance

The Colerick Test

After struggling to find a responsible contractor to use the product and monitor its performance, CMI persuaded Colerick Foundation Company of Baltimore, Maryland, to try its pads on a papermill expansion in Newark, Delaware. The job required 300 55-foot piles driven 50 feet into the ground. The piles were 10-inch and 14-inch steel H-beams; both used an 11 1/2-inch helmet and, thus, 11 1/2-inch cushion pads. The total contractor revenue from the job was $75,000 ($5 per foot of pile driven).

Colerick drove a number of piles using the conventional 1/4-inch thick asbestos cushion pads to determine their characteristics for the job. Eighteen were placed in the helmet and driven until they lost resiliency. Pads were added, and driving continued until a complete set of 24 were sitting in the helmet. After these were spent, the entire set was removed and the cycle repeated.

The rest of the job used the CMI pads. Four were initially installed and driven until 46 piles had been placed. One pad was added and the driving continued for 184 more piles. Another pad was placed in the helmet, and

---

[3]In calendering, curled metal ringlets were compressed between rollers to make a smooth, tight band.

[4]The managers at CMI were concerned that other manufacturers might discover this new application for curled metal and enter the business before CMI could get patent protection. The company had a number of competitors, most of whom were substantially smaller than CMI and none of whom had shown a strong interest or competence in technical, market, or product development.

the job was completed. Comparable performances for the entire job were extrapolated as follows:

	Asbestos	CMI
1. Feet driven per hour while pile driver was at work (does not consider downtime)	150	200
2. Piles driven per set of pads	15	300
3. Number of pads per set	24	6
4. Number of sets required	20	1
5. Number of set changes	20	1
6. Time required for change per set	20 mins.	4 mins.
7. Colerick cost per set	$50	Not charged

Although the CMI pads drove piles 33% faster than the asbestos and lasted for the entire job, Simpson felt these results were unusual. He believed that a curled metal–set life of 10 times more than asbestos and a per-formance increase of 20% were probably more reasonable, because he was uncertain that the CMI pads in larger sizes would perform as well.

Industry Practice

Industry sources indicated that as many as 75% of pile-driving contractors owned their hammers, and most owned at least one crane and set of leads. To determine the contractors' cost of doing business, CMI studied expenses of small contractors who rented equipment for pile-driving jobs. These numbers were readily available and avoided the problem of allocating the cost of a purchased crane or hammer to a particular job.

Standard industry practice for equipment rental used a three-week month and a three-day workweek.[5] There was no explanation for this, other than tradition, but most equipment renters set their rates this way. The cost of renting the necessary equipment and the labor cost for a job similar to that performed by Colerick were estimated as shown in Table A.

Table A Equipment Rental, Labor, and Overhead Costs

	Per Standard			Average Cost per Real Hour[a]
	Month	Week	Per Hour	
1. Diesel hammer	$4,500–7,200	$1,500–2,400	$62.50–100.00	$34
2. Crane	8,000–10,000	2,667–3,334	111.00–140.00	52
3. Leads @ $20 per foot per month (assume 70 feet)	1,400	467	19.44	8
4. Labor[b] 3 laborers @ $6–8 per hour each 1 crane operator 1 foreman			18.00–24.00 8.00–12.00 12.00–14.00	21 10 13
5. Overhead[c] (office, trucks, oil/gas, tools, etc.)			100.00	100

(Casewriter's note: Please use average cost per real hour in all calculations, for uniformity in class discussion.)
[a]These costs were calculated from a rounded midpoint of the estimates. Hammer, crane, and lead costs were obtained by dividing standard monthly costs by 4.33 weeks per month and 40 hours per week.
[b]Labor was paid on a 40-hour week, and a 4.33-week month. One-shift operation (40 hours per week) was standard in the industry.
[c]Most contractors calculated overhead on the basis of "working" hours, not standard hours.

[5]This means that a contractor who rented equipment for one calendar month was charged only the "three-week" price, but had the equipment for the whole calendar month. The same was true of the "three-day week." Contractors generally tried to use the equipment for as much time per week or per month as possible. Thus they rented it on a "three-week" month but used it on a "4.33-week" month.

Hidden costs also played an important role. For every hour actually spent driving piles, a contractor could spend 20 to 40 minutes moving the crane into position. Another 10% to 15% was added to cover scheduling delays, mistakes, and other unavoidable problems. Thus, the real cost per hour was usually substantially more than the initial figures showed. Reducing the driving time or pad changing time did not usually affect the time lost on delays and moving.

All these figures were based on a job that utilized 55-foot piles and 11 1/2-inch pads. Although this was a common size, much larger jobs requiring substantially bigger material were frequent. A stack of 11 1/2-inch asbestos pads weighed between 30 and 40 pounds; the 30-inch size could weigh seven to eight times more. Each 11 1/2-inch CMI pad weighed 15 1/2 pounds. The bigger sizes, being much more difficult to handle, could contribute significantly to unproductive time on a job. (See Exhibit 5.)

Most contracts were awarded on a revenue-per-foot basis. Thus, contractors bid by estimating the amount of time it would take to drive the specified piles the distance required by the architectural engineers. After totaling costs and adding a percentage for profit, they submitted figures broken down into dollars per foot. The cost depended on the size of the piles and the type of soil to be penetrated. The $5 per foot that Colerick charged was not atypical, but prices could be considerably greater.

Test Results

The management of CMI was extremely pleased by how well its cushion pads had performed. Not only had they lasted the entire job, eliminating the downtime required for changeover, but other advantages had become apparent. For example, after 500 feet of driving, the average temperature for the asbestos pads was between 600°F and 700°F, which created great difficulty when they had to be replaced. The crew handling them was endangered, and substantial time was wasted waiting for them to cool. (This accounted for a major portion of the time lost to changeovers.)

The CMI pads, in contrast, never went above 250°F and could be handled almost immediately with protective gloves. This indicated that substantial energy lost in heat by the asbestos pads was being used more efficiently to drive the piles with CMI pads. In addition, the outstanding resiliency of the CMI product seemed to account for a 33% faster driving time, which translated into significant savings.

In talking with construction site personnel, CMI researchers also found that most were becoming wary of the asbestos pads' well-publicized health dangers. Many had expressed a desire to use some other material and were pleased that the new pads contained no asbestos.

The CMI management was quite happy with these results; Colerick was ecstatic. Understandably, Colerick became quite anxious to buy more pads and began pressing Tom Simpson to quote prices.

A Second Test

To confirm the results from the Colerick test, CMI asked Fazio Construction to try the pads on a job in New Brighton, Pennsylvania. This job required 300 45-foot concrete piles to be driven 40 feet into the ground. Asbestos pads (11 1/2 inches) were again used for comparison. Total job revenue was $108,000, or $9 per foot, and Fazio would have paid $40 for each set of 12 asbestos pads used. The results from this test are shown as follows:

	Asbestos	CMI
1. Feet driven per hour while pile driver was at work (does not consider downtime)	160	200
2. Piles driven per set of pads	6	300
3. Number of pads per set	12	5
4. Number of sets required	50	1
5. Number of set changes	50	1
6. Time required for change per set	20 mins.	4 mins.
7. Fazio cost per set	$40	Not charged

The Market

Projected Size

There were virtually no statistics from which a potential U.S. market for cushion pads could be determined, so Simpson had to make several assumptions based on the information he could gather. A 1977 report by *Construction Engineering* magazine estimated that approximately 13,000 pile hammers were owned by companies directly involved in pile driving. Industry sources estimated that another 6,500 to 13,000 were leased. He assumed that this total of 19,500 to 26,000 hammers would operate about 25 weeks per year (because of seasonality) and that they would be used 30 hours per week (because of moving time, repairs, scheduling problems, and other factors).

Simpson further assumed that an average actual driving figure (including time to change pads and so on) for most jobs was 20 feet per hour, which amounted to between 290 million and 390 million feet of piles driven annually. To be conservative, he also assumed that a set of curled metal pads (four initially installed, plus two added after the originals lost some resiliency) would drive 10,000 feet.

Purchase Influences

In the pile-driving business, as in other parts of the construction industry, a number of entities participated in purchases. The CMI management was able to identify six types of influences.

1. *Pile hammer manufacturers.* A number of manufacturers sold hammers in the United States although many were imported from Western Europe and Japan. The leading domestic producer in 1979 was Vulcan Iron Works of New Orleans, whose Model #1 had become the standard used by architectural engineers specifying equipment for a job. Simpson did not feel these manufacturers would purchase a large dollar volume of cushion pads, but they could be very influential in recommendations.

2. *Architectural/Consulting engineers.* Pile driving required significant expertise in determining the needs of a construction project. Thorough stress analysis and other mathematical analysis were necessary. Because of the risks in building the expensive projects usually supported by piles, the industry looked to architectural/consulting engineers as the ultimate authorities on all aspects of the business. Consequently, these firms were very detailed in specifying the materials and techniques to be used on a project. They always specified hammers and frequently mentioned pads. The CMI management felt that, although no sales would come from these people, they could be one of the most important purchase influences.

3. *Soil consultants.* These consultants were similar to the architectural/consulting engineers, but were consulted only on extraordinary conditions.

4. *Pile hammer distributing/renting companies.* This group was an important influence because it provided pads to the contractors. In fact, renting companies often included the first set of pads free. CMI management felt that these companies would handle the cushion pads they could most easily sell and might even hesitate to provide pads that enabled a contractor to return equipment faster.

5. *Engineering/Construction contractors.* The contracting portion of the industry was divided among large international firms and smaller independents. The former almost always participated in the bigger, more sophisticated jobs. Companies like Conmaco and Raymond International not only contracted to drive piles, but also designed jobs, specified material, and even manufactured their own equipment. It was clear to Simpson that if he was to succeed in getting CMI pads used on bigger, complex construction projects, CMI would have to solicit this group actively on a very sophisticated level.

6. *Independent pile-driving contractors.* These contractors represented the "frontline buying influence." Their primary objective was to make money. They were very knowledgeable about the practical aspects of pile driving, but not very sophisticated.

No national industry associations influenced this business, but some regional organizations played a minor part. Contractors and others talked freely, although few were willing to reveal competitive secrets. The company was unsure how important word-of-mouth communication would be. Very little was published about the pile-driving industry, although construction-oriented magazines like *Louisiana Contractor* occasionally reported on pile-driving contractors and their jobs. These magazines featured advertising by suppliers to the trade, mostly equipment dealers and supply houses. One industry supplier, Associated Pile and Fitting Corporation, sponsored professional-level "Piletalk" seminars in various cities, bringing designers, contractors, and equipment developers together "to discuss practical aspects of installation of driven piles."

Another potential influence was Professor R. Stephen McCormack of Pennsylvania A&M University. He had established a department to study pile driving and had become a respected authority on its theoretical aspects. Sophisticated engineering/construction firms and many architectural consultants were familiar with his work and helped support it. Cumberland management felt that his endorsement of the operational performance of CMI cushion pads would greatly enhance industry acceptance. The company submitted the pads for testing by Dr. McCormack in the fall of 1979, and although the final results were not yet available he had expressed considerable enthusiasm. Final results were expected by early 1980.

Competitive Products and Channels of Distribution

The pile-driving industry had paid very little attention to cushion pads before CMI's involvement. Everyone used them and took them for granted, but no one attempted to promote pads. No manufacturers dominated the business. In fact, most pads came unbranded, having been cut from larger pieces of asbestos or micarta by small, anonymous job shops.

Distribution of pads was also ambiguous. Hammer sales and rental outlets provided them, heavy construction supply houses carried them, pile manufacturers sometimes offered them, and a miscellaneous assortment of other outlets occasionally sold them as a service.[6] The smaller pads sold for $2 to $3 each; larger ones sold for between $5 and $10. Three dollars each was typical for 11 1/2 inch pads. The profit margin for a distributor was usually adequate—in the area of 30% to 40%—but the dollar profit did not compare well with that of other equipment lines. Most outlets carried pads as a necessary part of the business, but none featured them as a work-saving tool.

The CMI management felt it could be totally flexible in establishing an organization to approach the market. It toyed with the idea of a direct sales force and its own distribution outlets, but eventually began to settle on signing construction-oriented manufacturers' representatives,[7] who would sell to a variety of distributors and supply houses. The company feared an uphill struggle to convince the sales and distribution channels that there really was a market for the new pad. Management expected considerable difficulty in finding outlets willing to devote the attention necessary for success, but it also felt that once the initial barriers had been penetrated, most of the marketplace would be anxious to handle the product.

The Pricing Decision

Simpson had projected cost data developed by his manufacturing engineers. Exhibit 6 shows two sets of numbers: one utilized existing equipment; the other reflected the purchase of $50,000 of permanent tooling. In both cases, the estimated volume was 250 cushion pads per month. Additional equipment could be added at a cost of $75,000 per 250 pads per month of capacity, including permanent tooling like that which could be purchased for $50,000.

Both sets of numbers were based on the assumption that only one pad size would be manufactured; in other words, the numbers in the 11 1/2-inch size were based on manufacturing only this size for a year. This was done because CMI had no idea of the potential sales mix among product sizes. Management knew that 11 1/2 inches was the most popular size, but the information available on popularity of the other sizes was vague. CMI accounting personnel believed these numbers would not vary dramatically with a mix of sizes.

Corporate management usually burdened CMI products with a charge equal to 360% of direct labor to cover the overhead of its large engineering staff. Simpson was uncertain how this would apply to the new product, because little engineering had been done and excess capacity was to be used initially for manufacturing. Although it was allocated on a variable basis, he thought he might consider the overhead "fixed" for his analysis. Corporate management expected a contribution margin after all manufacturing costs of 40% to 50% of selling price.

Simpson was enthusiastic about the potential success of this new product. The Engineered Products Division was particularly pleased to offer something with such high dollar potential, especially since in the past, a "large customer" of the division had purchased only about $10,000 per year.

He was still uncertain how to market the pads and how to reach the various purchase influences. Advertising and promotion also concerned him because there were no precedents for this product or market.

For the moment, however, Simpson's primary consideration was pricing. He had promised to call Colerick Foundation Company by the end of the week, and Minicucci was anxious to review his decision with him. He hoped other prospects would be calling as soon as

---

[6]Supply houses were "hardware stores" for contractors and carried a general line of products, including lubricants, work gloves, and maintenance supplies. Distributors, in contrast, tended to be more equipment oriented and to sell a narrower line of merchandise.

[7]Manufacturers' representatives were agents (sometimes single people, sometimes organizations) who sold non-competing products for commission. They typically did *not* take title to the merchandise and did *not* extend credit.

Exhibit 1 Engineered Products Division Organization Chart

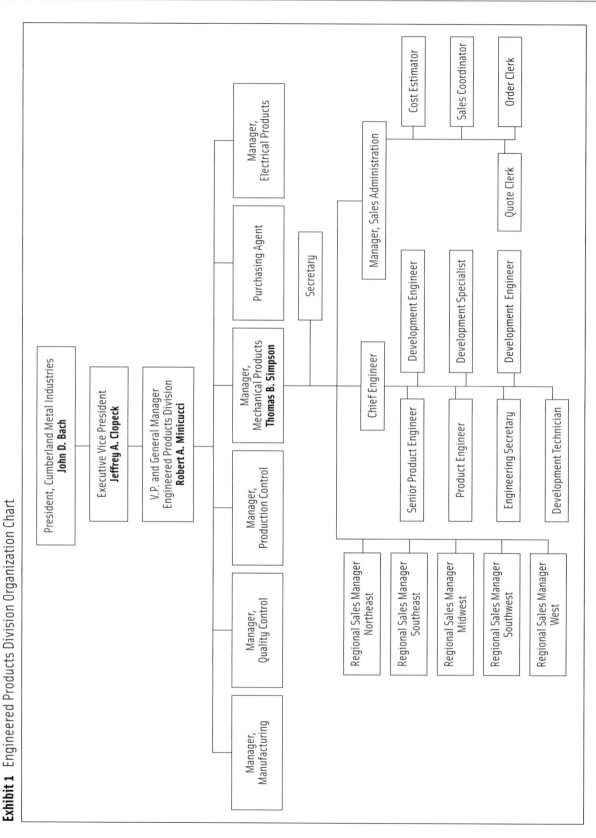

Exhibit 2 Income Statement

December 31	1979	1978
– *Net sales*	$18,524,428	$20,465,057
– *Costs and expenses*		
– Cost of sales	11,254,927	11,759,681
– Selling expenses	2,976,396	2,711,320
– General and administrative expenses	2,204,291	2,362,528
	16,435,614	16,833,529
Income from operations	2,088,814	3,631,528
– *Other income (expense)*		
– Dividend income	208,952	—
– Interest income	72,966	186,611
– Interest expense	(40,636)	(31,376)
	241,282	155,235
Income before income taxes	2,330,096	3,786,763
– *Provision for income taxes*	1,168,830	1,893,282
– Net income	1,161,266	1,893,481
– *Net income per share*	*$1.39*	*$2.16*

Exhibit 3 Typical Steam- or Air-Operated Pile Driver with Helmet and Cushion Pad

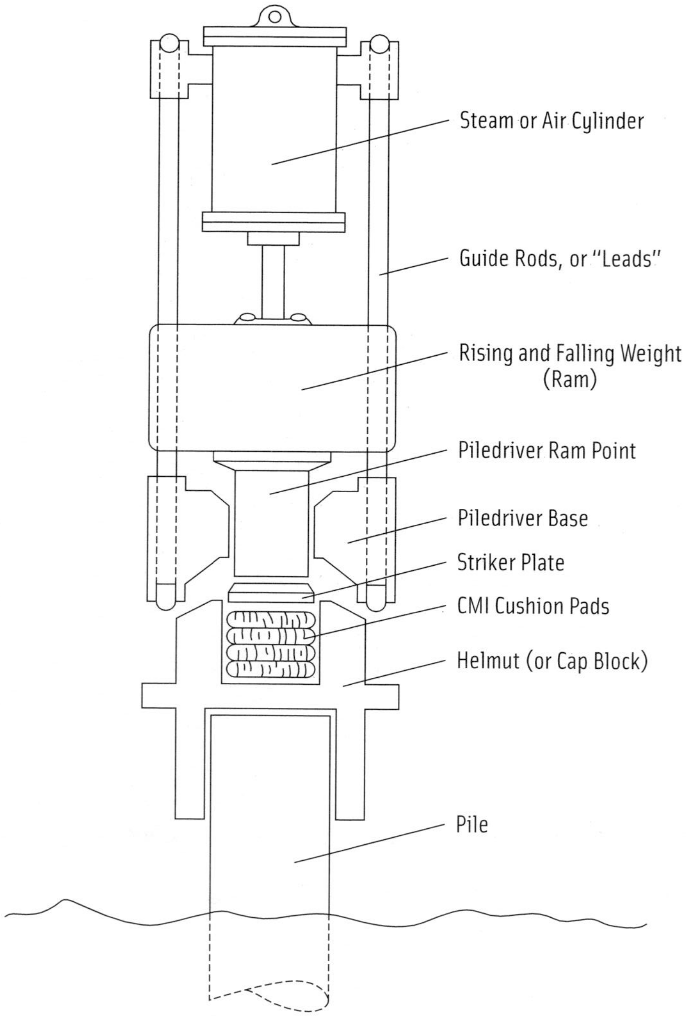

Pile hammer inside leads driving a steel H-beam into the ground

Steam or Air Cylinder

Guide Rods, or "Leads"

Rising and Falling Weight (Ram)

Piledriver Ram Point

Piledriver Base

Striker Plate

CMI Cushion Pads

Helmut (or Cap Block)

Pile

A schematic diagram of typical piledriver

Exhibit 3 Typical Steam- or Air-Operated Pile Driver with Helmet and Cushion Pad *(continued)*

CMI pile-driving pad in position in helmet

Close-up of hammer driving pile (most of the pile is already in the ground)

Exhibit 4 Close-up of CMI Curled Metal Cushion Pad for Pile Driving

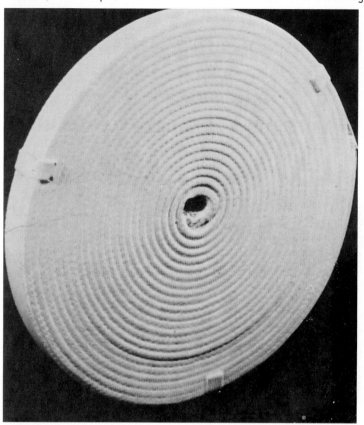

The calendered curled metal is wound tightly around the central point of a flat metallic disk. (The disk is on the back side of the pad from this view.) Soldered tabs secure the curled metal to the disk. The entire structure is coated with polyvinyl-chloride.

Exhibit 5 Curled Metal Cushion Pad Standard Sizes

Diameter (inches)	Thickness (inches)	Weight (pounds)
11 1/2	1	15 1/2
14	1	23
17 1/2	1	36
19 3/4	1	48
23	1	64
30	1	110

Exhibit 6 Two Sets of Projected Manufacturing Costs

	Size					
	$11\frac{1}{2}''$	$14''$	$17\frac{1}{2}''$	$19\frac{3}{4}''$	$23''$	$30''$
Estimates per Pad with Existing Equipment						
– *Variable*						
– Material	$15.64	$20.57	$31.81	$40.39	$53.16	$95.69
– Labor	28.80	33.07	50.02	57.07	69.16	118.36
– **Total variable**	44.44	53.64	81.83	97.46	122.32	214.05
– *Fixed factory overhead*						
– @ 360% direct labor	103.68	119.05	180.07	205.45	248.98	426.10
– **Total manufacturing cost**	$148.12	$172.69	$261.90	$302.91	$371.30	$640.15
Estimated with Purchase of $50,000 of Permanent Tooling						
– *Variable*						
– Material	$15.64	$20.57	$31.81	$40.39	$53.16	$95.69
– Labor	11.64	15.25	21.85	26.95	30.57	56.09
– **Total variable**	27.28	35.82	53.66	67.34	83.73	151.78
– *Fixed factory overhead*						
– @ 360% direct labor	41.90	54.90	78.66	97.02	110.05	201.92
– **Total manufacturing cost**	$69.18	$90.72	$132.32	$164.36	$193.78	$353.70

Note: Estimated volume was 250 cushion pads per month.

EASTMAN KODAK COMPANY

Eastman Kodak Company lost 8% of its market value between January 17 and 24, 1994. Investors had become increasingly concerned about Kodak's declining position in the photographic film market.

Holding 70% share of the U.S. market and worldwide leadership, Kodak was still the dominant player in the market. But five years earlier Kodak's U.S. share had been 76% and ten years earlier—over 80%. Kodak had long enjoyed status as one of the most powerful brands in the United States. Dating back to 1887, Kodak advertising and promotion had made the brand a household name in the United States. Such was the presence of Kodak that many people referred to happy times at weddings, graduations and the like as "Kodak moments" to be preserved on film. While new camera and film technologies from Kodak and others were on the horizon, Kodak depended on the contribution from conventional film to help fund these developmental efforts. Kodak's first response to low-price competition from Fuji and private label manufacturers had been to introduce a superpremium brand called Ektar, targeted at professionals. However, Kodak's overall share continued to decline. In the wake of continued share loss and the market's attention to it, Kodak had to develop a response. It hoped to find a plan which would stem the loss in market share, maintain the cash flow from the business, and preserve the brand equity.

Alexander Wasilov, vice president and general manager of Kodak Consumer Imaging in the U.S. and Canada, advocated a strategy built around the introduction of a new brand to address the price-oriented segment. This new product would be priced about 20% less than Kodak's current main item in the film line. Others

felt the real problem was the price premium Kodak had charged and favored addressing it directly. Still others recognized the inherently emotional nature of the category—capturing "once-in-a-lifetime" events on film. They favored a response dominated by focus on advertising to communicate the value proposition; e.g., "why trust less than Kodak?" Kodak management was open to any well-reasoned, well-supported plan which would help attain their market share, profit, and brand equity objectives.

Kodak manufactured and marketed many components of imaging systems. To amateurs, Kodak supplied films, photographic papers, processing services, photographic chemicals, cameras and projectors. Kodak also served professional photofinishers, professional photographers and customers in motion picture, television, and government markets. In addition to imaging systems Kodak sold information systems and health products. On December 31, 1993, the company spun off its worldwide chemicals business.

The U.S. Photo Film Market

In 1993, consumers made approximately 16 billion color exposures in the United States—the equivalent of 670 million 24-exposure rolls. Typically, a consumer paid between $2.50 and $3.50 for a 24-exposure roll. Over the past five years, the market's annual unit growth rate averaged only 2%. Major suppliers besides Kodak were Fuji of Japan, Agfa of Germany, and 3M. Kodak and Fuji sold only branded products. Because of a 1921 consent decree still in force, Kodak could not sell film on a private label basis.[1] Both Agfa and 3M sold their film to consumers as branded product and to other firms for sale under a private label. Polaroid, the leader in instant photography, had entered the conventional film market in 1989 with

Professor Robert Dolan prepared this case as the basis for class discussion rather than to illustrate either effective or ineffective handling of an administrative situation. This is a rewritten version of an earlier HBS Case—#594-111, Eastman Kodak Company: Funtime Film.

[1]Private labels are products marketed not under a name controlled by the manufacturer but under a name controlled by a member of the channel of distribution. A private label is sometimes called a store brand if it bears the name of store itself, e.g., CVS Film. In 1993, private label goods accounted for about 20% of the units sold in U.S. grocery stores. This represented 15% of supermarket dollar volume. Private labels typically sold at a lower price than the branded competitors.

Table A Approximate Unit Market Shares in 1993 (U.S. Market)

Kodak	70%
Fuji	11%
Polaroid	4%
Private label	10%
Other	5%

its branded product, which it sourced from 3M. Film was intensively distributed through discount and department stores (32% of industry sales), drug stores (24%), camera shops (14%), supermarkets and convenience stores (13%), wholesale clubs (9%) and mail order (2%).

Estimated unit market shares by manufacturer are shown in Table A.

Fuji and Kodak were locked in a global battle for dominance of the worldwide photographic market. Like Kodak, Fuji sold cameras and other imaging products as well as film. Fuji's worldwide sales were about $10 billion. See Exhibit 1 for Kodak sales and earning figures, 1991–93. Fuji started its serious incursion into Kodak territory in 1984, when it captured consumers' attention, particularly in the United States, by becoming the Official Film of the 1984 Summer Olympics in Los Angeles.

Both Fuji's and Polaroid's U.S. dollar sales grew at over 15% in the past year, compared with Kodak's 3% growth rate. An industry expert opined, "Fuji's gains can be largely attributed to the marketer's ability to keep the line on price, an area where Kodak has suffered."[2] Private labels as a group grew about 10%.

Category Pricing

Kodak offered two brands: Ektar and Gold Plus. Its Gold Plus brand was the leader of the industry. Exhibit 2 shows the average retail prices for a single 24-exposure roll of ISO 100 film for leading suppliers. (ISO refers to the "speed" or light sensitivity of the film. Amateurs typically use 100, 200, or 400, with 100 being the most popular. Higher-ISO films performed in lower light conditions, but were more expensive.)

As shown in Exhibit 2, there were four segments in the market. Kodak Gold Plus, the largest-selling brand

by far, set the Premium Brand price at $3.49. Dealers earned about 20% margins off the Kodak prices in Exhibit 2. Kodak's gross margins were believed to be about 70% on each of its two brands. Kodak's super-premium brand Ektar was targeted very narrowly at advanced amateurs and professionals. Fuji had a similar positioning for its Reala brand. These superpremium products were distributed mainly through camera shops and were not major sellers, representing less than 5% of units sold.

Fuji's key brand, Fujicolor Super G, anchored the Economy Brand tier at a price 17% below the Premium tier. Dealers earned a 25% margin on Fuji typically. Fuji's gross margin was believed to be about 55%. Konica and 3M's ScotchColor brand were other competitors in this tier. Finally, film procured from either Agfa or 3M and sold under another name made up the Price Brand tier. Representative products are shown in Exhibit 2. While most of the film in this group was a "store brand" marketed under the name of the retail outlet selling it (e.g., Kmart, a major mass merchant, and Walgreen's, a major drug chain), Polaroid, the dominant firm in instant cameras and film, marketed conventional film it sourced from 3M in this tier. Dealer percentage margins were typically higher for private label products.[3]

Consumer Behavior

Film usage rates varied widely across households but averaged 15 rolls per year. The *Wolfman Report*[4] estimated that 20% of households bought less than 5 rolls per year, 22% bought between 5 and 9 rolls, 28% bought 10 to 15 rolls, 16% bought 16 to 25 rolls, and 13%

---

[2]Ricardo Davis, "Fuji Makes Gains in 35MM Film Sales Using Price Strategy," *Advertising Age,* October 18, 1993, p. 48.

[3]Casewriter Note: For purposes of calculations in the case analysis, a good approximation is that dealer margins on Kodak film averaged 20%; other suppliers' film yielded a 25% dealer margin.

[4]*1992–93 Wolfman Report on the Photographic and Imaging Industry in the United States,* p. 31.

bought more than 25 rolls. Often, these rolls were purchased in "multipacs" containing 2–3 rolls of film.

Kodak advertising spending was approximately $50 million on cameras and film in the United States in 1993. (This was about four times Fuji's U.S. advertising spending.) Typical advertising copy was a presentation developed for the 1994 Olympic Winter Games television broadcast. Contrasted against the Olympic competition from Norway broadcast around the world, the ad portrayed a young boy in his own competition in his backyard falling into a snowbank to make a "snow angel." The voice-over noted, "Some of the best events happen in your own backyard . . . why trust them to less than Kodak film." A history of heavy spending behind an emotional message made Kodak one of the most powerful brands in the U.S.

Actual quality differences among films were unclear. Both Kodak and Fuji tried to position themselves as providing superior quality film through their advanced technology. However, *Consumer Reports*[5] conducted a test of films and reported, "We found most films to be no better or worse than their competitors of the same speed. The top six ISO 100 films scored so similarly that we think all will yield prints of comparable quality." In order of overall quality score (score out of 100 in parenthesis), these top six films were:

1. Polaroid High Definition (95)
2. Fujicolor Super G (94)
3. Kodak Gold Plus (93)
4. Konica Super SR (93)
5. Kodak Ektar (92)
6. ScotchColor (92)

ScotchColor was also sold as private label from Kmart, Kroeger, Target, and York, among others as shown in Exhibit 2. Fuji Superpremium brand Reala had a score of 90, and Agfacolor XRG scored 88. *Consumer Reports* regarded score differences of less than 5 points as "not significant."

According to a 1991 survey cited in *Discount Merchandiser*, more than half of the picture takers in the United States claim to know "little or nothing about photography."[6] As a result the article claimed, "Consumers tend to view film as a commodity, often buying

on price alone." Neither top player accepted the judgment that price was key however. A Fuji spokesperson noted that if price were the deciding factor, private label would be a stronger seller. Jim Van Senus, Kodak's manager of general merchandise marketing said: "The importance of brand name in consumer decision making is still strong. On the other hand, there is a growing body of price-sensitive consumers there. We are seeing growth in private label film activity." Kodak research had shown that 50% of buyers were "Kodak-loyal," 40% were "samplers" switching between brands but relying heavily on Kodak, and 10% shopped on price.

Strategic Alternatives

One proposal was for a major repositioning of Kodak's film product line, expanding the number of offerings to three:

1. Gold Plus—would remain the flagship brand at a price unchanged from 1993 levels.

2. Royal Gold—the Ektar product would be renamed Royal Gold, in the Superpremium segment. Whereas Ektar had been targeted to professionals and serious amateurs, Royal Gold would be targeted to a consumer audience for "very special" occasions. Offering richer color saturation and sharper pictures than Gold Plus, it would be positioned as especially appropriate for those occasions when the consumer may wish to make enlargements. It would be priced lower than Ektar had been, selling to the trade at only a 9% premium over Gold Plus. Cooperative advertising allowances were to be offered to the trade to provide the incentive to maintain Royal Gold *retail* prices at 20% above Gold Plus, thereby offering superior trade margins.[7]

3. A new brand would be introduced to give Kodak a presence in the Economy Brand Tier, at a price approximately 20% below Gold Plus on a per roll basis. One proposal was to call the new brand "Funtime" and position it as being "For Casual

[5]*Consumer Reports,* November 1993, p. 712.
[6]R. Lee Sullivan, "Photogoods on the Upgrade," *Discount Merchandiser,* September 1991, pp. 64 ff.

[7]In cooperative advertising, a manufacturer agrees to pay a portion of a retailer's advertising cost. For example, it might agree to reimburse 50% of advertising cost up to 2% of sales. Terms of the cooperative advertising program often specified conditions under which payments would be made, e.g., the ad could not feature the item below a certain price.

Picture Taking." The manufacturing cost for this product would be about the same as for the current Gold Plus product.

Alexander Wasilov advocated this strategy as: "intelligent risk taking that will drive both our market share and earnings."[8] He described it as a way to target customer segments more precisely, with Royal Gold for "very special moments" and Gold for "those unexpected moments—the baby smiling, the father and son playing catch." The risk of new economy film could be limited by making it available only in limited quantities or at certain times of the year. If this strategy were followed, Kodak would have to decide how to allocate advertising spending across the three products.

Others were less convinced of the product line extension strategy. One argued that this category and Kodak's historical success were all about communicating the emotional bond between the consumer and the brand and, hence, Kodak should return to a strength: advertising. Perhaps even added spending was warranted despite recent declines in share.

Another felt it was time to face the fact the *Consumer Reports* had documented, i.e., that there was not much difference between films anymore and, hence, Kodak was just not entitled to as great a price premium as it enjoyed in the past. Those in this camp argued that the pricing action should be taken now before market share slipped even further.

Decisions

George Fisher, the recently appointed CEO of Kodak who came from Motorola, prepared to meet analysts and large investor houses in the wake of Kodak's one week 8% loss in market value. He hoped to present a film strategy which would "drive both market share and earnings." This required setting out a detailed marketing plan and describing the expected results for Kodak.

---

[8]Wendy Bounds, "Kodak Develops Economy-Brand Film That Is Focused on Low-Priced Rivals," *Wall Street Journal,* January 26, 1994, p. A3.

Exhibit 1 Kodak Sales and Earnings, 1991–93 ($ in millions)

Company	1993	1992	1991
Sales from Continuing Operations	$16,364	$16,545	$15,951
Earnings (loss) from Continuing Operations			
Before Extraordinary Item and Cumulative Effect			
Of Changes in Accounting Principle	$475	$727	($302)
For Imaging Segment			
Sales from Continuing Operations	$7,257	$7,415	$7,075

Exhibit 2 Price Tiers in Film Market Defined by Average Retail Price Paid

Superpremium Brands		
Fujicolor Reala	$4.69	(134)
Kodak Ektar	$4.27	(122)
Premium Brands		
Kodak Gold Plus	$3.49	(100)
Agfacolor XRG	$3.49	(100)
Economy Brands		
Fujicolor Super G	$2.91	(83)
Konica Super SR	$2.91	(83)
ScotchColor	$2.69	(77)
Price Brands[a]		
(S) Polaroid High Definition	$2.49	(71)
(S) Kroeger	$2.49	(71)
(A) Walgreen's	$2.49	(71)
(S) York	$2.40	(69)
(A) Clark Color	$2.35	(67)
(S) Kmart Focal	$2.29	(66)
(S) Target	$2.19	(63)

Source: National Survey reported in *Consumer Reports,* November 1993, pp. 711–715.
Note: Numbers in ( ) are indices indicating price relative to Kodak Gold Plus.
[a](S) designates the film was procured from 3M and was equivalent to ScotchColor.
(A) designates the film was procured from Bayer's Agfa and was equivalent to AgfaColor XRG.

BECTON DICKINSON & COMPANY: VACUTAINER® SYSTEMS DIVISION (CONDENSED)

On Thursday, August 1, 1985, William Kozy, national sales director for Becton Dickinson VACUTAINER® Systems (BDVS), and Hank Smith, BDVS's vice president of marketing and sales, slumped into their seats on the evening flight from Chicago to Newark. They had just completed their fifth round of negotiations in as many months with the materials manager of Affiliated Purchasing Group (APG), a large hospital buying group. Historically, BDVS had supplied most blood collection products bought by individual APG-member hospitals. But in April, APG had announced its intention of initiating group purchasing of one brand of blood collection products for all member hospitals. Since then, Kozy and Smith had represented BDVS in repeated negotiations with APG, while APG had also been negotiating with BDVS's competitors.

The subject of the negotiations was the pricing and delivery terms of a proposed purchasing agreement between APG and BDVS. Traditionally, all of BDVS's products had been sold through its distributors, who also negotiated prices for those (and other) products directly with hospital customers. In recent years, however, BDVS had begun a new form of sales agreement, known as a "Z contract," in which BDVS negotiated prices and quantities directly with large accounts but supplied its products through one or more of its authorized distributors.

The August 1 meeting with APG had been an all-day session, at the end of which both sides agreed that BDVS would submit its final proposal by August 15. At issue were the specific prices and terms for BDVS's two major products. In addition, there were questions raised regarding which distributors would be used to service the contract, and APG negotiators had urged BDVS to consider manufacturing a private label for APG.

"They're bringing out the big guns this time," noted Kozy as the plane began to taxi down the runway. "They certainly are," agreed Smith, "and we'll have to decide what we do about that. Al Battaglia wants to meet with us tomorrow at 1 p.m. about the APG contract. Let's review the situation one more time and make our recommendations."

Company Background

Becton Dickinson (BD) manufactured medical, diagnostic, and industrial safety products for health care professionals, medical research institutions, industry, and the general public. Sales in 1984 were $1.127 billion, with 75% coming from U.S. operations (see Exhibit 1). The company had three business segments—Laboratory, Industrial Safety, and Medical Products—each a profit center with separate marketing responsibilities. Medical Products had three divisions: (1) needles, syringes, and diabetic products, (2) pharmaceutical systems, and (3) VACUTAINER blood collection systems.

Becton Dickinson VACUTAINER® Systems Division (BDVS)[1]

See Exhibit 2 for a BD organization chart. Reporting to Hank Smith, vice president for marketing and sales, were three product managers, each responsible for one of the division's product groups, and a sales director, William Kozy, responsible for achieving sales targets through six regional managers. Alfred Battaglia had held several financial functions before assuming the role of division president.

Prof. Frank Cespedes and Prof. V. Kasturi Rangan prepared this case as the basis for class discussion rather than to illustrate either effective or ineffective handling of an administrative situation.

---

[1]Both VACUTAINER® and MICROTAINER® are registered trademarks of Becton Dickinson and Company.

Products

BD introduced blood collection products in the late 1940s. BDVS was formed as a business unit in 1980 with three major product groups having total 1984 sales of $90 million: venous blood collection (about 70% of BDVS sales) consisting of VACUTAINER tubes and needles; capillary blood collection consisting of MICRO-TAINER tubes and lancets; and microbiology systems consisting of culture tubes and specimen collectors. Each product group accounted for about 33% of BDVS's 1984 operating income.

Venous blood collection systems consisted of a needle and vacuum tube used for collecting blood from a patient's veins. VACUTAINER was the BD brand name for a broad line of tubes and needles designed to meet hundreds of differing needs in hospitals, medical laboratories, and physicians' offices. (See Exhibit 3 for sample products.)

In venous blood collection, the tubes were coated with reagents to preserve the integrity of the specimen (the stoppers on the tubes were color coded to indicate the specific reagent inside). The laboratory technician, known as a phlebotomist, collected blood in different tubes depending on the type of test required by the patient's doctor.

Evacuated-tube blood collection was considered superior to the older needle-and-syringe method in providing specimen integrity, convenience, and lower costs. BD was the pioneer in converting the market to evacuated tubes. According to industry sources, BD had an estimated 80% market share in the United States, where nearly 100% of venous blood collection had been converted to evacuated-tube methods (worldwide, evacuated tube methods accounted for less than 40% of blood collection).

Capillary blood collection systems consisted of a lancet for pricking the patient's finger and a tube (MICRO-TAINER® was the BD brand name) used for blood collection and testing. MICROTAINER tubes used capillary action and gravity for collecting blood samples of smaller volumes than those generally collected by the venous method. MICROTAINER systems could be used for the same blood tests administered through VACU-TAINER systems, but the common applications for MICROTAINER were in single-tube collections for infants, children, and geriatric patients.

The division marketed VACUTAINER and MICRO-TAINER systems as complete blood collection systems, but other suppliers' needles and lancets could be used on BD tubes and vice versa. On average, about 2.5 tubes were used per needle, with an estimated 1985 U.S. market, in units, of 800 million tubes and 320 million needles.

Microbiology systems provided a sterile environment for transferring blood specimens from the collection to the testing site. The division's microbiology tubes and collectors were all marketed under the VACUTAINER brand name.

BDVS had the broadest line of blood collection products in the industry. Peter Trow, sales representative for BDVS, noted:

> In this business, quality is not merely a function of needle sharpness or the integrity of the reagents. We also offer the widest range of tubes, and that's crucial. Big hospitals and labs run a multitude of tests, and they require product assortment and color-coding schemes to make their jobs easier. That is part of their definition of quality.

Cost-containment pressures resulted in a 1.0% compounded annual decline in hospital blood testing between 1983 and 1985. Forecasts indicated hospital blood testing would decline through 1987, but an aging U.S. population should increase testing somewhat in subsequent years. Testing in commercial labs and physicians' offices was expected to be 40% of total blood testing by 1990.

Total microcollections were forecast to increase 5% annually through 1990 as less-expensive, easier-to-use equipment motivated physicians to do more testing in their offices rather than via a hospital or commercial lab. Battaglia also noted that blood collection technology was changing rapidly:

> The clear technological trend is to enable end-users to do more of the diagnostic testing. This means more testing can be done in nonlaboratory settings such as doctors' offices. In turn, that has implications for our distribution network, which tends to be built around lab distributors rather than the medical/surgical distributors who sell to nonlab locations. The technological developments also place more technical selling demands on our sales force.

Industry Background

Blood collection products were used in hospitals, commercial laboratories, and many nonhospital health care centers.

Hospitals. In 1985 approximately 7,000 U.S. hospitals performed 70% of all blood tests. Blood collection was generally performed at the patient's bedside and the sample then sent to a hospital laboratory for testing. The 1,800 largest hospitals (200 or more beds each) accounted for 50% of the market for medical equipment and supplies.

Within hospitals, the buying process for medical supplies, including blood collection products, was complex and changing. The primary contact of a BD salesperson varied depending upon usage requirements and the purchasing process in an individual hospital. Robert Giardino, senior sales representative for BD, noted:

> Blood collection tubes are a key product for a hospital lab: if the specimen is not collected properly, the lab has many problems. Hospitals order tubes frequently; most have a standing weekly order with one or more distributors for tubes.

> The hospital's chief lab technician is usually the person responsible for testing, ordering supplies, and handling administrative matters. In a large teaching hospital, this person might have an M.D. or a Ph.D.; in other hospitals, it would be someone who came up through the lab ranks. On average, there are six subsidiary lab departments, each headed by a supervisor who reports to the chief lab technician.

> Purchasing influences vary, depending on the specific product. In general, the "bench people" [i.e., medical technicians in the lab] have product preferences, and these people tend to be concerned with the best quality and not price. Among the bench people, VACUTAINER is the best-known brand of blood collection tubes. But the department heads and chief lab technicians have budgets to meet. Increasingly, upper levels of hospital administration, and especially the materials managers [who perform a role analogous to that of purchasing agents in industrial concerns] are more influential. These people tend to come from different backgrounds than the lab people do, and they are always price sensitive.

In most hospitals, medical supplies accounted for 10% to 15% of a hospital's total costs, while the logistical expenses associated with supplies made up another 10% to 15%. Labor costs usually accounted for at least 70%. Blood collection products typically accounted for less than 5% of the total supplies purchased. A smaller, 100-bed hospital might purchase 40 cases of tubes (each case contained 1,000 tubes) and 20 cases of needles (each case contained 1,000 needles) annually, while a large 1,100-bed hospital, such as Massachusetts General Hospital, purchased about 1,700 cases of tubes and 800 cases of needles annually.

Commercial Laboratories. In 1985, 700 commercial labs in the United States performed about 25% of all blood tests. Larger national labs had 15 to 20 lab locations for which the company purchased blood collection products centrally. In these labs, the purchase process for blood collection products was similar to that in large hospitals. Most commercial labs, however, were smaller, single-location companies where the owner-manager often supervised all purchases personally. In both large and small labs, according to Giardino, "the purchasers are cost conscious, because commercial labs compete with each other primarily on price."

Commercial labs analyzed blood samples sent to them by physicians or small health care centers that had collected the blood but lacked either equipment or expertise to perform tests. Many commercial labs also performed blood tests for hospitals for a fee. A significant percentage of a commercial lab's total revenues came from blood collection and testing.

Nonhospital Health Care Centers. In 1985 these accounted for about 5% of blood collection and testing in the United States. But easier-to-use and less expensive technology, as well as changing patterns in health care, indicated that nonhospital centers would account for increased proportions of blood testing in coming years.

In 1985 there were approximately 250,000 physicians in 180,000 offices throughout the United States. A number of physicians—often 50 to 60 per group—were affiliated with forms of group medical care. These physicians were increasingly performing in their offices many medical activities previously subcontracted to commercial labs or hospitals.

Other nonhospital sites—such as surgicenters, emergency centers, and free-standing diagnostic centers—were also increasing in number. They were expected to perform a higher proportion of medical activities during the coming decade, including blood collection and testing.

Market Trends

A *Newsweek* article stated:

> Few industries have gone through such intense trauma in the past two years as the market for health care. New cost containment pressures have forced a wave of cutbacks: hospital use has dropped precipitously, hospitals have shaved their own costs dramatically, and an estimated 100,000 jobs have been lost in

a range of health care fields. Out of such chaos new order seems destined to emerge.[2]

In 1983 a change in how the U.S. government reimbursed hospitals for Medicare patients (40% of all hospital patient days) affected the entire health care industry. Previously, hospitals had been reimbursed for all costs incurred in serving those patients. Most observers agreed this cost-plus system did not reward hospitals for efficiency. Federal legislation in April 1983 provided for a change (over a four-year period) to a payment approach based on diagnosis-related groups (DRGs).

Under the new system, the payment to a hospital was based on national and regional costs for each DRG, not on the hospital's costs. Moreover, the national and regional averages were to be updated, so that if hospitals improved their cost performance, they would be subject to stricter DRG-related payment limits.

By 1985 the impact had been dramatic. In 1984, hospital admissions fell 4%—the largest drop on record, according to the American Hospital Association; the average length of a patient's hospital stay fell 5% to 6.7 days, also the largest drop ever. For the first time, admission of people over the age of 65 fell. Nonhospital treatment—especially in-home treatment—was expected to account for larger proportions of health care. Conversely, estimates[3] indicated that the number of hospital beds would fall to 650,000 in 1990 from one million in 1983. In their place, it was expected that a variety of smaller, short-term health care facilities would proliferate.

Thus, in 1985, many hospital administrators felt that, for the first time, they faced effective, increasing competition and a need to reduce costs. One response was the acceleration of a trend toward the formation of multihospital chains and multihospital buying groups. Both types of organization were intended to increase the purchasing power of hospitals for equipment and supplies. In 1985, about 45% of all U.S. hospitals were affiliated with multihospital chains, and it was predicted that 65% would be so affiliated by 1990. Similarly, in 1985 most hospitals were members of buying groups.

Multihospital chains were usually for-profit hospitals that purchased most supplies and equipment through centralized buying organizations. In these chains, individual hospitals submitted purchase requirements and preferences for specific products, but price and delivery terms were negotiated centrally. Buying groups were looser affiliations of not-for-profit hospitals. Like chains, purchases for buying groups were handled centrally; but individual hospitals were often free to accept or reject the terms negotiated on a specific item by the central buying group. Thus, if a given hospital's administration or lab personnel had a strong preference for a given brand, and the buying group had negotiated a volume discount for a different brand, that hospital might purchase its tubes separately while purchasing other items through the centralized buying group. In addition, many hospitals belonged to several buying groups, purchasing different items through different buying groups depending upon the product, specific prices, and other factors. One BD manager noted:

> The chains and buying groups structure negotiations on the premise that they can deliver so many thousands of beds to the manufacturer with the best price. But the actual strength of these groups varies. In some, all of their hospitals purchase through the centralized procedure. In others, a large percentage of the member hospitals do not adhere to the centralized procedure. The result is that the purchasing leverage differs from one group to the next.
>
> In addition, individual hospitals belong to a number of different buying groups, and often switch from one group to the next. The result is that the various buying-group headquarters organizations in effect compete actively with each other to attract and retain hospital clients. Nonetheless, there is no doubt that chains and buying groups have increased the pricing pressures on both manufacturers and distributors of health care products in recent years.

Competition

Competition in the blood collection market was primarily among BD and two other firms. Terumo, a Japanese company, was a global competitor with a 1984 U.S. market share of about 18% in evacuated blood collection tubes and nearly 50% in blood collection needles. Sherwood Medical Corporation's Monoject Division was predominantly a U.S. competitor with a U.S. market share of about 2% in tubes and 15% in needles.

Over the past seven years, BDVS had maintained about an 80% share of the U.S. evacuated blood collection tube market while increasing its average unit price from about 6 cents to 8 cents. During that time, Terumo had increased its share from 10% to 20% while main-

[2]*Newsweek*, April 15, 1986, p. 79.
[3]Cited in "Hospital Suppliers Strike Back," *The New York Times*, March 31, 1985.

taining its price at about 6.5 cents per unit. In blood collection needles, however, BDVS's share had dropped from 40% to 30% during this period, while Terumo had doubled its share from 25% to 50%. In needles, BDVS and Terumo charged approximately 7.5 cents per unit, while Sherwood charged about 10 cents per unit.

A primary objective for BD in both tubes and needles was to maintain a leading market share. Management believed that Terumo was also committed to increasing its share in all segments and would continue to price aggressively. BD planned to combat such competition through accelerated new product developments and annual improvements in product quality, while using its strong market share to become the lowest-cost producer in all product segments.

An important element in BD's marketing strategy was what one executive termed "quality aggression." Since BD had vertically integrated into the production of components such as glass tubes and rubber stoppers, it could keep a tight hold on quality. In addition, BD could process reagents and chemicals in its own plants to especially demanding specifications and pioneer in new tube sterilization techniques that demanded large capital investments in radiation equipment. As one manager noted, "This raises our costs but also forces our competitors to raise their costs even more, since our higher volume allows us to amortize the capital investments over a larger base."

In the past, major companies, including Corning Glass, Abbott Labs, and Johnson & Johnson, had participated in the blood collection market but had then withdrawn. However, BDVS management believed new technologies could provoke renewed competition from these firms as well as from companies that might enter the market from a base in computer equipment, other forms of medical diagnostic equipment, or biotechnology.

BOUS Marketing and Sales Program

BD's blood collection products were initially sold through the Medical Products group pooled salesforce. In 1980, however, separate sales forces were established for VACUTAINER products and a number of other Medical Products divisions. Battaglia explained:

The basic reason for the reorganization was that the different products were sold to different buyers within hospitals and had different selling requirements. Our division's products require our salespeople to speak with phlebotomists, nurses, physicians, and other technical people as well as the administrators and materials managers at an account. The salespeople must also know a great deal about the people and procedures in the various hospital labs.

In addition, developments in blood collection technology also made our product line wider and required salespeople to learn more about more complex products. Our new product development plans also supported a move toward a separate VACUTAINER sales force.

In 1985 BDVS had 55 sales representatives organized into territories based on the number of hospital beds in a given area. Territories ranged from 10,000 to 20,000 beds. All hospital, commercial lab, and distributor accounts within a territory were the responsibility of that territory rep. Territory reps reported to one of six regional managers, who in turn reported to William Kozy, the national sales director.

Each BDVS sales rep had about 100 accounts and typically made five sales calls daily: four on hospital labs and one on either a distributor or nonhospital lab. A large metropolitan hospital might receive two or three calls monthly, while a small rural hospital might receive one or two calls annually. One rep noted:

Our sales strategy has traditionally been to sell from the bottom up: we try to work with as many of the bench people as possible—that is, the lab technicians who actually use blood collection products, who care about the quality of what they use, and who will complain to the administrators if they do not get the product they want. BD has a reputation for being more responsive than other firms are to end-users.

I think we've maintained our market share because of this philosophy. In recent years, I've seen a number of instances where materials managers wanted to standardize their purchases around a less-expensive blood collection product, but the lab people complained and insisted on our product.

During the past year the division had introduced a new needle and had placed major emphasis on converting accounts from competing needle brands. Several sales promotions in 1985 for VACUTAINER needles gave sales reps cash awards for conversions. Results had been very positive, including the conversion of nearly 66,000 beds from competitive needles and a substantial increase in market share for VACUTAINER needles during a four-month promotion campaign (11/1/84 through 2/28/85).

Distribution

BDVS sold its products through 474 independent distributors who fell into two categories: laboratory products distributors and medical-surgical products distributors. A laboratory products distributor called on hospital and commercial labs and carried a range of items such as glassware, chemicals, spectrometers, lab coats, and thousands of other supply items as well as tubes and needles. According to one BDVS executive, "Lab products distributors feel they must carry blood collection products, which hospitals order regularly, because hospitals often order the more expensive, higher-margin items along with those staple products." According to industry trade journals, price competition for large volumes had reduced distributor gross margins on blood collection products from an average of 25% down to about 12%. Medical-surgical products distributors, on the other hand, called on physicians' offices and other nonhospital sites and carried items such as gowns, wheelchairs, examination tables, and other products in addition to tubes and needles. Their margins on blood collection items rarely dropped below acceptable levels.

Battaglia noted that the distribution policies of BDVS and other BD divisions were developed and executed separately:

> We use many of the same distributors other BD divisions do, but the importance of various distributors to different divisions can vary significantly. For example, most of our sales are through lab products distributors, while other divisions sell more of their products through medical-surgical distributors. Those two types of distributors attend different conventions and speak different languages. In addition, we sell nearly all of our products through distributors, but some other BD divisions have a greater percentage of direct sales.

Nationally, there were over 1,000 distributors of hospital/medical supplies, but the 10 largest accounted for nearly 80% of hospital supply sales made through distributors. At BDVS, its 6 largest distributors accounted for more than 65% of division sales, the 50 largest for 85%, and 67 of the division's 474 dealers for nearly 95% of division sales.

BDVS's largest distributor was American Scientific Products (ASP), a division of American Hospital Supply Corporation (AHS), which in 1984 had total sales of $3.45 billion.[4] ASP was the largest lab products distributor in the United States, with an estimated 40% market share among distributors of products to hospital and commercial laboratories. In 1984, ASP accounted for a similar share of BDVS's sales.

ASP had 21 warehouse locations in the United States. It had installed computer terminals in major hospitals and become an important part of their logistical systems for purchasing supplies. According to ASP, for every dollar a hospital spent on a product, the hospital also spent nearly an additional dollar on acquiring and storing that item. Thus, less costly order entry and delivery could have a significant impact for supply items.

ASP paid higher commissions to its salespeople for selling AHS products. One AHS vice president was quoted as saying: "We manufacture 45% of what we distribute, but our manufactured products represented 70% of our profits last year. Before long, we hope to manufacture 65% of what we distribute."[5]

Terumo and Sherwood products were also distributed by ASP. Between 1979 and 1981, according to estimates by industry sources, over 70% of Terumo's U.S. sales went through ASP. Beginning in 1981, BDVS managers sought to build its relationship with ASP. BDVS managers held frequent meetings with ASP management, and BDVS salespeople were encouraged to devote more time to sales meetings and product training sessions with ASP branches. In addition, as one BDVS manager noted, "We made clear to ASP our commitment to maintaining our market share and product leadership in blood collection systems and hoped they would support that objective." In 1985, BDVS was ASP's number-one supplier of blood collection products. It was estimated that all BDVS products accounted for about 10% of ASP's sales (making BDVS one of ASP's top suppliers) and that BDVS products accounted for about 25% of the BDVS products sold by ASP.

Other major distributors for BDVS were Curtin-Matheson Scientific (CMS), which had 20 warehouse locations and sold primarily to hospital labs, and Fisher Scientific, which had 20 warehouse locations and sold primarily to medical schools, research centers, and industrial labs.

In total, BDVS sold through six national distributors, with the remainder of its distribution network composed of regional chains and small local distributors. In most market areas, four or five different distributors sold BDVS products. One manager commented:

---

[4]In 1985, American Hospital Supply merged with Baxter-Travenol, Inc., a manufacturer of medical equipment. The merged company was known as Baxter-Travenol and had 1985 sales of approximately $5 billion.

[5]"Hospital Suppliers Strike Back," *The New York Times,* March 31, 1985.

Our relatively intensive distribution is a result of several factors. One is a legacy from when we were part of the BD division. Because BD sells syringes to a very fragmented physicians' market, intensive distribution is important there, and we retain many distributors that began selling VACUTAINER products when we were not a separate division. Another factor is that established relationships between a small local distributor and a lab have traditionally been important in the blood collection products area. As a result, you sometimes must sell through a certain local distributor to break into an account.

Also, since the DRG regulations, hospitals are more conscious of inventory carrying costs. As they cut stocking levels and order more frequently, some hospitals look more favorably on a supplier whose products are available from a number of different distributors in the area. If there is ever a problem with getting product from one distributor, the hospital knows there is back-up stock available at another in the area.

By contrast, Terumo sold its products primarily through ASP and CMS, the two largest national distributors. Terumo initially entered the U.S. market with needles in 1970 and tubes in 1972, selling through smaller West Coast distributors. In the mid-1970s, however, Terumo established a joint marketing agreement with Kimball Glass, one of ASP's major suppliers of lab products. Smith explained:

Kimball opened the door for Terumo at ASP, which had been reluctant to take on an unknown line of blood collection products. ASP soon found, however, that Terumo's line provided them with an alternative to VACUTAINER. Terumo developed the relationship by focusing on individual ASP reps in individual branches: they worked closely with those reps to create a champion for their products in the branch.

Changing Buyer Behavior

During the 1980s, the distributor and end-user marketplace was changing significantly. According to a senior executive of one large national distributor of hospital supply products:

In the past, our customer was the pathologist, chief technologist, or lab manager. This person's responsibility was to produce quality diagnostic tests on specimens brought into the lab and to do it as fast as possible. A key was to ensure that an adequate supply of products was on hand at all times. It was also the element that these people were least prepared to deal with. Most lab managers and chief technologists had risen to their positions on the basis of their clinical skills, not their purchasing skills. In addition, they didn't particularly enjoy the purchasing part of their jobs.

Major national distributors flourished in this environment, with the distributor-served portion of the market growing at 10% to 17% annually throughout the 1970s. Also, distributors generally paid little attention to costs, because customers primarily wanted service and were willing to pay for it. After all, the lab was a true profit center then: hospital reimbursement procedures allowed any increased operating expenses to be passed on to customers.

Those days are gone. First, the customer is different. Buying influence has moved out of the lab in most hospitals. Most decisions on products purchased from distributors are now made by professional purchasing people, who require that traditional levels of service be provided along with lower costs. In addition, the buying influence is in many instances moving beyond the hospital's purchasing department to the corporate purchasing department of national multihospital systems. Some distributors probably have over half of their total sales in these national accounts.

Finally, while most distributors currently serve the hospital and commercial lab markets, little attention has been paid by distributors to the fastest growing customer segment, the physicians' market, which includes surgicenters, emergency centers, and diagnostic centers as well as the offices of individual doctors. All trends point toward more volume in these locations and less in the hospital.

In this environment, distributors must lower costs. I believe many distributors will carry only two—or even one—vendors' brands in many product categories in exchange for lower prices from those vendors. Moreover, distributors can reduce inventory, transportation, and some administrative costs through consolidation of their product lines.

BDVS Response

BDVS instituted a Z contract, in which prices and order quantities were negotiated directly with hospitals but still delivered through distributors. Often Z-contract prices with large buying groups were 30% to 40% lower than list prices. Under a Z contract, as with other BDVS contracts, BDVS's distributors received a set commission from the company for stocking, shipping, and billing the hospital.

One BDVS manager explained that "some hospitals negotiate with us and then shop among our distributors for the best price at that level of the chain. They force our distributors to compete away a portion of their commission on Z-contract orders." With Z-contract customers, a BDVS sales rep called on the buyer 30 to 60 days before the contract expiration date to gather information about the customer's product requirements and any competitive inroads at the account. This information was entered on a Critical Information Questionnaire, which suggested a selling price and which the rep submitted to the regional manager. One sales rep estimated he spent 25% of his time on contract negotiations:

> Until recent years, only four or five of my accounts were on Z contracts, but now almost all are. That means more paperwork and legwork. It also means less time spent with the bench people and more time with purchasing people. I've also been spending more time in negotiating seminars, since these contract sessions can be difficult and tense. I've been in the business for nearly 15 years; selling in the health care industry is more complicated, and less fun, than it used to be.

By 1985, most BDVS venous blood collection products and approximately 20% of the division's capillary and microbiology products were sold through Z contracts. Many of BDVS's hospital customers were affiliated with several different buying groups, each of which had separate Z contracts with BDVS. While there were approximately one million hospital beds in the United States, Z contracts encompassed nearly 2.8 million hospital beds by 1985.

Affiliated Purchasing Group

Affiliated Purchasing Group (APG) was founded in 1975. A group of independent, not-for-profit hospitals were affiliated as shareholders with a central organization that provided various services for member hospitals, including purchasing programs. APG's motto was "In Unity There Is Strength," and the group sought to use the power of centralized purchasing while maintaining local autonomy among member hospitals.

APG headquarters personnel negotiated national purchasing agreements with suppliers, but member hospitals were free to make individual purchases separately with manufacturers or distributors of the products. APG purchasing staff monitored national and regional costs, and these data became the basis for their contract negotiations with manufacturers and distributors. The aim, according to one APG manager, was to "pay the lowest price available."

From a group of 20 hospitals in 1975, APG included more than 500 hospitals by 1985, accounting for more than 10% of all U.S. hospital beds and nearly 2 million annual admissions. Many large, prestigious hospitals affiliated with medical schools were APG members. In 1985, APG had national purchasing agreements with about 100 medical equipment suppliers, and the number of such agreements had grown consistently in recent years.

In addition to group purchasing, APG offered other services to member hospitals, especially for hospital administrative personnel. APG maintained a database on department administrators at APG-member hospitals, and this database was made available to APG hospitals seeking new managers. The intent was to offer administrators an opportunity to move among APG hospitals while retaining quality administrators within APG-affiliated hospitals. APG maintained a similar database on doctors. The group also coordinated a program that brought together doctors, nurses, and administrators from different APG-affiliated hospitals to discuss cost-reduction opportunities and develop specific action plans. The program allowed member hospitals to compare their costs by product line, therapy type, and department.

APG had been aggressive and innovative in other areas. It had recently established a private-label program in which it sought to have its suppliers use the APG trademark on products sold through APG purchasing agreements. By mid-1985, this private-label program encompassed a dozen product categories, and APG expected to add 30 to 40 additional products by 1986. According to James Wilson, APG's vice president for materials management and the person who had initiated many of APG's recent programs, APG eventually hoped to private-label "virtually all" products sold through APG purchasing agreements.

In early 1985, Wilson also announced APG's intention of establishing its own distribution network. Throughout 1985, APG negotiated with a number of smaller, regional medical products distributors to provide warehousing, trucking, and related functions for hospitals that purchased under APG agreements. APG then sought to have its suppliers distribute their products to

APG-affiliated distributors who, in return for a larger share of the high-volume APG contracts, distributed products for lower margins than hospital supply distributors had traditionally received.

Wilson announced that the program would eventually involve a national order-entry system linking these distributors with APG-affiliated hospitals. He expected that, if the system could achieve sufficient utilization by suppliers and APG member hospitals, it could lower the hospital's costs by 3% to 12% on most supply items.

By mid-1985, both the private-label and distribution programs were being aggressively promoted by APG materials management. Some manufacturers had agreed to participate in these programs, while others had rejected participation. BDVS's management knew of at least two manufacturers that had not been awarded APG contracts after rejecting participation in these programs. At the same time, distributors not part of the APG distribution network, including the large national distributors of hospital supply products, were reportedly ready to stop supporting (and perhaps sever agreements with) manufacturers that agreed to the program.

Negotiations with APG

In 1982, APG had first sought to standardize its purchase of needles and tubes and had demanded substantial price reductions from BDVS. BDVS had resisted negotiating prices and terms directly with APG headquarters and had continued dealing separately with individual hospitals. Then APG established a national purchasing agreement with Terumo. BDVS's field salespeople were able to retain most sales of BDVS tubes at individual APG-affiliated hospitals, in part by lowering prices when necessary on a hospital-by-hospital basis.

APG subsequently established a group of field personnel charged with promoting the importance of compliance with APG-negotiated contracts at member hospitals. In turn, BDVS field salespeople soon reported that their Z relationships with many accounts in the APG system seemed to be suffering. One salesperson noted:

There was a period in which I couldn't get phone calls returned from people I had done business with for years. This was especially true of certain administrators who had introduced APG programs in their hospitals. The word on the street was that APG personnel were bad-mouthing us with their numbers. I don't think this appreciably affected my actual volume with individual departments in hospitals, but it certainly

made life uncomfortable. In addition, the experience made the whole issue of compliance by member hospitals with national purchasing agreements more visible and important for APG.

In response, BDVS managers sought to mend fences with certain administrators and with APG headquarters personnel. One manager recalled:

We held meetings with these people in different regions and explained over dinner that our actions had been based on a reasonable business decision intended to retain our presence in those accounts and nothing personal had been intended. There is definitely an emotional dimension to business situations like this, and it's important to establish lines of communications with important individuals.

Following this series of meetings, BDVS field salespeople reported a "better atmosphere" at certain hospitals.

In April 1985, Wilson announced his intention of establishing a new national purchasing agreement for blood collection products. He asserted that the supplier awarded the contract would receive 90% of the business in these product lines from APG-affiliated hospitals. Informally, one APG manager also informed BDVS that APG considered the blood collection agreement to be a "showcase program in which a high degree of compliance by member hospitals is important to us: we'll work for that." BDVS management estimated that VACU-TAINER products currently represented more than 80% of the venous blood collection tubes and 40% of the needles purchased by APG hospitals, totaling about $6 million in 1984 purchases from BDVS.

In contrast to 1982, BDVS management in 1985 decided to negotiate directly with APG headquarters. Management felt that the APG system had grown considerably during the past three years, the central purchasing organization had increased its strength with member hospitals, and there was more risk in refusing to negotiate. Kozy recalled:

These meetings with APG in Chicago were tense. At the first meeting, they dramatically announced that 90% of their business was available to the vendor with the right price. We then surveyed our sales force and, based on their contacts with users at APG affiliates, concluded that a substantial portion, but not 90%, of our business with these hospitals was at risk.

At the next meeting, the APG manager pulled out a thick binder with the price of *every* item purchased by *every* member from *every* supplier. At the third meeting, out came another binder with their estimates of prices in our product category to all other hospital-buying groups in the United States. This is a difference from previous negotiations: they are very well prepared this time around.

At a fourth meeting, they announced they had received bids from our competitors and wanted to know if we would meet their prices, which were considerably lower than our list prices and, because of the volume involved, lower than our prices on other Z-contract accounts.

Traditionally, BDVS products were sold through its authorized distributors, such as ASP, to APG-affiliated hospitals. At the start of the new negotiations with APG, Kozy noted:

> We told our distributors we were negotiating a potential contract with APG and that the negotiations had the potential to be bloody: if we lost the contract, we would be very aggressive in seeking to retain business at end-user accounts and wanted their support, even if the contract went to another supplier whose products they also distributed. Since then, our distributors, who do lots of business with APG-member hospitals, have sought ongoing information about developments.

The Guns of August

At the fifth meeting on August 1, Kozy and Smith proposed a Z contract with prices approximately 20% higher than competitors' proposals. The proposal required APG to deliver within 90 days of the initial contract date 95% of their member hospitals' purchases of venous blood collection tubes and 90% of their purchases of blood collection needles. If these targets were not achieved within 90 days, prices on BD products covered by the contract would automatically increase by 5% during the remaining 21 months of the proposed two-year contract agreement.

APG negotiators rejected this proposal and gave BDVS until August 15 to submit a new proposal. They also announced that they wanted all blood collection products covered by a national purchasing agreement to be part of the private-label program and thus carry the APG logo. They also wanted all products covered by the agreement to be supplied through distributors affiliated with APG, and they provided a list of these distributors. The list did not include most of BDVS's major distributors. According to the APG negotiators, moreover, BDVS's competitors had maintained their original pricing proposals and had agreed to both the private-label and distribution demands.

Exhibit 1 Summary of Selected Financial Data (years ending September 30, thousands of dollars, except per-share data)

	1984	1983	1982
– *Operations*			
– Net sales	$1,126,845	$1,119,520	$1,113,921
– Gross profit	498,128	469,077	478,291
– Gross profit margin	44.2%	41.9%	42.9%
– Interest income	23,824	18,211	15,147
– Interest expense	22,757	32,511	32,336
– Income before income taxes[a]	92,908	33,652	106,198
– Income tax provision (credit)	29,505	(2,278)	29,506
– Net income	63,403	35,930	76,692
– *Financial Position*			
– Current assets	$ 565,526	$ 553,281	$ 557,242
– Current liabilities	245,794	190,222	229,523
– Current ratio	2.3	2.9	2.4
– Pretax income as percent of sales	8.2%	3.0%	9.5%
– Net income as a percent of sales	5.6%	3.2%	6.9%
– Return on net operating assets	8.2%	5.8%	10.6%
– Return on equity	10.5%	6.1%	13.3%
– *Additional Data*			
– Capital expenditures	$82,324	$91,031	$130,008
– Research and development expense	57,735	55,149	49,308
– Number of employees	17,700	19,000	21,200
Summary by Business Segment			
– *Health Care*			
– Medical product sales	$668,757	$685,275	$ 685,553
– Laboratory product sales	260,828	264,234	266,425
– Total health care sales	929,585	949,509	951,978
– Segment operating income	108,178	100,069	130,342
– Percentage of income to sales	11.6%	10.5%	13.7%
– *Industrial Safety*			
– Sales	$ 197,260	$ 170,011	$ 161,943
– Segment operating income	22,635	4,616	15,839
– Percentage of income to sales	11.5%	10.5%	13.7%

Source: Company annual reports

[a]1983 income was significantly affected by a one-time nonrecurring charge.

Exhibit 2 Blood Collection Systems Division

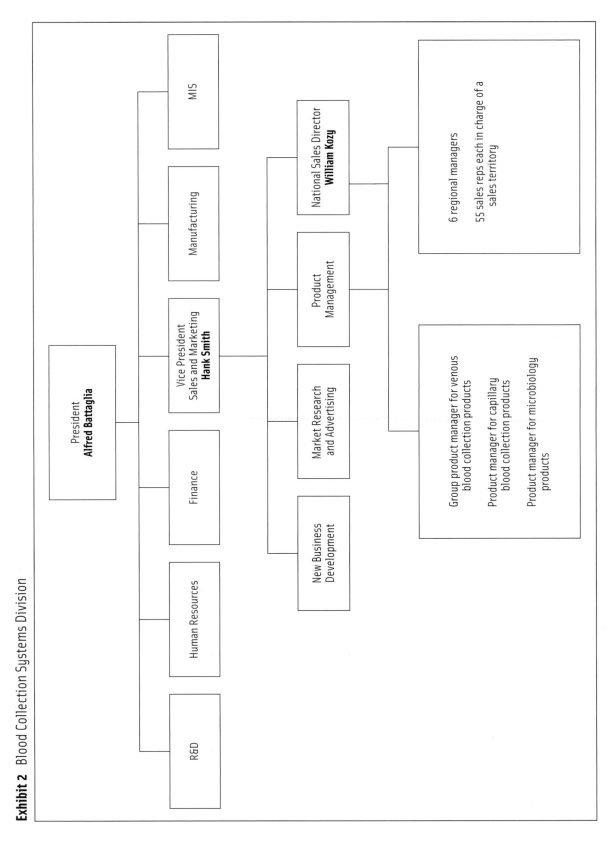

Exhibit 3 Sample Products

STERILE **VACUTAINER** BRAND EVACUATED TUBES

After 40 years, the goals and achievements of the VACUTAINER Brand Tube line are still unique. VACUTAINER Brand products offer unique benefits for the laboratory valuing the most extensive research and development program…an unequalled depth of product line…and an unrivaled commitment to specialized service. It's all here, exclusively with VACUTAINER Tubes.

Here is the most comprehensive line of evacuated blood collection tubes available today All sterile for safety. And featuring the widest array of tube sizes, draw and approved formulations…for chemistry, hematology, coagulation studies, special procedures and blood banking.

Here are the most extensively researched and documented tubes you'll find They have to be. That's the extra commitment we bring as the people who not only manufacture them, but pioneer their development as well. Every VACUTAINER Tube is backed by in-depth clinical and/or research studies. Data is available on request.

Here are the most significant tube introductions and improvements seen anywhere in recent years We improved blood collection tubes for trace element studies, therapeutic drug monitoring and coagulation studies. We've developed new tubes for special procedures like activated clotting time (ACT), LE cell preps and STAT tests. We've expanded our choice of tubes for serum preparation. Starting with our top-of-the-line SST™ (Serum Separator Tube with gel barrier material), we added our new CAT™ (Clot Activator Tube), and then improved our standard red-top tube with a new hemorepellent stopper. For laboratories that prefer their own labeling system, we now offer a new line of VACUTAINER Tubes with SeeThru labeling that provides all the essential information without impeding visibility of the specimen.

Here is the caliber of service support available only through VACUTAINER Systems…the company that stands behind every tube you use. Becton Dickinson VACUTAINER Systems is capable of meeting your special needs because we're not just a manufacturer, but researchers and originators ready to anticipate and respond to changes in your diagnostic procedures. Our sales representatives are accessible specialists in the laboratory field. Our nationwide distribution network is always ready to get you the supplies you need, when you need them. Our technical service team is available for immediate consultation (call toll free 800-631-0174). And, to help you train your staff for the best venous blood collection techniques, our educational materials—publications, films, and sound/slide programs—are at your disposal.

The following pages contain the latest information on our complete line of Sterile VACUTAINER Tubes and VACUTAINER Needles.

Exhibit 3 Sample Products (continued)

VACUTAINER BRAND NEEDLES AND ACCESSORIES

The VACUTAINER System offers a wide selection of blood collection needles and accessories that meet both demanding technical requirements and patient needs during venipuncture. Sterile needles are available for single sample or multiple sample collection, with standard or thin-wall cannulae, in peel-apart packages or plastic cases, and in lengths and gauges you require.

Improved VACUTAINER Multiple Sample Needles feature the most up-to-date improvements for sharpness and ease of use. A new point configuration, special polishing and a new lubrication process allow extra smooth vein entry and reduce "drag." Laser inspection of *every needle* detects even microscopic flaws for virtually flawless quality control. All needle hubs and shields are color-coded for quick identification of gauge. New tamper-evident labels protect against inadvertent use of an already opened needle.

There is a VACUTAINER Holder/Needle Combination designed to fit any VACUTAINER Blood Collection Tube or VACUTAINER Culture Tube. Available with choice of single sample or multiple sample needles, with standard or small diameter holder. VACUTAINER Holder/Needle Combinations are sterile, single-use units that assure protection of the sterile pathway from patient to blood collection tube. Preassembled, they offer the additional advantage of eliminating assembly and clean-up time requirements. Also available are VACUTAINER Reusable Holders in three sizes to meet any need. And sterile, single-use Luer Adapters—unique to the VACUTAINER System—that allow the use of a variety of attachments (needle holders, catheters) under a single venipuncture, sparing the patient unnecessary trauma.

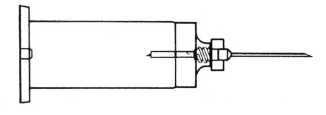

ONSALE, INC.

Jerry Kaplan had an idea. Over the past few years, Onsale had been a pioneer in electronic commerce, offering excess and refurbished goods using an online auction format. Originally the company's focus had been on computer goods, although shoppers could now bid on home and office equipment, sporting goods, and even travel and vacation packages at the Onsale website.

By all accounts, the business had been a success. The company had turned a profit in 1996; its revenues in December 1998 were up to $4 million a week and growing steadily.

Onsale's CEO, however, had even bigger plans for 1999. Although the company had made its mark by providing a market for close-out and refurbished computer merchandise, Kaplan, 45, was now planning to become a player in the highly competitive world of first-run computer merchandise as well. The twist? Unlike other computer resellers whose business models were based on gross margins, Kaplan had created his new business model around the idea of fixed commissions. Kaplan would cut his "best deal" with manufacturers and distributors based on the site's buying power. He would then add a fixed fee of $5–10 to his cost to get his price to consumers. He called this his "at-cost" model:

> I'd like to believe that the future of at least some retailing on the Internet is going to be transformed, much the way that the brokerage business has been transformed in recent years. The economics of online brokerage transformed the economics of the brokerage business. We're trying to do the same thing to the retail business.

In addition, Onsale planned to make "full disclosure" an explicit part of its merchandising efforts: Onsale would "unbundle" the price, so that the buyer understood exactly what the manufacturer or distributor got, how much Onsale took in, and the shipping and handling costs. The price components would carry a Price Waterhouse Coopers' seal of certification. Kaplan commented:

> I think that this is going to create a revolution between the retailer and the customer. In a margin-based model, it's often in the retailer's interest to get prices up. When you move to a commission-style model, a fee-based model, then the retailer's interest is to get the price down. And since the customer is also interested in getting the price down, the customer and the retailer have the same goals. The retailer becomes the customer's advocate back to the distribution channels and sources of supply, in order to achieve the best possible price. I look at it as a way for buyers to collectively bargain with the supply channel.

Of course, the new business plan created a number of challenges for Kaplan and his team. For one thing, in the Internet buying community, the Onsale brand name was practically synonymous with online auctioning. Since Kaplan planned to continue his auctions, he wondered about the fit between the new "at-cost" model and his established brand image. In addition, there was already a profusion of strong competitors in the online world of computer retail, including manufacturers such as Dell selling their own products and intermediaries such as CDW. To date, Onsale had been able to avoid direct competition with these companies because of its focus on excess goods. With the at-cost model, this would no longer be the case. Would Onsale be able to divert a significant amount of online buying traffic away from entrenched online retailers? And finally, the success of the at-cost model depended heavily on close integration with suppliers and distributors. How enthusiastic would these partners be when presented with Onsale's plan?

Professor Youngme Moon prepared this case as the basis for class discussion rather than to illustrate either effective or ineffective handling of an administrative situation.

Company Background

In 1994, Jerry Kaplan had already established a reputation in the computer industry as an entrepreneur and technical innovator. Unlike many entrepreneurs, however, his reputation had largely been built on failure. His previous startup, Go Corporation (a pen-based computing company), had been considered one of Silicon Valley's biggest flops, burning up more than $75 million dollars in venture capital before being sold to AT&T at a fire sale price in early 1994. But the failure hadn't discouraged Kaplan in the least; in fact, he had promptly turned the story of his experience at Go into a best-selling book entitled, "Startup: A Silicon Valley Adventure."[1]

For his next venture, he hooked up with long-time friend Alan Fisher, a successful entrepreneur who had more than 16 years of software development expertise and had, among other things, helped develop online trading software for Charles Schwab & Co. Together, they began looking for a business that would operate on the Internet.

They weren't alone. In 1994, an increasing number of businesses—including catalog and mail order firms such as L. L. Bean and Lands' End—were establishing a presence on the web. However, the merchandise available online was usually identical to that available through the merchants' own catalogs and retail stores. Moreover, there was often no price advantage to online merchandise because retailers didn't wish to undercut their existing channels. Thus, in Kaplan and Fisher's minds, existing Internet merchants failed to exploit some of the benefits of the medium, including the ability to dynamically change product mix, pricing, and visual presentation.

The two decided to come up with a business plan that would allow them to leverage two key characteristics of the Internet: (1) its ability to broadcast real-time, dynamic information very cheaply, and (2) its ability to allow people to create real-time communities, or interactive forums with multi-directional channels of communication. The product of their brainstorming was Onsale, an Internet auction house that created an electronic market for consumer goods, with prices set by supply and demand. Kaplan again:

> We realized that we could create a new form of retailing that exploited the unique characteristics of the Net. The big picture is that this was really a way in which there could be a negotiation between buyer and seller in the large, so that a group of people could be setting prices on goods and getting immediate feedback on demand.

From the beginning, the plan was to focus on "excess" merchandise, i.e., close-out, refurbished or "end-of-life"

computer and consumer electronic goods. Close-out merchandise usually consisted of slightly older models that had been withdrawn from the primary channels of distribution because of the introduction of newer models. Refurbished products were those that typically required a nominal amount of service, such as minor repairs, cleaning and repackaging, before being resold.

The market for excess goods was difficult to measure. However, the PC and consumer electronics markets had significant quantities of such merchandise due to short product life cycles and high return rates through the consumer retailing channel. Kaplan knew that the total PC market in the United States was estimated to be greater than $65 billion dollars a year; he thus estimated that the portion of this market that ended up as refurbished and close-out goods exceeded $10 billion.

Moreover, the disposal of this excess merchandise often created a burden for the manufacturers, who ended up unloading the goods through a fragmented distribution system consisting of auction houses, swap meets, catalogs, company "outlets," specialized retailers, and large superstores and mass merchants. None of these outlets were particularly committed to the resale of these goods and generally sold them as a supplementary product line or a "loss leader."

Onsale, on the other hand, was offering vendors a way to bring excess goods to market very quickly, which obviated some of the inventory price erosion typical in other channels. Its frequently updated electronic format could accommodate unpredictable, odd lot quantities on short notice. And its exclusive focus on excess goods would allow vendors to avoid the channel conflicts inherent in other channels where similar or identical goods sold at different prices.

From a buyer perspective, the founders of Onsale believed that excess goods were particularly well-suited for the online auction format because there was no widely accepted fair market value for such goods. In contrast to the market for new merchandise where vendors traditionally set a fixed price, Kaplan believed that both the vendors and customers for excess goods would accept variability in pricing.

After lining up manufacturers to provide merchandise, Onsale conducted its first auction in May of 1995.

The Auction Process

In the auction process, the company posted online descriptions and images of merchandise for sale on its website on a continuing basis. By 1996, it was operating

---

[1]Kaplan, Jerry (1996), "Startup: A Silicon Valley Adventure," Penguin USA.

three auctions per week in two-day auction cycles. By 1998, it was operating seven auctions a week in one-day cycles. Several hundred items would be available at any given time, in quantities ranging from one to several hundred. Prices ranged widely, from $25 to several thousand dollars, depending on the item and the bidding dynamics.

Customers could bid 24 hours a day, 7 days a week. To become a registered user of the site, customers completed a simple electronic registration form (which included an email address and other demographic information) on Onsale's website. More than half of all registered users also agreed to be put on Onsale's direct mailing list. To bid, customers had to take the additional step of establishing an online "ID," as well as submitting credit card information. After establishing their IDs, customers could bid and buy at will. Once the bid was received, Onsale's webpages were instantly updated to display the current high bidders' initials, city and state, and an optional comment from the bidder that served to personalize the bidding. When customers were outbid, they would receive an email message alerting them and giving them an opportunity to increase their bid by return email or by returning to the company's website. Customers could also monitor their bid status at the website. At the designated closing time, the "winning" bidders were determined and email messages were sent to them confirming their purchases. An order was created, the winners' credit cards were charged, and the merchandise was shipped either by Onsale or the original vendor.

Onsale's auctions were specifically designed to be fun and exciting. The auction format created a sense of scarcity and time limits among customers; Onsale's customers did not simply purchase merchandise—they "won" it. This competition and gamesmanship were evident in the spirited bidding that would often take place on the site. On each merchandise page, bidders were allowed to place brief comments that accompanied the display of their bids. Bidders would use these comments to communicate with other bidders. Sometimes they were explicit attempts to "psyche out" the competition; other times they were attempts to form cooperative alliances with other bidders. And because the comments were generally good-natured and humorous, they contributed to the overall sense of "community" on the company's website.

Exhibit 1, taken from an Onsale promotional piece, provides a detailed description of a sample auction. As shown on the "Product Page" of this exhibit, five NEC computers will be sold in a "Yankee auction." Customer CK of Jackson Heights, NY places a bid on an NEC computer, bumping customer MP of Shreveport, LA off of the "Current High Bidders" list. MP's bid is now replaced with CK's bid and comment: "My 486 is in pieces in my room!" Meanwhile, MP automatically receives a "You've been outbid!" email. MP responds by increasing his bid, bumping CK off the "Current High Bidders" list. When CK receives the "You've been outbid" email, he immediately logs back on, increases his bid, adding the comment "Mine!" Finally, after several rounds of bidding, the auction is closed. The winner? CK!

From Kaplan's perspective, this social dynamic was key:

> The competitive environment, the fact that it is a bit of a game, that it's skill—we like to call it "the lure of the bargain and the thrill of the hunt"—is what motivates our customers.[2]

In addition, Onsale went to great lengths to keep the "game" interesting for bidders, by constantly rotating the merchandise mix and by providing a variety of auction formats for participants to try their hand at. In the "Yankee auction" format (used in the example in Exhibit 1), a number of identical items were offered for sale at the same time. When the auction closed, the highest bidders would win the available inventory at their bid prices. Thus, each winning bidder might end up paying a price that was different from the prices paid by other winning bidders. Other auction formats included the "Dutch auction," in which Onsale offered a number of identical items for sale at the same time and the highest bidders would win the available inventory at the lowest successful bidder's price; the "Standard auction," in which a single item of merchandise would simply be sold to the highest bidder; the "Buy or Bid" auction, in which Onsale permitted customers to bid on an item either at the posted asking price, or below the asking price in the hope of receiving the item at a lower price; and the "Straight Sale," in which Onsale would post an item at a listed price and customers' orders were immediately accepted at that price. This variety allowed customers to develop a number of strategies for the different auctions that made the bidding process interesting and challenging. As Kaplan put it:

> We wanted to bring people the bargains that they typically find at Costco, married to the entertainment value of something like QVC, a little bit of skill in the style of the stock market, and an element of luck in the spirit of

---

[2]"CEO Interview: Jerry Kaplan, Onsale," *Wall Street Journal*, July 1, 1998.

Las Vegas.[3] So it's really a form of entertainment retailing and specialty retailing, where we are selling goods through this very unique online mechanism.

The entire auction process, from the posting of the items for auction through the notification of the winners, was run by internally developed proprietary software. Onsale's salesfront, display inventory, salespeople, order-takers, and catalog-printing operation are shown in Exhibit 2. The result of all of this technology was a retail system that was fully automated, almost infinitely scaleable, and provided an exciting sales format for shoppers.

The Installed Customer Base

By the end of 1998, Onsale's registered customer base numbered close to a million. Most tended to be somewhat regular customers, bidding an average of 20 times a year. Exhibit 3 provides a profile of Onsale's customer base.

The average bidder spent approximately 42 minutes per visit, either bidding or simply watching the auction process. In addition, although the average buyer was spending about $800 a year at the Onsale website, about 10% of Onsale's buyers were spending as much as $4,400 a year at Onsale. One buyer commented:

> I bought one computer, then another, then a monitor, then a scanner, and then my wife cut off my credit card. I love to outbid people. It's entertaining and I love a good bargain.[4]

Based on surveys conducted by the company, 66% of visitors tended to come to Onsale with a specific purchase in mind. Most purchases (over 80%) were made for either personal use or gifts; the rest tended to be made by small businesses.[5]

In addition, the Onsale website was steadily growing in popularity. By the end of 1998, it was generating over 150,000 unique visitors a day, and over half of these were first-time visitors. About 10% of Onsale's traffic was "trackable," i.e., could be electronically traced back to a paid referral site.[6] The remaining 90% of their traffic was not trackable; rather, it came from the user simply typing "www.onsale.com" into their browser. See Exhibit 4 for traffic and customer performance data.

Onsale also actively marketed to its existing customer base using email. By the end of 1998, Onsale was sending more than half a million email messages a week, announcing new items available at auction. The response or "clickthrough" rate[7] from these messages was high by Internet standards, averaging about 4%–6%. Onsale coupled these generic emails with very specific, highly targeted emails, in which buyers would be sent customized messages based on their prior bids, purchases, and stated preferences. The response rate from these targeted messages was about 30%.

Finally, Onsale generated revenue from paid advertisers. It was one of the few Internet commerce sites that was "sticky"[8] by design, since bidders had to browse the site thoroughly to look for new auctions involving items of interest, to check bid status, or to re-bid. The company began accepting ads on its own site in August of 1997 and generated $75,000 in revenue the first quarter. To Kaplan, this revenue stream was like "money from heaven."

The Product Mix

About a year after the launch, the site had two "stores," a "Computer Products Supersite" consisting primarily of refurbished and close-out computers, peripherals, printers, networking equipment, and software, and a "Consumer Electronics Supersite." Brand names included AST, AT&T, Aiwa, Apple, Canon, Compaq, Dell, Hewlett-Packard, Intel, JVC, Kenwood, NEC, Packard Bell, Sanyo, Seagate, Toshiba, and Uniden.

In October 1997, the company added a "Sports and Fitness Supersite," which included products ranging from sports memorabilia and sporting goods, to an

---

[3]QVC is the nation's most profitable televised shopping service, marketing a wide variety of brand name products in such categories as home furnishings, fashion and beauty, electronics and fine jewelry. Themed shopping programs are telecast live, 24 hours a day, seven days a week, to over 64 million households in the U.S. Costco is the largest wholesale club operator in the U.S., operating huge warehouse stores that offer products ranging from alcoholic beverages to pharmaceuticals at sharply discounted prices. It carries a tenth of the inventory offered by regular discount retailers, but it competes by stocking the fastest-selling, highest-volume products.

[4]"Going . . . Going . . . Downloaded: How Onsale, the Leading Web Auctioneer, Outsmarts Rivals," *Business Week,* September 29, 1997.

[5]Small businesses were defined as those with annual sales less than $20 million a year and fewer than 100 employees. According to a CRN/Gallup poll, these companies tended to spend between $3000 and $6000 a month on IT-related purchases.

[6]Onsale was spending about $1.2 million a quarter on advertising at various online sites. By 1998 they had entered into agreements and partnerships with various Internet companies including Yahoo, Excite, America Online, and Netscape.

[7]This rate refers to the percentage of times these messages were successful in getting recipients to visit the Onsale website.

[8]"Stickiness" refers to the tendency for customers accessing a site to remain at that site (i.e., "stick" with it) for an extended period of time.

ongoing supply of tee times at more than 200 golf facilities. A year later, Onsale launched a "Vacation and Travel Supersite," at which customers could bid for resort condominium vacations. Despite this expanded product mix, about 80% of their revenues still derived from the sale of computer-related equipment, and computer auctions were attracting the bulk of first-time buyers.

Onsale also continued to tinker with new types of auction formats. For example, in April of 1998 it launched QuickBuy, a new sales format that offered customers a quick and convenient way to buy goods at a fixed price. Company surveys had found that after customers purchased a new computer or printer, they often wanted to be able to purchase additional memory or printer cartridges without having to bargain. QuickBuy was designed to offer customers this opportunity; it thus featured consumer electronic accessories and consumables.

Interestingly, Onsale had tried this format (the "Straight Sale") many months before with very little success. This time, however, QuickBuy was extremely successful, particularly among new buyers. As a result, the company expanded the range of goods available via QuickBuy, eventually offering higher priced goods from every product category it carried. Soon, Onsale found that the average order value was three times as high for QuickBuy as it was on the auction site. This was partly due to the higher ticket prices of these items, but it also indicated to Barry Peters, Director of Customer Acquisition, that:

> First-time buyers are willing to step up for higher ticket goods, higher priced goods, when it's in a straight sale format. Whereas in an auction, they're not really comfortable going to that thousand dollar desktop. If it's QuickBuy, they know they're going to have it on the spot, and they're more comfortable.

By the end of 1998, more than 10% of Onsale's revenue was coming from QuickBuy sales; roughly half of this was coming from new buyers.

In June 1998, Onsale introduced "Express Auctions," one-hour auctions with bids starting at one dollar. Products offered under this format included computer products (e.g., PCs and modems), consumer electronics (e.g., CD players), and sports and fitness equipment. The idea was to provide bidders with more "instant gratification," particularly those bidders who were pressed for time and didn't want to wait 24 hours to learn whether they had won a product. These were also an instant success with new visitors to the site.

Vendor Relationships

The company had no long-term contracts with vendors. The company was originally organized as a sales agent for manufacturers, generating orders for manufacturers which were fulfilled directly by those manufacturers. But after encountering frequent delays and other problems with vendors, Onsale began buying some merchandise for resale. By purchasing the merchandise, Onsale assumed the full inventory and price risk involved in selling the merchandise.

For some products, the company still acted as a sales agent for vendors. At the conclusion of an auction Onsale would forward the order information to the vendor, which would then charge the customer's credit card. Onsale would not take title to the merchandise; it would simply receive a commission based on a percentage of the price. This category consisted almost exclusively of products from the "Vacation and Travel" auctions, such as condominium rentals where there was no shipping of a product to a customer.

In 1996, the company turned a profit (see Exhibit 5). (The company subsequently began operating at a loss in order to invest in its marketing and infrastructure.) And by 1998, Onsale's sales revenues were rivaling those of major Internet companies such as Yahoo!, although they still couldn't compare with powerhouse e-tailers such as Amazon or Dell. (Exhibit 6 provides a comparison to some of these companies.) Onsale's sales revenues were also beating the combined sales revenue from three of Onsale's biggest competitors in the online auction business, Surplus Auction, WebAuction, and Ubid. Kaplan no longer felt threatened by these competitors because, as he put it:

> There just isn't enough supply to go around and the supply tends to go to the biggest player. So while it looks like there is competition . . . and there are certainly hundreds of auctions sites . . . if you look at what they're selling and the prices they're getting, the fact is that I don't think they're making a significant dent in the business we're currently doing.

In fact, in Kaplan's view, the biggest obstacle to growth as the company geared up for 1999 was not the competition; rather, it was getting adequate supply. Several factors contributed to the company's supply constraints. First, given the nature of their business, Onsale's supply of excess goods tended to be "lumpy," i.e., heavy with respect to particular models but practically nonexistent with respect to other models. Second, supply was often unpredictable since it was created by vendors' miscalculations regarding demand. And finally, Onsale had discovered that many manufacturers had developed entrenched channels for distributing excess goods, usually handled by a low-ranking manager in the company who was deeply vested in existing relationships. Thus, even when Onsale was able to convince manufacturers of the value it could offer, the liquidation of end-of-life goods was simply not a big enough priority to warrant their "rocking the boat." According to Merle McIntosh, VP of Merchandise Acquisition:

> In the computer business in particular, all the senior level executives are concerned with their new products. It's a matter of priority. It's not that they don't see the value. They tend to see the wisdom in what we're telling them, but it's a matter of priority.

The At-Cost Model

Faced with this situation, Kaplan was considering a new direction, i.e., the addition of first-run computer merchandise to its website. Onsale had no plans to jettison the existing business; rather, the plan was to run two separate businesses on a single website. Customers who were interested in purchasing excess goods could either bid for or "QuickBuy" those goods in the traditional auction section. Customers who were interested in first-run merchandise could purchase those goods in the "at-cost" section of the website.

Under the at-cost model, the customer would be offered the merchandise at a price equal to Onsale's cost of goods from the distributor or manufacturer, plus a fixed commission of $5–$10, regardless of the cost of the merchandise. Moreover, Onsale was planning on "unbundling" and certifying (using the Price Waterhouse Coopers' certification) the price, such that the customer could verify each element of Onsale's purchase order. Customers would be billed separately for shipping and handling fees.

Three issues sparked debate within the company:

1. To date, Onsale had been able to avoid direct competition with the biggest players in the online world of computer retail because of its exclusive focus on excess goods. With the at-cost model, this would no longer be the case. How would Onsale fare against this stiffer competition? (See Exhibit 7 for a brief description of the online computer retail industry.) Would Onsale be able to divert a significant amount of online buying traffic away from these bigger retailers? Were online customers likely to switch from a company they knew and trusted, just because Onsale was offering a slightly lower price?

2. Onsale's brand image had been built around the concept of the online auction; indeed, it had leveraged the psycho-social dynamics associated with the auction format to build a loyal customer base. Because a large part of their past growth had been due to word-of-mouth among bargain-hunting "wire-heads," Onsale had been able to grow its business without substantial marketing expenditures. In order to compete against well-established online retailers, Onsale would probably have to step up its marketing efforts. Manufacturers typically put between 3–10% of sales in marketing development funds (MDFs) and cooperative advertising funds[9] for a retailer's use in marketing and promoting their products; how should Onsale spend these dollars? Complicating matters was the fact that many current online retailers were selling various models at a loss (loss leaders). Thus, Onsale couldn't claim to have the lowest prices all the time, although it believed that its prices would be the lowest about 80% of the time.

3. The success of the at-cost model depended heavily on close integration with suppliers. It was unclear how manufacturers would respond to Onsale's plan to offer first-run goods. Onsale had not been a priority player for them in this area in the past. What should Onsale's approach be? In addition, some products would have to be sourced by Onsale from the three major distributors that dominated the computer industry: Ingram, Tech Data, and Merisel. Onsale had never dealt with distributors before, and getting at least one of these brokers on-board seemed key to some Onsale executives.

As he considered these matters, a more long-term question in Kaplan's mind had to do with diversification. The immediate plan was to offer wholesale prices for computer equipment; however, there was no reason that the at-cost model couldn't eventually be extended to

---

[9]These were monies a manufacturer set aside to support a reseller's marketing efforts for that manufacturer's products. MDFs and co-op advertising funds were often used to help defray the cost of mailing catalogs and placing space ads.

other types of products. The company was already offering everything from office supplies to golfing vacations on their auction site. Did this type of diversification make sense?

These were some of the questions in Kaplan's mind as 1998 drew to a close. Nonetheless, he was confident that, given the proper execution, the at-cost model would signal a new era in Internet retail, led by Onsale:

> We're obviously moving into an entirely different competitive landscape. But I think we're in the unique position to make this successful because we have a different proposition, one that has only become possible because of the efficiencies of the Internet. And the new reality is that this is not going to be a margin-based business, it's going to be a fee-based business. You could look at us as simply an order generation machine. But there's a lot more to it than that. What we're doing is we're reducing the friction in the channels; we're improving the flow of information back and forth, which makes it possible for us to provide a consistent and efficient shopping experience for customers.

Exhibit 1 Onsale's Bidding Process

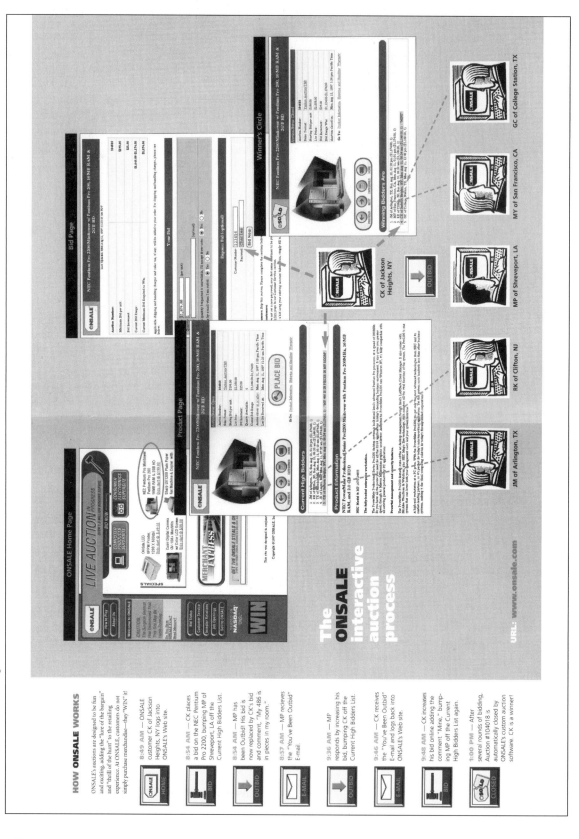

Exhibit 2 Onsale's Sales Staff, Retail Showroom, Display Inventory, Catalog, Mail Center, and Order Takers

Exhibit 3 Demographic Profile of Onsale Customers[10]

Gender of Customers	Male	Female			
	80.3%	19.7%			
Age of Customers	18–24	25–34	35–44	45–54	55+
	16.1%	32.4%	25.5%	15.1%	10.9%
Occupation of Customers	Professional/ Managerial	IS/IT	Self- Employed	Other	
	58.2%	13.8%	12%	16%	
Primary Reason for Purchase	Personal Use/Gifts	Business Use	Resale		
	81%	15%	4%		

[10]Source: Internal company survey, based on a random sample of several hundred visitors/buyers at the site in September 1998.

Exhibit 4 Onsale Traffic and Customer Performance Analysis, 1998

	Q2	Q3	Q4 (Est.)
Unique Daily Visitors	97,000	114,000	139,000
Daily Page Views	1,062,000	1,100,000	1,220,000
Registered Customers	667,000	822,000	1,000,000
Orders Placed	331,000	350,000	355,000
Average Order Size	$186	$193	$190

Exhibit 5 Financial Performance of Onsale ($ in millions)

	1996	1997	1998–Q1	1998–Q2	1998–Q3
– *Gross merchandise sales*[11]	30.7	115.9	50.3	58.6	63.3
– Merchandise revenue	12.6	86.0	39.3	50.1	57.2
– Commission revenue	1.7	2.9	0.7	0.5	0.6
– Advertising revenue		0.1	0.2	0.2	0.3
– *Net revenue*	14.3	89.0	40.2	50.8	58.1
– *Cost of revenue*	11.5	77.7	35.9	46.1	51.7
– *Gross profit*	2.7	11.3	4.3	4.7	6.4
– *Operating expenses*					
– Sales and marketing	0.9	6.3	4.0	4.8	6.5
– General and administrative	0.8	5.5	3.3	3.4	2.1
– Engineering	0.7	2.9	1.1	1.3	1.3
– Total operating expenses	2.4	14.6	8.4	9.4	9.9
– *Operating income*	0.4	(3.4)	(4.1)	(4.9)	(3.5)
– *Net income*	0.4	(2.5)	(3.4)	(4.0)	(3.0)

[11]Gross merchandise sales represent what Onsale's total revenue would have been if all sales had been made as principal sales.

Exhibit 6 Onsale versus Other Public E-Tailers

	Onsale	Amazon	EBay	Dell	Yahoo
Business	Direct auction	Books, etc.	P-to-P auction	Computer products	Portal
Installed Base (Reg. Users in millions)	.95	4.5	1.2	10	25
1998–Q3 Sales	57.8	153.7	12.9	4331.0	53.6
No. of Employees	190	1000	80	16,000	400

Source: Company records. Dell's Q3 sales include non-Internet sales.

Exhibit 7 The Online Computer Retail Industry

In 1998, there were two primary channels of computer product distribution on the Internet: direct selling by manufacturers, and direct marketing by resellers (see Table 7A). (Most of these companies also engaged in direct selling/marketing through catalogs and telemarketing.) Customer loyalty in these channels tended to be high; for most companies, between 50–90% of their sales came from repeat customers.

Table 7A Two Channels of Internet Distribution

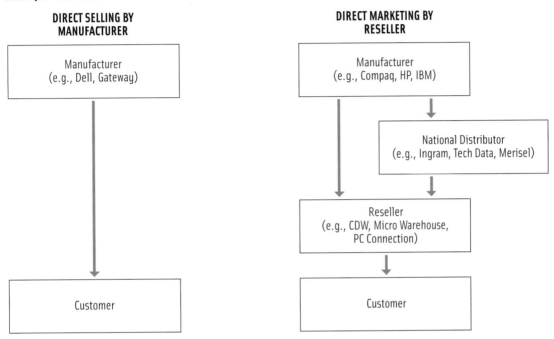

The leading direct seller of computers was Dell, which held roughly 9% market share of the entire PC market. Dell's built-to-order boxes resulted in lower inventories, which translated into lower costs and higher margins. Dell's website, which featured more than 40 country-specific pages, claimed up to $10 million in computer sales daily, and was expected to process half of Dell's transactions by the year 2000. Roughly 90% of its products were sold to large businesses, institutions, educational and government entities. By 1998, Dell had also developed customized "Premier Pages" on its website for over 500 of its corporate customers. Gateway was the #2 direct seller, averaging up to $4 million in computer sales from its website. A recent push into the large corporate market had been unsuccessful for this company; since then, it had refocused efforts on small-medium businesses (18% of sales) and high-end consumer customers (35% of sales). Table 7B provides a comparison of Dell and Gateway.

Table 7B A Comparison of Dell and Gateway*

	Quarterly Sales Revenues	Internet Sales as % of Total Sales	Annual Sales Growth	Gross Margins	Number of Employees
Dell	$4.8 billion	20%	51%	22.5%	16,000
Gateway	$1.8 billion	15%	21%	20.8%	13,300

*Based on company reports, Q3, 1998. Gross margins are for all sales, including non-Internet sales.

Exhibit 7 The Online Computer Retail Industry (continued)

The leading direct marketers included CDW Computer Centers, Micro Warehouse, and PC Connection. According to industry data, the direct marketing channel was the fastest-growing segment of the U.S. PC market; sales through this distribution channel were expected to increase from $16.1 billion in 1996 to $36 billion by 2000. For the larger companies, the most frequently consumed products in each product category were typically purchased directly from manufacturers such as Compaq and IBM,[12] and tended to turn over rapidly. Slower-moving items were typically sourced on an as-needed basis (usually same day) from wholesale distributors. The mix between manufacturer direct and wholesale distribution sourcing was (roughly) split evenly between the two. The larger companies in this channel had customer databases of about 2 million. Table 7C provides a comparison of CDW, Micro Warehouse, and PC Connection.

Table 7C A Comparison of CDW, Micro Warehouse, and PC Connection*

	Quarterly Sales Revenues	Internet Sales as % of Total Sales	Annual Sales Growth	Gross Margins	Number of Employees
CDW	$462.7 million	6%	42.9%	12.7%	1000
Micro Warehouse	$551.8 million	9%	5.7%	16.3%	4100
PC Connection	$169.1 million	15%	21.5%	13.0%	900

*Based on company reports, Q3, 1998. Gross margins are for all sales, including non-Internet sales.

[12]Many of the top manufacturers, such as Compaq, IBM, and HP, were moving toward adopting some form of direct selling in order to stay competitive.

COCA-COLA'S NEW VENDING MACHINE (A): PRICING TO CAPTURE VALUE, OR NOT?

On December 17, 1999, *The Wall Street Journal* ran a front page story headlined "*Tone Deaf:* Ivester Has All Skills of a CEO but One: Ear for Political Nuance." The article detailed how Coca-Cola Chairman and Chief Executive Officer M. Douglas Ivester's handling of one flap after another cost him the Coke Board's confidence, eventually leading him to abruptly announce that he would step down from his position in April 2000.

One of the many events highlighted concerned Ivester's comments about Coke's new vending machine technology. The article reported:

A few months later came another public relations gaffe. Asked by a Brazilian newsmagazine about Coke's testing of vending machines that could change prices according to the weather, Mr. Ivester gave a theoretical response that came across as both a defense of the technology and a confirmation that it would hit the streets. "Coca-Cola is a product whose utility varies from moment to moment," he said. "In a final summer championship, when people meet in a stadium to have fun, the utility of a cold Coca-Cola is very high. So it is fair that it should be more expensive. The machine will simply make this process automatic."

A Coke spokesman says the remarks were taken out of context. Though the company had tested the technology in a lab, it never had an intention of introducing it, the spokesman says, and [Coke] bottlers confirm this. Nevertheless, the CEO's answer created a flap, seeming to cast the company as one that wasn't customer-friendly.

The article also pointed out that:

To Mr. Ivester, the accountant, the concept [of changing prices based on the ambient temperature] was just the law of supply and demand in action. To the board, the ensuing flap was Murphy's Law at work.

For a consumer-product company that, in the words of a person close to the board, "is a giant image machine," the pummeling of Coke's image was increasingly intolerable.

Earlier, on October 28, 1999, *The New York Times* (*NYT*) had reported that Coke was testing vending machines that could raise prices in hot weather (see Exhibit 1). The *NYT* story precipitated an immediate response from the Coca-Cola Company (see Exhibit 2 for the company press release posted on the firm's website on the same day), triggered a lampoon in *The Philadelphia Inquirer* on October 31, 1999 (see Exhibit 3), and generated national and international controversy (see Exhibit 4).

Professors Charles King III and Das Narayandas prepared this case using publicly available sources as the basis for class discussion rather than to illustrate either effective or ineffective handling of an administrative situation.

Exhibit 1 Text of *The New York Times* Article, October 28, 1999

Coke Tests Vending Unit That Can Hike Prices in Hot Weather

by Constance L. Hays

[T]aking full advantage of the law of supply and demand, Coca-Cola Co. has quietly begun testing a vending machine that can automatically raise prices for its drinks in hot weather.

"This technology is something the Coca-Cola Co. has been looking at for more than a year," said Rob Baskin, a company spokesman, adding that it had not yet been placed in any consumer market.

The potential was heralded, though, by the company's chairman and chief executive in an interview earlier this month with a Brazilian newsmagazine. Chairman M. Douglas Ivester described how desire for a cold drink can increase during a sports championship final held in the summer heat. "So, it is fair that it should be more expensive," Ivester was quoted as saying in the magazine, *Veja*. "The machine will simply make this process automatic."

The process appears to be done simply through a temperature sensor and a computer chip, not any breakthrough technology, though Coca-Cola refused to provide any details Wednesday.

While the concept might seem unfair to a thirsty person, it essentially extends to another industry what has become the practice for airlines and other companies that sell products and services to consumers. The falling price of computer chips and the increasing ease of connecting to the Internet has made it practical for companies to pair daily and hourly fluctuations in demand with fluctuations in price—even if the product is a can of soda that sells for just 75 cents.

The potential for other types of innovations is great. Other modifications under discussion at Coca-Cola, Baskin said, include adjusting prices based on demand at a specific machine. "What could you do to boost sales at off-hours?" he asked. "You might be able to lower the price. It might be discounted at a vending machine in a building during the evening or when there's less traffic."

Vending machines have become an increasingly important source of profits for Coca-Cola and its archrival, Pepsico. Over the last three years, the soft-drink giants have watched their earnings erode as they waged a price war in supermarkets. Vending machines have remained largely untouched by the discounting. Now, Coca-Cola aims to tweak what has been a golden goose to extract even more profits.

"There are a number of initiatives under way in Japan, the United States and in other parts of the world where the technology in vending is rapidly improving, not only from a temperature-scanning capability but also to understand when a machine is out of stock," said Andrew Conway, a beverage analyst for Morgan Stanley. "The increase in the rate of technology breakthrough in vending is pretty dramatic."

Bill Hurley, a spokesman for the National Automatic Merchandising Association in Washington, added: "You are only limited by your creativity, since electronic components are becoming more and more versatile."

Machines are already in place that can accept credit cards and debit cards for payment. In Australia and in North Carolina, Coke bottlers use machines to relay, via wireless signal or telephone, information about which drinks are selling and at what rates in a particular location. The technology is known as intelligent vending, Baskin said, and the information gathered and relayed by Internet helps salespeople to figure out which drinks will sell best in which locations.

"It all feeds into their strategy of micro-marketing and understanding the local consumer," Conway said. "If you can understand brand preferences by geography, that has implications for other places with similar geography."

Coca-Cola and its bottlers have invested heavily in vending machines, refrigerated display cases, coolers and other equipment to sell their drinks cold. Over the last five years, Coca-Cola Enterprises, Coke's biggest bottler, has spent more than $1.8 billion on such equipment. In support, Coca-Cola has spent millions more on employees who monitor and service the equipment. In 1998 alone, it spent $324 million on such support to its biggest bottler.

And last week, Coke's chief marketing officer unveiled the company's plan to pump more sales of its flagship soft drink, Coca-Cola Classic. The program includes a pronounced emphasis on Coke served cold.

Sales of soft drinks from vending machines have risen steadily over the last few years, though most sales still take place in supermarkets. Last year, about 11.9 percent of soft-drink sales worldwide came from vending machines, said John Sicher, the editor of *Beverage Digest,* an industry newsletter. In the United States, about 1.2 billion cases of soft drinks were sold through vending machines.

In Japan, some vending machines already adjust their prices based on the temperature outside, using wireless modems, said Gad Elmoznino, director of the Trisignal division of Eicon Technology, a Montreal-based modem maker. "They are going to be using more and more communications in these machines to do interactive price setting," he said.

Industry reactions to the heat-sensitive Coke machine ranged from enthusiastic to sanctimonious. "It's another reason to move to Sweden," one beverage industry executive sniffed. "What's next? A machine that X-rays people's pockets to find out how much change they have and raises the price accordingly?"

Bill Pecoriello, a stock analyst with Sanford C. Bernstein, applauded the move to increase profits in the vending-machine business. "This is already the most profitable channel for the beverage companies, so any effort to get higher profits when demand is higher obviously can enhance the profitability of the system further," he said.

He pointed to a possible downside as well. "You don't want to have a price war in this channel, where you have discounting over a holiday weekend, for example," he said. "Once the capability is out there to vary the pricing, you can take the price down."

A Pepsi spokesman said no similar innovation was being tested at the No. 2 soft-drink company. "We believe that machines that raise prices in hot weather exploit consumers who live in warm climates," declared the spokesman, Jeff Brown. "At Pepsi, we are focused on innovations that make it easier for consumers to buy a soft drink, not harder."

STATEMENT ON VENDING MACHINE TECHNOLOGY

ATLANTA, October 28, 1999—Contrary to some erroneous press reports, The Coca-Cola Company is not introducing vending machines that raise the price of soft drinks in hot weather.

We are exploring innovative technology and communication systems that can actually improve product availability, promotional activity, and even offer consumers an interactive experience when they purchase a soft drink from a vending machine.

Our commitment for 113 years has been to putting our products within an arm's reach of desire. Offering the products that people want at affordable prices is precisely why Coca-Cola is the favorite soft drink of people in nearly 200 countries around the world.

The new technologies we're exploring will only enhance our ability to deliver on that promise.

Source: Coca-Cola Company Website: http://www.coke.com

Exhibit 3 Text of the *Philadelphia Inquirer* Article, October 31, 1999

Have a Coke, and Big Brother is sure to smile

by Jeff Brown

Now for the latest evidence that the world is going to hell in a handbasket: The Coca Cola Co., seeking new ways to make thirst pay, is working on a weather-sensing vending machine that will raise prices when it's hot. Isn't that immoral? I mean, if a man crawls in from the desert dying of thirst, would you demand a C-note for a glass of water?

No, but a Coke . . . that's different. It's just an indulgence. So what's wrong with charging what the market will bear—more when it's hot, less when it's cold?

In fact, computer chips may soon enable vending machines to constantly adjust prices according to any number of factors that cause momentary fluctuations in supply and demand, not just weather.

So, some busy fall evening in the not-too-distant future, you sidle up to a well-lit Coke machine in South Philly. The box has no buttons, does not display any prices. A spotlight shines on your face as sensors zoom in on your vital signs. A head-high video screen flickers on.

The machine sees you're in jeans, not a suit, so it scans its library of personalities, skipping the erudite Englishman and the slinky French model. It displays the good-natured face of Sylvester Stallone.

"Yo!" the Coke machine calls. "What can I do ya for?" Sly smiles, thinking of his royalty, perhaps.

"A Coke Classic, please."

"No problem. Four bucks."

"Whoa! They're 50 cents at the supermarket."

The machine pauses while its accent analyzer determines you aren't from the neighborhood.

"You see a supermarket around here?" it says. "Four dollars."

You decide to bluff. "Look, the machine around the corner gave me a Pepsi for half that."

"When?"

"A couple of hours ago."

"Yeah, it's rush hour now. You won't get a two-dollar soda anywhere." The head on the screen shakes from side to side sympathetically. Then the red and white machine goes silent, letting you sweat. This is going to be tougher than you'd thought. You pull out your Palm Pilot X, link to the Internet, and go to sodamachines.com.

"There are 14 soda machines within four blocks," you report, holding up the Palm Pilot for the machine to see. "You're telling me I can't beat four dollars?"

The Coke machine tallies the 90 seconds it has expended on this negotiation. Its motion sensor detects two customers moving around impatiently behind you. Its atomic clock reports that rush hour is winding down.

"Okay, three dollars," it offers, peeved.

"No way." You stuff your wallet into your pants and step back.

The Coke machine focuses an infrared scanner on your lips, calibrating your thirst. It counts its inventory and finds a surplus of Diet Coke. Its hard drive whirs for a second.

"I'll give you a Coke Lite for $2.50," it offers resentfully.

"Terrible aftertaste," you say.

"With a bag of nuts."

"Nah."

"Look, pal, if you're not buyin' move along."

Traffic is getting lighter. The two people behind you give up and leave.

"All right," the box grumbles.

You deposit two dollars, get your can, and turn to go.

"How about those peanuts?" the machine asks hopefully. "Fifty cents."

"I'm allergic," you answer.

The machine pauses a nanosecond while electrons zip around its circuits. It's a week day. Rush hour. Statistics suggest you work nearby. You'll be back. The machine activates its customer relations software.

"Have a nice evening, bud," it calls as you turn away, the face smiling widely.

"Hey!" it calls. "I'm a soft touch today. Just got my circuits cleaned. Don't expect a deal like this next time!"

As you disappear around the corner, the machine counts its remaining cans, assesses the odds of making a sale this late in the day, and looks at how it's doing on its sales goal—a little behind. It cranks up the volume on its Rocky voice and calls out to the nearly empty street.

"Coke Classic! Get your Coke Classic here!

"Only a dollar!"

Source: Philadelphia Newspapers Inc.

Mean Vending Machines

by John S. Irons

This past weekend the news wires were all buzzing about the latest idea to come from the world of soft drinks. Coca-Cola is apparently considering creating a new kind of vending machine that would test the outside temperature and adjust the price of a can of soda upwards when it is warmer outside. Here's some of the typical reactions to the idea:

- "a cynical ploy to exploit the thirst of faithful customers" (*San Francisco Chronicle*)
- "lunk-headed idea" (*Honolulu Star-Bulletin*)
- "Soda jerks" (*Miami Herald*)
- "latest evidence that the world is going to hell in a handbasket" (*Philadelphia Inquirer*)
- "ticks me off" (*Edmonton Sun*)

What did they think the Coca-Cola company was doing anyway? Selflessly providing the world with a glorious beverage to further the goals of all mankind? Why should all these people be suddenly offended by a company trying to maximize profits?

"Price discrimination" is the term economists use to describe the practice of selling the same good to different groups of buyers at different prices. In the Coke case, the groups of buyers are segmented by the outside temperature (i.e. Jill when it is hot outside vs. Jill when it is cold). If possible, a company would like to charge a high price to those who place a high value on the good, while charging less to those that do not.

So, are you personally offended by Coke's plan to charge more for sodas when it is warm outside? Well, you had better get over it pretty quickly, there is already plenty of price discrimination out there, and there is MUCH more to come.

Rampant Price Discrimination

Price discrimination is quite common. Ever wonder why hardcover books are produced first and are so much more expensive than paperback books? Or, why it is so much cheaper to buy airline tickets far in advance? Or, why there are student discounts? Or, why matinee prices are cheaper for movies? Ever tried to buy a soda from a vending machine at a hotel or at a movie theater?

All these examples are attempts by sellers to charge different people different prices for the same good.

Much of the price discrimination in the economy may in fact be quite hidden. How do you know that the Crate and Barrel catalogue you just received has the same price for you as for someone living in another zip code? Those with a 90210 zip code see higher prices on their catalogues.

Why Is the Vending Machine Different?

In principle, [at least,] the temperature-sensitive vending machine is no different from any other form of price discrimination.

Although, I do think the idea that the process is automatic generates some additional discomfort—it is the idea that technology can effectively gauge our buying interests. The heat sensitive machine is a small step toward applying machine "intelligence" to profit maximization.

If you think that the vending machine idea is worrisome, just wait—the internet will be the most sophisticated price discriminator the world has ever seen. Smart vending machines will be the least of your worries. Online vendors such as Amazon.com may know quite a lot about you—your past purchasing habits, your internet preferences, your zip code, etc,—and they may want to use this information to adjust prices. Did you buy a Stephen King book last month? Maybe you'd like to buy another, more expensive, Grisham novel this month with a smaller "discount" chosen just for you.

The internet is much better than the "real world" at price discrimination, because it is so much easier to change prices. In fact they can set a price just for you. It's hard to imagine a traditional store doing this ("Hey, here comes John. Quick, raise the price of the new Krugman Book."). But for an on-line e-commerce store, this is feasible and, with a clever programmer on the payroll, quite easy.

Not all bad: Discrimination means increased efficiency. Actually, price discrimination can actually increase the overall efficiency of a market.

A loss of economic efficiency may occur when a company has some ability to set prices and there is no discrimination. The seller must pick a price that balances their desire to charge a high price to those that really want a product, with their desire to sell a higher overall quantity to those that are not willing to pay very much for it. Because of this, there are trades which would benefit both buyer and seller that do not happen—the resulting price is "too high" and the total quantity traded is "too low".

By identifying individual groups of consumers, a seller can provide an additional unit at a lower price to someone who before would have been priced out of the market. The company would now be willing to do this since they would not have to sacrifice profits by lowering prices for the high-demand group.

In the Coke case, some consumers—those who drink Cokes on hot days—will be worse off since they must pay a higher price, while some consumers—those who drink Coke on cold days—will be better off since they will receive a lower price. The Coca-Cola company, of course, will be better off. The sum total will be positive (pick your favorite Introduction to Economics textbook to see why).

Would you really be as offended if it was described as a discount on cold days?

So, if you are still stewing about the potential of higher Coke prices, I suggest you stock up the refrigerator and put some of that retirement money into Coca-Cola stock.